THE PSYCHOLOGY AND SCIENCE OF PSEUDOSCIENCE

THE PSYCHOLOGY AND SCIENCE OF PSEUDOSCIENCE

TERENCE HINES
Pace University and
New York Medical College

ROWMAN & LITTLEFIELD
Lanham • Boulder • New York • London

Executive Acquisitions Editor: Jonathan Joyce
Assistant Acquisitions Editor: Sarah Rinehart
Sales and Marketing Inquiries: RLtextbooks@bloomsbury.com

Bloomsbury Publishing Inc, 1385 Broadway, New York, NY 10018, USA
Bloomsbury Publishing Plc, 50 Bedford Square, London, WC1B 3DP, UK
Bloomsbury Publishing Ireland, 29 Earlsfort Terrace, Dublin 2, D02 AY28, Ireland
www.rowman.com

British Library Cataloguing in Publication Information Available

Library of Congress Cataloging-in-Publication Data Available

ISBN: 978-1-5381-9465-2 (cloth : alk. paper)
ISBN: 978-1-5381-9466-9 (pbk. : alk. paper)
ISBN: 978-1-5381-9467-6 (ebook)

∞™ The paper used in this publication meets the minimum requirements of American National Standard for Information Sciences—Permanence of Paper for Printed Library Materials, ANSI/NISO Z39.48-1992.

This book is dedicated with love to
my lovely wife
Sarah Johnson

BRIEF CONTENTS

CONTENTS

PREFACE

Like so many other people, when I was young, I was fascinated with all things paranormal, parapsychological, and cryptozoological, although that last term didn't yet exist. I read *Fate* magazine and books by Frank Edwards, a great promoter of such things in the 1960s. I believed that flying saucers were real visitors from other planets and even wrote a letter to my local newspaper, in ninth grade if memory serves, arguing for the reality of UFOs.

College was Duke University, where in the 1930s J. B. Rhine had conducted experiments (described in chapter 4) that he believed proved the reality of extrasensory perception. At a Duke faculty picnic, I had the pleasure of meeting Rhine, then retired from parapsychological research. My impression was of a perfectly charming elderly gentleman. My time at Duke neither strengthened nor weakened my beliefs—I was quite busy learning experimental/cognitive psychology, which would later morph into my chosen field of cognitive neuroscience.

It is evident that people accept, often very deeply, belief systems that have no validity. By the late 1960s, there had been little research in cognitive psychology aimed at understanding the cognitive processes that led people to believe in the sorts of paranormal things I found so compelling. That changed during the 1970s. Research revealed that processes of memory and perception were much more complex and malleable than previously thought. I began to learn about this research in graduate school at the University of Oregon, where Ray Hyman taught a course in "pseudopsychologies" and introduced me to the psychology behind false beliefs. It was extremely exciting to learn that there were explanations for such erroneous beliefs, memories, and perceptions and that these could be investigated rigorously. Research on the cognitive biases and illusions that lead to belief in things paranormal and pseudoscientific took off in the last decades of the twentieth century, and it is this research that forms the core ideas of this book.

To briefly summarize what is said at much greater length in the following chapters, there are three major processes involved. First, the naïve view that memory and perception are almost always accurate is, while usually correct, incorrect in important ways. Both of these important psychological processes can be deeply influenced by a person's expectations and preexisting beliefs, even when these are wrong. In other words, memory and perception are constructive processes and not just passive reflections of reality. These constructive processes help to account for many of the reports of flying saucers, bigfoots, sea monsters, ghosts, and the like. Second, the human brain is a pattern-seeking device, and it will find patterns even in randomness, especially if heightened expectations for patterns are present. Such pattern seeking, especially when combined with perceptual constructions, can lead to belief in the paranormal when people see "meaningful" patterns in random events. Third, a process called agency can cause people to believe in ghosts and other phenomena. Being in a creepy old house can lead to expectations of hauntings. Then when a door silently moves shut, seemingly on its own, or a tiny sound is heard, such things may not be attributed to the normal events and sounds in an old house but to some spirit whose intention, whose agency, is believed to cause the events.

To the above three cognitive processes that lead to the acceptance of bizarre and unfounded beliefs one needs to add a fourth to account for why some obviously intelligent people continue to accept such beliefs in spite of the overwhelming evidence that they are wrong. Shermer (2011), in his book *The Believing Brain*, noted that intelligent people are very good at coming up with arguments to support their beliefs, no matter how crazy those beliefs are. This is especially the case when they live in an echo chamber where they hear only input from others that hold the same beliefs and are not exposed to contrary information. Religious beliefs are prime examples of this sort of process, but the same can be said for many of the beliefs discussed in this book.

Earlier research did not address the cognitive bases of false belief but simply examined the validity of such beliefs. Such research can date back to before the twentieth century and provides important information on whether a particular claim was correct or not. One example is the twentieth-century work examining the validity of concepts central to Freudian psychoanalysis. Psychoanalysis has largely, and properly, been relegated to the "dust bin of history" in academic circles and, as such, receives very little current research attention. However, it still commands considerable interest outside academia, so it is important to discuss the historical record of relevant research, even if that research was done over fifty years ago. Such older research can be just as relevant and informative as that done last year.

No one book can cover all the areas of pseudoscience and related topics and stay at a reasonable size. So there will be some topics that could have been included but were not. One area that I explicitly decided to exclude from this book is what might be called the earth science pseudosciences. These include beliefs that the earth is flat, that the sun circles the earth, that it is hollow, that the moon landing was a hoax, and that Atlantis, Lemuria, and ley lines are, or were, real. I did this because my knowledge of the science in this area is limited. Happily, Donald Prothero's excellent 2020 book *Weird Earth* covers all these topics and more.

Especially in these times of misinformation and denial of facts, I think it is especially important to back up one's contentions with specific references. To this end there are copious references throughout the text. This will allow the reader curious to find the primary sources on which I have relied easy access to the relevant literature.

Terence Hines

ACKNOWLEDGMENTS

An author is always helped by numerous people who contribute to the finished book. In my case, I am delighted to acknowledge help that stretches back to graduate school, and even high school. In my senior year at Hanover (NH) High School, I sat in on Rogers Elliott's Dartmouth College Psychology 10 (Personality) class. There, I had my first encounter with skepticism as Rogers delightfully skewered the nonsense that was Freud. In graduate school, Ray Hyman introduced me to the constructive nature of memory and perception and the reasons why people accept unsubstantiated beliefs. Ray's approach had a huge impact on my thinking.

My editor, Sarah Rinehart, has been knowledgeable and extremely helpful at all stages of the process of transforming my manuscript into a finished product.

The staff at Pace University's Mortola Library were invaluable in helping me with the research for this book. Shelia Hu, the interlibrary loan librarian, was a wonder at finding the numerous, often obscure, articles that I needed.

Several anonymous reviewers of the original manuscript made useful suggestions about which topics to add, revise, or remove. An anonymous copy editor spotted my too-many bibliographic errors and made several excellent suggestions (which I took) to improve my wording in several important places.

Finally, and most importantly, my wife Sarah has been a loving, patient, and steadfast supporter while I spent so much time on this project.

1

THE NATURE OF PSEUDOSCIENCE

What is pseudoscience? It is difficult to come up with a strict definition. In the real world things are not clearly delineated but surrounded by gray areas that doom any hard distinction. As the term implies, a pseudoscience is a doctrine or belief system that pretends to be a science. What distinguishes pseudoscience from real science? This question is known as the demarcation problem by philosophers, and the answer has been the source of much interest and debate (i.e., Pigliucci and Boudry 2013). Some philosophers, notably Laudan (1983), have argued that a distinction between real and pseudosciences cannot be made. This position is easily answered by reference to a comment attributed to the American sensory psychologist Stanley Smith Stevens (1906–1973), who pointed out that just because there is no clear dividing line between day and night does not mean that the two cannot be distinguished (Stevens 1968).

If one wants a short definition of pseudoscience, one could not do better than the one from Kendrick Frazier (2024, 27). A pseudoscience is a "set of strong ideas and assertions about the natural world unsupported or even contradicted by the best available scientific evidence and advanced without applying scientific methodologies." In chapter 8 of Frazier's book, he provides an excellent discussion of the philosophical debate over the demarcation problem.

An early criterion for identifying pseudoscience and distinguishing it from real science was proposed by the Austrian philosopher Karl Popper (1902–1994) in 1957. He identified nonfalsifiability as an important characteristic of a pseudoscience. A nonfalsifiable hypothesis is one against which there can be no evidence—that is, no evidence can show the hypothesis to be wrong. It might at first seem that such a hypothesis must be true, but a bit of reflection and several examples will demonstrate just the opposite. Consider the following hypothesis: "I, Terence Michael Hines, am God incarnate, and I created the universe thirty seconds ago." Now, you probably don't believe this hypothesis, but how would you go about disproving it? You could argue, "You say you created the universe thirty seconds ago, but I have memories from *years* ago. So, you're not God." But I reply, "When I created the universe, I created everyone complete with memories." We could go on like this for some time, and you would never be able to prove that I'm not God. Nonetheless, this hypothesis is clearly absurd! Creationists, who have recently renamed themselves "intelligent design" proponents to avoid the religious connotations of the term *creationism* and believe that the biblical story of creation is literal truth, adopt a similar nonfalsifiable hypothesis. They claim that the world was created about six thousand years ago. As will be seen in chapter 13, vast amounts of physical evidence clearly refute this claim. All one has to do is point to something older than six thousand years. Backed into a corner by such evidence, creationists rephrase their hypothesis in a nonfalsifiable form. They explain the clear geological and fossil evidence that dates back millions of years by claiming that God put that evidence there to test our faith. An alternative version is that the evidence was manufactured by Satan to tempt us from the true path of redemption. No evidence can refute either of these versions of the hypothesis since any new piece of geological or fossil evidence can be dismissed as having been placed there by God or Satan. This does not make the hypothesis true—it just makes it nonfalsifiable. Such a hypothesis contributes nothing to our understanding of the physical world.

Another example of a nonfalsifiable hypothesis comes from psychoanalysis, a belief system replete with pseudoscientific characteristics (chapter 5). Sigmund Freud believed that all males had latent homosexual tendencies but that in most males these tendencies were repressed. Clearly, homosexual males have homosexual tendencies. But what about heterosexual males? To determine whether the hypothesis that all males have repressed homosexual tendencies is false, you could give some sort of test for homosexual tendencies. What if you failed to find such tendencies? The standard Freudian reply is that the tendencies have been so completely repressed that they don't show up on the test. Given this nonfalsifiable hypothesis, no test could show that heterosexual males don't have latent homosexual urges. No matter how sensitive the test, the reply can always be made that the urges are so deeply repressed that they don't show up on the test.

Those who are skeptical about pseudoscientific and paranormal claims are frequently accused of being closed-minded in demanding adequate evidence and proof before accepting such a claim. But who is really being closed-minded? As a scientist, I can specify exactly the type of evidence I would require to make me change my mind and accept the reality of astrology, UFOs as extraterrestrial spacecraft, or any other topic considered in this book. But it is the believers, who like to paint themselves as open-minded and accepting of new possibilities, that are closed-minded. The nonfalsifiable hypothesis is really saying, "There is no conceivable piece of evidence that will cause me to change my mind!" This is true closed-mindedness.

Further on nonfalsifiable hypotheses, consider the theory of gravity. Gravitational theory, both Newtonian and Einsteinian, makes the very strong prediction that when a person standing on the surface of planet Earth holds a pencil in their hand and then lets go of it, it will fall to the ground, and of course this is exactly what happens. However, one can *imagine* that the pencil does not drop. Thus, the theory of gravity is conceptually falsifiable because there is an outcome of this little experiment that *could* show the theory to be false. In reality the predications of gravitational theory are consistently borne out so one can have great confidence that the theory is correct.

Another point regarding nonfalsifiable hypotheses is important. Although they are nonfalsifiable, they could, in principle, be verified and shown to be true. The Freudian hypothesis about males' latent homosexual urges could be verified if all males did show such urges on some sensitive measure of sexual interest. So nonfalsifiable hypotheses are only that—nonfalsifiable. They could be verified if the evidence to support them existed. The promoters of such hypotheses have been forced to fall back on them precisely because of the lack of supporting evidence.

One way to make a hypothesis nonfalsifiable is to simply declare, "I don't believe it," when confronted with evidence contrary to one's beliefs. This is a common tactic among proponents of some of the more extreme pseudoscientific beliefs out there. Such beliefs include that the earth is flat or is enclosed in a dome, that aircraft contrails are poisons, and that the hurricanes of 2024 were caused by government control of the weather.

Since Popper's proposal, it has become clear that there are several other criteria for demarking the boundary between real and pseudosciences. These are listed in textbox 1.1. It is important to keep in mind that the boundary between the two is not absolute and that a given system of beliefs may fall into a gray area between the two ends of the continuum.

TEXTBOX 1.1. MAJOR CHARACTERISTICS OF A PSEUDOSCIENCE

1. Supported by nonfalsifiable hypotheses.
2. Contributes nothing to the advancement of knowledge.
3. Does not look closely at the data or use methods that would show the idea(s) to be correct.
4. Does not change in the light of new, contrary, evidence.
5. Makes up post-hoc excuses for why studies and experiments fail to generate support for the claim(s).
6. Uses the "argument from ignorance" in place of supporting evidence.

Some belief systems that are falsifiable can still be readily classified as pseudoscientific. Two examples are astrology and biorhythm theory. Both these systems make predictions that can be, and have been, clearly falsified. This alone does not make them scientific. Hansson (2017) has reviewed the philosophical approaches to the science-versus-pseudoscience distinction. He notes that another important characteristic of a pseudoscience is a failure to progress or to contribute to the advancement of knowledge. The falsification of the predictions of astrology and biorhythm theory have never resulted in astrologers or biorhythmists changing the basic tenants of their beliefs. That is, such failed predictions do not result in revisions of the basic idea and the generation of new ideas that can be tested. In contrast, in real science failed predictions can, and should, lead to such revisions and progress. Like any working scientist, I have done my share of experiments where my hypothesis was shown to be wrong. Such a negative result generates an interesting "puzzle" to be solved. One tries to figure out what went wrong, to change one's theory to accommodate the negative results and move on to generate a theory more in line with reality. None of that happens in a pseudoscience. As a consequence of pseudosciences not changing in light of new evidence, they are stale and stagnant, adding nothing to the sum total of human knowledge, while real sciences constantly advance. The astrology of 2024 is essentially identical to that of 1024. Every area of science, on the other hand, has seen huge advances in knowledge in just the last fifty, or even twenty, years.

A third characteristic of pseudoscience is the proponents' unwillingness to look closely at the phenomenon they claim exists. In other words, careful, controlled experiments that would demonstrate the existence of the phenomenon—if it were real—are not conducted. The reality of the phenomenon is uncritically accepted, and the need for hard data and facts is belittled. MacRobert (1982) gave an example in the work of George Leonard (1976), who believed that official photographs from the National Aeronautics and Space Administration (NASA) show that "somebody else is on the moon." Leonard contended that he discovered this secret and tried to inform the public about it in spite of a massive conspiracy of silence. Leonard's evidence consists of low-resolution NASA photographs, many of them poor reproductions rather than crisp originals. The objects Leonard claimed to see, such as huge bridges and construction equipment of various types, are all just at the limit of resolution of the photos he used. MacRobert pointed out that

> when he had a chance to get better photos and see the terrain more clearly, he didn't. One of his pictures is supposed to show miles-long bridges. The photo is a very distant shot, and the bridges are the vaguest smudges. Equally good close-ups have been taken of the bridge areas, and if the bridges were there, they would reach from one side of the photos to the other like a wall poster of the Golden Gate. For some reason Leonard did not get those particular close-ups, readily available from NASA. He was unwilling to look carefully. (p. 47)

Oberg (1982) discussed Leonard's errors in detail.

The burden of proof should rest squarely on the one who is making the extraordinary claim. This is because, as we have seen, it is often impossible to disprove even a clearly ridiculous claim. Consider the claim that fairies actually existed in the English countryside. The testimony of two little girls and some photographs that they faked convinced none other than Sir Arthur Conan Doyle, the creator of the fictional detective Sherlock Holmes, that fairies really existed in the English countryside. The story is important because it illustrates how reversal of the burden of proof can lead to the uncritical acceptance of the most absurd claims.

The story starts in Cottingley, England, in 1917. Two girls—Elsie Wright, thirteen, and a cousin, Frances Griffiths, ten—claimed to have taken two photographs of fairies who played with them. Three more photos were apparently taken in the summer of 1920 (Sheaffer 1977–1978). It was Doyle who brought the photos to the public's awareness, and later wrote a book arguing for the real existence of fairies based largely on these photos (Doyle 1922). The photographs, one of which is shown in figure 1.1, have always looked fake.

Figure 1.1. One of the Cottingley Fairy photographs. Photo by Elsie Wright, 1917 (https://en.wikipedia.org/wiki/File:Cottingley_Fairies_1.jpg)

But neither this nor the inherent absurdity of the claim stopped many people, including Doyle, from taking the existence of fairies seriously. UFOlogists have been interested in fairy sightings, believing they may be related to the UFO phenomenon and extraterrestrials (Sheaffer 1978). Various reports of fairies, leprechauns, and the like are all brought together to argue that maybe there really is some substance to the reports. And, again, the skeptic is challenged to explain away each and every report. However, it's impossible to explain every case. No one could ever track down whatever it was that led to each individual report. The Cottingley photos can be explained. They were—and this should come as no great surprise to the reader—a hoax. The "fairies" were cutouts from a children's book, and many years later Frances and Elsie admitted the hoax (Cooper 1982). Crawley (2000) has described the creation of the photos and the hoax in detail. Finally, Sheaffer (1978) subjected the photographs to computer enhancement and found evidence of a string that was used to hang the cutouts from shrubs while the photos were taken. So what began as a hoax and concerned a clearly absurd hypothesis—that fairies really exist—turned into pseudoscientific belief that required sixty years and much effort to put to rest. And none of this would have happened if the burden of proof had been on the proponents in the first place to provide adequate evidence of their claim—such as a fairy or a leprechaun in a cage. Instead, the burden was shifted to the skeptics, who were told, "If you can't explain away every photo and every report, then fairies must exist."

This is an example of the logical fallacy known as the "argument from ignorance." Its general form is to argue that "If you (the skeptic) can't explain some specific event or phenomenon, it must be because of (fairies, aliens, bigfoot, astrology, sea monsters, or whatever)." As will be seen in chapters 6 and 7, this argument is probably most commonly made in regard to UFOs, where if a specific sighting of an unexplained light in the sky can't be traced to a known cause, then it "must be an alien craft."

Proponents of pseudoscience often complain that skeptics are unfair in demanding more proof for pseudoscientific claims than for the claims of "establishment" sciences. This is both true and reasonable. As Carl Sagan was fond of saying, "extraordinary claims demand extraordinary proof." For example, consider the following two claims about transcendental meditation (TM): (1) TM can make you feel better; (2) TM can teach you how to defy the law of gravity and float in the air at will. Most people would accept the validity of the first claim based simply on the testimony of several people who say that they felt better after they learned how to meditate. Clearly, one would demand more proof for the second claim. Most people wouldn't accept mere statements from several people that they knew how to levitate at will. Additional evidence would be needed. Pictures wouldn't do because the TM movement has been known to fake photos of people levitating (Randi 1982a). You'd probably demand that someone actually levitate right in front of you. And you'd want a professional magician present as an observer to ensure that no trickery was involved.

In short, you would demand more rigorous confirmation of the second claim than of the first. So not only is the burden of proof on the proponents of pseudoscience to prove their claims, but the burden on them is greater than on someone making a claim that does not challenge the bulk of known facts.

Myths of various cultures are sometimes used as support for pseudoscientific claims. Myths are commonly agreed on stories that play important roles in a culture's perception of itself and its history. Origin myths are a major example and show how fundamental myths can be. Myths typically feature supernatural characters and events. They are also attempts to explain natural phenomena before scientific explanations became available. An example here would be the notion that volcanoes erupt because some volcano god or spirit is angry. Proponents of some pseudosciences argue that because myths have been around for a long time, they must contain a kernel of truth. An example is the vision of Ezekiel in which a flaming chariot appears in the sky and four-faced human-like creatures appear and then God speaks to Ezekiel directing him to preach to the Judeans about how sinful they have been. "The idea that Ezekiel witnessed an extraterrestrial visit has been floated repeatedly since the UFO era began" (Halperin 2020, 122).

Some native peoples worldwide had myths and legends regarding giants, "hairy men," or similar frightening semihuman creatures. Especially for such myths from native cultures in the North American Pacific Northwest, it has been argued that such stories are support for the reality of Bigfoot (chapter 13). Such "indigenous histories are ripe for plunder by cryptozoologists seeking confirmation of their beliefs" (Dickey 2020) by taking literally entities that have spiritual and metaphorical meanings. Dickey spoke to Snxakila, a First Nations "orator and historian" from the Nuxalk culture of British Columbia regarding the culture's myths of supernatural creatures. He learned that entities like "the sk'amtsk [a water monster] are not beings that can be pulled out of the fabric of the world and talked about in isolation. They are woven into all of time, and any history that recounts their existence or purpose is interconnected with every other aspect of creation," and "they also provide guidance and perspective on contemporary matters" (Dickey 2020, 110).

In 1950 Immanuel Velikovsky put forward his theory of "worlds in collision." It was based in large part on myths. Among other things, he believed that a comet was ejected from Jupiter and became the planet Venus around 1500 BCE. To get from Jupiter to its present orbit, the comet approached Earth, which passed through the tail of the comet. This caused a variety of effects, including a fall of red dust from the comet. The rivers thus turned blood red. Petroleum fell from the sky in great quantities, creating the vast oil reserves of the Middle East. As Earth passed deeper and deeper into the tail of the comet, the sun disappeared, and the planet was plunged into darkness that lasted for days. Due to the gravitational influence of Venus, Earth's rotation slowed, causing earthquakes. New mountain ranges were created. Hurricane-strength winds and huge tidal waves left some areas dry. This is Velikovsky's explanation for the biblical story of the parting of the Red Sea that allowed Moses to lead the Israelites out of the land of Pharaoh.

Basic knowledge about planetary science is much more common now than it was in the 1950s, so it's obvious now that Velikovsky was a world-class crackpot. Nonetheless, his ideas attracted considerable support from nonscientists at the time. It was even necessary for scientists to spend some effort in debunking his ideas (Goldsmith 1979; Sagan 1977).

Velikovsky demonstrates another characteristic of a pseudoscience—the failure to change or update the theory in light of new evidence. In terms of willingness to change ideas based on new evidence, the Velikovsky episode is telling. In a 1972 speech at Harvard University, Velikovsky correctly stated that science textbooks from the 1950s, when his theories first appeared, were now "antiquated." He went on to say that his theories were just as valid in 1972 as they had been in 1950. In other words, the great advances in knowledge of astronomy, astrophysics, planetary geology, and related fields that had taken place in that twenty-two-year span were irrelevant to the validity of his theories. If the facts don't fit the theory, proponents of pseudoscience ignore the facts.

Velikovsky's attitude can be contrasted with those of real scientists. For example, in the 1980s there were large changes in astronomers' views on how the moon was formed. The view now widely held is that the moon was the result of a collision about 4.5 billion years ago between then-cooling Earth and another, smaller, planet about the size of Mars. A typical response to this change in views about the moon's origin was very well expressed by Dr. H. J. Melosh of the University of Arizona in a *New York Times* article (Gleick 1986):

> I was sort of an expert on impact cratering, and people hadn't really looked at what happens during impact. So I decided to do it and get rid of this insane idea [that the Moon resulted from planetary impact] once and for all. Instead, what I found within weeks is that the physics of what happened during an impact event agrees extremely well [with the impact theory]. The more I looked, the more I thought that the giant impact theory was the only one that could explain what we saw.

Why was this impact theory accepted by scientists, while Velikovsky's was not? Velikovsky presented no evidence to support his ideas. He merely surrounded them with a forest of obscure citations, many from myths and legends and many of which were inaccurate. The impact theory of lunar formation made testable predictions that were found to be correct when tested.

This is rather ironic, as I suspect the general public's impression is that scientists are closed-minded, stodgy folk who rarely change their minds. In fact, nothing could be further from the truth. In the last thirty years all areas of scientific investigation have undergone radical changes. New theories have appeared, been useful for a time, then given way to even newer theories as new data and facts have demonstrated that the old theories were incomplete. Not wrong, just incomplete. Science changes so rapidly, it is frequently difficult to keep up with the changes even in one's own field. This is in contrast, of course, to the pseudoscientists, whose theories almost never change. Again, if one looks at the actual *behavior* of scientists and pseudoscientists, it is clear which is really the more open-minded of the two groups.

It occasionally happens that psychics or other paranormal claimants agree to be tested scientifically. When they fail the test, they often show another characteristic of a pseudoscience by claiming that the reason for their failure wasn't because their claims were wrong. No, it was a "bad day" or there were "bad vibrations" about that blocked their ability.

The characteristics of pseudoscience discussed in this chapter offer useful guidelines for distinguishing pseudosciences from the real thing. Some object that because there can be no strict demarcation between real science and pseudoscience, classifying something as a pseudoscience is illegitimate. But as I've already noted in this regard, echoing S. S. Stevens—the fact that day shades into night and vice versa does not mean that day and night cannot be told apart.

THE PARANORMAL

The paranormal can best be thought of as a subset of pseudoscience. What sets the paranormal apart from other pseudosciences is a reliance on explanations for alleged phenomena that are well outside the bounds of established science. Thus, paranormal phenomena include extrasensory perception (ESP), telekinesis, ghosts, poltergeists, life after death, reincarnation, faith healing, human auras, and so forth. The explanations for these allied phenomena are phrased in vague terms of "psychic forces," "human energy fields," and so on. This contrasts with many pseudoscientific explanations for other nonparanormal phenomena, which, although very bad science, are still couched in acceptable scientific terms. Thus, chelation therapy, a popular bit of medical quackery, is said to remove calcium from clogged arteries when the chemical ethylenediamine tetraacetate (EDTA) is given. The specific claim is that EDTA binds to calcium, thus destroying material blocking arteries. Binding of one substance to another is a real and very important biochemical process. However, it has long been known that the claims of the chelation therapists are simply wrong (Green and Sampson 2002) and the therapy is not effective. So the claims for chelation therapy are pseudoscientific but not paranormal.

However, the boundary between paranormal and nonparanormal pseudosciences is often fuzzy. Different individuals may give different types of explanations for the same alleged phenomena. Thus, the claims that UFOs are extraterrestrial spacecraft is generally a pseudoscientific one (see chapters 7 and 8). But some UFOlogists, such as Vallee (1975) argued that UFOs are really some sort of psychic projection. This transforms the phenomenon into a paranormal one. Similarly, Mack (1999) argues that we live in a universe of many dimensions and that UFO aliens are spirits (or some such) from these other dimensions.

Another example concerns biorhythm theory, which became popular in the 1970s. It postulated three biorhythms lasting twenty-three, twenty-eight, and thirty-three days. These started at the moment of birth and ran sinusoidally and totally unchanged throughout one's life. The sinusoidal nature of the rhythms meant that each rhythm was divided in half—into an "up" and a "down" phase. The twenty-three-day rhythm controlled physical abilities, the twenty-eight-day rhythm one's emotional level, and the thirty-three-day rhythm intellectual abilities. The theory made specific predictions. For example, people would be better at intellectual tasks like taking a test on the up days of their intellectual rhythm. They would do worse on physical activity, like sports performance, on the down phase of the physical rhythm. Biorhythms were promoted in books (e.g., Gittelson 1982) that contained lists of events that seemed to correspond with biorhythm predictions. Typical were lists of great sports performances that took place when the athlete was on an up day, or sports failures when the athlete was on a down day. Accidents, such as airline crashes or traffic accidents, were said to be much more common when the pilot or the driver were on a down phase of the physical rhythm. Worse than the down days were the "critical" days, when a rhythm was changing from the up to the down phase or vice versa. Accidents and poor performance generally were said to be especially common on such days.

The predictions of the theory were easy to test. All one had to know was the individual's birth date and the date on which the event in question took place. This resulted in a plethora of papers putting biorhythm to the test. In a 1998 paper I reviewed 134 published studies of biorhythm theory and found no evidence whatsoever in the validity of the theory. What I did find were a subset of papers claiming evidence for the theory that contained such egregious errors in statistical analysis that they were almost funny.

The pseudoscientific explanation of these alleged biorhythm effects was that the rhythms are set at the moment of birth in the individual's brain (Mallardi 1978). Attempts are then made to tie the claims for biorhythms in with what is known about real biological rhythms in humans and animals (Gittelson 1982). On the other hand, a "biorhythmist" in Oregon explained that the concept of biorhythms works because "it concerns itself with rhythmic flows of energy, relating to the conscious levels of our being, to the subconscious levels of creativity and intuition, and to superconscious levels that relate to the spiritual tendencies of the human condition" (Holden 1977, 5). I would classify this as a paranormal explanation. It could also be reasonably classified as gibberish.

PATHOLOGICAL SCIENCE: N-RAYS, POLYWATER, AND COLD FUSION

In a 1953 lecture Irving Langmuir (1881–1957) was probably the first person to try to set out criteria for what he termed pathological science or the science of "things that aren't so," a concept closely related to pseudoscience. Langmuir was a chemist who won the 1932 Nobel Prize in Chemistry for his work on oil films. The criteria included an effect so small that it is very difficult to detect from background random noise in whatever measurement is being used. Fantastic theories are then proposed to explain the effect. Objections are replied to not with better data and theories but with made-up excuses and post-hoc rationalizations (number 5 in textbox 1.1). Finally, while there are initially quite a few proponents of the pathological science, as more and better experiments are done and the effect remains at the very borderline of detectability, the number of proponents drops and only a few diehards remain.

Langmuir gave several examples of pathological science in his 1953 presentation. These included some now justifiably obscure claims in physics. But he included N-rays and ESP and gave a passing comment on UFOs as examples. In my view these latter two fall more in the category of pseudoscience and will be discussed in detail later on. However, the N-ray episode certainly fits, as do two post-1953 claims, polywater and cold fusion.

Pathological sciences provide important cautionary tales. It is often instructive to examine how and why an incorrect conclusion has been reached because then one can see the mistakes to be avoided in the future. The stories of N-rays, polywater, and cold fusion are classic examples of scientific mistakes. In all cases, initial claims for the existence of a new phenomenon seemed to garner impressive experimental support. Much interest was thereby generated until it became clear, on further experimentation, that the phenomena had never really existed. Once this was clear, most scientists expended no further effort investigating the phenomena and these scientific dead ends were abandoned.

These stories are important for a discussion of pseudoscience and the paranormal for several reasons. First, they demonstrate once again, this time in a scientific context, that attempting to shift the burden of proof to the skeptic is not a legitimate means of defending otherwise untenable hypotheses. Second, when contrasted with claims about ESP (discussed in chapter 4), these cases show how most incorrect ideas in science are handled. Finally, they show that, under some circumstances, scientists who become strongly attached to a particular claim will resort to some of the same techniques used by proponents of pseudoscientific claims, such as nonfalsifiable hypotheses. The following discussion of N-rays is based on the excellent articles by Klotz (1980) and Nye (1980). The discussion of polywater is based on the book by Franks (1981). The reader should refer to these sources for much more detail on these fascinating episodes in the history of science.

René Blondlot (1849–1930) bears the dubious distinction of being the "discoverer" of N-rays. Blondlot was an outstanding physicist at the University of Nancy in France. He made many important contributions to physics in the late 1800s. The late 1800s and early 1900s were exciting times in physics. In 1895 X-rays had been discovered, and in the next few years other types of radiation were found: alpha, beta, and gamma rays. Thus, as Klotz (1980, 168) points out, when Blondlot made known his discovery of N-rays (named after the University of Nancy) in 1903, physics was psychologically prepared for the discovery of another new type of radiation.

One of the properties of N-rays was that they increased the brightness of an electric spark. Blondlot used subjective judgments of spark brightness as a measure of the presence of N-rays in his experiments. No instruments were used that could have given objective measures of brightness. Blondlot's reputation in physics was such that, once he had reported N-rays, other physicists rushed to study this new phenomenon. In the next few years, a stream of papers appeared, largely from other French laboratories, confirming that N-rays did exist and detailing additional properties. Blondlot's own laboratory led the research effort. By this time, Blondlot had adopted a new method for determining the presence of N-rays. A screen was painted with a chemical that became more luminous when N-rays were projected onto it. Again, the judgments of luminosity were purely subjective; Blondlot even specified that observers should "not look directly at the screen" (Nye 1980, 132) but observe it out of the corner of their eye.

In the course of further investigation, it was found that the sun, flames, and incandescent objects were all sources of N-rays. Another French investigator, Auguste Charpentier, found that the human nervous system emitted N-rays, and this finding was soon "confirmed" in Blondlot's laboratory. Further, when a portion of the nervous system was active, that portion was said to emit more N-rays. Blondlot also discovered "secondary" sources of N-rays. These were sources that absorbed N-rays and then reemitted them. The fluids of the human eye were alleged to be such secondary sources and, amazingly, when the eye was exposed to N-rays, it became more sensitive to dim illumination. Text that could not ordinarily be read in dim light could be read after the eye was exposed to N-rays.

Here, then, was an important new phenomenon, confirmed by dozens of independent studies in many different laboratories, many of the studies conducted by well-known and highly respected scientists.

But other physicists, especially those working outside France, were skeptical about the existence of N-rays. They objected to the conclusions of Blondlot and others, who based their results on subjective judgments of brightness. Such judgments, which are liable to be influenced by the observer's beliefs, are poor sources of data. One experiment allegedly showing that N-rays increased visual sensitivity was faulted as being due to nothing more than dark adaptation—the phenomenon that accounts for the increase in ability to see in a dark room the longer one spends in such a room. More devastating to the claims about N-rays was the failure of other physicists outside France to repeat Blondlot's results. These failures were most striking when objective as opposed to subjective measures of brightness were used. Nye (1980) chronicles the numerous failures to replicate Blondlot's results in the few years following his initial report.

One of the most telling pieces of evidence against the existence of N-rays came in 1904, when American physicist Robert W. Wood (1868–1955) decided to visit Blondlot's laboratory to see for himself whether Blondlot's experiments were valid. Wood was an extraordinary man, with many interests outside physics (Seabrook 1941). One of his interests was exposing fraudulent spiritualist mediums; Wood's experiences in this endeavor must have helped him when he came to evaluate Blondlot's N-ray experiments. Blondlot had found that N-rays were blocked by lead. Wood observed demonstrations of N-ray effects in Blondlot's laboratory and concluded, as had other critics, that the reported changes in brightness that Blondlot used to argue for the reality of N-rays were figments of Blondlot's imagination and a result of his desire to validate the existence of N-rays.

N-ray experiments had to be carried out in a darkened laboratory so the changes in brightness due to the rays' presence could be observed. This gave Wood an opportunity to make several observations that proved Blondlot's judgments of brightness changes were a function of his beliefs and not of the presence or absence of N-rays. In one experiment, Wood was to block an N-ray source by inserting a sheet of lead between the source and a card with luminous paint on it. Blondlot, acting as observer, made judgments about the paint's brightness and, therefore, about the presence or absence of N-rays. Without telling Blondlot, Wood changed the experiment in one slight but vitally important way. He would indicate to Blondlot that the lead sheet was blocking the N-ray source when it really wasn't, and vice versa. If N-rays really existed, Blondlot's judgments of the brightness of the luminous paint should be a function of whether the lead screen really was between the card and the N-ray source and should have had no relationship to whether or not he believed the sheet was blocking the source. Wood found that Blondlot's judgments depended on whether he believed the screen to be present or not. For example, if he believed the screen was present (blocking N-rays) but it wasn't, he reported the paint to be less luminous. If he was told the screen was not present (allowing N-rays to pass) but it really was, he reported the paint to be more luminous.

In two other situations, Wood showed Blondlot's subjective brightness judgments to be a function of his belief. Blondlot had claimed that an aluminum prism would produce a spectrum of N-rays of different wavelengths, just as a glass prism produces a spectrum of visible light of different wavelengths. Wood found he could remove the aluminum prism from the path of the N-rays without interfering with Blondlot's ability to see the N-ray spectrum. Later, when Blondlot's laboratory assistant became suspicious of Wood, Wood pretended to remove the prism, while leaving it in place. This caused the assistant to report that the N-ray spectrum was not present. Finally, Wood performed a similar substitution in an experiment designed to show that N-rays increased visual sensitivity in dim light. An N-ray source was placed near a subject's eyes. The "subject of the experiment assured Wood that the hands of a clock, which were normally not clearly visible to him, became brighter and much more distinct" (Klotz 1980, 174) when the N-ray source was held near. Wood then replaced the N-ray source with a similarly shaped piece of wood, a substance that was not an N-ray source. Nonetheless, as long as the subject was unaware of the switch, he continued to report that objects were brighter and more distinct when the piece of wood, which he believed to be an N-ray source, was close to his eyes.

Wood's report, published in the British journal *Nature* in 1904 (reprinted with a short commentary in Hines 1996), along with the failures of other laboratories to verify the existence of N-rays, led to the conclusion that N-rays do not exist. No further papers appeared on the topic after about 1907. Only Blondlot, convinced until the end that N-rays were real, pursued his research on the topic until he died in 1930. But he never used objective measures.

At the height of the debate over the existence of N-rays, proponents made up excuses and adopted a nonfalsifiable hypothesis to account for critics' inability to observe the rays: the critics' eyes weren't sensitive enough. When Wood initially told Blondlot that he couldn't see any brightness difference on a screen when the rays were or were not present, he was told "that was because my eyes were not sensitive enough, so that proved nothing" (Seabrook 1941, 238). Years later, one of the early proponents of N-rays made a similar point: "If an observer (who is not convinced) sees nothing, you conclude that he does not have sensitive eyes" (Becquerel 1934, cited in Nye 1980, 153). For a more detailed account of N-rays and Blondlot, see Collins's (2001, chapter 4) excellent book.

It is vital to note that Blondlot and the other proponents of N-rays were not lying when they reported that they saw a brighter spark or luminous screen when they believed that N-rays were present. Nor were they stupid or unintelligent. Sparks and luminous screens vary in brightness from moment to moment for several reasons. Random changes in brightness that confirm an observer's belief are more likely to be noted than those that go against the belief. Numerous similar instances where a belief can profoundly change the way someone perceives a stimulus will be noted throughout this book. The case of N-rays also illustrates how science handles the burden of proof. (Compare this to the discussion of academic studies of ESP in chapter 4.) Assume that someone wished to argue, today, that N-rays really do exist. To bolster the case, they go back to the physics journals of 1903–1907 and assemble all the papers that argued that N-rays are real. The proponent then challenges the skeptic to explain in detail what was wrong in each of the published papers favorable to the existence of N-rays. Could the skeptic meet this challenge? Certainly not—there is simply not sufficient detail in the papers to pinpoint precisely what led the author to mistakenly conclude that N-rays existed.

Polywater, initially known as anomalous water, was "discovered" in the early 1960s by a Russian scientist named Nikdlai Fedyakin, working at a laboratory about one hundred miles from Moscow. This form of water had several extremely strange qualities. It boiled at a temperature well above water's normal boiling point and froze at a point well below water's normal freezing point. Further, polywater was said to be a more stable form of the H_2O molecule. This led to at least one scientist making the dire prediction that, if even the smallest amount of polywater was allowed to contaminate natural water supplies, natural water molecules would spontaneously change into the more stable polywater form, thus ending all life on Earth due to the radically different characteristics of polywater. (Readers familiar with the work of Kurt Vonnegut Jr. will recognize at once the similarity between polywater and the mythical substance "ice nine" created in Vonnegut's 1963 novel *Cat's Cradle*.)

Russian research on polywater quickly moved from the provinces to a prestigious laboratory in Moscow. At first polywater attracted little attention in Western scientific circles. When it did, however, there was an explosion of papers on the topic in numerous scientific journals. Between 1962 and 1975 several hundred papers on polywater appeared. For various technical reasons, polywater could be produced only in minute quantities inside sealed glass tubes with equally minute diameters. The debate over the existence of polywater turned on one crucial point—whether the water produced in these tubes was pure H_2O or impure, the impurities leaching out of the glass and changing the properties of the pure water. Proponents of polywater claimed they had produced pure polywater, with no impurities. Other scientists who tried to produce polywater in their laboratories consistently ended up with nothing more than impure water of the normal molecular configuration. The proponents responded that the reason the skeptics couldn't produce true polywater was that they hadn't learned how to do it just right. While such a rejoinder was appropriate at first, it quickly became little more than a nonfalsifiable hypothesis in the form of a desperate excuse that proponents used to explain away every failure by the skeptics to produce "true" polywater. As the 1960s faded into the 1970s, it became clear that polywater did not exist and claims for its reality were based on impure water, as the skeptics had argued from the first. By the mid-1970s polywater was a dead issue.

The similarities between the N-ray and polywater episodes are instructive. One similarity was the use by proponents of both phenomena of post-hoc excuses in the form of nonfalsifiable hypotheses in the defense of their claims. Thus, such techniques for defending untenable claims are not limited to pseudosciences and the paranormal. They appear in legitimate science in those—happily rather rare—situations where commitment to the reality of a certain phenomenon is stronger than the data on which that commitment is based. The much more common use of nonfalsifiable hypotheses in pseudosciences and the paranormal is due simply to the near-total lack of real phenomena in these areas to begin with.

As was the case with N-rays, it would be impossible to pinpoint the exact procedural errors made in every experiment that seemed to produce evidence of polywater. We know, of course, the general nature of the errors made, but that is different from an exact explanation for every case on record. However, as in the case of N-rays, it is not necessary for the skeptic to explain away every seemingly positive instance of a claimed phenomenon before rejecting the phenomenon. In the polywater case, as well as in the case of N-rays, the total failure of careful experimentation to turn up evidence for the reality of the phenomenon, combined with a general explanation for what went wrong, was more than sufficient for scientists to reject the existence of the phenomenon.

The same principle of rejecting a finding even if no scientific flaw can be found in the experiment, on the grounds that the result cannot be replicated, is universal in science. Science is littered with experiments reporting some particular result that, upon later attempts, fails to replicate.

In the cases of N-rays and polywater, one cannot specify the exact date on which these aberrations came to the attention of the scientific community, much less the public at large. Such is not the case with cold fusion, the final scientific mistake to be considered here. On Thursday, March 23, 1989, chemists Stanley Pons and Martin Fleischmann held a news conference at the University of Utah that was widely covered on the national news programs that evening. They announced that they had discovered a method for producing nuclear fusion using simple equipment at room temperature. The term *cold fusion* was immediately coined to describe this phenomenon. Over the next few years great controversy raged over whether or not cold fusion was real or illusory. The history of the controversy has been examined in detail in three books (Close 1991; Huizenga 1992; Taubes 1993). Of the three, that by Gary Taubes is probably the most comprehensive. Rothman (1989–1990) has published an article-length summary.

Nuclear fusion occurs when atomic nuclei are brought so close together that they stick to each other. The mass of the stuck-together nuclei is less than that of the separate individual nuclei. The "extra" mass is converted into energy, with the amount of energy determined by Einstein's famous equation $E = mc^2$, where E is energy, m is mass, and c is the speed of light. Since c^2 is a huge number, even a very small mass, such as that of atomic nuclei, will result in the release of a great amount of energy.

If this was all there was to it, fusion would be easy. However, in order to get atomic nuclei close enough to actually fuse, the natural repulsive force that exists between nuclei when they are brought close together must be overcome. This takes a huge amount of energy. The conventional method of achieving fusion is to use heat on the order of hundreds of millions of degrees to sufficiently speed up the nuclei so that the repulsive forces will be overcome. Needless to say, this is both difficult and expensive. Still, since fusion would be a relatively clean source of energy (it produces little of the radioactive waste that nuclear fission does), it has been the object of considerable research funding. Given the clean nature of fusion energy and the great expense of obtaining it using the conventional superheated methods, one can understand how attractive a method would be for obtaining this sort of energy using a cheap apparatus at room temperature. This is exactly what Pons and Fleischmann claimed at their news conference to have done.

The news conference immediately raised suspicions on the part of many scientists. The absolutely standard way to announce a new scientific result is to first publish it in a professional scientific journal in the relevant field. Before a paper can be published in such a journal, it is carefully reviewed by other scientists who are experts in the area of research the paper concerns. These experts point out any flaws in the paper in terms of methodology, statistical analysis, citation of the relevant scientific literature, and the like. Only after a paper has passed this type of scrutiny, called *peer review*, will it be accepted for publication and finally published. Peer review is one major, but certainly not foolproof, guard against the publication of the results of scientific mistakes and faulty experiments. The time to hold the news conference is after the paper has been published, and it is generally considered unethical to "go public" with one's results before publication, let alone before even submitting a paper to a journal, which Pons and Fleischmann had done.

What did Pons and Fleischmann point to at their news conference to argue that they had actually achieved cold fusion? There were two measures that led them to the conclusion that fusion was taking place in their small fusion "cells," which were really little more than large jars that held electrodes of palladium or platinum in a bath of heavy water (D_2O). One was heat. It was claimed that the cells produced more heat than would be expected if no fusion was occurring. The other measure was gamma rays. Fusion produces gamma rays, and Pons and Fleischmann claimed to have found gamma rays coming from their fusion cells. One might think that it is an easy matter to measure these two variables, especially heat. One would be wrong. Both variables require very sensitive measurements requiring much experience. Scientists with real experience in the measurement of these two variables in the conditions under which Pons and Fleischmann were operating were nuclear physicists. Pons and Fleischmann, as chemists, had relatively little experience with such measurements. Working outside one's area of specialization can be dangerous because one will probably be less aware of the subtleties and pitfalls of experimentation and measurement in a field in which one is not an expert. The history of parapsychology, for example, is littered with scientists respected in their own fields who embarrassed themselves by making blunders when they assumed, incorrectly, that they were also experts in other areas of experimentation. Pons and Fleischmann's unfamiliarity with the details of measurement of heat and gamma rays led them into serious error.

A second factor that caused scientists to be suspicious of Pons and Fleischmann's claims at the news conference was the fact that if the claims of cold fusion were true, several basic laws of physics would have been in jeopardy. Recalling that extraordinary claims demand extraordinary proof, it was obviously going to take more than claims unsubstantiated by published results to convince scientists that cold fusion had been demonstrated. However, since the apparatus used was relatively straightforward and was visible in the background in a videotape shown at the news conference, and since Pons and Fleischmann did give a general description of their basic method, for the next several months numerous laboratories around the world tried to replicate the results.

When groups of researchers attempt to replicate an exciting new finding, even if that finding is artifactual, some will "succeed" in the replication, while some will correctly fail to replicate. The seeming successes may be due to various types of errors of experimentation. In the heated atmosphere of the first few months following Pons and Fleischmann's news conference, it was the allegedly successful replications that got the lion's share of attention, both from the popular media and from Pons and Fleischmann, who tended to dismiss failures as being due to "not doing it right." Alas, they failed to be explicit about what "doing it right" consisted of in terms of exact methodology. As time passed, it was established that the seemingly successful replications were due to various sources of errors, some quite subtle. When these sources of error were eliminated, so too was evidence for cold fusion. Close (1991) reviewed many of these replications and showed what went wrong to mislead the researchers into thinking that they had obtained fusion.

One laboratory in particular seemed to be especially able to replicate Pons and Fleischmann's findings of excess heat in their fusion cells—and to find tritium as well. Standard physical theory requires that tritium be produced as a result of fusion. Pons and Fleischmann had never reported finding any tritium, but tritium, as well as heat, was reported in cold fusion cells in the laboratory of John Bockris at Texas A&M University. The combined finding of tritium and heat was taken as strong support for the reality of cold fusion. Alas, the tritium appeared only sporadically and, like other cold fusion findings, could not be reproduced. The actual pattern of the appearance of tritium suggested the possibility that it was fraudulently being added to some cold fusion cells (Taubes 1993).

The finding of excess heat in the fusion cells in Bockris's lab has a particularly interesting explanation. It is a perfect example of how disregard for the basic rules of scientific evidence kept the cold fusion debate going. Even in the total absence of cold fusion, sometimes a cold fusion cell would run a little hotter than expected, while others would run slightly cooler. That is, not each cell would be at exactly the same temperature. The temperature of all the cells taken as a group would vary around some average. Cells running cooler than expected were negative results, and Bockris wasn't interested in negative results, which he said "can be obtained without skill and experience" (quoted in Taubes 1993, 322). Such negative results were simply tossed in a drawer and not considered. When a cell ran slightly warmer than expected, this was taken as evidence for cold fusion.

N-rays and polywater died fairly quiet deaths once the scientific community realized the nature of the flaws in the experiments said to support these phenomena. And neither had any following among the general public. Such is not the case with cold fusion. Disgraced in the eyes of the scientific community, cold fusion became the topic of cartoons (figure 1.2).

Pons left the academic world in 1992 to work for a private industrial concern still looking for evidence of cold fusion. The Japanese Ministry of Trade and Industry continued to support cold fusion work for a few years in the mid-1990s. The attention that the Internet continues to give cold fusion ensures that it will live on forever, supported by a small group of true believers who will always insist that the ultimate proof of cold fusion is just around the corner, with that one more crucial experiment that has to be done. Or with just another infusion of money from some lucky investors given the opportunity of a lifetime to fund the latest huckster's honest-to-god, guaranteed cold fusion gimmick. Given the well-earned sleazy reputation of cold fusion, it is no longer referred to as such by those who claim it exists. The new name, which sounds much more sciencey, is "low energy nuclear reactions."

The interest in cold fusion faded away by the early 1990s. Since then "isolated groups [of scientists] have continued its pursuit, but have yet to produce a credible 'reference experiment' that provides unambiguous evidence" of any cold fusion effects (Berlinguette et al. 2019, 45.) The term *cold fusion* was replaced by *low*

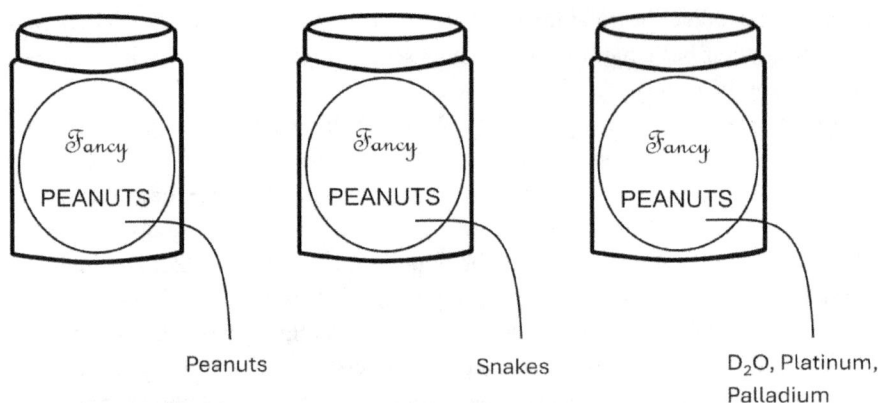

Figure 1.2. Cold fusion: Evolution of a practical joke. Cartoon by Karen Hopkin

energy nuclear reactions to hide the failure to find any evidence for cold fusion. In 2016 Berlinguette and colleagues undertook to use state-of-the-art technology, and develop new technology, to see if they could finally find any evidence for cold fusion. They kept a "low profile to avoid distraction" (Berlinguette et al. 2019, 45) and, one presumes, to avoid negative input from the broader scientific community. Funded by Google (Gibney 2019), the group consisted of experts from several major universities. Their goal was to "re-evaluate cold fusion to a high standard of scientific rigour" (Berlinguette et al. 2019, 45). The groups spent two years trying to find evidence for cold fusion. The results were negative—no evidence for cold fusion was found. But the effort was not in vain. In the course of the research, new technologies were developed to study "materials and phenomena that we otherwise might not have considered. We set out looking for cold fusion, and instead benefited contemporary research topics in unexpected ways" (49). So, in the end, the cold fusion debacle turned out to have been beneficial, even though the original sought-after effect does not exist.

In the cases of scientific mistakes, or pathological science, described above, those making the claims were blinded by their excitement about their, alleged, revolutionary discoveries. One famous scientist showed how such discoveries should be approached. When Wilhelm Rontgen first noticed the phenomenon that would lead him to the discovery of X-rays, he didn't believe it. As Kean (2010, 271) tells the story in his wonderful book *The Disappearing Spoon*, "Rontgen assumed he'd made a mistake somewhere" and spent weeks "determined to prove himself wrong." Only when he had convinced himself, using objective methods, that what he had seen was real did he announce his findings. Rontgen, a scientific hero, won the first Nobel Prize in Physics in 1901. Figure 1.3 shows Rontgen on a 1951 commemorative postage stamp from Germany.

CONSPIRACY THEORIES

The term *conspiracy theory* is usually taken to refer to some more-or-less crazy, crackpot belief that would be rejected by sane, thinking individuals. This is too limited a definition. There really have been and are conspiracies. Shermer (2022, xi–xii, emphasis in original) makes a distinction between two types of conspiracy theories. Specifically, between "*paranoid conspiracy theories*, involving ultra-secret and uber-powerful entities, for which there is little or no evidence and which are largely driven by paranoia and *realistic conspiracy theories* pertaining to normal public institutions and corporate entities that are conspiring to manipulate the system to gain an unfair, immoral, and sometimes illegal advantage over others." The conspiracy theories pertaining to things such as UFO cover-ups, hiding evidence that vaccines

Figure 1.3. Wilhelm Rontgen on a 1951 West German stamp, Scott Catalog # 686. Author's collection

cause autism, that the medical establishment is hiding a cure for cancer, or that COVID is a hoax are examples of the paranoid type discussed in this book.

A major theme of this book is that the normal operation of the human perceptual and cognitive systems is responsible for the acceptance of many pseudoscientific and paranormal beliefs. It is not that a person who honestly believes that they saw a flying saucer (or Bigfoot or a ghost) has some sort of deficiency in their perceptual/cognitive systems. Rather, these systems were working normally but under difficult conditions that did not allow the systems to return a correct interpretation of what was actually present.

The same can be said to a certain extent of believers in paranoid conspiracy theories. It is not that they are generally deficient in intelligence or cognitive abilities. Rather, they are in social situations where those normally operating systems are provided with limited or distorted inputs that, almost inevitably, lead to the acceptance of even the most outlandish paranoid type of conspiracy theories. It is a situation of "garbage in, garbage out." Nonetheless, research does show that there are some differences between those who accept and those who do not accept paranoid-type conspiracy theories.

In general, whether they concern pseudoscientific or paranormal topics or not, the paranoid conspiracy theory belief systems do share a major component with the belief systems of pseudoscientific proponents: inherent nonfalsifiability. When the alleged evidence for a particular conspiracy has been refuted, the proponent will often point to the very lack of evidence for the theory as evidence for the theory! That is, it is argued that the lack of evidence is not because the theory is false but instead is due to the supreme effectiveness of the conspiracy itself in seeing to it that no convincing evidence for the conspiracy can be found. In this sort of cloud-cuckoo-land, any belief, no matter how absurd, can be sustained for a very long time indeed.

A good way to evaluate conspiracy theories is to ask, "If there really had been such a conspiracy, how could it actually have been carried out? How many people would have to be involved?" When the answer to the first question is "with great difficulty" and the answer to the second is "hundreds, maybe thousands" and no one, not a single sane person, has come forth to say something like, "Yes, I was part of the fifty-person team that took care of the alien bodies found at Roswell," then the conspiracy claim can safely be consigned to the rubbish heap.

As to why some people accept even the craziest conspiracy theories, paranormal or otherwise, Brian Dunning (2017) says it well in his podcast on the (originally) satirical theory that Finland doesn't exist. He notes that a conspiracy theory "offers its believers the most tantalizing of rewards: an insider's perspective on forbidden knowledge. The superpower of knowing what the sheeple don't. A superior position, intellectual empowerment, bought cheaply through nothing more than a willingness to dismiss reality in favor of a spectral alternative." Supporting Dunning's hypothesis is a positive relationship, consistent albeit rather weak, between acceptance of conspiracy theories and one's need to see oneself as somehow unique (Imhoff and Lamberty 2017; Hart and Graether 2018).

People are more likely to accept conspiracy theories, paranormal or not, when they perceive themselves as having less control over their situation. Conversely, they are less likely to accept such theories when they believe that they have more control (Van Prooijen and Acker 2015). This effect seems to apply even to perception. Whitson and Galinsky (2008) found that experiencing a lack of control increased peoples' tendency to see visual patterns where none existed. Van Prooijen, Douglas, and De Inocencio (2018) studied the perception of illusory patterns, that is, the tendency to see patterns where none really exist. They found that those who were more likely to perceive nonexistent patterns in visual stimuli or in a series of random coin tosses were also more likely to accept paranormal beliefs and conspiracy theories. They concluded that "illusory pattern perception is a central cognitive mechanism accounting for conspiracy theories and supernatural beliefs" (320).

Believers in conspiracy theories are more likely to commit conjunction fallacy errors. These are errors where "people overestimate the likelihood of co-occurring events" (Brotherton and French 2014, 238). This results in believing that unrelated events are causally related when they are not. This, in turn, results in a search for the cause of the (nonexistent) relationships, and a conspiracy theory is born. Given this sequence of cognitive processes, it would be predicted that believers in conspiracy theories would be more likely to see "agency"—some conscious entity responsible for the cooccurrence involved. This is what Brotherton and French found.

Brotherton and French's (2014) findings were confirmed and extended by Douglas and colleagues (2016). These authors found that individuals who accepted more conspiracy theories were more likely to attribute agency to nonliving things. They were also more likely to attribute conscious intentions to geometric objects moving around in a short video clip. These findings relate belief in conspiracy theories to paranormal belief since such beliefs are also highly correlated with acceptance of conspiracy theories (Darwin, Neave, and Holmes, 2011). As discussed further on (page 19), attributing agency to nonexistent entities (i.e., ghosts) or inanimate objects is a characteristic of paranormal belief.

Bowes and colleagues (2021) took a slightly different tack on belief in conspiracy theories. They studied whether different personality traits, both normal and abnormal, as opposed to perceptual or cognitive mechanisms, could predict acceptance of such theories. They used a large sample and several measures of personality and what they termed "conspiratorial ideation." They found a "mixture of narcissism, immodesty, and undue intellectual certainty, on the one hand, conjoined with poor impulse control, angst, interpersonal alienation, and reduced inquisitiveness, on the other" (433–34) in those prone to conspiracy beliefs. They further suggested that this pattern "may provide a personological recipe for a tendency to impetuously latch on to spurious but confidently held causal narratives that account for one's distress and resentment" (434).

Bowes, Costello, and Tasimi (2023) performed a meta-analysis of 170 studies of the personality characteristics of conspiracy theorists. This huge number shows how much research has been devoted to this question. As will be seen throughout this book, one characteristic that is common in those who accept various paranormal and pseudoscientific claims, but not necessarily conspiracy theories, is a tendency to perceive meaningful patterns in randomness. So it is especially interesting in the present context that "seeing patterns in their absence" (281) was common among conspiracy theorists. This effect in the meta-analysis confirmed the same finding in the earlier paper by Bowes and colleagues (2021).

WHY STUDY PSEUDOSCIENTIFIC CLAIMS?

The serious examination of pseudoscientific and paranormal claims by scientists and scholars who are skeptical about the existence of such phenomena is not a recent development. In the late nineteenth and early twentieth centuries, the claims of spiritualists were carefully scrutinized by several scientists (see chapter 2). A new interest in evaluating pseudoscientific claims arose during the early 1970s as scientists and educators became concerned with the public's uncritical acceptance of almost every type of pseudoscientific claim. This resulted in the formation in 1976 of the Committee for the Scientific Investigation of Claims of the Paranormal (CSICOP). CSICOP changed its name in 2006 to the Committee for Skeptical Inquiry (CSI). The members of CSICOP, including scientists, writers, educators, journalists, and philosophers, founded the organization because of the concern about the "uncritical acceptance by wide sections of the public of many claims of 'paranormal' phenomena as true, even without testing" (Kurtz 1976–1977, 6). The objectives of CSICOP/CSI included critical, unbiased, objective research into pseudoscientific claims; the publication of the results of these studies; and a commitment not "to reject on a priori grounds, antecedent to inquiry, any or all [paranormal] claims, but rather to examine them openly, completely, objectively, and carefully" (Kurtz 1976–1977, 6).

This is very different from a common approach of scientists and scholars, whose response to pseudoscientific claims is simply to dismiss them as nonsense. This latter is a most unfortunate attitude. It is important to examine these claims objectively for at least four reasons. First, the claim might be true. Failure to examine it would then delay the acquisition of new, perhaps important, knowledge. Second, if the claim is false, the scientific community, which is heavily supported by the public through taxes, has a responsibility to inform the public. Ignoring a claim and not testing it leaves the field to the promoters of such claims and deprives the public of the information needed to make informed choices. Third, several important psychological issues relate to the study of pseudoscience and the paranormal. Why, for example, do people so strongly believe in theories that not only have no evidence to support them but also have been shown time and again to be flat wrong? Fourth, and finally, the unthinking acceptance of pseudoscientific claims poses real dangers. Believers may act on their beliefs and cause physical harm, even death, to themselves and others. This is most evident in the case of alternative medicine (chapter 11). In addition, as our society becomes more dependent on science and technology, we are all threatened by an increase in the uncritical acceptance of clearly incorrect, nonscientific superstitions and related beliefs.

The past decades have seen a great increase in the rejection of the basic scientific approach to establishing what is real and what isn't. This trend is seen in the refusal of parents to vaccinate their children (chapter 13) and, incredibly, in the renewed popularity of the belief that planet Earth is flat. Nichols (2017) has warned about "the death of expertise," where those with little or no knowledge of a particular topic consider themselves as knowledgeable about the topic as a true expert who has spent years studying the topic in question. Thus the antivaccination parents who have spent the total of a couple of days surfing antivax websites and now feel that their opinions are just as valid as those of a scientist who has spent years getting advanced degrees and doing research on the topic.

Belief in superstitions, many of which like astrology would now be called pseudosciences, and simple unfounded claims have probably been around as long as humanity. Objections to such beliefs also have a long history. The Jewish philosopher Maimonides (1135–1204) was a strong critic of astrology and might thus be thought of as an early critic of pseudoscience. However, his objections to astrology were not based on any actual evidence regarding the lack of validity of astrology. Rather, he objected only to "judicial" astrology, which was concerned with predicting human behavior and was not, as the name incorrectly implies, used in court. His objection was based on the fact that if astrology was true then it deprived humans of free will and this would render religious dictates and commandments "superfluous" (Lerner 1968, 155). Maimonides did not object to "medical" astrology, which was used to diagnose illnesses. So his objections were not evidence based.

Giovanni Pico Della Mirandola (1463–1494) came closer to a modern rejection of astrology (Rabin 2008). He argued that the association of the planet Mars with aggressiveness was what would now be called associative magical thinking. Mars was the god of war. War is obviously associated with aggression. Therefore, someone born when Mars was astrologically important would be more aggressive. Further, the association of the planet with Mars was specific to Western culture. The planet had different associations in different cultures. Such modern-sounding rejections of pseudosciences were very rare until the twentieth century. Nonetheless, such criticisms even of witchcraft (e.g., Henningsen 1980) sprang up from time to time through the Middle Ages and into the nineteenth century.

It is one thing to criticize beliefs in pseudosciences and related beliefs. But simple criticism is not sufficient. This first became clear to me when, back in the early 1980s, I started teaching a course on pseudoscience and the paranormal at Pace University. As important as careful criticism was, and is, it is equally important and more interesting to, where possible, test the claims that grow out of such beliefs. It was not until well into the twentieth century that the full array of experimental methods and their associated statistical techniques were brought to bear to evaluate such claims.

Also lacking in mere criticism is any attempt to explain why people accept false claims in the first place, especially when the evidence clearly contradicts the belief. Platitudes about a "will to believe" traditionally have been used to explain belief. But such a "will" is really not an explanation at all as it now requires an explanation of why the "will" exists in the first place. It's like saying that I collect stamps because I have a "will to collect stamps." That doesn't exactly clear up the situation!

This state of affairs changed around the 1970s when cognitive psychologists began to wonder about why people believed in claims that were clearly false. In a surprisingly short period of time research on basic cognitive and perceptual processes showed that several factors were responsible for belief in pseudoscientific and related theories and phenomena. First, it became clear that perception was not a simple process by which some external stimulus is transferred, without much change, and experienced in the brain. Rather, it was found that perception is a highly constructive process. This basic concept had been known since the late nineteenth century, but it was not applied to the understanding of paranormal-type experiences until the 1960s and 1970s. Because the incoming sensory information is not sufficient in and of itself to generate an accurate perception of the world, the brain must combine that information with knowledge and beliefs built up through experience. If such knowledge or beliefs are incorrect, perception can also be incorrect. This effect is most evident when the incoming sensory input is minimal, thus allowing beliefs and knowledge to have an inordinate influence on perceptual experience. Perception is a process during which the final perception of the world is constructed from both the sensory input and knowledge and beliefs already stored in the brain.

The brain evolved to be a pattern-recognizing device. Our brains, and animal brains as well, have a strong tendency to perceive patterns even when no pattern actually exists. This might seem to be a disadvantage in evolutionary terms, but it is definitely not. It is far better to incorrectly perceive that some danger (say a saber-toothed tiger hiding in the brush) is present when it isn't than to miss one that is present. When this pattern-detecting process detects patterns that are not present, it is termed pareidolia. Pareidolia produces perceptions of UFOs, lake monsters, Bigfoots, ghosts, images of Christ on toast and in window stains. It is very important to make it clear that people who perceive such things are not stupid, crazy, intoxicated, or lying. Rather they have been misled by a perfectly natural brain process that usually produces an accurate perception of the world but, for the moment, just went a bit off the rails. These experiences can and do seem very real and can and do produce powerful emotional reactions. That does not in any way mean that the ghosts, UFOs, or images of Jesus were really there.

Memory is now known to be a far more complex, and less accurate, process than once believed. In much the same way that false perceptions can be constructed, so can false, and even bizarre and terrifying, memories. One aspect of memory that is especially involved in the maintenance of false beliefs is confirmation bias, also known as "myside bias" to reflect the fact that the bias may result in the disconfirmation of beliefs one does not accept (Mercier 2017). This is the very human tendency to seek out and selectively remember information that is consistent with our beliefs. Equally, we tend to explain away or simply ignore information that runs contrary tour beliefs. Closely related to confirmation bias is the availability heuristic. This is the tendency to judge as more frequent events that are more easily retrieved from long-term memory (Reber 2017). Thus people tend to think that flying on a commercial airline is more dangerous than driving a car when just the opposite is the case. It is easier to remember cases of horrible airline crashes that kill many people at once than car accidents that kill a few at a time and get less wide publicity. The latter is judged as being more dangerous. In terms of pseudosciences, a believer in astrology will be more likely to store in memory examples that confirm their belief, and thus it will be easier for the believer to retrieve confirmatory examples. The combination of false perceptions and memory illusions provides a powerful explanation for false beliefs, whether pseudoscientific or otherwise.

More recently a third factor has been recognized as important for creating and maintaining false beliefs. This is the concept of agency, which is the idea that the behavior of sentient beings can be explained through understanding the reasons why they do things. More basically, the behavior of such beings happens because they have agency—intentions to behave in a certain way. The problem comes because humans have a strong tendency to attribute agency to inanimate objects. Or to assume that when an inanimate object moves in a way that is not immediately explainable, some entity that had agency must have caused it to move. As French and Stone (2014, 273) put it, agency is the "tendency to assume that events happen because some intentional agent makes them happen." This was demonstrated by Heider and Simmel in 1944. They showed that when individuals saw a short film of geometric shapes (triangles and a circle) moving about, there was a very strong tendency to attribute personality traits to the shapes and emotional reasons for the shapes' actions. This sort of result has generated additional research (see Rutherford and Kuhlmeier 2014 for a review), much of which shows that the tendency to attribute agency to moving but inanimate objects is innate. This is probably a spillover for a very adaptive bias to see certain kinds of movement in the environment as due to some living entity, perhaps one with dangerous intentions. Biological motion, that is, motion caused by actual living entities in the environment, tends to easily and rapidly "pop out" from random background movement. Thus when a door swings shut and we don't feel any breeze, it is easy to assume that a ghost—an entity with agency—caused the door to move. Humans are loath to conclude that something "just happened" and leave it at that. We look for agency and are very likely to find it even if it isn't there.

Finally, humans are terrible intuitive statisticians. Our brains did not evolve to take careful note of the relative frequency of events and make a rational decision based on such data. As noted, we greatly overemphasize events that come easily to mind even when they are not at all representative of the true situation. This is especially true for the evaluation of risks. If the study of the cognitive processes underlying the acceptance of incorrect beliefs can be summarized succinctly, it would be to say that one cannot always rely on personal observations, experience, and emotions as a guide to reality. The world is just too complex for that, and one must rely instead on objective data, not subjective beliefs, to determine what is or isn't true. This is the approach taken throughout this book. For each topic, the evidence is reviewed and then the cognitive processes that led to acceptance of the belief under discussion are examined. The specific processes will vary from topic to topic, and in some cases a topic may be driven by a process or combination of processes unique to that belief.

Alcock (2018) has covered the research on why beliefs that are wrong are often accepted in the face of evidence to the contrary. He goes into considerable detail on the psychological mechanisms involved, many of which support belief in pseudoscientific and paranormal claims. One thing that is not a factor is intelligence—those who espouse such beliefs are not any less intelligent than average. However, some personality factors play a role in individual differences in the degree of acceptance of pseudoscientific, paranormal, and related beliefs. Bouvet and Bonnefon (2015) studied differences between individuals who differed on the personality dimension of reflective thinking. Reflective thinkers take more time to evaluate a situation before making a judgment. Nonreflective thinkers are more likely to arrive at their conclusions without much careful evaluation. In a series of clever experiments, the authors set up situations where people were exposed to what were described as "uncanny experiences," such as witnessing what appeared to be a real ESP experience. They found that "irrespective of their prior beliefs in the supernatural, non-reflective thinkers are more likely than reflective thinkers to accept supernatural causation" for the uncanny experience (Bouvet and Bonnefon 2015, 955). The wide acceptance in society of such claims also raises important sociological issues, which have been discussed by Goode (2000).

It is my hope that combining discussions of the actual evidence on a wide variety of different beliefs with descriptions of the cognitive fallacies that led to their acceptance will promote a better understanding of why so many beliefs can be both incorrect but often widely accepted. It is also hoped that this type of analysis will enable readers to protect themselves against current as well as new fallacious claims that will undoubtedly crop up in the future.

Responsibility to Inform the Public about the Truth of Paranormal Claims

A glance at the occult books section in any moderately large bookstore is all that is needed to convince one of the huge market for pseudoscientific and paranormal claims in this country. A 2005 Gallup poll found that 24 percent of Americans believed that aliens had visited Earth, 25 percent believed in astrology, 32 percent accepted the reality of ghosts, and 41 percent believed in ESP. John Mack's (1997) book *Abduction: Human Encounters with Aliens* was a bestseller when it was published. Every kind of pseudoscientific claim finds eager buyers. Psychics, palm readers, tarot card readers, mediums, and the like rarely lack for victims willing to shell out even thousands of dollars for readings and advice. Those who claim that Earth was visited in historical times by ancient astronauts, or that there is a mysterious area off Florida's east coast where ships and planes have disappeared, or that they can bend keys with sheer mind power, can make millions from books, films, and the lecture circuit. In short, the public spends a lot of time and money supporting the proponents of pseudoscience and the paranormal. As will be seen in the following chapters, there is not one bit of acceptable evidence to support these pseudoscientific claims, and much evidence exists that flatly contradicts them. This being the case, the continued claims by proponents of pseudoscience constitute nothing short of consumer fraud that costs the American public billions of dollars each year. In this situation, scientists have a strong responsibility to investigate pseudoscientific claims and to speak out vigorously when those claims are shown to be false.

Unfortunately, communication of the real data on the truth of pseudoscientific claims is often hampered by the media and grossly inaccurate websites. Online media, television programs, and newspapers are frequently more interested in presenting sensational claims than in carefully evaluating the truth of such claims. The media, both print and electronic, often act with extreme irresponsibility in covering pseudoscience and the paranormal. In the case of uncritical coverage of faith healers and psychic surgeons, this lack of responsibility on the part of the media has resulted in injury and death. Journalists often feel the need to cover "both sides" of a claim as if both are equally valid when one is total bunk.

The case for speaking out is even clearer regarding modern health and nutrition quackery, now known as "alternative medicine," which in the early 1980s was a ten-billion-dollar-a-year problem in the United States (Pepper 1984). The figure must be much higher now. The quacks' and charlatans' victims are most likely to be those least able to defend themselves—the desperate, the elderly, and the poor. However, in the last few years, the healthy worried well have become popular targets. Why rip off relatively poor victims when you can scam the wealthy worried well? A classic example is Gwyneth Paltrow's company Goop. Back in 2017 she started promoting healing stickers that you'd stick to your skin that would "rebalance the energy frequency in our bodies" (quoted in Salzberg 2017). These were initially said to have been made from the same material that NASA uses to make space suits. They weren't. But they were expensive: sixty dollars for ten. Almost identical stickers can be purchased at any toy store for a few pennies each.

Only through careful evaluation of pseudoscientific claims and seeing that the results of those evaluations are reported by the popular media can the public be fully informed. The proponents of pseudoscience and the paranormal, who make vast sums of money selling their wares, are unlikely to provide the public with accurate information. Scientists, then, have a responsibility to inform the public.

Dangers of Paranormal and Pseudoscientific Beliefs

Skeptics are often asked, "Who cares if there really isn't anything to astrology? What does it hurt if someone believes in it?" I've found that this question is frequently asked by proponents of pseudoscientific claims when they have been backed into a corner by the evidence. The answer can be made at three levels. At a philosophical level, most people would agree that it is harmful to hold invalid beliefs and that one should base one's life on a correct view of how the world operates. To do otherwise is to be deluded.

In the past thirty years there has been growing public acceptance of several pseudoscientific beliefs that have been, or have a real potential to be, harmful. One is the antivaccine movement, which got started in a serious way after the 1998 publication by Andrew Wakefield and colleagues of a fraudulent paper claiming that childhood vaccination causes autism. This has caused at least millions of parents to refuse to have their children vaccinated, leading to outbreaks of measles and increased risks of diseases that were once thought largely conquered. As of June 2018, there have been over one thousand cases of measles in the United States, a level not seen in decades. Although measles can be fatal, no deaths have been reported so far. These cases are almost entirely due to individuals refusing to be vaccinated or to have their children vaccinated.

The antivaccine movement has more than a bit of conspiracy theory paranoia in it. The numerous studies (described in chapter 13) that show the antivaccine claims to be simply false are dismissed as part of a conspiracy and cover-up orchestrated by big pharma with almost all medical doctors, medical researchers, and academics involved. On the face of it, this is an absurd theory since "big pharma" and the medical establishment would make a great deal more money treating the diseases vaccines prevent than they do selling vaccines.

Nowhere are the dangers of acceptance of false beliefs clearer than in the area of quack or "complementary and alternative" medicine (chapter 11). Numerous individuals who could have been treated successfully by real medicine have turned to quacks and their quack cures and have died as a result. These cases are especially tragic when parents subject their children to such treatments and the children die as a result. Charlatans and frauds take advantage of desperate people, and it is especially easy for them to do so with desperate parents. It may be understandable that one would want to avoid the obvious unpleasantness of chemical and radiation therapies for cancer. But these therapies actually work. And work quite well. In 1962 the five-year survival rate for children with acute lymphoblastic leukemia was 4 percent. Now it is 94 percent. For neuroblastoma, a brain tumor, the five-year survival rate went from 10 percent to 75 percent during the same period. Other childhood cancers show similar dramatic increases in survival. This was due to the work of real scientists applying strict rules of evidence to determine, scientifically, whether a proposed cure worked or not. Real medicine works. No quack can make anything close to such a claim.

These dramatic increases in the cure rates for cancer put the lie to the silly claims of those who believe that some sort of "real" cure for cancer is being kept secret by the pharmaceutical industry to continue making profits by selling cancer drugs. There will never be a single, one-size-fits-all cure for cancer. *Cancer* is a term covering hundreds of different specific diseases with different specific causes, genetic or environmental or both, and different symptoms. Each type needs to be attacked with treatments specific for that type.

Mental health quackery in the form of useless psychotherapies does not result in as many deaths as quack medicine, although such deaths do occur. However, fringe psychotherapies, of which there seem to be an unending number, cause untold misery to those who could be helped by truly effective, evidence-based therapeutic approaches. The reasons why both patients and therapists continue to believe that objectively useless or actually harmful therapies are effective makes a fascinating story that will be discussed in chapters 5 and 11.

The personal damage done by uncritical acceptance of paranormal claims can be clearly seen in faith healing and psychic surgery (chapter 10). People go to these fraudulent healers and often are convinced, incorrectly, that they have been cured. Thus, they may not seek legitimate medical help. By the time they realize that they have not, in fact, been cured, they may be beyond even medical help. Years ago Nolen (1974) documented such cases. Of all the proponents of pseudoscience, faith healers and psychic surgeons are the most dangerous—they kill people. The magician Jamy Ian Swiss attended a faith healing program and saw this sort of thing in action. His description of one person's reaction to the healer is very moving:

> A woman came to the microphone. She was shy, and awkward, and spoke quietly, and with what was clearly great gratitude and an overwhelming sense of relief. She stepped up and began to speak, explaining that recently she had detected a lump in her breast that frightened her. She had eventually seen her doctor, who wanted to run some tests. But she was afraid of the tests, she said to us, through her tears, and she had waited, and she had not returned to the doctor, because she was afraid. But now, she said, trembling with the release from the weight of her fear, she knew that on *this very night* she had felt it—she had come to be healed and indeed now she *knew that she had* been healed, and that she knew this with such certainty, praise be, that she knew that she *did not have to* return to her doctor again. (Swiss 2020, 153, emphasis in original).

From the point of view of society at large, uncritical acceptance of paranormal belief systems can be extremely damaging. The classic example is the witchcraft craze that swept Europe between approximately the middle of the fourteenth and the beginning of the eighteenth centuries. During that period, well over two hundred thousand people were burned, tortured, or hanged as witches (Robbins 1959). The belief in the reality of witches is a classic example of a paranormal belief. It shares many characteristics with modern-day paranormal belief systems. We will see, for example, in chapters 7 and 8 that proponents of the reality of UFOs as extraterrestrial spacecraft argue that some of the strongest evidence for the reality of UFOs is the many reports of UFOs that have been seen and reported by reliable, trained, sane observers. Yet even a short perusal of the literature on witchcraft will reveal hundreds of similar reports of witches turned in by reliable, trustworthy witnesses. Of course, not one of these reports was true.

Another similarity between the belief in witchcraft and the belief in numerous modern pseudoscientific claims is the presence of a nonfalsifiable hypothesis as a cornerstone of the belief system. For the poor individual accused of being a witch, the hypothesis often spelled a slow and lingering death. There was no possible piece of evidence that could show that the accused was not a witch. Even an accusation based on extremely flimsy evidence could result in an arrest. At this point, the accused was asked to confess to the charges. If the confession was not made, the accused could be tortured. If a confession was still not made, the torture continued. Johannes Junius, the burgomaster of Bamberg, made this point in his last letter to his daughter before he was executed as a witch in August 1628. He described the several days of torture he endured without confessing and then said, "When at last the executioner led me back into the cell, he said to me, 'Sir, I beg you, confess something, whether it be true or not. Invent something, for you cannot endure the torture which you will be put to; and even if you bear it all, yet you will not escape, not even if you were an earl, but one torture will follow another until you say you are a witch'" (Robbins 1959, 292–93). There was no way out. If one confessed without torture to being a witch, one was executed. If one did not confess at once, one was tortured until one did—and was then executed. If one confessed and later recanted the confession, the torture started anew. To make matters worse for the accused, who might be willing to confess at once simply to escape torture, one was asked to name acquaintances who had also engaged in witchcraft. If names were not forthcoming, they were extracted, again, under torture. These other individuals were then rounded up and tortured into confessing and naming still more "witches," and so the horrible cycle went on.

It should not be thought that in our modern and "enlightened" age witch hunts are a thing of the past. In the 1980s and 1990s, hysteria over bizarre claims of mass abuse and killings, usually of children, by a well-organized and highly secret group of Satan worshipers swept the United States and other countries (chapter 12). Innocent parents and teachers were accused, and many went to prison. As in the medieval witch trials, there was no physical evidence. The victims of this modern witch hunt were not convicted on the basis of testimony extracted under torture but by something eerily similar: the testimony of children who had been subjected to interrogation techniques such that many of them came to truly believe the fantastic accusations they were making.

The medieval witch delusion also provides what is presumably one of the first reported cases of "special pleading" for a pseudoscientific claim. Proponents of pseudoscience often claim that the usual rules of science are too strict (tacitly admitting that their evidence is scientifically inadequate to prove their claims) and that less stringent criteria of proof should be allowed for this or that pseudoscientific idea. In this vein, Robbins (1959) noted a "distinguished professor of law at the University of Toulouse advocate[d] the suspension of rules in witch trials, because 'not one out of a million witches would be accused or punished, if regular legal procedure were followed'" (34). In more modern times, special pleading is often seen in areas of pseudoscience such as psychotherapies and alternative medicine.

An even more terrible pseudoscience, the phony racial theories of the Nazis in the twentieth century, resulted in loss of life on a scale vastly greater than that caused by the witchcraft delusion. Although the role of the occult per se in the rise of Nazism has been overestimated, it is clear that the racial theories on which Hitler built the Holocaust were pure pseudoscience.

Another commonly heard defense of paranormal claims goes like this: "Reality is relative. If I decide to believe in astrology, then it becomes real in my own reality and works for me." In other words, belief determines the structure of reality. An extreme version of this rather silly position is held by many parapsychologists who try to explain their critics' repeated failures to find any evidence confirming the existence of ESP by saying that the critics don't believe the phenomenon to be real and, therefore, for the critics it isn't. We'll see in chapter 4 that a much better explanation is that the critics conduct better, more tightly controlled experiments than do the believers. In any event, this position that belief determines reality puts its proponents in a rather unpleasant position. In Nazi Germany millions of people really believed that Jews were subhuman. If belief determines reality, then this belief must really have been true. Those who hold that belief determines reality have never bothered to think their notion through to its repellent logical conclusions.

Unfortunately, the idea that belief determines reality is an integral part of much of the "new age" belief system. This is exemplified by the 2006 book *The Secret* by Rhonda Byrne. The "secret" is the "law of attraction," which simply states that if you wish for something enough it will come to you. A person's desires can directly influence the outcome of events. While on the surface this may sound simply silly, the book was a huge bestseller in the United States and spawned several additional books and films. A little thought reveals a very dark side to the secret. If it is true that wanting something (money, fame, love, health, etc.) hard enough will bring it to you, it must also be the case that when bad things happen it was because the individual didn't want them not to happen hard enough. So people who die of cancer do so because they just didn't have enough desire to live. I view this as a fundamentally evil idea. Truth is independent of belief. When the proponents of a pseudoscientific claim maintain that belief determines reality, it's a safe bet that they can't prove their point using legitimate rules of evidence.

The examples of the witch delusion and the Nazi horrors show the great damage done by the uncritical acceptance of pseudoscientific claims. Others will be encountered throughout this book. All might well have been avoided if the public had been educated in critical scientific thinking and had simply asked, "What evidence is there that what you are telling me is really true?"

Of course, not all pseudosciences have the vast potential for damage of the witch mania and Nazi racial theories. However, if one accepts faulty evidence, intellectual shoddiness and fraud, and twisted logic in the case of relatively benign pseudosciences, it becomes much easier to accept the same type of evidence when it is presented in support of much more damaging pseudosciences.

PSYCHICS AND PSYCHIC PHENOMENA

The term *psychic phenomena* conjures up an image of a psychic foretelling the future with great accuracy, of a psychic crime fighter leading police straight to where a body has been hidden, of a spiritualistic medium like John Edward contacting the dead and relaying to the living information only the dead could have known, or of an ordinary individual having a dream that later turns out to have correctly predicted an important event. This chapter will discuss the origins of spiritualism and examine contemporary claims for such phenomena. The more scientific sounding study of ESP, clairvoyance, and psychokinesis in parapsychological laboratories will be discussed in chapter 4, which will also discuss the psychic Uri Geller, as his alleged abilities were extensively tested in parapsychological laboratories. That Geller could equally well have been discussed in the present chapter points up the often fuzzy distinction between spectacular psychic claims and laboratory parapsychology.

SPIRITUALISM

Scientific investigation of psychic phenomena began in the mid-1800s as a result of the worldwide interest in spiritualism. Spiritualism was born in 1848 in the small New York town of Hydesville, about twenty-five miles southeast of Rochester. Two sisters, Kate and Margaret Fox (eleven and thirteen years old, respectively), produced strange knocks and rapping in their home, which were interpreted as messages from the dead. The effects were produced by various simple tricks, as the sisters later admitted (Kurtz 1985; Brandon 1983). An older sister took the young girls on tour, and a nationwide interest in spiritualism and communication with the dead sprang up in their wake. This interest quickly spread overseas. As interest in spiritualism grew, so did the number of spiritualistic mediums who claimed to be able to contact the spirit world and communicate with the dead. Mediums could be found in every city.

Communication with the dead typically took place at a seance, in which the medium and "sitters" would hold hands while seated around a table in the dark. Various phenomena occurred during the seance, varying from rather mundane rappings and knockings, through table tipping (in which the table seemed to move of its own accord), up to the most spectacular seances where "ectoplasm" would flow from the medium's body, actual spirits would appear, and objects would materialize out of thin air, presumably "apported" from the spirit world. Photographs of disembodied spirits floating near mediums were also produced in some quantity. It was these sorts of phenomena that convinced so many people of the truth of spiritualists' claims and of the reality of communication with the dead.

The rage for spiritualism attracted the attention of some of the period's leading scientists. Most were highly skeptical and critical of spiritualism, but several attended seances and came away convinced of the reality of spiritualistic phenomena. A few then instituted often impressive studies of individual spiritualists which, they claimed, gave solid scientific support to the claims of spiritualism. This type of research and interest led to the founding in England in 1882 of the Society for Psychical Research (SPR). The goal of the SPR was scientific investigation of spiritualistic and other psychic phenomena. As such, it represented an alliance between the spiritualists and the small portion of the scientific community that accepted their claims. As time passed, however, the alliance weakened and finally split. The split came about not because of doubt on the part of the scientists who belonged to the SPR but because of a fundamental difference with spiritualists over the correct interpretation of the phenomena that took place at seances (Cerullo 1982).

The spiritualists felt that these phenomena proved the existence of an afterlife and the reality of the individual soul, and demonstrated that they were in communication with the dead. For the spiritualists, these claims did not have any particular religious implications, and hence spiritualists were attacked as vehemently by organized religion as by scientists. Their claims, however, were still too nonmaterialistic for many of the scientists in the SPR. As Cerullo (1982) points out in his excellent history of the development of psychical research in Britain during this period, the SPR came more and more to interpret spiritualistic phenomena in terms of telepathy (what would now be termed ESP) and psychokinesis (PK). Thus, if a medium told someone at a seance something that medium could not have known through normal channels, she (most mediums were female) was not getting the information from the spirits of the dead but rather through her own power of ESP. Similarly, when an object was apported during a seance, it was not being transported from the "other side" by spirits of the dead but was being moved by the medium through PK. This latter explanation for spiritualistic phenomena prevailed in the SPR. These phenomena constitute the first pieces of evidence for the reality of paranormal claims.

The debate over the validity of spiritualistic phenomena, however they were interpreted, raged well into the early twentieth century. Some of the most famous names in science and literature were involved, including Michael Faraday, the discoverer of electromagnetism; Sir Arthur Conan Doyle; and magician Harry Houdini. Brandon (1983) has written an excellent account of the history of spiritualism and the debate surrounding it. (Modern spiritualists, who still exist and still claim to be in communication with the dead, will be considered later in this book.) Much of the material in the following sections is drawn from Ray Hyman's (1985a) "A Critical Historical Overview of Parapsychology."

Probably the most famous scientist to become involved in the investigation of spiritualistic phenomena was Michael Faraday. Faraday investigated table moving, which was frequently observed at seances. The table at which the seance was held, and on which the sitters rested their hands, would move about, seemingly under its own power. When the seance was conducted by a professional medium, it was easy to attribute the movement to conscious shoving of the table by the medium—one of many types of cheating practiced by mediums. What made table movement so convincing and fascinating, however, was that it sometimes took place at informal, private seances where only a group of friends was in attendance and cheating could usually be ruled out. It was even possible for a single individual to sit at a table and have it move about—yet the individual would swear that no conscious attempt had been made to move the table. The key word here is *conscious*. Through several ingenious experiments, Faraday (1853, cited in Hyman 1985a) demonstrated that the movement of the table was due to consciously imperceptible muscle exertions on the part of sitters. This is known as the ideomotor effect (Spitz 1997; Hyman 2007). After satisfying himself that the table movements were not due to any type of electromagnetic forces, Faraday constructed special tables that would reveal unconscious muscle exertions. Hyman (1985a) describes one such experiment, in which Faraday

> placed four or five pieces of slippery cardboard, one over the other, on the table top. The pieces were attached to one another by little pellets of a soft cement. The lowest piece was attached to a piece of sandpaper that rested on the table top. The edges of the sheets overlapped slightly, and on the undersurface Faraday drew a pencil line to indicate the position. The table turner then placed his hands upon the upper card and waited for the table to move in the previously agreed upon direction. (10)

When the sheets of cardboard were examined after the table movement, it was found that the top sheet had moved to the right relative to the sheets under it. This indicated that the movement was caused by the hands pushing on the table. If the table had moved to the right of its own accord, the top sheet would have moved to the *left* relative to the lower sheets, as the table dragged the hand along with it, as shown in figure 2.1. Faraday also demonstrated that when a feedback device was arranged that showed the subject he was exerting a force to make the table move, the table promptly ceased to move "of its own accord."

The ideomotor effect of unconscious muscle movements is also responsible for another spiritualistic phenomenon, the Ouija board. Figure 2.2 shows such a board from the late nineteenth century. Modern boards have fancier designs. This well-known board is marked with numbers, the letters of the alphabet, and special "yes" and "no" locations. Users put their hands on a moveable planchette that is supposedly

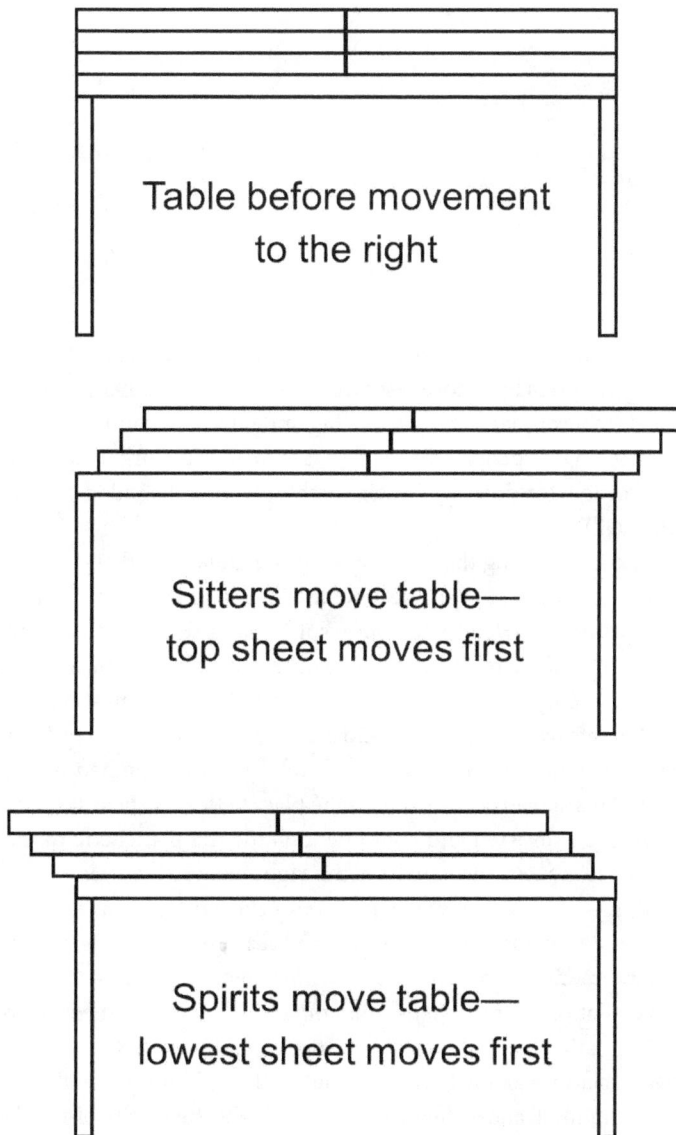

Figure 2.1. Faraday's table experiment. From "Michael Faraday's Researches in Spiritualism," *Scientific Monthly* 83 (1956): 145–50

Figure 2.2. 1890s Ouija board. Photo by Elijah Bond and Charles Kennard, c. 1890, Museum of Talking Boards (https://museumoftalkingboards.com/factory.html)

guided by the spirits around the board to spell out answers to questions. In fact, the planchette is guided by unconscious muscular exertions like those responsible for table movement. Nonetheless, in both cases, the illusion that the object (table or planchette) is moving under its own control is often extremely powerful and sufficient to convince many people that spirits are truly at work. Such unconscious muscular movements are also responsible for dowsing (water witching), as explained in chapter 13, and the "magic pendulum" effect (Spitz 1997).

The fact that it is the people moving the planchette on the Ouija board and not spirits was made clear in a very clever demonstration shown in episode 12 of the 2003 first season of Penn and Teller's Showtime program *Bullshit*. Participants first tried to contact a spirit using the board normally. And it seemed to work as expected—the spirit of the late TV actor William Frawley, best known for his role as Fred Mertz in the famous TV show *I Love Lucy*, came through and answered various questions correctly. After the first successful run, the participants were blindfolded and asked again to contact Mr. Frawley. Then, unknown to them, the board was turned around such that where the "yes" location had been was now where "no" was and vice versa. If Frawley's spirit was controlling the planchette, his spirit should easily have been able to see that the board had been reversed and continue to guide the planchette to the proper answer. But nothing of the sort occurred. Questions to which the right answer was yes resulted in the planchette moving to the "no" location—the location where the sitters believed "yes" was to be found. Similarly, when the correct answer was no, the planchette moved to the "yes" position. This shows that the beliefs and expectations of the sitters, mediated by tiny muscle movements of which the sitters are unaware, are responsible for the movement of the planchette, not contact from the spirits of the dead or some sort of ESP.

Many, perhaps the vast majority, of mediums were out-and-out frauds who faked everything associated with their seances, including the trances they entered to contact the spirits of the dead. Some mediums, however, experienced what appeared to be genuine trances. The medium was actually in a psychological condition known as a dissociative state. Other "personalities" emerged and took control of the medium's body. These other personalities were interpreted, by both the medium and the sitters at the seance, as genuine manifestations of spirit control. Viewing a medium in a genuine trance state is compelling. The medium's voice may change dramatically as different "spirits" take control. The medium's facial expression may also change. It is obvious that something is happening in such situations. The important question as far as paranormal claims are concerned is whether whatever is going on provides evidence for the paranormal. The answer is no. Mediums who experienced genuine dissociative trance states were no better able to provide valid proof of their contact with the dead than were other mediums. If the true dissociative state did put the medium into contact with the dead, one would expect the spirits of the dead to be able to provide evidence of their identity. While the spirits often claimed to be famous people, they were unable to provide evidence to support such claims.

The case of one famous medium clearly shows the action of a dissociative state. This is the case of Hélène Smith (1861–1929; real name Catherine-Elise Muller), a French medium who was active at the end of the nineteenth century. Smith had numerous spirit guides who took over her body while she was in a trance. One of her most famous guides was the "spirit" of someone who could not possibly have existed. For a considerable time, she was said to be under the control of the spirit of a dead Martian. When this Martian was in control, she would speak and write in "Martian" and produce drawings of Martian landscapes, shown in figures 2.3a and 2.3b. Flournoy (1900) discusses the case at length and

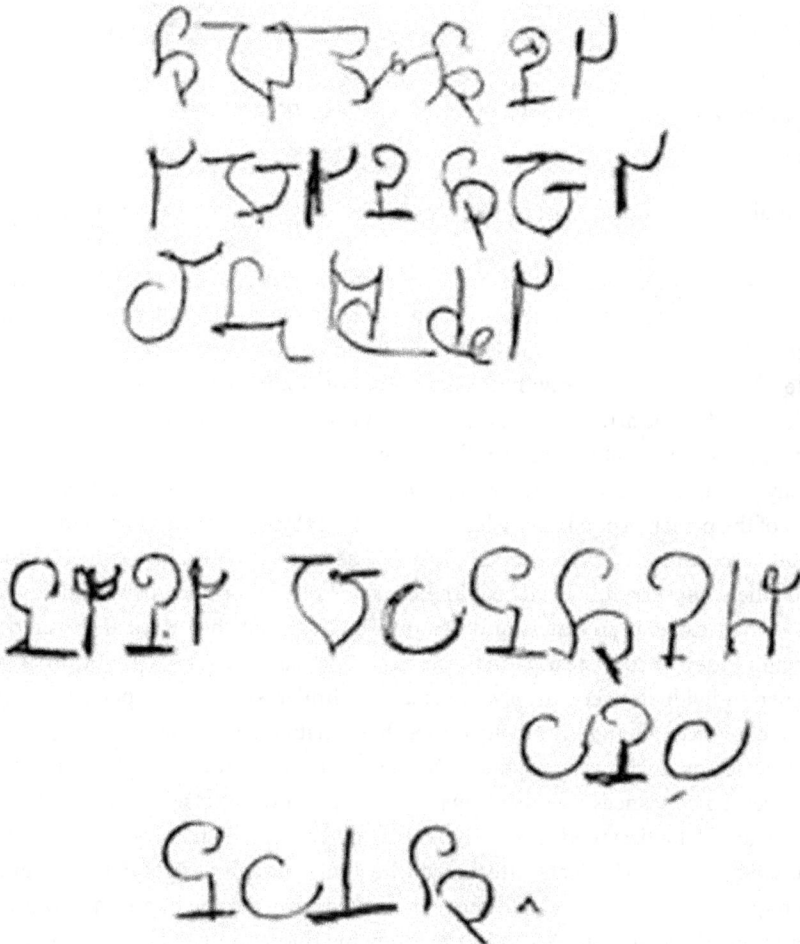

Figure 2.3a. Example of Hélène Smith's writing. From *Des Indes à la planète Mars* by Théodore Flournoy, 1897, figure 21, Wikimedia Commons (https://en.m.wikipedia.org/wiki/File:H%C3%A9l%C3%A8neSmith_martien01.jpg). PD-US

Figure 2.3b. Example of Hélène Smith's drawing. From Hélène Smith, 1896, Wikimedia Commons (https://commons .wikimedia.org/wiki/File:LaM_helene_smith_paysage_ultramartien.jpg). PD-US

reproduces several of Smith's drawings of Martian landscapes and buildings as well as examples of her Martian writing.

The Smith case shows that other manifestations of the dissociative state exist than simply speaking as if a different personality is in control. Smith also wrote while in her trances, allegedly under the guidance of the spirit control. This is known as automatic writing; it can be produced by some individuals who are not in a trance state. The arm, in such individuals, seems to write on its own. It is easy to understand how the feeling could develop that the arm was "possessed," perhaps by a spirit of the dead.

Phenomena that took place at seances run by professional mediums were sometimes spectacular and were not so easily put to the test as table moving. For example, Alfred Russel Wallace, a codiscoverer with Charles Darwin of the principle of natural selection, reported (Wallace 1878, quoted in Hyman 1985a) that at a seance he attended with five close friends the entire seance table became covered with "fresh flowers and ferns" while the sitters carefully watched. The flora appeared from nowhere, and "the first thing that struck us all was their extreme freshness and beauty. The next that they were all covered, especially the ferns, with a delicate dew" (20). Clearly, unconscious muscular exertions will not do as an explanation here. Many other individuals were deeply affected by similar spectacular personal experiences with mediums, which convinced them beyond any doubt that spiritualism was real.

One prominent scientist who was convinced of the reality of spiritualistic phenomena on the basis of the events he observed at seances was the American chemist Robert Hare. To further test the reality of spirit communication, Hare designed an experiment in which tipping and movement of a table at which a medium sat caused a pointer to indicate letters on a wheel that was out of sight of the medium. Hare would ask the medium questions, the table would move, and the answer to the questions would be spelled out. The results were very impressive, as shown in the following quotation from Hyman's (1985a) description of Hare's experiment, reported first in Hare (1855):

Hare then began by asking if any spirits were present to indicate so by causing the letter Y to be under the pointer. Immediately the pointer moved to the letter Y. Hare next asked, "Will the spirit do us the favor to give the initials of his name?" The index pointed first to R and next to H. Hare immediately asked, "My honoured father?" The index pointed to Y. After a few more tests such as these, the onlookers urged that Hare admit the reality of spiritual agency. Hare must have still shown some hesitation, because the index spelled out, "Oh, my son, listen to reason!" (14)

This type of report seems convincing. Highly trained scientists conducting experiments that seemed to verify their initial impressions concluded that spirit communication was real. The evidential value of these impressions and experiments is destroyed, however, when it is revealed that mediums accomplished their seeming miracles by cheating and using illusion and sleight of hand at every possible opportunity.

Remember that the reports of what occurred at seances—the reports that convinced so many of the reality of spiritualist phenomena—were eyewitness testimony. Such testimony is unreliable even when the object of the testimony is not making conscious or skillful efforts to deceive, mislead, and distract witnesses from what is really taking place. Of course, mediums were doing just that, so eyewitness reports of what happened at seances, given by individuals totally unfamiliar with the deceptive techniques used, are even less reliable than most eyewitness reports. The literature on spiritualism is replete with stories of mediums being caught red-handed during a seance, cheating to produce some wonder or another. One of the greatest exposers of mediumistic fraud was the famous magician and escape artist Harry Houdini, who wrote of his experiences in his classic 1924 book *A Magician among the Spirits*. Here Houdini described in detail the methods used by many mediums. Tompkin's (2019) book *The Spectacle of Illusion* describes and illustrates many of the techniques used by mediums.

Houdini (figure 2.4) deserves special mention here. Perhaps more than any other single person, he was responsible for the decline in public acceptance of spiritualistic claims. The public recognized both his name and his expertise as a magician and exposer of fraudulent mediums. That he never found a single genuine medium was very powerful evidence against spiritualism. Houdini himself was a skeptic but one who badly wanted to be able to believe, but the constant string of frauds he saw prevented him from doing so. His desire was to communicate with the spirit of his mother, whom he loved (Brandon 1983). Even in death, Houdini continued to expose the sham of spiritualism. Before he died suddenly in 1926 at the age of fifty-two, Houdini had arranged a secret code with his wife that he would transmit from the spirit world. If she received it, this would prove that the medium giving the code was truly in contact with Houdini's spirit. In spite of years of attempts, no medium was ever able to give the code, although many claimed to be in contact with the great magician.

Some mediums confessed their fraud. An apparently very accomplished medium wrote the anonymous *Confessions of a Medium* in 1882. Margaret Fox herself confessed, in 1888 (the confession is reprinted in Kurtz 1985), that the origins of spiritualism were fraudulent. The mysterious rapping at the Fox home in 1848 had been produced by Kate and Margaret tying an apple to a string and bouncing it up and down on the floor in order to frighten their mother. Margaret Fox stated that those, and all subsequent phenomena she and her sister Kate had produced, were fraudulent.

The methods used by mediums are many and varied. At some seances seemingly disembodied voices would move about the room, responding to the medium's or the sitters' questions. This was easy to accomplish as seances were almost always held in the dark. An assistant of the medium, or sometimes the medium in person, completely dressed in black clothing, head covered, would move invisibly about the darkened room. This general gimmick could be adapted to have the black-clothed individual hold some bright object that would then appear to float mysteriously about the room. On more than one occasion, a skeptical sitter would spring out of their chair and grab the "spirit," only to find that they had grabbed a very angry and embarrassed medium or assistant. Cumberland (1888) reports spraying red dye in the face of the spirit and later discovering

Figure 2.4. Houdini in handcuffs. From Bettmann/Corbis, through the *New York Times* photo archive, 1918, Wikimedia Commons (https://en.m.wikipedia.org/wiki/File:Houdini_in_Handcuffs,_1918.JPG). PD-US

the very same dye on the face of the medium. So-called spirit photographs, in which the head or the entire form of a spirit seemed to float about the medium, were easily produced by trick photography—usually double or multiple exposures of the same plate. These were produced as early as 1855 (Finefield 2011). The spirit photo shown in figure 2.5 was taken in 1931 by William Hope (1863–1933), a major producer of spirit photographs. These photos seem astonishingly crude today and were easily duplicated.

Figure 2.5. Typical spirit photo from 1931 by William Hope. Photo by William Hope and the Crewe Circle, 1931, Wikimedia Commons (https://en.m.wikipedia.org/wiki/File:Williamhopehoax4.jpg)

Some female mediums went so far as to conceal in their vagina or anus objects to be "apported" during the seance and gauzy fabric that would become "ectoplasm." These were places that Victorian gentlemen, no matter how skeptical, were highly unlikely to ask to search.

Does the critical literature on mediums and spiritualism contain an explanation for every single apparently wondrous phenomenon reported by sitters at the thousands of seances held over the years? Of course not. Many reports, such as medium D. H. Home's levitation (Brandon 1983, 71–73), the dewy flowers reported by Wallace, and the results of Hare's (1855) experiments, remain to my knowledge without specific explanations. Should the lack of such explanations convince anyone that spiritualistic phenomena and claims are valid? Certainly not. The burden of proof must rest on the medium and not on the skeptic. This conclusion is strengthened by the fact that, when rigorous experimental conditions that truly excluded cheating were imposed on mediums, no spiritualistic phenomena were seen (Houdini 1924; Brandon 1983).

What of scientists such as Hare and Wallace who were convinced by what they saw at seances? Were they incompetent scientists, dupes, or just plain gullible? The answer is none of the above. They had simply ventured out of their own area of expertise—a common source of error. They assumed that if one is a good observer in the laboratory, one is also qualified to observe in the seance. This is simply not true. Mediums were known to cheat, using the magicians' tricks of sleight of hand and distraction. Magic is a skilled trade requiring years of experience and practice. The training of a chemist, physicist, or psychologist confers no ability to spot magicians' tricks. To detect such cheating requires a magician. This is one of the most important requirements in research into paranormal claims. In the investigation of any type of psychic, a magician is best able to spot the tricks that mediums and other psychics use. This is why Houdini was so successful in exposing mediums. He was a magician and knew exactly what to look for. Magicians will also be of immense help in any psychic investigation in designing procedures to eliminate trickery and sleight of hand, as will be seen in the next chapter.

The repeated revelations of fraud and trickery on the part of even the most famous mediums had surprisingly little immediate effect on believers in spiritualism. One common response, which presaged the responses of believers in psychic phenomena to similar revelations even today, was to admit that a particular medium did cheat sometimes but that at other times the phenomena were real. This argument, of course, was an attempt to shift the burden of proof back to the skeptic by requiring that the skeptic explain away every single allegedly miraculous event before a medium, or spiritualism in general, would be considered discredited.

In the 1980s a new, simpler form of mediumship became quite popular. Known as *channeling*, it dispensed with the sleight of hand and other gimmickry associated with classical mediumship. There are no floating, disembodied apparitions and no apported objects in channeling. The medium simply sits and allows some entity to speak through him or her, becoming a channel for the entity's communication. Depending on the channel, the entity may be from the past, the future, another planet, or even another dimension. Mrs. J. Z. Knight, a California channel highly thought of by Shirley MacLaine, channeled Ramtha, who conquered the world thirty-five thousand years ago. Ramtha was born on Atlantis. Mrs. Knight certainly doesn't channel for free. A session of listening to Ramtha cost four hundred dollars. The fee was $1,500 for a two-day seminar (Gardner 1987a). What sort of wisdom do the channels impart? It consisted largely of new age platitudes about getting in touch with yourself, loving yourself, and the lack of reality.

PSYCHIC READINGS

Repeated exposés of fraud had a cumulative effect over the years, and spiritualism was largely discredited by the 1920s. Classic mediumistic spiritualism is, however, still with us, although it now has a much smaller following. Proponents support at least one spiritualist "camp," Camp Chesterfield in Chesterfield, Indiana. Camp Silver Belle in Ephrata, Pennsylvania, another spiritualist camp, closed in the mid-1990s. Just as youngsters might go to a tennis camp to improve their tennis game or to a computer camp to learn coding, thousands of mostly elderly people go to spiritualist camps to communicate with their dead relatives and friends. M. Lamar Keene was for years a leading medium at Camp Chesterfield. He revealed the inner workings of modern spiritualism in his book *The Psychic Mafia* (Keene and Spraggett 1997; first published in 1976).

Spiritualism became big business, raking in millions of dollars annually from the lonely, the elderly, and the bereaved who believed that they were being put in touch with the spirits of their loved ones. As Keene and Spraggett (1997) make clear, spiritualism was a lucrative racket. (It still is, as the case of John Edward, described later, shows.) Keene and his partner took in between ten and twenty thousand dollars "in one night of services" (65) at their small spiritualist church in Tampa, Florida. Another time, "I collected one Sunday $15,000 in contributions, most of them cash, for our building fund" (71). Of course, there never was any plan to build anything with the money—other than Keene's personal bank account. Keene states that "one woman, who wasn't particularly well-off, gave more than $40,000 to the church—to my partner and me—during the four years or so she attended" (69). Sitters would leave money to Camp Chesterfield in their wills, one man leaving $100,000 and another estate worth more than $500,000.

Keene and Spraggett (1997) reveal in detail the tricks of the medium's trade, several of which are worth repeating here. One of Keene's specialties was apporting lost objects during a seance, or having the spirits tell the sitter where a lost object would be found, even if the sitter wasn't aware that the object was missing. Imagine sitting at a seance and having the college ring you lost months ago fall onto the table. Or having the spirits tell you that the earring you lost will be found at a particular place in the local shopping mall where, you are told, you lost it. You go to the specified location and find the earring. A miracle? Not quite. Here's one way to do this sort of trick.

The spiritualist hires an accomplice to deliver a bouquet of flowers, tightly tied, to someone, usually a widow, who is a sitter at the spiritualist's seances. The ultimate object is to get the victim to increase the contributions to the spiritualist's "church." The flowers are lovely; the card with them indicates that they are from an anonymous admirer. Such a lovely and mysterious gift will thrill most people. At this point, the phony delivery man makes his move. By any of a number of ruses, he gains access to the victim's home. One technique that almost always works is to ask permission to use the bathroom. Few people will refuse such a request, especially considering that the fellow has just brought such a pleasant surprise. While the victim takes time to undo the tightly tied bouquet and put it in a vase, the accomplice quickly scans the bathroom and the bedroom—which is frequently located near the bathroom—looking for any small piece of jewelry, ideally one that is likely to be of more sentimental than monetary value. The item is pocketed and the accomplice leaves and gives the object to the spiritualist. Why not take something of monetary value? The victim is likely to report such a loss to the police, the last thing the spiritualist wants. The loss of an item of little monetary value, even if it has great sentimental value, is much less likely to be reported. However, it is quite likely that at some point in time the victim will ask the spirits for help in finding the object. Once the spiritualist has the object, a number of variations can be worked on this basic theme. In one, the object is apported at a later seance, to the victim's amazement. In another, the object is hidden somewhere in the victim's own house or elsewhere. Later the spirits tell the victim where to look for it. The reader can probably think of other variations on this technique.

Once you know how it's done, the whole thing seems extremely simple. But almost no one, unless they are familiar with the methods of spiritualists and similar con artists, will figure out on their own what happened. They are much more likely to attribute it to the powers of the spirits and the spiritualists. As a result, they may increase their donations.

Another favorite spiritualist trick, used when facing large groups, is *billet reading*. The basic technique is familiar to anyone who is old enough to have seen Johnny Carson's often hilarious "Carnac the Magnificent" routine on his *Tonight Show*. Clips of this routine are on YouTube and are worth watching. The trick is also called the "old one ahead" in the trade. The idea is to convince the congregation that the spirits are providing the spiritualist with information that the spiritualist would otherwise be unable to obtain. At the start of the spiritualist service (not a seance but a service similar to those in established churches), the people present are asked to write a question for the spirits on a card and seal it in an envelope. The sealed envelopes are then collected. Later in the service, the spiritualist holds them up one at a time and, without opening them, reads the question, which is presumably being communicated to him by the spirits. At this point, someone in the congregation will usually exclaim that that was his or her question. The spiritualist then answers the question, tears open the envelope to satisfy himself that the spirits communicated the correct question and answer, then picks up the next envelope and continues. Again, it's a simple trick, once you know how.

Before the "reading" starts, the spiritualist finds out what is inside one of the envelopes and memorizes that question. There are several ways of finding out even if the envelopes are in full view of the audience at all times (google "billet reading" for a more detailed explanation). Once the spiritualist has read the first question, the rest is easy. The spiritualist picks what the audience thinks is the first envelope (it's really a second envelope), holds it up, recites from memory the question that was in the envelope that was really first, but which the audience didn't see, and gives an answer to that question like, "Betty, your mother's lumbago will be cured." He then rips open the envelope he's holding. The audience thinks the spiritualist is simply verifying that the first envelope really contained the question he just obtained an answer to from the spirits. In fact, the spiritualist has just opened the second envelope and is reading a second question. He then picks up a third envelope (the audience thinks it's the second) and reads off the question that was in the previous envelope. A simple trick, but very effective if done well.

In addition to the use of stage magic techniques, spiritualists and psychics use other, more mundane techniques to convince their victims that they have extraordinary powers. Spiritualists and more expensive psychics don't just see anyone who walks in off the street; instead, new clients must make an appointment. This allows time for the accumulation of information. One way of obtaining information about a new client is through a private detective. A detective is especially likely to be used when the victim is wealthy enough to justify the expense involved. However, a great deal of information about an individual can be obtained through other, less expensive sources. A slow drive past the house will reveal much—the type of house, the color, the number and type of cars in the driveway, the presence of children's toys on the lawn. In the Internet age, of course, there is a cornucopia of personal information available online. All this information, available essentially for free, can be fed back to the victim, who will likely be amazed that the psychic could know such details about his or her life. The victim will almost always accept the psychic's knowledge of this information as proof of his or her powers. Modern spiritualists and psychics keep detailed files on their victims. As might be expected, these files can be very valuable and are often passed on from one medium or psychic to another when one retires or dies.

Even if a psychic doesn't use a private detective or have immediate access to any other source of information, there is still a very powerful technique that will allow the psychic to convince people that the psychic knows all about them, their problems, and their deep personal secrets, fears, and desires. The technique is called *cold reading* and is probably as old as charlatanism itself. The technique has been described in detail by Hyman (1976–1977).

Because the majority of human problems fall into one of three general categories—sex, money, or health—the reader already has some idea of the nature of the victim's problem. Of course, the nature of the problem can, to some extent, be predicted by carefully observing the age, mode of speech, style of dress, and physical appearance of the victim. If the victim is young, health problems are less likely to be the reason for the consultation. Sex or personal problems are much more likely to be the reason for the visit. If the victim is a college student—this can be ascertained by simply asking during prereading chitchat, another extremely valuable source of information, or by noting a college ring or fraternity pin—concern about grades is also a strong possibility. In any case, information obtained by careful observation of the victim is then used to guide the reading toward the most likely problem area. For example, if a woman comes in wearing an expensive dress and lots of jewelry, money is probably not the problem she's come to talk about. Elderly people are more likely to have health problems, and many of these can be spotted simply by looking at the victim—the tremors of Parkinson's disease, the hobbling caused by arthritis, and the types of paralysis caused by some strokes can all be readily observed.

As an exercise, put yourself in the position of a cold reader and see what you make of this: A middle-aged man, good-looking and well dressed, walks in. During idle chat before the reading, you discover he's in town for a week or so on business. You also note that there is a white area of skin at the base of his ring finger. What do you conclude?

Students often answer that the fellow has been recently divorced and thus no longer wears a wedding ring. A logical response, and perhaps right, but there is another, seamier, possibility: Perhaps the man is playing around while he's away from his wife and that's why he's not wearing his ring. How do you tell which alternative is true, or whether neither is true? (After all, his wife could have died recently.) Finding out is simple—you ask, but in such a way that he's not aware you're asking and isn't aware he's given you the information. You then, later in the reading, feed the information he's given you back to him, and he's probably amazed at your psychic powers.

One of the most powerful sources of information for a cold reader is vague statements inflected in the form of questions. For example, you could say something like, "I see a recent loss in your life," and inflect the end of the sentence like a question. Because of the inflection, the victim will almost always respond as to a question. He may answer right out, "Yes, my wife just died," or "My wife and I were separated last month." Or the response may be more subtle and almost unconscious—a nod of the head, for example. Even such subtle responses confirm that you're on the right track. If you get a puzzled look and a shake of the head, you know you're on the wrong track. He hasn't suffered a recent loss, so the "fooling around" hypothesis is more likely. At this point, don't come out and say, "I see you cheating on your wife." Never make a specific statement like that in a cold reading. For one thing, it may get you a fist in your face. For another, it may start the victim wondering how you obtained such specific information, and he *may* be able to figure it out for himself. Instead, make it a bit vague: "The spirits point to less than total satisfaction with a woman in your life." Note that you don't say "your wife" here. By being vague, you're protecting yourself: You may be wrong after all. Maybe his wife *did* just die. How embarrassing it would be for you to say "your wife" and use the present tense.

In any event, when you make the comment and watch for the victim's response, you'll learn more. Let's assume the victim's response is a sigh and a nod. This is evidence that the "fooling around" hypothesis is correct. But again, don't make a specific statement. In fact, a good strategy at this point would be to drop the topic and move on to other areas, perhaps doing a little fishing about financial matters. Later, when the victim has probably forgotten the details of your comments about his marital affairs, vague as they were, pop in something like, "I'm getting part of a word or a name. Frank? Frank something? Does that mean anything to you?" Note that you're asking him, not telling him, but that won't be noticed. Let us assume, for this example, that several notorious pickup bars in town are on Franklin Avenue so, if your "fooling around" hypothesis is right, the partial name "Frank" will mean something to him. (A good cold reader must keep up on the locations of such places, and much else besides.)

If you're good, this fellow will leave wondering how you knew he was planning to go to that pickup place on Franklin and hoping that his wife never develops psychic powers, of which he has just seen such an impressive demonstration.

Another technique used by psychics is the *multiple out*. Many magician's tricks depend on this technique as well. The basic idea is to make statements or predictions that are vague and nebulous so that they can be interpreted, after the fact, to fit almost any outcome. Thus one of the great powers of the cold reading is the very vagueness of the statements the reader makes. In the above example, the victim would be just as impressed with the reader's "psychic" powers if he were planning to go to Franklin Avenue that night, if he had thought about going but decided against it, or if he had gone some previous night or during a previous trip. In other words, because of the vague nature of the reading, there are numerous real-life situations that are consistent with it, and the reader gets credit for being psychic if any of them have taken place, have been thought about, or occur in the future. The victim will almost never realize that numerous other events could have taken place that would have made the reading seem to have come true. This characteristic of the cold reading is actively enhanced by the reader, who will often preface the reading by saying something like, "The messages I get are often symbolic and have to be fitted into your particular life."

One sometimes hears of people who have consulted psychics and claim to have been told extremely specific facts about themselves and their friends that the psychic "couldn't possibly have known." Again, it's simple, once you know the gimmick. The reader asks questions about initials and common names: "I see the initial J—is there an important J in your life?" If not, little is lost, but since the victim has been instructed to interpret what the reader says, he or she will search around in memory for someone with a first or last name beginning with J. Note also that "important" is itself a vague term. Important how? A lover, a colleague, a fellow student, a child, a friend? There are dozens of possibilities.

The reader can run the same trick with a full name: "Does the name Fred mean anything to you?" To which the response will often be something like, "My God, Fred Black, how did you ever know about him? Why, I haven't seen Fred since that football game back in college." Of course, the reader didn't know about Fred Black, the football game, or college. But the victim is now convinced that he did and will swear that the psychic told him about Fred Black, even though he had no way of knowing about him. Sometimes it's not even necessary to supply the name; the victim will do it himself. A statement like, "I see in the cards that you're not happy with your personal relationships," can elicit the response, "How did you ever know that Sally and I were having problems?" The reader didn't know, but the victim will have missed that.

What does the reader do next? A good cold reader tells victims what they want to hear: "Don't worry, the tea leaves tell me that it will all work out for the best in the end." This doesn't really mean anything, but the victim, convinced of the psychic's powers, will believe the reader has foretold a pleasant outcome. The victim may be back again, money in hand, the next time he or she has a problem.

One of the most fascinating effects of cold readings is that they not only convince the victim that the reader has paranormal powers; they can also convince the reader of the same thing. Ray Hyman, a psychologist who studies why people believe in the paranormal, became interested in the issue when, as a student, he became convinced that he really could divine amazing information from the lines in people's palms. Let Hyman (1976–1977) tell the story in his own words:

> One danger of playing the role of reader is that you will persuade yourself that you are really divining true character. This happened to me. I started reading palms in my teens as a way to supplement my income from doing magic and mental shows. When I started I did not believe in palmistry. But I knew that to "sell" it I had to act as if I did. After a few years I became a firm believer in palmistry. One day the late Dr. Stanley Jaks, who was a professional mentalist and a man I respected, tactfully suggested that it would make an interesting experiment if I deliberately gave readings opposite to what the lines indicated. I tried this out with a few clients. To my surprise and horror my readings were just as successful as ever. (27)

Several self-proclaimed psychics (they would have been called spiritualists earlier in the twentieth century) became very popular in the late 1990s. James van Praagh was probably the most widely seen, popping up on numerous TV and radio talk shows, followed by Sylvia Browne. Then there was John Edward, who had his own TV program, *Crossing Over*, from 1999 to 2004 on the Sci-Fi Channel. Several authors (Christopher 2001; Posner 1998; Randi 2000; Shermer 1998) have noted that these three were using nothing more than the standard cold-reading technique, combined in John Edward's case with a bit of "twenty questions" and a clever editing of what viewers see on his TV program. The program that airs is a cutdown version of a much longer studio session. And what airs does not include the numerous misses Edward makes (Jaroff 2001). The viewers see only the amazed reactions of the audience members when he does make a "hit." Van Praagh also uses a version of the cold-reading technique in which he'll make a statement (i.e., "I'm getting an image of green dinner plates") and will then ask "Do you understand?" The answer is almost always "yes" because the person being asked does understand the concept of green dinner plates. But the "yes" is taken by van Praagh, and many people who see or hear him, to mean that green dinner plates were something meaningful or important to the dead person van Praagh is supposedly in contact with.

If John Edward, or any of the other self-proclaimed speakers with the dead, really could communicate with the dead, it would be a trivial matter to prove it. All that would be necessary would be for them to contact any of the thousands of missing persons who are presumed dead—famous (e.g., Jimmy Hoffa, Judge Crater) or otherwise—and correctly report where the body is. Of course, this is never done. All we get, instead, are platitudes to the effect that Aunt Millie, who liked green dinner plates, is happy on the other side.

Shortly after the terrorist attacks of September 11, 2001, Edward taped "readings" with several victims' families, which he planned to air on a special edition of his television show. Even by Edward's standards, this was an especially despicable attempt to cash in on the grief of the victims' families. Fearing it might offend viewers, the producers of *Crossing Over* scrapped the idea (de Moraes 2001).

Another factor plays an important role in convincing reader and victim that the cold reading is accurate. This is known as the *P. T. Barnum effect*. It permits victims to believe that a vague stock spiel, with few or no specifics, is an accurate description of their own individual personality. The Barnum effect (so named because the famous quip "There's a sucker born every minute" is usually attributed to P. T. Barnum; in fact, the phrase didn't originate with Barnum, and credit should go to an 1880s con man named Joseph Bessimer [Saxon 1989]) can be demonstrated easily in a classroom. The instructor gives a personality test to each student, telling the class that the test gives an accurate picture of an individual's personality. About a week after the students have taken the test, they receive typed personality sketches, complete with their names at the top, based on their test responses. Students are then asked to judge how accurate the sketches are as a description of their own, individual personality and how accurate they would be if applied to the "average" person. Invariably, the sketch is seen as a very accurate portrayal of the individual's personality but a very poor portrayal of the personality of the "average" person (Hyman 1976–1977). This would be unsurprising, except for one thing: the personality test was a fake. All the students were given the same personality sketch, differing only in the name at the top of the page. Thus, the belief that the fake personality test was valid resulted in the acceptance of the sketch as highly accurate by each individual. This is known as the fallacy of personal validation. It is due to the selective nature of human memory. People will use the vague statements in the personality descriptions to retrieve from memory specific examples from their lives and will then credit the test or psychic with being highly accurate.

John Edward was the topic of an investigation on the television program *Dateline NBC* in 2001. In that program, he was caught cheating—doing what is called a hot reading in addition to the better-known cold reading technique. In a hot reading the medium explicitly obtains information on the client beforehand. This can be done in a number of ways, even hiring a private detective to gather information on a wealthy victim, as described earlier. In the case of Edward on *Dateline NBC*, he chatted up a member of the studio crew before the program started and then acted as if the information had come to him from the spirit world (Nickell, 2001a). Edward was parodied in a hilarious 2002 episode of the Comedy Central cartoon series *South Park* titled "The Biggest Douche in the Universe" (season 6, episode 15) in which he was, without his knowledge, entered into a universe-wide contest for the title of, well, you know. (Spoiler alert: He wins.)

Edward was studied by University of Arizona psychologist Gary Schwartz, who has investigated several mediums. Schwartz (2002) claims that he has proven that they actually do communicate with the dead. However, Schwartz's experiments are shot through with amateurish methodological errors that allow him to interpret the mediums' cold readings as actual communication from the dead. Larsen (2015), Wiseman and O'Keeffe (2001), and Hyman (2003) have detailed these problems at some length. Hyman states that "probably no other extended program in psychical research deviates so much from accepted norms of scientific methodology as this one does" (22). For example, Schwartz's experiments were not done in a double-blind manner and often relied on the interpretations of the sitters, the individuals for whom the mediums were doing their readings, as valid indicators of the medium's accuracy. For example, if a medium said, "I get the impression of a G-type name—George, Gretchen, G something," and the sitter's father's name was Greg and the sitter classified that as a highly accurate hit on the part of the medium, Schwartz accepted it as such.

Relying on sitters' subjective judgments about the accuracy of a medium's readings is highly problematic. Parapsychologist Susan Blackmore (1983) used tarot cards, which date back to at least the fourteenth century (Hargrave 1966), to test the accuracy of such judgments. Blackmore, who had "eight years' experience using the cards for divination" (97), found that when she gave her reading "face to face," subjects rated the readings as highly accurate. However, when she asked other subjects to pick their own readings from among nine others, they were unable to do so and "tended to choose readings which were most general."

Another problematic aspect of Schwartz's research program is that he has been made fully aware of the problems with his methodology, problems that can easily be fixed. Hyman (2003) reports pointing out these problems to Schwartz personally several times. Any competent scientist, when given advice on how to improve his or her methodology, would be happy to take it. But Schwartz didn't do this and simply tried to shift the burden of proof to skeptics, a standard trick of pseudoscientists. A 2007 paper by Beischel and Schwartz still suffered from serious methodological flaws (Battista, Gauvrit, and LeBel 2015).

Psychics, astrologers, graphologists (who claim to be able to determine personality from handwriting), and tarot card readers all benefit greatly from the Barnum effect. For a review of the research on this effect, see Furnham and Schofield (1987). The vast majority of mediums' clients are already, to some extent, believers. Thus, even a vague description that could apply to nearly anyone will be seen as highly specific to the individual. The psychic will then be given credit for amazing, perhaps even paranormal, insights.

These vague descriptions can come in the form of a "stock spiel," a set of general statements that will apply to almost anyone. Two stock spiels that have been shown to be effective illustrate just how vague such statements really are. The following are taken from Hyman (1976–1977) and Snyder and Shenkel (1975), respectively.

> You appear to be a cheerful, well-balanced person. You may have some alternation of happy and unhappy moods, but they are not extreme now. You have few or no problems with your health. You are sociable and mix well with others. You are adaptable to social situations. You tend to be adventurous. Your interests are wide. You are fairly self-confident and usually think clearly. (Hyman 1976–1977, 23)

> Some of your aspirations tend to be pretty unrealistic. At times you are extroverted, affable, sociable, while at other times you are introverted, wary and reserved. You have found it unwise to be too frank in revealing yourself to others. You pride yourself on being an independent thinker and do not accept others' opinions without satisfactory proof. You prefer a certain amount of change and variety, and become dissatisfied when hemmed in by restrictions and limitations. At times you have serious doubts as to whether you have made the right decision or done the right thing. Disciplined and controlled on the outside, you tend to be worrisome and insecure on the inside.
> Your sexual adjustment has presented some problems for you. While you have some personality weaknesses, you are generally able to compensate for them. You have a great deal of unused capacity which you have not turned to your advantage. You have a tendency to be critical of yourself. You have a strong need for other people to like you and for them to admire you. (Snyder and Shenkel 1975, 53)

When one is forewarned about the vagueness of these spiels, the ploy becomes fairly obvious. Why is the vagueness overlooked when the victim is not forewarned? The answer lies in the active role victims adopt when they consult a psychic. The psychic is likely to say that the readings are symbolic and that clients must try to apply what is said to their own life. Thus, when victims are told, "Your sexual adjustment has presented some problems for you," they are likely to recall a specific instance of this sort. They then credit the psychic with telling them not the vague statement but the details of the specific instance.

A good stock spiel will have what are called "double-headed" statements (Dickson and Kelly 1985). For example: "Often extroverted and outgoing, you are sometimes retiring and unsure of yourself in social situations." The stock spiel is not totally flattering. Flattery in a cold reading should not be overdone. Everyone has some bad points, and if the reader makes vague statements that seem to match some of them, the victim won't think, "Well, I'm just being flattered." Putting negative points into the spiel enhances its credibility even further.

It's one thing to describe in writing how psychics con their victims with vague statements, cold readings, and multiple outs as well as the other tricks of the trade. But seeing these techniques in action really brings the point home. The first episode of the first (2003) season of Penn and Teller's excellent HBO television program *Bullshit* shows several psychics using their tricks. And being caught doing it by Penn and Teller. It is an eye-opening experience to watch these con artists at work. In one case Penn and Teller caught the noted psychic Rosemary Altea pumping audience members for information before her on-camera performance and then recycling that information as if she had obtained it through psychic means, much as John Edward did in the *Dateline* exposé.

Psychics' con artistry can go far beyond simply convincing the grief stricken that they have been in contact with the dead. Psychics prey on all sorts of sorrows. In 2014 a man in New York City was conned out of over $700,000 by a psychic who claimed that she could unite him with the women whom he had met online and fallen in love with but who had no serious interest in him (Wilson 2015). The man was not an idiot but had a good education and a job in marketing that paid well enough for him to be able to give the psychic that huge amount.

Another psychic scam that is far more common than one would imagine, or hope, takes advantage of parents with children with serious illnesses. Think of a couple whose child has been diagnosed with some deadly form of cancer or other life-threatening disease. The prognosis is grim, to say the least. Some will visit a psychic, initially, simply to try to find out what the future holds. But the psychic will take full advantage of the parents' fears. A common trick is to tell the parents the child's illness stems from a curse that has been placed on the parents' money. The psychic says that he or she can remove the curse and the child will recover. The "removal" entails the parents bringing the psychic a large sum of money, such as ten thousand dollars, in cash. The parents are also asked to bring a fresh egg with them. When they arrive at the psychic's location, an elaborate ritual begins. The cash is wrapped in a cloth—perhaps a fine silk scarf. The egg is placed on top of the bundle of money. The psychic then chants, sings, or otherwise communicates with the spirits. The purpose of this is to take the curse off the money and move the evilness of the curse into the egg.

At the end of the performance, the parents are asked to break the egg they brought. When they do so they find a stinking rotten egg. The psychic points to this as proof that the curse has been lifted from the money. The parents are instructed that they can take their money home but it must stay wrapped in the scarf for twenty-four hours. (Hey—don't get ahead of me here. I know what you're thinking and you're wrong.) So twenty-four hours later the parents unwrap the wrapped bundle and find—their money. (Weren't expecting that were you?) Probably the parents were just a tiny bit surprised too—they may well have had some lingering doubt about the psychic's honesty and might have thought there was just a chance that the money would be gone. But it wasn't, proving the psychic's integrity.

This is called "putting in the hook"—getting the parents' trust. Does the child get better following the removal of the curse? Maybe, but often not. What's a parent to do? Go back to the psychic, obviously. The psychic pronounces that the curse on the money must have been very powerful, more powerful than expected. So the parents are instructed once again to bring money—something like twenty-five thousand dollars this time. And two eggs. The entire sham is repeated. The two eggs mysteriously become rotten and smelly. The parents are told to take their money home and unwrap it in twenty-four hours. Filled with hope, because the psychic was obviously honest, they do so. Only to find a bunch of newspapers cut to the shape and size of their twenty-five thousand dollars cash. The psychic is long gone. This sort of scam is despicable enough to begin with, but when it persuades parents to forgo real medical treatments that could have helped the child, it is especially vile.

How did the psychic manage to make the eggs turn rotten? During the performance, simple sleight of hand was used to switch the good eggs for ones already rotten. The same technique was used to switch the bundle of real money for the bundle of cut-up newspapers.

It's important to realize that parents, and others, who fall for these sorts of psychic scams aren't fools. They're in a desperate time in their lives that makes them throw critical thinking to the side, so they're ripe for the picking by psychics. Like the case noted above of the man who spent over $700,000 on a psychic, these scams usually start when the desperate visit one of those innocent-looking psychic storefronts that can be found in almost every large community.

One of the most famous psychics of the twenty-first century was Sylvia Browne (1936–2013), who appeared numerous times on such highly rated TV shows as *Larry King Live* and the *Montel Williams Show*. She was a regular guest on the latter. She had a huge money-making empire based on her nonexistent psychic abilities. A telephone consultation with her cost $850.

During her television appearances, she made hundreds of predictions in response to questions she received both from guests brought in to consult with her and about missing persons cases. Shaffer (Shaffer and Jadwiszczok 2010; Shaffer 2013) compiled a set of 116 cases in which Browne made predictions that were specific enough to be evaluated as true or false if enough information about the outcome of the case was available. Her record is truly impressive—for her consistent failure to be correct. Out of these 116 cases, she was wrong, usually completely wrong, in thirty-three. In the other eighty-three, the predictions could not be evaluated because the cases remained unsolved.

It is the nature of Browne's abject failures that tells the story. She would tell grieving parents that their missing child was dead when this was not the case. Or the opposite—that the child was alive when they weren't. It's hard to imagine the amount of grief this pious fraud caused, abetted by ratings-hungry TV talk show hosts lacking in basic ethics and common decency.

One of Browne's most astonishing errors came in 2006 when she was on the *Montel Williams Show* and commented about the case of Shawn Hornbeck, a missing child. According to Browne, the child had been murdered and his body would be found in the woods. The child was alive, having been kidnapped. He and another boy were rescued in 2007, four years after going missing. Not only had Browne got the alive/dead thing wrong, she had said that the nonexistent murderer was Black or Hispanic with dreadlocks. In fact, the kidnapper was White. Stooping low even for a psychic, after her comments on the program Browne offered to continue consulting on the case with the Hornbeck family, for a seven-hundred-dollar fee (Radford 2007).

In 2004 Browne was on the *Montel Williams Show* with Louwana Berry, the mother of Amanda Berry, who had been kidnapped in 2003. Browne informed Ms. Berry that her daughter was dead and that her killer was in his early twenties. But, again, she was wrong. Amanda was alive but being held along with two other women by her kidnapper, Ariel Castro. Castro was in his early forties when the kidnapping took place. On May 6, 2013, Amanda Berry escaped from Castro and helped rescue her two captive companions. Very sadly, Berry's mother had died several years earlier, going to her death believing her daughter was dead. When in captivity, Amanda Berry had actually seen her mom on the *Montel Williams Show* and had heard Browne's statement that she was dead. As might be expected, she was devastated by this. In 2015 Williams, in an uncharacteristic act of honesty, issued an apology to Berry about what Browne had said on his show.

Browne is also noteworthy for being the person who stalled for the longest time after agreeing to take James Randi's One Million Dollar Paranormal Challenge. In 1996 the James Randi Educational Foundation (JREF) raised the one-million-dollar prize money for anyone demonstrating any sort of psychic or paranormal ability or phenomenon under conditions set up to eliminate the possibility of cheating. On the *Larry King Live* program in 2001, Browne accepted the challenge. She died twelve years later, never having put her self-proclaimed abilities to the test. Persons attempting to win the money had to work in advance with scientists to come up with a test that both the scientists and the individual agreed was a fair test. If the amazing powers so many claim to have were real, the million dollars should be long gone. Between 1996 and 2015, when the prize was discontinued, only a few even attempted to win the prize, and none succeeded.

Reasons given for not even trying for the money include claims that the money isn't real, that the very act of testing a claim will make the claimant's ability vanish, and that the claimant doesn't need the money. Those few people who have tried for the prize and failed usually argue that, although they had agreed beforehand to the procedure, something (i.e., the presence of skepticism, stage lights, or what have you) made their powers disappear. In 2020 the Center for Inquiry (www.centerforinquiry.org) announced a $250,000 "Paranormal Challenge" prize, like the JREF challenge, for anyone who could prove that they had paranormal powers. So far, the money has not been won in spite of several attempts.

And then there are the pet psychics, people who say they can read the minds of dogs, cats, horses, goldfish, and maybe your pet tarantula. No pet psychic has ever submitted to a very simple test to prove their abilities, a procedure proposed by Radford (2012a). Give your pet a treat or do something specific with it—play ball, rub its tummy, or some such totally out of sight and sound of the pet psychic. Then have the pet psychic do their thing and see if they can tell specifically what you and the pet did. Don't hold your breath waiting for any pet psychic to agree to this simple test. Some pet psychics even say they can contact dead pets. Like unscrupulous human psychics, these reprehensible people take advantage of grieving pet owners just like human psychics take advantage of grieving people who have lost human loved ones.

The COVID-19 crisis and the social isolation it created also created a new venue for psychics. Susan Gerbic (2020) described how these online scams work. The psychic sets up online meetings using Zoom or some other platform and either charges, or asks for a donation, of, say, thirty dollars. Since Zoom can easily accommodate hundreds of people, that is a great deal of money right up front. It's important to realize that the host of a Zoom meeting can see the names of the attendees, and something of their location if they have their camera on, as psychics often require. Seeing inside the attendees' homes can provide valuable clues for the readings. The con starts when the psychic does a standard cold reading—throwing out vague statements and then following up by talking to people who have seen meaning in such statements. Zoom also affords an excellent way to do hot readings. It's a trivial matter to enter the attendee names into Facebook or do a Google search on them during the reading. There are also more sophisticated search services like Intelius that can dredge up much more information than either Facebook or Google. The information gleaned from the online searches, done by the psychic's assistant(s), is then fed back to the victim and presented as coming from the psychic's paranormal powers.

Gerbic (2020) described how the psychic Thomas John used such searches in his online Zoom performances. Thomas John said he was looking for a mother whose son had passed in the last few years. Something to do with Disneyland and Mitchell and a woman who had diabetes. This mother—we will call her Annie—claimed

> Mitchell as her poor son who had just started to find happiness when he died. The family had been planning a trip to Disneyland and grandma had passed before Mitchell and was welcoming him. Yep, we confirmed all this information [that Thomas John claimed was obtained paranormally] from an [online] obituary for Mitchell and grandma. I should mention that Annie's last name made finding her information pretty quick, maybe three minutes.

Psychics continue to use Zoom and similar platforms. They offer numerous advantages, financial and otherwise. There is no need to pay rent on a physical meeting place, a major expense for any in-person performance. The Zoom fees for a large meeting are very small compared to such costs. Nor does the psychic have to physically travel to different meeting places, a huge additional savings. The cost for the commercial search services are tiny. Intelius charges $22 a month. Since the attendees can only see what the host psychic wants them to see, they do not see the psychic's accomplices using other computers to search for detailed information on audience members. The profits can be huge. Assume each audience member paid thirty dollars and there were five hundred in the audience. That's fifteen thousand dollars for a few hours of work, minus the small costs noted above.

PSYCHIC PREDICTIONS OF THE FUTURE

Every year psychics make predictions about the events that will take place in the coming year(s). And every year these predictions include numerous events that never took place, all the while missing the truly important and surprising events that did take place. It is a common tactic of psychics to make predictions that are too vague to be verified one way or the other such as "the risk of earthquakes will increase next year." Here, if there are more earthquakes, the psychic can claim a hit. But if there are not more earthquakes, the prediction wasn't wrong because the prediction was about "risk," not the actual number of quakes. This is another example of a multiple out.

There is not room here to list all, or even a small portion, of the wrong predictions famous psychics have made over the past decades. However, a Google search for "failed psychic predictions" will turn up a plethora of these. One of the best web pages documenting such failed predictions is http:/www.relativelyi nteresting.com/2017-failed-forgotten-psychic-predictions/. They also have a listing for failed 2013 and 2014 predictions. These very recent psychic failings are nothing new. Such failures have been well documented in the past (Anonymous 2002; Ellis 1998, 2001; Saxon 1974).

In 2022 the Australian Skeptics organization published the results of their comprehensive examination of predictions made by over two hundred Australian psychics from the years 2000 to 2020. The Great Australian Psychic Prediction Project examined more than 3,800 predictions and scored each for accuracy (Palmer 2022). The results were as expected—the psychics were astonishingly bad at predicting the future. They were excellent at predicting things that, had they occurred, would have been very surprising. But they didn't happen. They failed to predict many surprising real events such as the COVID epidemic, the 9/11 attacks on the United States, and the 2003 U.S. Space Shuttle disaster, to name but a few. Many predictions were couched in the usual vague terms used by psychics. The results of this biggest-ever examination of the accuracy of psychic predictions show, again, that psychics and their predictions are bogus.

People continue to believe in the accuracy of such predictions because of several psychological factors. One is, again, selective memory. People will remember even a vague prediction as being much more specific when something close to it takes place. Thus, people will falsely remember that a psychic made a very accurate prediction of a specific terrorist event in the Middle East when all that was predicted was "continuing trouble in the Middle East." The fact that the media publishes such predictions also plays a role. People assume that since these predictions get so much publicity, there must be something to them.

One famous future-predicting psychic was Michel de Notredame, commonly known as Nostradamus (1503–1566), whose predictions have been the topic of numerous books and a 1981 television documentary, *The Man Who Saw Tomorrow*, narrated by Orson Welles.

Nostradamus was certainly a most prolific prophet. His prophecies fill more than 175 pages in Edgar Leoni's (1982) *Nostradamus and His Prophecies*. Leoni provides not only the English translations of all Nostradamus's prophecies but also the original French text, along with a bibliography of the work of

Nostradamus. The English translations of Nostradamus's predictions in this chapter are all taken from Leoni. For an excellent biography of Nostradamus placing him in historical context, see Randi (1993). Nostradamus has been credited with predicting nearly every major historical event to take place since his death, as well as many minor events (Hoebens 1982–1983; Randi 1982–1983b, 1993). Among his alleged correct predictions have been the rise of Napoleon, the rise and fall of Adolf Hitler, World Wars I and II, the invention of fighter aircraft, the atomic bomb, and the deaths of John F. and Robert Kennedy, to name a few. He is even said to have *named* Hitler, getting his name correct to within a single letter.

However, these prophecies are only seen to be accurate *after the fact*.

No one has ever used them to make correct predictions about what is going to occur before it happens. Rather, after an event occurs, people go back to Nostradamus's thousands of predictions and find a passage that seems, now that the event is known, to have foretold its occurrence. For example, after World War II, many people claimed that Nostradamus had foreseen the details of that war. But no one had been able to see such predictions in his writings before the war.

Nostradamus's prophecies are far from the sharp, clear predictions most people believe them to be. He left a total of one thousand verses, divided into ten "centuries," each with one hundred verses, as well as some additional predictions. Each of the one thousand verses can contain multiple predictions, so his writing contains literally thousands of "prophecies." In the best traditions of the multiple out, the verses are vague, sometimes to the point of being little more than gibberish. Two examples will give a flavor of these verses:

An Emperor will be born near Italy,
One who will cost his Empire a high price:
They will say that from the sort of people who surround him
He is to be found less prince than butcher. (Century I, verse 60)

Ruin for the Volcae [people of southern France] so very terrible with fear,
Their great city stained, pestilential deed:
To plunder Sun and Moon and to violate their temples:
And to redden the two rivers flowing with blood. (Century VI, verse 98)

Such vague passages can be interpreted in many ways. The first one quoted above has been seen as a prediction of the rise of Napoleon, but, as Randi (1982–1983b) points out, it applies as well to Hitler and Ferdinand II, a Holy Roman emperor. In fact, it applies to any European ruler born "near" (an extremely vague term) Italy between the fifteenth and twentieth centuries (and beyond) who associated with unsavory individuals and involved his country in any sort of costly adventure, whether war or some sort of economic disaster that resulted from poor policy. As such, it probably applies, with enough creative interpretation, to almost any ruler of this period. In short, Nostradamus was predicting that at some unspecified time, in some unspecified European country, there would be a ruler in some way involved in killing people or whose policies would somehow prove costly to his country.

What about claims that Nostradamus predicted specific developments that have taken place in the twentieth century, such as fighter aircraft and the atomic bomb? Consider the verse said to predict both of these:

They will think they have seen the Sun at night
When they will see the pig half-man:
Noise, song, battle, fighting in the sky perceived,
And one will hear brute beasts talking. (Century I, verse 64)

This is certainly a far cry from any truly specific prediction of fighter aircraft and atomic weapons!

Nostradamus's greatest, and most specific, prediction is said to be his almost perfectly accurate naming of Adolf Hitler. In fact, the word *Hister* does occur in the prophecies three times. It is clear, however, that this in no way refers to Adolf Hitler. *Hister* is the Latin name of the lower Danube River. The translations of the three verses that contain the word *Hister* make it obvious that Nostradamus was not accurately predicting Adolf Hitler's rise and fall, for they are still more gibberish. Here is one example:

> Beasts ferocious from hunger will swim across rivers:
> The greater part of the region will be against the Hister,
> The great one will cause it to be dragged in an iron cage,
> When the German child will observe nothing. (Century II, verse 24)

The other two "Hister" verses (IV 68 and V 29) are equally obscure.

Immediately following the September 11, 2001, terrorist attacks on the United States, the Internet was alive with claims that Nostradamus had predicted the destruction of the World Trade Center. Several different versions of the specific quatrain said to make this prediction were in circulation. But it was not written by him—it appeared on the web page of a Canadian student, who wrote it in 1997 as an example of the style of Nostradamus's quatrains. It was embellished after the fact to make it appear more specific to the World Trade Center.

It was a vague prediction, retroactively made much more specific, that launched the success of Jeane Dixon (1904–1997), probably the best-known psychic of her era. Dixon and her admirers claimed that she correctly predicted not only John F. Kennedy's 1960 election to the presidency but also his assassination (Montgomery 1965). Impressive, if it were true—but it's not. Dixon's actual prediction appeared in the May 13, 1956, *Parade* magazine. It stated, "As for the 1960 election, Mrs. Dixon thinks it will be dominated by labor and won by a Democrat. But he will be assassinated or die in office, although not necessarily in his first term." Now that prediction covers a lot of ground. The portion about a Democrat winning the election would have about a 50 percent chance of coming true. There are numerous possible outcomes that would be consistent with the second portion of the prediction, regarding assassination or dying in office. The president, whose name is never mentioned, could be assassinated in his first or his second term. He could die during his first or second term. Dixon would undoubtedly have claimed a hit if Kennedy had had a serious illness during either the first or the second term, or if an assassination attempt—whether or not the president had been injured—had taken place during the first or second term. However, the coup de grâce to Dixon's claim to have foretold the Kennedy assassination is that in 1960 she predicted that "John F. Kennedy would fail to win the presidency" (Tyler 1977).

Another way to make a prediction seem surprisingly accurate is to make the entire, specific prediction after the event has taken place and then try to con the public into believing that it was made before the event. A blatant example of this psychic technique took place in 1981 when Los Angeles psychic Tamara Rand claimed to have predicted the attempt on President Reagan's life. Her "prediction" included the details that the assassin would have the initials "J. H.," which John Hinkley did, and that the last name would be something like "Humley," which is pretty close to Hinkley. She further "saw" that the president would be shot in the chest in a "hail of bullets" and that the assassin would come from a wealthy family and have sandy hair. All of these descriptions are correct. She even got the time of the assassination right, saying it would take place in the last week of March or the first week of April 1981. The attempt actually took place on March 30, 1981. These predictions were said to have been made on a talk show taped on January 6, 1981, on KTNV-TV, Las Vegas.

Such astonishingly accurate predictions were impressive stuff, and ABC, NBC, and CNN all broadcast the videotape of the January 6 program on April 2, 1981, four days after the assassination attempt. Alas, these major news-gathering organizations made no attempt to verify the accuracy of Rand's claims before broadcasting her videotaped "predictions." In fact, the tape was a fake. Rand and KTNV talk show host Dick Maurice had conspired to produce the fake tape, which was actually filmed in the KTNV studios on March 31, the day *after* the assassination attempt (Frazier and Randi 1981–1982). The hoax was exposed when Associated Press reporter Paul Simon, who was skeptical of the story, investigated and turned up the truth.

One important point should be noted here about the nature of Rand's phony predictions. She took pains to make her predictions less than perfect. She did not say, "I foresee that on March 30 an attempt will be made on the life of President Reagan by a man named John Wayne Hinkley. Hinkley will attempt to assassinate the president as he emerges from the Sheraton Washington Hotel at 1:48 p.m." No one would have believed such a specific prediction. So Rand purposely made her "prediction" somewhat vague, although consistent with what had happened.

PSYCHIC CRIME DETECTION

Many people believe that psychics can help police solve crimes and find missing persons. Certainly, psychics' claims in these areas attract considerable media attention. When examined, however, these claims turn out to be as groundless as claims to predict the future.

Nancy Weber is one psychic who has made such claims. Radford (2012b) investigated one claim of hers—that she provided important information in a 1982 New Jersey case that is sometimes cited as the "best evidence" for the reality of psychic crime fighting abilities. A young woman had been murdered, and Weber was said to have given the police specific details about the identity of the killer. Radford tracked down the facts of the case and found that both Weber and the police officers who had vouched for her accuracy had made numerous conflicting statements about what Weber had said during the initial investigation. Weber, on purpose or otherwise, had retrofitted her original vague statements in such a way that they appeared, after the fact, to be much more accurate.

One interesting fact about Weber's allegedly highly accurate initial statements was that, had she really made them, it would have been child's play for the police to track down the killer. Radford (2012b) used only those retrofitted statements and within twenty minutes, using only sources available in 1982 when the crime was committed, was able to find the name, phone number, and address of the killer. The police, by their own admission, didn't use any of Weber's information but instead caught the killer by chance almost two months later.

In another "best case," as proclaimed by psychics (Radford 2013), a psychic named Pam Ragland said that visions she had led her to the discovery of the body of a murdered boy. The case took place in Menifee, California, in 2013. The visions were of a particular house that turned out to be a real house more than fifty miles from where Ragland lived. When she and several others visited Menifee, they found the house and, poking around the lot, found the body of the missing boy.

Pretty impressive, eh? Well, not really. Ragland claimed that she had never seen the house and had never even been in the area. True enough. But the house was the one in which the missing boy had lived and had been featured on television stories about the child. So she either had forgotten that she'd seen the house before or lied about it. As to finding the body, this too might sound very unlikely. But a very large percentage of bodies of missing individuals are found close to their homes, not hundreds of miles away. So if you poke around the location where someone went missing, chances are good that you'll find the body.

In these and other such cases, it is common for the media to highlight the "mysterious" and "unexplained" nature of the psychics' abilities. In the cases noted above, once Radford published his findings there wasn't even the slightest attempt by local media to correct the impression that they had given that something truly psychic had taken place. This is characteristic of the media's cavalier attitude toward the truth regarding psychics and another reason why people continue to believe that individuals with psychic powers exist—they've heard about it often, and the misleading stories are never corrected.

One of the most famous psychic "crime fighters" was Dorothy Allison (1924–1999) of Nutley, New Jersey. She claimed to have helped dozens of police forces solve crimes, including a string of murders of African American children in Atlanta in 1980–1981. She appeared on the television talk show *Donahue* in 1981, which resulted in the citizens of Atlanta bringing pressure on the police to invite her to try her hand at solving the children's murders. Allison's trip to Atlanta was widely covered on the local television news in both New York and Atlanta, as well as many other cities. The results of her trip, however, received much less coverage. A Sgt. Gundlach of the Atlanta police force, quoted by Randi (1982–1983a), revealed that Allison produced a total of forty-two different names for the murderer or murderers—she believed that there were two murderers. Thus, she was of no help whatever in solving the murders.

The multiple out was the heart of Allison's method. She produced so many "feelings," "impressions," and "hunches" that, after the fact, some were bound to have been correct. This effect is accentuated by the fact that she often took a Nutley, New Jersey, detective with her to "interpret" what she said. With sufficient "interpretation," almost anything can be transformed after the fact into a "correct" prediction. An excellent example of this technique was Allison's prediction in the case of a missing teenager whose parents turned to her for help. She sadly informed the parents that the boy was dead and his body would be found "near an airport." Now, that sounds pretty specific. After all, dead is dead—except when psychics are trying to cover up their blunders. The teenager had, in fact, joined a religious cult and was living in New York City's Pan Am Building (now the MetLife Building). Allison claimed she was right because the boy was "emotionally dead" and there is a heliport on the roof of the building. With such leeway, it's almost impossible to imagine any statement about the boy that couldn't be made to fit the situation after the fact.

Allison blundered in another famous case in New York City. On May 25, 1979, Etan Patz, a six-year-old boy, disappeared while walking to school in the Greenwich Village section of Manhattan. His disappearance set off the national concern over missing children in the early 1980s. In 1980 Allison was prominently featured on at least one major New York television station predicting that little Etan would be found "alive and well in six months." She was flat wrong, but what one did *not* hear six or seven months or even a year later on that television station was a story that started: "Dorothy Allison, the famed New York psychic, was wrong in her prediction about Etan Patz made on this program last year." Years later investigations concluded that Etan had been murdered the day he vanished.

The Dutch clairvoyant Gerard Croiset, who died in 1980, was another famed psychic crime fighter. Pollack (1964) recounts many of his exploits, relying for his information on Dutch parapsychologist Prof. W. Tenhaeff, who was a promoter of Croiset. Hoebens (1981–1982a, 1981–1982b) reviewed the claims made for Croiset, both in Pollack's book and in the European literature. He found that the claims are not supported by the facts. For example, Pollack describes a 1953 case in which Croiset allegedly saw, psychically and in detail, what had happened to ten-year-old Dirk Zwenne, who disappeared while playing and was later found dead in a canal. Pollack's account, taken from Tenhaeff, contains many specific statements and predictions that Croiset is said to have made, which were said to have come true. In fact, Croiset never made such statements. Hoebens (1981–1982b) tracked down the original report of the Zwenne case and found that Croiset made the same type of vague statements that are typical of the multiple out. In addition, several of his statements were simply wrong. At one point, Croiset said the body would be found at a particular location. When taken to a second location to see if he "saw" anything there, he indicated that he did not. The body was found at this second location, not the first. Croiset also said that when discovered, the body would bear a fatal wound on the left side of the forehead. There was no such wound. Of course, these errors are not mentioned in Pollack's book. The Zwenne case is just another example of psychics and their promoters claiming great accuracy and slyly changing the predictions after the fact.

In the only study of its type to date, Reiser and colleagues (1979) studied whether, in a controlled situation, psychics could provide any information about a crime. They examined twelve psychics: eight professionals who make all or part of their living from selling psychic services and four amateur psychics. Physical evidence from four crimes, two solved and two unsolved, was presented to the psychics, who were to give their impressions of the crimes. The psychics were told nothing else about the crimes. The psychics, both individually and as a group, scored no better than chance on any of the four crimes. They showed very poor consistency in their impressions of the same crime and made flagrant errors. The most common error was to believe that the crimes had something to do with the "Hillside Strangler" murders, which were taking place at the time in Los Angeles, where the study was conducted. In fact, none of the cases had anything to do with the "Strangler" series of killings.

Psychics can fool the police with the same tricks they use to fool others. Posner (1998) has shown that the claims of great accuracy by Florida "psychic detective" Noreen Renier are way off base. Nickell's (1994) classic book *Psychic Sleuths* contains eleven chapters carefully examining the claims of numerous police psychics. These claims do not hold up well to close scrutiny.

Self-proclaimed psychics like Sylvia Browne, Nancy Weber, and all the others make or made their living preying on grief-stricken people and exploiting the understandable desire to learn what happened to their loved ones. But when their claims for accuracy are carefully investigated, they are found to be false.

In-person or via television or Zoom are not the only ways psychic con artists operate. Another avenue of activity is by direct mail. A victim receives what appears to be a personal letter from a psychic promising that if they send in a donation, or "offering," the psychic will help them with whatever life problems they are facing. Such operations are big business, as Ellis and Hicken (2018) revealed in their exposé of one such operation that lasted for over twenty years starting in the late twentieth century. The "personal" letters of course are not. But they contain personal information such as age, marital condition, interests, and the like that will convince the victim that the letter is for them alone. Such data can be gathered in a variety of ways and added to the letters to make them appear highly specific. Hundreds of thousands of letters are mailed at a time. Sometimes little gifts are included, said to be blessed or otherwise endowed with mystic qualities and powers. It is far from a trivial matter to organize such an operation. Copy writers are hired to write the letters, getting either a flat rate for their work or a percentage of the money the letters bring in. Commercial printing firms print the letters. Firms specializing in the manufacture of cheap trinkets provide the gifts. Direct mailing companies do the mailing. Front companies process the cash or checks that come in, take their cut, and forward the rest of the money to the criminals behind the scheme. The victims are usually the most vulnerable members of society—the elderly, often with cognitive impairment; the sick; the poor, for whom promises of money are enticing; and the lonely.

Sometimes the scam doesn't involve a letter but a less ambitious post card. An example is shown in figure 2.6. This was addressed to my father and states that the psychic is "very much concerned about you" because a "major event may soon change your life" perhaps "before November 18," 1996, and that there is "an urgent message awaiting you." Obviously this "certified Psychic" wasn't all that psychic. My father had died six years previously.

PROPHETIC DREAMS AND HUNCHES

People can become convinced of the reality of psychic phenomena because of some seemingly psychic personal experience they have had like going to a psychic who does a good cold reading. Having what seems to be a prophetic dream can also be convincing. Many people can describe dreams that they, a friend, or a relative have had that later "came true." In some rare instances, the dream seemed to contain detailed information about the event that later took place, information that the dreamer really had no way of knowing. Take a hypothetical example: Late one night John is awakened by a nightmare in which his beloved Great Aunt Petunia is driving a brand-new shocking pink Porsche down the San Diego Freeway. Suddenly, the engine of a 747 flying over the freeway to make a landing at San Diego Airport falls off and crushes the Porsche, killing Aunt Petunia instantly. Shaken by the dream, John worries for a while and then goes back to sleep. He is stunned to learn later that day that, in fact, Aunt Petunia was killed in just the way he had dreamed a few hours after he had had his dream.

Name	Telephone Time Credit (No. Of Minutes)	RATE
Lawrence G Hines	Two (2)	Free

Reason

The free time indicated above has been requested by the psychic whose name appears below because of urgent message awaiting you!

Urgent!!

Call Us **FREE** At:
1-800-371-1923

Name of Psychic

Paulette

MESSAGE AREA

Very much concerned about you. Since we spoke short time ago, I keep thinking major event may soon change your life. Could happen before November 18th. Also want to discuss possible favorable shifting in your money situation and future trip. What I have to tell you so important, I requested and was granted two minutes FREE telephone time for you to use. Also, urgent you immediately concentrate hard on eliminating problem that is bothering you. But, don't wait, if I'm not available when you call -- get the very next available certified Psychic -- Believe me -- they'll know what to do!

...I care for you, Paulette

P.S. Forgive this
form, but is   *Love & luck, always!!*
quickest way of
alerting you of
your situation.
I will be awaiting
your call.
Use number above.

TTC
PF1009 33-42

Figure 2.6. Letter card to the author's father. Author's collection

Is such a dream not compelling evidence that, at least sometimes, dreams can psychically foretell the future? Most people would answer yes to that question. But I will argue that such dreams are simply coincidences. That argument may sound quite implausible at first, simply because most people are unaware of the vast number of dreams that take place. Dreams have been the target of a huge amount of research over the past many years. Much has been learned about dreaming from this research. What is relevant here is that dreaming does not occur throughout the night but mostly during periods of REM (rapid eye movement) sleep. There are about five such REM periods in a normal night's sleep. Each REM period lasts about fifteen to twenty minutes in adults. In a single REM period, there are upwards of possibly as many as fifty dream "themes" or events, any one of which could, in some way, "come true." Thus, a normal individual will have about 250 (five REM periods times fifty dream themes per period) dream themes per night. That may not sound like many, but multiply that figure by the approximately 331 million people in the United States, as of the 2020 census. This means that there are over 80 billion dream themes dreamed every night in the United States. In one year there are over 2.9×10^{13} dream themes dreamed in the United States alone. The number of dream events dreamed around the world each year is unimaginably vast. What Hand (2014) calls the Law of Truly Large Numbers states, in essence, that if an event is given enough opportunities to occur, sooner or later it will occur. Thus, if you flip a coin long enough, sooner or later you will have a run of twenty heads, even though the probability of that event is tiny. Similarly, with the huge number of opportunities for dreams to come true afforded by the vast number of dream themes that occur each year, some will turn out to be impressively "prophetic" by chance alone.

The convincing nature of prophetic dreams is enhanced by the fact that we don't recall the vast majority of our dreams. In fact, some people never recall any dreams. But they do dream. When these individuals are brought into a sleep laboratory and awakened during a REM period, they report normal dreams. The dreams that are most likely to be remembered are ones that take place just before awakening in the morning or, more to the point of the present discussion, those that "come true." If a dream doesn't "come true," there is little chance that it will be recalled spontaneously. We have all had the experience of awakening and not remembering any dreams. Then, sometime later during the day, something happens to us, or we see or hear something that retrieves from long-term memory a dream we had had, but which, until we were exposed to what is called a *retrieval cue*, we were unable to recall voluntarily. Of course, if we had not been exposed to the retrieval cue, we would never have been aware that the dream had occurred. Thus, the nature of memory for dreams introduces a strong bias that makes dreams appear to be much more reliably prophetic than they are—we selectively remember those dreams that "come true."

Another familiar factor works to make dreams appear more prophetic than they are—the multiple out. People will frequently count a dream as "coming true" even if the events in the dream and the events in real life are only somewhat similar. A personal example: One night when I was living in Boston, I had a dream about a horrible accident on the Boston subway system's Green Line. In my dream the accident took place underground (a large part of the Green Line is above ground). There were many dead, much blood, and a great number of injured. I mentioned the dream to a friend. A few months later, there was an accident on the Green Line. A car empty of passengers was traveling on the section of track above ground. It derailed and rolled down a small embankment. No one was hurt and, since it was a Saturday, no one was really very much inconvenienced. Yet my friend was convinced that my dream had been a psychic prophecy that had come true. She was a bit miffed that I didn't immediately agree that psychic phenomena were real.

Of course, the accident in my dream and the real-life accident were entirely different. To count the two as a "match" and classify my dream as prophetic would mean my dream almost had to come true: sooner or later, some type of accident, large or small, will occur on any subway line. Further, dreams don't come with disclaimers at the end stating "this dream invalid for purposes of prophecy in thirty days." Thus, they have practically an endless amount of time to come true. Given this, it's hardly surprising that some seem to.

Alcock (1981) reports an experiment that shows that eliminating the opportunity for multiple outs in dreams eliminates their seemingly prophetic nature. He is often confronted by people who report that their dreams "always come true." I have had people make similar reports to me. Alcock simply asks these people to keep a dream diary, in which they write down their dreams upon awakening. When this is done, the dreams all at once stop being accurate. The diary is a written record of the dream, and it prevents the dreams from being "misremembered" as more accurate than they really were.

Hunches, intuition, and "feelings" that something is going to happen seem to be accurate more often than would be expected by chance, for similar reasons. We forget the hunches that don't come true but remember the ones that do. I used to own a secondhand Pinto. I often had hunches that something would go wrong with the car. Not surprisingly, eventually one of the hunches came true. Consider how multiple outs can operate to inflate the "hit rate" of hunches or dreams. A wife has a strong feeling that her husband has been involved in a serious car accident and becomes very worried. Upon returning from work, she finds her husband in perfect health. Was the hunch wrong? A believer in the prophetic power of hunches would be very likely to count the hunch as a hit if (1) the husband had been in a minor accident, (2) had *seen* a serious accident, (3) had *seen* a fender bender or minor accident, (4) had seen what was *almost* a serious accident, or (5) any number of other events related to accidents. After all, the believer in the prophetic nature of hunches or dreams will tell you, these things aren't precise—they must be interpreted to make them meaningful. The interpretation always takes place after the fact.

Seemingly amazing coincidences that have convinced some people of the reality of ESP are due to similar memory-biasing mechanisms. A classic example is to be thinking of someone and, minutes later, have them call or otherwise make contact. Is this sort of instance amazing proof of direct mind-to-mind communication? No—it's just a coincidence. It seems amazing because we normally don't think about the millions of telephone calls, emails, and such made each day, and we don't remember the thousands of times we have thought of someone when they *haven't* contacted us a few minutes, hours, days, weeks, or months later.

Hintzman, Asher, and Stern (1978) nicely demonstrated selective memory for coincidences in a laboratory setting where the coincidences were under strict control. In one experiment, subjects rated a list of nouns on various characteristics (size and attractiveness). They were not told that they would later be asked to recall the words. After a brief "filler task" designed to pass the time and occupy the subjects' attention, a set of pictures of objects was rated. Some of the pictures corresponded to some of the words that had been rated in the first part of the experiment, and this correspondence was what was defined as a coincidence for the purposes of the experiment. When the subjects, without previous warning, had to recall as many of the words they had previously rated as they could, their memory was much better for words if that word's corresponding picture had been rated in the picture-rating portion of the study. This occurred even if the subject didn't notice that some of the pictures corresponded with the words.

In a second experiment, Hintzman, Asher, and Stern (1978) showed that the same effect was found if the pictures were rated first. Finally, in a third experiment, it was found that the effect of the coincidence was maintained over a period of twenty-four hours. In this final study, a set of words was rated, then came a filler task, then a set of pictures was rated. Memory was not tested—again unexpectedly—until the next day. This series of experiments demonstrates that coincidences are better remembered than noncoincidences.

Related to hunches is the phenomenon of déjà vu, which means "already seen" in French. In a déjà vu experience, a place or situation seems familiar even though the person having the experience knows that they have never been in that place or situation before. Such experiences have led some people to conclude that they had visited the familiar location in a past life. One need not resort to reincarnation for an understanding of déjà vu; it can be understood in terms of normal memory function. Specifically, déjà vu results when two different memory processes that normally occur together occur separately. Usually, when we find ourselves in a familiar location, we have both a conscious memory of the previous experience or experiences at that location and a feeling of familiarity. In the déjà vu situation, the feeling of familiarity is present, but the memory of previous experience is not, either because it is too weak or because there was no previous experience. In these situations, the mechanism that generates the feeling of familiarity has briefly been activated without the corresponding conscious memory. Déjà vu is a fascinating topic on which Brown (2004) has written a book-length review.

There is much laboratory evidence for the dissociability of retrieval of a memory and a feeling of familiarity (Gardiner and Richardson-Klavehn 2000). In the "tip of the tongue" situation (Brown and

McNeill 1966; Gruneberg and Sykes 1978) you know you know the answer to a question—that is, you are familiar with it—but you cannot retrieve it. This effect is especially annoying when it occurs when one is taking an exam or playing a game. The reverse situation can also be shown to occur. People may have no consciously retrievable memory of learning, for example, a list of words, but will relearn the words faster than if they had never learned them in the first place (Nelson 1978).

LIFE AFTER DEATH

The idea that the human spirit survives after the physical death of the body is probably as old as humanity and plays an extremely important role in nearly all of the world's great religions. Occult sections of bookstores are filled with sensational paperbacks alleged to contain true reports of ghosts and postdeath survival. Ghost-hunting tours and "reality" TV shows have exploded in popularity in the past decades. Hill (2017, 40) describes these shows as "hyperreality" TV in that the shows are "a manufactured reality, an enhanced, more dramatic, condensed, and concentrated version of reality. The hazard that viewers may mistake hyperreality for reality . . . happens! People visit paranormal hotspots looking for their own experiences." And when they do visit, almost anything that happens will be taken as evidence for some type of paranormal, or ghostly, encounter.

This chapter will examine several phenomena that are said to provide evidence for the reality of life, or some sort of survival, after death.

The best evidence for survival after death would be contact between the living and the spirits of the dead. Such contact was the goal of spiritualism. However, as was discussed in chapter 2, the spiritualistic movement failed to produce evidence for such survival. Modern psychical researchers have thus generally turned away from mediums and spiritualism and looked for evidence of survival after death in other phenomena.

Belief in ghosts is widespread, even in modern culture. A 2021 Stastica Poll found that 36 percent of Americans reported that they believed in ghosts, 43 percent did not, and 20 percent weren't sure. Ghost-hunting tours have been quite popular in the past decades. These are often run by commercial companies that have a vested interest in not investigating ghost claims carefully. They hype any little thing that happens during a tour as evidence of ghosts. There is clearly big money to be made in commercial ghost hunting. Unfortunately, the lure of such money has led some colleges and universities to abandon their role as guardians of rationalism by offering uncritical ghost-hunting experiences and courses.

GHOSTS

The most dramatic and seemingly convincing evidence for the existence of ghosts comes from thousands of eyewitness reports of ghosts and apparitions. Less convincing, and much more common, are the odd noises (creaks and knockings) and movements of objects (such as doors closing "under their own power") that many people interpret as the activity of ghosts or spirits. As noted in chapter 1, humans have a strong tendency to explain such events as due to some entity with "agency"—a motivation to make the door close, the light flicker, or the floor creak. When such things happen in a "haunted" house, people are especially likely to attribute them to ghosts and reject nonparanormal explanations. The aforementioned ghost-hunter TV shows and tours further encourage people to misinterpret such creaks, cold spots, and small movements as evidence of ghosts.

Hallucinations are another important factor leading to ghost reports. Ghosts are usually seen at night by someone who has just retired to bed. After going to bed, people fall into a sort of "in-between" state where they are neither fully awake nor fully asleep. During this period, *hypnagogic hallucinations* are quite common. These hallucinations are distinct from dreams in that they may seem to the individual to be real. If you've ever heard your name called as you were falling asleep, but you know that no one really called you, you've had a hypnagogic hallucination. Auditory hallucinations are most common, but visual imagery is enhanced as well in this state, and highly realistic visual hallucinations, as well as combined visual and auditory hallucinations, do occur. A similar type of hallucination occurs when one awakens, called a *hypnopompic hallucination* (Sharpless and Doghramji 2015). These two types of hallucinations are responsible for a great number of impressive reports of ghosts and similar apparitions.

The common occurrence of hypnagogic and hypnopompic hallucinations is not well known. Despite how common they are, they are almost never covered in introductory psychology textbooks. I know of only one modern Western cultural reference to them, the theme song of the original (1979) *Muppet Movie*, "Rainbow Connection," with music and words by Paul Williams and Kenneth Ascher. One verse contains the words, "Have you been half asleep and have you heard voices? I've heard them calling my name." Such hallucinations can run from the rather mundane, just hearing your name called, to very detailed and dramatic. The fact that one is paralyzed while the hallucinations occur makes the experience even more frightening if one isn't aware of the real cause of the experience. Many cultures have names for such hallucinations, and the experiences are interpreted in the context of the time and culture of the experiencer (Baker 1996), such as the "Old Hag" in Newfoundland and Scandinavia. Historically these experiences have led to reports of such things as witches (Hufford 1982; Ellis 1988; Sharpless and Doghramji 2015). More recently, as will be seen in chapter 8, these hallucinations have led to the belief in being kidnapped by aliens.

As in other areas of the paranormal, such as prophetic dreams, a reporting bias exists that spuriously increases the frequency of dramatic ghostly encounters. Unspectacular hypnagogic hallucinations, such as hearing one's name called, are likely to go unreported or even unremembered. However, a spectacular hallucination of a ghost, perhaps complete with groans and other auditory "special effects," is very likely to arouse one into full wakefulness, so the hallucination will be firmly planted in memory. Research has shown that a very large percentage of normal individuals have experienced auditory hallucinations even when fully awake. Posey and Losch (1983–1984) found that more than 70 percent of a sample of 375 college students had at some time experienced an auditory hallucination of hearing voices while they were awake. Such hallucinations may readily be mistaken for ghosts or taken as evidence of the paranormal by those experiencing them. It is the commonness of such hallucinations that helps to account for the large percent of Americans who report that they believe in ghosts.

Fraud and hoax have long played a role in reports of ghosts and hauntings, especially in the most dramatic cases. MacKay (1980) describes numerous cases of faked hauntings, including a 1649 case in England in which a series of dreadful ghostly occurrences drove a group of Oliver Cromwell's administrators from a manor in Woodstock. The haunting was later revealed to have been the work of a royal loyalist. In spite of the fact that the cases MacKay relates were fraudulent, hundreds—perhaps even thousands—of people were convinced of their legitimacy before the real causes were determined.

Two of the most frightening and allegedly well-documented modern cases of hauntings have likewise turned out to be fraudulent. The cases in question are those of Borley Rectory in England and the "Amityville Horror" in Amityville, New York.

Borley Rectory (figure 3.1) in Essex became popularly known as "the most haunted house in England" after a book of that title was published in 1940 by Harry Price (1881–1948). Price's book purported to document a series of astonishing hauntings and manifestations from the time the rectory was built in 1863. The manifestations Price reported included the ghosts of a nun and several other individuals; all sorts of

Figure 3.1. Borley Rectory. From Wikimedia Commons, 1892 (https://en.wikipedia.org/wiki/File:BorleyRectory1892 .jpg). PD-US

noises in and around the rectory that, according to Price, could not have been due to normal causes; spontaneous fires; mysterious cold spots; unexplained ringing of electrical bells that had been installed in the rectory; crockery flying through the air without any human assistance; and even mysterious messages written on the walls by the ghosts.

The phenomena Price reported in his book were said to have been witnessed by many of the inhabitants of the rectory over the years, and Price interviewed many of them for the book. He also visited the rectory on many occasions and, from May 1937 to May 1938, rented it himself, relating his own experiences at the rectory in the book.

The book was very well received, and many readers found it convincing. One reader, Sir Albion Richard, K.C., C.B.E., said of the book:

> The evidence which he [i.e., Mr. Price] has collected of the phenomena which appeared there is as conclusive as human testimony can ever be and is admirably marshalled.
>
> I have not met anyone who has read the book—and it is mainly with legal friends of long experience in the weighing and sifting of evidence that I have discussed it—(many of them, like myself, previously sceptical) who has not been satisfied that the manifestations therein disclosed are proved by the evidence, to the point of moral certainty. (Quoted in Dingwall, Goldney, and Hall 1956, 171)

Another famous English jurist, Sir Ernest Jelf, then senior master of the Supreme Court, was equally impressed with the evidence in Price's book (Dingwall, Goldney, and Hall 1956).

In the early 1950s the Society for Psychical Research in England undertook a complete investigation of the haunting. The result is a painstaking and scrupulous book, *The Haunting of Borley Rectory*, by parapsychologists Dingwall, Goldney, and Hall, published in 1956. Unfortunately the book is long out of print, but a short summary can be found in Hall (1985).

Dingwall, Goldney, and Hall (1956) demolish the claim that Borley Rectory was ever haunted. They find, by comparing reports in Price's books to the actual statements that witnesses made to Price—which are still preserved—that Price distorted and embellished reports to make them much more dramatic than they actually were. Their investigation also made it clear that during the period in which the seemingly paranormal goings-on were at their peak, Mrs. Marianne Foyster, wife of the Rev. Lionel Foyster, who lived at the rectory from 1930 to 1935, was actively engaged in fraudulently creating these phenomena. Price himself "salted the mine" and faked several phenomena while he was at the rectory. When such phenomena were seen by others, as in one case where a glass of water mysteriously turned to ink, they were embellished and entered Price's books as further evidence of the reality of the haunting.

Dingwall, Goldney, and Hall (1956) found nonparanormal explanations for nearly every incident reported from Borley. The very few that go unexplained do not constitute support for the reality of the haunting. Rather, they are merely cases about which not enough is known to arrive at the correct explanation. In any case, as was shown in chapter 1, the burden of proof should not rest on the skeptic. In their conclusion, Dingwall, Goldney, and Hall state that "when analysed, the evidence for haunting and poltergeist activity for each and every period appears to diminish in force and finally to vanish away" (168).

Harry Price was well known as a ghost hunter and psychic investigator before his first book on Borley Rectory appeared. Hall (1978) has shown that Price's regard for the truth was as poor in other paranormal occurrences that he reported as it was in the case of Borley Rectory.

If Borley Rectory is the most famous haunted house in England, the "Amityville Horror" house in Amityville, New York, is probably the most famous haunted house in the United States. This house has a much more gruesome history than the rectory. In late 1974 six members of the DeFeo family were shot to death by a seventh member of the family, twenty-three-year-old Ronald DeFeo, who was convicted on six counts of second-degree murder in late 1975. In 1975 the house was purchased by George and Kathy Lutz. Within hours of their moving in, they were witness to the most astonishing and horrible hauntings in the history of parapsychology, according to Jay Anson's 1977 book *The Amityville Horror*. It was so bad that the Lutzes stayed in the house only twenty-eight days.

What happened while they were in the house? The incidents read like the script for a horror movie—one with lots of special effects. And the book did, starting in 1979, spawn a series of dreadful, low-budget horror films and made-for-TV movies. Large statues moved about the house with no human assistance. Kathy Lutz levitated in her sleep. Green slime oozed from the walls. Mysterious voices were heard, sometimes saying, "Get out, get out." A large door was ripped off its hinges. Hundreds of flies appeared seemingly from nowhere.

The book was a hoax from start to finish, dreamed up by the Lutzes for the sole purpose of making money. In a long review, Morris (1977–1978) pointed out numerous problems with the claims in the book even before it was known to be a hoax. Moran and Jordan (1978) investigated some of the incidents reported in the book and found that the events described never happened. For example, a Father Mancuse is said in the book to have attempted to rid the house of its ghosts by using holy water. He is said to have had a mysterious car accident very shortly thereafter and to have had his hands break out in a terrible rash. His own living quarters began to reek so badly that he and other priests couldn't stand to live there. This entire story was made up, as Moran and Jordan show. Not only did none of these dramatic incidents happen to Father Mancuse, he never entered the Lutzes' house. Other incidents reported in the book were also revealed to be fictitious when subjected to Moran's and Jordan's investigation.

In the summer of 1979 lawyer William Weber, who defended murderer Ronald DeFeo, revealed the origin of the hoax. Weber had been planning to write a book about the case when the Lutzes contacted him regarding their experiences in the house. Thinking that these might make an interesting addition to his book, Weber spoke with the Lutzes at length. In a United Press interview in July 1979 (see Frazier 1979–1980) Weber said, "We created this horror story over many bottles of wine that George Lutz was drinking. We were really playing with each other. We were creating something the public would want to hear about."

Figure 3.2. Amityville Horror House. Photo by Seulatr, 2005, Wikimedia Commons (https://en.m.wikipedia.org/wiki/File :Amityville_house.JPG)

When Weber mentioned that the murders took place at around 3 a.m., Kathy Lutz said, "Well, that's good. I can say I'm awakened by noises at that hour . . . and I could say I had dreams at that hour of the day about the DeFeo family."

Owners of the house since the Lutzes moved out did not have a single incident of anything out of the ordinary. Barbara Cromarty, who lived in the house after the Lutzes left, said, "We know everything was a hoax" (Frazier 1979–1980, 3). The Cromartys, however, were troubled by another type of manifestation: the curious people and crackpots who came from miles around to gawk or to look for ghosts. The house as it was at the time of the murders is shown in figure 3.2. The façade has since been changed to discourage unwanted gawkers.

Another hoax like the Amityville Horror house was the claimed haunting of a house in Southington, Connecticut, that was the basis for a 1992 book (Warren et al., 1992) and the "based on a true story" movie *A Haunting in Connecticut*, released in 2009. Joe Nickell (2009) tracked down the facts behind the events shown in the movie. Although the film was released in 2009, the events it depicts took place in the mid-1980s.

The Snedeker family rented a house in Southington that had been a funeral home. Then all sorts of horrible things began to happen, according to the story. One of the sons saw ghosts. The Snedeker parents both claimed to have been raped by demons. A young female relative in the house reported being touched by a mysterious hand in the night. Chains clanked. Power failed.

Pretty awful, right? Wrong. Coincident with these dramatic reports the Snedekers were involved in a deal to produce a book about the events—the book noted above. They appeared on television shows to promote the book, telling their tales. Nickell's (2009) article reveals what was really going on, and it wasn't paranormal at all. Ed and Lorraine Warren, who lived in the house for several weeks, were well-known ghost and demon finders who had been involved with the Amityville Horror hoax. Some of the events in the house were fabrications, such as the rapes of the adult Snedekers. Others had real causes, which were, willfully or otherwise, misrepresented as being paranormal in nature. The clanking chains were due to large trucks passing by. The power failures were, wait for it, just regular power failures. The cause of the young girl who was touched by a mysterious hand in the night was more troubling. One of the Snedekers' sons, later diagnosed with schizophrenia, had fondled her and actually tried to rape her while she slept. Even Ray Garton, a professional writer brought in to help with the Warrens' book, pretty much abandoned any claim that the book was other than a made-up ghost story (Nickell 2009).

The Amityville Horror movie spawned numerous awful sequels. So far, *The Haunting in Connecticut* has spawned only one—*The Haunting in Connecticut 2: Ghosts of Georgia*. This is based on the supposedly true experiences of the Wyrick family in their haunted house. It was based on a book by Cathey and Harrington (2007). To my knowledge, the claims made in the book have not been carefully checked by any serious investigator. But it is relevant to point out that they have been endorsed by William Roll, a parapsychological investigator who was conned by Tina Resch (page 64) back in 1984.

Wondering about another haunted house movie "based on a true story"—2013's *The Conjuring*? Joe Nickell (2014) has investigated the claims made for that case as well and found them to be based on "folktales," "waking dreams, contagion (the spreading of belief from person to person by suggestion), and probably pranking by one or more of the five girls" involved. Also involved were "a phony demonologist and clairvoyant" (25)—the Warrens again. Another one bites the dust due to careful investigation. This film introduced the world to Annabelle, the haunted Raggedy Ann doll, which was in the Warrens' occult museum. She has "starred" in at least three films since then.

Claims of real hauntings don't have to originate through conscious hoaxes, as did the Amityville and Southington stories. They can start with simple misremembering and then grow into what appears, in the absence of careful investigation, to be a really impressive case of haunting. So it was with the haunting of the Kimo Theater in Albuquerque, New Mexico, a seemingly dramatic haunting that has been investigated by Radford (2009). On August 2, 1951, an explosion at the Kimo killed a six-year-old boy, Robert Darnall.

The whole ghost story started when Dennis Potter, a former technical director at the theater, told a tale about a disastrous performance of Dickens's *Christmas Carol* that took place on December 25, 1974, twenty-three years earlier. It seems that sometime before the performance a plate of doughnuts that was a sort of shrine to Bobby's memory had been removed. The shrine was in the theater because it was believed that Bobby had died there. According to the legend that developed out of Mr. Potter's story, the removal of the pastries angered the boy ghost. He took his revenge by causing all sorts of mishaps and mayhem to take place during the Christmas performance. As Radford (2009) notes, the story of these events spread far and wide, often plagiarized from one writer to the next and often exaggerated and embellished. This is frequently the case with writers of allegedly true paranormal events—they fail to do any real research, copy from others without checking, and add new made-up events to the story. Radford, unlike any other writer, actually investigated the reported events, starting by asking the stunningly obvious question—did they even happen at all? The answer, it turns out, is no.

A check of the local paper in Albuquerque for the date of December 25, 1974, the day all hell was said to have broken out at the theater, was quite revealing. The theater wasn't showing live productions then. It was an adult movie house showing a porn film called *Teenage Fantasies*. Further search of Albuquerque papers turned up no mention, in the form of reviews, advertisements, or notices of any production of the Dickins classic at the Kimo from the 1970s. There was a production in 1986, but Radford interviewed members of the cast and they reported that nothing abnormal had happened. Careful reading of the newspapers also showed that Robert Darnall didn't even die in the theater. He died in an ambulance on the way to the hospital.

Was Dennis Potter lying when he told his story of the haunting of the Kimo? Probably not. Human memory is highly fallible, as will be seen in detail in chapter 7. I suspect that Potter had simply misremembered several innocuous events, exaggerated them in his own mind with numerous retellings until the full tale was created. It's something that happens to all of us. When I was in high school, I was fishing in a lake in northern Maine. I caught an eel—much to my surprise since I didn't then know that eels lived in freshwater lakes far inland. Through the years I'd tell the tale of the eel, which I remembered (and still do!) as being about four or five feet long. Imagine my great surprise when, many years later, I came across a photo my dad had taken of me holding the eel. Four or five feet long? Not a chance. It was about a foot long.

Ghosts and ghostly phenomena are most often reported and experienced in creepy old houses and other buildings and places like graveyards. Most reports of hauntings derive from mundane phenomena such as odd noises, a cold spot, or a door swinging shut when no one is around and the like. These are often interpreted as being the work of a ghostly presence even if no apparition is seen. It is certainly a huge leap from a few odd noises to a ghost. It is understandable that people might make such a leap. As noted earlier, there is a natural tendency to attribute agency to a ghost or spirit that is then seen as responsible for whatever phenomenon cannot be immediately explained. And, like the size of my eel, the inexplicableness of the phenomenon grows with the passage of time.

Back in the 1970s a fictitious London ghost, the "Phantom Vicar of Ratcliffe Wharf" (Wiseman 2011), demonstrated how expectations can create vivid ghost reports. Journalist Frank Smyth published an entirely made-up story of a murderous nineteenth-century vicar and his continued ghostly presence in a British magazine. Some years later a television program on the BBC found many people who reported having seen the ghost. Some of the reported encounters with the ghost were dramatic—being watched while getting undressed, for example. I have no doubt that these people were reporting feelings they genuinely had. It's just that the ghost to which they attributed these feelings had never existed.

Several years ago two students in my pseudoscience class did something similar to the vicar hoax. One requirement of the class is for students to do either a traditional term paper or some sort of project. For their project, these two made up a tragic, and totally false, story of a teenage girl who had killed herself. Her ghost haunted the local graveyard where she was buried. According to the story, the girl's ghost could be seen at night (would you expect to see a ghost at high noon?) around her tomb. The students took friends (not in the class) to the graveyard at night and filmed the result. It's both instructive and hilarious. With only a bit of prodding, a few became quite frightened because they felt the ghostly presence and how frightening it was. You might try something like this yourself to see how easy it is to get dramatic reports of ghosts on demand.

The nonexistent vicar and graveyard ghost were informative demonstrations, but a more formal demonstration of the effect of expectations would be nice. One has been provided by Lange and Houran (1997), who had people report any feelings and sensations they felt when in an abandoned theater. In one condition people were told that the place had a history of haunting. In a second condition the theater was simply said to be undergoing repair. The results were not at all surprising. Many more strange sensations and perceptions were reported by those who had been told of the (nonexistent) haunting than by those who believed they were just in an old building.

Perhaps people are just more likely to notice such things in a supposedly haunted location. To test this idea, Houran and Lange (1996) found a totally nonhaunted home. They had the residents keep a record of any strange or unusual events that took place over a period of thirty days. Sure enough, during that period there were numerous events that were characterized as odd or unusual. Had a troop of ghosts come to visit for the duration of the study? No—the couple was just paying more attention to things that they would normally have not thought anything of. But if those same minor events had taken place in a supposedly haunted location where every creak, slight breeze, and feeling of cold are immediately noticed and attributed to a haunting, this would have been interpreted as proof of ghostly presence.

Given what has been discussed above, we are now in a good position to understand what is going on when ghost hunters slink around various spooky old ruins in search of ghostly happenings. Are they going to find them? Of course they are! And all that fancy equipment such as electromagnetic field detectors, night vision goggles, and such is just window dressing that can give rise to more spurious signals of "something spooky." Take the electromagnetic field (EMF) detector. These are rather complex devices, and any number of nonghostly sources can give rise to signals. But in the context of a creepy deserted house, such signals will certainly be interpreted as due to something paranormal.

One piece of ghost-hunting equipment regularly generates what is claimed to be proof of hauntings. In past years it was a tape recorder. Now cell phones serve the same purpose. These produce what in the ghost-hunting business is called "electronic voice phenomenon" or EVP. One puts a recorder on "record," ideally in a graveyard or some other supposedly haunted place, and waits silently for a while and then plays back whatever sounds were caught. Typically, vague hissing noises are heard. These are interpreted as being the voices of the dead. This is an excellent example of pareidolia—the tendency to see or hear meaningful patterns in random noise.

The ghost hunters on TV use fairly cheap recorders, like their phones, to find EVP, which are said to have been generated by spirits trying to communicate. To do so, the spirits would have to alter the structure of whatever recording medium is being used. These devices aren't particularly sensitive. So why is it that the professional sound guys, who are right there behind the camera recording the sound with their extremely sensitive and very expensive state-of-the-art sound recording devices, never get anything like EVP?

If EVP was real, that is, the actual voices of ghosts or spirits, then individuals listening to the same EVP example should show a high degree of agreement about what the voice said. However, if EVP is just a case of auditory pareidolia, there should be little or no agreement. Ness and Phillips (2015) carried out a clever experiment to test whether people agreed about what was in examples of EVPs. They used as their stimuli actual EVPs taken from several ghost-hunter-type TV programs that claimed that the EVPs were real examples of communication from the dead. The people who listened to the EVPs were simply asked to report what they heard the voices say. The results were clear. There was no agreement between individuals about what the supposed voices were saying.

A nonparanormal example of auditory pareidolia demonstrates how powerful this effect can be. Back in the 1970s there were claims that, if you played certain phonograph records backward, you could hear evil, even satanic, hidden messages. Or just plain old dirty words. People would sit around and spin records in reverse to listen for such words and phrases. And, not surprisingly, they heard them, even though they weren't there. They were a construction of the pattern recognition processes in the brain. Vokey and Read (1985) played listeners a tape recording of a passage from *Alice in Wonderland* backward. When listeners were told just to listen but not to expect any specific coherent message, they only heard gibberish. But when they were asked to listen for a particular phrase, that phrase just popped right out of the background noise.

Photographs are also a common source of supposed evidence of ghosts or something paranormal. Spooky spirit photos were common in the nineteenth and early twentieth centuries, as noted in chapter 2. A popular modern type of photographic evidence of things that go bump in the night is the seemingly ever-present orbs. Orbs are bright round or roundish shapes that show up on photographs to the surprise of those who took the photographs because at the time they saw nothing like the things that later appeared. There are many interpretations of the orbs. One is that they are evidence of ghosts, although why ghosts would adopt such a small round form is never made clear. A slightly more outlandish view is that orbs are intelligent, perhaps alien, living beings. In reality, orbs are caused when the light of a camera flash reflects off of tiny dust particles in the air that the photographer was unaware of. Many amateur photographers jump to the conclusion that, since they didn't see the minute particles that caused the orbs, the images in their pictures must be evidence of something paranormal. Figure 3.3 shows a photo with an impressive number of orbs. It is reproduced from an article by Nickell and Biddle (2020) that describes how orbs and other normal, but unfamiliar, photographic effects are mistaken for ghosts.

Figure 3.3. Orbs. From Joe Nickell and Kenny Biddle, "So You Have a Ghost in Your Photo," *Skeptical Inquirer* 44, no. 4 (July/August 2020), figure 1 (https://skepticalinquirer.org/2020/06/so-you-have-a-ghost-in-your-photo/)

Hill (2012, 2017) surveyed the websites of one thousand amateur paranormal investigation groups in the United States. She found that a great majority of these groups used various types of scientific-sounding equipment to look for ghosts. But the websites showed that these amateurs had little idea of how to use the equipment or how to interpret the data the equipment generated. The results of these investigations were "ineffectual and without a sound foundation in scientific principles" and lacked the "specialized skills and high standards [that] characterize scientific work" (Hill 2012, 41). All these sorts of amateur investigators produce is a lot of meaningless "sciencey" sounding fluff. But they fill up lots of ghost-hunting "reality" shows.

Radford (2017a), in his book *Investigating Ghosts: The Scientific Search for Spirits*, also found that ghost hunters used all sorts of fancy gadgets such as infrared cameras, EMF detectors, and night vision goggles but had no real rationale as to why these things should detect ghosts. Ghost hunts are almost always conducted in the dark. It certainly makes it spookier than walking around an old house or fort in the light. But it also would make it much more difficult to detect something if that something was there. Radford describes going along on a ghost-hunting expedition being filmed for a TV show. These ghost-hunting TV shows never come up with anything other than, as I've said before, the usual suspects of odd noises, subjective feelings of unease or coldness, or sensed movement. Nor did the ghost hunters that Radford accompanied find anything concrete. It's almost as if the ghost hunters don't want to look too carefully for ghosts because that might show that there was nothing to ghost reports. Radford's book gives excellent advice on how to carefully and scientifically look for evidence of ghosts. If ghosts really existed, Radford's techniques would be much more likely to find evidence for them than having a bunch of amateurs stumbling around at night in some old house with all the lights out.

POLTERGEIST

Closely related to classical hauntings is the poltergeist, which comes from the German for "playful spirit." The two are sometimes reported together, as was the case at Borley Rectory. Some of the goings on in the

Amityville Horror house could have been classified as poltergeists had they not been revealed as part of a hoax. The vast majority of the thousands of poltergeist reports that have accumulated over the years are of mild, even humorous, events such as objects moving about when no one is watching, breaking of crockery, spontaneous small fires, and showers of pebbles and small stones, the latter often being inflicted on some particular adult such as a priest. Poltergeists, when they occur alone, are almost invariably associated with adolescent children. This association has led some parapsychologists (i.e., Fodor 1964) to propose that the approach of puberty and attendant increase in sexual energy and feelings in adolescents cause a release of psychic energy that is responsible for the poltergeist activity. This association between adolescents and poltergeist activity causes the more skeptical to reflect on adolescents' well-known love of pranks and practical jokes—particularly when played on adults. Those who believe poltergeists are a paranormal phenomenon will quickly point to many cases, mostly decades old, that "have never been explained." This is quite true but is merely another example of the logical fallacy so common among the proponents of the paranormal—saying that "if you can't explain it, it must be due to" whatever paranormal claim is being made.

A good example is a March 1984 poltergeist occurrence in Columbus, Ohio, which received nationwide and even worldwide media attention. Typically, the coverage was totally uncritical. In New York City, for example, WCBS-TV used the phrase "Poltergeist for real!" as the teaser for the story on the evening news. At the center of the incident was a fourteen-year-old girl named Tina Resch.

Shortly after Tina, an emotionally disturbed adoptee, saw the movie *Poltergeist*, objects began to fly about in the Resch household. This phenomenon quickly came to the attention of the *Columbus Dispatch*, which published several photos showing, allegedly, a telephone flying through the air under its own power while Tina looked on in horror. Parapsychologist William Roll of the Psychical Research Foundation in Chapel Hill, North Carolina, stayed in the Resch house to investigate the case. He concluded that "when I felt I had Tina under close observation" she demonstrated "genuine recurrent spontaneous psychokinesis" (quoted in Randi 1984–1985, 232). "Recurrent spontaneous psychokinesis," or RSPK, is Roll's term for the poltergeist phenomenon.

Randi, a well-known magician and fellow of the then named Committee for the Scientific Investigation of Claims of the Paranormal, also came to Columbus with a team of scientists to investigate the case but was denied entrance to the Resch house. Nonetheless, their investigation, reported in Randi (1984–1985), revealed that Tina had faked the entire string of occurrences. Not only were the media easily duped by Tina, but in several cases the media knew about the fraud but failed to report it.

The Resch poltergeist turned out to be so elusive that no one ever actually saw a single object even start to move of its own accord. This included the newspaper photographer, who found that if he watched an object, it stubbornly refused to budge. So he would hold up his camera and look away. "While Tina sat in a soft chair with two telephones within easy reach, Shannon (the photographer) looked away. When he saw a movement from the corner of his eye, he pressed the shutter" (Randi 1984–1985, 224). One of the photos obtained in this way was distributed by the Associated Press and touted widely as proof of the reality of the phenomenon. Examined closely, the photographic evidence in this case strongly suggested that Tina was faking the occurrences by simply throwing the phone and other "flying" objects when no one was looking. Randi's careful analysis of the other photos, many unpublished, of Tina and her flying phone strengthen the conclusion that she was faking. Interestingly, the editor of the *Columbus Dispatch*, Luke Feck, embarrassed by the revelation that he and his paper were taken in by so obvious a fake, refused Randi permission to print the photos he had given him earlier, in an apparent attempt to suppress the evidence of Tina's trickery and the newspaper's credulity.

This refusal came only after Randi had uncovered even more direct evidence of Tina's faking: she was caught faking on videotape. A camera crew from WTVN-TV in Cincinnati had been filming in the Resch home. While the crew was packing up to leave, a camera pointed at Tina was accidentally left on and recording. Randi (1984–1985) describes what the camera caught: "Seated at one end of the sofa, near an end-table, and believing the camera was no longer active, she watched carefully until she was unobserved, then reached up and pulled a table lamp toward herself, simultaneously jumping away, letting out a series of bleating noises, and feigning, quite effectively, a reaction of stark terror" (228). This all was revealed when the tape was processed. When confronted with the evidence, Tina said she had only done it to get the television crew to leave. Typically, this incident and Tina's explanation led some to conclude that Tina only cheated "sometimes"; the rest of the time the paranormal phenomena were genuine. For example, Mike Harden, the reporter who first reported the poltergeist, wrote in the *Columbus Dispatch* that the same day that Tina had been caught cheating the television crew had witnessed a true poltergeist occurrence in the form of a moving table. But WTVN crew member Robb Forest saw Tina move the table with her foot.

What of parapsychologist Roll's statement as to Tina's genuineness? It turned out that he, like others, had not actually seen any object start to move. In one incident, he was facing away from a picture when it fell from the wall. This took place upstairs in the Resch house and Tina had been up there, apparently alone, for half an hour before this event. As Roll was attempting to rehang the photograph, using a pair of pliers to drive in the nail, a small tape recorder flew some feet from the dresser where it had been left. The layout of the room shows that Roll had his back to the recorder when it made its short journey and, attending to the task of rehanging the fallen photograph, couldn't have been watching Tina closely at all. Randi (1984–1985) further points out that "Roll is myopic and wears thick glasses; he is a poor observer" (233).

So the Tina Resch case crashes in flames. But how many television stations and newspapers that initially reported it as verified evidence of the reality of poltergeists have informed their viewers or readers of the results of the full investigation of the case? Not many, as you might expect. Randi (1984–1985) makes an important point in his discussion of the Resch case, saying:

> I have long believed that the major difference between the skeptic and the parapsychologist is one of expectation. The former does not believe that validation of paranormal claims is imminent; the latter depends upon that event for justification. Also, the skeptic will invoke parsimony—the simplest explanation consistent with the facts—where the parapsychologist eschews it. Personally, I find it much more reasonable, when objects fly around the room in the vicinity of an unhappy 14-year-old, to suspect poor reporting and observation rather than a repeal of the basic laws of physics. (222)

Perception and memory being constructive, the expectations of the parapsychologist are frequently met.

NEAR-DEATH AND OUT-OF-BODY EXPERIENCES

The badly injured victim of an automobile accident is rushed to the nearest hospital emergency room. Working frantically, the doctors manage to save him. Later, after his recovery, he tells a strange story. He saw, from a vantage point near the ceiling of the emergency room, the entire scene as the doctors worked to save him. It was as if he were floating above his physical body, looking down on it. Then he found himself moving down a tunnel with a blazing white light at the end. As he neared the end of the tunnel, a being dressed in white, together with a dead relative, came toward him and told him his time had not yet come. During the entire experience, he felt a great sense of unity and profound understanding and a total lack of anxiety.

Reports such as this have been collected by several investigators, who argue that they represent true reports of an afterlife (Ring 1980; Moody 1976; Osis and Haraldsson 1977). These investigators started the modern interest in near-death experiences (NDEs). Some make a point of the great similarity of these "deathbed" visions, even across different cultures. This is what would be expected if the visions were really memories of a trip to the threshold of the afterlife. However, proponents of the afterlife interpretation of these reports grossly underestimate the variability among reports. One researcher (Rawlings 1978), for example, found that the patients he talked to often reported visiting hell. In Ring's reports, the tunnel imagery is rarely found. Moody has explicitly called attention to the great variability in the reports: "There is an enormously wide spectrum of experiences, with some people having only one or two of the elements, and others most of them" (1976, 87). In addition, reports of this type are quite rare. Most people lying critically injured in the emergency room don't experience them.

The way the reports are collected poses another serious problem for those who want to take them seriously as evidence of an afterlife. Osis and Haraldsson's (1977) study was based on replies received from ten thousand questionnaires sent to doctors and nurses in the United States and India. Only 6.4 percent were returned. Since it was the doctors and nurses who were giving the reports, not the patients who, presumably, actually had the experience, the reports were secondhand. This means they had passed through two highly fallible and constructive human memory systems (the doctor's or nurse's and the actual patient's) before reaching Osis and Haraldsson. In other cases (e.g., Moody 1976) the reports were given by the patients themselves but months and years after the event. Such reports are hardly sufficient to argue for the reality of an afterlife.

Near-death visions are actually hallucinations. Siegel (1980) described the high degree of similarity between near-death visions and other types of hallucinations (such as drug-induced hallucinations) in both form and content. Hallucinations caused by drugs frequently contain images of long tunnels, blinding light, otherworldly beings, friends and relatives (alive and dead), and so forth. However, most of the individuals who experience deathbed visions are not drugged. What, then, is responsible for their hallucinations? The answer is *cerebral anoxia*. When the body is badly injured—especially if the heart stops, even if only for a brief period—the brain is deprived of oxygen. Even a very brief period of cerebral anoxia, such as sixty to ninety seconds, can result in impaired neural function (Brierley and Graham 1984) and can result in experiences very similar to NDEs. Braithwaite and Dewe (2015) show that even syncopal episodes, common fainting spells, in which blood supply to the brain is temporarily reduced, can produce hallucinations very much like those experienced in NDEs. The effects of cerebral anoxia are well known. Initially there is a feeling of well-being and power. As the anoxia continues and more neurons become impaired, reality becomes vague and hallucinations, often visual, appear.

The response of the proponents of life after death to this argument is to admit that cerebral anoxia, drugs, and brain damage can cause hallucinations that are essentially identical to deathbed visions. But the hallucination hypothesis, they claim, is not sufficient to explain the visions because not every patient who has ever had such a vision has been conclusively shown to have been anoxic, brain damaged, or drugged. Again, the "irreducible minimum" number of allegedly unexplainable reports is thrown up as proof of the paranormal hypothesis after the initial mass of supposedly supportive evidence that the proponents started with has been whittled down to almost nothing by careful inspection. Certainly, there will always be cases in which, because of incomplete medical information, it is not possible to show that a particular patient was anoxic or intoxicated. However, the fact that anoxia and drug intoxication are known to produce hallucinations just like the report given by the patient would suggest the rational conclusion that the patient was anoxic or drugged, not that the patient had visited the threshold of the afterlife.

After recovery, patients sometimes report comments and bits of conversation that took place while they were presumably unconscious, either due to the severity of injuries or to anesthesia. Should this be seen as convincing evidence for some sort of "astral" body being detached from the physical body and observing the situation? No. Even during unconsciousness, the brain is able to register sensory impressions. The registration of stimuli in anesthetized patients was demonstrated decades ago by Millar and Watkinson (1983). While patients who were undergoing surgery were anesthetized, a tape-recorded list of words was presented to them. After recovery from anesthesia, their memory was tested. When asked to recall the words on the list, they were unable to do so. However, when they were asked simply to recognize which of two words had been presented to them, they were correct at a rate significantly above chance. Thus, even while under general anesthetic, the brain does retain some capacity to store new information, although it may be difficult to retrieve this information later. This is very likely the source of the snippets of conversation that sometimes turn up in deathbed visions.

The content of an NDE where the experiencer visits the other side varies as a function of the culture and religion of that person (Marsh 2010; Augustine 2015). This is not what would be expected if the person was actually visiting some afterlife that will be the same for all humans when we die. I found it especially amusing to learn, from Marsh's excellent book, that some NDE reports from India involve the individual ending up in a bureaucratic waiting room and finding out that they're there due to a paperwork error and are being sent back. Great—you've gone to all the trouble of almost dying only to arrive in the afterlife to find that it's run by the spiritual equivalent of incompetent clerks in the Department of Motor Vehicles! Happily, Marsh reports, the spirits responsible for the paperwork errors are sometimes punished.

More seriously, Augustine (2015) notes that NDEs often include components that clearly show they aren't real. Experiencers may meet people who are not even dead yet. Or they may report seeing dramatic things that supposedly happened while they were unconscious and on their way to the afterlife that, in fact, didn't happen. One patient returned from his experience to find a team of medical personnel around him. They had been responsible for saving his life. He thanked them profusely, especially the team leader, whom he had seen taking charge of the procedures that brought him back. The problem was that this particular doctor, although he was the team leader and was present when the patient regained consciousness, had not been present during the actual event. He had been in a completely different part of the hospital and had had nothing whatsoever to do with the patient's recovery.

Another problem with reports of NDEs is a selection bias as to what is, and is not, reported. Proponents of the reality of such experiences such as Moody and Ring have rather specific ideas about what the experiences should contain. It is very likely that people who have experiences that correspond to those expectations will be more likely to report them. And those whose experiences do not match the expectations will be less likely to report what happened to them.

Two book-length descriptions of NDEs seemed both highly detailed and initially convincing. In 2004 a six-year-old boy with the highly appropriate name of Alex Malarkey was seriously injured in a car accident that left him in a coma for several months. When he came out of the coma, he told a tale of going to heaven, meeting Christ and Satan, and gave vivid descriptions of what heaven was like. The story was turned into a book, *The Boy Who Came Back from Heaven*, written by Alex and his father, Kevin, in 2010. The book sold nearly six million copies before Kevin, who was left quadriplegic by the accident, admitted in early 2015 that he'd made the whole thing up to get attention.

A somewhat similar tale was told by neurosurgeon Ebon Alexander, who in his bestselling 2012 book *Proof of Heaven* told of visiting the afterlife and acquiring all sorts of esoteric wisdom while he was in a coma due to a bacterial infection of his brain. Dittrich (2012) has examined Alexander's claims and found them wanting. Alexander's story has him in a coma, but the physician on his case states that he was "awake but hallucinating." Alexander became more of a tent show evangelical promoting his view of heaven than a neurosurgeon. In the book and elsewhere, he keeps promising to share the great spiritual insights he gained while cavorting about in the afterlife, but he never quite delivers on these promises. We'll all just have to buy his next book!

In contrast to NDEs, out-of-body experiences (OBEs) take place when the experiencer is very much alive and in no danger. Some individuals claim that they can leave their physical bodies at will and travel through space (and time!) using their "astral" bodies, thus the term *astral projection*. Such claims have attracted a good deal of interest on the part of parapsychologists. At least conceptually, testing for the reality of OBEs would seem to be quite easy. You just find someone who claims to be able to have an OBE at will, place them is a secure room, and ask them to read, for example, the serial number of a dollar bill sealed in a different room.

Augustine and Fishman (2015) summarized the studies attempting to verify the reality of OBEs. In these studies, people are asked to identify some sort of visual target supposedly hidden from them. These studies have serious flaws. For example, self-proclaimed OBE-er Ingo Swann was asked to draw pictures of objects hidden from him on a shelf ten feet high. He seemed to be very successful. However, there was one little problem. Swann was allowed to be in the same room as the objects on the shelf without any supervision. How many different ways can you think of to cheat under those circumstances? The conclusion of the careful examination of the empirical studies of OBEs is that, while they certainly may seem very real to the experiencer, they are not real in the sense that nothing actually leaves the body.

Studies of neurological patients have suggested a brain-related cause of out-of-body experiences. In an important paper, Blanke and colleagues (2002) reported the case of a forty-three-year-old epileptic woman who, for diagnostic reasons, had a grid of electrodes placed on the surface of her brain. With these electrodes, it was possible not only to record brain electrical activity but to stimulate different parts of the cortex. Stimulation of one area of the cortex, the right angular gyrus, reliably caused an out-of-body experience. Part of an out-of-body experience is a feeling of floating outside and above one's body. This is likely due to a disturbance of the vestibular sensory system, the system that tells us where in space our body is. The angular gyrus stimulation reported by Blanke and colleagues resulted in "whole body displacements (vestibular responses), indicating that out-of-body experiences may reflect a failure by the brain to integrate complex somato-sensory and vestibular information" (269). A major component of an out-of-body experience can thus be generated by artificial stimulation of the brain. This suggests that spontaneous such experiences are due to temporary, minor brain processes, not by people's spirit (or soul or whatever) actually leaving the body.

Blanke and colleagues (2004) described six patients who had out-of-body experiences secondary to either epileptic seizures or other neurological disorders. The authors were able to specify the area of brain disturbance in five of the six patients. These were distributed over the more posterior parts of the brain on both the left and the right sides but seemed to be centered around the junction of the temporal, occipital, and parietal lobes, an area known to be involved in processing of information about the body and body part locations in space. In these patients the OBE occurred spontaneously rather than due to outside stimulation, as in the case reported by Blanke and colleagues (2002).

DeRidder and colleagues (2007) studied one patient who had had electrodes implanted in the brain in a (sadly unsuccessful) attempt to treat tinnitus. Stimulation using these electrodes caused an OBE. But this group went a bit further in their study of the OBE phenomenon by using PET scanning, a technique that allows the visualization of activity of the cortex of the brain. They found that when the patient had an OBE, specific cortical areas in the right hemisphere became active. These included areas of the parietal, temporal, and a bit of the occipital lobe. This anatomical location is similar to that observed by Blanke and colleagues (2004).

These studies of neurological patients do not mean, of course, that people who spontaneously have OBEs are suffering from brain damage. It does suggest that certain areas of the brain are spontaneously active in those normal individuals who have OBEs. As noted above, some people claim to be able to have OBEs at will. It would be very interesting to have them produce an OBE while their brains are being scanned to see which areas become active during their experience.

Smith and Messier (2014) did such a study. They used functional neuroimaging to study a normal individual who was "able, at will, to produce somatosensory sensations that are experienced as her body moving outside the boundaries of her physical body" (5). Among the brain areas activated during these voluntary OBEs was the junction between the left temporal and parietal lobes. This area is important for integrating information about bodily feelings and the location of the body from the several sensory systems. Blanke and Arzy (2005) have reviewed findings suggesting that OBEs are due to impaired processing at this location in the brain. Smith and Messier concluded that the brain activation pattern of the individual they studied showed that she had a very "unusual type of kinesthetic imagery" (2014, 5). This study is important because it shows that one can have vivid out-of-body experiences without either brain damage or any paranormal aspect to the experience.

When all is said and done, the evidence for ghosts, OBEs, NDEs, and the whole panoply of such claims in no way, shape, or form adds up to anything even close to support for the reality of any sort of disembodied spirit or consciousness, after our death or before it. This is not to say that OBEs and NDEs do not have real and powerful emotional impact on many who experience them. They can be life changing. NDEs can have psychological effects on those who experience them. The individuals may become more secure or more religious and may adopt a generally more mystical and "spiritual" worldview (Irwin 1985). These personality changes testify to the power of the misinterpretation of what is actually happening to the individual. Similarly, although less dramatic, changes may take place in those who experience auditory hallucinations that they misinterpret as evidence for life after death or see an object in the sky that they can't identify at once and so believe it to be a flying saucer guided by aliens. The personality changes and extreme conviction with which people hold to their new beliefs, such as those engendered by NDEs, convince many that the new beliefs are valid. It is important to remember, however, that the strength of a belief is no guide to its validity.

The NDE and OBE hallucinations seem so real and are so powerful because, as Oliver Sacks (2015) explains, "they deploy the very same systems in the brain that actual perceptions do. When one hallucinates voices, the auditory pathways are activated; when one hallucinates a face, the fusiform face area, normally used to perceive and identify faces in the environment, is stimulated." Since higher brain areas, such as the frontal lobes, may be impaired in these situations, they are not available to help the experiencer realize that the experience is not real. This is very similar to the dream state. When we're dreaming, we're (usually) not aware that the dream is not real. But when we wake up, and these higher areas come back online, most of us realize that we didn't really swim to France in a red Volkswagen, have a chat with President Lincoln, or hear a pterodactyl quote Shakespeare.

There is another tack to take in evaluating arguments for disembodied consciousness. This involves examining the role of the brain not just in consciousness but in the basic cognitive processes that allow humans, as well as other animals, to communicate, remember, and perceive. OBEs, NDEs, and ghosts are by definition examples of consciousness and cognitive processing outside a physical body. This is a spinoff of that ancient philosophical position known as dualism, which contends that the mind (spirit, soul, whatever) is separate from the physical body. The mind is, somehow, just "out there" away from the body. Before there was much, if any, understanding of how the brain is required for cognition and consciousness, dualism was a respectable position. That is no longer the case. While there is a great deal about how the brain produces consciousness and cognition that is not yet understood, there is also a great deal about this issue that is well understood. It is clear that different anatomical circuits in the brain are responsible for language, memory, and perception. Each of these basic cognitive processes is a combination of many subprocesses, each mediated by different brain areas.

The reality of these different areas is testified to by thousands of studies of brain scans of normal individuals. Studies of patients with brain damage to specific brain areas tell the same tale—different brain areas do different things. Damage to different brain areas causes specific cognitive impairments. In one of the most devastating types of brain damage, that seen in dementing diseases like Alzheimer's, cognitive functions may be lost almost entirely. If there is mind "out there" independent of the body, then why doesn't that disembodied mind pick up the slack and overcome the effects of brain damage? It sure isn't doing the demented any good!

Ghosts and spirits, with no bodies at all, are said to engage in the full range of human cognitive activities. How can they do this without a brain? One answer is that the brain is just sort of a transmitter/receiver that passes information to and from the extracorporeal mind that is "out there." In this view, all the complex cognition is done outside the brain. But this answer doesn't work. If the brain really were just some sort of transmitter/receiver, it would not have evolved the extremely complex circuitry that allows the processing of language, memory, and perception. This argument is developed in more detail in Hines (2015), Gennaro and Fishman (2015), and Piccinini and Bahar (2015).

As has been mentioned before, the burden of proof falls on the proponents of paranormal claims like ghosts and their kin. It is, of course, impossible to prove that there is *not* a disembodied mind out there somewhere. The great mathematician Pierre Simon LaPlace was asked by Napoleon what role God played in mathematics. LaPlace's response is perfect here as well in regard to the question of the existence of a noncorporeal mind: "Sir, I have no need of that hypothesis."

A phenomenological point is sometimes raised to argue that OBEs really are due to something leaving the body: People reporting OBEs almost always report seeing their own body from a vantage point somewhere above it. If the OBE were nothing more than a hallucination combined with bits and pieces of memories acquired during the event, wouldn't one expect the result to be seen from the perspective of the physical body—for example, with the doctors looking down on the patient? In fact, there is nothing at all unusual about the vantage point seen in OBEs. Remember the last time you were at the beach? Or the dinner you had last night? Try to form a visual image of some such occasion. The overwhelming majority of people see the scene from a vantage point above where they actually were. They, and presumably you, "see" themselves in the scene. This is in spite of the fact that all the information used to construct the image comes from memory.

In her book-length review of the literature on the psychology (as opposed to neurology) of OBE experiences, parapsychologist Susan Blackmore (1992) concluded that the OBE experience, while extremely interesting from a psychological point of view, provides no evidence for any type of paranormal event. Irwin (1985) reached the same conclusion. Both Blackmore and Irwin focused on psychological differences between those who have and have not experienced OBEs (OBE-ers and non-OBE-ers). Blackmore hypothesized that OBE-ers would be better than non-OBE-ers at forming visual images and that OBE-ers would be poorer at distinguishing reality from fantasy than non-OBE-ers. Research on the psychological differences between OBE-ers and non-OBE-ers has confirmed Blackmore's hypotheses. OBE-ers are more likely to remember dreams from a bird's-eye perspective and are better at forming visual images from that perspective than are non-OBE-ers (Blackmore 1986a). It is this bird's-eye perspective that is so common in OBEs and is one of the aspects of the experience that OBE-ers find so compelling. People who have experienced OBEs are also more susceptible to hypnosis than are non-OBE-ers (see Irwin 1985 for a brief review). OBE-ers also show greater suggestibility and become deeply absorbed more easily than non-OBE-ers (Irwin 1985). Individuals who can be hypnotized are more likely to experience imagined or suggested events as real, even when not hypnotized (Irwin 1985). Thus, the individual who has become convinced that some nonphysical aspect of their personality has left their physical body differs from the individual who has not had such an experience in that they are less able to distinguish reality from fantasy.

REINCARNATION

Arguments that reincarnation is a real phenomenon are based on reports of people who, either spontaneously or under hypnosis, remember past lives and details of those lives that they would have, supposedly, no other way of knowing. Cases allegedly proving reincarnation are numerous, and it has proved impossible to conduct detailed investigations of all of them. However, when the most dramatic cases are investigated carefully, evidence for the reality of reincarnation evaporates. The investigation of alleged cases of reincarnation reveals the normal sources of the information that the individuals supposedly could have obtained only in a previous life. Proponents of reincarnation often conduct poor investigations and hence miss the true explanations.

One famous, and typical, alleged case of reincarnation is that of Bridey Murphy. In 1952 a woman named Virginia Tighe was hypnotized. She reported details of a previous life in Cork, Ireland, as "Bridey Murphy." While hypnotized, she spoke in a distinct Irish accent that she did not have normally and described her life in Cork in great detail. Her case was reported as proof of reincarnation in Bernstein's (1956) best-selling book *The Search for Bridey Murphy*.

The case was thoroughly investigated several years later. It was discovered that, as a child, Mrs. Tighe had had a neighbor across the street who had grown up in Ireland and used to tell her stories about life there. The woman's maiden name? You guessed it—Bridey Murphy. Further, it was revealed that Mrs. Tighe had been involved in theater in high school and had "learned several Irish monologues, which she had delivered in what her former teacher referred to as a heavy Irish brogue" (Alcock 1978–1979, 38; see also Gardner 1957 for more on the debunking of the Bridey Murphy case).

Iverson (1977) reported the case of Jane Evans, among others, in a book claiming to prove the existence of reincarnation. Evans was a housewife living in Wales who, under hypnosis, gave details of six past lives. The great amount of historically accurate detail in Evans's accounts led Iverson to argue that her case was excellent proof of reincarnation. For example, in one of her past lives she was a maid of Jacques Coeur, an extremely wealthy and powerful merchant in fifteenth-century France. Evans "was able to fully describe the exteriors and interiors of Coeur's magnificent house—she even gave details of the carvings over the fireplace in his main banquet hall" (Harris 1986, 21). Impressive stuff, to be sure, until it is realized that Coeur's house is "one of the most photographed houses in all of France" (22), interior and exterior.

Evans's account of her life in Coeur's house contains one most puzzling, and significant, error. She says he was not married and had no children. But he was married and had five children—not the sort of thing the maid would be likely to overlook. This omission on Evans's part is most illuminating. *The Moneyman*, a novel based on Coeur's life by Thomas B. Costain, contains great detail about Coeur's life but makes no mention of his wife or children. Harris (1986, 22), who investigated Iverson's (1977) cases, states that "there is overwhelmingly strong evidence" that this book provided the basis for Evans's "memories" of her life in fifteenth-century France.

Evans's tales of her other lives contained similar errors and historical inconsistencies. She also reported a life as a Jew in the twelfth century in York, England. In that life she remembered being forced to wear a badge of yellow circles denoting that she was Jewish. However, badges for Jews were not used in England until the thirteenth century and then were not made of yellow circles but white stripes (Harris 1986).

In yet another life, Evans was a woman living in the time of the Roman occupation of England. Her knowledge of that period was quite detailed. It was this detail that allowed Harris (1986) to trace the origin of her information. It came from a best-selling novel set in that time period titled *The Living Wood* (De Wohl 1947). Harris notes that "*every single piece of information* given by Jane Evans can be traced to De Wohl's fictional account. She uses his fictional sequences in exactly the same order and even speaks of his fictional characters, such as Curio and Valerius, as if they were real people" (1986, 23).

Are cases like those of Bridey Murphy and Jane Evans hoaxes? Not in the usual sense that a conscious attempt was made to deceive. Tighe and Evans (and the hundreds of others who report past-life memories) presumably really believe that these memories come from a past life. In just the same way, people who see a strange light at night often come to believe passionately that they have seen a flying saucer, complete with all the details one would expect on such a craft. Such belief can be extremely convincing to others, even though the belief is wrong.

Ian Stevenson (1918–2007), a parapsychologist at the University of Virginia in Charlottesville, was a leading proponent of reincarnation. In his writings on the subject (Stevenson 1975, 1977), he presents case studies of people who have what he considers memories of past lives that they could not have obtained in any normal way. In one report (Stevenson 1975) he described Indian children with alleged past-life memories. Barker (1979b), a colleague of Stevenson, has investigated similar Indian cases. In one he considered the "most authentic, evidential and thoroughly investigated" (269), he concluded that the child had acquired through normal means the information that others could take as evidence of reincarnation.

Stevenson's work has been widely criticized, even in parapsychological circles (see Edwards 1996 for a fuller discussion). The major problem is that the methods he used to investigate alleged cases of reincarnation are inadequate to rule out simple, imaginative storytelling on the part of the children claiming to be reincarnations of dead individuals. In the seemingly most impressive cases Stevenson (1975, 1977) reported, the children claiming to be reincarnated knew friends and relatives of the dead individual. The children's knowledge of facts about these individuals is, then, somewhat less than conclusive evidence for reincarnation.

Many proponents of reincarnation use hypnosis to elicit past-life memories. This technique produces highly unreliable reports because hypnotized individuals will readily respond to leading questions, make up stories, fantasize, and thus report nonexistent past lives in detail. They may often truly believe that their "memories" are evidence for past lives, but, as has been seen, the strength of a belief is a very poor guide to its truth. Even claims that hypnosis can regress individuals back to their own childhoods are unfounded (Nash 1987).

The same type of process may take place even when people are not under hypnosis. When asked to relax and "imagine" themselves in some past life, they begin to make up a story set in the appropriate time and place. Some fantasy-prone individuals have difficulty separating reality from fantasy, and the self-generated past-life story may take on so much reality that they believe it to be a real past-life memory.

Proponents of reincarnation sometimes claim that individuals can speak languages they have not learned in their present lives. This is said to occur especially under age-regression hypnosis. Thomason (1984, 1986–1987), a linguist, investigated three such cases. As far as I know, these are the only three such cases to have been investigated by a qualified linguist. In the first of the three cases, a hypnotist claimed that one of his patients was speaking Bulgarian while hypnotized. The hypnotist himself did not know any Bulgarian and apparently made the judgment based on the general "sound" of the patient's utterances. In fact, the "language" was not only not Bulgarian but wasn't any language at all. It was merely run together sets of syllables that had a Slavic sound. The second case was similar. A patient claimed to be speaking Gaelic and to be a fourteenth-century Frenchman. Analysis of his speech showed that it combined modern French and Latin in a hodge-podge. Further undermining this patient's claim to regression to a past life are the facts that Gaelic was never spoken in France and the patient made many historically incorrect statements about fourteenth-century France while under hypnosis. The third case was of a woman who claimed to have been an Apache in a previous life. Her speech was almost all Hollywood-style pidgin English, for example: "He ride ponies for white man. I no care. He [white man] spoil my Dwaytskem [her husband]. I no like. He scout for white man. I go to happy hunting ground" (1984, 547). Thomason (1984) comments on an earlier analysis by Ian Stevenson (1974) of a woman known as "TE" who was supposed to be able to speak Swedish, learned in a past life. She notes that "Stevenson is . . . unsophisticated about language, and TE's 'Swedish' is as unconvincing as" the Bulgarian, Gaelic, and Apache in the other cases she examined (347).

Ransom (2015), a former research assistant for Stevenson, specifically asked Stevenson for details of those cases where, according to Stevenson, the "investigation had begun *before* the families of the present personality and the 'previous' one had met and probably talked among themselves about the details" (574) of the events in the life of the "previous" individual. Out of 1,114 cases, only eleven fit this requirement. Ransom reports that seven had "serious flaws" and the other four had "weaknesses" common to the rest of the cases reported by Stevenson.

Descriptions of other impressive-sounding evidence for reincarnation that disappeared upon close examination can be found in Harris (1986) and Edwards (1996). Edwards (1986) comments on Wilson's (1982) book, saying that when "all the most famous reincarnation cases [in it] are minutely examined and on the basis of meticulous research[,] all of them are found wanting" (34). For more philosophical criticisms of reincarnation theory, Edwards (1996) has a good discussion.

Mary Roach, in her very amusing but highly informative book *Spook* (2005) has chronicled her adventures in investigating all aspects of research on life after death. Her chapter on reincarnation is especially revealing of the problems with the claims made by Stevenson and similar researchers.

According to the new age movement, humankind is just on the threshold of a so-called new age of psychic enlightenment in which all psychic powers will be verified as real; all humans will possess such powers; people will all love one another; war, disease, and hunger will be forever banished from the earth; and, in short, the earth will be transformed into a near-paradise. A particularly bizarre element of the new age vision is the claim that just such a world is seen when people are hypnotically sent into the future ("progressed" as opposed to "regressed"). Another claim is that people who have near-death experiences report being told of such a world by "others" during the experience. Unfortunately, those who have "progressed" have been sent far into the future, between 2100 and about 2600—too far ahead, of course, to enable one who is "progressed" to bring back specific information with which to test the claim that they really stepped into the future.

VAMPIRES AND ZOMBIES

One can hardly go to the movies or watch TV without coming across vampires and zombies in great number and innumerable situations. I doubt whether anyone, today, really believes that vampires exist. But clearly that belief was once widespread, especially in Europe in the Middle Ages, and it is instructive to examine the bases of that belief. Before the modern routine use of embalming and sturdy coffins, bodies, especially those of the poor or who died of a feared disease, were often hastily and shallowly buried. This was quite common in rural areas, areas where large animals such as wolves, bears, wild dogs, and coyotes acted as scavengers and could dig up a body. At that time not much was known about the natural process of decomposition of corpses. Often a corpse will bloat as gas is produced during decomposition. The top layer of skin may slough off, leaving the deeper layers, which look reddish, exposed. The people of the Middle Ages were excellent observers of what happens as a corpse decomposes. The problem was that they misinterpreted what they observed. The bloated, ruddy-looking features of the corpse were seen as evidence that the body had been well fed since it now looked "fatter" and "healthier" with its new ruddy complexion. The case for the body having returned from the dead and getting nourishment was obvious—people get fatter by eating more, so that corpse must have been eating because it was now "fatter." And what was the vampire eating? Blood of course. This was proven when attempts were made to slay the vampire by driving a stake through its heart. One would often see a reddish liquid coming out of the mouth. It wasn't new blood but the liquefied remains of the decomposed internal organs along with some blood from the body itself. But no one knew that then. Finally, the vampire could speak—when the stake was pounded in, the corpse would let out a low moan. This was caused by gasses being forced up through the larynx by the pressure on the chest. It must have been terrifying to hear. Barber (2010) has discussed the history of vampires and the reasons for the belief in their existence much more extensively in his excellent, witty, and a bit morbid book *Vampires, Burial, and Death*.

There are, however, individuals who adopt a vampire "lifestyle," in some cases drinking small amounts of human blood from time to time. The blood is obtained from consenting donors. These are the "sanguinarian" vampires. Less extreme followers of vampirism seem to be an extension of the goth culture.

They are perfectly able to go out in the sun, eat normal food; they do not believe they can transform into bats and fly about at night (Laycock 2009).

If no one believes in real vampires anymore, such is not the case for zombies. The claim has been made by Wade Davis (1985) in his popular book *The Serpent and the Rainbow* that not only do zombies really exist but the method of making them is known and used by Haitian witch doctors. According to Davis, the witch doctors use a poison called tetrodotoxin (TTX), which is found in local puffer fish, as one ingredient of a "zombie powder" that is said to make zombies. The powder contains other interesting ingredients, such as, sometimes, rotting human brains. The idea is that the TTX renders victims mindless pawns of whomever has control. In fact, as I've discussed in detail elsewhere (Hines 2008), this is all total nonsense. TTX is a poison, and its effects are well known. It blocks nerve conduction in the peripheral nervous system. In smaller doses it can cause nausea, vomiting, and weakness. If enough is ingested, it can be fatal. But it doesn't get into the brain, so it does not affect cognition—it doesn't turn one into a mindless slave. Thus, the idea that voodoo sorcerers use it to turn out slave field hands is preposterous. A bunch of puking, half-paralyzed guys aren't going to be particularly efficient workers!

LABORATORY PARAPSYCHOLOGY

Parapsychology is the study of extrasensory perception (ESP), precognition or clairvoyance (the ability to see into the future), and psychokinesis (the ability to move objects with psychic powers). Collectively, these are often referred to as psi or psi phenomena. The experimental literature in parapsychology is vast. Forty years ago Hyman (1985a) estimated that it consisted of approximately three thousand experiments. That number has only increased since then. These experiments have been largely carried out by competent, honest, rational investigators who are convinced that the data support the existence of psi phenomena. Nonetheless, the experimental work conducted to date has left the great majority of scientists unconvinced, to say the least, that ESP or any other such phenomenon has been demonstrated.

It is well beyond the scope of this chapter to review the entire corpus of experimental work in parapsychology, so the chapter will focus on the categories of experiments that are considered by proponents to show the best evidence for the reality of psi phenomena. Proponents might object to this approach on the grounds that it fails to consider certain specific experiments that proponents believe clearly establish the reality of ESP and related phenomena. Several points made earlier answer this type of objection. It will be recalled that in the cases of N-rays, polywater, and cold fusion, it was not necessary for skeptics to explain away every experimental result that seemed to support the existence of these phenomena. What convinced almost everyone that these phenomena were spurious was their failure to replicate, combined with a powerful common factor that would explain, in general, the seemingly supportive results. In the case of N-rays, this factor was the use of subjective measures of N-ray effects. In the polywater case, it was the inadequate examination of the "polywater" for impurities.

Further, the demand that every experiment in parapsychology must be considered and explained away in detail before one can reject the existence of psi phenomena is identical to the position of UFO proponents that skeptics must be able to attribute every UFO report to some known object or phenomenon before the extraterrestrial hypothesis of UFOs can be rejected. As will be seen in chapters 7 and 8, there will always be some "irreducible minimum" number of unexplained UFO sightings. This in no way proves the claim that UFOs are extraterrestrial spacecraft; it simply means that investigators will never have all the information needed to find the causes of each sighting.

Applying this logic to the parapsychological literature, the present chapter will focus on the failure of parapsychological studies to replicate, and the multiple and general procedural errors that have led to results seemingly supportive of psi phenomena. The reasons why many parapsychologists remain convinced of the reality of such phenomena, in spite of extremely poor evidence, will also be discussed.

Parapsychologists often complain that their critics require higher standards of proof for claims of psi phenomena than for other types of claims. They argue that critics reject as proof of the reality of psi evidence that they would accept as sufficient to prove more mundane claims. As was shown in chapter 1, this is both true and reasonable, as extraordinary claims demand extraordinary proof.

THE NATURE OF THE EVIDENCE

Historically, the first type of evidence used to argue for the reality of ESP and related phenomena was drawn from spiritualism. As was noted in chapter 2, such evidence was inadequate because of widespread fraud and the fact that witnesses who reported impressive spiritualistic phenomena were untrained in magic and sleight of hand.

In the 1930s a new, more laboratory-oriented approach to the study of ESP gained popularity among parapsychologists. Subjects were to identify long series of hidden objects; their "hit rate" would be compared to that expected by chance. The objects to be guessed were usually cards, dice, or numbers. The percent of correct guesses was the dependent measure. The most famous practitioners of this type of experimental parapsychology were J. B. Rhine of Duke University in Durham, North Carolina, and S. C. Soal in England. Rhine's experiments are well known in this country, and his procedures for studying ESP have come to form the popular view of a typical ESP experiment. Rhine actually coined the term *extrasensory perception* in 1934 and popularized the use of the now-famous Zener ESP cards. These cards were named for a Duke University psychology professor, Carl Zener, who developed them when working with Rhine. Zener cards consist of a deck of twenty-five cards, five each with a different design printed on the face: square, circle, star, cross, and three wavy lines.

In the standard ESP experiment using Zener cards, the cards are arranged in random sequence, then shown—face down and one at a time—to the subject, who must identify which of the five designs is on the card. Since there are five possible designs, the rate of correct responses (the "hit rate") expected by chance is 20 percent. Hit rates significantly above chance are taken as evidence for ESP. So are results significantly below chance. This latter claim will strike readers with some statistical background as, well, odd, as it should. More on this later.

The results of Rhine's experiments can be fairly easily summarized. For the most part, subjects scored at chance levels. That is, the hit rate when guessing which design was on the card was the 20 percent expected by chance. Occasionally, however, a few subjects were found to score significantly above chance for at least some period of time. This effect typically declined as testing of these "gifted" subjects continued.

Many people, having heard about ESP and related phenomena in the popular media, tend to think there is a considerable body of scientific evidence for such phenomena. This is simply not so. The major problem in parapsychology is the lack of any repeatable paranormal phenomenon. Occasionally, seemingly impressive results pop up, but they have the curious property of not being repeatable in other laboratories—at least not when procedural, statistical, or other flaws in the construction of the experiment are corrected. Several examples of this will be discussed below. As in the case of N-rays and polywater, lack of repeatability is a sign that the alleged phenomenon is merely an artifact, the result of some experimental flaw, and not a real effect. It is this lack of repeatability of paranormal phenomena that has convinced the great majority of the scientific community that psi phenomena are nonexistent.

The ubiquity of negative results has been troubling to parapsychologists as well as to their critics. Dommeyer (1975) commented that

> the reader inexperienced in parapsychology is likely to believe . . . that psi phenomena are relatively commonplace. The scientific investigator knows that this is not so. . . . The present reviewer, after spending the greater part of two summers in the 1960s at the Parapsychology Laboratory at Duke University, was unable to observe over those months a single identifiable instance of ESP or PK. (11)

Crumbaugh (1966) made a similar point, but his experience covered a much longer period of time:

> At the time [1938] of performing the experiments involved I fully expected that they would yield easily all the final answers. I did not imagine that after 28 years I would still be in as much doubt as when I had begun. I repeated a number of the then current Duke techniques, but the results of 3,024 runs [one run

consists of [twenty-five guesses] of the ESP cards, as much work as Rhine reported in his first book, were all negative. In 1940 I utilized further methods with high school students, again with negative results. (524)

Beloff (1973) made the same point:

I recently completed a seven-year programme of parapsychological research with the help of one full time research assistant. No one would have been more delighted to obtain positive results than we, but for all the success we achieved ESP might just as well not have existed. I have not found on comparing notes with other parapsychologists . . . that my experience is in any way out of the ordinary.

These and additional testimony making the same point can be found in Alcock (1981).

The most common rationale offered by parapsychologists to explain the lack of a repeatable demonstration of ESP or other psi phenomena is to say that ESP in particular and psi phenomena in general are elusive or jealous phenomena. This means the phenomena go away when a skeptic is present or when skeptical "vibrations" are present. This argument seems nicely to explain away some of the major problems facing parapsychology until it is realized that it is nothing more than a classic nonfalsifiable hypothesis, like those discussed in chapter 1.

It is common in parapsychology for a new method of studying psi phenomena to be reported with much initial optimism that finally a way has been found to obtain a repeatable demonstration of the phenomena. Often the initial report is accompanied by seemingly impressive results. But when attempts are made by other laboratories to use the new technique, no hint of paranormal phenomena is found. Examples of this pattern of events will be discussed in the next section. Skeptics argue that the reason for the lack of evidence for psi phenomena when an experiment is repeated are such mundane things as better experimental controls and procedures and better statistical analysis. Proponents, however, are likely to say that others failed to obtain evidence for psi phenomena because they didn't believe in them. And so, since such phenomena are jealous, they promptly went away.

A related finding in parapsychology is the oft-noted negative correlation between the quality of a parapsychological experiment (measured by the degree and rigor of controls, use of appropriate statistical tests, and so forth) and the probability of obtaining results favorable to the existence of psi phenomena. In other words, the better controlled the experiment, the less likely it is to show evidence for psi phenomena (see Hyman 1985b for one example). The skeptical explanation of this correlation is quite simple: the better and more rigorous the controls in an experiment, the less the chance for artifactual findings to occur. If psi doesn't exist, then when one removes the various sources of artifacts in an experiment, evidence for psi phenomena will also disappear. The proponent who accepts the "jealous phenomena" point of view (and not all do) has a different explanation: the use of strict controls is evidence of a lack of belief in the phenomena, and this causes the phenomena to go away. This approach is used to explain even the failure of believers to obtain good evidence of psi phenomena. Even for strong believers, the use of strict controls means they have at least some degree of doubt, and that doubt causes the phenomena to vanish.

A case in point is that of Susan Blackmore, an English parapsychologist of long standing who become skeptical after years of parapsychological research (Blackmore 1986b, 1986–1987). In a 1986 article in *Fate* magazine, she outlined the reasons for her increasing skepticism, which constitute a familiar theme. In sixteen years of research in parapsychology, she was never able to obtain any evidence for psi phenomena. Another parapsychologist, the late Scott Rogo (author of a book called *Phone Calls from the Dead*) replied to Blackmore's article (Rogo 1986). In his reply, Rogo attributed Blackmore's continued failure to find evidence of psi phenomena not to the nonexistence of such phenomena but to Blackmore's unconscious motives. "Is Blackmore using her own ESP to block her subjects' functioning during her tests? Is she psychically sabotaging her own experiments?" he asked (78). Later he stated that "I believe that a sense of deep personal conviction may be the key to achieving good results in the lab," and "In the course of my conversations with Blackmore I have come to suspect that she resists—at a deeply unconscious level—the idea that psychic phenomena exist" (80).

The view that ESP and related phenomena are "jealous" has been carried even further by other writers. It has been argued that skepticism can act backward in time to change the initially positive results of parapsychological experiments (Collins and Pinch 1982). The argument runs as follows: When good evidence for psi phenomena is found, it is written up and published. If, after publication, a lot of skeptics read the paper, their skepticism will act in the past to change the outcome of the experiment. It is a tribute to the lack of demonstrable psi phenomena that some proponents have had to resort to such explanations for the overwhelming failure to demonstrate the existence of the phenomena they believe in. There are no phenomena in science that depend on the belief of the researcher for their demonstration.

EARLY RESEARCH: J. B. RHINE AND S. C. SOAL

The work of J. B. Rhine and his wife, Louisa, at Duke University and of S. C. Soal in England marks the beginning of modern experimental parapsychology. This line of research, and its recent descendants, claims to have provided evidence for the existence of ESP and related phenomena. Such claims, however, do not stand up to critical evaluations.

The basic card-guessing method used by the Rhines and others failed to provide adequate evidence for ESP. A major problem was the very poor experimental control used in these experiments. For example, the cards that first gave such seeming success were poorly printed—the designs were often stamped on the cards with such force that embossing resulted and the design could sometimes be seen from the back of the card (Randi 1982b; Zusne and Jones 1982). Some of the cards were transparent enough that some designs could be seen through the cards (Zusne and Jones 1982).

The methods the Rhines used to prevent subjects from gaining hints and clues as to the design on the cards were far from adequate. In many experiments, the cards were displayed face up but hidden behind a small wooden shield. Several ways of obtaining information about the design on the card remain even in the presence of the shield. For instance, the subject may be able sometimes to see the design on the face-up card reflected in the agent's glasses. Even if the agent isn't wearing glasses, it is possible to see the reflection in his cornea. Of course, this wouldn't be possible all the time, and certainly not every subject would take advantage of such information. But the Rhines' results showed that only certain subjects were able to score above chance—and then not a great deal above chance, although the difference was significant statistically. This is just what would be expected if a few subjects, some of the time, were able to make use of a slight advantage based on information from such sources. Other sources of information not controlled in the Rhines' experiments were the facial expressions and tone of voice of the agent. Such clues can be valuable sources of information.

Other nonparanormal sources of information existed about the design on the cards in the Rhines' experiments. The small shield between the subject and the agent did not eliminate clues when the agent wrote down which card was presented on each trial. The sound of a pencil writing provides information about what is being written. Try this experiment: Have someone write the numeral 2 and then the numeral 4 behind you while you listen carefully. Now have the person write "lines" and "square," names of two of the Zener cards. In both cases, you can hear the difference. Observing the top of a moving pencil or pen also provides information about what is being written. Magicians use this technique in several tricks; with a bit of practice, one can become quite good at it. Since there are only five alternatives in the Rhine experiments, even a little information based on such sources would boost a subject's score above chance, with no paranormal powers needed to explain the results.

Several procedural flaws in the Rhine experiments have been detailed by Zusne and Jones (1982) and Hansel (1966, 1980). Zusne and Jones pointed out that "the keeping of records in Rhine's experiments was inadequate. Sometimes, the subject would help with the checking of his or her calls against the order of cards. In some long-distance telepathy experiments, the order of the cards passed through the hands of the percipient [subject] before it got from Rhine to the agent" (375). In other words, the subject was given a list of the cards that he or she was later to attempt to guess. The opportunity for nonparanormal transfer of information in such situations is obvious. As early as 1939, Kennedy (1939) concluded that the vast majority of the seemingly positive experiments by the Rhines were due to poor experimental control. Three studies that Kennedy did not fault on procedural grounds have since been questioned on the basis of opportunity for cheating or use of clues that Kennedy was not aware of (Hansel 1966; Zusne and Jones 1982).

The procedural errors in the Rhine experiments have been extremely damaging to his claims to have demonstrated the existence of ESP. Equally damaging has been the fact that the results have not been replicated when the experiments have been conducted in other laboratories. The Rhines and ESP have been the Blondlot and N-rays of the middle part of the twentieth century. Crumbaugh's (1966) comments on his failure to repeat the Rhines' findings, even after years of effort, have been noted previously; other researchers fared little better when trying to repeat the Rhines' work. By 1940 "six different researchers, using some 500 subjects in experiments totaling about half a million trials demonstrated nothing but chance scores" (Zusne and Jones 1982, 375). See also Hansel (1966, 1980) for detailed accounts of the failures to replicate Rhine's findings.

Occasionally, of course, apparent replication would occur. It should be remembered, however, that replications were also reported of Blondlot's N-ray findings. As in the N-ray case, reports that seemed to support the Rhines' work were few and could be attributed to some of the same procedural problems as found in the original work. In addition, it should be remembered that what is taken as evidence for ESP is above-chance performance on some sort of card-guessing task. If one tests enough subjects long enough, sooner or later one of them will score above chance at a statistically significant level, for at least some set of trials. Does this mean that, for this brief time, the subject possessed ESP? No, it simply means that chance is operating as expected. Let us assume that out of two hundred subjects, one scores significantly above chance at the .01 level. That is, the deviation from chance would be expected to occur once in one hundred times. This will impress no one who has any knowledge of statistics, since the fact that an event that is expected to occur by chance once in one hundred times does so when you give it two hundred opportunities to occur is not evidence of anything extraordinary.

Real-world analogues to the card-guessing experiments occur frequently. One can consider every spin of the roulette wheel, every throw of the dice, every draw of the card in gambling casinos the world over as a single trial in a worldwide ongoing study in parapsychology. At gambling casinos, the odds are in favor of the house by only a tiny margin (if the margin were greater, people would lose much more frequently and be much less willing to play). Nonetheless, this tiny margin is enough to produce huge amounts of money for the house. Over the billions of "trials" in this real-world "experiment," there has been no hint of any deviation from the strict laws of chance. State-run lotteries offer another opportunity to look for ESP in real-world situations. Billions of state lottery tickets have been sold since New Hampshire introduced the modern state lottery in 1964. Skolnick (personal communication, 1985) examined the data from the New York State Lottery for several years. He found that New Yorkers were not winning the lottery at a rate higher than chance. If ESP had been operating, even in only a minority of players, the rate of winning would have been higher than chance.

The argument is often made by proponents of paranormal claims that these powers cannot be used for profit, so when one tries to use ESP to foresee the outcome of a spin of a roulette wheel, a football game, or the movement of a company's stock on Wall Street, psi powers promptly vanish. However, not all parapsychologists agree with this position. Rhine himself contended that highly motivated subjects did better in ESP experiments (Rhine and Pratt 1962). For most people, money is a strong motivating factor.

In England, S. C. Soal attempted to replicate the Rhines' findings. At first Soal believed he had failed, stating, "I have delivered a stunning blow to Dr. Rhine's work by my repetition of his experiments in England . . . there is no evidence that individuals guessing cards can beat the laws of chance" (Thouless 1974, quoted in Markwick 1985, 287). Soal's studies included 160 subjects and a total of 68,350 trials. Later, however, Soal reanalyzed his data for what has been termed a displacement effect. That is, he compared the card guessed, not with the card actually present on that trial, but with either the card that had been present on the previous trial or with the card that had appeared on the succeeding trial. When this was done, two subjects, Gloria Stewart and Basil Shackleton, out of 160 showed hit rates well above chance. Presumably, had Soal's reanalysis not produced results to his liking, he would have done further analyses, perhaps looking at the hit rate for cards two back or in front of the actual target card.

Soal's further work with Basil Shackleton lasted for forty sessions and totaled twelve thousand trials. Cards with a picture of one of five animals were used instead of Zener cards with symbols. Each design was coded with a digit from 1 through 5. Before a session, Soal reported, he would obtain a random list of the digits 1 through 5 from a book of logarithms. He described in detail the procedure he used to obtain these lists of digits. This was important, as it permitted other investigators, years later, to find the exact source of the random digits used. The random digits were written in a "target" column on the score sheets for the session and were used to determine the order in which the five different designs would be presented. Thus, if the digit 1 was the code for the elephant design, when a 1 appeared in the target column on a trial, the elephant design would be used. Shackleton would make his guess by naming the animal, not naming a digit. His guess was also coded into the appropriate digit and that digit recorded on the score sheet. Thus, if he guessed "elephant," a 1 would be recorded in the "guess" column.

Soal's work with Shackleton (reported in Soal and Goldney 1943) was extremely successful. It was long considered the best evidence for the existence of ESP by both proponents and skeptics. As might be expected, critics spent considerable time and effort attempting to refute the results. Frequently these attempts were unfair, distorted, or simply wrong (see Markwick 1985 for a brief review). Then in 1960 it was revealed (Soal and Goldney 1960) that in 1941 Soal had been charged with changing some of the 1's in the target column to 4's or 5's after a session. The accuser was a Mrs. Gretl Albert, who had taken part in the experiment as an "agent," the individual who attempted to send the identity of the card to Shackleton. Soal originally denied the charge and did not permit it to be published until 1960.

The publication of Mrs. Albert's charge heightened suspicion regarding the Shackleton studies. Medhurst (1971) examined a small portion of the data from Soal's sessions with Shackleton and found that there was an excess of hits when the target was a 4 or a 5. Scott and Haskell (1973, 1974) examined all the data and showed that not only were hits much more likely to occur than chance would predict when the target was a 4 or 5, but that there were far fewer 1's as target when a 4 or 5 was guessed than would be expected by chance. These results showed how Soal had been cheating. He filled the target digit sequence with extra 1's. When Shackleton guessed a 4 or 5 on a trial when the target was one of these supernumerary 1's, the target was changed to a 4 or 5, whichever was correct. This inflated the hit rate to above-chance levels. Markwick (1978, 1985) discovered that Soal (who died in 1975) had cheated in a second way. He had left blanks in the target column and had later filled in the digit corresponding to whatever animal Shackleton guessed.

The discoveries of how Soal had faked his results destroyed the credibility of his work in the eyes of skeptics and most parapsychologists. One parapsychologist, J. C. Pratt, who had worked with the Rhines at Duke, proposed an astonishing defense of Soal. According to Pratt (1978), Soal had powers of precognition and had inserted the extra digits in the target columns guided by his precognition. The desire to believe knows few bounds.

THE URI GELLER EPISODE

The Rhines had pioneered the study of parapsychology using card-guessing experiments. As the years passed, many became dissatisfied with this approach. It was dull for all involved, including the readers of the final papers. Worst of all, it failed to produce convincing evidence for ESP or other paranormal abilities. By the 1970s, then, the stage was set for something new to burst on the scene. This turned out to be an Israeli psychic named Uri Geller. Starting with his arrival in the United States, Geller quickly became the parapsychological sensation of the decade. Many parapsychologists became convinced that in Geller they finally had positive proof that psychic powers were real and that they could be demonstrated more or less on demand. Geller also became a darling of the media, appearing on multiple magazine covers and on talk show after talk show, where his powers were amply demonstrated and declared genuine. He convinced millions that he was, at last, the real thing.

Geller's alleged powers were truly amazing. He could bend solid metal objects with his mind alone. He could read minds. He could see inside sealed envelopes and boxes and tell what was in them. These powers were apparently verified when Geller was studied by physicists Russell Targ and Harold Puthoff at California's prestigious Stanford Research Institute (SRI), which is not affiliated with Stanford University. Targ and Puthoff (1974) published a paper in *Nature*, one of the world's leading scientific journals, in which they declared they had demonstrated that Geller's powers were real.

Unfortunately for Geller and his supporters, it soon became obvious that the truth about Geller was very different from his claims. Geller turned out to be nothing more than a magician using sleight of hand and considerable personal charm to fool his admirers. The tests at SRI turned out to have been run under conditions that can best be described as chaotic. Few limits were placed on Geller's behavior, and he was more or less in control of the procedures used to test him. Further, the results of the tests were incorrectly reported in Targ and Puthoff's *Nature* paper. Magician James ("The Amazing Randi") Randi's (1982b) book *The Truth about Uri Geller* is the definitive exposé of this alleged modern psychic. Marks's *The Psychology of the Psychic* (2000) also contains excellent material on Geller.

Geller was caught blatantly using sleight of hand on many occasions (Randi 1982b; Marks 2000). In early 1973 *Time* magazine was considering doing a story on Geller, and he was invited to give a demonstration of his powers for members of *Time*'s staff. Unknown to Geller, James Randi was present, posing as a *Time* employee. Strangely, for all Geller's professed powers, he failed to detect the presence of a trained professional magician and went on to give what Randi (1982b, 93) called "the saddest, most transparent act I've ever seen." From then on Geller never performed if there was a trained magician watching. They gave off "bad vibes" that made his powers go away.

It is interesting to describe how Geller did one of his better-known tricks. In his stage show, which convinced millions of paying customers that he was truly psychic, he did a simple mind-reading act (Marks and Kammann 1980; Hyman, personal communication, 2002). He asked members of the audience to think of one geometric figure inside another, often saying something like "don't think of a square—that's too easy for me." After a few moments, he says that he has received the mental impression of a circle inside a triangle, and asks how many in the audience were thinking of that design. Many amazed hands go up. He then typically says that he initially was going to say a triangle inside a circle, but changed his mind. How many in the audience were thinking of that combination? More hands go up in amazement until, perhaps, well over half the audience members have their hands up. Simple as it is, this can be an impressive gimmick in the excitement of a live performance. The trick is simple—after you've excluded the square, there really are only two "simple" geometric figures left, the circle and the triangle. There aren't going to be many geometric whizzes in the audience who think of a dodecahedron inside a rhombus.

In another easy trick you can do, the audience is asked to think of an odd two-digit number less than fifty, with the restriction that the two digits can't be the same. With much fanfare, you announce that you received the number 37. Typically, about one-third of the audience will have picked this number. You may then say you first were going to say 35, but changed your mind. How many were thinking of 35? More hands go up. While it may appear at first blush that there are lots of numbers to choose from, the restrictions placed on the choice narrow the number of possible choices down to just eighteen. And the specification to pick an odd number tends to steer people away from picking a number like 27, which is odd but has an even first digit. When such numbers are taken out, there are only eight numbers left to pick from. It has been shown that about 56 percent of a group of people will pick either 35 or 37 when given these instructions (Marks 2000). These response patterns are called population stereotypes, and the magician or phony psychic can make good use of them to convince people that their minds really are being read.

Geller's most famous trick was bending metal objects, supposedly by psychic energy. The bent objects were usually keys or spoons. Both are surprisingly easy to bend when you know how. Keys are easiest—all one needs to do is distract the audience for a moment and slip the key into some slot or press it on a solid surface and give it a good push. The audience, of course, won't have seen this since their attention has been distracted. Another way of bending a key is to use a second key that has a large enough hole in the top (figure 4.1) to insert the end of the key you want to bend. You do so and, while the audience is distracted, apply pressure. Geller, always a master of distraction, would perform such simple tricks on various television shows to amaze his hosts. Randi (1982b) reported that one could see him palm keys and bend them physically when one carefully viewed a videotape of the program later.

Bending spoons takes a bit more preparation if the trick is to work. One has to prepare the spoon beforehand. Let us assume that you are going to a party and wish to amaze those present with your psychic powers. When you arrive, go to the kitchen and borrow an all-metal spoon. (The trick doesn't work with plastic or nonmetal spoons.) Prepare the trick by bending the spoon back and forth at the point where the stem and bowl meet. At first, bend only a small bit, then gradually increase the angle of the bend. It's best to do this under running water, as the spoon becomes hot from the friction that occurs during the bending. You'll have to practice with many spoons before you'll be skilled enough to know when the spoon is just about ready to break at the junction between stem and bowl. There will be almost no visible sign on the top of the spoon that anything is amiss, although there will be a small crack on the underside. Now mark the spoon in some way so you can distinguish it from the others in the cutlery drawer (a small scratch will do

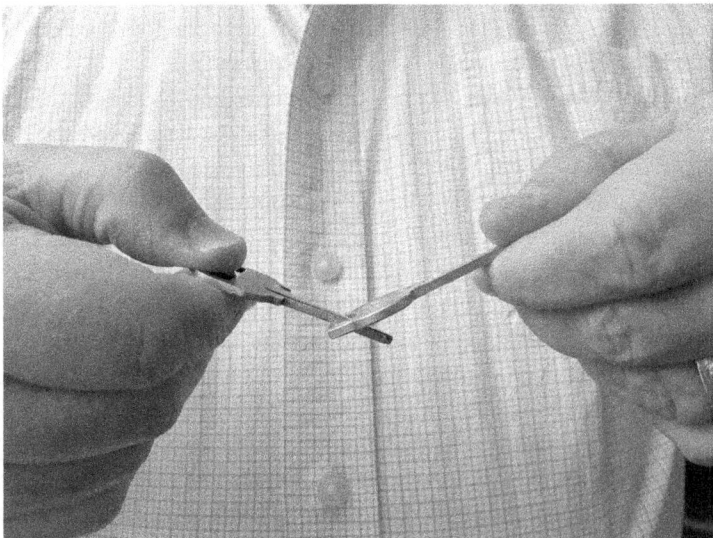

Figure 4.1. Key bending. Photo by Sarah Johnson

fine) and return it to the drawer. Then, mention casually in conversation that you have psychic powers. Don't be too loud about it—act modest and perhaps a little embarrassed. Usually, someone will take the bait and ask you to demonstrate. At this point, hedge—say the powers come and go, you're not sure, and so forth. Finally, allow yourself to be talked into giving a performance.

As you start, emphasize one point: your powers aren't 100 percent reliable. They depend not only on you but on those around you. Say something to the effect that everyone has such powers, and the audience has to help. That way, if you fail, whose fault is it? Not yours—the audience didn't help or didn't believe enough.

Don't start off with the spoon-bending act. Instead, do a little number-guessing mind reading, or the cold readings described in chapter 2, to warm up the group and convince them there is really something to your claim. Then trot out the spoon trick. But—and the importance of this point can't be overemphasized—fail at it the first time you try. That may seem strange, but as Randi has frequently pointed out, it is very important for psychics to fail some of the time when attempting a trick. After all, if the psychic were a magician doing tricks, the trick would always work. Therefore, if the trick fails, the person must be a real psychic. This way, psychics get "credit" both when the trick works and when it doesn't.

Ask someone to bring the drawer with the silverware or, better yet, go into the kitchen yourself, ask where the drawer is (even though you already know), open it, and "randomly" select the spoon you've previously worked on and marked. Or have a friend who is in on it with you pick the marked spoon. Ask another person to hold the spoon at points 1 and 2 (figure 4.2a). Tell the audience to concentrate on seeing the spoon bend. Have them chant, "Bend, bend, bend," if you think they'll go for it. Sweat will pop out on your forehead as you concentrate, focusing all your psychic powers on the spoon. Exclaim that you feel the spoon getting warm. Does the person holding it feel the same thing? (Of course it's getting warm, with one person holding it and you stroking it!) But, try as you will, the spoon doesn't bend; you've failed. Explain that your powers are weak at the moment, or that the mind reading drained you, and say you'll try to bend the spoon again later. Then, carefully and in view of everyone, put the spoon in some prominent place and state that no one should touch the spoon until you try to bend it again. This is to forestall any question of faking. Of course, you don't have to go near the spoon before your second attempt to bend it. The work has already been done. The audience doesn't know that, however, and it's an effective ploy.

When, about fifteen minutes later, you feel that your powers have recovered, it's time to try again to bend the spoon. Pick another person to hold the spoon at points 1 and 3 (figure 4.2b). This tiny difference in your method will go entirely unnoticed, but it is crucial. Now, stroke the spoon as before (or have someone else do so), between points 1 and 2. At first put no pressure on the spoon stem. You don't want it to bend right away. Strain some, and have the group chant, "Bend, bend, bend," again. After a half minute or so, apply gentle pressure to the stem as you stroke it. The spoon will start to bend! It will continue to

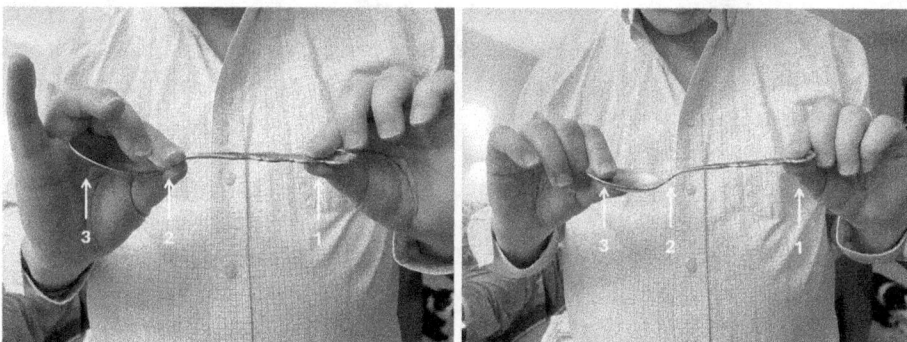

Figure 4.2a and 4.2b. One way to bend a spoon. Photo by Sarah Johnson

bend until, if you've worked it enough, the stem will fall off. The audience will be utterly amazed. Even people who already believe in psychic powers will be astonished at having seen such a powerful demonstration with their own eyes.

What makes this trick so very convincing is that the following three facts about what the audience sees are all true:

1. You failed to bend the spoon on the first attempt.

2. No one went near the spoon between the first and second attempts to bend it.

3. The spoon did bend on the second attempt.

The conclusion that almost everyone will draw is that your powers returned to full strength between the two attempts. Few will catch on to the trick. It's a simple trick, but it proved very effective for Uri Geller.

After your performance is over, you are ethically bound to tell people that what you did was just a trick. You are not, however, bound to tell them how it was done. Some will not believe that it was a trick. Randi, who has not only duplicated all of Geller's tricks but performed tricks that are far beyond Geller's rather limited abilities as a magician, has from time to time been accused by Geller's supporters of being a real psychic himself. They claim that Randi is a powerful psychic trying to convince the world that such powers don't exist so he can take the lead role in the psychic world.

Geller's well-publicized feats made psychic metal bending a popular addition to the repertoire of the would-be psychic. Even psychic children got into the act. Mathematics professor John Taylor of Kings College, University of London, was very impressed by one of Geller's performances and began investigating such psychic phenomena. He discovered that children have an amazing ability to bend metal psychically. It turned out, however, that children can't perform while anyone is watching them. But if you give one a spoon and turn away for a bit, when you look back, the spoon is bent. Taylor would even send pieces of silverware and other bits of metal home with the children, where they could use their psychic powers at their leisure. Oddly enough, objects sealed in containers were never bent. Taylor was later shocked to discover that his young subjects had been fooling him. Two other investigators placed some supposedly psychic children alone in a room with metal objects that were to be bent. Unknown to the children, they were being videotaped. They promptly proceeded to bend the objects with their hands or by placing them against the edges of tables (Randi 1982a).

At one point, Kent State University metallurgist Wilbur Franklin stated that a scanning electron microscope analysis of a ring Geller had broken, allegedly paranormally, showed that the break had not occurred by any normal, physical means (Franklin 1976). Later, Franklin (1977) reported that this was incorrect and that a more complete analysis showed evidence of metal fatigue of the type caused by repeated bending. In other words, Geller had simply "put in the work" on the ring.

It may seem hard to believe that so many people, including highly trained scientists, could be taken in by Geller's sleight of hand. Note, however, that very few people have been trained in the art of magic. If we go to a magic show, we usually have no idea how the tricks are being performed. We know they are tricks because the performer does not mislead us about it. But when someone claims to be psychic and does tricks that most people can't figure out, they assume that the individual really is psychic. Few people question the claim or consider the possibility that the person may be misleading them. The psychic helps this assumption along by using the techniques described above. Some parapsychologists, who may have impressive scientific credentials and a career of real distinction in those fields, seem to believe they can't be fooled. They fail to realize that a Ph.D. in physics, psychology, or chemistry does not confer expertise in detecting trickery. Thus, they are just as vulnerable, if not more so, to the magic tricks of a Geller as people who lack their scientific training. This was clearly demonstrated in the Geller case by Targ and Puthoff and more than a hundred years ago in the investigations of spiritualism described in chapter 2.

The Geller episode makes one vital point: in any investigation of psychics or psi phenomena, a trained magician must be part of the investigating team. Only such a person has the skill and training needed to spot sleight of hand and similar trickery. One would have thought this simple point would have been learned following the Geller incident, but one major parapsychology laboratory ignored it, to its shame and embarrassment.

To drive home the importance of having a professional magician involved in any investigations of psychics, and to investigate just how much could be gotten away with by someone posing as a psychic at a major parapsychology laboratory, Randi set up what he termed "Project Alpha." His detailed reports can be found in Randi (1982–1983c, 1983–1984).

In Project Alpha, two young magicians, Steve Shaw and Michael Edwards, with Randi's advice and training, went to the McDonnell Laboratory for Psychical Research at Washington University in St. Louis, Missouri. The McDonnell Laboratory was probably the best-funded psychical research laboratory in the world; it had been created with a $500,000 grant from James McDonnell, chairman of the board of the McDonnell-Douglas Aircraft Corporation.

Shaw and Edwards easily convinced the research staff at the McDonnell Laboratory that they had genuine psychic powers. They were tested by the laboratory for a period of three years. They rarely failed to achieve "psychic" feats. Metal was bent "paranormally," minds were read, the contents of sealed envelopes were mysteriously divined, fuses sealed in protective containers burned out, and mysterious pictures appeared "psychically" on film inside cameras.

Before Shaw and Edwards began to be tested at the McDonnell Laboratory, Randi wrote to the director, Dr. Peter Phillips, a physics professor at Washington University. Randi outlined the type of controls that the lab should use to guard against sleight of hand and other such trickery. He also offered to come to the lab, at his own expense and without public acknowledgment, to assist in the preparation of "trick-proof" experiments. Randi's offer was rejected and his advice ignored. The controls that were placed on Shaw and Edwards were totally inadequate to prevent their use of trickery. Even when videotapes of their feats showed fairly clearly, to anyone watching them carefully, how the trick had been done, the enthusiastic laboratory staff failed to catch on. When Shaw and Edwards were revealed to be magicians, the lab's claims to have demonstrated that psychic abilities existed collapsed.

In the last forty years a number of new methods have been introduced in parapsychology laboratories to study ESP and related phenomena. Unlike earlier experiments, such as those of Rhine and Soal, or the quite recent tests of "psychics" Shaw and Edwards, the new procedures are used largely to test "normal" individuals claiming no particular psychic powers. The remainder of this chapter will review these new techniques and the results they have achieved.

REMOTE VIEWING

The remote-viewing paradigm was developed by Russell Targ and Harold Puthoff (1977), the same investigators who were so thoroughly deceived by Uri Geller. Regarding their remote-viewing paradigm, Targ and Puthoff made a familiar claim: finally, they said, a method has been found that reliably provides strong evidence for psi phenomena.

The basic procedure in a remote-viewing experiment is simple. A subject sits in the laboratory with an experimenter. Another experimenter and one or two other people, who constitute the "demarcation team," visit randomly selected geographic locations outside the laboratory, such as airports, bridges, parks, or specific buildings. The team attempts to send information psychically about the location to the subject at a predetermined time. Thus, for example, the team might be scheduled to be at an airport at 10 a.m.

At 10 a.m. the subject back in the laboratory gives a description of the location based on any impressions he or she receives. Of course, neither the subject nor the experimenter back in the laboratory knows the locations the team will be visiting.

Following the completion of the experiment, which may include several different locations, the subject's tape-recorded impressions are transcribed. These are then given to an independent judge who, in Targ and Puthoff's experiments, visits each of the actual locations and rates each of the subjects' descriptions on how well it describes each location. If there were no ESP operating, the independent judge should not be able to match the subjects' descriptions to the actual locations at a rate better than chance. If, however, the subject is really picking up information from the team through ESP, then the descriptions should contain enough information to permit the judge to reliably associate a particular description with a particular location. Targ and Puthoff claimed they conducted more than one hundred such experiments and that "most" of them were successful (Targ and Puthoff 1977, 10). Several of their experiments seem to have been spectacularly successful (Targ and Puthoff 1977; Marks 2000). At least one subject, Targ and Puthoff reported, was able to demonstrate precognition in this procedure, describing the locations to be visited not only before they were visited but before they were even chosen.

Impressed with these seemingly powerful and consistent results, Marks and Kammann (1980) attempted to replicate Targ and Puthoff's remote-viewing results. In a series of thirty-five studies, they were unable to do so. Their results always showed chance performance. Naturally feeling that they were doing something wrong, they searched for differences in procedure between their studies and those of Targ and Puthoff that might explain the difference in results. The crucial variable turned out to be unexpected. Targ and Puthoff provided their judges with unedited transcripts of the subjects' impressions, and included the comments made by the experimenter who stayed with the subject. Marks and Kammann edited their transcripts to remove cues that would enable a judge to match the subjects' transcribed comments to the location. Such cues can provide a great deal of information.

Examination of the few actual transcripts published by Targ and Puthoff (1977; Wilhelm 1976) show that just such clues were present. To find out if the unpublished transcripts also contained cues, Marks and Kammann wrote to Targ and Puthoff requesting copies. It is almost unheard of for scientists to refuse to provide their data for independent examination when asked, but Targ and Puthoff consistently refused to allow Marks and Kammann to see copies of the transcripts. Marks and Kammann were, however, able to obtain copies of the transcripts from a judge who used them. The transcripts were found to contain a wealth of cues. In addition, the judge had also been given a list of the locations visited in the order in which they were visited. A simplified example will demonstrate how this information could easily have been used to correctly match the transcripts to the locations, with no paranormal powers needed. Suppose you are a judge in a remote-viewing experiment in which only three locations are visited by the demarcation team. You are given three transcripts, A, B, and C, which are in random order. You are also given—as was the judge in the Targ and Puthoff experiment—a list of the order in which the three target locations were visited: (1) university library, (2) supermarket, and (3) large bridge. Transcript A contains the phrase, "Third time's the charm." Transcript C contains the phrase, "Don't be nervous—you're just starting." You can now correctly assign each transcript to the correct location. Transcript A is the large bridge, B is the supermarket, and C is the library. You've achieved an accuracy of 100 percent without even reading any of the actual descriptions in the transcripts. It would be very difficult for a judge to ignore such cues, even if he or she were trying to do so.

Marks and Kammann (1980) showed, in a procedure they wryly called "remote judging," that subjects were able to match the transcripts to the correct locations using only the cues provided. When these cues were eliminated, but the description of the subjects' impressions remained intact, matching fell to a chance level.

In 1980 Charles Tart (Tart, Puthoff, and Targ 1980) claimed that a rejudging of now-edited transcripts from one of Targ and Puthoff's earlier experiments still resulted in above-chance performance. However,

Targ and Puthoff again refused to provide copies of the actual transcripts used in this study. They suppressed this vital evidence until July 1985, when it was finally made available. The transcripts still contained numerous cues, and Marks and Scott (1986) concluded that "considering the importance for the remote viewing hypothesis of adequate cue removal, Tart's failure to perform this basic task seems beyond comprehension. As previously concluded, remote viewing has not been demonstrated in the experiments conducted by Puthoff and Targ, only the repeated failure of the investigators to remove sensory cues" (444).

Another aspect of the remote viewing situation described by Marks and Kammann (1980) deserves mention. Their attempts to replicate the results of Targ and Puthoff were complete failures. But before the judging was done, the subjects were given feedback about what target location corresponded to which of their descriptions. They frequently became convinced that their descriptions had been extremely accurate. Descriptions in remote-viewing experiments are vague, mentioning trees, buildings, water, and sky. Given the vagueness of the descriptions, when subjects are told or shown the location, they will always be able to find some points of similarity between the location and the description. Thus, like cold readers becoming convinced that they can divine hidden knowledge from their clients, subjects in a remote viewing experiment become convinced that their descriptions are paranormally inspired.

The remote-viewing controversy lasted more than a decade. It is a sobering example of how sloppy experiments and the conclusions based on them can be accepted as evidence in parapsychology. It further demonstrates the great amount of hard work it takes to put such erroneous conclusions to rest.

GANZFELD STUDIES

The German word *ganzfeld* means "blank field." The procedure in a ganzfeld study of psi powers is in some ways similar to the procedure in a remote-viewing experiment. Both types of studies use a subject trying to pick up impressions telepathically and a sender trying to send them. In the ganzfeld study, however, the sender is thinking about an object (tree, orange, dollar bill, whatever) rather than a location. The subject is seated in the "blank field" trying to receive the sensory impressions. The blank field may be a large, opaque, white screen covering the subject's entire field of vision, or it may be simply a table tennis (ping pong) ball, cut in half and fixed in goggles over the subject's eyes. The idea is that the ganzfeld cuts out extraneous sensory inputs and permits the telepathic "message" to be perceived more clearly by subjects who, at the appointed time, give their impressions of the object the sender is concentrating on. The ganzfeld technique was developed in the 1970s, and proponents of psi phenomena contended that it represents a method that gives consistent and repeatable evidence for such phenomena. Sound familiar?

Hyman (1985b) reviewed forty-two studies using the technique (essentially the entire corpus of published studies up to the time of the review) and concluded,

> I believe that the ganzfeld psi data base, despite initial impressions, is inadequate either to support the contention of a repeatable study or to demonstrate the reality of psi. Whatever other value these studies may have for the parapsychological community, they have too many weaknesses to serve as the basis for confronting the rest of the scientific community. (38)

Hyman (1985b) found several different flaws in the ganzfeld studies. There was inadequate randomization of the targets in a large percentage of the studies. Opportunities for information on the target to inadvertently reach the subject and breaches in security that might have permitted cheating were also present in many of the studies. Many studies were not described in sufficient detail to allow evaluation of what actually happened in the study. Statistical problems were also common. These included the use of incorrect statistical tests and procedures and "multiple testing" errors in which the subjects' responses were tested several times against chance, using different criteria for scoring the responses for different tests. This increases the chance of spuriously obtaining a significant result. Further, the greater the number of flaws in a study, the more likely it was to find a significant effect. This is another example of the phenomenon noted earlier, that evidence for ESP and related phenomena disappears as the tightness of experimental controls is increased. On the basis of Hyman's review, the ganzfeld studies cannot be said to provide evidence for ESP, as claimed by proponents.

As might be expected, not everyone agreed with Hyman's (1985b) conclusions. Honorton (1985) reviewed the same set of experiments and concluded that there was no relationship between the presence of methodological errors and evidence of ESP, and that these studies did show the reality of some type of psychic phenomena. It is often the case in science that the data existing at a given time are not adequate to settle a particular dispute. In 1985 this seemed to be the case with the ganzfeld studies. Hyman and Honorton (1986) agreed to disagree about whether the studies up to that point were or were not supportive of ESP, and they called for additional studies with better, more precise methodologies that would help rule out nonparanormal sources of above-chance results. Eight years later Bem and Honorton (1994) published a review of ganzfeld studies not included in previous reviews that did not suffer from the type of methodological flaws noted by Hyman and Honorton. Bem and Honorton concluded that these new studies did, in fact, provide "replicable evidence for an anomalous process of information transfer" (1994, 4). In other words, they provided reliable evidence for the reality of ESP.

But it turned out that there was a serious problem with the Bem and Honorton (1994) review. In 1999 Milton and Wiseman published a critique of that review and an analysis of additional new ganzfeld studies. In their review Bem and Honorton (1994) had counted the results of some studies as being statistically significant when they actually were not significant. This error led Bem and Honorton to conclude that the studies they reviewed had shown, overall, that ESP was operating in the ganzfeld situation. Milton and Wiseman (1999) then reviewed thirty ganzfeld studies that had been designed to meet the rigorous methodological standards set forth in Hyman and Honorton (1986); these studies showed no effect greater than chance.

Another type of ESP study has strong similarities to the ganzfeld studies. These are studies of ESP during dreams. The procedure is like that used in the ganzfeld study, except the subject is asleep in a laboratory. The subjects' electroencephalogram (EEG) is monitored. When they are in a dream period (indicated by the presence of rapid eye movements [REM]), the agent is signaled to begin concentrating on a target object or picture. When the subjects' REM period ends, signaling an end of dreaming, they are awakened and report any dreams. The content of the dreams is then compared to the object or picture the agent was "sending." The basic procedure can easily be altered to study precognition or clairvoyance (see Child 1985 for a review). Such research is time consuming and expensive, like any sleep research. For one thing, a well-equipped sleep laboratory is needed. Thus, not a great deal of parapsychological research has used this paradigm.

Initial studies at the Maimonides Medical Center in Brooklyn, New York, in the 1960s and early 1970s seemed promising. Child (1985) correctly pointed out that these studies have sometimes been misdescribed by critics. Nonetheless, serious problems remain. Akers (1984) noted that there was a violation "of the experimental protocol" that "leaves doubts as to the rigor with which the experiment was conducted" (129). Further, as Child (1985) described, three attempts at replication failed (Belvedere and Foulkes 1971; Foulkes et al. 1972; Globus et al. 1968). In addition, some of the Maimonides studies failed to obtain significant results, although Child reported that the series, taken as a whole, still yielded statistical significance. In view of these problems, the Maimonides results cannot be taken as providing convincing evidence of psi phenomena.

RANDOM EVENTS AND REACTION TIME STUDIES

In the 1980s a series of studies by physicist Helmut Schmidt attracted the attention of parapsychologists and the field's critics. Schmidt used a random number generator to cause one of several lights to turn on.

In his precognition studies, subjects had to press a button to predict which light would turn on. After the button was pressed, the random number generator determined the light that would turn on. In clairvoyance studies, the light that turned on was determined before the subject's response. Schmidt's published reports (for reviews see Hansel 1980; Akers 1984; Rush 1982) claimed that subjects were able to show better-than-chance responses in these situations.

Schmidt's work faced problems, as was pointed out by critics (Hansel 1980; Hyman 1980–1981). For one thing, the details of the random number generator changed frequently in Schmidt's work, often from one experiment to the next. Thus, one cannot gather "cumulative experience with one particular generator to fully understand its peculiarities and . . . properly 'debug' it" (Hyman 1980–1981, 37). Further, there were problems with the control trials that Schmidt used. These were series of trials during which the random number generator was generating random numbers but no subjects were making attempts to predict what its output would be. This is an absolutely necessary procedure, but the control trials that Schmidt used were hundreds of times longer than the actual experimental series (Hyman 1980–1981). Thus, the various generators Schmidt used may show temporary deviations from randomness in the short run that are obscured by the very lengthy control runs. Comparing short experimental runs to very lengthy control runs would spuriously give significant results. Subjects could become aware of these deviations and adjust their predictions accordingly. This would especially be a problem in the psychokinesis (PK) studies, where subjects attempted to influence the counter so that one of two events occurs more than 50 percent of the time. Here the crucial comparison was between the probability of the two events in the short experimental runs and vastly longer control runs. Any short-term deviations from randomness due to the generator would likely be interpreted as significant PK effects. Another problem with Schmidt's work was that the subjects were left largely unobserved and unsupervised during the experiment. Randall (1975) has said of Schmidt's studies that they "provide us with the final proof of the reality of ESP" (131). But almost these exact words have been used many times in the past to describe the latest surefire demonstration of the existence of psi, which promptly fell to pieces upon close examination. In view of the problems with Schmidt's work, Randall was certainly premature in his evaluation.

Schmidt is not the first investigator to have used this sort of paradigm to investigate psi. As early as 1963 Smith and colleagues (cited in Hansel 1980), working for the U.S. Air Force, tried a similar experiment. It was a failure. Parapsychologist Charles Tart (1976) used a random number generator to study the possibility of training people to use psi. Subjects were given feedback on whether or not their responses were correct following each trial. Such feedback is extremely important and enhances learning greatly. Positive results were initially found, as subjects came to be able to match their responses to the numbers generated by the machine. It turned out, however, that the sequence of targets generated by the random number generator was not random. This finding renders highly problematic the contention that the experiment demonstrated psi. Tart's response (see Akers 1984 for a brief review of this controversy) to the discovery of nonrandomness was to suggest that it was partly due to PK. Thus, a serious procedural flaw in an experiment has itself been claimed as evidence for psi, in yet another example of the use of a nonfalsifiable hypothesis.

In a somewhat similar vein, the Princeton Engineering Anomalous Research (PEAR) group spent twenty-eight years attempting to show that it was possible for people to psychically influence the generation of random numbers. The group, based at Princeton University and headed by Robert Jahn, closed its doors in 2007. The group's studies involved a device that would produce electronic pulses at a variable rate. That is, the time between pulses would vary. If one examined a specific period of time, there would be a given number of pulses during that period. Sample another identical period of time and there would be a different number of pulses. After counting the number of pulses in thousands of time periods of identical length, one would have a distribution of numbers of pulses. That distribution would have an average and a standard deviation, the latter being a measure of how variable a distribution is. In the PEAR experiments subjects attempted to influence the average number of pulses generated in each period of time. In some conditions, they attempted to, psychically, make the machine generate more pulses. In another condition, the attempt was to lower the number of pulses. Typical of the history of parapsychological research, initial results of Jahn's work seemed to show barely detectable differences from what would be expected by chance. Attempts to replicate the effects by other laboratories failed (Jeffers 2003) and "even the PEAR group was unable to reproduce a credible effect" (Jeffers 2006, 56).

In the 1980s several of my students and I used a more sensitive method to look for ESP effects. This method uses reaction time as the major dependent variable or measure. Up through the 1980s, almost all studies of ESP used accuracy as their dependent measure, as can be seen from the studies described above or in reviews of psi research up through the 1980s (e.g., Akers 1984; Morris 1978, 1982; Palmer 1978, 1982). In cognitive psychology, which is the experimental study of human learning, memory, and higher mental processes, accuracy is rarely used as the sole dependent measure. The dependent measure of choice is reaction time. This is because reaction time is a much more sensitive indicator of cognitive processes and processing than is accuracy. In other words, phenomena that are easily shown using a reaction time measure are not revealed by an accuracy measure.

An example will make the difference between the two measures clear. In a lexical decision task, subjects see, in each of several hundred trials, a string of letters. The string either is a real word—such as *queen*—or is not a real word—such as *rarden*. The subjects' task is simple: press one button if the letter string is a word and another button if the letter string is not a word. Reaction time and accuracy are recorded. Consider the results in two situations. In the first, the subject sees the letter string *kind* in one trial, makes a response, sees *queen* in the next trial, and again responds. In the second situation, the first letter string is *king* and in the next *queen*. The reaction time to respond that queen is a word is faster by about fifty to one hundred milliseconds in the second situation. Thus, having processed one word speeds up subsequent processing of words that are associated with it in meaning. This is a highly replicable result and has served as the basis for thousands of published studies of reading, memory, bilingualism, and other cognitive processes. The important point here is that accuracy measures do not reveal the effect of having just processed an associated word. This is a common result in studies of cognition—accuracy measures are not precise enough to demonstrate the often small, but very important, effects studied.

The implications of this analysis for ESP should be obvious. Perhaps the repeated failure to find evidence for ESP is due to the almost universal use of a dependent measure that is just too crude to find the looked-for effects. With this in mind, my students and I (Hines and Dennison 1988; Hines, Lang, and Seroussi 1987) conducted a series of studies of ESP using reaction time as a dependent measure.

One of our studies (Hines and Dennison 1988) followed naturally from Schmidt's work described above. On each trial a computer generated, randomly, a 0 or a 1. In the ESP condition, this digit was stored in the computer's memory. The computer then generated another random 0 or 1 and displayed that digit on a television monitor in front of the subject. The subject had to decide, as quickly as possible, if the digit on the screen was the same as the digit stored in the computer's memory or not. Reaction time, measured from the onset of the digit on the monitor to the time the subject responded, was recorded, as was the accuracy of the subject's responses.

Even if ESP is a real phenomenon, the accuracy measure would be unlikely to demonstrate it. In line with this prediction, our subjects performed no better than chance when the accuracy measure was used. The real test, however, was the much more sensitive reaction time measure. If ESP exists, subjects should respond more quickly when they are correct than when they are incorrect. Whatever the source of the hypothesized extrasensory information, if it were getting to the brain, where it would have to be processed to have any effect at all on behavior, it would speed up the process of making a correct decision. However, we found no difference between correct and incorrect reaction times that even approached statistical significance, nor did providing feedback to the subjects regarding their accuracy on each trial change these results. Reaction times of correct and incorrect responses remained the same.

We also examined a precognition condition, again with and without feedback to subjects on their accuracy. In the precognition condition, the computer generated a random 0 or 1 and displayed it on the monitor. The subject then had to decide if the digit the computer would generate after he or she responded would be the same as or different from the one on the screen. After the subject responded, the computer generated another 0 or 1. As in the clairvoyance condition, subjects were no more accurate than expected by chance, nor were they any faster when their responses—predictions, in this condition—were correct than when they were incorrect. Again, the presence or absence of feedback to the subject did not alter this pattern.

Hines, Lang, and Seroussi (1987) adapted the lexical decision task described above to the study of ESP. There were two conditions. In both the control and the ESP conditions, a subject made a series of lexical decisions on letter strings presented on the right side of a television monitor controlled by a computer. In the control condition, the lone subject had no companion. In the ESP condition, there was a second subject who also made decisions about letter strings presented on the left side of the television monitor. The two subjects sat on opposite sides of a large divider that prevented either from seeing the other side of the monitor. In the ESP condition the subject who sat on the left side of the divider—the agent or "sender"—saw a letter string, and 400 milliseconds later the receiver—the subject on the right side of the screen—saw a letter string. Both subjects had to make lexical decisions on the letter strings they saw. On some of the trials in the ESP condition, the letter string the agent saw was the same one the receiver saw, 400 milliseconds later. In the standard lexical decision task, if the same subject sees the same letter string twice in a row, reaction time on the second presentation is greatly reduced. This is due to the fact that the location in memory that stores the concept, if the string is a word, is activated by the first presentation, and when the same word occurs again, that location is much more able or ready to be activated again. This activation decays after a few seconds. If there is extrasensory communication between individuals even of a very low level, it should show up in the reaction times of the receiver when the agent had just processed, 400 milliseconds previously, the same letter string that the receiver was processing. We found no hint of any such effect in our data.

Failure to find an effect is not conclusive evidence that the effect is not real. However, the fact that our studies using a highly sensitive reaction time measure have consistently failed to show any evidence for ESP seems to be convincing prima facie evidence against the reality of the phenomena.

One of the characteristics of a pseudoscience mentioned in chapter 1 is the failure of proponents to look closely at the evidence, or lack thereof, for the claims being made. When I first came up with the idea of using reaction time to study parapsychological effects, I was surprised that no one else in the field had ever used this measure. It seemed such an obvious idea since decades of research on normal cognition had shown reaction time to be a much, much more sensitive measure of even very subtle cognitive processes than accuracy (percent correct) measures. After we published the reaction time studies described above, I was, naively as it turned out, pretty sure that other researchers in parapsychology would begin using this much more sensitive method.

They might argue, I thought, that we had failed to find evidence of ESP because we had screwed up the studies somehow, or because we didn't go into the research as believers. But the method was so promising that it should have immediately appealed to researchers trying to find evidence of such an elusive and weak effect. But I was wrong. In the more than thirty-five years since our studies were published, only two studies (Bem 2011; Moulton and Kosslyn 2008, described on pages 92–94) using reaction time in the study of parapsychology have appeared. It's as if someone had been using a magnifying glass to look for some tiny objects and sort of thought that maybe, just maybe, they had seen them through the glass. Someone else comes along and uses a microscope and doesn't see the purported objects for whatever reason. But then the user of the magnifying glass ignores the existence of the much more powerful microscope and continues to vainly poke about with the magnifying glass. This is not the behavior of a field that really wants to separate fact from fantasy.

A similar criticism of studies of psychokinesis can be made. Psychokinesis is the alleged ability that certain individuals have to move objects with their mind alone. Many self-proclaimed psychics claim such an ability. Their abilities are demonstrated by showing that they can, it seems, move relatively heavy objects (i.e., pencils, dice) psychically. In one famous case psychic James Hydrick claimed to be able to flip pages of a telephone book with only his mind. He was put to the test on the December 29, 1980, episode of the TV Show *That's My Line*, which can be seen online on YouTube. At first, when he was allowed to perform the trick without any controls for trickery, all went well and the pages seemed to move magically. But then magician James Randi was brought onstage. Randi contended that Hydrick was simply blowing surreptitiously on the book's pages to make them move. To test this Randi sprinkled some light Styrofoam chips around the book. If Hydrick really had psychic powers, the Styrofoam shouldn't interfere with his abilities. But, if he was blowing on the pages, the Styrofoam would reveal all. With the foam scattered about Hydrick tried mightily to move the pages, but neither the pages nor the chips budged a bit.

Even telephone book pages are relatively heavy compared to the things that real scientists weigh in the laboratory. Sensitive microbalance scales can weigh objects with a mass of less than one millionth of a gram. That's pretty damn small! As Park (2008) first suggested, it would be a simple matter to ask anyone who claims psychokinetic powers to step into the local physics laboratory and try to move such a super-sensitive measuring device with their mind alone. These devices are sealed in glass containers as a matter of course, and this would make it easy to prevent trickery. To my knowledge, no one has ever used such a scale to study psychokinesis. Another example of the failure to look closely.

BEM'S STUDIES

In 2011 Daryl Bem published a paper in which he reported nine different experiments that, he argued, proved the reality of precognition. The experiments were highly creative in that they used methods taken from mainstream cognitive psychology but not previously used in psi research. Several used reaction time as the dependent measure, while the rest relied on the usual percent correct measure. Further, the paper was published in the prestigious *Journal of Personality and Social Psychology*.

An example of one of Bem's experiments will give the flavor of his approach to the topic. In experiment 8 he used a version of a technique widely used in the study of memory, the free recall method. This is a very simple technique in which the subjects of the experiment are given a list of items, usually words, to remember. At some later time, they must recall as many of the words as they can. One obvious finding is that the more practice people have with a list of words, the better they are later at recalling them.

But Bem cleverly reversed the usual procedure. In his experiment 8 he had subjects view a list of words and then recall as many as they could. As is always the case, some of the words were recalled better than others. But after the initial recall test, a computer randomly picked some words from the original list of words and subjects then practiced these words. Bem claims that words that were practiced after the initial memory test were more likely to be remembered on that test compared to words that were not practiced after the initial memory test. His explanation was that the post-memory-test practice was acting backward through time to improve performance on the initial memory test.

The results of Bem's (2011) nine experiments would have been a true breakthrough if they could be verified. But from the very first there were serious doubts about Bem's results. This is not the place to go into a mind-numbing discussion of statistical arcana. However, it is crucial to note that in his analyses of all his results Bem used a test called a *t*-test, one of the tests most commonly used in scientific research. (Interesting piece of statistical trivia: the *t*-test was developed by William Gosset, a brewer at the Guinness brewery in Dublin, to test differences in vats of beer brewed with different types of barley. Now you know.) Bem used the so-called one-tailed version of the *t*-test. This is a huge red flag (Wagenmakers et al. 2011). The use of the one-tailed *t*-test doubles the chances of a researcher finding a significant effect. Using a one-tailed test is basically saying that if a difference occurs, it could only occur in the direction predicted by the experimenter; it would be impossible for the difference to occur in the direction opposite from that predicted. In Bem's case, it is the equivalent of saying that it is impossible for subjects to score below chance in an ESP experiment. If there is a difference it *must* be in the direction of showing that ESP is real. But if ESP isn't real, there will be a distribution of deviations from chance, some above and some below. These will average out to no difference, as discussed earlier in regard to Rhine's research. By using a one-tailed test, a researcher increases the probability of finding a "significant" effect when there isn't one. The problem with the t-test was not the only methodological flaw in Bem's studies. Alcock (2011) has outlined numerous other flaws, as have Wagenmakers and colleagues (2011).

Even if Bem's results had stood up to proper statistical analyses, there still would have been the issue of replication. Just like one swallow does not make a summer, one paper does not prove a hypothesis. Replication by other, independent laboratories is essential before any new phenomenon is accepted as established. To his great credit, Bem made the exact stimuli and procedures used in all nine experiments available free to anyone who wished to attempt to replicate his results.

Very rapidly after Bem's initial (2011) publication, attempts at replication were made. They have not been successful. In one large study Galak and colleagues (2011) conducted seven experiments attempting to specifically replicate the results of Bem's studies of retroactive recall. Using a total of over three thousand subjects, they found no psi effects at all. Ritchie, Wiseman, and French (2012) also failed to replicate the retroactive recall effects. Other attempts to replicate Bem's findings have been failures as well (Reber and Alcock 2020) in spite of the finding of occasional, perhaps above-chance results—just what would be expected when dozens and dozens of studies chase after a nonexistent effect. In 2022 Muhmenthales, Dubravac, and Meier reported yet another failure to replicate using two of Bem's reaction time methods with over two thousand subjects. Worse, as reported by Reber and Alcock (2020, 6) in an interview, "Bem acknowledged that he never actually ran any of the experiments [reported in his 2011 paper] or directly supervised the data collection. He used student volunteers." Thus, Bem's results are yet another example of the pattern seen consistently in parapsychological research. A new technique is used and positive findings are reported with much enthusiasm. But replication attempts fail.

NEUROIMAGING STUDIES

The newest technique used to study ESP and related phenomenon is functional magnetic resonance imaging (fMRI) of the brain. The technique is widely used in mainstream cognitive neuroscience to study which areas of the brain are active when people perform particular cognitive (or motor) tasks. More sophisticated methods of analysis of fMRI data allows a description of the functional connections between different brain areas that underlie cognitive processing. The introduction of this type of technology has revolutionized the study of cognition and the brain almost as much as the microscope revolutionized biology and the telescope astronomy.

The fMRI equipment is far from inexpensive and requires a dedicated and highly trained laboratory staff to maintain and use. Data analysis is also complex. Given the expertise and expense required to do an fMRI study, it is not surprising that only a few such studies have been aimed at questions about paranormal abilities. The fMRI studies of ESP are following the usual pattern of ESP studies outlined above, specifically that when a new technique is introduced there is a flurry of seemingly positive results based on poorly done studies, followed by better done studies that show no effects. Acunzo, Evard, and Rabeyron (2013) have reviewed the six ESP/fMRI studies done to date. Of the six, five claimed to have found evidence for some sort of paranormal communication between individuals. Of these five, Acunzo, Evard, and Rabeyron identified serious methodological flaws in four, all of which claimed to find evidence of some type of paranormal information transfer. These flaws invalidate that claim.

Of the remaining two studies that Acunzo, Evard, and Rabeyron found acceptable in terms of methodology and data analysis, one (Bierman and Scholte 2002) found and the other (Moulton and Kosslyn 2008) did not find evidence of paranormal effects. The two studies used different experimental approaches to the issue. Bierman and Scholte had their subjects view either emotionally arousing or neutral pictures while in the scanner. It is well known that emotional pictures cause activation of brain areas involved in processing emotional information, and these authors found that as well. The paranormal aspect of their findings comes in that these emotion-responding areas seemed to respond to the emotional picture *before* the pictures were actually presented, suggesting to the authors some sort of precognitive effect.

Moulton and Kosslyn (2008) performed a more complex study. They recruited pairs of individuals who were emotionally close, such as lovers, close friends, and twins, since it is believed by parapsychologists that emotional closeness enhances psychic connections. One member of each pair was assigned the job of "sender" while the other was the "receiver." Half of the time the sender looked at emotional pictures and tried to transfer the picture to the receiver while the receiver was in the scanner having his or her brain scanned. At the same time as the sender was attempting to transfer an emotional picture, the receiver was shown two pictures. One was identical to the one the sender was looking at while the other was different. As a control, half of the time the receiver was shown a pair of pictures when the sender was not attempting to send anything. The basic idea was that, if there was any sort of psychic transfer of information, the brain of the receiver would respond more to the emotional pictures when the sender was sending than when this was not the case. There was also a reaction time component in the study. The receiver pressed a button to indicate which of the two pictures he or she thought was the one being sent.

Results of the Moulton and Kosslyn (2008) study were negative. Considering first the reaction results, the receivers were not faster (or more accurate) when the sender was attempting to send information than when no information was being sent. This confirms the results of Hines and Dennison (1988) and Hines, Lang, and Seroussi (1987), who also found no paranormal effects in their reaction time tasks. More importantly, there were no differences in brain activity when senders were sending compared to when they were not. This result, from a laboratory highly experienced in the use of fMRI technology, coupled with a sophisticated design and analyses, is a powerful piece of evidence against the existence of anomalous information exchange. It is often said that it is very difficult to prove that something does not exist, and this is certainly true. Nonetheless, the negative results of this experiment give great confidence that ESP-type phenomenon do not exist.

Psi phenomena of one sort or another have been systematically studied for more than one hundred years. This period of investigation shows a common, repeating pattern. A new method is found that "finally shows that psi is real," the skeptic is told. However, upon careful examination, the claim collapses. But by the time one method has been carefully investigated and found faulty, another method has come along that "once and for all shows psi to be real." And on it goes. First there was spiritualism, then card-guessing experiments, then individual psychics like Geller, then the ganzfeld studies, the random events studies of Schmidt and others, Bem's studies, and now brain scanning studies. In the entire history of parapsychological investigation, with its numerous methods, there has never been anything even close to a convincing demonstration of any real effect. As Reber and Alcock (2020, 395, emphasis in original) put it, in the entire over one-hundred-year history of parapsychological investigations *"nothing has been learned. Parapsychology is precisely where it was when the first efforts were mounted in the 1880"* to study ESP and related phenomenon.

The situation of parapsychology stands in stark contrast to the pattern of research and discovery in every other area of science. It is almost a general principle in real science that as research on a new phenomenon progresses from initial discovery to detailed analyses it becomes easier and easier to obtain demonstrations of and evidence for the phenomenon. At first, researchers aren't sure about just which variables affect the presence, absence, or strength of the phenomenon in question. But as research progresses, these variables become clearer and clearer as more studies are published that describe under just what specific conditions the phenomenon can be seen. Note how vastly different this pattern is from that seen in parapsychology.

Why, then, does the field of parapsychology continue to exist? Why has it not withered away, like the study of N-rays and polywater? I think that there are two major, and not unrelated, reasons. First, especially since the early 1960s, parapsychology has acquired a following that is made up of people—most of them not active investigators and most with almost no scientific training—who accept the reality of psi not because of any empirical evidence but simply because psi fits well with their view of what the world and reality ought to be like. This is a world in which the spiritual dominates over the scientific and rational; a world in which simply thinking good thoughts can make the world "right" again; a world in which what one feels to be true is, automatically and without effort, true; a world where there is no need to carefully consider evidence to arrive at the truth. This group is quite large and helps to support the enormous number of uncritical books, television programs, and newspaper articles about psi and other aspects of the paranormal. Thus, these topics are kept in the public eye. This, in turn, fuels the interest of the general public and helps to support parapsychological research, both in terms of funding and in terms of the publicity that is so rewarding to researchers in any field.

The second reason for the persistence of parapsychology as a discipline has to do with the type of logical arguments permitted within the field. The use of the nonfalsifiable hypothesis is permitted in parapsychology to a degree unheard of in any scientific discipline. To the extent that investigators accept this type of hypothesis, they will be immune to having their belief in psi disproved. No matter how many experiments fail to provide evidence for psi and no matter how good those experiments are, the nonfalsifiable hypothesis will always protect the belief. The investigator will thus persist in conducting experiment after experiment, even when none of them produces positive results. The nonfalsifiable hypothesis always permits, almost requires, the attribution of the experiments' failures to something other than the nonexistence of psi. This attitude is epitomized in the quotation from Rogo (1986) earlier in this chapter regarding the reasons for Blackmore's failure to find any evidence of psi in her numerous experiments. Rogo didn't even consider the possibility that psi doesn't exist. Rather, he put forth the totally untestable idea that Blackmore's failure to find evidence of psi was due to her deeply hidden, unconscious motives. In any other area of scientific research, it would be impossible for anyone to seriously propose such an "explanation" for the failure to find a hypothesized effect.

Wiseman (2010) has suggested additional reasons for the continued search for evidence of parapsychological effects in laboratory studies. One is the file drawer problem. Until the debacle of Bem's (2011) studies that failed to find evidence of parapsychological effects, negative studies were almost always relegated to the researchers' file drawers and never saw the light of day. This effect produced the illusion that negative findings were much rarer than they actually were.

There is also the "nullifying of null findings [that] permeates parapsychological literature (Wiseman 2010, 37). For example, Kanthamani and Broughton (1994) conducted a ganzfeld study that ran for six years and over three hundred experimental sessions. The overall results showed no effect. Any reasonable scientist would interpret such negative findings as at least highly suggestive that there was no effect to be found. The authors did not do any such thing. Rather, they interpreted their huge corpus of negative findings as simply showing that the specific stimuli they used were not the right ones to use when studying parapsychological effects.

Data mining is a technique that can be used to produce a seemingly positive result from what is actually negative data and thus reinforce the belief that parapsychological effects are real. In this procedure, after the initial negative effects are found, the data is "mined" by looking at any number of different variables to see if any yield evidence for a positive effect. This is also known as the multiple comparison fallacy, which will reappear in chapters 11 and 12. In this regard, Wiseman (2010) cites the ganzfeld studies of Willin

(1996), which spanned a period of fifteen months and hundreds of experimental sessions. The results were negative. But Willin ran numerous post-hoc (i.e., after-the-fact) analyses to see if any specific variable might show an effect. The variables examined included the "age, profession, hobbies, previous paranormal experiences and relationship with the person acting as the sender" and "the month and time of day each trial was conducted" (Wiseman 2010, 38). Only one of these numerous variables showed any effect—sessions conducted early in the fifteen-month study showed more of an effect than those conducted later. Even if there were no parapsychological effects whatsoever, if this sort of data mining is carried out on a sufficiently large number of variables, some of those variables will show what appears to be a confirming result just by chance alone.

The type of reasoning so frequently used in parapsychology, reasoning that is nearly invulnerable to empirical disproof, is much more characteristic of religion than of science. Alcock (1985) has persuasively argued that for many, but certainly not all, parapsychologists the search for psi has become an almost religious quest, a quest to dethrone materialistic science and reestablish the dominance of a spiritual approach to the world.

PSI THEORY

Many theories have been proposed by parapsychologists to explain how psi takes place. To skeptics, such theory building seems premature as the phenomena to be explained by the theories have not been demonstrated. Dobbs (1967, cited in Rao 1978) proposed the existence of subatomic particles with "imaginary" mass and energy called "psitrons," which are emitted in great numbers by the brain. Needless to say, there is not a bit of evidence to suggest that such particles actually exist.

A common ploy used by some parapsychologists (see Cardena 2018) is to resort to quantum mechanics to provide an explanation for psi. Quantum mechanics is a theory filled with, to say the least, unusual phenomenon. Quantum effects occur at the "microphysical level of individual [subatomic] particles" (Reber and Alcock 2020, 395), not at the level of everyday experience. It is also a cornerstone of modern physics and has over and over proved its validity by making predictions that are found to be amazingly accurate when put to an experimental test. It is the basis on which numerous modern devices such as GPS work.

Over forty years ago Gardner (1981) reviewed the use of quantum mechanics in parapsychology. He found that it was often used incorrectly or to hide, in complex terminology, old nonfalsifiable hypotheses. Thus, for example, the fact that psychics can't or won't perform their feats in front of skeptics is attributed to the fact that skeptics' "wills kept reducing wave packets the wrong way" (69). This sort of conceptualization does not provide much substance for a theory of psi. It's little more than quantum gibberish, as are other attempts to squeeze explanations of nonexistent parapsychological effects from quantum theory. To quote Reber and Alcock (2020, 395) in their paper on the current status of parapsychological research, "no matter how much one tries to weave in the strange, wonderful world of quantum mechanics . . . it cannot get a person to the paranormal."

Another bizarre theory has been proposed and has some popularity in parapsychology: the theory of *synchronicity*. This is a notion dreamed up by psychoanalyst Carl Jung in the 1950s (Jung and Pauli 1955). The idea is straightforward, if naive. According to synchronicity, there is no such thing as a coincidence. All "coincidences" are meaningful. Palmer (1978, 1982) and others (Rao 1978) have suggested that psi may not be due to transmission of information, but may be examples of such "meaningful coincidences."

BELIEF IN PSI

Why is the existence of ESP and related phenomena so widely accepted by the public and parapsychologists in spite of what is at best very poor evidence for its reality? One reason is that paranormal topics are constantly and uncritically discussed in the media, both print and electronic. Given the high visibility of paranormal topics in the media, it is natural for people to believe that there must be something to them. Another powerful factor influencing belief is the startling personal experiences that many people have. These convince them, on purely subjective grounds, that they have had an ESP experience and, therefore, that ESP is real. Hand's (2014) Law of Truly Large Numbers, mentioned in chapter 2, ensures that what seem, subjectively, extremely rare events are very likely to occur to someone at some time. It's just that when that event happens to that someone at that sometime, the someone sees it as extremely unlikely because people generally do not think about all the opportunities such an event has had to occur to others. The constructive nature of memory and related cognitive illusions combine forces to convince people of the reality of ESP and related phenomena.

What type of experiences occur in everyday life that are classified as being due to ESP? Very commonly, they are hunches or dreams that seem to come true. The cognitive illusions that operate to make this type of precognitive experience seem so real were discussed in chapter 2. A similar experience more directly related to ESP is that of thinking of a friend that one has not heard from in some time. Shortly after one has thought about the individual, one receives a phone call, letter, email, or some other form of communication from or about the person. This can be a striking experience. Such occurrences are, of course, coincidences. But most people are quite poor at estimating the probabilities of events and using probabilistic information in decision making.

Research on differences in terms of personality or information processing between those who believe in parapsychological phenomenon and those who do not have begun to show interesting results. Belief in the paranormal is a "psychological construct that, being conceptually complex and presenting a highly variable thematic spectrum" (Fasce and Pico 2018, 625), is difficult to study. As such, no single variable, or simple set of variables, will distinguish perfectly between believers and nonbelievers.

In an early study using an experimental task, Blackmore (1985) found that believers in ESP were worse than nonbelievers at making judgments of probability. In a coin-flipping experiment, believers significantly underestimated the number of heads or tails that would occur due to chance alone. Nonbelievers made more accurate estimates. Thus, when believers are faced with a sequence of random events, they, more than nonbelievers, will perceive it as nonchance and seek some explanation for the perceived nonchance nature of the sequence of events. ESP, or other paranormal effects, provide a perfect "explanation." This idea received support from a study by Dagnall, Parker, and Munley (2007) that found the believers were poor at judging randomness.

In a review of the relevant literature, Wiseman and Watt (2006, 333) found that the strongest difference between believers and nonbelievers was that believers "have consistently obtained higher scores on several measures of fantasy proneness, [and] the propensity to find correspondences in distantly related material." They also found that differences between the two groups in terms of variables such as intelligence and school performance were "inconsistent."

Riekki and colleagues (2013) studied differences between believers and skeptics in the tendency to see faces in natural objects with face-like patterns such as tree trunks or arrangements of objects like tools. The paranormal and religious believers were more likely to label nonface stimuli as faces than were skeptics. This result helps explain the finding that in pareidolia it is usually religious figures whose faces are seen in ambiguous patterns such as burned tacos and reflections from glass buildings. One seldom, if ever, finds skeptics seeing Darwin's face on a taco.

Regarding the specific issue of perception of agency, Elk (2013) found that believers in the paranormal were more likely than skeptics to detect human-like patterns of movement in ambiguous displays of moving lights—in other words, to see some nonrandom cause or agent behind the pattern of lights. This difference was not found with patterns of light that allowed little leeway to see human agency. In that condition believers were not more likely than skeptics to see a human agent behind the pattern of movement. But when the pattern at least allowed for some possibility of such an agent, then the believer-versus-skeptic difference appeared.

Taken together, the results of such studies support what Wiseman and Watt (2006) term the "misattribution hypothesis," wherein believers are more likely than nonbelievers to misattribute random events to some causal factor than are nonbelievers. This is quite similar to the notion of agency introduced in chapter 1. Here believers are more likely to attribute agency, some causative agent, to random events than are nonbelievers.

It is interesting that one of the characteristics of believers is a greater degree of fantasy proneness, which is also termed "suggestibility." Research approaching the question of how believers differ from the more skeptical from a neurobiological point of view have examined possible genetic differences between the two groups. The first study to do so (Raz et al. 2008) looked for correlations between alleles of the COMT gene and paranormal experiences. This gene codes for a neurochemical, COMT, that breaks down dopamine in synapses of the central nervous system that use dopamine. There are three alleles of the COMT gene that differ in the ability of their gene product to break down dopamine. Dopamine has many functions in the human brain, but one of them can be characterized as helping distinguish reality from fantasy. Higher levels of dopamine in certain brain circuits are linked to greater difficulty in telling reality from fantasy (see Krummenacher et al. 2010 for references). Raz and colleagues (2008) gave several paper-and-pencil tests of paranormal experience and belief to a sample of undergraduate students and genotyped each for their specific COMT allele. They hypothesized that individuals with the COMT allele that was less effective at breaking down dopamine would report more paranormal experiences and high belief. Alas, they found no such relationship. This was due to the fact that almost none of the students in the study had had any paranormal experiences and very few had any strong beliefs in paranormal phenomenon. However, Schmack and colleagues (2015), using a more sophisticated genetic analysis and a more varied sample, did find a relationship such that greater dopamine availability was associated with a "stronger propensity toward unfounded beliefs" (521).

In terms of processing new information, Russell and Jones (1980) showed that believers in ESP were less able to interpret and assimilate new information if that information was contrary to their belief in ESP than if it confirmed their belief in ESP. Believers and nonbelievers were given articles to read about ESP that were either supportive of the reality of ESP or argued that ESP didn't exist. Believers remembered the articles that supported their position very well. Believers' memories about the article that argued against ESP, however, were quite inaccurate, and more than 15 percent actually remembered the article, incorrectly, as favorable to the existence of ESP. Nonbelievers, on the other hand, showed excellent memory for both articles, regardless of whether the articles supported or argued against the nonbelievers' position.

The finding that believers are less willing or able than nonbelievers to deal with information that counters their preconceived belief is not limited to belief in ESP. It may be a general characteristic of believers. Glick and Snyder (1986) studied belief in astrology; their findings are relevant here as they take the results of the Russell and Jones's (1980) study one step further to ask what effects confirming or disconfirming information has on believers' and nonbelievers' beliefs. Glick and Snyder gave subjects, who were classified as believing or not believing in astrology, the opportunity to test a particular astrological prediction by asking an individual questions about his personality and habits. The "hypothesis" being tested was that this individual was, according to their horoscope, extroverted, friendly, and outgoing. Unknown to the subjects, the individual who was interviewed was a confederate of the experimenters and was instructed to provide responses of a particular type. If the question was such that it invited an "extroverted answer" (e.g., "Do you like to go to parties?"), the confederate gave an extroverted answer ("yes," in this case). If the question invited an introverted answer (e.g., "Do you like to stay at home alone and read?"), the confederate gave an introverted answer ("yes," in this case).

Glick and Snyder (1986) found that both believers and nonbelievers asked more questions that would tend to confirm the "hypothesis." Thus, both believers and nonbelievers got the same information from their questioning of the confederate. However, for the believers the information confirmed their belief while, for the nonbelievers, it disconfirmed their prior attitude. What effect did this information have on the attitudes toward astrology of the believers and nonbelievers? Nonbelievers were more likely than believers to see the specific astrological prediction as confirmed. That is, they used the information to modify their prior attitude. Believers did not use the information obtained to modify their belief in astrology. Within the group of believers, there was a variation in the number of confirmatory questions asked of the confederate and, therefore, variation in the amount of evidence the believers received that confirmed the astrological hypothesis. This made no difference in the believers' ratings of whether or not the hypothesis had been confirmed. No matter how much or how little confirming evidence they obtained, they saw the hypothesis as confirmed. The nonbelievers showed the opposite effect. The more confirming responses nonbelievers received, the more they believed the hypothesis had been confirmed. Nonbelievers were more willing than believers to assimilate new information that countered their preexisting attitudes and to use that information to change their attitudes.

The pattern that emerges from these studies is one in which believers in paranormal phenomena are more rigid and unchanging in their beliefs than are skeptics, who are more likely to change their attitudes when presented with evidence that shows their beliefs to be incorrect. In other words, believers appear to be considerably more closed-minded than nonbelievers.

PSEUDOPSYCHOLOGIES

Founded by Sigmund Freud in Vienna in the late 1800s, psychoanalysis, the best-known pseudopsychology, has had enormous influence on Western culture. For many people, Freud and psychoanalysis are still synonymous with psychology. Nonetheless, psychoanalysis is based in large part on pseudoscientific formulations that are inherently nonfalsifiable. This nonfalsifiability accounts for the popularity of psychoanalytic "explanations" in many fields. In some instances, psychoanalytic theory does make testable predictions; these predictions have usually been found to be incorrect.

The Freudian approach to psychology and psychotherapy went largely unquestioned until the 1950s. Then research began to appear showing that, where they could be tested, Freud's ideas were wrong. This line of research continued through the 1980s, when there was little left of the husk of Freudian pseudoscience to investigate further. More recent scholarship on Freud has concerned how he misrepresented his supposed therapeutic successes and how his successors and followers have hidden or downplayed his therapeutic and intellectual failings and deceptions. Freud based his claims for the validity of psychoanalysis on the supposed ability of the process to cure patients of various psychological problems. His writings are filled with descriptions of his patients, their problems, and how he was able to treat and cure them using the psychoanalytic approach. Unfortunately, such claims turned out to be bogus. Freud probably never cured many patients, but he certainly fraudulently claimed to have cured many. A more detailed discussion of Freud's misrepresentations is beyond the scope of this book, but an excellent treatment of them can be found in Crews's (2017) *Freud: The Making of an Illusion*.

The disconfirming research of the mid-twentieth century did not mean that Freudian theory was moribund. Far from it. Most introductory psychology textbooks still treat Freud's theories and psychoanalysis as important and Freud himself as a pioneer in psychology. Worse, in the 1980s a particularly virulent version of Freudian pseudoscience based on Freud's theory of repression appeared. This led to the repressed memory panic that started in the early 1980s and lasted into the twenty-first century and caused so much damage to innocent people.

FREUDIAN THEORY

One major aspect of Freud's theory was his division of the mind into three levels of consciousness. First, there was the conscious level; below this lay the preconscious, equivalent to a mental library and storing most of our memories. Freud believed these memories were available to consciousness, so the preconscious would thus correspond to what modern psychologists call long-term memory. Below the preconscious lay the unconscious. Freud believed this contained memories, desires, and feelings that had been repressed by the individual because they were too traumatic or painful to face directly. In addition, the unconscious contained "instinctual drives and infantile goals, hopes, wishes, and needs that have been repressed or concealed from conscious awareness, because they cause internal conflict" (Bootzin et al. 1986, 455). The Freudian unconscious is a seething cauldron of lusts, desires, and frustrations. The crucial question is whether such an unconscious exists. Research in cognitive psychology, the study of memory, perception, and language, has revealed a great deal about the nature of cognitive processes, both conscious and unconscious. A great deal of cognitive processing does go on without awareness. Cognitive psychologists prefer to use terms such as *automatic* or *reflexive* to describe these processes, in part to avoid any implication that they resemble the unconscious processes made up by Freud. To argue, as some do (e.g., Miller 1986), that modern cognitive research supports the Freudian view of the unconscious is like an astrologer pointing out, correctly, that both astrology and astronomy postulate the existence of stars and then arguing that because modern research in astronomy has proven that stars exist, that research also shows that astrology is valid. The Freudian unconscious is another Freudian fiction.

Freud believed that all children go through a period when they have active sexual desires for the parent of the opposite sex. He termed this the Oedipus complex. Since these incestuous desires would be considered perverted by most societies, they are repressed. Castration anxiety, discussed below, also results in the repression of Oedipal feelings. Highly traumatic events that take place in childhood or adulthood would also be repressed and relegated to the unconscious, because memories of these events would be too painful to face directly. Material in the unconscious is not available to consciousness but could still exert powerful influences on behavior. Thus, the repressed memory of some childhood trauma could result in severe psychological difficulties later in life, even though the patient would deny that the actual trauma had ever taken place. This theory about repression of traumatic memories led, in the 1980s and 1990s, to a horrific episode of psychological abuse of patients by naive and poorly trained psychotherapists, which will be described later in this chapter.

Psychoanalytic explanations for behavior are often unintentionally humorous. For example, Tourette's syndrome is an inherited neurological disorder in which the patient has difficulty, often great difficulty, controlling motor and vocal "tics." The latter sometimes include unwanted cursing. In prescientific times, patients suffering from Tourette's syndrome were sometimes thought to be possessed by evil spirits. The psychoanalytic explanations are no less absurd. They range from "displaced unconscious muscular eroticism toward the father" to "defense against auto-pleasurable thumb-sucking" (quotes from Garelik 1986, 79–80).

Symbolic Interpretation

According to Freud, the repressed contents of the unconscious could result in psychological disorders. It was the task of the psychoanalytic therapist to discover the repressed, hidden contents of the patient's unconscious and to help the patient achieve insight into the psychological roots of their problems. Once insight was achieved, the psychological problems would fade away because the insight eliminated the repressed cause of the problems. The problem for the therapist was how to get at the contents of the unconscious since the patient did not have conscious access to this material. Symbolic interpretations of various forms of behavior, from dreams to accidents, became the primary method by which psychoanalysts attempted to delve into the unconscious. Freud tried hypnosis for a time but abandoned it. A valuable source of information about the patient's hidden fears, anxieties, and desires was to be found in dreams. For Freud, a dream had two types of content, *manifest content* and *latent content*. Manifest content referred to the psychoanalytically uninteresting images of the dream itself. The latent content was the meaning hidden in those images. Latent content could be revealed only through the analyst's symbolic interpretation of the images in the dream. Thus, "all sharp and elongated weapons, knives, daggers, and pikes represent "the male member. . . . Small boxes, chests, cupboards, and ovens correspond to the female [sex] organ; also cavities, ships, and all kinds of vessels. A room in a dream generally represents a woman" (Freud 1950, 242). The symbolism could be much more complex: "a woman's hat may often be interpreted with certainty as the male genitals. In the dreams of men one often finds the necktie as a symbol for the penis" (243).

Everyday errors and slips of the tongue were also interpreted symbolically as reflecting hidden conflicts and motivations.

There is an extremely serious problem in symbolic interpretation, whether it is of behavior or anything else that is being interpreted: such interpretations are inherently nonfalsifiable. This is especially true in psychoanalytic theory, where the concept of repression can be used to protect any interpretation, no matter how absurd, against falsification. Consider a hypothetical example in which a woman dreams that a man forces his way into her apartment through the front door. Doors and other entrances are said to be symbolic representations of the vagina. Since the "entry" in the dream was forced, the easy interpretation of this dream is that it symbolizes rape. Perhaps the dreamer has a great fear of rape or perhaps she has a hidden desire to be raped or otherwise sexually abused. Is there any way to disprove either of these symbolic interpretations? Absolutely not—if we ask the woman, and she protests that she is neither abnormally afraid of rape nor desirous of being raped, it merely shows that her fear or desire is deeply hidden. In fact, her denial is interpreted as further evidence that the interpretation is true. Thus, no matter whether she agrees with the interpretation or argues against it, her behavior will be seen by the psychoanalyst as supporting the interpretation.

The nonfalsifiability of symbolic interpretations of dreams is not limited to psychoanalytic interpretations. Rather, it applies to any type of symbolic interpretation. In nonpsychoanalytic symbolic schemes, where repression does not play such a large role in protecting an interpretation from falsification, another mechanism operates to make the interpretation seem more valid than it is. This mechanism is highly similar to the fallacy of personal validation that was discussed in chapter 2. It will be recalled that this fallacy convinces people that the vague "predictions" of psychics are much more specific than they really are. Like psychic predictions, dreams are vague because a given dream can appear, after the fact, to be consistent with numerous outcomes. This characteristic of dreams has already been discussed in the context of prophetic dreams, but it applies with equal force to the symbolic interpretation of dream content. A major study of the effects of stress on dreaming (Breger, Hunter, and Lane 1971) illustrates this point.

Many nonpsychoanalytic psychologists reject the specific symbolic interpretations of psychoanalysis but still believe that dream content is at least partially symbolic. A common view is that stressful situations the dreamer is experiencing, or is about to experience, will be symbolically, but not explicitly, represented in the dream, presumably allowing the dreamer to deal with the stress at less than its full intensity. Breger, Hunter, and Lane (1971) set out to test this view by examining the dreams of a number of individuals who were about to undergo the very stressful experience of major surgery. Reports of their dreams were recorded during the nights before the surgery and were then analyzed to see if the content of the dreams symbolically reflected the impending surgery. The authors concluded that the upcoming surgery was featured symbolically in the dreams of the patients.

The Breger, Hunter, and Lane (1971) study was an influential one, but the conclusions are seriously flawed because of both the way the data were collected and the way they were presented in the published report. The authors, who collected the dream reports from the patients and later interpreted them, were well aware of the particular type of surgery that each patient was facing. Thus, it was an easy matter, given the vagueness of dreams, to find symbolic relationships between dream content and the specific surgery that the authors knew patients were facing. In the published report, the reader is first presented with a medical case history for each dreamer; only then are descriptions of the actual dreams provided, followed by the authors' interpretations of the dreams. Given such a sequence, it is not at all surprising that the reader will agree with the authors' interpretations. But the seeming correctness of the interpretation is biased by the previous knowledge the reader was given. This knowledge acts like mental "blinders" to prevent the reader from thinking of alternative interpretations. The authors' previous knowledge before they interpreted the dream prevented them, as well, from seeing alternative interpretations.

The biasing effects of previous information about the dreamers' surgery can be most clearly seen when that information is absent. If there really is a relationship between the symbolic dream content and the nature of the surgery, it should be possible to determine what type of surgery the patient is going to have from the dream itself, without any previous knowledge. Unfortunately, Breger, Hunter, and Lane (1971) made no attempt to find out whether such determinations could be made. Nor did they bother to assess objectively whether it was possible to distinguish between the dreams of stressed and nonstressed individuals if one did not already know which group the dreamer fell into.

The importance of the biasing effect of information about the dreamer and his surgery can be most clearly seen when such information is absent. As an example, read the following dream report from Breger, Hunter, and Lane (1971, 118–19), as edited by Antrobus (1978, 570–71), and try to determine the type of surgery this patient will undergo:

> We was working on a train . . . a work train . . . this Oregon crew came over on account of some washout or something. . . . So we saw them come down to that last station and do some switching. We figures . . . also they came across the bridge up there someplace and hooked over onto our railroad. We was . . . looking at this other engine and . . . we lined the switch, it seemed like our switch . . . it was a funny thing. They had to come off this private [rail] road onto ours and them switches weren't a standard switch. We had to dig some rocks out of the ground . . . and throw this switch over. And I was doing that, I was helping. . . . I can't tell you what a switch is, instead of them being flapped over and locked down to the padlock they was flapped over, the ends of two pipes together and there was a piece of this crooked zigzag piece of iron that was run first in one pipe and then the other so you couldn't lift the one out . . . and we was digging them things out of them pipes so we could throw the switch for them guys so they wouldn't have to stop . . . they hadn't used that switch it seemed like for years and naturally the sand and dust had blowed into these pipes and it was rusty. It took quite a while.

The salient features of the above dream, as far as its symbolic interpretation by Breger, Hunter, and Lane (1971) and Antrobus (1978) is concerned, are the train and train tracks, the switch, and the rocks and dust that seem to block the switch. Even knowing which "symbols" in the dream are considered important by those with knowledge of the dreamer's surgery does not at all constrain the possible interpretations if one does not have such knowledge. In fact, it is almost impossible to think of an operation that is not in some way consistent, after the fact, with the dream if symbolic interpretation of the dream content is permitted.

Perhaps the dreamer will have a brain tumor removed. In that case, the rocks and dust would symbolically reflect the tumor mass. The train and its tracks would represent the normal flow of cognition that was interrupted by the tumor. The switch could further represent the ability to change ("switch") from one type of cognitive process to another, an ability lost in many types of brain damage. Or perhaps the fellow had a kidney stone. Here the train would symbolically represent the fluid in the kidney that is blocked by the kidney stones. The stones and dust in the switch would, of course, represent the kidney stone itself. The train tracks would no doubt be interpreted as symbolic representations of the actual nephrons of the kidney, the tubular structures through which fluid actually moves. In the case of a gallstone, interpretation is almost identical except that, if the gallstone was at the junction of the cystic duct, which originates in the gall bladder, and the common hepatic duct, which originates in the liver, the blocked switch would almost certainly be interpreted as an elegant symbolic representation of the dreamer's particular anatomical problem. The dream could also be symbolically interpreted to represent a tumor of the intestinal tract; blockage of one of the major arteries of the brain; a stroke in which a blood vessel in the brain had become clogged; or atherosclerosis, a buildup of fatty materials in the blood vessels that, when it occurs in the arteries of the heart, can lead to coronary bypass surgery.

All of the possibilities given above could be seen as symbolically represented in the dream. But the dreamer was suffering from none of those conditions. Instead, he suffered from "vascular blockages in his legs" (Breger, Hunter, and Lane 1971, 106), and the surgery was to remove a portion of the blood vessel that was blocked. Naturally, Breger, Hunter, and Lane interpret this dream only in terms of the operation they already knew the patient was going to have, stating that the railroad tracks and switch represent the patient's "clogged blood vessels" (122). Antrobus (1978) gives an even more detailed symbolic interpretation, contending that "there is a double representation in this report of some features of the impending surgery. The veins are similar to the railroad track. Blood moving through the veins is similar to the train moving along the tracks" (571). Certainly, one must agree that some of the images in the dream are "similar," in one way or another, to certain features of the patient's disease. But they are also "similar," given a little creative interpretation, to some features of almost any other conceivable type of surgery. In summary, symbolic interpretation of dreams, whether the interpretation is explicitly Freudian or not, meets one of the major criteria for being considered a pseudoscience: the interpretations are nonfalsifiable.

It is appropriate to inquire here a bit further into the nature of the content of dreams. If the contents are not symbolic, what are they? Since dream content is so complex, it can be interpreted, after the fact, in a myriad number of different ways. Modern dream research has brought order out of this chaos. Dream content is partly due to random activation of material in memory during dreaming sleep, which accounts for its often-bizarre characteristics. But there are nonrandom aspects of dream content as well. What one has been doing during the period before sleep can impact dream content. If you've just seen a horror movie before sleeping, your dreams are likely to have a different aspect than if you'd watched a romantic comedy. Once, in college, when I was worried about final exams, I had a dream in which I was sitting in the room for a very, very important final. The professor walked through the room and passed out the final exam paper to everyone. Except me! Nothing symbolic in that. Children who are bullied are more likely to have a dream in which some sort of threatening figure appears. The issues that face us at different times in our lives influence dream content, but in fairly straightforward, nonsymbolic ways (McNamara 2019). Fanciful, after-the-fact symbolic dream interpretations may make for amusing cocktail party conversations, but they have no basis in reality.

Dreams were not the only aspect of behavior that Freud interpreted in symbolic fashion. His penchant—almost mania—for finding hidden, symbolic meanings nearly everywhere reveals the absurdity not only of his specific method of symbolic interpretation but also of the process in general. Freud was a very close friend of Wilhelm Fliess, the inventor of biorhythms, who was a surgeon in Berlin in the late 1800s. Fliess was a man of many peculiar ideas, biorhythms being just one of them. He believed that many of his patients suffered from what he termed the *nasal reflex neurosis*. This neurosis could manifest itself in any number of symptoms, and Fliess was "rarely at a loss to discover that one of his patients had a nasal reflex neurosis" (Crews 1995, 10). The treatment for this disorder? Application of cocaine to the inside of the nose—no doubt a popular treatment. Unfortunately, if the local application of cocaine didn't cure the neurosis, more drastic measures had to be taken. Fliess would cauterize the spots in the nose on which the sexual organs were represented (Fliess believed that the nose was a secondary sexual organ itself), and if that unpleasant procedure failed, one of the small bones inside the nose would be surgically removed.

So it was with Emma Eckstein, who was unfortunate enough to be a patient of both Fliess and Freud. Surgical skills and procedures in the late 1800s were not what they are now; nor, apparently, was Fliess what one might call a master surgeon. When he removed the bone from Emma Eckstein's nose, he left some gauze in the wound. Not surprisingly, this resulted in nasal hemorrhages. Freud, who was also treating Emma at the time, came to an astonishing conclusion about the nature of these hemorrhages. They were, Freud wrote to Fliess, symbolic representations of Emma's sexual "longing" for Freud and an attempt by her to seduce him (Crews 1984; letter to Fliess originally published in Schur 1966).

Crews (1984) has described another aspect of Freud's love of symbolic interpretation. Fliess believed, and apparently influenced Freud strongly in this regard, that all humans were inherently bisexual. Thus, all males had hidden, or "latent," homosexual tendencies. These tendencies, of course, had to be repressed if normal heterosexual activity was to take place and the species was to perpetuate itself. But in the distant past, males weren't so skilled at repressing their latent homosexual urges. Rather than actually having sexual intercourse with other males, they expressed their only partially repressed homosexual desires symbolically. How was this done? In his scathing essay "The Freudian Way of Knowledge," Crews (1984) summarizes Freud's view clearly: our male ancestors "went around dousing fires with urine, thus experiencing a homosexual gratification in vanquishing the phallic flames" (23). Civilization began to really develop, according to Freud, when fire was domesticated—when man "could sufficiently master his homosexuality to save and nurture a fire instead of obeying his drive to pee on it" (23).

Symbolic interpretation has been adopted with special vigor in the study of literature. Probably everyone who has ever taken a high school or college literature course has heard symbolic interpretations of stories or poems. Such interpretations are nonfalsifiable and can show an excess of interpretative zeal, sometimes becoming absurd. My personal favorite came from an instructor in my freshman year required college English course. We were reading James Joyce's set of short stories *Dubliners*. One question concerned the reason for the presence of snow in the stories. I suggested that this reflected the fact that it snows in Dublin, the setting of the stories, in the winter. To me, this seemed a logical response. I was informed, however, that my response revealed that I didn't understand the symbolic meaning of literature. Far from being a mere realistic representation of Dublin's climate, the instructor informed us, the snow was a psychosexual symbol. Snow is wet, white, and sticky; semen is also wet, white, and sticky. Therefore, snow is a symbol of semen, and from this one can deduce that Joyce had deep anxieties about his masculinity. I did not have the nerve then to point out that there is at least one major difference between snow and semen: one is cold, the other warm. However, I doubt that this would have presented any difficulty to the symbolic interpretation. In fact, I suspect that my instructor would have used the difference to support his symbolic interpretation, perhaps along the lines that Joyce's anxieties made him "cool" to sexual matters, and the coolness of the snow symbolically represented this.

In summary, the use of symbolic interpretations of behavior suffers from the same problems found in the symbolic interpretations of psychic predictions, as discussed in chapter 2. No matter what the prediction, or how the subject behaves, the symbolic interpretation will supply "evidence" that appears to validate the theory in question.

Theories of Psychosexual Development

Freud divided psychosexual development into four stages. One of the most important was the anal stage, because it was during this stage that toilet training took place. Freud believed that toilet training had great influence on the development of personality. According to Hall (1954, 107) in his classic introduction to Freudian theory, "the methods employed by the mother in training the child, and her attitudes about such matters as defecation, cleanliness, control, and responsibility, determine in large measure the exact nature of the influence that toilet training will have upon the personality and its development." It is Freud's view of toilet training that gives one of the best examples of the nonfalsifiable nature of what is one of the most important pillars of his psychoanalytic theory. If toilet training is strict, it may have one of two possible outcomes. First, the child may "get even with frustrating authority figures by being messy, irresponsible, disorderly, wasteful, and extravagant" (108). Second, strict toilet training may result in "meticulous neatness, fastidiousness, compulsive orderliness, frugality, disgust, fear of dirt, strict budgeting of time and money, and other over-controlled behaviors" (108). So strict toilet training can result in either a slob or a neat freak or, presumably, anything in between. Thus, the theory can "explain," post hoc, any degree of neatness or sloppiness as being due to strict toilet training.

The theory becomes doubly nonfalsifiable when one considers the effects of gentle toilet training can also have directly opposite effects. On the one hand, if the training is such that the mother pleads with the child to have a bowel movement and praises him extravagantly when he does, the child will come to regard the product he has made as being of great value. Later in life he may be motivated to produce or create things to please others or to please himself as he once made feces to please his mother. Generosity, giving presents, charity, and philanthropy may all be outgrowths of this basic experience. (Hall 1954, 108)

Does this mean that gentle toilet training will always result in this sort of behavior? Not at all:

If too much emphasis is placed on the value of feces, the child may feel that he has lost something valuable when he defecates. He will respond to the loss by feeling depressed, depleted, and anxious. He will try to prevent future loss by refusing to give up his feces. If this mode fixates and generalizes, the person will be thrifty, parsimonious, and economical. (108)

So gentle toilet training can result in either a generous person or a tightwad. Again, both styles of personality can be "explained" after the fact, but neither can be predicted.

Further, note that strict toilet training can be used to explain the "strict budgeting of time and money," while gentle toilet training can result in someone who is "thrifty, parsimonious, and economical." Also, gentle training can result in "generosity, giving presents, charity, and philanthropy," while strict training can produce "extravagant" behavior. Thus, the same behavior can be "explained" by opposite types of toilet training, and opposite types of behavior can be "explained" as being due to identical toilet training procedures.

Freud's fecal fascination does not end here. Hall (1954, 108) states that "the gentle pressure on the intestinal walls of the rectum is sensually satisfying" and "if a person gets fixated upon this form of erotic pleasure it may develop into a generalized interest in collecting, possessing, and retaining objects." But if a reaction formation develops, the "person will feel impelled to give away his possessions and money in a heedless manner or lose them by making foolish investments or by reckless gambling. Having things makes such people so anxious that they will do almost anything to get rid of them."

Repression and the Unconscious

The concept of repression is of great importance in Freudian theory. A defining feature of repression is that it is "motivated" forgetting; that is, it is an active process in which certain memories are blocked from reaching consciousness because of their emotionally negative content. Should such memories reach the conscious level, they could cause serious psychological disturbance.

One well-known phenomenon has long been used to argue for the reality of repression. This is *infant amnesia*, which refers to the fact that adults have very poor memories for the first few years of life. Freud proposed a characteristically creative explanation for this amnesia. The period of early childhood, according to psychoanalytic theory, is one during which children, both male and female, are awash with strong sexual desires, most of them incestuous. Since these desires cannot be fulfilled, they result in considerable frustration. Further, in the case of the boy, his lust for his mother may, he fears, result in his castration. These factors lead to a repression of early childhood memories when the Oedipus complex is resolved. Why are all childhood memories repressed and not just the ones dealing with the child's sexual desires? Because if any memory from this period came to consciousness, there would be a risk that memories of the perverted (by adult standards) and frustrating sexual desires the individual had as an infant would also emerge into consciousness, perhaps causing serious psychological damage.

There is no question that infant amnesia is a real phenomenon. However, research on memory and the brain has shown that its causes are very different from those proposed in psychoanalytic theory. In the 1970s Spear (1979) and Coulter, Collier, and Campbell (1976) showed that rats also show infant amnesia. Monkeys also show infant amnesia (Mishkin and Appenzeller 1987). It seems most unlikely that rat or monkey infant amnesia is due to the rats or monkeys repressing their incestuous childhood desires for their parents.

The real reason for infant amnesia in rats, monkeys, and humans lies in the nature of the brain of the immature organism (Alberini and Travaglia 2017). The immature brain is both anatomically and physiologically different from the mature brain. Deep in each temporal lobe of the vertebrate brain is a structure known as the *hippocampus*. Together, the two hippocampi (and, of course, other brain structures) are vital for normal memory function. The hippocampi in the human brain do not begin to undergo maturational changes until between four and five years of age (White and Pillemer 1979). Significantly, it is at about this time that the earliest memories adults can recall are found. Thus, it is the anatomical and physiological changes that take place in the brain, specifically in the hippocampi, that result in more lasting memories being formed by rats, monkeys, and humans who have passed the infant and very young child stages of development.

A second variable operates in the case of humans to make memories of events that took place during early childhood and infancy difficult to recall. This is the development of language. Infants and very young children have no—or at best very limited—language skills. As language develops, it becomes, among other things, a major way of storing information in memory. Adult human memory is language oriented. Memories of events that took place before language developed must be stored in some nonlinguistic fashion, if they are stored at all. Since the human adult typically uses language processes to code and retrieve memories, the mismatch between the type of coding of prelanguage (infant and early childhood) memories and postlanguage (later childhood and adult) memories will render the former difficult to retrieve (White and Pillemer 1979).

Many experimental studies have tried to validate the existence of repression. Holmes (1974) reviewed this large literature. He concluded that "there is no consistent research evidence to support the hypothesis" that repression actually exists (649). He further commented that the failure of numerous studies to support the reality of repression was "especially notable in view of the wide variety of approaches which have been tried and the persistent effort which has been made during the last half century to find support" for repression (649). Research done after Holmes's (1974) has been no more successful in turning up evidence in support of the concept (Clifasef, Garry, and Loftus 2007).

Recovered Memory and Satanic Ritual Abuse Claims

The Freudian concept of repression was the keystone of one of the most bizarre and damaging episodes in the history of psychotherapy: the *repressed* (or *recovered*) *memory* hysteria that broke out in the late 1980s. While this has now greatly abated, it has not totally passed from the scene. The episode grew out of a concern about a very real and serious problem—sexual abuse of children by parents, relatives, and other caregivers. However, as the legitimate recognition that such abuse had been underappreciated and underreported for years grew, so did fantastical claims that hundreds of thousands, even millions, of people, mostly women, had been abused as children but had repressed the memories of these hideous events. In some cases, the recovered memories included truly horrific accounts of satanic ritual abuse and the killing and eating of children. Several women "remembered" that they had been used as "baby factories" in their adolescence; the babies they gave birth to were then used for ritual torture and cannibalism. Many women, including the actress Rosanne Barr, "remembered" incidents of abuse that occurred when they were less than a year old, three months old in Barr's case. Another common finding was that therapists discovered that patients suffered from multiple personality disorder (MPD—now termed dissociative identity disorder, or DID). The 1988 publication of the book *Courage to Heal* by Ellen Bass and Laura Davis brought the recovered memory claims to wide public attention, as it soon became a bestseller. This and similar books stated that not only had millions of women repressed their memories of childhood abuse, but the unremembered abuse was the cause of numerous psychological problems these women suffered from. In her book *Secret Survivor*, E. Sue Blume (1990) argued that half of all women were sexually abused as children. Further—and this was the truly damaging and dangerous aspect of the ideology of what became known as "repressed memory therapy"—the only way to deal with and cure these psychological problems was for the patient to recover (i.e., bring back to consciousness) memories of the abuse and confront their abuser(s). This therapeutic approach was, in fact, based on fundamental misunderstandings about how human memory worked. As such, when implemented, it was a recipe for disaster.

The debate over repressed memory therapy generated a vast literature (McNally 2003; Brainerd and Reyna 2005). Loftus's early (1993) article is still an important review on the issue of the reality of the memories recovered by patients during therapy. Loftus is a leading researcher in the cognitive psychology of memory who has made major contributions to the understanding of how malleable human memory is even under nonextreme conditions. Her book *The Myth of Repressed Memory* (Loftus and Ketcham 1994) remains an excellent treatment of the repressed memory episode. Crews's (1995) book *The Memory Wars* is a chilling read that focuses more specifically on the role of Freudian psychology in the repressed memory movement.

If a woman had no memory of abuse during childhood, how was she to know that she had been abused? This was supposedly established by the psychological difficulties she suffered from. The first (1988) edition of *Courage to Heal* includes a checklist of symptoms that is so long and nonspecific that almost anyone reading it could convince themselves that they had been abused. As Crews (1995) pointed out, these checklists disappeared from later editions of the work, no doubt because of the serious criticism they engendered. But they were there at the beginning and contributed to the generation of what became a wave of near hysteria. In another early book on the topic, Blume (1990) warned readers that if they "speak too softly, or wear too many clothes, or have 'no awareness at all' of having been violated" (quoted in Crews 1995, 196), then they probably had been abused. A memory of a pleasant childhood with no hint of abuse was said to be a fantasy or "screen memory" created to help repress the memories of the actual events. This is typical Freudian doublespeak. If one has memories of abuse, one was abused. But if there were no memories of abuse, that also indicated that abuse had happened.

Usually the process of becoming convinced that one's symptoms were due to unremembered childhood sexual abuse began in a therapist's office. The patient would seek help for common psychological maladies such as depression, anxiety, or general difficulties in getting along with others and end up convinced that previously unsuspected and unremembered abuse was responsible. But at this point, while the patient may have accepted the abuse explanation, there was still no memory of the abuse. If it was the case that, in order to treat the psychological problems, the abuse had to be consciously remembered, this posed the problem of how to get the patient to recover those repressed memories.

Techniques used to recover memories included hypnosis, participation in support groups, something called guided imagery, and drugs such as sodium pentothal, also known as truth serum. Hypnosis is not a state that is conducive to obtaining accurate information from memory. Rather, it is a process that can create memories of events that never took place and cause the individual to strongly believe that the false memories are real. The use of hypnosis by therapists who believe that a patient's symptoms are due to unremembered sexual abuse will frequently be "successful" in that the therapist will be able to implant memories of abuse that never took place. Hypnosis was often combined with group therapy sessions, where patients who had already accepted the reality of their hypnotically induced abuse memories put pressure on other patients who had not yet done so. Such group pressure is very powerful and has also been used by UFO groups to "help" abductees come to accept the reality of their abduction experiences, as discussed in chapter 8.

One technique widely used to help recover repressed memories was guided imagery, also known as visualization. In this technique patients are trained in how to form vivid images, in visual, tactile, and other sensory modalities, of incidents of abuse. Consider, for example, a woman who suspects that she was abused by, say, her uncle but has no specific memories of such abuse. She would be instructed to go home, lie on her bed, and imagine that she is lying on her bed when she was a child. She should then imagine her uncle coming into her room and fondling her, forcing her to fondle him as, maybe, he undresses. She should then imagine the uncle climbing on top of her and entering her. This type of exercise is repeated until the patient is convinced that she has a real memory of her uncle's abuse. In some cases, the imagery takes place in the therapist's office with the therapist helping, or "guiding," the scenario. Obviously, such a procedure, along with the social pressure of the therapist, a "support" group of patients already convinced that their recovered memories are real, and hypnosis, forms a belief that the totally fictitious, albeit truly terrifying, memories are very real. In addition, it is now clear that the cases of DID reported in patients subjected to recovered memory "therapy" were caused by the same therapeutic techniques. This was especially true for hypnosis, where the hypnotized, and thus highly suggestible, patient had the different personalities encouraged to "come out" and "show themselves." The effects of such techniques are graphically illustrated in the episode of the PBS documentary series *Frontline* titled "The Search for Satan," first broadcast on October 24, 1995.

In some extreme cases, sodium pentothal was used to aid in recovering memories of abuse. This drug can be thought of as sort of a chemical hypnosis. It does not force the patient to tell the truth. Rather, like hypnosis, it induces a state in which the patient becomes highly suggestible (Piper 1993).

The results of such "therapy" were, as might be expected, disastrous. Although exact figures will never be known, at least thousands of families were torn apart by accusations of abuse recovered in therapy. Part of the treatment included getting angry at the abuser and confronting him or her. This led to both civil and criminal cases in which often elderly parents were charged with criminal activity or subject to damage suits, based on nothing more than the memories recovered in therapy.

The concept of human memory advocated by recovered memory therapists is totally contrary to what is known about how human memory actually works. As noted earlier, there is no evidence that repression is a real phenomenon. In the Freudian view of repression, memories of traumatic events are said to be stored away, in more or less complete form, somewhere deep in the unconscious where we cannot access them—until, of course, the recovered memory therapists dig them out. It was these repressed memories, festering away outside of consciousness, that were said to cause so many of the symptoms and problems that people sought therapy for in the first place. But it is clear now that the great majority of recovered memories of abuse were simply false and had been created by the interventions of the therapists. The fact that, for the patients, the recovered memories were frighteningly real and obviously engendered very real emotional reactions in no way proves that they were real. The memories created in UFO abductees by alien abductee therapists using similar techniques are also experienced as very real, frightening, and traumatic by the individuals in question, and these memories are clearly false.

If anything, memories of real traumatic events stick in our memory much more persistently than memories of more mundane events. This is the basis for posttraumatic stress disorder (PTSD), a condition in which someone who has suffered some traumatic event or situation can't stop remembering it. The event plays out in the mind again and again, terrifying each time, sometimes for years after the event. It might actually seem that it would be better if human memory did come with some sort of repression mechanism so that we wouldn't be haunted by troubling memories of highly unpleasant events. But as Daniel Schacter (2001) argued in his excellent book on human memory *The Seven Sins of Memory*, PTSD is actually a side effect of a valuable and useful aspect of normal memory functioning that highlights memories of dangerous events. For example, getting attacked by a saber-toothed tiger would certainly have been a traumatic event for early humans. And, assuming that the attack was survived, it would have been vital to remember the details of the attack—where it took place, visual or auditory cues that warned of the attack, and so forth. If there was a mechanism that repressed memories of traumatic events, our early ancestors would not have been able to learn from unpleasant experiences, certainly a vital part of survival. Repression makes no sense from an evolutionary point of view.

Recovered memory therapists also believe that it is possible to recover memories of events that took place when a person was very young—as young as three months in the case of Rosanne Barr. As the discussion of infant amnesia above shows, in the brain of a young child, the anatomical structures and circuitry needed for long-term retention of memories is not yet adequately developed. This is not to say, of course, that young children do not remember events from day to day. They do, but they lack the mechanisms that provide storage of these memories in forms that will make them retrievable years later.

The issue of the reliability of children's memories became one focal point in the debate about another aspect of claims about ritual abuse. In the early 1980s allegations began to appear that children were being subjected to truly ghastly forms of sexual abuse and torture by Satan worshippers. This abuse took place in private homes but also in schools and day care centers. It was argued that there was a huge, nationwide ring of satanists coordinating the abuse. Included were young women kept as "breeders" whose job was to have babies that were then used in ritual sacrifices and cannibalism. It was said that tens of thousands of people were being killed by satanic cults every year. But no bodies were ever found, leading an FBI agent who investigated some of the claims to write (Lanning 1991) that "it is up to mental health professionals, not law enforcement, to explain why victims are alleging things that don't seem to be true" (171). Why were no bodies ever found? Believers in the ritual abuse cults claimed that the bodies, bones and all, were either eaten in ritual cannibalism or cremated in portable crematoria hidden in semitrucks cruising the highways of America.

In a typical case, charges of abuse at some school came to the attention of the local authorities, who then intervened by interviewing the children said to have been abused. In some cases, these young children told the most chilling stories of abuse. It was believed by social workers and psychologists that the children couldn't be making up such horrible stories. They had to be telling the truth. The full story of the "satanic panic" that spread across America in the 1980s and early 1990s has been described in several books, specifically Victor's 1993 *Satanic Panic*, Carlson and Larue's 1989 *Satanism in America: How the Devil Got Much More Than His Due*, and Beck's 2015 *We Believe the Children*.

The McMartin Preschool case holds the dubious distinction of being the prototypical case of satanic ritual child abuse allegations in a school setting. Eberle and Eberle (1993) have written a book-length treatment of this tragic and informative case. Beck (2015) has placed the case in the context of the "moral panic" of the 1980s. The best article-length summary I have read is by Fischer (1989). The McMartin Preschool was located in a suburb of Los Angeles, California. In 1983 Judy Johnson, the mother of three-year-old Jeffrey Johnson, charged that her son had been sexually abused by a staff member at the school. Medical support for this charge was, at very best, flimsy, and no charges were brought. Then, in an astonishing move, the local police department sent a letter to every parent with a child in the McMartin school alleging that sexual abuse was taking place at the school. The letter asked that parents report anything suspicious. The effect of the letter was exactly what one would have expected: it started a panic. After all, parents assumed, if the police were sending such a letter, there must be real, solid evidence of something horrible going on at the school. Not surprisingly, soon after the letter went out, other reports of abuse appeared.

As parents reported their suspicions, their children were interviewed by police investigators as well as social workers. The interview techniques used on these children, and in other similar cases, did not involve hypnosis, visualization, or drugs, as is often the case with adults in repressed memory therapy. But the techniques that were used, when applied to children, were just as productive of false reports of abuse that, in the long term, became real memories of abuse that hadn't taken place.

One of the most notorious methods used in these cases was the use of anatomically correct dolls. These are dolls are complete with, as required, a penis or a vagina. When these dolls were first introduced in the investigation of child abuse in the 1970s, it was simply assumed that children who had been sexually abused would pay more attention to, and thus play more, with the "naughty bits" than would nonabused children. Thus, playing with the penis or vagina was seen as evidence of abuse, even if the child said he or she had not been abused and there was no physical evidence of abuse.

Unfortunately, it was years after the use of the dolls had begun that attempts were made to find out if the way children played with them was really a valid indication of whether a child had been abused. As summarized by Wolfner, Faust, and Dawes (1993), Dawes (1994), and Bruck and Ceci (1999), it is clear that the use of these sorts of dolls was useless as an indicator of abuse. For example, in one study (Bruck et al. 1995), the subjects were young children who had been given a regular physical checkup, including an examination of the genital area that did not involve any touching or penetration. When asked to use anatomically correct dolls to "show me on the doll how the doctor touched your genitals," a "significant proportion of the children (particularly the girls) showed touching on the doll even though they had not been touched" (Bruck and Ceci 1999, 428). Further, some children showed that they had been penetrated with the doctor's finger or a spoon or that a stethoscope had been used in the genital exam. This unreliability of the dolls means that not only were children who were not abused classified as having been abused by the dolls test, but the reverse occurred. Children who had been abused were missed by the test. The failure of the large number of psychologists and social workers who used these dolls without rigorous evidence that they were valid is inexcusable and resulted in much harm. Unfortunately, in some areas in social work and clinical psychology, there seems to be little appreciation of the fact that it is unethical to use a test without evidence that it actually works. The belief that it works is thought to be enough.

The doll test tended to classify more children as having been abused simply because children tend to play with the interesting new bits that they have not seen before. But the doll test, in and of itself, did not result in specific reports of abuse. Other techniques used by police, psychologists, child services personnel, and social workers, however, had exactly such an effect. In one simple example, a child would be told that he or she could not go home to their parents until the investigators were told the "truth." And it was made very clear to the child what the "truth" was, through the leading questions being asked. In another situation, investigators would determine that Sam and Betty were best friends. The two children would be interviewed separately. Betty might be asked if Mr. So-and-so had abused her in some way. Since he hadn't, the child would answer no. The rest of the interrogation would go something like the following:

Investigator: Is Sam your best friend?
Betty: Yes.
I: Is Sam an honest boy?
B: Yes, sure.
I: He wouldn't tell a lie?
B: No.
I: Then I don't understand—Sam told us that Mr. So-and-so did that thing to you. Is Sam lying to us?

Sam had said no such thing—but Betty has no way to know this and is way too young to consider that a friendly adult authority figure might be blatantly lying to her. This obviously put Betty in a bad position! Most adults (although not all!) would easily see through this ploy, but few children would be able to. So Betty has to choose between saying her best friend is a liar or agreeing that Mr. So-and-so did something to her that she probably doesn't really understand. Usually, it is clear what the friendly adult authority figures want her to say—and that she'll be rewarded for saying it by, as above, going home to her folks, or through other praise and rewards. It doesn't take much of such pressure to get children to tell some pretty fantastic stories. And in the McMartin case, tell stories they did. They told of being sexually abused in hot air balloons. Of being taken on airplane rides and photographed naked, then being flown back to the school. Of a great network of tunnels under the school in which abuse took place. Of seeing a horse killed with a baseball bat. Of going to graveyards and digging up corpses, where one child saw a teacher flying (Cockburn 1990). And of numerous instances of disgusting sexual abuse. But there was *no physical evidence* found. No balloons were found. No reports of anyone seeing balloons going to and from the school. No tunnels under the school. The case against all seven of the McMartin defendants rested on the uncorroborated testimony of the children. Such testimony was given after months and, as the trial dragged on, years of interviews and coaching that reinforced the children's beliefs that they truly had been abused. Obviously, the parents believed that their children had been abused, so that belief was strongly reinforced in the children's homes as well.

The trial dragged on for seven years. It remains the longest criminal trial in American history and was, when it ended, the most expensive. At the end of the first trial, the defendants were found not guilty on a great majority of the charges. The jury hung on the remaining charges. When two defendants were retried on the charges on which the original jury could not reach a verdict, they were found not guilty on most and the jury hung on the rest. These charges were dropped within a few months. Of course, during this time, the defendants had been in prison: some for five years, some for seven. By the time the trial ended, the children were now teenagers. Some had become absolutely convinced that they had been horribly abused when they were youngsters. They went on local TV shows with their parents to rail against the outcomes of the trials (Cockburn 1990). And, in a very sad way, they're right. They had been horribly abused. But not by anyone at the McMartin Preschool. They had been abused by the very people who should have been least likely to abuse them: the police, child protection workers, social workers, and psychologists. It was this group that had carefully, albeit in ignorance, created, maintained, and reinforced the false memories of abuse that these young individuals will probably carry with them for the rest of their lives.

The McMartin case was far from unique. There were similar cases around the country. As usual, there was no physical evidence of abuse. Teachers, school workers, and sometimes parents were convicted on the basis of the testimony of children—testimony elicited by the same tactics used on the McMartin children. How could such things happen in a modern, presumably sophisticated America? The sociologist Jeffrey Victor (1993) noted in his book *Satanic Panic* that rumor and the mass media played major roles. He said, "the ritual abuse scare is the social creation of a late twentieth century witch hunt. There is no verifiable evidence for claims about a satanic cult ritual abuse conspiracy. However, there is abundant evidence that an increasing number of moral crusaders are creating a form of deviant behavior, which exists only in their preconceptions" (117). Victor also reported that media sensationalism played a major role. The *Los Angeles Times*—after the McMartin trials were over, of course—was highly critical of its own reporting, noting, "Pack journalism. Laziness. Superficiality" and "a competitive zeal that sends reporters off in a frantic search to be the first with the latest shocking allegation, responsible journalism be damned" (quoted in Victor 1993, 116). Much "credit" for keeping the general "satanism in America" panic going in the 1980s belongs to that paragon of journalistic integrity Geraldo Rivera, whose special on NBC titled *Devil Worship: Exposing Satan's Underground*, aired on October 25, 1980 (just before Halloween!), was "watched by more people than any other television documentary in history," and "was distinguished by its almost total lack of credible information; it substituted sensationalism and hype for accurate investigation" (Alexander 1990, 10).

In the annals of the repressed memory horrors, the case of Paul Ingram is one of the most bizarre and telling. Ofshe and Watters (1994) describe the case in detail in *Making Monsters: False Memories, Psychotherapy, and Sexual Hysteria*, their book on repressed memory claims. In 1988 one of Ingram's daughters charged that she had been repeatedly raped by her father and some of his friends during her childhood. These accusations started when the daughter was at a religious camp and was told by a faith healer that she had been sexually abused by her father. Before this, she had no memories whatsoever of any abuse. The accusations grew to include claims that her father and mother were part of a satanic group responsible for the ritual killing of hundreds of babies.

Ingram was arrested and confessed to the abuse charges made against him, now by both his daughters. One might think that such a confession was proof positive that the abuse had taken place, but in fact false confessions are rather common, occurring in about 25 percent of cases where the confessor was proven innocent by DNA evidence (Perillo and Kassin 2011). In this case, however, the confessions included great detail about the crimes. Ingram was told, incorrectly, by the interrogating police officers that people often did not remember committing horrible crimes such as the ones he was charged with. A law enforcement officer himself, Ingram was very cooperative with his interrogators. They first got him to agree that his daughters wouldn't lie about such events. This, combined with his belief in repressed memories, allowed Ingram to believe that he had committed crimes of which he had no memory. He was then instructed in the process of visualization in order to "retrieve" his repressed memories. It is not surprising that this process led to very detailed and graphic memories of the abuse his daughters charged him with. Again, it might seem that such detail would be further evidence of the reality of his memories. But the memories were *too* detailed. In one instance Ingram claimed to remember the time on the watch he had seen during one of the episodes, which had purportedly taken place several years earlier.

As the investigation progressed, the local prosecutor's office called in psychologist Ofshe to consult on the case. As Ofshe (Ofshe and Watters 1994) says, he "began to suspect that Paul was not confessing to crimes he had actually committed but was self-inducing trance and imagining crimes suggested to him" (172). To verify this suspicion, Ofshe conducted a clever test. He made up an incident of abuse (forcing the daughter and her brother to have sex while Ingram watched) that Ingram's daughters had never alleged. He told Ingram that his daughter had made the charge. At first Ingram said he had no memory of such an event. But the next day, having used the same technique he had used to "recover" other memories, Ingram had a detailed, graphic description of the event that had never taken place.

This case shows the power of belief in repressed memories and the techniques used to "recover" memories of events that never took place. Not only can individuals become convinced they were victims of abuses that never took place; it is also possible for a person to convince himself that he committed terrible crimes when, in fact, he did not. At the time of Ingram's trial, little of this was known, so it could not be used in his defense. He was convicted and remained in jail in spite of appeals. He was released in 2003 at the end of his sentence.

During the moral panic over satanic ritual abuse, role-playing games like Dungeons and Dragons became targets of fundamentalist religious groups. The best known was Bothered About Dungeons and Dragons (BADD), which tried, with some initial success, to get such games banned from public schools. Game players were thought to be at risk because the games would seduce them into the occult and the arms of Satan. But the gamers fought back and showed how absurd these worries were (Laycock 2015, chap. 4).

Claims for satanic ritual abuse faded away by the early 2000s as the legal system became more familiar with the pitfalls of repressed memory. An important factor in educating the legal system was what Barden (2018) calls "multidisciplinary science litigation teams." These are legal teams that include "science-informed attorneys" as well as experts able to refute the testimony of social workers and psychotherapists trained badly (or not at all) in the basics of the science of memory and cognition.

The nature of human memory was a central issue in both the recovered/repressed memory controversy and the controversy over claims of satanic ritual abuse. As noted above, by the time the recovered/repressed memory issue came to the fore, memory researchers had long since abandoned the concept of repression as yet another Freudian myth. The therapists who accepted the reality of repression were simply unacquainted with anything approaching research on the real nature of human memory. This may seem surprising. One might think that a person trained in psychotherapy would have had to have obtained a solid background in the scientific study of how the mind works, and that this would have included much material on memory. In fact, many therapists, even those with doctoral degrees, obtain their degrees with essentially no training in the nature of memory. Many programs granting master's or doctoral degrees in psychotherapy require little or no coursework on the scientific understanding of how the mind actually works. It is rather as if programs training jet aircraft mechanics did not require the mechanics to know how a jet engine worked! In many cases, the only information about memory the therapists have will have come from a long-ago and mostly forgotten undergraduate course.

This lack of training in the scientific basis of how the mind and its various components function is the reflection of a sometimes hostile and frequently dismissive attitude on the part of therapists and would-be therapists that such information would be of any use to them. In my role as a college professor, I often advise students who want to be psychology majors. When I tell them that the psychology major at Pace University, like most others, requires that they take courses covering human cognitive and brain function, as well as statistical analysis and experimental design, an all-to-frequent reply is something like, "Gee, I want to be a psychotherapist. Why do I have to take all that science stuff?" This strikes me as the equivalent of someone who wants to be a surgeon whining about having to take "all that anatomy stuff." Certainly, the tragedy of the repressed/recovered memory debacle might well have been greatly reduced had therapists been better trained in the facts about memory so they could have avoided, from the outset, the trap of believing that the methods of "recovery" they used were producing memories of real events.

As of the mid-1980s, when the satanic ritual abuse hysteria was getting rolling, cognitive scientists and psychologists already knew a great deal about how memory worked—and about how it didn't. Among the things that were clear by then was that memory was often unreliable. But not just unreliable in the rather trivial sense that from time to time we can't pull out of memory information that we want or need. Rather, as the pioneering work of Loftus made clear, memory could be distorted by information presented in questions about an event. Leading questions, for example, added new (false) information to memory and resulted in the "rememberer" *really remembering events that never took place*. In a now famous study Loftus and Palmer (1974; Loftus 1975) showed subjects a film of a staged car accident. The subjects were then asked, among other things, how fast one car was going when it either "smashed" or "hit" the other car. Not surprisingly, the "smashed" question produced faster speed estimates. But what was very surprising was what happened a week later when the subjects were asked whether they had seen any broken glass in the film. There was no broken glass in the film. But people who had been asked the "smashed" question a week previously were much more likely to report seeing, and thus remembering, broken glass that wasn't there compared to those who had answered the "hit" question. So a very minor change in the wording of a question placed new, and incorrect, information into long-term memory. Studies like this, however, had been done with college-aged subjects, not children. The controversy over the reports and charges made by the child witnesses in the satanic ritual abuse cases motivated a large amount of research specifically aimed at assessing the reliability of children's memories and their susceptibility to various suggestive questioning techniques.

In a classic experiment Bruck, Ceci, and Hembrooke (1997) made up an event that they knew from talking to the parents had not happened to a child: for example, getting a finger trapped in a mouse trap and having to go to the hospital. Upon initial questioning, the children correctly reported that the event had not happened. But all it took was several repeated questionings, spaced several days apart, and the admonition to "think about it" to get a substantial percentage of the children to believe that the event had occurred. Some children came to "remember" the event with considerable detail and were resistant to acknowledging that it had never occurred when so informed. Note the ease with which a false memory of a very unpleasant event had been created—no high-pressure tactics were used. Obviously, with the high-pressure tactics used by the investigators in the satanic ritual abuse cases, the proportion of children reporting horrible events would be greater. In a related study using college-aged students, Loftus (1997) showed that the simple repetition of a question could create a memory of a childhood event that had never taken place, this being lost in a shopping mall. Again, all it took for memories of this nonevent to form was being asked about it several times in succession during questioning sessions spaced several days apart. These two studies serve to give the flavor of a much larger literature on this topic. For a review of this topic, see Brainerd and Reyna (2005).

Therapists often claim that they can easily tell the difference between children's real memories and false or created memories. But the evidence shows this not to be the case. Bruck and Ceci (1999) reviewed studies that show that "trained professionals in the fields of child development, mental health, and forensics . . . cannot reliably discriminate between children whose reports are accurate from those whose reports are inaccurate as the result of suggestive interviewing techniques" (432).

Most of the time, memory serves us well. But studies of the conditions under which it fails us— misleads us into believing that something happened when it did not, for example—have led to a view of memory very different from what might be called the "common view" of memory. In the common view, memory is likened to an old videotape recorder. The tape may be fuzzy, or even erased, but if an image appears on the tape, it must be real. In this view, the act of remembering is basically a passive process of retrieving some piece of information that is stored in memory. Research not only on the suggestibility of memory in adults and children but also on many other aspects of memory shows that the act of remembering is much more complex. Remembering is an interactive process in which the information that is stored can be altered in different ways (added to, made more or less specific, etc.) by the situation the "rememberer" finds herself in.

As noted above, Schacter (2021) has detailed the seven ways that memory is usually good enough to get us through the day, but it is far from perfect. Mild memory unreliability is common in everyday life. It is the conditions found in the therapy sessions of recovered/repressed memory therapists and the interrogation rooms of childcare workers, social workers, and psychologists that elicit the horrible, but false, reports of satanic and sexual abuse.

Another claim made by repressed memory therapists was that traumatic childhood abuse led to the development of multiple personality disorder (MPD), termed dissociative identity disorder (DID) since 1994. There is considerable doubt in the psychiatric community as to whether this disorder even exists in the first place. At one end of the spectrum, we all exhibit somewhat different personalities under different conditions. For example, I am quite outgoing, ebullient, and extraverted when I'm giving a lecture in class that's going really well. On the other hand, I can be quite dour, grumpy, and introverted when I'm in a meeting with a bunch of pettifogging university bureaucrats who have nothing better to do than waste my time. So even, presumably, normal people can show very different personalities under different conditions. If two different people observed me under these two conditions and described my behavior, others reading the descriptions might think that the two descriptions were of two different people.

What is clear is that the same psychological processes that create false memories can also create seemingly real multiple personalities (Brainerd and Reyna 2005). Through hypnosis, encouragement, and other methods, therapists can shape behavior, usually unknowingly, such that different identities will be attributed, by the patient and the therapist, to different patterns of behavior. Such different patterns can even be given different names. Of course, this is what actors do all the time when they assume a new role. The difference for actors is that they are consciously aware that they are taking on a role and that the role they are playing doesn't mean that they are really that person while they are playing the role. It is the use of suggestive psychotherapeutic techniques that creates an illusion that abuse creates multiple personalities.

One of the most famous cases of multiple personalities in history was created by a psychiatrist. Shirley Mason was better known as Sybil when a book by that name by Flora Schreiber was published in 1973. It was made into a popular movie in 1976 starring Sally Field as Sybil and Joanne Woodward as her psychiatrist, Connie Wilbur. Following the publication of the book and the release of the film, diagnoses of multiple personality disorder skyrocketed. It became the fad diagnosis de jour of the period. In reality, the case of Sybil was cooked up by psychiatrist Wilbur and journalist Schreiber. Using the standard tricks of the trade, including extensive hypnosis of Shirley Mason, Wilbur created as many as sixteen "alter" personalities in Mason. The whole sad story is told in Debbie Nathan's (2011) investigative book *Sybil Exposed*, for which she had access to extensive files and records unexamined previously.

Cognitive psychologists working on the basic science of memory were stunned in the 1980s when it became clear that clinical psychologists and social workers often had serious misunderstandings of the basic facts of how human memory works and doesn't work. This surprise led to a great deal of research on the conditions under which false memories can be created. These conditions were more widespread than previously realized and extended from the therapeutic interaction to police lineups. McNally (2003, 275) summarized the results of scientific research on memory for traumatic events: "The notion that the mind protects itself by repressing or dissociating memories of trauma, rendering them inaccessible to awareness, is a piece of psychiatric folklore devoid of convincing empirical support."

Unfortunately, in spite of the research, ill-informed psychotherapists continue to believe in repressed memories and the ability of hypnosis and related techniques to retrieve memories. They confuse simple forgetting, which is obviously real, with repression, which isn't. Patihis and colleagues (2014) found that very high percentages of fringe therapists believed that repressed memories were real and accurate and that various forms of psychotherapy could recover such memories. For example, 69 percent of psychoanalysts and 90 percent of neurolinguistic programmers believed in repressed memories. For those two groups 47 percent of 75 percent, respectively, believed that therapy could accurately recover repressed memories. For other practicing clinical psychologists, the figures were 60 percent and 43 percent. Obviously, practicing therapists have little interest in being informed about the reality of the beliefs they hold.

Otgaar and colleagues (2019) found that about 50 percent of psychotherapists continued to believe in repressed memories and that references to repressed or recovered memories was common in legal proceedings. Patihis and Pendergrast (2019) surveyed 2,326 adults in the United States and found that 46.5 percent had seen some type of psychotherapist during the period 1970–2017. For those seeing therapists during the most recent period studied, 2015–2017, almost 20 percent reported that their therapist raised the possibility that they had repressed memories of childhood abuse. About half of those individuals had actually recovered such memories. About 40 percent of these terminated relationships with family members due to the recovered memories. This is a real cost of this sort of therapy.

The continued acceptance of belief in recovered memories is not limited to the United States. Shaw and Vredeveldt (2019) found that such beliefs were widespread in Europe, especially in France and Germany, where the psychoanalytic approach to therapy is still very common. Probably in an attempt to disguise the unsavory history of repressed memory claims, proponents of the idea have begun to use an alternate term, *dissociative amnesia*. Whatever the name, "falsely recovered memories of abuse continue to pose a substantial risk in therapeutic settings, potentially leading to false accusations and associated miscarriages of justice" (Otgaar et al. 2019, 1089).

Neurolinguistic programming (NLP), mentioned above, is a therapeutic approach in which how an individual moves their eyes is said to reveal much about their personality and psychological problems. Initially it was claimed that by watching how a person's eyes move you could tell what they were thinking about. For example, if the eyes moved up to the (person's) left, they were doing visual recall. Down to the right? Kinesthetic processing. And so forth. In addition to its use as a type of psychotherapy, it is often used in social work and is said to be able to enhance training in sports and sales and even can be a treatment for neurological diseases such as Parkinson's disease. It has become quite popular in the alternative medicine (chapter 11) community. NLP practitioners are explicitly hostile to attempts to scientifically verify their claims, no doubt because they are aware that scientific studies have failed to do so (Sharpley 1987; Witkowski, 2010). In an amazingly revealing example of therapeutic arrogance, two NLP therapists stated, "We are not scientists, and what we do is not science, so we do not have to offer proof" (Clancy and Yorkshire 1989, 64).

The studies of the scientific status of Freud's theories started in the 1950s and 1960s when psychologists became more willing to challenge the then widespread acceptance of Freudian orthodoxy. As described above, these studies have shown that almost everything Freud claimed was either wrong or could not be tested. The scientific status, or lack thereof, of Freud's theories does not tell the whole story of the problems with Freud and psychoanalysis. Freud based his claims for the validity of psychoanalysis on the supposed ability of the process to cure patients of various psychological problems. His writings are filled with descriptions of his patients, their problems, and how the heroic Freud was able to treat and cure them using his psychoanalytic approach. Such claims have been revealed to be bogus. Freud probably never cured a single patient but fraudulently claimed in his writings to have cured many. Crews (2017) has described the level and consistency of Freud's duplicity. As early as Freud wrote about his cures, he misrepresented the results of his treatments by changing important details about the results, simply making up treatment effects and lying about patients' improvement.

Projective Tests

On projective tests, test takers are presented with some ambiguous stimulus that they must describe or make up a story about. Responses are interpreted, frequently symbolically, and are said to reflect the basic, stable personality characteristics of individuals. A related approach is to have the individual produce some output like a drawing of a person or a picture. These are then interpreted psychologically. The responses or drawings can be used, it is claimed, to reveal hidden psychological problems, desires, and anxieties, even if these are lodged in the unconscious. Thus, the term *projective*: the test taker is assumed to project information from their unconscious about their personality and any psychological disturbances onto the ambiguous stimulus or drawing. The conceptual basis for projective tests comes directly from Freudian psychoanalytic theory.

The classic example of a projective test is the Rorschach inkblot test (Rorschach 1942), in which test takers are presented with a series of inkblots and asked to tell what each reminds them of. Another type of projective test is one in which test takers produce some nonverbal response. This type of projective test is typified by the Draw-a-Person test, in which individuals are simply asked to draw a person. The drawings are then interpreted to reveal personality traits, anxieties, and so forth. Similarly, drawings and paintings that people produce outside of any therapeutic situation are interpreted psychologically.

Projective tests are widely used by psychiatrists, psychologists, and social workers. The important question is whether they really provide useful information. That is, do they "work" in any objective sense? For a test to work in this sense, it must possess two basic characteristics: it must be both reliable and valid. Briefly, a test is reliable if it gives the same individual close to the same score on two different test administrations. A test is valid if it can be shown to measure what it claims to measure. There are numerous ways of measuring reliability and validity that are beyond the scope of this section, but they can be found in any text on psychological testing. Projective tests lack both reliability and validity. As long ago as 1988, regarding the issue of validity, Anne Anastasi, an expert on psychological testing, said, "The accumulation of published studies that have *failed* to demonstrate any validity for such projective techniques as the Rorschach and the D-A-P (Draw A Person Test) is truly impressive. Yet after five decades of negative results, the status of projective techniques remains substantially unchanged" (Anastasi 1988, 621; emphasis in original). Twelve years later Lilienfeld, Wood, and Garb (2000) published a thorough review of the research on the most widely used projective tests—the Rorschach, the Thematic Apperception Test, and the Draw-a-Person techniques. Their conclusion was that these tests had such low validity that they were essentially useless. There are other problems with the Rorschach than mere low validity. For one thing it badly overpathologizes those who take the test. That is, it is likely to classify normal individuals as mentally disturbed in some way (Wood, Nezworski, and Garb 2023a, 2023b). Imagine a test for cancer that incorrectly identified even half of cancer-free individuals as having cancer. The continued use of such a test would be highly unethical. And yet the inkblot test continues to be used extensively by clinical psychologists and other mental health professionals who don't know any better.

Wood and colleagues (2003) suggest that the overpathologizing by the Rorschach is one of the reasons for its continued use. This may sound counterintuitive at first, but it stems from the fact that mental health professionals tend to see, and give the test, to people who do have some type of mental problem. So clinicians get the erroneous impression that the Rorschach is a useful source of information. The fallacy here becomes clear if one considers a medical diagnostic procedure. I claim that I have a procedure that is 100 percent accurate in diagnosing cancer. Really, I do have such a procedure and it really (I'm not joking) does correctly identify every single person with cancer, no matter how tiny the cancer, as having cancer. What is the procedure? When anyone comes to the Hines Miracle Cancer Diagnostic Clinic, I say that they have cancer. That's it. I label everyone as having cancer whether they do or not. That way my hit rate really is 100 percent; everyone with cancer is correctly labeled by the Hines Miracle Cancer Screen (HMCS). But, and it's a big but (yeah, I know, I probably should have reworded that), my false alarm rate is also 100 percent. Every single person who does *not* have cancer gets told they have cancer. So, while the HMCS really does have an impressive hit rate of 100 percent, that tells you nothing at all about how good the test is. A test that is actually useful would have a high hit rate *and* a low false alarm rate. However, since mental health professionals tend to see people who have mental health problems, they don't see the false alarms and are misled into thinking that the Rorschach's high hit rate means that it really is a good test. But the test adds very little, if anything, to the diagnostic procedure. In fact, as Wood and colleagues (2003) note, adding Rorschach data into a profile can actually reduce the accuracy of a diagnosis.

In the 1970s, it appeared that a method had been developed that rendered the Rorschach both reliable and valid. This was the Exner "Comprehensive System," a specialized system used to score a patient's descriptions of the inkblots. In some trivial sense it did make the test reliable. So can any such system. If the rule is that every time a patient says "I see a bird" you say "the patient is depressed," then the test is, trivially, reliable. That is, the same response will always get the same diagnosis. But the serious question about validity remained regarding Exner's system. By the 1990s the Comprehensive System had lost all credibility. Exner had been very uncooperative in sharing the research that he alleged supported the validity of the system, and it was discovered that studies Exner had claimed to be supportive didn't exist. Further, there had been a serious mistake in the initial norming of the scoring system. In norming a test one has to administer the test to a large group of normal people to find out what the normal responses are and how much they vary from person to person. Exner had claimed that the scoring system had been normed on seven hundred individuals. But it transpired that only five hundred had been used and the results of two hundred of those had been counted twice. Wood and colleagues (2003, chap. 9) provide details on what can only be termed scientific misconduct by Exner.

The Rorschach is sensitive to some psychological variables such as cognitive and perceptual abilities (Mihura et al. 2013; Wood et al. 2015). Thus, Rorschach responses can distinguish between cognitively impaired and nonimpaired individuals. Overall intelligence can also influence Rorschach responses, with more intelligent individuals giving more and more detailed responses. The test can also detect disorganized thought. Since there are numerous other instruments designed specifically to test for cognitive impairment and intelligence, the Rorschach is not useful for these purposes (Wood, Nezworski, and Garb 2023a, 2023b). Using the Rorschach in such a way would be like using a dirty low-power magnifying glass when a quality microscope was available. Similarly, schizophrenics tend to respond differently to the inkblots than nonschizophrenics. Again, this isn't saying much as differentiating schizophrenics is well done by other more reliable and valid assessments. Technically, the Rorschach has no incremental validity in these situations.

The Rorschach can also be useful as a technique to simply get an overall impression of someone. Interacting one on one while giving the test will certainly provide some information. But a general interview or simply interacting with the person for the same length of time it takes to give the test will also provide such an impression.

If projective techniques are so poor when measured objectively, why are they still so widely used? One reason is that in many cases the test results are interpreted symbolically. For example, in an unpublished report it was noted that one test taker "provided a Rorschach response of cells dividing, in the process of pulling apart, reflecting a lack of separateness and differentiation. Another subject's sense of incompletion and deficiency was illustrated in many anatomical responses, which indicate concerns over bodily integrity." The projective test essentially becomes the "gimmick" in a cold reading (see chapter 2), replacing the astrological chart, tea leaves, or palm lines that the storefront cold reader uses. Thus, it will always be possible for projective test users to convince themselves that the test has revealed something about the test taker.

Another, somewhat more subtle, mechanism also works to increase the perceived validity of projective tests. Known as *illusory correlation*, this mechanism was extensively studied by Chapman and Chapman (1967, 1969; Chapman 1967). Illusory correlation means that certain variables are perceived as co-occurring more frequently than they actually do. Chapman and Chapman (1967) demonstrated this in a series of studies using the projective Draw-a-Person (DAP) test. In these studies, college undergraduates with no knowledge of the DAP were presented with DAP drawings. Each drawing was paired with two statements that, the students were told, described the psychological symptoms of the man who had drawn each drawing. For example, a drawing would be accompanied with a statement such as "The man who drew this (1) is suspicious of other people (2) is worried about how manly he is." The statements that were presented with each drawing had nothing to do with actual symptoms since the drawings were done by symptom-free individuals. The drawings varied on a number of characteristics, several of which clinicians with experience using the DAP believe are signs of particular symptoms. For example, a drawing that has broad shoulders or is muscular or manly is said to be characteristic of a man who is worried about his masculinity. A man worried about his intelligence is said to draw a large or emphasized head. The actual set of drawings and symptom statements used by Chapman and Chapman was specifically constructed such that there was no correlation between any symptoms and any drawing characteristic. That is, the symptom "is worried about how manly he is" occurred equally often with drawings that were muscular and manly and with drawings that weren't.

After having examined the drawings and the pair of "symptoms" associated with each, subjects were asked to indicate which characteristics of the drawings went with each of the symptoms even though there were no such relationships. Nonetheless, the subjects' responses showed that they had perceived in the drawings relationships between drawing characteristics and symptoms that were not really there. They reported, for example, that men who worried about their masculinity draw figures with broad shoulders. Chapman and Chapman (1969) later showed that trained psychodiagnosticians showed similar illusory correlation effects. Additional research has shown that even explicit warnings about the illusory correlation effect fail to prevent it (Waller and Keeley 1978; Kurtz and Garfield 1978). Even trained clinicians "try to find something in the clinical material presented" (Kurtz and Garfield 1978, 1013). Even if no meaning is really there, it will be found.

Chapman and Chapman (1967; Chapman 1967) further found that the degree of the illusory correlation effect is due to what is termed the associative strength between variables that are perceived, incorrectly, to be correlated. Thus, the head and intelligence are logically associated. So are broad shoulders and masculinity. Based on these associations, people assume that a broad-shouldered drawing means that the individual worries about his masculinity and that people worried about their intelligence draw large-headed figures. Chapman showed the importance of associative strength in the genesis of illusory correlation in a study that used pairs of words. Subjects saw sets of word pairs, one pair at a time. Some of the pairs contained associated words (e.g., "lion tiger") and some pairs contained unassociated words (e.g., "lion notebook"). Although each word in the list of pairs that the subjects saw appeared equally often with each other word, subjects reported that words that were paired with a strongly associated word were more frequent than was actually the case. In the clinical situation with projective tests, these results show that the associative strength variable produces the illusory correlation. Selective memory is probably responsible for the continued acceptance of the correlations. When one finds an actual instance in which a man worried about his masculinity has drawn a broad-shouldered picture, that instance will stand out in memory much more than one in which a man worried about his masculinity doesn't draw a broad-shouldered picture. This will be recognized as the same process that maintains belief in psychic predictions, hunches, and prophetic dreams. Illusory correlations, license to make symbolic interpretations, and selective memory all combine to produce a strong belief that unreliable and invalid projective tests are accurate ways of discovering psychologically relevant information about people.

Some mental health professionals claim that children's drawings can be interpreted psychologically to reveal characteristics of the child's personality and psychological problems the child may have. Wimmer (2012, 9) states that "children's drawings offer a kind of map enabling you to navigate in the child's inner emotional world. Through the drawings, the child expresses his difficulties, as well as the solutions he requires." Wimmer's book is full of unsubstantiated claims about what certain characteristics of a child's drawing mean. On page 62 we are informed that "exaggerated use of blue represents cold, distant and restrained communication. It may also symbolize the child's lack of confidence, oversensitivity, vulnerability and even his tendency to suppress his feelings." Or . . . it may just mean that the kid likes blue. Regarding divorce, "One of the most common examples in drawings relating to divorce is drawing a house without an indication of separation" (179). One wonders how a child could include "indications of separation" in a drawing of a house.

Throughout the book, Wimmers interprets the drawings she shows *after* she knows the child's psychological situation. More to the point, could Wimmer or other believers in the psychological interpretation of children's drawings distinguish, without any knowledge beforehand, drawings of houses done by children whose parents were divorcing from those by children whose parents were in a happy, stable relationship? Such a study would be trivially easy to do, but the proponents of this type of pseudopsychology seem never to have even tried. What makes this sort of pseudopsychology so alarming is that, according to the back cover of her book, Wimmer is a "sought-after lecturer on this subject who also provides expert witness testimony to courts of law in cases of abuse and children at risk." The damage that this sort of unreliable and invalid testimony can do is obvious.

The failure of projective tests to achieve even minimal standards of adequacy has led Grove and colleagues (2002) to conclude that the results of these tests should not be admitted in the courtroom as they do not meet the legal standards of scientific evidence. In fact, Grove and Barden (1999) have argued that testimony of mental health experts (clinical psychologists, social workers, and other types of mental health therapists) in general is based so much on nonscientific methods that no such testimony meets the legal standards for admissibility. In the years since Grove and Barden's paper, nothing has changed in this regard.

Projective test results are still used in making life-changing decisions (e.g., child custody, parole, etc.) by clinicians and others not familiar with the evidence of their lack of validity. Dawes (1994, 152–53) gave excellent advice for anyone being asked to take a projective test:

> If a professional psychologist is "evaluating" you in a situation in which you are at risk and asks you for a response to ink blots . . . or for a drawing of anything, walk out of that psychologist's office. Going through with such an examination creates the danger of having a serious decision made about you on totally invalid

grounds. If your contact with the psychologist involves a legal matter, your civil liberties themselves may be at stake.

Returning to the topic of traumatic memories, Freudian psychology was not the only belief system to claim that repressed traumatic memories were important causes of psychological dysfunction. The pseudo-religion of Scientology, founded in the early 1950s by science fiction author L. Ron Hubbard, posits that repressed memories are the source of ills both physical and psychological. These memories can be from early childhood or even before birth or from past lives. Some such memories are implanted by alien spiritual beings called thetans. Thetans are sort of like human souls and can be good, but they can go bad and when they do so they implant these harmful memories. Scientology has a way of removing the harmful repressed memories. It is called auditing, and the goal is to "get clear" of the memories. Not surprisingly, auditing is an extremely expensive process. To aid the process a gimmick called an e-meter is used. This is nothing more than a simple device that measures electrical activity in the skin. By order number 71-2064 dated March 1, 1973, the U.S. District Court for the District of Columbia required that all e-meters carry a warning label that stated, among other things, that e-meters were not "capable of improving the health or bodily functions of anyone." Space does not permit a more detailed discussion of the truly bizarre aspects of Scientological "theology," but for those interested Wright's 2013 book *Going Clear* is excellent. The episode of *South Park* titled "Trapped in the Closet" (season 9, episode 12), which aired in 2005, gives a very humorous take on the theology of Scientology.

If the problems with psychoanalytic theory and therapy (see below for a discussion of psychoanalytic and other psychotherapies) are so great, why is it still so popular and presented in so matter-of-fact and uncritical a way in many texts of introductory and abnormal psychology? One answer is that the seductive pseudoscientific and nonfalsifiable nature of major parts of psychoanalytic theory make it very easy to accept, even for trained psychologists. Another answer is more historical in nature. It holds, generally correctly, that Freud's ideas have had major influences on Western thought and that, within psychology, it was Freud who brought the important concept of an unconscious to the notice of the field. Although, to be clear, Freud was certainly not the first person to posit some sort of unconscious. These two points provide weak support for the continued teaching of so faulty a theory as psychoanalysis. An analogy, first made by Dallenbach (1955), between psychoanalysis and phrenology is instructive in this regard. Phrenology was the nineteenth-century pseudoscience that held that an individual's personality could be determined by measuring the shape of his or her skull. Phrenology was founded by Franz Joseph Gall (1758–1828), a well-known physician, in the last years of the eighteenth century. According to phrenology, each area of the brain was specialized for some particular function. This theory was in sharp contrast to the then prevailing view that the brain was a mass of functionally homogeneous tissue. Gall further believed that if a particular "faculty" was well developed in an individual, the brain area that corresponded to that faculty would be enlarged. Therefore, the skull over the brain area that controlled the faculty would bulge outward. All that remained, then, was to measure the skull, find where the bulges were, and infer the individual's personality and abilities.

There were two great problems with phrenology. First, the faculties that the phrenologists believed were represented in specific brain areas were extremely vague, as can be seen from the phrenological "map" shown in figure 5.1. Second, even if the brain had been organized as the phrenologists believed, measuring the skull would have revealed nothing about personality. This is because the gross shape of the brain is the same even in people with very different personalities and abilities. In spite of these fatal problems, phrenology had considerable, and often positive, social influences (Davies 1955). In the 1800s phrenology was widely practiced all over the United States and Europe. Phrenological societies sprang up to work for needed reforms in education and treatment of prisoners, the mentally ill, and children. In the United States phrenology was a powerful enough movement to at least start many of these reforms. On the intellectual

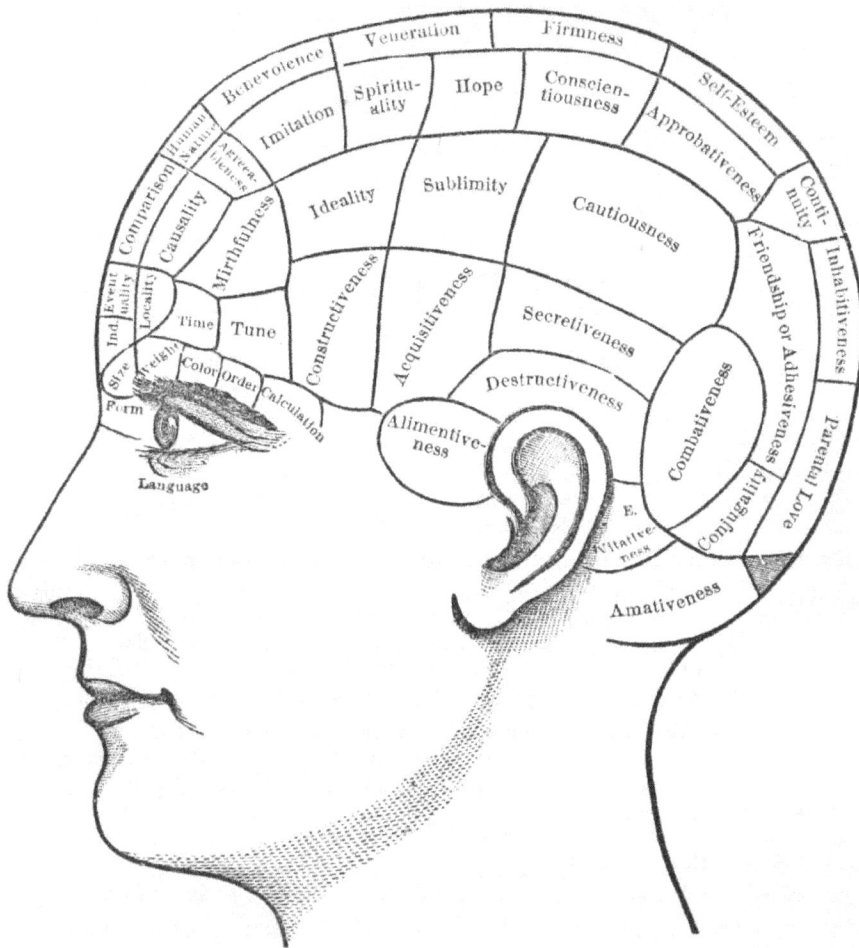

NUMBERING AND DEFINITION OF THE ORGANS.

1. AMATIVENESS, Love between the sexes.
A. CONJUGALITY, Matrimony—love of one. [etc.
2. PARENTAL LOVE, Regard for offspring, pets,
3. FRIENDSHIP, Adhesiveness—sociability.
4. INHABITIVENESS, Love of home.
5. CONTINUITY, One thing at a time.
E. VITATIVENESS, Love of life.
6. COMBATIVENESS, Resistance—defense.
7. DESTRUCTIVENESS, Executiveness—force.
8. ALIMENTIVENESS, Appetite—hunger.
9. ACQUISITIVENESS, Accumulation.
10. SECRETIVENESS, Policy—management.
11. CAUTIOUSNESS, Prudence—provision.
12. APPROBATIVENESS, Ambition—display.
13. SELF-ESTEEM, Self-respect—dignity.
14. FIRMNESS, Decision—perseverance.
15. CONSCIENTIOUSNESS, Justice equity.
16. HOPE, Expectation—enterprise.
17. SPIRITUALITY, Intuition—faith—credulity.
18. VENERATION, Devotion—respect.
19. BENEVOLENCE, Kindness—goodness.
20. CONSTRUCTIVENESS, Mechanical ingenuity.
21. IDEALITY, Refinement—taste—purity.
B. SUBLIMITY, Love of grandeur—infinitude.
22. IMITATION, Copying—patterning.
23. MIRTHFULNESS, Jocoseness—wit—fun.
24. INDIVIDUALITY, Observation.
25. FORM, Recollection of shape.
26. SIZE, Measuring by the eye.
27. WEIGHT, Balancing—climbing.
28. COLOR, Judgment of colors.
29. ORDER, Method—system—arrangement.
30. CALCULATION, Mental arithmetic.
31. LOCALITY, Recollection of places.
32. EVENTUALITY, Memory of facts.
33. TIME, Cognizance of duration.
34. TUNE, Sense of harmony and melody.
35. LANGUAGE, Expression of ideas.
36. CAUSALITY, Applying causes to effect. [tion.
37. COMPARISON, Inductive reasoning—illustra-
C. HUMAN NATURE, Perception of motives.
D. AGREEABLENESS, Pleasantness—suavity.

Figure 5.1. Phrenology head. From O. S. Fowler and L. N. Fowler, *The Illustrated Self-Instructor in Phrenology and Physiology* (New York: Fowler & Wells, 1859) (https://commons.wikimedia.org/wiki/File:Phrenology%E2%80%94Numbering_and_Definition_of_the_Organs.png)

front, phrenology also had great influence. Neurologists began to consider that perhaps the brain wasn't homogeneous in function but that different brain areas might control different functions. This view, known as *localizationism*, has been supported by more than one hundred years of experimentation. Unfortunately for phrenology, the functions that are actually localized in various areas of the brain bear no resemblance to those the phrenologists thought were localized. Specific aspects of sensory and motor function, as well as cognitive functions, such as speech, language, and attention, among others, can be localized to particular brain areas.

Although phrenology was a pseudoscience, it had an important effect on society and a large influence on the development of thought about brain function. However, today one does not find any treatment of phrenology, other than as a historical curiosity, in texts on psychology or neurology. This is an appropriate treatment for the pseudoscience of psychoanalysis. It belongs in the dust bin of history.

Graphology

Closely related to projective tests is the practice of graphology. The basic idea here is that a person's personality influences the structure of their handwriting. Thus, an examination of their handwriting can reveal facts about their personality. Graphology is often used, especially in Europe and Israel, in making decisions about personnel matters such as hiring. In this regard, it is sometimes used to evaluate how honest a job applicant is. Graphology meets many of the criteria for a pseudoscience (Beyerstein and Beyerstein 1992; Beyerstein 2007). Dean (1992) reviewed over two hundred experimental studies of graphology and found that the technique was neither reliable nor valid. Klimoski (1992) specifically addressed the research on whether graphology was useful in employment screening and found that it was not.

Myers-Briggs Type Indicator

The Myers-Briggs Type Indicator is not a projective test but deserves mention here because it is pure pseudopsychology. It is a self-report personality test that classifies people into one of sixteen different personality types based on their "agree/disagree" responses to a long series of statements (e.g., "You usually stay calm even under a lot of pressure"). An individual gets a score on four different dichotomous dimensions so that one's "type" is indicated by a four-letter sequence. This leads to astrology-like psychobabble. Instead of saying, "Oh, he's obviously an Aries," the Myers-Briggs aficionado might say "He's an INJT." The Myers-Briggs is the most popular and widely used personality test in the world and is frequently used in making hiring and other personnel decisions.

The Myers-Briggs test was created by two individuals who had no training or experience in psychology at all. Isabelle Briggs-Myers was a mystery writer. Her mother, Catherine Cook Briggs, was a magazine writer. They just made the test up in 1943 sort of based on the pseudoscientific theories of personality of the famous psychoanalyst Carl Jung, theories for which there is no scientific support (Emre 2018, and see below on Jung). Studies of the reliability and validity of the Myers-Briggs show that it lacks these fundamental characteristics (Durkman and Bjork 1991). No research since then has changed this conclusion. The lack of reliability means that if you take the test at one point in time and then again, say, six months later, there is an extremely good chance that the results will be very different the second time around. Stromberg and Caswell (2015) discuss "why the Myers-Briggs test is totally meaningless" and conclude that it has no place being used in any serious employment, or other, situations. At best, it's nothing more than a fun cocktail party game to label people, as amusingly dramatized in the episode of truTV's *Adam Ruins Everything* titled "Why the Myers-Briggs Test is Total B.S."

The Myers-Briggs is not the only bogus personality test that claims to be able to pigeonhole people into different types. The Enneagram classifies people into nine different types based on their responses to statements to which they are asked to agree or disagree. There are several different variations of the test available. The test has become popular in the business community, supposedly helping employees achieve greater insight into their personality and how they interact with others. There is no evidence that the Enneagram tests are either reliable or valid (Thyer and Pignotti 2015, chap. 2).

Psychotherapy

The question of whether any type of psychotherapy works or not is much more difficult to investigate than might be expected. One of the problems lies in the definition of "work." If by "work" one means only that the therapy is better than doing nothing at all, then nearly all types of psychotherapies "work." However, there is a very large placebo effect in psychotherapy. Simply believing that one is being treated can result in beneficial effects. A more rigorous definition of "work," then, requires that the therapy in question be more effective than a placebo therapy in which patients engage in some activity they believe is therapeutic, rather than receiving the actual type of psychotherapy being evaluated. Another problem in evaluating psychotherapeutic effectiveness is spontaneous remission. Many of the problems about which people consult psychotherapists will simply go away after a period of time if left untreated. If an individual is seeing a therapist during the period of time when the problem would have disappeared on its own, it is quite natural for both the therapist and the patient to attribute the elimination of the problem to the therapy, not to the passage of time. Such processes result in strong beliefs on the part of many psychotherapists, psychoanalytic as well as nonpsychoanalytic, that their particular brand of therapy works. These same processes also produce scores of testimonials for any type of psychotherapy one wishes to name.

The gold standard for evaluating whether a psychotherapy, or any type of therapy, psychological, medical, or sometimes even surgical, really works is the double-blind placebo controlled study. In such a study there should be three groups of patients matched for severity of their disorder and other relevant variables such as age, sex, race, socioeconomic class, and so on. Patients in the control group receive no therapy. This group is used to determine the frequency at which the problem simply goes away on its own—spontaneous remission. A second group receives some sort of placebo treatment, while the third group receives the actual treatment being evaluated. The crucial aspect of this procedure is that patients in the second and third groups both are told that they are receiving real therapy. Importantly, the people evaluating the patients in all three groups at the end of the study do not know which group an individual patient was in. This procedure controls for potential bias. If the evaluator knew which group a patient was in, he or she might expect more improvement in those in the "real" therapy group. It also controls for the very powerful effects of expectations whereby almost any sort of therapy will produce improvements if the patient is told that the therapy is effective. Placebo effects again.

The effects of expectation and the power of placebos have been known for hundreds of years. They were probably first demonstrated in the 1780s. At the time "animal magnetism," also known as mesmerism, after it's inventor Franz Anton Mesmer (1734–1815), was a huge craze in Europe. Mesmer claimed that he could cure people through animal magnetism. Thousands of people swore that he had cured them. When Mesmer "magnetized" people, they would fall into trances and have seizures. Surely something real was happening! The craze for animal magnetism became so great in France that in 1784 King Louis XVI ordered a royal commission assembled to study whether mesmerism was real or not. The commission included Benjamin Franklin, then in Paris representing the United States, and Antoine Lavoisier. They planned a test where a person would be told that Mesmer was behind a door and would then attempt to magnetize them. According to the doctrine of animal magnetism, the wooden door would in no way prevent the effects of animal magnetism. Sometimes Mesmer would really be behind the door doing his thing. But sometimes he would not be. But the individual would be told that he was there. Mesmer, like so many frauds, refused to participate in the study. Happily for science one of his top students, Charles Deslon, agreed to take part.

The results were clear. It didn't matter whether there was anybody behind the door or not. As long as the person believed they were being magnetized, they behaved (fainting and the like) as they knew people who were magnetized behaved. The Royal Commission concluded that mesmerism was due to suggestion and that animal magnetism did not exist. The original 1784 report of the commission has been translated into English by Salas and Salas (1996).

Another historical example from the late eighteenth century is Elisha Perkins and his "tractors." (See figure 5.2.) These had nothing to do with farming but were pairs of metal rods said to cure all varieties of disease. The rods were to be run from the head to the feet of the patient (never in the opposite direction!), and in some unspecified way, because of the powers of the metals of which they were constructed, they would draw out whatever was causing the patient's illness. As Walsh (1923) noted, these were extremely popular at the time and resulted in thousands upon thousands of testimonials from supposedly cured patients. But the tractors actually had no real effect at all. In a very early report of the power of placebos Haygarth (1800) reported a study he performed with a Dr. Falconer. They carved pieces of wood in the shape of Perkins's tractors and painted them to look like they were made of metal. You can guess what happened. The fake tractors were just as effective as the real ones. When this became generally known, the tractors amazingly lost their healing powers (see Hines 2017 for details).

Walsh (1923, 267) discusses numerous nineteenth-century placebo cures and concludes, correctly, that it "does not matter at all if the 'cure' has no physical effect or but the slightest. It may even be detrimental to some degree, but it will cure sufferers who have been complaining for years if they only once become persuaded that it will."

A therapy can be ethically said to work *only* if the patients in the real therapy group show more improvement compared to those in the placebo therapy group. Practitioners of questionable therapies are loath to subject their treatments to this kind of testing. It should be obvious why this is. They are afraid that the results will show that their wonderful new therapy is nothing more than a sham. Any therapist who claims that his or her therapy can't be validated by careful double-blind studies is likely a fraud and should be avoided.

The problems discussed above all operate to make it appear that various types of psychotherapy are more effective than they really are. Research on the effectiveness of psychotherapies as far back as the 1980s in general has shown that, as expected, so-called talk therapies are more effective than doing nothing (Smith, Glass, and Miller 1980). However, such psychotherapies showed little more effectiveness than placebo therapies (Prioleau, Murdock, and Brody 1983). Although these conclusions may at first seem surprising, they become more understandable after a bit of "demythologizing" of psychotherapy is done. Most people consult psychotherapists not because they suffer from major psychoses—such as schizophrenia or manic-depressive psychosis—but because of smaller neurotic problems or just because they are upset by the "slings and arrows of outrageous fortune" that beset everyone from time to time. Gross (1978), in an excellent and much overlooked book, cogently argued that we are becoming a "psychological society" in which we are led to define every little disappointment, setback, and depression as something to be treated by some mental health professional. Albert Ellis, founder of rational emotive therapy, pungently commented on this trend: "I find that increasingly in our society much of what we call emotional disturbance is whining" (quoted in Gross 1978, 315). Salerno (2005) in his book *Sham* makes the point more strongly than Gross, arguing that the "self-help and actualization movement" has led people to seek psychotherapy for every minor emotional "ouchie" and that the movement has led to the shifting of blame for bad behavior from the individual to some vague "disease." Sommers and Satel (2005) also criticize the overreliance on psychotherapies and self-help gurus in their book *One Nation under Therapy*. They are especially critical of the flocks of grief therapists that show up after any disaster,

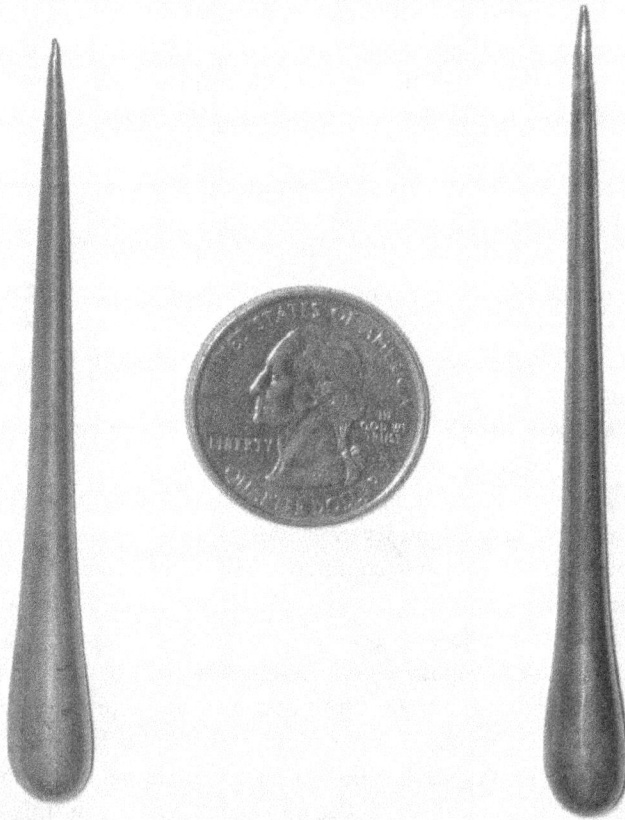

Figure 5.2. Perkins's tractors. Image courtesy of the Duke University Archives

usually promoting psychotherapies that not only are ineffective but can cause real harm, as described below.

The type of problems for which many people now consult a psychotherapist, then, are frequently minor in terms of true psychopathology. In past years, such problems would have been talked over with a trusted friend, relative, or clergyman—people who would have had no psychotherapeutic training. It is certainly true that talking about problems with someone else can be very beneficial. The other person may be able to propose solutions not previously thought of, may see the problem from a different perspective, or may simply provide moral support for a difficult and troubling course of action already decided on. These are real and important benefits of what is generally called "advice." Psychotherapists, no matter what particular type of therapy they practice, usually provide advice to their patients, in addition to the special ministrations their own brand of therapy calls for. It is this advice component of every psychotherapy that helps account for the general effectiveness of psychotherapy over doing nothing.

If psychotherapies in general are more effective than doing nothing because the therapist is providing advice to patients, one would expect that professional advice givers (i.e., trained professional psychotherapists) would not be much more effective than individuals lacking formal therapeutic training. This issue has been the focus of considerable research. Two older reviews of the literature on this issue (Durlak 1979; Hattie, Sharpley, and Rogers 1984) found that patients treated by trained professionals do *worse* than those treated by untrained "paraprofessionals." Berman and Norton (1985) criticized the Hattie, Sharpley, and Rogers review on statistical grounds and reanalyzed the literature that the original study reviewed. In their reanalysis Berman and Norton found no difference in therapeutic effectiveness between trained professionals and untrained paraprofessionals. Dawes (1994) penned an especially trenchant critique of the practice of psychotherapy that exposed the many empirical and logical failings of claims that underlie many psychotherapeutic beliefs and techniques. His 1994 analysis is as applicable today as it was when first published.

In a classic paper Shanteau (1992) argued that psychotherapy was an occupation where greater experience did not lead to greater expertise or effectiveness. It is still widely recognized that this is the case. Tracey and colleagues (2014, 218) termed demonstrating expertise in psychotherapy "an elusive goal." The authors made important suggestions about how to improve the effectiveness of psychotherapists (Tracey et al. 2014, 2015). These include providing psychotherapists with more and better feedback about whether their therapy was or was not effective. Psychotherapists rarely get such feedback. Feedback about the success or failure of any intervention is vital for the continued improvement of the process. Without feedback, the therapist is nearly flying blind. However, feedback alone is not enough. According to Tracey and colleagues (2014, 225), "psychotherapists fail to develop clinical expertise because of their failure to adopt a disconfirming scientific process in practice even when there is quality feedback information." In other words, psychotherapists have adopted various nonfalsifiable hypotheses and cognitive strategies such as confirmation bias that allow them to continue to believe their therapy is effective even in the face of disconfirming evidence.

Speaking to the issue of lack of feedback as a cause of the inability of psychotherapists to become experts, Westra and DiBartolomeo (2024) propose that training in "process coding" can provide such feedback. Process coding refers to paying close attention to the moment-to-moment subtle behaviors of both the client and the therapist. By doing so, the therapist presumably can guide his or her behavior to be more positive and responsive to the client's situation. The skills needed to recognize the subtle cues about whether the therapist is having a negative or positive effect on the client can be taught. This, then, will result in more effective therapeutic outcomes. Maybe. The authors acknowledge that there is, as of the time of their writing, little objective evidence that becoming skilled process coders will result in better therapeutic outcomes in the long run. Even if such training changes an ineffective therapist into an effective one (aka, an expert), it will not transform an ineffective therapy into an effective one, a point the authors do not make.

Concerning the specific issue of the effectiveness of psychoanalytic therapies, what is true for psychotherapies in general is true for psychoanalytic therapies in particular. Repeated reviews of the literature have failed to show any solid evidence that psychoanalytic therapy is superior to placebo therapy (Rachman 1971; Rachman and Wilson 1980; Erwin 1980, 1986). It is, however, clearly more expensive and time consuming, sometimes taking years with little effect other than increasing the psychoanalyst's bank account.

The whole question of whether psychotherapy works or not, and what "works" means, began in 1952 with the publication of Hans J. Eysenck's provocative paper "The Effects of Psychotherapy." Eysenck concluded that the results of studies did not "support the hypothesis that psychotherapy facilitates recovery from neurotic disorder" (Eysenck 1952, 319). The response of the psychotherapeutic community was a hostile "Hurumph—how *dare* anyone even suggest that psychotherapy should be required to prove its effectiveness. We therapists simply *know* that it works." This was the first time that anyone had dared to suggest that (1) psychotherapy could actually be evaluated scientifically and (2) the results of such evaluations could show that it was not effective. At the time Eysenck wrote his paper, all psychotherapies were basically one form or another of psychoanalysis so that people with very different psychological disorders (phobias, depression, addictions, obsessive compulsive disorder, etc.) got essentially the same treatment. In this context it is relevant to point out that, when stripped of excess Freudian (or Jungian) psychobabble, the psychoanalytic therapists were really claiming that the same treatment could be used for a multitude of different disorders. As will be seen in detail in chapter 11, this "one therapy fits all" claim is a diagnostic characteristic of a quack treatment.

With the emergence of many different types of psychotherapies since 1952, it no longer makes sense to ask whether "psychotherapy" works or not. To do so would be like asking whether "pills" work or not. The issue now is what types of psychotherapy work for which types of psychological disorders. In this regard, a major change has taken place since 1952. There is now a much greater emphasis on evidence-based psychotherapies—therapies that can demonstrate empirically that they are effective and better than a placebo therapy. This approach did not, and still does not, sit well with many therapists. The opposition on the part of many psychotherapists to requiring that psychotherapies prove their effectiveness is often fierce. In an early twenty-first-century review of the topic, Chambless and Ollendick (2001) devoted several pages of their paper to refuting arguments against examining the actual effectiveness of psychotherapies. Many psychotherapists argued that the mere fact that they believed that their therapies were effective was sufficient proof that it was. However, the degree of personal belief on the part of a therapist in the effectiveness of any type of therapy, psychological, medical, or pharmacological, should never be taken as evidence that the therapy is really effective. There are too many cognitive illusions and other effects such as spontaneous remission and confirmation bias, among others (see below) that lead even well-meaning therapists to incorrect conclusions that their therapy is working when it is not.

One problem in the evaluation of psychotherapies of whatever type has been to define what constitutes a placebo therapy (Blease and Kirsch 2016). Most, if not all, psychotherapies have specific practices and procedures that clients are encouraged to engage in or trained to do in order to get better. But in the process of encouraging and training, the therapist will obviously have to interact with the client on a personal level. So a proper placebo would provide the personal interaction without the specific advice, training, or encouragement given the client. A good candidate for such a placebo therapy is nondirective supportive therapy (NDST). In NDST the "therapist refrains from giving advice or making interpretations, and the therapy typically is not aimed at providing solutions or acquiring new skills" (Cuijpers et al. 2012, 281). This sounds very much like simply talking to a caring friend or acquaintance, or even a stranger, about one's problems. But in the case of NDST the therapist is identified as a therapist, and such an identification can in and of itself engender placebo effects (Torrey 1986). Brody (2010) speaks of healing as a ritual. When a treatment is real, there is real improvement. A placebo treatment includes the aspects of the ritual except, of course, an effective treatment. One aspect of the ritual is the identification of the therapist as a healer. Thus a placebo will seem to the patient to show better "effects" than doing nothing. And placebo psychotherapies are no doubt better than just sitting around and stewing in one's own juices.

The effects of NDST can be considered nonspecific in the sense that there are aspects of the NDST therapeutic experience that are common to all psychotherapies. Nonplacebo psychotherapies add on to the NDST situation specific practices unique to the specific type of psychotherapy. Thus, when a psychotherapy is shown to be effective in the sense that it is better than doing nothing, one can ask whether this is due to the nonspecific components of the psychotherapeutic situation or to the specific features of the psychotherapy's approach. Perhaps not surprisingly, the answer depends on what psychological disorder is being treated. Thus Cuijpers and colleagues (2012) found that, for adult depression, nonspecific aspects of the therapeutic interaction accounted for a large percentage of psychotherapeutic effects. Another way of putting this is that, for a disorder as serious as adult depression, almost any kind of psychotherapy works— is better than doing nothing. However, for a very different problem, obsessive compulsive disorder, Strauss and colleagues (2018) found that specific factors, cognitive behavior therapy in their study, were much more important than nonspecific factors.

With the existence of so many different types of psychotherapy, a major focus of research has been to investigate which types are effective for which disorders. This has spawned a huge amount of research literature that now includes a regularly updated book titled *A Guide to Treatments That Work*, with the fourth edition (Nathan and Gorman 2015) containing twenty-eight chapters and over nine hundred pages. The results of this research show that the therapies with the highest rate of success are the various cognitive behavior therapies. Developed as an alternative to the ineffective psychoanalytic treatments in the early 1960s, early behavior therapies concentrated on classical and instrumental (or operant) conditioning as the explanation of disordered behavior. The idea was that such behavior was learned and could be eliminated using the techniques of reinforcement, punishment, and extinction drawn from work on conditioning animals. As the field of behavioral therapies has matured, it has become much more cognitive since patients' cognitions play an important role in disordered behavior and must be addressed by any therapy. Thus, Lazarus (1986) noted that "terms such as 'expectancies,' 'encoding,' 'plans,' 'values,' and 'self-regulatory systems,' all operationally defined, have crept into the behavior literature" (251). It has been shown that versions of behavior modification are effective in treating major depression (Hollon and Ponniah 2010; Hollon, Thase, and Markowitz 2002). Pharmacological treatment is effective for depression as well, but a combination of behaviorally and cognitively oriented therapies with drug treatment may be more effective in many cases (Kramer 2016).

The advent of behavioral modification techniques that focus on the disordered behavior itself, rather than on hypothetical psychological causes such as unresolved Oedipal complexes and the like, provided an opportunity to test one strong prediction made by psychoanalytic theory. According to psychoanalytic theory, the overt disordered behavior a patient displays is merely a symptom of some hidden, deep psychological cause. Given this, it would not be sufficient to simply eliminate the symptom (i.e., the behavior), because the underlying cause of the disorder would still be there and would only cause some other problem behavior (i.e., symptom) in the future. This is known as the *symptom substitution hypothesis*. Studies of patients who have been treated behaviorally have shown no evidence of symptom substitution (Bandura 1969; Franks 1969).

The evidence indicates that the belief that psychotherapies other than behaviorally oriented ones actually work is a myth. Another myth held dear by psychologists is what Dawes (1994) termed the "myth of expertise." This is the deeply held belief that clinical judgments based on interviews and personal interaction with patients or clients results in better judgments about such variables as dangerousness, psychopathology, neuropsychological status, and so on than do judgments based only on the results of valid and reliable empirical tests. It has been known since the early 1950s that this belief is simply wrong. Not only are judgments based on what is often termed "clinical experience" no better than those based purely on statistical calculations; they are almost always worse (Meehl 1954; Faust and Ziskin 1988; Dawes, Faust, and Meehl 1989; Dawes 1994; Ziskin 1995). Clinicians continue to believe that their experience-based judgments are superior because of effects such as selective memory and, as noted above, confirmation bias. They are much more likely to remember the instances in which their judgments happened to be correct than those in which they were not. This is precisely the sort of cognitive illusion that supports beliefs in other invalid belief systems such as ESP, astrology, moon madness, and even, in part, racial and ethnic biases. The realization of the "myth of expertise" has led some (e.g., Dawes 1994; Hagen 1997) to question whether evaluations by psychologists and psychiatrists based on interviews, projective tests, and other invalid techniques are anything other than junk science.

THE PSYCHOLOGY OF JUNG

Carl Gustav Jung (1875–1961) was a devoted follower of Freud who later broke with strictly Freudian psychoanalysis over several theoretical issues. He was rather a mystic, and two of his ideas have entered the mainstream of paranormal thinking. Jung was interested in astrology and actually conducted some astrological research. He was not particularly a believer in astrology but felt that astrologers were occasionally accurate through what would now be called clairvoyance or ESP. Jung also had a lifelong interest in coincidences that resulted in the development of his concept of *synchronicity* or *meaningful coincidences*. According to this view, some events that would be considered just coincidences were actually meaningful, although they were not related through cause and effect. Von Franz (1964) gives an example: "If I bought a blue frock and, by mistake, the shop delivered a black one on the day one of my near relatives died, this would be a meaningful coincidence. The two events are not causally related, but they are connected by the symbolic meaning that our society gives to the color black" (211). The coincidental events are not causally related, but the meaning, according to Jung, is not just meaning imposed by the individual who experiences the coincidence. Jung believed that such coincidences do not occur at random. Rather, they tend to take place at psychologically important times in an individual's life.

Such coincidences are a manifestation of various *archetypes*, basic ideas or concepts stored in the *collective unconscious*, another Jungian concept. The collective unconscious was the storehouse of the accumulated memories and forms of behavior that date back to the dawn of the human species. The archetypes can express themselves via meaningful coincidences. To continue with von Franz's example: "To illustrate this in the case of the black frock: In such a case the person who receives the black frock might also have had a dream on the theme of death. It seems as if the underlying archetype is manifesting itself simultaneously in inner and external events. The common denominator is a symbolically expressed message—in this case a message about death" (211). It is no trick at all to find "meaningful coincidences" if you look for them, and as always in this sort of theory, you are permitted to interpret the "meaning" of the event through symbolism. Thus, the concept that Jung felt was equal in importance to the notion of causality itself turns out to be yet another example of confirmation bias and selective memory and perception.

A great lover of symbolic interpretation, although the nature of his symbols differed greatly from those of Freud, Jung found in the myths and legends of numerous cultures evidence for the various archetypes he believed to exist in the collective unconscious. Jung was fond of pointing out that myths and legends of cultures around the globe had symbols and meanings in common. This he interpreted as evidence for the collective unconscious. One need not, however, postulate a collective unconscious to explain the similarities of the myths and legends of different peoples. All human cultures have existed on the same planet and have faced the same basic problems, such as finding food and a mate, avoiding predators and enemies, securing protection from terrible weather and geologic phenomena, raising children, and so forth. Thus, it is inevitable that the myths and legends of all peoples will share common features (Vitaliano 1973). This is true even if one looks only at the obvious (nonsymbolic) characteristics of myths and legends and does not further enhance the seeming number and psychological significance of the common features by using spurious symbolic interpretation, as Jung did.

Another psychoanalyst who, like Jung, broke with Freud was Wilhelm Reich (1897–1957), who believed that an energy called "orgone energy," the energy of the orgasm, could cure mental and physical diseases. Reich also believed that dowsing rods operated because of orgone energy and that orgone energy was blue (Gardner 1957). Happily for Reich, orgone energy could be accumulated in special phone-booth-sized boxes in which the patient who wished to take the cure would sit. Reich rented these for about $250 a month until the government put this particular fraud out of business in the mid-1950s (Janssen 1980). Reich died in federal prison in 1957.

HUMANISTIC PSYCHOLOGY

Humanistic psychology, which became popular in the 1960s and 1970s, grew out of a dissatisfaction with both psychoanalytic and behavioral approaches, especially where therapy was concerned. Both psychoanalytic and behavioral approaches are deterministic in that both view human behavior as determined and controlled—either by ids, egos, and various complexes, in the case of psychoanalysis, or by reinforcers, punishers, and cognitive processes in the case of behavioral approaches. Neither approach, the humanistic psychologists felt, gave any attention to human free will, which became a focal point for humanistic psychology and therapy. Humanistic therapy is said to be "client centered" or "nondirective." The best description of this approach I've seen comes from a textbook I used in my introductory psychology classes some years ago. The therapist is supposed to give "unconditional positive regard, supporting the client regardless of what she or he says or does. Instead of interpreting or instructing, the therapist clarifies the client's feelings by restating what has been said" (Bootzin et al. 1986, 590). If all this sounds vague, vagueness is one of the major characteristics of humanistic psychology. Out of this vagueness has grown most of the hollow and vacuous "psychobabble" that makes up current pop psychology. For example, one major concept in humanistic psychology is that of "self-actualization," a term coined by Abraham Maslow (1966). Stripped of its psychobabble, the term boils down to "be happy in your work and play and be nice to others." It's hard to argue with that as a goal, but it is not very helpful in dealing with real problems of human beings. This sort of psychobabble is characteristic of humanistic psychology and reveals its intellectual sterility.

Since its founding, humanistic psychology has spewed forth literally hundreds of different brands of "therapy," all couched in layers of meaningless psychobabble and containing considerable amounts of pseudoscience. The "human potential" movement, with its emphasis on self-actualization and "getting in touch with yourself," is an outgrowth of humanistic psychology. In an early critical book, Rosen (1977) examined several of the better-known therapies that grew out of humanistic psychology. Arthur Janov's primal therapy, which involves screaming about your anger and frustration, is one example. Another is "rebirthing," which involves reexperiencing the birth process by means of tubs of warm water and shallow breathing. Sadly, in April 2000 ten-year-old Candice Newmaker in Colorado was killed while being subjected to a version of rebirthing therapy known as coercive restraint. The therapist and the girl's adoptive mother wrapped her so tightly in blankets that she suffocated. The idea was that she had to fight to get out of the blankets to prove that she wanted to live. Rebirthing therapy is a type of "attachment therapy" (Mercer, Sarner, and Rosa 2003). The Candice Newmaker tragedy shows that some fringe therapies are not just harmless diversions for the worried well. They can be—and are—deadly.

The idea that psychotherapies can be actively harmful may seem counterintuitive. However, attachment therapies are not the only harmful psychotherapies. Repressed memory therapies, already mentioned, clearly fall into this category. Lilienfeld (2017) discussed several other harmful psychotherapies. Facilitated communication, discussed in chapter 13, is also among them. "Alter reification" therapy aims to bring out different "personalities" in patients who may suffer from dissociative identity disorder. Hypnosis is used, as are various techniques to strengthen the differentiation between the different personalities such as naming them and having them communicate with each other. It's rather as if a doctor, suspecting a patient to have a broken right leg, breaks the patient's left arm.

Various trauma-reducing therapies can also induce harm by making the patient more traumatized. These therapies, like "critical incident stress debriefing" (Lilienfeld 2017), encourage patients to reexperience the traumatic events but include few if any components to reduce the induced anxiety. In addition, many trauma therapists seem to believe that humans are very fragile psychological creatures that can only rarely get through even serious trauma without some form of therapy. For example, after the 9/11 terrorist attacks, these therapists predicted a wave of suicides and an increase in major stress-related psychological disorders. It didn't happen. There is now a large "grief industry" devoted to the idea that some sort of psychological intervention is required for people to overcome their normal responses to trauma and loss. This industry consists of hordes of often minimally trained grief "counselors" who show up after a tragedy to help people "get in touch with their grief," "vent their feelings," and similar vague therapeutic-sounding platitudes (Sommers and Satel 2005).

Contrary to the self-serving claims of the trauma industry that humans are fragile creatures who need the help of specialized (and expensive) therapists to get through the aftermath of almost any trauma is the research on resilience. One of the most trauma-inducing experiences one can go through is military combat. But the rate of PTSD in combat veterans was around 7 percent in a study of those deployed to Iraq and Afghanistan (Bonanno et al. 2012). Further, "about 83 percent of respondents showed a pattern of resilience: they exhibited a normal-range ability to cope with stress both before *and* after deployment" (Mancini 2012, A23, emphasis in original).

Another unfortunate and harmful spawn of humanistic psychology has been the self-help industry that spews forth hundreds of books, gurus, and seminars aimed at repeat customers who become addicted to such therapies and end up spending a great deal of time and money chasing just the right self-help gimmick that will do something for them. The ninth episode of the first season of Penn and Teller's Showtime program *Bullshit* shows much more effectively than anything I could write the type of con artists who prey on this type of unfortunate individual. The self-help industry does nothing so much as encourage useless navel-gazing and self-absorption and defines the slings and arrows of everyday life as events that can't be dealt with without the intervention of some type of therapy. It preys on people who have trouble making simple decisions in life and need a "life coach" to get through even slightly difficult situations. In other words, it encourages whining. It also focuses on self-esteem and assumes that increasing self-esteem will more or less automatically make one's problems go away. In fact, self-esteem is a much overrated construct. It's nice to have, but it does not correlate highly with important variables such as success in school (Sommers and Satel 2005). The emphasis on self-esteem has led to those silly situations where children receive awards no matter how well, or badly, they do or the outright elimination of awards for good performance for fear that those who didn't win will suffer from lowered self-esteem. It also leads to those absurd and elaborate "graduation" ceremonies from kindergarten, first grade, and such. The attitude among some in educational circles is that children and students should never feel bad about their performance. Such an attitude is the first step to creating individuals who have difficulty coping on their own with the problems of everyday life.

The focus of the self-help movement, ironically, does nothing to help people actually become more self-reliant. For example, after the 9/11 attack, the University Counseling Center at Pace University in Pleasantville, New York, where I teach, sent faculty a memo telling us *not* to urge students to be strong, to face the problem, and to get on with their lives. Presumably, then, students should focus on the grief, wallowing in sorrow, and not move forward. This type of advice was commonly given by university counseling offices at the time (Sommers and Satel 2005).

Steve Salerno's (2005) book *Sham: How the Self-Help Movement Made America Helpless* ends with some very wise words (141): "Today as never before—given the genuinely apocalyptic threats unfolding around us—Americans have an obligation to themselves, their families, and society to quit whining, stop comparing notes on who is more diseased, addicted, or dysfunctional, and just get down to business." Perhaps the most absurd approach to come out of the self-help movement was the book *The Secret* (Byrne 2006) and its various spin-off products mentioned previously. The book was highly promoted by Oprah Winfrey, well known for her love of crackpot ideas and promoter of the famous quack Dr. Mehmet Oz, aka Dr. Oz (more on him in chapter 11). The "secret" boils down to a simple and childish idea of wish fulfillment. If only you want something hard enough, the universe will provide it. To any rational individual, a bit of thought about this would reveal it to be utter bunk.

One sure sign that an author is a charlatan is references to quantum mechanics by someone who has no background in the topic. New age/humanistic psychology types love to toss around quantum mechanics—it makes them sound so sciencey. And, sure enough, *The Secret* makes reference to quantum mechanics often. Now, quantum mechanics is a field which requires considerable mathematical skill and knowledge of physics to master. But author Byrne claims that she was able to master it, with no background in physics whatsoever, just because she wanted to through the use of *The Secret*. It would be fun to have her take the final exam in a third-year undergraduate course in quantum mechanics. Then we'd see just how much of the topic she'd mastered! DeBakesy (2014) has discussed the misuse of quantum mechanical jargon by new age charlatans.

Much of the idea behind *The Secret* is just plain silly. But there is a very unpleasant undertone to the claims made therein. If you can get what you want by just wanting it enough, that means that if you didn't get something you wanted, it was because you didn't want it hard enough, even though that lack of wanting may have been unconscious. This leads to victim blaming. Why did that cancer patient die of cancer? He or she just didn't want to live hard enough. What utter, vile rubbish.

While not strictly speaking a psychotherapy, it is worth mentioning here a major intervention program that claims to prevent drug abuse in adolescents. This is the Drug Abuse Resistance Education (DARE) program, which aims to teach adolescents about the dangers of drug abuse. It's a great idea. Sadly, neither the original DARE program nor the revised program work (Singh et al. 2011). It may actually make DARE graduates slightly more likely to experiment with drugs. The entire program is a waste of taxpayer money that should be used on more effective drug treatment programs. Social programs should be subject to the same objective criteria of success as therapies for individuals. In a similar vein is the Scared Straight program where teenage offenders are exposed to how terrifying life in prison really would be with the hope that it will deter them from future crime. Lilienfeld (2017, 7) summarizes the research on such programs by saying that "delinquency programs that emphasize harsh discipline without providing adolescents with constructive coping skills tend to be ineffective or harmful (Lipsey 2009)."

6

ASTROLOGY AND THE LUNAR EFFECT

Ancient people must have learned well before the dawn of recorded history that observations of the stars and planets could predict the coming of the seasons, when to plant crops, when certain animals would give birth, and numerous other events vital to their survival. It must have seemed reasonable, then, that the positions of the heavenly bodies could predict and influence human behavior. Thus, astrology, the oldest pseudoscience, was born.

Astrology's history goes back more than four thousand years and testifies to people's unending fascination with the stars and attempts to predict the future. The first written records of astrology come from Mesopotamia, located between the Tigris and Euphrates Rivers in the area that is now Iraq and Syria (Campion 2008). The early astrology of the Mesopotamians was an "omen" astrology and was much simpler than later astrology. Ancient people saw omens in everything, not just the stars. Almost anything that happened could be interpreted as an omen of something that was going to take place in the future. Examples of astrological omens from this period include

When Mars approaches the star Shu.gi there will be uprising in Amurru and hostility; one will kill another. When Venus stands high, there will be pleasure of copulation.

Nonastrological omens were of essentially the same character and were rather unlikely to have been based on empirical study, as the following examples illustrate:

If a woman gives birth to a pig, a woman will seize the throne.
If a woman gives birth to an elephant, the land will be laid to waste.
If an ewe gives birth to a lion and it has two horns on the left, an enemy will take your fortress.
If a man goes on an errand and a falcon passes from his right to his left, he will achieve his goal.

The sources for these omens are Van der Waerden (1974) and Leichty (1975).

Modern astrologers claim their "science" is not based on magical associations, but the history of astrology shows this to be false. Astrology flourished in ancient Greece, where the magical influence is clear. The Greeks deified the planets, and each of their gods had certain characteristics. For example, Aphrodite (Venus) was the goddess of love and beauty, so the planet Venus was assumed to magically make one sensitive, emotional, and appreciative of beauty. Similarly, Hermes (Mercury) was the messenger of the gods. Because the actual planet was hard to see and moved rapidly, by purely magical association (Campion 2008) Mercury was said to make someone difficult to predict, deceitful, and yet skillful. These associations were obviously not based on empirical research but simply on ancient magical associations. They still form the basis for modern astrological predictions.

The grouping of stars into the constellations that make up the twelve signs of the zodiac is arbitrary. The stars in a constellation seem to be grouped together not because they are actually close together in space but because they appear to be close together when seen from Earth. Two stars that appear close to each other because they are both in the same area of the night sky may be hundreds of thousands of light-years apart from each other. Highlighting the arbitrary nature of the Western arrangement of the stars into constellations is the fact that different cultures group the stars in different ways and see different constellations in the sky. The only way these apparent groupings of stars could have any special influence over human beings is through some unspecified sort of magic.

Ptolemy, the great astronomer and astrologer who lived in the second century CE, also based his astrology on magical associations between the stars and planets and human behavior (Campion 2008). During the Middle Ages in Europe, great emphasis was placed on the authority of previous writers. Ptolemy was considered to be the greatest astrologer of the ancient world, so his writings on astrology were accepted and passed down in this way. Thus, modern astrologers' claims that their "science" is based on thousands of years of experimental and empirical observation are simply untrue. Modern Western astrology rests largely on Ptolemy's writings.

Certainly, views about the exact nature of the hypothesized influences of specific stars and planets on human behavior have changed over the centuries, and differences of opinion did and do exist among astrologers. Speaking of the Renaissance period, Shumaker (1972) states: "There has never, perhaps, been a time when conflicting opinions [about how astrology should be practiced] were not held and practices were not being modified. If at first glance such tinkering might be thought to imply constant experimental rectification, no one who has read much [medieval or Renaissance] astrological literature is likely to believe this was the cause of the alterations" (11). Shumaker has found no experimental studies of astrology. Instead, astrology was justified by appeal "regularly to authorities . . . or to abstract reason" (11). It is only in the twentieth century that statistical tests of astrological predictions have been attempted. These are reviewed later in this chapter.

ASTROLOGY AND ASTRONOMY

Astrologers are fond of claiming that their craft is a science and that astronomy is merely an offshoot of astrology. As seen from the above, however, the basic structure of Western astrological hypotheses has hardly changed at all over the last twenty-five hundred years. The associations the Greek astrologers believed, based on magical associations, are still accepted by Western astrologers today. This in spite of the fact that in the four-thousand-year history of astrology, no astrologer, until very recently, ever tried to see if the hypothesized relationships between heavenly bodies and human behavior really existed. In chapter 1 it was pointed out that one of the chief characteristics of a pseudoscience is a refusal to change in the light of new evidence. Knowledge of astronomy has changed immensely since the Greeks looked up at the stars and saw their gods there. In spite of this, astrology has not changed at all—it is a static, stale pseudoscience.

On those few occasions when astrologers have made attempts to change astrological practice and theory, the nature of the attempts further reveals the pseudoscientific nature of astrology. In 1970, for example, astrologer Steven Schmidt argued that there are really fourteen signs of the zodiac, not twelve. According to Schmidt, the constellations Cetus and Ophiuchus should be added to the familiar set of twelve. From a purely astronomical point of view, there is much to recommend this change. The sun does, in fact, pass through these two constellations in addition to the twelve accepted signs of the zodiac. Schmidt's problem was to determine the character traits associated with these two "new" signs of the zodiac. Nowhere in his book did he present any data or suggest an adequate method of discovering what these traits might be. Rather, he simply "collected people" and "examined their character traits" (Schmidt 1970, 18). The people he examined were hardly a representative or random sample since they included movie stars, past presidents (dead and alive), famous politicians, and so forth. The method used is utterly worthless scientifically.

One of the best examples of astrology's refusal to change in the light of new knowledge is its failure to take into account the astronomical phenomenon of precession. The assignment of certain dates to certain signs of the zodiac (e.g., Aries ruling the period from March 21 to April 19) was made two thousand years ago and has been followed by astrologers ever since. When it is said that the sun is "in" Aries between March 21 and April 19, this means that the sun, as seen from Earth, is in the same part of the sky as is the constellation Aries. The correspondences between the twelve constellations of the zodiac and their assigned dates were correct two thousand years ago—but not today. Earth "wobbles" slowly as it rotates, and because of this the position of the sun relative to the constellations of the zodiac (as seen from Earth) changes over the centuries. By now, the difference is almost one complete sign—so the sun is not in Aries from March 21 to April 19 but in Pisces for most of that period. Thus, if you are an Aries (born between March 21 and April 19), the sun was almost certainly not in Aries when you were born but in Pisces! Most astrologers have been making predictions and casting horoscopes for the wrong signs for all these years. Many so-called tropical astrologers are aware of precession but choose to ignore it, arguing that somehow the "signs remember the influence of the constellations that corresponded to them two thousand years ago" (Abell 1981a, 86). This does not explain "why those same signs do not also recall the influence of other constellations that corresponded with them in even earlier millennia" (86).

When confronted with the fact that their "science" has hardly changed at all in the last two thousand years, astrologers respond that astrology was so well established twenty centuries ago that there has never been any need to change, in spite of the vast changes that have taken place in our knowledge of the universe over the same period of time. Linda Goodman, a best-selling author of popular books on astrology in the 1970s, summed up the astrologers' position by saying, "Alone among the sciences, astrology has spanned the centuries and made the journey intact. We shouldn't be surprised that it remains with us, unchanged by time—because astrology is truth—and truth is eternal" (Goodman 1971, 475).

Unfortunately for astrologers and their "ancient truths," these "truths" are not true. An excellent example is the ancient astrological teaching that there are only seven heavenly bodies, other than Earth, in the solar system—the sun, the moon, Mercury, Venus, Mars, Jupiter, and Saturn. All ancient astrological teachings, the same that have been handed down to the likes of Linda Goodman, had this as a basic tenet. These teachings are wrong. Two additional planets have been discovered since the eighteenth century—Uranus in 1781 and Neptune in 1846, not to mention Pluto, now a "dwarf planet," discovered in 1930. These cannot be seen with the naked eye and were unknown to the ancient astrologers.

The ability to derive, test, and verify or falsify predictions is one of the most important characteristics of science. Astrologers never predicted the existence of the three other bodies and never even had the slightest hint that they existed—until astronomers discovered them. On the other hand, astronomers predicted the existence of Neptune twelve years before it was first identified through observation, and also predicted with great accuracy just where in the sky it could be found. It is in the discovery of Neptune that the contrast between the pseudoscience of astrology and the science of astronomy is most clearly seen. The exciting intellectual detective story of the discovery of Neptune is told in Standage's (2000) *The Neptune File* and more recently and in more detail by Sheehan (2021). It will be briefly summarized here to further highlight the differences between astrology and astronomy.

The prediction of the existence of a planet beyond Uranus was based on observed irregularities in Uranus's orbit. Uranus was discovered in 1781, and astronomers soon found that its orbit was irregular and could not be predicted, based on Newton's laws of gravitation, with the same precision as the orbits of the other planets. In 1834 the skilled British amateur astronomer Thomas Hussey (1792–1866?—he disappeared mysteriously in 1866) was the first to suggest that the perturbations of Uranus's orbit were caused by the gravitational influence of an as-yet-unknown planet. In the early 1840s two scientists, the English mathematician John Couch Adams (1819–1892), still an undergraduate at Cambridge University, and the French astronomer Urbain Jean Joseph Le Verrier (1811–1877), independently began working on the problem of Uranus's orbit with the goal of finding the unknown planet that was responsible for the perturbations. Their predictions were tested in 1846, and the previously unknown planet was found by the German astronomers Johann Gottfried Galle (1812–1910) and Heinrich Louis d'Arrest (1822–1875) where Adams and Le Verrier said it would be. Figure 6.1 shows Adams in his later years, and figure 6.2 shows Le Verrier on a 1958 French stamp.

Today, astrologers have assigned astrological influences to the new planets. The addition of the new planets didn't even cause much fuss among astrologers when they were discovered. But for nearly two thousand years, not one astrologer ever noticed a planetary influence where there was no known planet or was able to predict the existence or location of additional planets. Again, the history of astrological practice is inconsistent with the astrologers' claims that astrology is a precise science. If, as astrologers claim, each planet has an influence on human behavior, even a small one, and if that influence varies according to where the planet is located, then predictions of at least the existence of the new planets should have been made long ago. But one will search the writings of Ptolemy and later astrologers in vain for any hint of such a prediction. Goodman (1968) explained astrology's failure to note the influences of the "new" planets

John Couch Adams.

Figure 6.1. John Couch Adams. From Robert S. Ball, *Great Astronomers* (London: Isbister, 1895), National Library of Poland (https://commons.wikimedia.org/wiki/File:John_Couch_Adams_%28Great_astronomers_1895_%28151751965%29_%28cropped%29%29.jpg)

Figure 6.2. Urbain John Joseph Le Verrier, shown on a 1958 French stamp, Scott Catalog # 870. Author's collection

before their discovery in a most creative way by saying that a planet doesn't have any astrological influence until it is discovered!

Uranus wasn't the only planet that was uncooperative and didn't follow Newton's laws particularly well. Mercury's orbit also deviated from what these laws predicted. Given the explanation for the abnormalities in the orbit of Uranus, it was natural to try to explain those in Mercury's orbit as being due to the influence of another undiscovered planet, this one being closer to the sun than Mercury. Astronomers postulated such a planet and named it Vulcan. In 1859 Le Verrier published a prediction about where Vulcan would be found. In the next few years sightings of the planet were made, but these were due to "hoaxes or wishful thinking at the telescope" (Culver and Ianna 1984, 164) as well as the normal perceptual processes that lead to errors, as discussed in chapter 7.

The deviations in Mercury's orbit turned out not to be due to the gravitational effects of a planet but were explained by Einstein's general theory of relativity, as was confirmed by observations of the solar eclipse of 1919 (Kennefick 2019). The fascinating story of the search for Vulcan, the erroneous sightings of the planet, and the final resolution of the deviation of Mercury's orbit by Einstein is told by Baum and Sheehan (1997) in their *In Search of Planet Vulcan*. Levenson (2015) in his equally well-written *The Hunt for Vulcan* covers much of the same ground but places the search for Vulcan in the greater historical context of astronomy and physics.

Astrologers, not wanting to be caught out over Vulcan as they had been about Uranus, added Vulcan to the pantheon of planets that have astrological influences. As late as 1968, Linda Goodman said that "it's important to mention here the still unseen planet Vulcan, the planet of thunder, will become visible through telescopes in a few years" (203). By 1968 any well-read person would have known that Vulcan never existed in the first place.

Before moving on to a discussion of the studies that have empirically examined the claims of astrologers, a theoretical problem of major proportions has to be discussed: the mechanism by which any alleged astrological influence would occur. In other words, how would the stars and planets make their influence felt? Several answers to this question have been proposed: gravity, tidal or electromagnetic forces, magnetic fields, or emission of some sort of particles.

All these hypothesized mechanisms for astrological influence are far too weak to have any influence on human infants, let alone the massive influence that is required by astrology. The effects of gravity, for instance, decrease as the square of the distance between two objects. If planet A is twice as far from planet B as it is from planet C, the gravitational effect of A on B will be four times ($2^2 = 4$) less than the gravitational effect of A on C. The practical import of this is that the gravitational effects of the stars and planets on a newborn are essentially nonexistent. A mother holding her infant in her arms exerts a gravitational influence on the child that is much greater than the gravitational influence of the planet Mars. Mars is much more massive than the mother, but it is also a great deal farther away from the child.

The case is even worse for tidal forces. These decrease as the cube of the distance between two objects. In the example above, the tidal forces of planet A on planet B are eight times less ($2^3 = 8$) than the tidal forces of A on C. This means that, when one takes into account the other factors that go into the equation used to calculate tidal forces, the mother's tidal influence on the child is trillions of times greater than that of the planet Mars.

Electromagnetic and magnetic forces are equally unlikely to be the influence astrology requires. Electromagnetic forces are well understood, and they are not responsible for astrological influence. Magnetic fields certainly exist, but some planets of great importance in astrology don't have any. For example, the Moon, Venus, and Mars are devoid of such fields. As for emitted particles, in the solar system only the sun emits particles; the planets do not. Other stars also emit particles, but by the time they reach Earth they are so diffuse that they cannot influence individuals in the way that astrology requires.

Note also that astrology does not take into account any physical characteristics of the planets or stars. Their astrological influences are independent of size, mass, shape, temperature, age, composition, distance, and rotation. This disregard of physical characteristics is just what would be expected from a system based on magic, but not from a scientific system.

TESTING ASTROLOGICAL PREDICTIONS

In spite of the historical, logical, and theoretical shortcomings of astrology, it is still important to ask the purely empirical question: Does astrology work? That is, can it make accurate predictions about, for example, personality, personal destiny, mate selection, or any of dozens of other possible variables that astrologers claim are influenced by the sun, moon, and stars. Tests of the accuracy of astrology date back at least to the sixteenth century. During that period an astrologer named Sixtus ab Hemminga (1533–1586) lost his belief in astrology when he discovered that the predictions he had made based on astrology for thirty famous people for whom he had cast horoscopes were simply wrong. After this realization, he "came to know it [astrology] better, to be impossible, not worthy of dignity, and useless" (Dean et al. 2023, 105).

Studies from the later twentieth century show the efforts of researchers to approach the question of astrology from an empirical point of view. These studies have stood the test of time because of their simple and elegant methodology and results and, in one case, the demonstration of an important confounding factor that led to a false finding that astrological factors could influence personality. These studies have been summarized and described in Dean and colleagues (2016, 2023). The treatment in these sources is more thorough than is possible here. Dean and colleagues (2023) is over nine hundred pages long. After years of testing and thousands of tests, the evidence shows overwhelmingly that astrology does not have any validity.

According to astrologers, the most important astrological influence on personality is the sun sign, the sign of the zodiac in which the sun is located on the day of one's birth. Linda Goodman (1971) said that "an individual's sun sign will be approximately 80 percent accurate" as a description of personality (xvi). There are hundreds of ways of classifying human personality, but one common method is to dichotomize personality types and then assign individuals to one or the other type. While this is a gross oversimplification, it is popular with many psychologists. One of the most popular ways of dichotomizing personality is into extroverts and introverts. The characteristic personality of the extrovert seems to be nicely defined by the typical description of Aries: bold, assertive, aggressive, self-confident, and determined (Dean 1977; Eysenck and Nias 1982). An obvious astrological prediction, then, is that more extroverts than introverts should be born under Aries. If there are no astrological influences on personality, then the number of extroverts and introverts born under Aries should be about the same.

The hypothesis that there are astrological influences on extroversion and introversion has often been raised. Dean (1977) reviewed studies of this hypothesis. They offer no support for any proposed astrological influence. As early as 1941, Forlano and Ehrlich examined the birth dates of 7,527 male college students and found no effect of any sun sign on extroversion and introversion. Lim (1975) studied 163 people and found no correlation between extroversion and introversion and sun signs. Nor did Lim find any influence of moon signs on this personality variable.

Mayo, White, and Eysenck (1978) reported a study of 2,324 individuals that seemed to give impressive support to the hypothesis of astrological influence on extroversion and introversion. In this study, subjects filled out a personality questionnaire; the results of that questionnaire were correlated with the subjects' birth dates. Later work by Eysenck, reported in Eysenck and Nias (1982), showed that the original result was artifactual but in a very interesting way. Specifically, the subjects had knowledge of their astrological sign and the type of personality that is supposed to correlate with each sign. Eysenck and Nias studied 1,160 children, who were presumably unaware of astrological theory. There was no correlation between extroversion or introversion and astrological sign in these children. Another study reported by Eysenck and Nias was designed to test directly the prediction that subjects who had specific knowledge of the alleged astrological relationships between birth date and sign and personality would show greater correlation between sign and personality than those who didn't. One hundred and twenty-two subjects were divided into three groups: those who were knowledgeable about astrological claims about personality, those who had a "borderline" knowledge, and those who had no knowledge about the alleged relationships. Both the "no knowledge" and "borderline" groups showed no correlation between astrological sign and extroversion or introversion. However, "the knowledgeable group . . . showed a marked tendency to assess themselves in accordance with astrological predictions" (Eysenck and Nias 1982, 56). Thus, the original Mayo, White, and Eysenck (1978) results were due to the subjects' astrological knowledge, which was apparently extensive (Eysenck and Nias 1982). This knowledge biased at least some subjects in the way they reported their personality on the questionnaire. If subjects knew, for instance, that people born under Aries are supposed to be extroverted and knew that they had been born under Aries, they reported a more extroverted personality.

An earlier study by Delaney and Woodward (1974) also demonstrated such behavior. In this study, fifty-five high school students read personality descriptions based on their birth dates. Half received descriptions that were consistent with traditional astrological teachings ("Aries are extroverted," for example) and half received descriptions that were just the reverse (e.g., "Aries are introverted"). After reading the descriptions, they were asked to fill out a personality questionnaire. They were told that the purpose of the study was to "attempt to see if astrology has any real predictive value" and that the questionnaire was "concerned with your personality not the personality which was astrologically predicted" (1214). The responses on the questionnaire were influenced by the descriptions of personality that had been read, whether or not those descriptions were those of classical astrology. That is, if a subject was an Aries and had read that Aries individuals are extroverted, the responses on the subject's personality questionnaire showed a more extroverted personality. If an Aries was told that Aries individuals are introverted, the subject's questionnaire responses showed a tendency toward introversion. In addition to showing that the original Mayo, White, and Eysenck (1978) results were not due to astrological influence, these studies further demonstrate how subtle uncontrolled experimental variables can produce results that look as if they support astrological influences.

Eysenck and Nias (1982) also failed to find any astrological influence on another major personality variable, emotionality versus stability, although subjects' knowledge at first resulted in spurious correlations between astrological sign and this personality variable as well.

Astrologers commonly assert that a couple's compatibility is determined, at least in large part, by their sun signs. That is, two people who have "compatible" sun signs will have a better chance of making a successful marriage than two people whose sun signs are "incompatible." Several studies have shown that sun signs have no influence on marriage or divorce (Dean 1977; Culver and Ianna 1984). In these studies the birth dates for divorced and nondivorced couples were obtained. If sun signs have any influence, pairs with incompatible sun signs should be overrepresented among divorced couples and underrepresented among nondivorced couples. The studies reviewed in these two references reveal no influence of sun signs on marriage or divorce rates.

Astrologers disagree widely on which sun signs are compatible. Figure 6.3, taken from Culver and Ianna (1984, 132–33), shows the sun signs that Righter (1977), King (1973), Norvell (1975), and Omarr

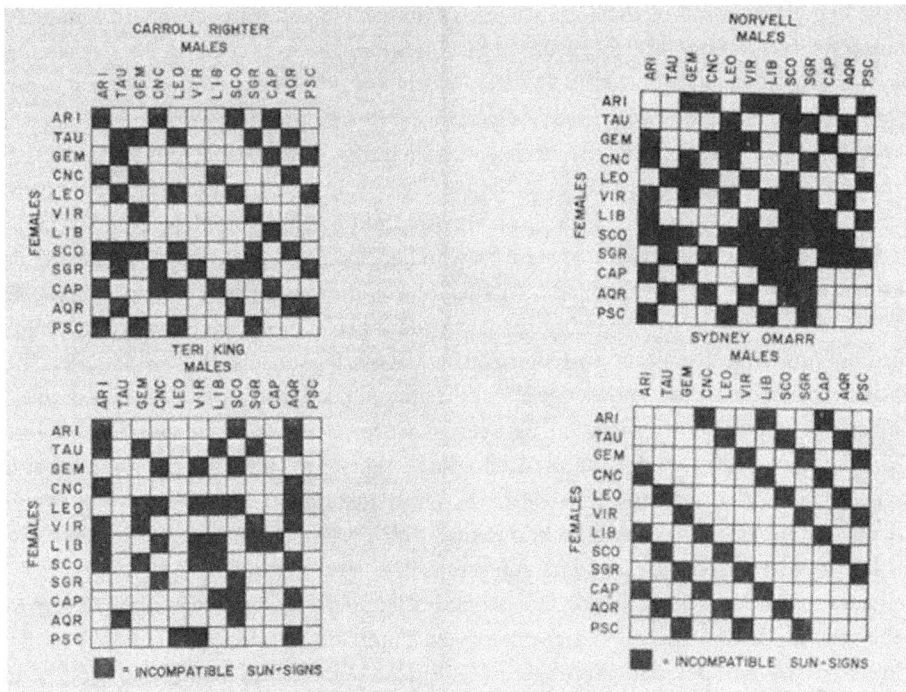

Figure 6.3. Vastly different patterns of compatible and incompatible sun signs by four leading astrologers. From R. B. Culver and P. A. Ianna, *The Gemini Syndrome: A Scientific Evaluation of Astrology* (Amherst, NY: Prometheus Books, 1984)

(1972) consider compatible and incompatible. Inspection of the figure shows the great degree of disagreement among these four popular astrologers, each of whom claims validity for their system, but not on the basis of any real data. The lack of agreement among astrologers should not be seen as reducing the importance of the research findings on sun signs and rates of marriage and divorce. These studies show that no combination of sun signs was associated with marriages or divorces. In other words, these studies examined all possible relationships between sun sign and compatibility and found that in no case was there any relationship. They did not simply test the few specific predictions made by astrologers.

In a similar vein, Helgertz and Scott (2020) examined marriage and divorce records for over sixty-five thousand married and divorced couples from Sweden. They found no astrological effects on either pairing of marriage partners or on divorce rates.

Carlson (1985) performed an extremely thorough and well-designed study of astrological predictions. This study is unique in that the help and cooperation of the astrological "profession" was sought and obtained. "So that the participating astrologers should be respected by the astrological community, we sought the advice of the National Council for Geocosmic Research" (420). Further, the astrologers involved agreed before the study was conducted that the procedures and design constituted a fair test of astrological predictions.

In the first part of the study, 177 subjects were recruited through newspaper ads. Based on their birth date, time, and place, their horoscopes were constructed and then interpreted by the astrologers associated with the study. Each subject was given an interpretation of three different horoscopes. One of the interpretations was of their own horoscope, while the other two were interpretations of horoscopes of two other randomly chosen participants in the study. If astrologers were able to divine personal information from a horoscope, then the subjects should have been able to choose the interpretation of their own horoscope over the interpretations of other individuals' horoscopes at a rate better than chance.

In the second part of the study, 116 subjects took the California Psychological Inventory (CPI), a widely used reliable and valid test of personality in normal (nonpathological) individuals (Megargie 1972). The astrologers were then given one individual's horoscope and the CPI personality profile of three subjects. One of the CPI profiles was that of the subject whose horoscope was given to the astrologer. The astrologers' task in this part of the study was to pick the CPI profile that matched the horoscope. The results of both parts of the study provide no support for astrology. Subjects in the first part of the study were unable to pick the interpretation of their horoscope from the interpretation of two other individuals' horoscopes at a rate above chance. In the second part of the study, the astrologers were not able to match the horoscope of an individual to his or her CPI personality profile at a rate higher than chance. Given two opportunities to provide impressive empirical support for the reality of astrological claims, in a test that respected astrologers agreed beforehand was fair, astrology failed.

According to astrology, numerous other personality traits—in addition to physical characteristics, occupation, and medical disorders—are influenced by one's sun sign. The predictions have been shown to be wrong (Dean 1977; Dean et al. 2016, 2023). For example, of sixty different occupations studied, not one showed any influence of sun signs. That is, members of these sixty occupations were no more or less likely to be born under one sun sign than another. Among the occupations examined were those of actor, pilot, artist, astronomer, banker, baseball player, chemist, teacher, journalist, lawyer, doctor, opera singer, poet, politician, psychologist, and priest. Among the physical characteristics not related to sun sign were blood type, baldness, hair color, height, sex, handedness, and weight. Medical disorders found to be unrelated to sun sign included acne, allergies, diabetes, Down syndrome, heart attack, infant death, leukemia, lung cancer, multiple sclerosis, stillbirths, stroke, and muscular dystrophy. Age at death is also not related to sun sign. Finally, the following personality traits are not related to sun sign: aggression, ambition, creativity, feelings of inferiority, integrity, intelligence, leadership, self-expression, sociability, tough-mindedness, understanding, and wisdom. All these findings are in strong contrast to the empirically unsubstantiated claims of astrologers. Those claims can now be seen to be simply wrong.

The studies on the accuracy of astrology described above have been based on the astrological prediction that different people born under the same astrological conditions (i.e., under the same sun sign) will show greater similarities than expected by chance on any number of traits and characteristics. Those predictions were not born out by the studies. Astrology makes an even stronger prediction that individuals born close together in place and time, but who are not biologically related (called "time twins") should share more common personality traits than biologically unrelated people who are not time twins. This prediction was tested by Dean and Kelly (2003). They took data on 110 cognitive, physical, and personality variables from 2,101 people born in London between March 3 and 9, 1958. The data came from the British National Child Development Study. The authors found no support for astrology in this very large dataset.

In the book by Dean and colleagues (2023) just over ninety pages are devoted to reviewing studies of the accuracy of astrological predictions about personality. In none of the dozens of such studies was any relationship found. In one amusing study, individuals went to astrologers and gave, not their actual birth date, but the birth date of the notorious serial killer John Wayne Gacy. Not one astrologer even suggested that there might be some negative aspects to the individuals' personality.

There is more to astrology than sun signs. Numerous other variables are said to influence the individual. Among these are planetary conjunctions, houses, ascendants, the relationship between the planets, and the planets' positions in the various signs. Culver and Ianna (1984) calculated that there are some 10^{35} possible astrological predictions. This huge number compares with only about 10^{27} grains of sand on the earth. Some of the predictions involving factors more complicated than sun signs have been tested (Dean 1977, 1986–1987a, 1986–1987b; Dean et al. 2016, 2023), but, again, these tests provided no support for astrological claims. It is worth noting that some of the tests described in the above-cited volumes used very sophisticated statistical techniques to look for astrological effects and found none.

With the advent of large computer databases, it has been possible to study astrological predictions in ways previously impossible. Dean (2016) and Dean and colleagues (2016, 2023) have reviewed these studies. In one such study Voas (2008) examined the birth dates of ten million (yes, million) married couples in England and Wales using official census data. If, as astrology claims, certain sun signs are more compatible than others, this should certainly show up in such a huge sample. That is, some allegedly compatible sun sign pairings should be much more common than other less or noncompatible ones. Voas noted that if "only one pair in a thousand is influenced by the stars, we would see ten thousand more couples than expected with certain combinations of signs" (53). Voas found absolutely no hint of any such effect. Nor did any of the other numerous studies reviewed by Dean and colleagues (2016, 2023).

While modern studies of the validity of astrological predictions are rarely published in the mainstream scientific literature, such studies continue to be done. They are often done by astrologers themselves and published in obscure astrological journals or are found in unpublished sources such as theses and dissertations. Dean and colleagues (2023) have reviewed these studies in their definitive compendium of astrological research. A strength of their book is that they subject all the astrological studies they review to critiques of methodology and statistical issues. They find that there is no evidence for the validity of astrology whatsoever.

It is revealing to look at the reaction of the astrologers to the disconfirmation of their claims and predictions. One tack is to say that astrological effects are just too subtle and esoteric to be verified by science. But if an astrologer can determine them by casting a horoscope, how subtle can they be? Related is the idea that the stars don't compel but merely guide, and thus astrological effects are small. Well, if that's true, why bother going to an astrologer if the effects are so small? And it should be remembered that science is very, very good at detecting extremely small, even minuscule, effects.

Another argument is that one cannot reject astrology until all, or at least a majority, of its predictions have been tested and found wanting. But, as just noted, there is an enormous number of possible predictions. It would take forever to test even a large fraction of these. It is unnecessary to test every possible prediction of a theory if the theory's major predictions are not verified.

A third defense of astrology is that personal experience is better than scientific knowledge as a guide to reality. So if your horoscope seems accurate, that's all you need to know to validate astrology's reality. This, of course, is another example of the fallacy of personal validation. Personal experience can sometimes be a good starting point for investigating the nature of reality. But it's clear that personal experience is often a terrible guide to reality. As noted throughout this book there are numerous ways personal experience can fool us and lead us to false, even harmful, beliefs.

Finally, one can make the "it doesn't matter that it doesn't really work because it provides psychological benefits" argument. An example of this comes from Lobell (1975, 223): "Astrology offers people what science does not: a psychologically meaningful link between the individual and the cosmos." The problem is the phrase "psychologically meaningful." Any deeply held belief, right or wrong, can be "psychologically meaningful" to the believer. The strength of that belief bears no relation to the truth of the belief.

The latest fad in astrology is the idea that when "Mercury is in retrograde" all sorts of bad things will happen. The term refers to the fact that several times every year it appears that Mercury is moving backward across the sky. It isn't of course—this is merely a sort of optical illusion. Nonetheless, believers worry that for the few days that this illusion occurs they should avoid such things as making important decisions, traveling, or starting a medical procedure. It would be very easy to test the idea that bad things are more likely to happen when Mercury seems to be moving backward than when it is seen to be moving forward. To my knowledge, no such tests have yet been done.

MOON MADNESS

The basic idea behind the lunar effect—or "moon madness" or the "Transylvania hypothesis" as some more lyrical writers term it—is that the moon in its different phases exerts a strong influence on human behavior. It is especially held that the full moon accentuates or increases the probability of all sorts of odd and troublesome behaviors. Suicides, admissions to mental hospitals, arrests for public drunkenness, and crimes of various sorts are all said to increase when the moon is full (Lieber and Agel 1978). It is also widely believed, especially among maternity ward personnel, that more babies are born when the moon is full than during the other phases of the moon (Abell and Greenspan 1979). The moon's gravitational influence is usually the mechanism used to explain the alleged effects of the full moon. After all, proponents say, the moon's gravity influences the oceans, which are largely water. Therefore, since the human body contains a great deal of water, the moon's gravity must also influence the human body. This, in some unspecified way, results in moon madness. But in fact the moon's gravitational influence on the human body is infinitesimal—equivalent to the weight of a single mosquito being added to the weight of a normal individual. Gravity is a weak force. As you hold this book, you are outpulling the entire planet Earth.

Campbell and Beets (1978), Abell (1981b), and Rotton and Kelly (1985) reviewed the considerable number of studies done to that time that examined the effects of the phases of the moon, especially the full moon, on human behavior. All three reviews concluded unequivocally that the phase of the moon does not influence human behavior. For example, Abell and Greenspan (1979) studied all the births that took place at the University of California Hospital, Los Angeles, from March 17, 1974, through April 30, 1978. During this period there were 11,691 live births, of which 8,142 were natural in that neither drugs nor caesarean section were used. There were 141 multiple births among the live births and 168 stillbirths. Analysis of this huge number of births showed no effect of phase of the moon in any of the four groups of births, all live births, natural births, multiple births, and stillbirths.

Studies of other variables have also failed to find any effect of the full moon. Rotton and Kelly's (1985) article reviews numerous published studies that showed the full moon did not influence (1) homicide rate, (2) other criminal offenses, (3) suicides, (4) psychiatric disturbances, or (5) psychiatric admissions to hospital.

Occasionally, of course, a study will report some sort of relation between the full moon and some variable. These studies require close examination. Under such examination, methodological or statistical flaws have appeared that invalidate the conclusions. Templer, Veleber, and Brooner (1982) found that highway accidents at night were more frequent when the moon was full. But their data showed no effect of the phase of the moon on daytime accidents. They devised a rather fanciful explanation of these results based on the effect of moonlight on the human pineal gland. However, as Rotton and Kelly (1985) point out, "a disproportionate number of full-moon nights fell on weekends" during the period studied by Templer, Veleber, and Brooner (292). Templer, Brooner, and Corgiat (1983) reanalyzed their data and, this time, took into account such variables as weekends, holidays, and such. They found that the supposed effect of the full moon on accidents disappeared. Thus, their original finding was due to the effect of weekends on accident rates, not to any effect of the full moon. Redelmeier and Shafir (2017) found significantly more motorcycle fatalities on full moon nights. They did control for day-of-the-week effects. They explained this effect as being due to the distracting effect of a full moon on drivers of motorcycles. In contrast to drivers of automobiles, motorcyclists have an unobstructed view of their environment and are more likely to have their attention diverted by a stimulus as striking as a full moon. It may also be the case that the better visibility afforded by a full moon leads motorcyclists to increase their speed and thus the risk of a fatal accident. Such an effect may not be important for automobile drivers, who are driving a much more stable vehicle. In a large analysis of lunar effects, Kelly, Rotton, and Culver (1985–1986) reviewed over forty studies that "examined lunar variables and mental behavior" and found "that there is no causal relationship between lunar phenomena and human behavior" (139).

Arnold Lieber and Jerome Agel (1978) have been strong proponents of the reality of lunar influence on human behavior. They reportedly found a relationship between homicide rates and the full moon in Dade County, Florida, and Cuyahoga County, Ohio, with more homicides taking place when the moon was full. There was a fatal flaw in this study (Rotton and Kelly 1985). In attempting to find an effect of the full moon, Lieber and Sherin (1972) conducted ninety-six different statistical tests on their data, a classic example of the multiple comparison fallacy. They tested the effect of the moon on homicide rates by looking at these rates for, among others, "the three days before and after, the three days before, the three days after, two days before and after, two days before, two days after, one day before and after, one day before, one to two days after, and one to three days after full moons" (Rotton and Kelly 1985, 293). Of the ninety-six analyses, three reached the accepted .05 level of significance, meaning that such a result would be expected by chance only one time in twenty, or five times out of one hundred. But, if one conducts ninety-six statistical tests, one would expect that 4.8 of them (96 x .05) would reach the .05 level by chance alone. Lieber and Sherin's (1972) data would provide evidence for the reality of lunar effects on homicide rates only if about ten of their ninety-six different tests showed a significant result. Sanduleak (1984–1985) analyzed all 3,370 homicides that took place in Cuyahoga County from 1971 through 1981 and found no lunar influences.

The empirical data on the lunar effect shows that the moon's phases have no effect on human behavior. Why do so many people continue to believe that "moon madness" exists? A clue can be found in a study by Angus (1973). This study revealed that nurses who believed in the reality of the moon's influence on behavior made more notes of patients' "unusual" behavior when the moon was full than did nurses who did not believe the moon influenced behavior. Nurses who believed that the moon influenced behavior knew when the moon was full and at those times expected, looked for, and, not surprisingly, found more noteworthy behavior. Other nurses, who did not believe that the moon influences behavior, did not search for incidents to validate their belief. Once again selective memory and confirmation bias appear and account for the belief in two more phenomena that do not exist.

Astrology and moon madness are both falsifiable and have been falsified, as the above discussion shows. Yet they remain pseudosciences because they meet two other characteristics of a pseudoscience. Their proponents do not change their beliefs in the face of disconfirming evidence, and neither contributes to the advancement of human knowledge.

7

UFOs I
Close Encounters of the First Kind

The belief that unidentified flying objects (UFOs) are some sort of extraterrestrial spacecraft is certainly one of the most prevalent pseudoscientific beliefs in Western culture. Dozens of movies have reinforced the view that "flying saucers," or UFOs, are alien craft. UFOs are largely a post–World War II phenomenon, although sightings of what would now be called UFOs did occur earlier (Bartholomew and Howard 1998). One particularly spectacular series of sightings consisted of reports of a UFO in the United States between late 1896 and early 1897. The airship was almost always reported to have been a dark, cigar-shaped object. This turned out to be the earliest known UFO "flap" (Cohen 1981). A UFO "flap" refers to a wave of UFO sightings in a particular place or time. Several factors contributed to the airship flap. First, newspaper editors made up hoax stories about the airship to fill space in their publications. Nearby editors would copy the stories for their papers. Newspaper ethics were different in the late nineteenth and early twentieth centuries from what they are today. Second, at the end of the nineteenth century the "social climate" was such that "almost any invention seemed possible, and an exaggerated optimism developed in the belief that the perfection of the world's first heavier-than-air ship was imminent" (Bartholomew 1998). Thus the public was primed for the airship.

During World War II both Allied and Axis pilots reported seeing "foo-fighters," strange lights that followed their aircraft, but these reports attracted little attention (Jacobs 1975). The modern era for UFOs began on June 24, 1947, when private pilot Kenneth Arnold was flying near the Cascade Mountains in Washington State and saw nine unidentified flying objects that he described flying "like a saucer skipping over water" (36–37). The term *flying saucer*, and the public's interest in the phenomenon, was born.

After Arnold's sighting was reported, the number of other sightings around the country and the world grew. There was a major wave of sightings in 1952. That year also saw the first reported contact between earthman and spaceman, or *close encounter of the third kind*. The first "contactee" was George Adamski, a handyman and failed mystic who met a visitor from Venus in the California desert on November 20, 1952. Contactee stories of this era contain several common elements (Jacobs 1975). A lone earthman was given a ride in the UFO. The occupants described their advanced culture to him and explained the workings of the craft. One contactee, Howard Menger, was lucky enough to have the aliens show him how to construct a "free-energy motor" (Menger 1959), although this marvelous invention somehow failed to forestall the energy crisis of the 1970s. The aliens would also predict dire happenings on Earth, such as atomic war, that would affect other planets. The contactee was usually given a mission to prevent this disaster and set the stage for final contact between the human and extraterrestrial civilizations. Somehow, the aliens always forgot to give their contacts any proof that they existed. They also must have been very bad psychologists, because the people they chose to carry their messages were almost invariably crackpots, lunatics, or charlatans. Thus, close encounters of the third kind were not taken seriously by many people until the 1970s, when such reports cropped up again, in rather different form. These encounters will be covered in the next chapter.

As the 1950s wore on, UFO reports continued and the U.S. Air Force became concerned. After all, people were reporting strange things in the skies—often reporting them directly to the Air Force. The fear was that they might be some type of new Soviet weapon. This was the period of the Cold War and McCarthy anticommunist paranoia. There was legitimate concern about whether the Soviet Union had the military capability to strike the United States using aircraft armed with its newly developed nuclear weapons. Thus, Project Blue Book was set up in 1952 by the Air Force to investigate UFO reports. However, the Air Force appears not to have taken the project too seriously; it had a small staff with little technical competence. Predictably, Project Blue Book was heavily criticized by those who felt there was really something to the UFO reports. In 1954 the National Investigations Committee on Aerial Phenomena (NICAP) was formed by retired Marine Corps Maj. Donald Keyhoe. It was the first private UFO research group and the most conservative. NICAP correctly dismissed as crackpots or frauds the various contactees of the 1950s, when other private UFO investigating organizations often took at least some of these stories seriously.

From about 1958 to 1965 came a period of controversy over UFOs. The several private UFO groups battled with each other over who was the best, and with the Air Force, since they were convinced that the Air Force knew that UFOs were alien spacecraft but was keeping this truth from the American public. There were constant calls for congressional investigations of UFO sightings, the Air Force itself, and its handling of UFO reports.

By 1966 the Air Force had concluded that there was nothing to UFO reports, either as a concern of national security or as extraterrestrial contact. Devoutly wishing to be rid of the entire matter, the Air Force contracted with a group of independent scientists to investigate all aspects of the UFO question. This group, headed by University of Colorado professor of physics Edward Condon, came to be known as the Condon Committee. Creation of the Condon Committee was greeted with optimism by all sides (Jacobs 1975). However, pro-UFO groups quickly became dissatisfied with the committee's investigation. Factions within the committee fought over how to approach the problem. One group felt that the focus of the investigation should be the extraterrestrial hypothesis, while another faction "thought the extraterrestrial theory was nonsense and believed the solution to the UFO mystery was to be found in the psychological makeup of the witnesses" (230). This dispute led to much internal dissension and fueled the private UFO groups' discontent with the committee. The Condon Committee issued its report in 1969 and concluded that there was no evidence that UFOs were of extraterrestrial origin. In December 1969 the Air Force officially got out of the UFO business, closing down Project Blue Book for good.

The conclusions of the Condon Committee and the government's official withdrawal from UFO investigations did not end public interest in UFOs. A 1973 Gallup poll showed that 11 percent of American adults believed that they had seen a UFO. Another Gallup poll conducted in 1978 showed that 57 percent of Americans believe that UFOs are "something real." Klass (1978–1979) was rightly critical of the wording of the UFO-related questions on the Gallup polls, pointing out that "something real" does not necessarily mean "something extraterrestrial" and that even skeptics would agree that UFOs represent *something* real. A 2015 Gallup poll supported Klass's criticism with better phrased questions. In this poll, 46 percent of respondents said flying saucers were "something real" but only 7 percent thought they were some type of alien craft. Most people didn't venture an opinion as to what they were. Nonetheless, these figures testify to the high degree of interest in UFOs on the part of the American public.

After the issuance of the Condon Report, several pro-UFO groups continued to investigate UFO sightings and to claim that there was good evidence for their extraterrestrial origin. A major argument put forth for the reality of extraterrestrial UFOs is the large number of reports that continue to be made. Astronomer J. Allen Hynek (1910–1986), a former skeptic where UFOs were concerned, changed his mind and came to support the extraterrestrial hypothesis (he also coined the term *close encounters of the third kind* and was an adviser for the film of the same name) based on the large number of sightings (Hynek 1972). Hynek frequently emphasized not only the large number of sightings but the fact that they come "trom all parts of the world and in many instances from remarkably competent witnesses" (Hynek 1976–1977, 77). This is a theme sounded over and over again in the UFO movement. The fact that many UFO witnesses are trained pilots, radar operators, or other professionals and that they are not crazy, drunk, or on drugs leads UFO proponents to conclude that they must have seen just what they say they saw. This conclusion is fundamentally wrong. The great failure of the pro-UFO movement has been its unwillingness to accept the fact that human perception and memory are not only unreliable under a variety of conditions (and these conditions are exactly those under which most UFOs are reported) but that perception and memory are also *constructive*. That is, perception is a function not only of the actual sensory stimulus that is picked up by the eye or the ear but also of what a witness knows and believes about the world, even if that knowledge and belief are wrong. The constructive nature of perception is greatest when the actual sensory input is weak, unclear, or ambiguous—just the type of sensory input present in most UFO sightings. Memory, too, is constructive, as described below.

The combination of the constructive nature of both memory and perception means that eyewitnesses can truthfully remember and testify to seeing or hearing events that never took place. Not only does this help explain seemingly impressive UFO reports; it has important implications for the criminal justice system as well.

THE CONSTRUCTIVE NATURE OF HUMAN PERCEPTION

The fact that knowledge influences how we perceive the world, that it influences how we interpret the sensory input received from the sense organs, is of vital importance: it allows us to make sense of what would otherwise be a very confusing world. Perceptual psychologists have studied so-called *perceptual constancies* for more than one hundred years. These constancies are among the best examples of the constructive nature of perception.

Consider color perception. A red apple will look red under a wide variety of lighting conditions, a phenomenon known as color constancy. Under normal white light, the apple looks red because the red wavelengths of light are reflected from the apple skin to the eye. By changing the light that falls on the apple, the composition of the light that is reflected from the apple skin to the eye changes. But, except for extreme cases, changes in reflected light do not result in a change in the perceived color of the apple. It is still perceived as red. This effect depends on the perceiver's knowledge that the object is a red apple. If that knowledge is removed, the color does not appear the same under different lighting conditions. This can be demonstrated by placing a red apple in a box that has a small hole that permits the viewer to see only a small section of the apple skin but not enough for the observer to see that the object is an apple. As far as observers are concerned, all they are looking at is a spot of color. If the light is changed in the box, the color seen through the tiny hole will appear to observers to change. In this situation, an observer doesn't know the color is that of a red apple, and with this knowledge eliminated, the perceived color is just a function of the actual wavelengths of light reflected to the observers' eyes. However, if the hole is big enough for observers to see that the object is a red apple, changing the illumination will change the perception of the red color very little, if at all. Hence, knowledge plays a major role in determining what color is perceived. It must be emphasized that color constancy is not a conscious process on the part of the observer; rather, the brain automatically takes into account what is known about the object and adjusts the perception accordingly.

A second example of constructive perception also concerns color vision. People who have normal color vision perceive the entire visual world as colored. This is taken for granted. But in spite of this, the cells in the retina of the eye that enable us to see color are found mostly in the very center of the retina, in an area called the *fovea*. If we depended only on retinal input for color perception, we would perceive a small central area of color, while the rest of the visual field would be black and white. This can easily be demonstrated: have a friend look straight ahead, then slowly move some colored object (a colored magic marker is ideal) into his or her field of vision. There will be a point at which the person will be able to see something in peripheral vision and will even be able to identify it but will not be able to say what color it is.

Another example may clarify this point. As I sit here in my office writing this, there is an orange-red door off to my left. I can just see the door out of the corner of my eye and I clearly perceive it as colored, in spite of the fact that the light being reflected off the door to my retina is falling on a part of the retina where there are no color receptors. Since I know what color the door is—it is very familiar to me—my brain constructs a perception of the color. How the brain manages this is not known, but the phenomenon demonstrates the great importance of knowledge in even the simplest types of perception.

Perception of size is also constant. That is, we perceive a familiar object as staying constant in size as it moves toward or away from us. This is in spite of the fact that as an object moves away from us, the image it casts on the retina gets much smaller. But, for the purposes of perceiving size, the brain ignores the retinal image size. It would be almost impossible to survive in the real world if size constancy did not exist. If it didn't exist, we would perceive large objects far away from us as small ones. Our ability to recognize that a large object really is a large object allows the brain to plan for such things as avoiding a charging predator when it's seen from a distance. While size constancy is largely innate, there is a learning component. Young children have poorer size constancy than adults. And native people who live in a jungle environment also have poorer size constancy, presumably because in their environment larger objects far away are obscured by the jungle. When individuals who grew up in such an environment are shown an object far away, they misjudge its size. After a few days' experience, they develop normal size constancy (Turnbull 1961).

Perception of an object's shape is also constant. A chair, for example, viewed from many different angles projects many different shapes onto the viewer's retina. But the brain ignores that, and the result is a constant perception of a chair, albeit perhaps moving in three dimensional space.

Color, size, and shape constancy are just three examples of many perceptual constancies. Others include *position constancy*, and *brightness constancy*. Details can be found in most introductory psychology texts and any textbook on perception. The constancies ensure that we perceive the world as it actually exists, not as just a flat expanse of color and shapes. The important point about these constancies is that they demonstrate that even in such straightforward tasks as judging color or shape or size, knowledge plays an extremely important role in influencing the way an object is perceived. The brain takes into account what is known about the object and constructs a perception based both on the actual sensory input and on knowledge. However, knowledge can be wrong. When it is, perception can also be wrong. Perceptual experience is especially vulnerable to wrong expectations and knowledge when the sensory input to the brain is minimal or when the thing one is trying to identify is far away and few details can be seen. It is not due to chance that UFOs are mostly seen at night and that things like sea monsters, Bigfoots, and other cryptozoological creatures (chapter 13) are usually perceived when, whatever the actual object is, it is far away—just at the limits of visibility. Bigfoot is not known for strolling down Main Street at lunchtime on a sunny weekday.

Other perceptual processes contribute to the constructive nature of perception. Look at the object in figure 7.1, then close the book and make a copy of it from memory. Chances are very high that you drew a triangle and did not include the small gap at one corner. If you had been asked to describe the figure to someone, you would almost certainly have left out that small gap. This is an example of *perceptual closure*, one of the Gestalt laws of perception. The Gestalt psychologists (*Gestalt* is a German word meaning form, pattern, or configuration), working in the early twentieth century, developed a number of laws describing how the brain interprets incoming sensory input to result in a final perception of the world that is usually accurate. It is the Gestalt psychologists who coined the phrase "the whole is more than the sum of its parts"

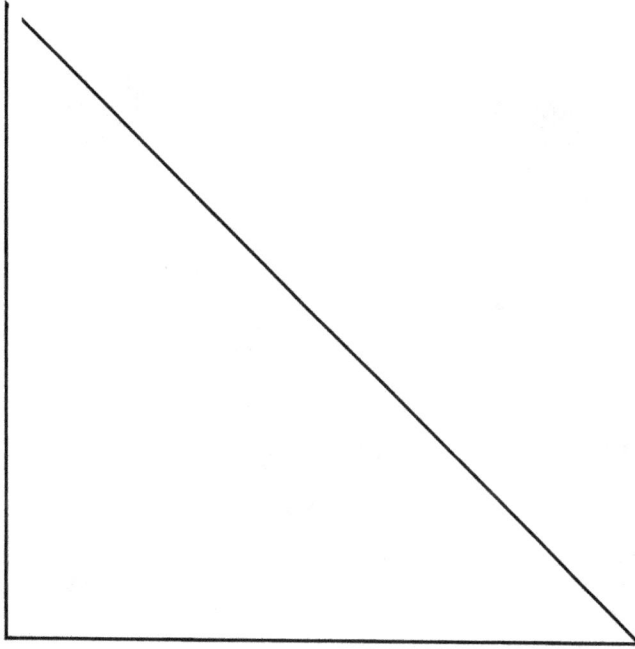

Figure 7.1. What is this figure?

to reflect the fact that the brain organizes sensory inputs into meaningful patterns. Another Gestalt law is the law of *continuity*, sometimes called *good continuation*. This law describes the fact that objects arranged together will tend to be seen as organized together even if they are not. Along with several related processes, the processes described by these laws tend to "clean up" sensory input, with the result being a perception of a more complete object, even if the stimulus was not such an object in the first place. A related example of constructive perception is that of *illusory contours*, seen in figure 7.2. The white triangular shape you see isn't really there; the brain constructs it.

Anatomically, the constructive nature of perception is mediated by the extensive connections from higher brain centers back to earlier sensory processing areas. This means that expectations produced in these higher (more forward) centers can influence the information passed on from earlier processing structures to the higher centers. Muckli and colleagues (2015) have demonstrated such an influence in the visual areas of the brain.

The constructive nature of perception and the Gestalt laws noted above account for a famous astronomical illusion—the canals of Mars. These were depicted in detail on a map of Mars in 1877 by the Italian astronomer Giovanni Schiaparelli (1835–1910). They were popularized in the early twentieth century by the American astronomer Percival Lowell (1855–1916). Figure 7.3 shows a map of the canals from Lowell's 1908 book *Mars as the Abode of Life*. In this book Lowell argued that the canals were constructed by an advanced Martian civilization. Certainly not all astronomers of the day saw the canals, and a lively debate swirled around the issue of their existence for years (Crowe 1986, chap. 10). It turns out that the canals of Mars do not exist. Sagan and Fox (1975) compared the photos taken by *Mariner 9*, which photographed the entire Martian surface, with maps of the canals. When the real Martian surface is examined, there are no canals or other physical features that could account for what Schiaparelli and Lowell reported. So where did the canals come from? Sagan and Fox state that "the vast majority of the canals appear to be largely self-generated by the visual observers of the canal school and stand as monuments to the imprecision of the human eye-brain-hand system under difficult observing conditions"

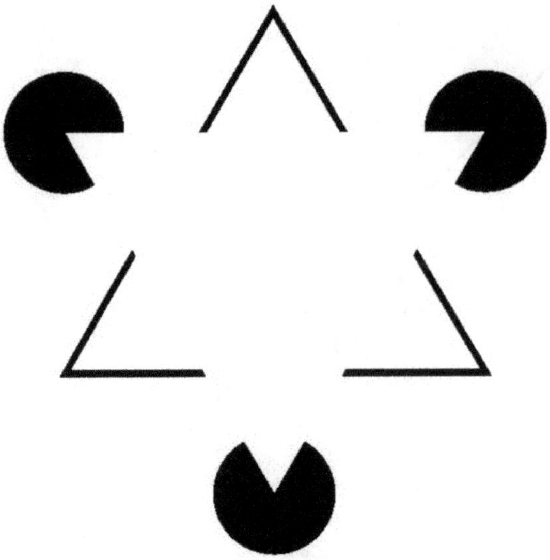

Figure 7.2. Illusory contours: the brain creates the contours of a white triangle that isn't really there. Kanizsa Triangle by Fibonacci (user), 2007, Wikimedia Commons (https://commons.wikimedia.org/wiki/File:Kanizsa_triangle.svg)

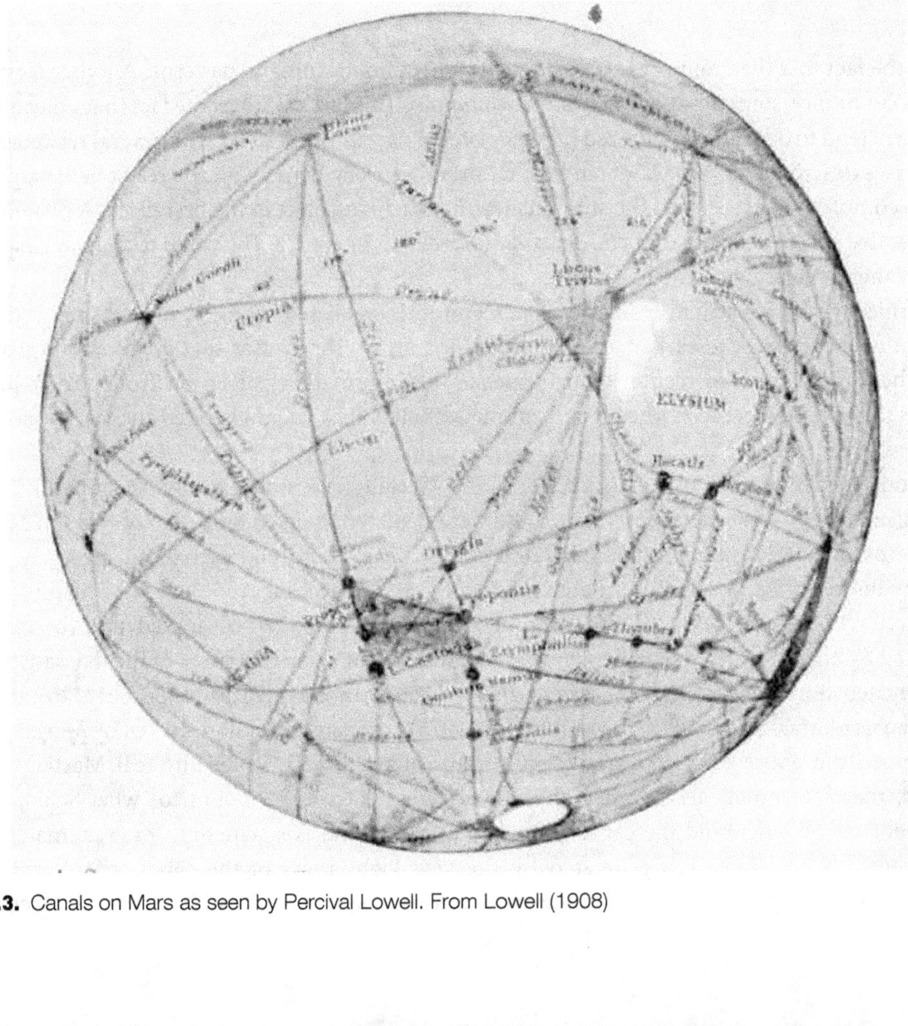

Figure 7.3. Canals on Mars as seen by Percival Lowell. From Lowell (1908)

(609). Sheehan (1988) expands on this idea in his excellent book *Planets and Perception*. He traces the history of trained professional astronomers falling prey to constructive perception and seeing nonexistent patterns on the moon, Mercury, Venus, as well as Mars from the time of the invention of the telescope. Lowell was just following an old tradition, albeit carrying it a bit further by asserting that the patterns he saw were the work of intelligent beings.

Sharps (2018) is more specific in describing how the laws of closure and continuity helped Lowell and other astronomers see canals that were not there. The Martian surface is littered with objects such as "craters and rocks very close together. These astronomers, with their human nervous systems, tended to see these things as contiguous. The contours thus created frequently formed lines, hence the canals" (45–46). There was no incompetence or psychopathology involved in seeing the canals—it was due to the normal working of the human perceptual systems.

A number of well-known visual illusions play a role in what witnesses report in UFO sightings, especially those that take place at night. One is the *autokinetic effect*. This effect refers to the fact that, if one views a small source of light in a completely dark room, the light will appear to move, even if both it and the observer's head are stationary. Otani and Dixon (1976) showed that social influence can affect the degree of the autokinetic effect—that is, one person saying he or she sees the light moving in a particular direction can induce others to make similar reports.

Another illusion is that of *apparent motion*. Consider two positions in a totally dark room, A and B. A small light is turned on at A, then turned off. Moments later, a second light is turned on at B. What does the observer perceive? The obvious answer would be that the perception is of one light going on and going off, followed by a second light in a different position going on. But this is not what the observer sees at all. What is perceived is a *single* light appearing at point A, moving to point B. The brain creates a perception of movement where none exists. It also creates a perception of light where none exists—between positions A and B.

A moving object is often obscured by clutter in the visual environment. It is important for the brain to be able to track an object as it moves behind obscuring clutter and not to conclude that the object simply vanishes immediately when it's out of sight. Apparent motion is a result of a brain mechanism that allows the tracking of objects that may disappear from view occasionally and then reappear.

Apparent motion is not due to any conscious expectations on the part of the perceiver. In Beck, Elsner, and Silverstein's (1977) study, subjects saw a central light go on. It then disappeared and one of two lights in different locations came on at random. Subjects had no way of predicting which one of the two lights would go on. And yet apparent motion was still clearly perceived. Apparent motion and other perceptual illusions exist because of the way the brain is wired.

Two other perceptual phenomena can lead people to perceive and remember UFO events as more detailed and compelling than they actually were. *Representational momentum* (Hubbard 2005) refers to the fact that when people observe an object that is, or seems to be, moving, they remember the extent of its movement as greater than it actually was. So a light observed moving across the night sky and disappearing (as happened in the Cradle Hill sightings described below) will be perceived to have traversed a greater distance than it did.

Boundary extension (Hubbard, Hutchison, and Courtney 2010) is observed when people are asked to remember a visual scene. When the scene has clear boundaries, people will falsely remember the boundaries as being extended beyond the actual size of the scene. They will also include in their memories objects not in the scene but inferred from what was in the actual scene. This can lead witnesses to include in their memories details that were not actually present but the addition of which can make the memory seem more real and compelling.

These constructive phenomena are extremely important for our survival in the real world. The constancies and other mechanisms described evolved because they help organisms interact with the world.

It would be very difficult to survive without these mechanisms. However, when the sensory input is minimal and only our knowledge and beliefs remain, our resultant perceptions and memories can be quite misleading. In these situations, we can perceive complex objects that are not there at all and be absolutely convinced that they were there. People who report seeing impressive flying saucers are not lying. They really perceive them, even though they weren't there: the objects were a construction of their brains and seem just as real as if they had been there.

Before moving on to the numerous UFO sightings that prove this point, it is important to discuss briefly the fallibility of human memory. You don't need expertise in cognitive psychology to know that human memory is fallible. Anyone who has ever taken an exam or tried unsuccessfully to remember someone's name or telephone number knows that human memory doesn't always work perfectly. The most important insight into the fallibility of human memory to come from cognitive psychology over the past decades is that memory is fallible in a very special way. It can be changed after the fact by new information, and the resultant memory may be very different from what took place—yet the person will swear that his or her memory is accurate. In some sense, it is. The witness is not lying in the usual sense of that word: the reported memory is really a memory, but due to the nature of memory, the reported memory differs from what really happened.

The best examples of this process come from the early work of Elizabeth Loftus (1979), whose work was also described in chapter 5. In her first experiment (Loftus and Palmer 1974), it will be recalled, she showed that a leading question asked after witnesses have seen a film of a staged car accident led to an increase in the frequency of false memories of broken glass that was implied by the leading question.

Loftus demonstrated how powerful this effect can be in a later experiment (Loftus, Miller, and Burns 1978) especially relevant to UFO sightings. In a series of five experiments, the authors showed that asking a leading question following the viewing of a slide show showing a car stopped at an intersection with either no sign, a yield sign, or a stop sign could change a significant number of subjects' memories about what sign they had seen. This task tapped recognition memory rather than recall memory. This is an important distinction because recognition tests are much more sensitive measures of memory than recall tests. The leading question had implanted a memory of a stop sign in the subjects' memories, even though none had been there. As before, the subjects were not lying—they really remembered seeing a sign, even though it had never been there.

CLOSE ENCOUNTERS OF THE FIRST KIND

The most common type of UFO report is the so-called *close encounter of the first kind* (CE I). It consists of a sighting of a UFO but with no physical evidence of the object left behind. Nonetheless, a CE I can be quite impressive, especially when the witnesses are trained, reliable, stable individuals.

The earliest wave of UFO sightings, those of the "mysterious airship" mentioned earlier between November 1896 and April 1897, are in the best traditions of constructive perception. What was usually seen in the sky was not a dark, cigar-shaped object but merely a light. It was "simply assumed that the lights were attached to the mystery airship. People sometimes added that they thought they saw a dark shape above the light which they took to be the body of the airship, but most witnesses seemed to indicate that this dark body, if they saw it at all, was vague and indistinct" (Cohen 1981, 186). The light itself was probably often the planet Venus. Venus is the brightest of all the planets in the night sky and is responsible for more UFO reports than any other single object (Hendry 1979). Sheaffer (cited in Cohen 1981) has calculated that Venus was at its brightest in March 1897. The mysterious airship sightings were most numerous just a few weeks later, in April 1897.

One of the major arguments put forward by proponents of the view that UFOs are extraterrestrial in origin is the large number of reports by reliable witnesses. However, such witnesses are just as liable as anyone else to the processes of constructive perception and thus to the attendant misidentification of known objects as UFOs. Klass (1981) described several instructive cases that demonstrate how badly wrong even honest, well-trained eyewitnesses can be when they are confronted with an ambiguous visual "something" and there is not sufficient sensory information to identify it. For example, who better to correctly identify objects in the sky than an experienced astronomer? One Arizona astronomer with "thousands of hours of experience in observing the night sky" (312) saw, on the night of October 5, 1973, a most "striking and unusual" UFO. He wrote a description of what he had seen and, being unable to identify it immediately, attempted to discover what it might have been. His investigation revealed that he had seen "the rocket-engine plume from a large air-force *Titan 2* intercontinental ballistic missile being launched from Vandenberg Air Force Base, California; *more than five hundred miles away*" (312). Not only had this experienced astronomer failed to recognize what he was seeing, he also found that his written report contained "several inaccuracies and inconsistencies" due to "the usual difficulties of perceiving and remembering an unusual, rapidly changing phenomenon. This report . . . is perhaps typical of the reliability of a UFO observation by a trained observer" (312).

Another case reported by Klass (1981) is illustrative. There were multiple independent witnesses, several UFOs appeared, and, in one instance, the presence of the UFOs seemed to terrify the dog of one of the witnesses. These strange events occurred on the night of March 3, 1968, in Columbus, Ohio. That night a science teacher walking her dog saw three small UFOs, which she observed through binoculars.

They were flying in formation, she reported, and seemed to be "under intelligent control." Her dog appeared to be "frightened to death" and lay on the ground whimpering. On the same night three witnesses in Nashville, Tennessee, reported seeing a huge metal saucer with many square windows glowing from the inside. The estimated altitude was about one thousand feet. The third report for this active evening came from Indiana, where a cigar-shaped UFO was seen that had a rocket-type exhaust and windows.

These reports seem to indicate an impressive phenomenon. What was going on in the sky that night? On that night a Russian *Zond 4* rocket reentered the atmosphere. It "reentered on a southwest-to-northeast trajectory that took it across Tennessee, Ohio, Pennsylvania, and southwestern New York State. As the rocket reentered it broke up into many luminous fragments as it traversed the atmosphere at very high speed" (Klass 1981, 314). Many other people saw this spectacular reentry that night. It is important to note that the UFO witnesses did not see the reentry in addition to the UFOs. In this case we see the power of constructive perception. The witnesses reported windows, an exhaust, and a huge saucer—all details that weren't there. These additions and embellishments were purely the creation of the witnesses' minds—not because they were crazy, drunk, or stupid, but because that is the way the human brain works. These witnesses did perceive what they said they did. This doesn't mean, however, that what they perceived was the same as what was really there. Note, too, how inaccurate was the estimate of the object's altitude made by the witness from Nashville, Tennessee. The witnesses estimated about one thousand feet while, in fact, the reentering rocket was miles high and scores of miles away. This type of gross inaccuracy frequently occurs when one sees a light in the sky with no background, as is the case at night. Under these circumstances, the many cues the brain uses to judge distance are not present, so no accurate basis for the judgment exists.

But what about the science teacher's dog, whimpering on the ground? This witness certainly attributed the dog's behavior to the three UFOs she saw through her binoculars. But if the objects she really saw were miles away, how can one explain the dog's behavior? Actually, it can be explained very simply: it was a cold night and, as the witness stated later, her dog hated the cold. Given the extra time no doubt taken by the witness to watch the UFOs, the dog was most probably cold and simply wanted to go home. UFO witnesses commonly attribute to the UFO almost anything that happens while they are observing a UFO, ignoring more prosaic explanations.

On December 9, 1965, a large fireball (aka meteor) was seen over much of northeastern Canada and the United States. It was well described as such at the time (Sheaffer 2016). It disintegrated in the atmosphere somewhere over Ontario. But that didn't stop scores of people from reporting that a UFO had actually landed somewhere very near them. This is understandable because it is extremely difficult, if not impossible, to judge the distance of a bright light in the night sky with no frames of reference. Thus, when the fireball disappeared behind a nearby building or forest, it was natural for the eyewitnesses to assume that the object had crashed just behind the buildings or trees.

In one location, Kecksburg, Pennsylvania, misperception of the December 9, 1965, meteor resulted in a claim of a crashed flying saucer. The Kecksburg event has been transformed, through sensationalistic reporting on TV, into a crashed saucer story (Young 1990–1991). The original witnesses turn out to have been a pair of children under ten years of age. But the September 19, 1990, broadcast of the mystery-mongering NBC program *Unsolved Mysteries* presented this as an event in which a flying saucer had crashed and the debris has been recovered by military personnel. Then in 2003 the Science Fiction Channel (now Syfy) broadcast a program touting Kecksburg as "The New Roswell." This is a classic example of how so-called documentaries on UFOs, as well as other paranormal topics, are designed to mislead and sensationalize rather than present the facts. The producers of both programs must have known going in that there was nothing in the slightest bit mysterious about the events of December 9, 1965. But they chose to lie to their viewers for better ratings. This tradition of misleading viewers is being continued by the numerous programs on UFOs (and other paranormal topics) on the History and Syfy channels.

Pilots are often thought to be among the most reliable witnesses when it comes to reporting things seen in the skies. On June 5, 1969, near St. Louis, Missouri, a UFO sighting occurred that involved pilot witnesses in three separate aircraft. A "squadron" of UFOs was reported, and two UFOs were seen on radar at the same time. A Federal Aviation Administration observer in one of the commercial aircraft involved estimated that the group of UFOs was only several hundred feet away from his aircraft and that they were going to strike the aircraft. He reported that the UFOs were colored like "burnished aluminum." They were said to be shaped like a "hydroplane." After this alarming incident was over, it was reported to the tower at St. Louis airport. The tower reported that there were two "unidentified targets" on radar. These targets were to the west of the first aircraft; the UFOs had been heading west. At this point a second commercial aircraft called to report that the UFOs had passed the aircraft moments previously and were still headed west. According to the pilot, the squadron of UFOs had "nearly collided with the aircraft," but avoided disaster at the last second by maneuvers that suggested they were "under intelligent control."

Can any nonextraordinary occurrence account for these simultaneous visual and radar reports? Klass's (1981) investigation revealed that the visual reports were due to a meteor and associated fireball "with a long, luminous tail of electrified air, followed by a smaller flaming fragment, also with a long tail, flying in trail behind" (315). The fireball was moving from east to west and was the source of a large number of reports from all over the Iowa-Illinois-Missouri area. Thus, the actual object was more than one hundred miles north of the reporting aircraft. Yet pilots in all three aircraft mistakenly perceived the object as extremely near—in two cases only hundreds of feet away.

But what about the radar report of two unidentified targets? Amusingly, it turns out that the targets were two of the aircraft that reported the UFOs in the first place. In 1969 airport radar did not automatically identify planes that appeared on the screen. The operator had to place a written note next to the screen identifying each "blip." Aircraft that were passing over rather than landing at a particular airport were not honored with such a written identification. None of the three aircraft that reported the UFOs was landing at St. Louis. Thus, when the first aircraft reported seeing the UFOs, the tower at St. Louis correctly reported that there were two "unidentified" targets in the area. There were—the two other aircraft that, moments later, also reported the UFOs. Modern airport radars now automatically identify all aircraft in their area by picking up a special signal from each aircraft's transponder. Klass (1984–1985) noted that, as radar technology became more sophisticated at correctly identifying aircraft and filtering out sources of error, the number of radar UFO reports has dropped dramatically. Of course, if UFOs were real, one would expect the increased sophistication and sensitivity of modern radar to *increase* the number of UFOs seen on radar. By the 1990s the continued advances in radar technology had reduced the number of UFOs seen on radar essentially to zero. They remain so today. This while, as will be seen in the next chapter, UFOs were claimed to be swooping down left and right and kidnapping people.

A frightening CE I took place on April 17, 1966, that illustrates the power of constructive perception. Two policemen chased a UFO at high speed for about sixty-five miles from eastern Ohio into western Pennsylvania, between 5 a.m. and 6 a.m. (Sheaffer 1981, chap. 19). This case is a classic demonstration of how a commonplace object, such as Venus in the dawn sky, can be misidentified as a UFO and endowed with the ability to move under intelligent control, creating the belief on the part of trained observers that they are witnessing something outside the realm of normal explanation. The most astonishing thing about this UFO, from the police officers' point of view, was that it appeared to be "teasing" them. When they first saw the object, it was stationary in the sky. When they got into their cruiser and slowly moved toward it, it slowly moved away. When they increased their speed, the UFO increased its speed. When they slowed down, it slowed down too, always keeping a constant distance from them. This is exactly the type of behavior that can convince UFO witnesses that the object is "under intelligent control"—it seems to be pacing them and responding to their own movements in a purposeful manner. This type of behavior is also characteristic of celestial bodies. The moon, for example, seems to pace a car as the car drives along a road at night. This happens because the moon is so far away that the movement of the car produces no change in the perceived position of the moon. Adult observers know that the moon is not really following the car, although children are often fooled by this illusion and may ask, "Why is the moon following us?" The situation is much the same for an object such as the planet Venus. Venus is much too far away to change its position perceptibly as an automobile moves. However, Venus lacks the obvious visual features that make the moon so easy to identify. Venus is little more than a very bright, steady light in the sky. Further, the lack of visual features on Venus—such as the patterns of craters that exist on the moon—means an observer has no way to correctly judge the size of the object. Such size judgments are especially difficult at dawn when the stars are no longer visible. Venus may then be the only object visible in the sky. This situation provides none of the usual cues that permit the brain to calculate how large and how far away an object is. The object could be something the size of an aircraft less than a mile away, or it could be something very large but much farther away. When the seeming motion of the object following the car is added, the illusion that it is an object the size of an aircraft and that it is deliberately "following" the observer can be very powerful.

This is exactly what happened in the case of the two policemen. During the entire hour-long chase, although the officers' attention was riveted to the sky and the UFO they were chasing, they never once saw Venus. Further, the position of the UFO that they reported was the same as the position that Venus occupied that morning. As dawn came on, Venus rose higher in the sky, and the UFO was reported to do the same. Finally, as the sun brightened, Venus faded from view—as did the UFO. A few moments later, the UFO was reported to reappear, but to have dropped about ten degrees in altitude. It then rose slowly. Sheaffer (1981) identifies this second object as a research balloon because the object's behavior as reported by the officers is just what one would expect of such a balloon. As the chase progressed, a second police car joined. Now, if two police cars really were chasing a large UFO only hundreds of feet above the road, one might reasonably expect that other independent witnesses would have seen the same object. In fact, the chase was twice slowed by early morning traffic. Yet none of the hundreds of people who saw the speeding police cars reported seeing the UFO they were chasing.

Although it might initially seem ridiculous to claim that an object like Venus could be mistaken for a large spacecraft that chased an automobile, this case clearly shows that such gross misidentification is possible. It also shows that people can and will attribute apparent movement to "intelligent control" when no such control exists.

Hendry (1979) provided even more examples of the unreliability of witnesses' reports—witnesses who are sane, sober individuals who have no reason to lie about what they saw—or, to be more precise, what they think they saw. Another source of false, but very impressive, UFO reports was advertising aircraft. These were small, usually single-engine, aircraft that carried beneath them an array of small lights that spelled out an advertising message. For obvious reasons, these aircraft flew only after dusk and at night. Such flights no longer take place due to the 9/11 attacks. If one saw such an aircraft from any vantage point other than directly underneath, it was difficult to read the message. On a dark night it might have been almost impossible to see the aircraft itself. One was left with an ambiguous visual stimulus—a bunch of disembodied lights in the sky—that was virtually guaranteed to result in UFO reports. Shown in figure 7.4 are drawings made by people who reported seeing UFOs. All these UFOs were positively identified by Hendry as advertising aircraft. In each case, the eyewitnesses who saw the flying saucer did not report seeing the advertising aircraft itself.

Look at the additions the witnesses have made to the known stimulus of a more or less random set of lights in the sky. All the objects are more or less saucer shaped, all have some sort of windows, many have some sort of device on top (propellers in one case!). In all cases the perception is more elaborate and detailed than was the actual stimulus. It must be emphasized that these witnesses were not consciously "making up" their reports. Rather, the knowledge they had about what a UFO, or "flying saucer," ought to look like greatly influenced the way their brains interpreted the ambiguous stimulus of lights in the night sky.

Hendry (1979, 85) reports another example of the power of constructive perception. The actual stimulus was, again, the planet Venus. The woman who reported the UFO described it as a "star," only much brighter. It was positioned low in the southwest sky, starting around seven o'clock in the evening on January 30, 1976—exactly where Venus was located at that time. She did not see Venus in addition to this "object." She then watched the light descend gradually to the horizon during an hour's period of time, which is exactly what Venus would do. This setting motion was perceived by her as being "jerky"; her husband thought that it was only a star, but she encouraged him to perceive the "jerky" descent, too, which got him excited. After staring at it for a sufficiently long time, the woman became convinced that she was looking at the illuminated window of a UFO and that she could see the round heads of the occupants inside, heads with silvery-colored faces. She then proceeded to see this apparition in the same place every night for successive nights. Yes, she was told that it was Venus. Her reply: "You are talking to a woman fifty-four years old. I know what stars look like."

People's conviction that they have seen a real flying saucer, when they've seen nothing of the kind, can be very convincing to others. No one is so likely to be believed as someone who truly believes what they are saying. Such belief sometimes pushes believers to absurd lengths to maintain their beliefs. This effect is seen in the series of UFO sightings in Westchester County, New York, from early 1983 through late 1984. The sighting reports were impressive, as is often the case. People who were pillars of the local communities reported seeing UFOs the size of a football field with multicolored lights. These UFOs could not have been aircraft since, according to the reports of numerous witnesses, they were too big, made no sound, hovered for minutes at a time in one spot, made perfect right-angle turns in the air, and winked in and out of existence, first appearing at one place, then disappearing, only to reappear suddenly, moments later, somewhere else. The late J. Allen Hynek, who was director of the Center for UFO Studies, said in the

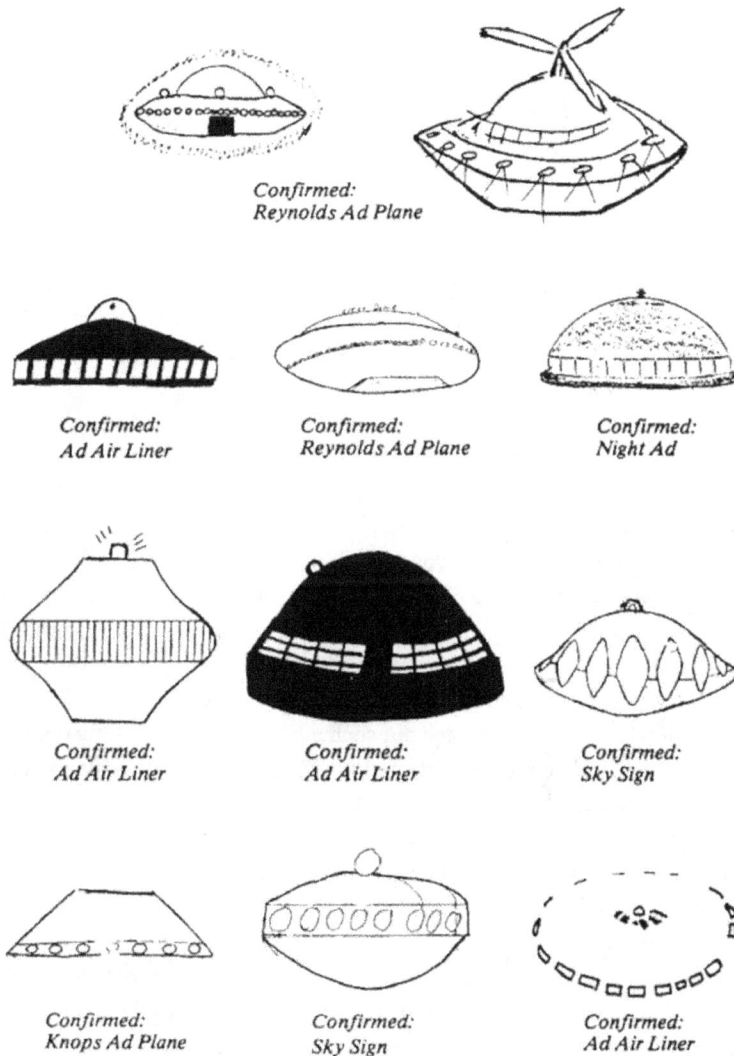

Figure 7.4. Drawings of UFOs by witnesses. All these sightings were actually due to misperceptions of advertising aircraft. From Hendry (1979)

center's publication, *International UFO Reporter*, that these sightings were among the most impressive in the history of UFO reports (Hynek, Imbrogno, and Pratt 1987). He felt there was no possible way to "explain away" these sightings by scores of witnesses. The reports did have a prosaic explanation: they were all a hoax. A group of private pilots flying from a small airport in Stormville, New York (in the mid–Hudson River Valley) had been flying in formation at night. They would fly along with all their lights out and then, on cue, turn on both the red and green wing lights and the bright white landing light. They flew in a boomerang formation, and many of the witnesses reported that the UFO had a boomerang shape. The appearing-disappearing trick was easy to pull off too. When all the lights were turned off at once, the UFO vanished. Thirty seconds later, after the planes had flown about one mile, the lights were all turned back on at once, so the UFO appeared to have moved from one spot to another in the twinkle of an eye.

The reports of the UFO hovering motionless for minutes were based, as the reader might by now expect, on the lack of cues available to the witnesses to tell them how far away the planes were. All the witnesses saw were lights in the night sky. In the absence of any other cues, the brain uses the size of the actual retinal image to judge movement and distance. Small lights on aircraft don't significantly change retinal image size as the plane moves toward or away from the eye. Thus, the perception is of unchanged distance, even though the planes are moving. As far as the lack of noise is concerned, many modern private aircraft are quiet and are only heard when directly overhead. They may not be heard even when overhead if they are above one thousand feet, depending on the wind conditions and the presence of other noises on the ground.

The pilots at Stormville Airport had a good time with their hoax. That it was a hoax was revealed by the local paper (Walzer 1984) and in a long investigative article in the November 1984 issue of *Discover* magazine (Garelik 1984). The response of several of the local UFO buffs was interesting. Not willing to admit they were fooled, they devised a bizarre and elaborate conspiracy theory to explain what happened: the night-flying pilots were put up to their tricks by the occupants of *real UFOs* who wanted the hoax to cover up the existence of their activities and to obscure the *real* sightings!

Although I lived and worked in Westchester County, New York, during the time of the Stormville hoax, I never had the pleasure of seeing the UFO myself. However, the power of constructive perception was brought home to me several years ago when I saw a giant thirty-foot-tall silver sparkling Christmas tree that didn't exist. I'd moved north to Putnam County, New York, and lived in a condo in a small development built charmingly out in the woods. One cold December night I was sitting at home reading and chanced to look out through the tall glass doors to the balcony that faces into the miles of forest behind my unit. The land slopes up gently to a ridge line about a third of a mile away. There was nothing back there except forest and a long-abandoned apple orchard. Yet I saw something odd shining through the forest. I looked at it and realized it was a very, very large silver Christmas tree that had been set up at the top of the ridge. I was baffled as to why (and how) anyone would have put such a tree there. So I got my boots (there was about a foot of snow on the ground) and coat on and started walking through the forest to get a better look. As I got closer to the tree it became clearer—it was very large, all in silver, and shimmering. It was quite beautiful. And it seemed very real. Then, suddenly, just as I was about to cross a small dry stream bed, I realized what was really there. It was the full moon, rising over the ridge line and shining through the trees at the top of the ridge. My brain had created a compelling perception of a complex object, a Christmas tree, from a much simpler set of inputs.

Simpson (1979–1980) described a controlled UFO hoax set up to determine just how distorted witnesses' reports of a UFO can become. The hoax was carried out on Cradle Hill in Warminster, England, on the night of March 28, 1970. Simpson describes the stimulus for the hoax:

> At 11 P.M. a 12-volt high-intensity purple spotlamp was directed from a neighboring hill toward a group of about 30 sky-watchers on Cradle Hill, three-quarters of a mile away. The lamp was switched on for 5, and then 25, seconds, with a 5-second pause between. During the second "on" period, a bogus magnetic field sensor, operated among the skywatchers by a colleague, sounded its alarm buzzer, apparently indicating the presence of a strong magnetic field. (UFO folklore states that strong magnetic fields are a characteristic of UFOs, so this sensor was not an unusual sight.) In practice, the alarm was simply synchronized to sound while the distant spotlamp was on. The "strangeness" of the purple light was thereby enhanced. (33)

One important aspect of this hoax was the production of fake photographs of the UFO. Four exposures were produced, but two had been taken months previously and doctored to show UFOs that did not look at all like the "UFO" produced by the purple lamp. The UFO in these two photos was much more saucer shaped. It was in a different position in each of the two photos, indicating movement. In one photo it was above the hill: in the other, below it. Another point about the first two photos is that, because they were taken months before the actual hoax, they showed a specific pattern of streetlights along a road running at the base of the hill. Due to repairs on some of the lights, that pattern changed between the time these photos were taken and the night of the hoax. Two additional photographs were taken on the night of the hoax, after the sighting. They did not show any UFO, but they did show the then current pattern of streetlights. This difference in the pattern of the streetlights was an obvious clue to the fake nature of the photographs. The important question was whether anyone would spot it.

The film was given to *Flying Saucer Review*, then a major international UFO magazine. *Flying Saucer Review* stated that the negatives had proven "genuine beyond all doubt" (Simpson 1979–1980, 34). The photographs were submitted to several experts, who declared them genuine. Consider the opinion of Pierre Guerin, director of research at the Astrophysical Institute of the French National Center for Scientific Research: "In my opinion there is no question of the object photographed being in any possible way the result of faking" (Guerin 1970, 6). Guerin did spend some effort to explain why the UFO in the photographs was so different in appearance from the UFO that was seen. Impressive scientific jargon abounds in his statement: "The object photographed was emitting ultraviolet light, which the eye does not see. Around the object, however, a ruby-red halo, probably of monochromatic color and doubtless due to some phenomenon of air ionisation, was visible only to the eye and in actual fact made no impression on the film" (6). Now, if someone with the title of director of research at an astrophysical institute told you something in an area seemingly related to astrophysics, it would be natural to believe him. But in this case an expert was misled by a rather obvious hoax. He failed to spot the clues in the photographs and went on to a grandiose pseudoscientific explanation of a phenomenon that never really existed in the first place. This sort of carelessness is, it turns out, a hallmark of investigations by UFO proponents, a point we will return to later. The photographs contained yet another clue to the fact that they were faked. The first two photos were shot at a 10 percent greater magnification than the second two, yet a land surveyor who attempted to determine the position of the UFO in the photos failed to notice this large discrepancy (Simpson 1979–1980).

How do the witnesses' reports of the UFO that was seen compare to the actual stimulus? Great differences show up between what actually took place and what the witnesses reported. These differences cover almost every aspect of the situation. The actual light was stationed on top of the nearby hill. The witnesses' reports had the light twenty degrees above the hill, in the air. The actual light was purple, but reports said it was purple and crimson. The light was stationary, but reports indicated that it moved slowly to the right and lost altitude. The light was said to dim considerably during the movement, a dimming that lasted twenty to thirty seconds. When it stopped moving, it increased in intensity. Ten to twenty seconds later, the UFO disappeared. According to the witnesses, the total duration of the sighting was one to one-and-a-half minutes (Ben 1970). In actuality, the time from the first onset of the light to its final disappearance was thirty-five seconds. In addition, the witnesses failed to note that the light went out for five seconds. They only reported that it "dimmed." The similarity to the autokinetic illusion here is obvious. Aside from the partially correct report of the light's color, nothing else in the witnesses' reports was accurate. This is especially important when one recalls that these were not random witnesses taken by surprise. They were UFO buffs expecting—and prepared for—a UFO sighting. It is also relevant that all the inaccuracies in the eyewitnesses' reports functioned to make the sighting more dramatic than the stimulus actually was.

The 1970 Warminster hoax was not the only one engineered to examine how people misperceived lights in the sky. In 1972, two years after the original Warminster hoax, UFO aficionados believed that there would be a landing of a UFO there. In the book *How UFOs Conquered the World*, Clarke (2015) describes, for the first time, a second Warminster hoax. Late at night when there were many UFO watchers in attendance, along with a BBC film crew, hoaxers sent two balloons into the air with two small lightbulbs powered by two small batteries. Each bulb had one side painted out so that, as the bulbs moved in the breeze, they would appear to flicker on and off. In addition, two photo flash bulbs (remember those?) were also attached to the balloons and set to flash two minutes after the balloons were released.

The results were spectacular and amusing. The UFO watchers were convinced that they had seen visitors from outer space. One man, Rex Dutta, a leading UFOlogist, believed that "the UFO occupants were 'appealing mind to mind to intelligent people . . . the intense brightness which came [from the flash bulbs] and the alternation was random yet significant'" (Clarke 2015, 89). The hoaxers later revealed the hoax on the BBC news program *Nationwide*. But the true believers soldiered on, arguing that the story of the hoax was itself a hoax, designed to cover up a real sighting.

UFO proponents claim that governments have super-secret information that proves UFOs are real and extraterrestrial. If true, this would mean that these governments have sophisticated plans to deal with flying saucers should they crash on Earth. Further, it is believed that the government would attempt to censor reporting of any crash. Such claims form the heart of stories of crashed saucers at places like Roswell. A hoax was mounted in 1967 to see if this was true. Six objects designed to look like alien spacecraft were constructed. They were:

> 54 inches long and 30 inches wide. Their shells were moulded from fiberglass and were given a graphite sheen. Each contained a mini loudspeaker powered by batteries. These had been carefully prepared to emit an unearthly bleeping noise when disturbed. The team filled the interiors of their interplanetary craft with a foul-smelling concoction of flour and water that was boiled to make it resemble an alien substance. (Clarke 2015, 166)

Six of these devises were deposited across southern England on the night of September 3–4.

The response of the authorities was nothing like what would be expected if there were well-organized plans in place to deal with alien spaceship crashes:

> Early on 4 September 1967 the police and RAF were flooded with calls from members of the public reporting the discovery of six landed "flying saucers" across southern England. For the twelve hours that followed, the British Army's southern command, along with bomb disposal units, RAF helicopters and four police forces, were drawn into the hoax. (Clarke 2015, 166)

An officer who was then with the Ministry of Defense secret air intelligence branch, that would have presumably been well in the know about any secret alien contacts and plans for dealing with crashes, said that the reaction at the ministry was "Shit. What shall we do?" "The farce that followed . . . was crowned by a bureaucratic dispute over which department [of the Ministry of Defense] was responsible for the requisition of a staff car" (Clarke 2015, 167).

The several cases described above are only a fraction of the numerous cases in which careful investigation has resulted in straightforward natural explanations for even very impressive-sounding UFO reports. Details of additional cases can be found in Hendry (1979), Klass (1974, 1983), Sheaffer (1981), Oberg (1982), and Menzel and Taves (1977). All these cases make clear the unreliability of eyewitness reports. In almost every case, the witnesses' reports differed substantially from the actual stimulus, but in only a very few cases were the witnesses willfully lying. Their knowledge about what UFOs "ought" to look like, the effects of visual illusions, and of course constructive perception influenced their reports.

UFO reports have certainly not gone away in the years since the classic cases described above took place. They are some of the most thoroughly investigated and thus most informative about how unreliable eyewitness reports can be. Such eyewitness sightings continue. MUFON, the Mutual UFO Network, a loosely organized volunteer network that tracks and tries to investigate UFO sightings, reported over 5,700 UFO sightings in a yearlong period ending July 23, 2020. These modern reports have not yielded any better evidence for the extraterrestrial hypothesis than the earlier well-investigated cases. As science writer Sharon Hill (2013b) put it, "The UFO research field is having a bit of a crisis these days. Reports come in by the hundreds. There are not enough people to investigate them. Yet decades of UFO research by private and military organizations have resulted in disappointment for those who surely thought there was something out there to reveal."

As said before, it emerges from a study of these explained cases that UFO organizations do a terrible job of investigating UFO reports. They are likely to naively accept witnesses' reports at face value and to fail to look carefully for possible natural explanations. The prevailing attitude assumes that witnesses' reports accurately reflect what was actually present, so there is no need to look for an explanation other than that of an extraterrestrial spacecraft. Thus, time and time again, impressive-sounding UFO reports are "investigated" by one or more of the major UFO organizations, declared to be genuine and verified, and highly touted in UFO publications, the popular press, and sensationalistic TV programs. Then, if a careful investigation is done and the case is shown to have been due to some natural phenomenon or is revealed as a hoax, the results of that investigation almost never appear in the venues that presented the sensational false claims when the sighting was first stated to be "genuine."

Proponents of extraterrestrial UFOs reply to this sort of criticism by claiming that although many, even a great majority, of UFO sightings are due to some type of natural or man-made phenomenon, there is an "irreducible minimum" number of sightings that skeptics cannot explain away. This is quite true—and a totally unconvincing argument. There will always be sightings that can never be attributed with certainty to any specific natural or man-made phenomenon, simply because the information needed to find the correct explanation is no longer available. Hendry (1979, 8) provided an excellent example here. As editor of the *International UFO Reporter*, published by the Center for UFO Studies, he reported a sighting that took place in Nevada in 1977. In trying to track down an explanation he was "by sheer luck . . . put in touch with the EPA [Environmental Protection Agency]." The EPA had sent aloft a balloon that was the source of the sighting. Had Hendry not had the good fortune to make contact with the EPA, that particular sighting would probably never have been explained. It would have become one of the "irreducible minimum" that the supporters of the extraterrestrial hypothesis claim proves their position.

Eyewitness reports of UFOs are inadequate as support for the extraterrestrial hypothesis, although the prosaic "lights in the sky" type of sighting will probably always be with us. A good example comes from my own Putnam County, New York. In February 2012 strange lights seen in the skies around Carmel, New York, generated a spate of UFO reports. Happily, the cause was rapidly tracked down. The strange lights in the sky were Chinese lanterns that had been sent aloft as part of a memorial service for a gentleman who had been killed in a traffic accident the previous year. These lanterns can make very dramatic flying saucer reports. Had the memorial program not been identified as the source of the reports, the "Carmel UFOs" might well have become an unexplained case that the credulous would cite as evidence for the reality of extraterrestrial visitation. This is the classic logical fallacy of the "argument from ignorance." In other words, the lack of an ironclad explanation permits one to assert that any explanation they make up is the correct one. Many times, there is simply no way to know exactly what caused mysterious lights in the sky—or shapes in the water. This does not give license to claim that the lack of a rational explanation means that some extraordinary explanation is correct.

UFOs II
Photographs, Physical Evidence, and Abductions

If eyewitness reports are unconvincing evidence for the reality of UFOs as extraterrestrial visitors, some sort of physical evidence could certainly settle the case. If, as UFO proponents claim, Earth is being visited frequently by extraterrestrials, physical evidence in some form or another should exist. This chapter examines the status of the claims that such physical evidence has been found. Also examined are UFO photos and reports of humans being abducted by UFO occupants.

PHOTOGRAPHIC EVIDENCE

Authenticated, clear photographs of a UFO would be excellent evidence for UFOs as something other than hoaxes and perceptual constructions. UFO photographs certainly abound; the question is whether the photos are genuine. Even before the advent of digital image manipulation techniques such as Photoshop, UFO photographs were extraordinarily easy to fake with old-fashioned double exposures and other types of trick photography. Several simple but impressive fake UFO photos produced by Robert Sheaffer (Sheaffer 1981, 1998b) are shown in figure 8.1. Most people don't realize how simple trick photography was even in the nineteenth century and will accept photos such as those shown here as convincing evidence. As was noted in the case of the controlled UFO hoax described in chapter 7, UFO organizations are notoriously poor at spotting hoaxes, being inclined to accept statements that photos are genuine with little further investigation. Like the highly publicized UFO sightings that turn out to be explainable upon careful investigation, we will see in this section that highly publicized UFO photos said to prove the reality of the phenomenon turn out to be fakes when examined with a little care. Just as investigations of psychics need a professional magician to be included, investigations of UFO photos and films need a professional photographer with expertise in trick photography to be included. Such a person will be much more able than the average photographer to spot tricks and deceptions.

Most UFO photos, whether from film cameras or cell phones, show nothing more than indistinct blobs of light. Many such blobs appear only when the film is developed, although the photographer didn't see any UFOs when the pictures were taken. Such blobs are defects in the film, lens flares, or by-products of film development. The numerous UFO pictures of vague "strange lights in the sky" turn out to be photos of aircraft, seagulls, or balloons. Under certain viewing conditions, such familiar objects lose their distinctive and familiar features and appear "mysterious," often resulting in a UFO report and photographs. Night photos of blobs of light can easily be caused by aircraft, the planet Venus, and other such objects (Sheaffer 1981; Menzel and Taves 1977). To be of value, a UFO picture should show at least some structure to the UFO and should have enough background to permit one to judge the relative size of the UFO, its distance from other objects in the picture, and—especially if successive photos are obtained—its speed and direction.

The period of UFO photography before digital cameras became popular is filled with cases of photos once touted as genuine and convincing only to be discredited when examined carefully. Three case histories emphasize this point.

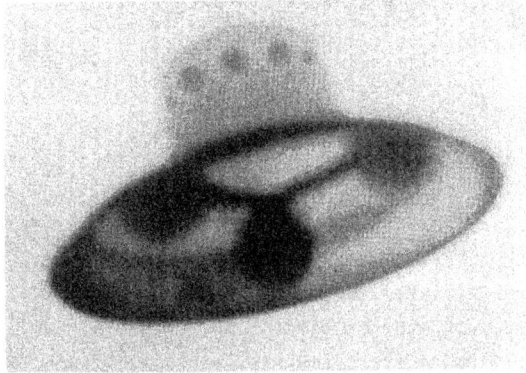

Figure 8.1. Impressive-looking, but faked, UFO photos. From R. Sheaffer, *The UFO Verdict: Examining the Evidence* (Amherst, NY: Prometheus Books, 1981)

Figure 8.2. The fake Brazil UFO photo. Photo taken from naval training vessel *Almirante Saldanha*, 1958, Trindade Island, Brazil

One famous early UFO photo is reproduced in figure 8.2. It is widely cited by pro-UFO groups as excellent evidence for UFOs. It would be—if it were genuine. But this photograph is a fake. The photo was allegedly taken from a Brazilian naval training ship in January 1958. The photographed UFO was said to be seen by many of the vessel's crew. The photographer was one Almiro Barauna, who, by an amazing coincidence, was a trick photographer who had previously made fake UFO photos to illustrate an article titled "A Flying Saucer Haunted Me at Home" (Sheaffer 1981). The crew of the vessel, upon investigation, said they had not seen the photographed object. Much was made of the fact that the film was developed aboard the ship and under supervision, but this would not have prevented a double exposure in which the UFO image was photographed before boarding the ship, the film rewound, and the terrain photographed from the ship.

A set of UFO photos taken in August 1965 by Rex Heflin in Santa Ana, California, follows the pattern of seeming impressive at first but falling apart upon investigation. One is shown in figure 8.3. The photos were allegedly taken through the window of Heflin's truck. At first, he reported shooting only three photos, but several weeks later a fourth turned up. His explanation was that three photos were "enough for one day" (Sheaffer 1981, 57). This is very suspicious behavior and a strong hint of a hoax. After all, if four photos were taken originally, there would be no reason not to show them all when making the report. Other aspects of this case were also suspicious. The photos were taken with a Polaroid camera, but the original prints disappeared. Heflin claimed that they were taken away by men from the North American Air Defense Command (NORAD) two days after he reported the sighting. NORAD denied sending any investigators to take the photographs, and Heflin did not ask for a receipt for photographs that, if genuine, would be among the most important in the history of science. Further, the road with cars on it seen in the photograph is the Santa Ana Freeway—hardly a deserted stretch. Yet no one else reported seeing this UFO, which, if the photographs were genuine, was flying and hovering in plain view almost directly over the road.

Figure 8.3. One of the fake Heflin UFO photos. Photo by Rex Heflin, 1965 (https://www.telegraph.co.uk/news/picturegalleries/howaboutthat/3447508/UFO-sightings-140-years-of-UFO-pictures.html)

One UFO organization, Ground Saucer Watch (GSW), did a good technical investigation and branded the Heflin photos a deliberate hoax, based on computer enhancement of the photos (Sheaffer 1981). The enhancement of a set of excellent duplicate prints revealed that "in the first of the three UFO photos, which shows the object at its minimum distance from the camera, the object is not in focus, as it is in the other two. Distant objects, however, are in focus in all three. This strongly suggests that the object was small and extremely close to the camera" (57). The enhancement also showed similar findings for two other photos. Finally, and most damningly, the enhancement showed traces of a very thin string from which the UFO is hanging. Once again, careful investigation showed that what once was accepted as genuine UFO photographs were fakes. This case showed the importance of considering all available evidence before reaching a decision about the genuineness of alleged UFO photos. The suspicious behavior of the photographer and the lack of confirming sightings—which should have been present in abundance if the UFO was really there—both point to a hoax.

Another early famous and, according to UFO proponents, compelling piece of photographic evidence for UFOs was a set of photographs taken in McMinnville, Oregon, on May 11, 1950, by members of the Trent family. One of the two photos is shown in figure 8.4. Hall (1964, 88) calls the Trent photos "two of the clearest UFO photographs on record." Before considering the photographs themselves, the behavior of the Trents in regard to the photos is enough to arouse considerable suspicion. The roll of film with the two UFO photographs was not developed immediately. Rather, the Trents waited until the few remaining exposures had been used up to develop the roll. In addition, Sheaffer (1981) reports that the precious negatives were left lying around and that one interviewer found them "on the floor under the davenport where the Trent children had been playing with them" (60). There were other inconsistencies in the Trents' story of how the photos were taken. The Trents were *repeaters*—people who claim to have sighted UFOs on several occasions. Mrs. Trent in particular claimed to have seen UFOs several times before the photos were taken and several times since. Even UFO proponents are generally suspicious of photos taken by such

Figure 8.4. One of the fake Trent UFO photos. Photo by Paul Trent, 1950, McMinnville, Oregon (https://commons
.wikimedia.org/wiki/File:Trent1_600dpi.jpg)

repeaters, and NICAP usually refused to accept any such photos as genuine. On behavioral grounds alone, the Trent photos must be viewed as a probable hoax.

An analysis of the Trent photos themselves clinches the case as a hoax. According to the Trents' story, the photos were taken around 8 p.m. The pattern of light and shadow in the photographs shows they were really taken at about 7:30 a.m. Further, the UFO is under the same spot in the telephone wires at the top of both pictures, in spite of the fact that the camera has been moved from one picture to the next. As the camera moved away from these wires, the wires and the UFO shrank in size by about the same amount. This is just the result one would obtain if one took a photograph of a small model hung from the wires. The Trent photos are about the clearest early photos known and stood, at the time, as good photographic evidence for UFOs. This merely showed, however, the extremely poor quality of the classical photographic evidence. After more than forty years since the 1947 sightings by Kenneth Arnold and thousands of subsequent sightings, by the 1980s the best photographic evidence consisted of a few grainy shots taken by trick photographers or people who claimed to have had repeated UFO experiences.

In the late 1980s a seemingly spectacular set of UFO photos appeared from the town of Gulf Breeze, Florida. These showed a flying saucer with much visible detail. That these photos were hoaxes was strongly suspected at the time. This suspicion was confirmed a few years later when the house that had belonged to the photographer was being renovated by new owners. Hidden away behind a partition was a model that looked just like the saucer in the photos! (See Sheaffer 1998b, 100ff., for more details on this case.)

Even before cell phones, excellent photographs existed of rare events. The photos of the airline crashes in Chicago in 1979 and San Diego in 1978 clearly show airliners falling from the sky—an extremely rare event, but the photos are sharp and clear and show every horrible detail. Film UFO photographs that show anything other than vague shapes or blobs of light are fakes. Those showing vague shapes and blobs of light are evidence of nothing. If UFOs were really some sort of extraterrestrial craft, there should have been quality pictures of them by the 1990s. But there weren't.

Cell phone cameras have become ubiquitous—everyone has one. There are billions more people carrying cameras around with them every waking minute than carried film cameras twenty years ago. So where are all the cell phone UFO pictures? If UFOs are flying around with the frequency that proponents claim, there should be piles of good nonfaked UFO cell phone photos. There are not, but the fakes have certainly not gone away. As technology marches on, it has become increasingly easy to produce fake UFO pictures and videos on cell phones and related devices. Several apps are available that are designed specifically to allow the addition of UFO images to one's videos. At this point it is important to consider what would constitute a believable cell phone UFO photo (or film). Given the ease with which technology can be used to fake such things, expert analyses of the relevant data files would be, of course, an extremely important step in authenticating any claimed photos. But equally important would be the nature of the non-UFO images in the pictures. Imagine a highly realistic film allegedly showing a UFO, or group of UFOs, over some city or town. The photographer saw these things in the sky and was excited enough to take the pictures. What are the other people in the pictures doing? If the UFOs had been there, the other people should be looking at them, pointing and generally acting as any of us would if we see something so interesting in the sky, including taking their own pictures. But if no one other than the photographer is paying any attention to the UFOs, they probably weren't there in the first place. Similarly, if the photos show UFOs over a populated area but there are no other reports, no other witnesses, the photos are likely hoaxes or misidentifications. Remember the Carmel, New York, 2012 UFO sightings referred to earlier (chapter 7). The Chinese lanterns in that case generated numerous reports from many different people, as well as cell phone photos.

A good case in point here is a UFO film from 2011 seeming to show a UFO mother ship and several small UFOs over London. These were posted anonymously online. In this case the film starts by showing a group of people who really are looking up into the sky, followed by images of the UFO formation in action. But the film was the first, and only, evidence for this event. There were no independent reports from all of London of what would have been an impressive UFO appearance had it actually taken place.

To the skeptic, this impressive lack of photographic evidence points to one conclusion—UFOs don't exist.

UFO proponents, however, interpret the situation differently. Admitting that the lack of photographic evidence is most odd, Hynek and Vallee (1975) concluded that UFOs are a "jealous phenomenon" that doesn't *want* to be photographed. Further, UFOs somehow know when someone has a camera and selectively appear only to those who have left their Nikons or cell phones at home. It should be obvious that this is yet another example of a nonfalsifiable hypothesis. Said hypothesis becomes even harder to accept given the proliferation of cell phones with cameras over that past twenty years (see Randall Munroe's comic "Settled": https://xkcd.com/1235/).

Astronaut and Military Pilot Sightings and Photos

It is difficult to think of a more highly trained and credible potential UFO witness than an astronaut. UFOs seen in space would be even more impressive than ground sightings since several possible sources of misidentification are not found in space (e.g., aircraft and weather balloons). The UFO literature is replete with alleged astronaut UFO sightings and alleged pictures of UFOs taken by astronauts. Nowhere else in the UFO literature, however, does one find such a high level of outright fraud and deception, not on the astronauts' part, but on the part of those who have knowingly distorted astronauts' reports and doctored official pictures. Oberg (1977b, 1978–1979a, 1982) conducted extensive research on the astronaut UFO sightings and pictures and concluded that "the compelling conclusion of the first serious analysis of all the astronaut UFO reports is that every one of them is false. Those that originated from the astronauts themselves were distorted in the UFO press, even as ordinary explanations became obvious" (Oberg 1977a, 7). Several representative astronaut sightings and photos will be described here. The interested reader should consult Oberg's work for further details and explanations for the other sightings.

Hynek and Vallee (1975, 64) reprint a list of astronaut UFO sightings compiled by UFO researcher Jim Fawcett. The following report is of a sighting said to have taken place during the *Gemini 12* mission in November 1966. "Jim Lovell and Edwin Aldrin saw four UFOs linked in a row. Both spacemen said the objects were not stars." The objects certainly weren't stars, but that doesn't mean they were UFOs or flying saucers. Oberg (1977a) traced this alleged sighting and found the original debriefing document that gave the entire report of this event. The following quotation is from the document titled "GT-12 Astronaut Debriefing" and occurs on pages K/3, 4: "During the last EVA we discarded, in addition to the ELSE [life support system], three bags. About 2, maybe 3 or possibly 4 orbits later at sunrise condition, we looked out again and saw 4 objects lined up in a row and they weren't stars I know. They must have been these same things we tossed overboard." By selectively eliminating the astronauts' own explanation for what they saw, Fawcett, as well as Hynek and Vallee, misled their readers into thinking that the sighting is more mysterious than it was.

Oberg (1977a) gave another example of the unreliability of those who manufacture astronaut UFO sightings. This sighting is said to have taken place during the *Mercury 7* mission of May 1962 and to have resulted in a photograph. "Scott Carpenter reported that he had what looked like a good shot of a saucer," we are told, and the photograph was "of a classical saucer-shaped UFO with a dome that followed his capsule" (23). Oberg comments, "In fact, the photographs show an entirely ordinary object: a space balloon ejected from the capsule for tracking practice. The balloon did not inflate but spun in a limp oblong sack. The flight schedule and the voice transmissions confirm this unexciting explanation" (23). Again, the sensational reports of astronaut UFO sightings and photos turn out to be the product of deliberate deceit on the part of some UFO proponents.

Usually, such deceit was limited to small-circulation UFO magazines and books published by UFO enthusiasts who don't bother to check their facts. However, one forged astronaut UFO photo made its way into a then major American science magazine. The magazine was *Science Digest*, now defunct, published by the Hearst Corporation. The phony photograph appeared in an article alleging a massive UFO cover-up by the government (Berlinger 1977). As a photograph, it doesn't show much—just a view of the northern hemisphere taken from *Apollo 11* during its July 1969 mission. At the top of the picture, above the planet, is a small white blob that is described as an "unidentified object." The picture is said to have been obtained from the National Aeronautics and Space Administration (NASA) and to be evidence of an official UFO cover-up because current prints of the same shot obtained from NASA do not show the white blob. They do show a piece of insulation debris in another location, but this piece of insulation does not appear in the *Science Digest* photo. *Science Digest* editor Daniel Button believed the article caused NASA to retouch the photos. He said, "My suspicion is right now that NASA has changed its story and altered its negatives and prints" (Oberg and Sheaffer 1977–1978, 44). There is one major problem with this theory: NASA prints of this shot obtained well *before* the *Science Digest* article don't show the white blob either. They do show the piece of debris. Has NASA somehow been able to locate and change every print of this shot ever released? What an effective cover-up! With the advent of the space shuttles and the international space station, UFO proponents occasionally claim that shuttle or station crew have seen or interacted with UFOs. The claims are as bogus as were those that the early astronauts saw flying saucers.

After years of essentially no new reports of interesting UFO photos, films, or videos, what appeared to be dramatic UFO videos, taken by military aircraft, began to come to light in the early twenty-first century. In November 2014 the crew of a Chilean navy helicopter used an infrared camera to film a mysterious object. The Chilean authorities undertook an extensive investigation of what the object could be. The investigation called on experts from numerous fields, including astronomy, engineering, psychology, and meteorology. After two years of effort, the investigation was unable to identify the object, and a true-blue UFO was born.

The Chilean video and failed investigation became public in an article by Leslie Kean in the *Huffington Post* on January 5, 2017. Kean is a "dedicated UFO promoter" who once argued that a "video of what was in fact a fly buzzing around" was "great proof of high-performance UFOs" (Sheaffer 2019, 14). By January 11, just six days later, the no-longer-so-mysterious object had been identified by an online group of amateur investigators using public online sources that the Chilean investigators could have used to solve the mystery, had they known about them (West 2017).

When he first saw the Chilean video, Mike West, the leader of the online investigators, thought that the image resembled commercial jet contrails he had seen from his home east of San Francisco. So he put the puzzle of identifying the Chilean object to the subreddit group Skydentify, which is described, not surprisingly, as "dedicated to identifying objects in the sky." The group started with what was known about the object, including the date, time, and place of the sighting and the orientation of the object relative to the helicopter. They then used the ADS-B system, an online source that tracks and keeps records of most commercial, military, and civilian flights all over the world, to see if there were any aircraft in the place and at the time of the reported object. And there was—Iberia Airlines flight 6830, Santiago to Madrid, was in the same place and at the same time as the UFO. West (2017) describes several other instances where crowdsourcing a UFO mystery led to positive identification.

How could the original, highly professional investigators have missed such an obvious solution to the puzzle? They made unwarranted assumptions. For example, since the object didn't appear on the helicopter's radar, they assumed that it couldn't be a normal aircraft since aircraft do appear on radar. But not on all radar. The radar in the helicopter had a short range, and the plane was too far away to register on its radar.

Supposed videos of UFO encounters by U.S. military aircraft in 2004 came to light in 2017. The otherwise respectable *New York Times* ran a story in the December 16, 2017, edition on mysterious "glowing auras" that came to be known as the Tic Tac UFO. The article, titled "Glowing Auras and 'Black Money': The Pentagon's Mysterious U.F.O. Program" (Cooper, Blumenthal, and Kean 2017), also revealed the existence of a supposedly secret military program to investigate UFOs.

Sheaffer (2019) investigated the origins of the Tic Tac UFO sightings. As usual, all is not what it is claimed to be by the popular media. The video images from 2004 do show something that is not identified and is in the air, so in the most trivial sense it is a UFO. But it is a gigantic leap from this to the idea that the object is an extraterrestrial spacecraft. Sheaffer reported that the system that generated the videos, known as ATFLIR, was at the time a brand-new system that used new infrared imaging technology. As anyone who has tried to install even relatively simple new software or hardware is well aware, there are almost always glitches when a new system is first installed. It takes some time and experience to get the system running properly. When the new ATFLIR system was first put into use on Navy F/A-18 jets in 2004, numerous anomalous objects, aka UFOs, were seen, including the Tic Tac object. A navy pilot was dispatched to the location of the Tic Tac sighting to see if anything was actually there. He saw nothing unusual in the air and had no radar contacts in the area. After time passed and there was more experience with the ATFLIR system, the sightings of anomalous objects vanished, suggesting that the Tic Tac object wasn't a real object but simply the result of a system glitch. Glitches, not being real objects, don't have to behave like real objects. Thus arguments by UFO proponents of the Tic Tac object doing un-object-like things such as "instantaneous acceleration" are more consistent with the glitch hypothesis than a mysterious physical object not obeying the basic laws of physics. About ten years after the Tic Tac UFO appeared, Navy "Carrier Air Wing One got its radar upgrade, and soon they, too, were reporting UFOs galore" (Sheaffer 2019, 16). But as time passed such reports of anomalous signals also faded away.

On May 26, 2019, the *New York Times* published another story by Cooper, Blumenthal, and Kean claiming that "strange objects" had "appeared almost daily" between "the summer of 2014 and March 2015." These new objects were said to have been seen by navy pilots, one of whom the story quoted as saying that the objects would "be out there all day." Sheaffer (2019, 14) properly wondered why, in the face of mysterious objects that stayed around for long and so consistently, "we don't have overwhelming video, photographic, and instrumentational evidence of them?"

None of the three authors of the *New York Times* articles noted above were science journalists. Blumenthal had written an article in 2013 suggesting that alien abductions were real. Kean's views on UFOs were described above. Cooper is a *Times* Pentagon correspondent and had previously written extensively on trade and foreign policy.

In addition to the military UFO sightings, both *Times* articles discussed a supposedly secret Pentagon program to investigate UFOs. The program was called the Advanced Aerospace Threat Identification Program—AATIP for short. It lasted from 2007 to 2012. The existence of AATIP has been touted as evidence that the Pentagon was seriously interested in UFOs as flying saucers—alien spacecraft.

Scoles (2020) tells the story of the origins of AATIP. It starts with Robert Bigelow, a wealthy businessman who was a major donor to the coffers of then Nevada senator Harry Reid, who served in the Senate from 1987 to 2017. Bigelow had a serious interest in UFOs and things paranormal. In 1995 he created the National Institute for Discovery Science (NIDS), which was to investigate everything from "UFOs to the possibility that consciousness survives death . . . with real scientists, real instruments, real experiments" (Scoles 2020, 83). One of the "real scientists" whom Bigelow put on the NIDS advisory board was Harold Puthoff, who had been conned by Uri Geller, as described in chapter 4. In 1996 or 1997 Bigelow purchased the Skinwalker (or Sherman) Ranch in Ballard, Utah. The ranch had a reputation for being a "hotbed" of paranormal and UFO activity and events. Bigelow's plan was to use all the scientific expertise of the NIDS to investigate and verify these events. In spite of all the serious investigative equipment and experience that was brought to the ranch, nothing paranormal or UFO related was ever found, no doubt because nothing of the kind had existed there in the first place. Bigelow gave up the investigation in 2004.

Around 2004 Bigelow spoke to Senator Reid about their mutual interest in UFOs. Reid "thought the government should be studying those [UFOs]" and "pushed a potential project forward" (Scoles 2020, 11), which resulted in the AATIP with funding of $22 million. Scoles (2020, 11) points out that the December 16, 2017, *New York Times* story that described AATIP was "all but a declaration not just that UFOs are extant, but also that they are extraterrestrial. They have landed, the Pentagon knows about them, and they may have had measurable effects on human beings." This is rather a stretch given the lack of evidence for any such thing. It is interesting to note that the great majority of the $22 million in funding for AATIP went to the Bigelow Aerospace Company. This might lead one to conclude that Robert Bigelow made his fortune in and had a great deal of experience with the aerospace industry. This would be wrong. Bigelow got rich in the cut-rate hotel industry.

UFO believer Bigelow was behind the creation of AATIP and profited from it directly. Another company was founded in 2017 by some of the same people involved in Bigelow's operations. This was the To the Stars Academy of Arts and Science. Harold Puthoff was the vice president for science and technology. Scoles (2020) found that many of the sources for the *Times* December 16, 2017, story on UFOs were from or associated with the To the Stars company. The *Times* articles turn out to be misleading pieces by journalists writing well outside of their areas of expertise. They failed to take a properly critical approach to claims made by UFO proponents. The *Times* articles treated the AATIP as a serious military approach to alien craft and thus lent it unjustified credibility. Thus "major media now ran countless stories [about it] citing the *Times* as excuse with little mention of space ghosts or anything that might make the program seem unserious" (Colavito 2021, 7).

Although the AATIP ended in 2012, the influence of Bigelow and the To the Stars Academy continued and resulted in the creation of the Unidentified Aerial Phenomena Task Force (UAPTF) in 2020. This group was to analyze UAPs, as UFOs were now officially labeled, to see if they posed any threat to national security. It was made up of a number of experts in diverse but relevant fields. The task force's preliminary report was released in 2021. Out of 144 sightings, this band of experts was able to identify only one. It's hard not to be reminded here of the committee of experts that failed to identify the source of the Chilean navy helicopter sighting described above.

In 2020 and 2021 several videos of seemingly mysterious objects taken by U.S. military aviators became public. One famous such video is known as the green triangle or green pyramid. West (2021, 3) "pointed out [that] it looked exactly like an out-of-focus airliner shot in night vision with a triangular aperture" on the camera. A video labeled "gimbal" (frame in figure 8.5) was taken in 2015 and released in 2020. What made this video so impressive to UFO enthusiasts was the way part of the image, the glare, is seen to rotate while other parts did not, seeming to defy the laws of physics. So does it show an extraterrestrial spaceship flying about some clouds? Well, maybe. But also maybe not. West found the details of the type of camera used to take the images by checking the patent files for that camera. It had a "de-rotation mechanism used to correct for 'gimbal roll.'" This is a type of mechanism that allows a camera to stay fixed in relation to an external object. This would "inevitably mean glares [in the video] would rotate in the manner seen in the video" (West 2021, 3; 2022).

An October 29, 2022, article in the *New York Times* by Julian Barnes cites military officials who have access to classified information about the imaging system involved in the gimbal video. They suggest an additional reason for the strange-appearing behavior of the image. These officials "now believe that the optics of the classified image sensor, designed to help target weapons, make the object appear like it is moving in a strange way" (Barnes 2022, A17). The article, titled "Many U.F.O. Sightings Are Just Drones or Trash," takes a very skeptical slant on UFO reports. This isn't surprising since Barnes is a legitimate *Times* national security reporter and not a UFO promoter, as were the authors of the more credulous *Times* articles published previously. Of course, the UFO enthusiasts will claim that the above is all part of a

Figure 8.5. "Gimbal" video. From "GIMBAL.wmv," Naval Air Systems Command FOIA, U.S. Department of Defense, 2020 (https://www.defense.gov/News/Releases/Release/Article/2165713/statement-by-the-department-of-defense-on -the-release-of-historical-navy-videos/)

massive government conspiracy to cover up the truth that aliens are all over the place. But they've been singing that tired old song so long that no one should take it seriously.

PHYSICAL EVIDENCE

Even better than photographs as evidence for the reality of UFOs as spacecraft would be a chunk of metal from one, preferably inscribed in some unknown writing, "Planet #5, Alpha Centauri." As the reader might expect by now, claims have been made that pieces of UFOs have been found. The reader will not be surprised to learn that these claims are unfounded. Sheaffer (1981, 25–26) described a piece of magnesium that was said to come from a UFO seen in Brazil in 1957. The Aerial Phenomena Research Organization (APRO) had the metal tested and stated it was so pure that it could not possibly have been of human or earthly manufacture. The Condon Committee tested the metal later and found that, in fact, it was much less pure than magnesium that could be produced by technology available as far back as 1940. This fact did not prevent UFO proponents from continuing to claim the metal as evidence for the extraterrestrial hypothesis. Sheaffer (1981) reported that APRO's research director claimed that "we can say it is an authentic fragment, beyond any reasonable doubt, of a UFO" because the sample contains no mercury, and a 1940 sample of industrial magnesium did (26). Where did the sample come from in the first place? It was sent anonymously to the society columnist of a Rio de Janeiro newspaper with a note describing the explosion of a UFO over a nearby beach.

Other physical evidence is sometimes said to accompany UFO sightings. "Angel hair," a soft, wispy, diaphanous material made up of extremely fine strands, is one such piece of evidence that is reported from time to time. It turns out to be masses of spiderweb used by some species of spider to allow their young to travel on the wind over great distances (Menzel 1972). The size of these webs can often be quite large—so the webs themselves are responsible for both a UFO sighting and the so-called physical evidence.

Physical effects, as well as hard evidence, have been attributed to UFOs by witnesses. A stalled car is one of the most common. The usual scenario is that a UFO appears and the witness reports that the car he or she was driving stalled at about the same time. UFO proponents explain that, somehow, the strong magnetic field that powers the UFO interferes with the car's electrical system, causing the stall. It is possible to test such an explanation. Any magnetic field strong enough to cause such a disruption of an automobile's electrical system would leave clear traces in the metal of the engine. The Condon Committee (Condon 1969) studied two cars that allegedly stalled because of proximity to UFOs. In neither case could any change in the magnetic characteristics of the metal of the engine be found. Had the automobiles actually been exposed to magnetic fields strong enough to cause electrical system failure, such changes would have been clear and easy to detect.

What causes these seemingly UFO-related stalls? Most likely the excitement of the witness. Emotional arousal leads to poorer performance of many manual tasks. Under the conditions of extreme emotional arousal experienced by many UFO witnesses, people become much less able to engage in manual tasks such as shifting gears properly. Improper shifting can result in a stall.

Another explanation for the stalls is that witnesses incorrectly attribute normal engine failures to the UFO. Perhaps the car stalls every now and then. When no UFO is present, the stall isn't thought to be anything other than an annoyance. But when the stall coincidentally happens when a UFO is seen, then the stall is suddenly transformed into something mysterious and is attributed to the UFO. Similar incorrect attributions of engine failures were noted in England during World War II in areas where radar was being used. Radar was then top secret, and residents living near radar towers had no idea what the towers were for. They began complaining that the towers were causing their cars to stall, although it is impossible for radar to cause engine failure. When the true purpose of the radar towers was revealed, the reports of mysterious stalling promptly stopped (Condon 1969).

THE TUNGUSKA EVENT

An interstellar ship develops engine trouble. It drops out of hyperspace and the captain finds himself (herself? itself?) near a planet. A quick scan shows that the planet is inhabited by intelligent beings who have not yet learned the secret of space flight. Nonetheless, the situation is desperate, so the decision is made to land in a relatively uninhabited area to make repairs. Just as the ship is entering the planet's atmosphere, a catastrophe occurs, and the ship explodes with the force of many nuclear bombs. The few primitive inhabitants in the area look up in wonder. Years later, scientific expeditions to the site reveal to the natives of the planet clear evidence of the spaceship's explosion and, thereby, of the existence of extraterrestrial space-traveling beings.

UFO enthusiasts claim this story is not science fiction but a true description of what happened over Siberia on June 30, 1908. (Some authors give the date as June 22, which was the Russian date. In 1908 Russia had not yet converted to the Gregorian calendar.)

Something clearly happened in Siberia that day in 1908. When the first scientific expedition arrived in the area in the late 1920s, much devastation was found—even after nearly twenty years. Trees had been blown down for miles around "ground zero." But those who argue that the Tunguska event was caused by an exploding UFO fabricate evidence to support their explanation and selectively omit evidence that argues against the UFO explanation.

If a nuclear-powered UFO were the cause of the Tunguska event, one would expect to find abnormally high levels of radioactivity in the area. In their 1976 book *The Fire Came By*, television drama critics Thomas Atkins and John Baxter state that high levels of radioactivity consistent with the exploding-UFO hypothesis have been found at the site. Erich von Däniken (1970) says the explosion "must have been a nuclear one" (147). Oberg (1978–1979b) and Story (1976, chap. 10) have both reviewed the evidence on this point. Their reviews show that no abnormal radioactivity is present at the Tunguska site. Reports of high levels of radioactivity are due to Russian physicist Aleksey Zolotov, who has "organized several college expeditions to the Tunguska site and made a series of announcements of 'abnormal radioactivity,' followed by embarrassed retractions" (Oberg 1978–1979b, 52). No scientific publications support his claim.

The scientific explanation of the Tunguska explosion is that a meteorite entered Earth's atmosphere and exploded before striking the ground. This explanation would demand that a crater be found, and UFO proponents point out that no single crater was found. That's true. But a group of ten craters was found, all at the center of the blast area, with sizes ranging from 30 to 160 feet across and an average depth of 10 feet (Story 1976). This is just what would be expected from the explosion of a large meteorite that produced smaller chunks that then struck the ground.

UFO proponents also claim that no trace of a meteorite has ever been found. But meteorites are generally composed of nickel and iron, and a high concentration of tiny nickel-iron fragments about 0.1 mm in size has been found at the center of the blast zone (Buchwald 1975, 9–10). Kvasnytsya and colleagues (2013) found additional evidence for a meteor at Tunguska.

CLOSE ENCOUNTERS OF THE THIRD KIND AND ALIEN ABDUCTIONS

UFO reports in which the witnesses either see the occupants of the UFO or are actually abducted by a UFO are certainly dramatic. In the 1950s such individuals were referred to as "contactees" and their stories were not taken seriously even by most UFO organizations. Things changed in the early 1960s with what is still the most famous CE III—Betty (1919–2004) and Barney (1922–1969) Hill's alleged abduction by UFO occupants. This case was brought to the public's attention by John Fuller's (1966) *The Interrupted Journey* and his sensational series of articles in *Look* magazine.

The standard version of what has become almost a legend in UFO circles has the Hills driving back to their home in Exeter, New Hampshire, from Montreal on the night of September 19, 1961. While driving through New Hampshire's White Mountains, they spot a UFO. It begins to follow their car. Barney Hill stops the car to get a better look at the UFO and sees windows in the object. Through the windows he sees the faces of the occupants. Frightened, he climbs back in the car and drives home, fearing capture. The Hills arrive home two hours later than normal and cannot account for the missing two hours. A week or so later Betty Hill begins to dream about being abducted and physically examined by UFO occupants. Several years later the Hills consulted a psychiatrist because of marital problems. Under hypnosis, both the Hills tell separate, but mutually confirming, stories of being abducted and examined by the occupants of the UFO that had chased them several years before. This period of examination accounts for the lost two hours. Betty is able to draw a "star map" that shows the major trade routes through the stars used by the civilization that built the UFO that abducted them. The map is said to be almost identical to a group of stars that Betty could not have known about. Finally, the legend goes, government records show that the UFO was tracked on several different radars that night. Betty Hill claimed that seven separate radar confirmations of the UFO are known (Sheaffer 1981, 38).

This report would be impressive, if true. But as is so often the case with UFO reports, the description presented to the public by credulous writers and investigators is very different from that which emerges after careful investigation.

The first question one can ask about this report concerns the identity of the object Betty first saw and later concluded was a UFO following the car. Sheaffer (1981) shows quite convincingly that it was the planet Jupiter. He points out that on the night of September 19, 1961, there were three bright objects visible in the night sky in northern New Hampshire. One was the moon; the other two were the planets Saturn and Jupiter. In her report, Betty Hill says that she saw the moon, one bright "star," and the UFO. She does not report seeing two bright "stars." This is a crucial point. If a real UFO had been present that night, she would have seen *four* objects in the sky—the moon, the two "stars," and the UFO. But she saw only three objects.

What about the "lost" two hours that later take on so much importance as the time during which the abduction took place? An examination of the Hills' reports regarding their time of arrival home in the months and years following the incident shows them to be extremely inconsistent (Sheaffer 1981; Klass 1974). The fact that two hours were allegedly missing from their lives was not even noticed by the Hills until a few weeks after the incident, following extensive questioning by pro-UFO investigators (Sheaffer 1981).

How does one account for the Hills' reports of the abduction that were revealed under hypnosis? It is commonly believed that hypnosis allows lost memories to be retrieved. But as described previously (chapter 5), research on hypnosis shows a far different picture: memories retrieved under hypnosis are even more unreliable than normal memories. Hilgard (1980–1981) reported that he "implanted in a subject a false memory of an experience connected with a bank robbery that never occurred, and the person found the experience so vivid that he was able to select from a series of photographs a picture of the man he thought had robbed the bank" (25). Similar fictitious memories can be created in hypnotized subjects simply by asking leading questions that presume that an event occurred, even if it didn't (Laurence and Perry 1983). Claims that hypnosis enhances memory in real-world situations, such as crime reports, also turn out to be incorrect (Smith 1983). Hypnosis is sometimes used in crime situations after several nonhypnotic sessions have been conducted with the witness to try to retrieve more details from memory. Such repeated attempts at recall themselves enhance memory, and hypnosis adds nothing to this enhancement (Dywan and Bowers 1983; Nogrady, McConkey, and Perry 1985). What hypnosis does do— and this is especially relevant to the UFO cases—is to greatly increase hypnotized subjects' confidence that their hypnotically induced memories are true. This increase in confidence occurs for both correct and incorrect memories (Nogrady, McConkey, and Perry 1985). For a good review of hypnosis effects, see Schacter (2021) and the references therein. Thus, hypnosis can create false memories, but the individual will be especially convinced that those memories are true. People repeating such false memories will seem credible because they really believe their false memories to be true. Their belief, of course, does not indicate whether the memory is true or false. Hilgard (1980–1981) concluded that "the use of hypnotic recall as evidence in UFO abduction cases is an abuse of hypnosis" because "abundant evidence exists that fabrication can take place under hypnosis" (25). Klass (1980–1981) described examples of such fabrication in several abduction stories.

Dr. Benjamin Simon, the psychiatrist who hypnotized the Hills, was asked whether he believed their abduction and examination stories were true. He replied, "Absolutely not!" (Klass 1974, 253). Dr. Simon had told John Fuller the same thing, but Fuller somehow failed to include this relevant expert opinion in his book or articles. The reports elicited under hypnosis were very likely simply the retelling of the dreams that Betty had had and which she had described to Barney in some detail. Betty had also read some sensational UFO literature after the incident, and the reports therein could easily have formed the basis for her "memories" related under hypnosis. In a letter dated October 28, 1975, to UFO investigator Philip Klass, Dr. Simon specifically stated that "the abduction did not take place but was a reproduction of Betty's dream which occurred right after the sighting" (Sheaffer 2015).

Betty Hill's claim of multiple radar confirmations of the UFO doesn't hold up when examined closely. The documents that she says prove this have mysteriously disappeared, if they ever really existed in the first place. Only one radar report of an unknown target took place that night. This was at Pease Air Force Base in Portsmouth, New Hampshire, on the coast—miles from the place where the Hills saw the UFO. The one unidentified contact that night at Pease was on the base's Precision Approach Radar, which looks directly down a runway and is used to guide planes landing on the runway. The object was four miles out and was described as a "weak" target. Sheaffer (1981) points out that this type of radar is so sensitive that it sometimes detects birds. More importantly, the base Airport Surveillance Radar, which scans the entire area, showed no unidentified target that night.

Betty Hill's "star map" is often claimed to be the best evidence for the reality of the Hills' close encounter. How could Betty possibly have drawn such an accurate map of stars that she didn't even know existed unless, as she claimed, she saw the map when she was aboard the UFO? The map consists of twenty-six dots representing stars, some of which are connected by lines representing trade routes between the stars. Several attempts have been made to match the pattern of dots on the map to patterns of actual stars. Great success has been claimed for these attempts but, as usual, the claims fall short upon examination.

Saunders (1975) reported that one attempt to match the map to a pattern of actual stars was so accurate that such a match would be expected to occur by chance only once in one thousand times. What Saunders fails to mention to his readers is that the seemingly impressive match uses only fifteen (57 percent) of the twenty-six stars. Eleven (43 percent) of the stars on the original map are simply ignored, apparently because they don't fit. Errors occur in this match as well (Sheaffer 1981). There is an incorrect orientation between the supposed "home star" of the UFO occupants and a nearby star in the match. That is, the orientation in the match turns out to be quite different from that on Betty Hill's original map. There is a further problem with the match proposed by Saunders (Soter and Sagan 1975). If one removes the drawn-in lines on both the match and the original map, the resemblance disappears. The lines impose an illusory similarity that is not present when considering the actual stars alone.

The Milky Way Galaxy consists of approximately one hundred billion stars. Out of that number, there will be, by pure chance alone, many sets of twenty-six stars that match the pattern on Betty Hill's map with impressive accuracy. If enough time were spent, one could probably find thousands of such matches. They would, of course, prove nothing, as the same number of matches could be made to a random pattern of twenty-six dots on paper. The much-discussed "star map" appears, after close inspection, to be nothing more than just such a random pattern produced by Betty Hill's fertile imagination.

In the years since her close encounter Betty Hill became a guru of the UFO movement. Her close encounters continued, multiplied, and are described in a short item in the fall 1978 issue of the *Skeptical Inquirer*:

> Now that Mrs. Hill is retired, she divides her time between giving UFO lectures and watching UFOs land at the semi-secret "landing spot" she claims to have discovered in New Hampshire. Mrs. Hill's recent claims are straining even the almost boundless credulity of the UFO groups. Mrs. Hill claims that the UFOs come in to land several times a week; they have become such a familiar sight that she is now calling them by name. Sometimes the aliens get out and do calisthenics before taking off again, she asserts. One UFO reportedly zapped a beam at her that was so powerful that it "blistered the paint on my car." Mrs. Hill also reports that window-peeping flying saucers sometimes fly from house to house late at night in New England, shine lights in the windows, and then move on when the occupants wake up and turn on the lights. (14)

The same item reports that when at her secret UFO landing site, Mrs. Hill was unable to distinguish streetlights from UFOs.

On October 20, 1975, NBC-TV broadcast a made-for-television movie based on the Hills' close encounter called *The UFO Incident*. In the months following this broadcast, numerous similar close encounters were reported (Sheaffer 1981) containing the same major elements as those found in the Hill story and in the movie: abduction and medical examination by aliens. (I've always wondered why the aliens were so interested in and ignorant of human anatomy and physiology. A species capable of sending ships across the galaxy certainly ought to be able to obtain a few basic anatomy and physiology texts without kidnapping innocent earthlings.) The cases also featured missing periods of time, just as in the Hill case. Sheaffer (1981, chap. 5) described several of these cases. It is difficult to take them seriously, but they are taken very seriously by the UFO groups. In their book *Abducted*, James and Coral Lorenzen, founders of APRO, worry that too many teenagers are spending too much time in deserted areas. This is dangerous because it is from just such areas that most UFO abductions occur. "Each and every inhabitant of this earth is a potential victim" (Lorenzen and Lorenzen 1980, 210), we are told.

Sporadic reports of UFO abductions continued to be made in the early 1980s. One of the most productive finders of abducted individuals was Dr. Leo Sprinkle, a psychologist at the University of Wyoming. He hypnotized witnesses who had seen UFOs and found, in a surprisingly high number of cases, that the witnesses had been abducted. Strangely, the witnesses usually were unaware of having been abducted until Dr. Sprinkle, who is apparently unaware of the problems with hypnosis, hypnotized them.

As the 1980s progressed, UFO abduction reports became the new standard in the UFO movement. Just plain old sightings were way too mundane to be very exciting anymore, what with people being abducted so frequently. Several books claimed that humans were being abducted by the tens of thousands and subjected to various invasive medical procedures. These included having an eyeball removed (but, happily for the victim, it was reattached before the return to Earth) and the insertion of probes into various bodily orifices. Sexual contact was also reported. The goal of all this, according to Budd Hopkins (1931–2011), a New York artist and one of the leading proponents of the reality of abductions, was to create a new race of human/alien crossbreeds.

The wave of claimed alien abductions got a slow start at the beginning of the 1980s. Hopkins published the first major book on the topic, *Missing Time*, in 1981. His list of "symptoms" of being abducted includes things that have happened to almost everyone. For example, have you ever looked at the time and noticed that it is either later or earlier than you thought? Guess what—that shows you've been abducted. The aliens have altered your sense of the passage of time. In 1985 Ruth Montgomery (1912–2001), who had earlier described that psychic wonder Jeane Dixon (Montgomery 1965), published the little-noticed book *Aliens among Us*. She contended, based on numerous personal reports she had received, that the "space brothers" had already arrived and were on Earth disguised as humans. Montgomery's aliens were of a very different character than the aliens that became the popular image of the abductors as the 1980s wore on. Her aliens were beneficent fellows, here to do good works for humanity. They did not abduct anyone. The stereotypical aliens in Hopkins's *Missing Time* are anything but beneficent—they are cruel, subjecting humans to various unpleasant medical procedures for their own ends with no concern about the pain inflicted. Montgomery's aliens promptly vanished from the popular scene to be replaced as part of popular culture by Hopkins's version.

UFO abduction claims, which had been a fringe element of the UFO movement, quickly became the major focus of that movement and came to the attention of the public by the late 1980s. This was due to the publication in 1987 of two major books touting abduction claims as real. One was Hopkins's *Intruders* and the other Whitley Strieber's *Communion*. As these books appeared, claims of alien abduction began to be featured on the numerous TV talk shows, always on the lookout for ever more bizarre topics to keep their ratings up. The average abductee who appeared on a talk show was not an obvious crazed psychotic but appeared to be a reasonable human being who truly believed that he had been abducted and was genuinely frightened by what had happened. The abductees were usually genuine in these respects. They really did believe that they had been abducted and that they had been cruelly used by the aliens. And they were frightened, sometimes terrified, that it might happen again.

The alien abduction story took a surprising turn in 1994 when John Mack (1929–2004), a psychiatrist at Harvard University, published his book *Abduction: Human Encounters with Aliens*, in which he argued that the abduction events were real and could not be explained by science. What most impressed Mack, as he reiterated later, were the "strange consistencies and unbelievable aspects of the abduction phenomenon" (McLeod, Corbisier, and Mack 1996, 166).

Despite the large number of the alleged abductions, there has never been a single piece of physical evidence produced by any abductee. No bits of alien technology from the spacecraft. No recovered implants such as the aliens are sometimes said to use. Nothing. Rumors and claims for real alien artifacts have floated around for years in the abduction community, but no artifact has ever been produced for independent study. Of course, should a genuine alien artifact be found, it would immediately be produced as positive proof by those so intent on showing that the abduction experiences are real. Such artifacts are conspicuous by their absence.

This absence of physical evidence strongly suggests that the abduction experiences are not real. But if they aren't, how can it be that so many seemingly sane individuals have come to believe that such a horrible event befell them? An event for which, as noted above, they seem to have real memories, memories that cause a great deal of fear and psychological suffering. It is important to make it clear that in the great majority of these cases, the explanation is not that the individuals are lying to get attention or to take on the status of victim, nor are they suffering from any psychopathology (e.g., schizophrenia). Rather, the explanation lies in the power of multiple persuasive techniques to create powerful false memories in humans. Variations within the normal range of the personality trait called fantasy proneness can enhance susceptibility to these techniques, but one of the important insights to emerge from the UFO abduction claims (as well as claims of recovered memories of childhood sexual abuse or ritual satanic abuse—see chapter 5) is that many more normal people are susceptible to these techniques than was previously realized. Another important factor is that one usually thinks of "techniques of persuasion" being used on those who don't want to be persuaded of something, as in the case of "brainwashing" for political reasons. Especially in the case of UFO abductees, the individual on whom the persuasive techniques are used is often an active and willing participant in the process of creating the false memories.

An important factor in understanding the psychology of the abduction experience is that the great majority of these experiences take place at night, often when the abductee is in bed or asleep. Some abductees even initially describe their experiences as dreams. The common phenomenon of hypnagogia was described previously in the context of ghosts and hauntings. It also plays a major role in reports of UFO abduction experiences.

Of course, not everyone who has a frightening hypnopompic experience involving aliens will interpret it as being a real alien visitation and kidnapping. But some will, especially since they have no alternative explanation to fall back on, hypnagogia being little known to the general public. As publicity about alien abductions became more and more widespread in the 1980s, abductions became more and more available to people seeking an explanation for their experiences. After all, here were thousands of other people, some going on national television with their experiences, almost all fully believing they had been abducted. Those on TV, as noted, came across as quite normal—perhaps traumatized, and understandably so, but normal nonetheless. If that is what happened to them, it was quite natural to adopt abduction as an explanation for one's own experience.

As the 1980s progressed, the abduction experience became part of American cultural knowledge. It had been around the fringes for some time. It had been a theme in science fiction for decades. Kottmeyer (1989, cited in Newman and Baumeister 1996) traced the themes in abduction reports as far back as those of the Hills to science fiction films and television programs. Some abduction experiences have the victim "transported" up to the alien ship in a beam of light (which no one else ever sees, of course), very much as in *Star Trek*. The 1993 release of the film *Fire in the Sky* elevated Travis Walton's tall tale to the silver screen. In addition, there were numerous television programs, both fictional and labeled as nonfiction, that acquainted viewers with the details of what is likely to happen when one gets abducted.

In 1996 the PBS series *Nova* presented an examination of abduction claims titled "Kidnapped by UFOs?" In one telling sequence, Budd Hopkins goes to Florida to investigate a presumed abduction case involving a young couple and their two children. The wife tells of a late-night experience in which she had what she later interprets as an abduction experience. She is very explicit about how she concluded that she had been abducted. She says she couldn't figure out what had happened to her until, by chance, she read Hopkins's book *Intruders*—and then it all "just fit so perfectly" and she contacted Hopkins to ask him to investigate. It's fascinating to watch him do so as he hypnotizes her and then conducts interviews with her two young children. Using not-too-subtle leading questions and other techniques, he elicits what, for him, is strong evidence that this family has suffered from abductions. The absurdity of the conclusions that Hopkins draws from his obviously flawed methods, which I think he employed in good faith, is astonishing. The reader who has any interest in this topic should get a copy of the program and watch it.

In another sequence in "Kidnapped by UFOs?" a woman who had gone undercover to investigate what goes on in John Mack's UFO abduction support groups reported that before she even met him he had sent her a package of literature about what happens during an abduction and that it was very obvious from that literature what an abduction experience was supposed to be like. Many people who contacted Hopkins as well as other alien abduction gurus were very familiar with the "script" of an abduction well before they meet the guru and are often hypnotized to obtain more memories. Hypnosis, that excellent means for producing false memories, especially when leading questions are asked and the hypnotist is a strong authority figure, was commonly used to elicit abduction reports.

"Kidnapped by UFOs?" also documents the use of another technique of persuasion—group pressure in the context of group therapy. Hopkins and Mack, among others, ran support groups for abduction "survivors." In a taped sequence of one such group meeting, it was obvious that some group members were pressuring others to accept the "reality" of their memories of the experience. Over time, such group pressure, and the considerable social rewards the group can use to reinforce the acceptance of belief in one's own abduction experiences, can lead to a powerful belief in their reality.

Budd Hopkins and John Mack were two of the best-known names in the UFO abduction business. Whitley Strieber, an author of horror fiction whose best-known book *Wolfen* (1978) was made into a movie in 1980, is a third. His 1987 book *Communion* is the "true story" of his encounters with and abduction by some type of alien beings. During these terrifying experiences, which began in December 1986, a needle was inserted into his head and an instrument of some sort was inserted into his anus.

Both Klass (1988) and Swords (1987) critiqued Strieber's accounts of his experience. Klass's book is especially valuable, as it covers the entire subject of UFO abductions. Both critiques note that Strieber's life has been filled with highly unusual and bizarre occurrences. When he was twelve, for example, he was assaulted by a skeleton on a motorcycle; earlier, he had had a threatening encounter with Mr. Peanut. In the early 1970s, he awoke one night and saw a tiny humanoid figure run by him holding a red light. In 1985 he was awakened while staying at his cabin in the Catskills and found the place surrounded by a strange blue light glowing in the fog. In all, Swords lists thirty-three separate highly unusual experiences of this sort reported as fact in *Communion* and finds no independent confirmation for fully thirty of them. For three experiences, the "confirmations" confirm only the most mundane aspects of the event. For example, Strieber reported that in 1982 he had a series of encounters with a mysterious white figure. A baby-sitter confirmed seeing a youngster in a white sheet outside a window. Strieber's wife, Anne, "clearly says that she didn't see anyone or anything, just was poked while asleep; and that W.S. first started talking about little white things. All her subsequent 'description' of a being was in response to imagining what it might look like" (Swords 1987, 5). Strieber used as further confirmation of some of the events he claims to have experienced the testimony of his son, born in 1979 and seven years old in 1986. Swords properly excludes the child's comments from the class of confirming evidence "because of the powerful potential for idea suggestibility which exists" between father and son (5).

Strieber is clearly obsessed with intruders, an obsession that apparently began long before he had his encounter with the aliens in 1986. He admits that late at night he often searches for possible intruders by "opening closets and looking under beds" and "especially [in] corners and crannies. I always looked down low in the closets, seeking something small" (Strieber 1987a, 101). He also has elaborate burglar alarms in both his New York City apartment and his cabin in the mountains.

Klass (1988) showed that Strieber has a history of telling stories he claims to be true but which turn out to be false. In an interview published in Winter's (1985) book of interviews with famous horror fiction writers, Strieber described in graphic detail being present and nearly shot on August 1, 1966, when Charles Whitman killed fourteen people in his sniper attack from the Texas Tower on the campus of the University of Texas in Austin. In *Communion*, however, Strieber admits that he was not present at the tragedy. Sprinkled throughout the book are other recantations of stories Strieber previously held out as true.

From reading *Communion* and hearing Strieber on several television and radio talk shows, I believe that he really believes that the encounters he says he had with the aliens were real. He is, however, not at all sure that the creatures are "only" members of an advanced civilization. He thinks they represent something even stranger, perhaps "mankind's first encounter with a quantum reality in the new macrocosm" (Strieber 1987b, 8). He also feels that "the abduction experience is *primarily* a mystical experience" and that following the experience "spiritual and paranormal life events" become more common (7).

In the forty-plus years since the start of the alien abduction reports in the 1980s, much has been learned about the psychology behind these reports. At first it might seem, as it did to me, that anyone who would report such an abduction, and believe that it really occurred, must be truly crazy. Research over the past years has shown that this is not the case. The most parsimonious explanation of the alien abduction experiences is that they are vivid false memories created by a combination of variables, including exposure to the alien abduction "script," hypnopompic experiences, hypnosis, and group pressure from self-appointed abduction therapists and other abductees, combined with a fantasy-prone personality. Not all these factors will be present in every case, and the "mix" of causative agents will vary from person to person. An entire issue of the journal *Psychological Inquiry* (Pervin 1996) was devoted to the issue of the psychology behind alien abduction claims. It contains thirteen papers covering a range of explanations for this phenomenon. The papers by Clark and Loftus (1996) and Orne and colleagues (1996) are especially relevant to the idea advanced here that abduction reports are due to false memories created by various psychological processes. Bartholomew and Howard (1998) discussed the psychology of alien abduction experiences at some length. Their discussion is especially valuable in putting this modern phenomenon in historical perspective by noting the high degree of similarities between the alien abductions and experiences with demons, incubi, witches, fairies, and ghosts in ages past.

Susan Clancy has extensively studied and interviewed many abductees. She has summarized her work beautifully in her 2005 book *Abducted: How People Come to Believe They Were Kidnapped by Aliens*. The first paragraph of her book (Clancy 2005, 1) gives a good feel for a typical abductee:

> Will Andrews is an articulate, handsome forty-two-year-old. He's a successful chiropractor, lives in a wealthy American suburb, and has a strikingly attractive wife and twin boys, age eight. The only glitch in this picture of domestic bliss is that his children are not his wife's—they are the product of an earlier infidelity. To complicate matters further, the biological mother is an extraterrestrial.

Abduction experiences don't just come out of nowhere. People who end up believing they have been abducted have a history of belief in UFOs and related phenomenon. Clancy (2005, 138) sums up by noting that "alien abduction memories are best understood as resulting from a blend of fantasy proneness, memory distortion, culturally available scripts, sleep hallucinations, and scientific illiteracy, aided and abetted by the suggestions and reinforcement of hypnotherapy." I doubt very much whether, back in the 1980s, anyone would have predicted that such vivid experiences could be created in this way. It sheds extremely interesting light on the malleability of human memory. It has led to important research on the cognitive and even genetic factors that facilitate certain people having these experiences. French and colleagues (2008) studied a group of British abductees. They found that, compared to nonabductees, those who believed that they had been kidnapped by alien beings showed "higher levels of dissociativity, absorption, paranormal belief, paranormal experience, self-reported psychic ability, fantasy proneness, tendency to hallucinate, and self-reported incidence of sleep paralysis" (1387).

The fantasy-proneness finding is crucial in suggesting that these individuals had a harder time telling reality from fantasy than did those who had not claimed to be kidnapped. There may even be a genetic component to the tendency to believe one has been abducted. Schmack and colleagues (2015) have found that genetically determined individual differences in levels of the neurotransmitter dopamine were associated with greater acceptance of what they termed "unfounded" beliefs.

Even individuals who are not terribly fantasy prone may become abductees (Spanos et al. 1993; Newman and Baumeister 1996; Orne et al. 1996). Orne and colleagues (1996) suggest that a normal degree of fantasy proneness and hypnotizability may itself be sufficient to produce dramatic abduction false memories when people are subjected to the types of social and psychological pressures that generate abduction false memories in more fantasy-prone individuals.

The alien abduction episode did have some beneficial fallout. It greatly increased the understanding of sleep paralysis, hypnogogic hallucinations, the psychology of how memory can be manipulated, and the individual differences that are responsible for differing susceptibility to such manipulations.

THE END OF THE WORLD, THE HOLLOW EARTH, AND CATTLE MUTILATION

Insiders in the UFO business sometimes say that the belief that UFOs are extraterrestrial craft is silly. There is insufficient evidence to justify such a belief. Further, the logistics of space travel from distant stars are too difficult. In this they agree, surprisingly, with Carl Sagan (1972) when he described the difficulties in overcoming such obstacles to space travel as the speed of light and the amount of fuel needed. Do these "avant-garde" UFOlogists conclude from all this that UFOs exist only as perceptual constructions, false memories, misidentifications, and hoaxes? Not at all. Instead, bizarre new hypotheses have sprung up to save the dedicated UFOlogist from having to admit that there is no foundation to the reports. One UFO group called Samisdat, based in Toronto, Ontario, believed that UFOs are really secret Nazi aircraft. Supposedly, just as World War II ended in May 1945, Hitler and all the other missing leaders of the Third Reich were whisked away by a UFO to a secret Nazi hideout in the Antarctic, where they resided, plotting the rise of a Fourth Reich. This same group also marketed Nazi propaganda.

Some fundamentalist Christian groups believe that UFOs are really angels and foretell the Second Coming or Judgment Day. Of course, only those who truly believe in the UFOs will be saved when the world ends. Actually, this type of group has a longer history than might be suspected. Even in the 1950s there were groups who believed that UFOs were harbingers of the end of the world, sent to save believers. One such group was infiltrated and studied by several social psychologists who wrote a classic book on the dynamics of the group and the group's response when the end of the world did not come as predicted (Festinger, Riecken, and Schachter 1956). The failure of the world to end on schedule did not suggest to several members of the group that their belief was wrong. Instead, they rationalized events to convince themselves that they had simply miscalculated. That particular group is no longer in existence, but another group that has suffered several failed end-of-the-world predictions is still around: the Seventh-day Adventist Church. This sect was founded in the 1840s when William Miller predicted that the world would end on March 21, 1843. It didn't, so Miller promptly recalculated that the end would come on October 22, 1844 (Randi 1982a; Numbers and Butler 1987). It didn't. Nonetheless, the church is still in business. They now contend that the end of the world is near, although they are wise enough to avoid making specific predictions about the date.

Occasionally these end-of-the-world movements are, at least in part, financially motivated. In the western United States in the late 1970s, two people, variously called "Bo and Peep" or "The Two," convinced several hundred people that the world would soon end. They told their followers that they would be saved by UFOs, that to purify themselves they should give up all their worldly goods (by transferring them to Bo and Peep), and that they should follow "The Two" into the Montana wilderness.

Alas, Bo and Peep did not just vanish into the Montana wilderness to live happily ever after on the money they had scammed from their gullible victims. Rather, they reappeared in the mid-1990s as leaders of what was to become the deadliest UFO cult in history. This was the Heaven's Gate cult. Led by Bo, its members believed that there was a flying saucer in the tail of the comet Hale-Bopp, that superior beings were aboard that craft, and that earthlings who chose to voluntarily leave the primitive "vehicles" of their bodies would be transported to the UFO and to the next level of existence. They also believed that Christ had been an alien and that deemphasizing the mundane, earthly pleasures of existence—such as sexual pleasure—would help them reach the next level. Several male members believed this to the extent that they had themselves castrated. The cult came to a horrible end in March 1997 when Bo and thirty-eight followers committed suicide by taking poison and tying plastic bags over their heads. They were all spiffily attired, including Nike running shoes, and their bodies were covered with purple cloaks. Videotapes left behind documented that they were looking forward to dying. "I just can't wait to get up there," one member said on tape (Kurtz 1997; Gardner 1997). If ever there was any doubt about the harmful effects of naive, uncritical belief in such things as UFOs, the Heaven's Gate episode should remove it.

My own favorite way-out theory of UFOs is that they come from an advanced civilization not somewhere in space but right here on Earth. Where might such a civilization be hiding? Where else but inside the earth? The earth is hollow, this theory maintains, and an advanced civilization is hiding there, complete with UFOs. This hollow-earth theory is the creation of the late Ray Palmer, a science fiction writer who believed not only that the earth is hollow but also that it has a hole at the north pole through which the flying saucers come and go. And how has this hole and the hollowness of the earth escaped the notice of geologists, explorers, airline pilots, and governments? Palmer maintained that they all know about it and are involved in a giant cover-up to hide this important knowledge from the rest of the world's people. Only those few who have managed to penetrate the curtain of silence and who are trying to bring this momentous news to the public can be trusted. Gardner (1987b) described the origin of the hollow-earth theory in some detail. Nadis (2013) has written an excellent biography of Palmer that covers his role in creating the hollow-earth fantasy as well as his significant contribution to keeping the flying saucer craze alive in the 1950s. Nadis argues convincingly that without Palmer, interest in UFOs would not have grown as it did in the 1950s and 1960s.

The case of the hollow earth is not the only time that science fiction and pseudoscience have crossed paths. In a wonderful book Andrew May (2017) describes the many contributions that pseudosciences, from parapsychology to UFOlogy and cryptozoology, have made to science fiction.

A case of collective delusion that covered a large part of the western United States was, and sometimes still is, blamed on UFOs and their occupants. This is the so-called cattle mutilation mystery. Starting in 1969 and gathering steam over the next few years, reports of mysteriously mutilated cattle found on the range in the West became quite common. What was causing these deaths? The deaths could not have been due to natural causes, people believed, because there were surgically sharp incisions on the bodies— incisions in very strange places—the anus was often cored like an apple, and the eyes, vagina, penis and testicles, tongue, and other soft parts of the body were removed. In addition to the UFO hypothesis, some felt that satanic cults or supernatural forces were at work. As reports increased in numbers, there was a call for the government to take action. In April 1979 the Justice Department funded an investigation of the problem by a former FBI agent. His report (Rommel 1980) and Kagan and Summers's (1983) book set to rest the claims for UFO or paranormal causes of the mutilations. The cattle were dying of natural causes, such as eating poisonous plants, and the bodies were being attacked by scavengers. Scavengers find it difficult to chew through tough cowhide. Instead, they attack the soft areas of the body, and these were just the areas found missing in the "mutilated" cattle. What about the surgical precision of the incisions? The incisions weren't surgically precise at all. This was easily seen when an actual scalpel was used to make an incision on the body of a dead cow, as was done as part of Rommel's investigation. Figure 8.6 shows an actual surgical incision in an animal's hide (lower image) and a supposedly "surgically precise" wound (top image). The two images are from Rommel's report. The scavenger-caused wounds simply had a sharper edge than one would expect. Few ranchers, coming on the dead and partly rotted body of one of their cattle, would bother to get close enough to inspect the wounds for the small tooth marks that would be visible. As a body decomposes, gases build up within and the body swells. The edges of any wounds are thereby stretched and come to appear sharper than they originally were.

In an article gruesomely titled "Maggots, Mutilation and Myth" veterinarians Nation and Williams (1989) reviewed the pathology of what happens when large animals die in the wild. The damage done by scavengers and predators is exactly like that said to have been done by aliens or other mysterious agents. The media played a role in the hysteria over the cattle mutilation reports. Sensational reporting that played up the outlandish speculations and ignored the true explanation probably prolonged this episode.

THE GREAT UFO COVER-UP

The basic idea is that the government has conclusive evidence that UFOs are real extraterrestrial spacecraft and that it has had this evidence since shortly after the first modern UFOs were seen in 1947. Further, the government is hiding this evidence from the American public. Only a few dedicated UFOlogists have managed to penetrate the cloak of government secrecy to find the truth, often at considerable risk, and

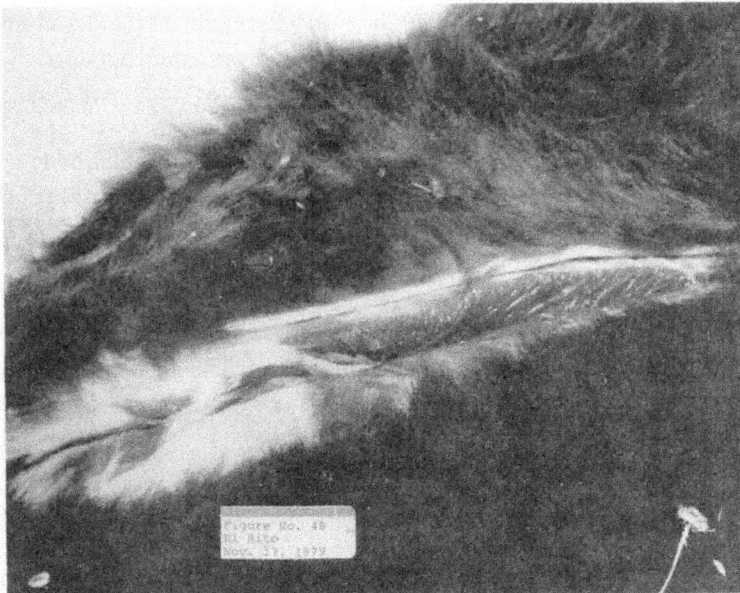

Figure 8.6. From Rommel (1980)

bring it to the attention of the public. The Central Intelligence Agency (CIA) is said to be heavily involved, along with the military and almost every other branch of government.

Before considering the evidence put forth to support this conspiracy theory, let us examine it on purely logical grounds. Over the past several decades the government has shown its inability to keep even extremely important secrets. The Pentagon Papers were leaked to the press. The power of the presidency was not enough to keep the secret of Watergate. The secret bombings in Cambodia at the end of the

Vietnam War weren't secret for long. In the late 1980s, the Iran-Contra arms-for-hostages deal was revealed. And yet, over more than seventy years, what would be the biggest news story of the century—the discovery that we are being visited by beings from another planet—has somehow been successfully kept by thousands of military personnel and untold numbers of federal bureaucrats who would have had to been involved. If the cover-up idea were not so widely held, it could be dismissed as the paranoid fantasy that it is.

However, since it is so widely believed and used by UFO groups to explain the lack of good evidence for the existence of UFOs, the cover-up story calls for detailed examination. The alleged cover-up started in the 1950s. Those individuals lucky enough to get a good look at a UFO or to learn the "truth" about UFOs were often visited by the dreaded Men in Black ("MIBs," in the UFOlogical literature). At first it was felt that MIBs were agents of some secret U.S. government agency. They certainly were frightening fellows, according to UFO proponent Gray Barker (1956, 92). Those visited by MIBs were so frightened by them that they "turned pale and got awfully sick" and "couldn't get anything to stay on [their] stomach for three long days." The 1976 *UFO Annual* says: "This much is *known* about those mysterious Men in Black who show up after almost every important saucer sighting or landing; they do not represent any known government; their basic purpose is to discredit or terrorize eyewitnesses; and they have seized or obliterated all UFO evidence for more than 27 years!" (16, emphasis in original). Efficient fellows, these—and what a nifty excuse for the otherwise totally unimpressive evidence for the reality of UFOs. Obviously, this is yet another nonfalsifiable hypothesis. The major contribution of the Men in Black has been several highly entertaining movies.

Throughout the 1950s and 1960s the UFO movement repeatedly charged that the U.S. Air Force was hiding secret files and documents that proved that UFOs were real, that is, extraterrestrial. Later, the CIA became the alleged repository for the secret files. The most far-fetched claim is that the Air Force has an entire crashed flying saucer, complete with frozen (or embalmed) remains of the occupants, hidden at Wright-Patterson Air Force Base in Ohio. Just how the UFOlogists managed to discover this secret, in spite of the MIBs and government secrecy, and why the government permits them to "blow the cover" on the most sensational secret of the century, is never made clear.

In 1977 Ground Saucer Watch filed a Freedom of Information Act suit against the CIA in an attempt to force the agency to reveal all its secret UFO files. This resulted in the release of nearly one thousand pages of materials from CIA files related to UFOs. The genesis of CIA interest in the UFO issue in the 1950s was the fear that Russia, "with its growing fleet of long-range bombers and its newly acquired atomic bomb, could conceivably exploit UFO-mania within the U.S. to stage a surprise attack" (Klass 1983, chap. 2). Not a very realistic fear, perhaps, but it certainly indicates that the CIA never took seriously the idea that UFOs are extraterrestrial.

Klass (1983) obtained copies of all the released CIA documents. The 997 pages of documents covered a thirty-year period, from 1949 to 1979. This works out to about three pages of material per month on the topic. Of the total material, about 350 pages had been classified. This means that the CIA generated "an average of only one page of classified UFO-related material per month" (14). If the CIA was involved in some sort of massive cover-up, the amount of material generated would have been much greater.

The actual contents of the released documents further destroy any claims of a government cover-up. The documents included letters to and from the CIA regarding UFOs, among them letters from people inquiring about the CIA's role in the UFO cover-up and the replies. Also included were miscellaneous newspaper clippings relating to UFOs, a Russian bibliography on parapsychology, and interoffice memos on the topic.

More revealing were several secret briefings for high-level CIA officials on the topic of UFOs. One such briefing took place in August 1952 and covered several theories about the nature of UFOs. The following quotation is relevant:

The third theory is the man from Mars—space ships—interplanetary travellers. Even though we might admit that intelligent life may exist elsewhere and that space travel is possible, there is no shred of evidence to support this theory at present. . . .

The fourth theory is that now held by the Air Force, that the sightings, given adequate data, can be explained either on the basis of misinterpretation of known objects, or of as yet little understood natural phenomena.

Remember that this was a secret briefing for high-level CIA officials. As Klass puts it, it is "inconceivable" that the Air Force could have knowledge of a crashed flying saucer and still convince the CIA that it believed sightings were the result of misidentifications and such. Another declassified secret briefing paper from August 1952 states that "no debris or material evidence has ever been recovered" from a UFO sighting (Klass 1997, 205). Obviously such statements would not have been made in 1952 if real flying saucers had been recovered at Roswell in 1947.

It is true that certain items were censored by the CIA before the documents were released. But this is hardly evidence for a cover-up; what was censored were the names of individuals making UFO reports and individual employees in the government whose names appeared on the released documents. The censoring conformed with Privacy Act requirements to protect the privacy of individuals who had communicated with the CIA on the topic. Communications on any other topic would have been treated in the same way.

An examination of the secret CIA papers and documents on UFOs reveals an agency mildly interested in the phenomenon but skeptical of the extraterrestrial hypothesis. These documents also contradict the silly claims that the Air Force (or the CIA, the National Security Agency, or the Boy Scouts) have a flying saucer hidden somewhere. They also contradict the oft-repeated claims of a government cover-up of the "truth" about UFOs.

Roswell

Roswell! No other UFO incident in history has so entered the public mind as what allegedly happened near the little town of Roswell, New Mexico, in July 1947. It was there, according to the standard version of the legend, that one or more flying saucers crashed in the desert. The military recovered not only the debris of the craft but the bodies of the alien occupants. The local military initially is said to have at first admitted the recovery of the flying saucers, but higher authorities quickly clamped down tight security. The debris and remains were taken to a secret laboratory somewhere (often said to be at Wright-Patterson Air Force Base in Ohio, known as Wright Army Airfield at the time) for analysis. From that day to this, the government has denied that the incident ever happened and that it is hiding the truth from the American people. In fact, there is not just one "standard" Roswell story. Saler, Ziegler, and Moore (1997) identified six different versions of the story. The Roswell incident has generated a huge amount of published literature in the form of articles and books, to say nothing of at least two movies that I know of (*Hangar 18* from 1980 and the 1994 TV movie *Roswell*) and one television series (NBC's *Roswell*, which ran from 1999 to 2002). Interestingly, the wide interest in the Roswell incident is a recent development, dating from the 1980s, compared to when it supposedly took place.

The Roswell incident took place just a few weeks after Kenneth Arnold's first modern report of "flying saucers" hit the news. "The flying saucer myth was defined against a background of conspiracy, fear and espionage," and this is certainly true of Roswell as well (Peebles 1994, 46). At the time, in 1947, World War II was just two years past and the Cold War was starting. It was becoming clear that the Soviet Union, our WWII ally, was now our chief antagonist on the world stage. The real cause of the events at Roswell was a secret government project aimed at keeping an eye (an ear would be more accurate) on nuclear weapons development in the Soviet Union.

Roswell turns out to be a most spectacular case of initial mistaken identity, followed years later by an explosion of media hype. Saler, Ziegler, and Moore (1997) provided the most detailed analysis of what happened near Roswell in that summer of 1947. By 1946 the United States government had come to recognize the Soviet Union as a possible military threat. At that time, the United States was the only nation with nuclear weapons, but the Soviets were certainly making every attempt to achieve their own nuclear capacity. The U.S. military put several measures in place to keep tabs on Soviet nuclear-testing programs. One of these, known as Project Mogul, was the development of very sensitive devices that, when sent into the upper atmosphere, would hopefully be able to detect Soviet nuclear weapons tests. Project Mogul was highly secret. The United States did not want the Soviets to have any idea that it might have the ability to detect such tests. But how to get these instruments so high in the air and keep them there? The answer was obvious—balloons. But then-existing balloons wouldn't do because they wouldn't keep the instruments at the stable high altitude needed for accurate monitoring. So the military funded development of balloons that could. The efforts to develop the balloons themselves were not secret, as they would have many scientific as well as intelligence uses.

Charles B. Moore, the engineer for the balloon development project, has written a detailed history of the project (Moore 1997). After initial testing of balloons in Pennsylvania, testing was moved in the spring of 1947 to an army base near Alamogordo, New Mexico, about one hundred miles from Roswell. The weather there was better suited for the testing. On June 4, 1947, one of the balloons, complete with a radar reflector used to track the balloons, went missing during a test launch. Moore argues convincingly that it was the crashed debris of this test balloon that started the entire Roswell ball rolling.

This raises an important question—how could the remains of a small balloon and radar reflector be mistaken for a flying saucer? The answer is simple—at the time, it wasn't. The debris was found initially on June 14 by a rancher named Mack Brazel and his son, Bill. They didn't think much of it at first and only returned to the location weeks later to collect it. Now, if someone had come across the remains of a real crashed flying saucer, it is highly doubtful that they would have simply gone about their business for several weeks. It is clear from Brazel's description of what he found that it was in no way the remains of a flying saucer. In an interview in the *Roswell Daily Record* of July 9, 1947, Brazel described what he found as "bright wreckage made up of rubber strips, tinfoil, a rather tough paper, and sticks" (quoted in Ziegler 1997, 6). This description turns out to be quite accurate. Such a collection is hardly what would be expected from the results of the crash of an interstellar spacecraft. Kenneth Arnold had reported seeing his flying discs only a few days before the interview (on June 24), and the story was given extensive media attention. In his interview Brazel did speculate that the debris "might be remnants" of such a disc. But it must be recalled that at this time, less than two weeks after the Arnold report, the idea that the flying discs or saucers were metal extraterrestrial craft piloted by beings from other planets had not yet been widely suggested. So, while Brazel did mention the flying discs, he was certainly not arguing that he had found the wreckage of anything remotely similar to the "flying saucers" of later fame. Rather, as Ziegler notes, "because he lived in the vicinity of an army airfield, Brazel apparently suspected that the wreckage he had found was associated with a military project," as indeed it was (6). Supporting this view is a Gallup poll that showed that during the period of the initial events at Roswell, "virtually no one thought of associating flying disks with extraterrestrial spaceships" (cited by Ziegler 1997, 6).

The debris was turned over to Army Air Corps authorities, who tried to figure out just what they had on their hands. Since this was clearly not the remains of a standard weather balloon, these authorities were unable to identify the source. The real identity of the debris stayed unidentified until Moore's (1997) paper because, as the authorities were taking possession of the remains, the staff of the balloon project was on the way back to the East Coast. "Thus, the people in the area who were most competent to recognize the debris as the wreckage of a balloon train and a radar reflector were unavailable, and no one at Roswell Air Field was able to identify the debris when it arrived there" (Ziegler 1997, 9). A Roswell base public relations officer then issued a press release in which he made reference to the acquisition by the base of a "flying disc," again in the non-extraterrestrial-spacecraft sense of the term. The rubber, foil, paper, and sticks that would years later cause so much commotion were then delivered to the commanding officer of the 8th Army Air Corps, Brig. Gen. Roger M. Ramey. In a radio interview on July 8, Ramey identified the remains correctly and stated that "the wreckage is in my office now and as far as I can see there is nothing to get excited about" (quoted in Ziegler 1997, 9). Following wide reporting of this and other statements of Brig. Gen. Ramey, "the historical Roswell incident faded quickly from public memory and entered the limbo of over-publicized nonevents, where it remained for more than 30 years." Then, with the 1980 publication of *The Roswell Incident* by Charles Berlitz (yes, the same Charles Berlitz who made up the Bermuda Triangle nonmystery as described in the next chapter) and William L. Moore, Roswell reentered the UFO world—and it has never left. The history of the Roswell myth since 1980 is a history of ever-growing distortions, made-up events, deliberate misinterpretations, and previously unknown "witnesses" with ever more fantastic stories to tell. Readers interested in detailed analyses of these can consult books by Saler, Ziegler, and Moore (1997); Klass (1997); and McAndrews (1997). The latter is the official report of an investigation conducted in 1994 by the United States Air Force.

MJ-12 Documents and Area 51

In May 1987 another chapter in the continuing saga of claims that the federal government knows "all about" UFOs and is hiding the truth from the American public unfolded with the announcement by UFO proponents William Moore (one of the authors of *The Roswell Incident*) and Stanton Friedman that new secret government documents had come to light proving that the government knew that UFOs were of extraterrestrial origin. The documents concerned an alleged super-secret project called Majestic 12 (MJ-12). According to the documents, MJ-12 was set up to further the investigation of UFOs because the government had recovered crashed saucers at Roswell. The documents were not found in government archives. Physical copies of the documents have never been found. What Moore and Friedman claimed to have received in the mail was an undeveloped roll of film that, when developed, had photographs of the new evidence. Included were photographs of three different documents: a 1947 memo from President Harry Truman to Secretary of Defense James Forrestal; a 1952 briefing paper for President Elect Dwight D. Eisenhower; and a July 14, 1954, memo from Robert Cutler, a special assistant to President Eisenhower, to Air Force general Nathan Twining. The briefing paper describes the recovery of alien spacecraft and bodies at Roswell in 1947. The last memo informed the general that a briefing at the White House on MJ-12 would take place on July 16.

The MJ-12 documents immediately generated huge interest. Here, at last, there seemed to be real proof that the government had been keeping the existence of UFO debris secret all these years. But almost at once serious problems were noted with the documents. Klass (1987–1988a, 1987–1988b) pointed out several of these. For example, the second document, the briefing paper, used a format for the dates that was never used by the military. Specifically, throughout, dates are given thus: "07 July, 1947." Authentic documents from the period never use a "0" in front of a single digit in a date and never use a comma following the month. The date format used in the MJ-12 documents is one that William Moore used in his own correspondence. Another problem is that real secret documents later declassified show that one of the alleged members of the MJ-12 team, Lloyd Berkner, took part in a real CIA assessment of the nature of UFOs. This assessment "concluded that there was no evidence that any UFOs were extraterrestrial craft or posed any threat to national security" (Klass 1987–1988c, 283). This assessment was conducted years after the alleged creation of MJ-12. If the government in general, and Berkner in particular, already knew about UFOs, there would have been no need to conduct the highly secret assessment.

The July 14 memo from Cutler to General Twining has to be a forgery. This is due to the simple fact that Cutler couldn't have written it because he was out of the country from July 3 to July 15 (Klass 1987–1988b). Finally, the 1947 Truman memo is also clearly a fake. Analysis of the type style showed that the memo was written using a typewriter model that was first produced in 1963. Further, the signature on the memo was a modified photocopy of a real Truman signature taken from a genuine document (Klass 1987–1988c).

In 1994 another batch of supposed MJ-12 documents turned up, again in the form of an undeveloped roll of film sent anonymously to a UFO proponent. Klass (2000) showed that these also are fakes. For example, one of the new documents, dated 1954, refers to the now famous Area 51 in Nevada. But the term "Area 51" (at Nellis Air Force Base in Nevada) was not assigned until years later. The brief description above of a few of the problems with the MJ-12 documents does not do justice to the detailed analyses that Klass provided in his several articles, cited above, which give a fuller appreciation of the scope of the fakery.

Mentioned above, Area 51 is a location in the Nevada desert said to be a hotbed of UFO activity. In UFO lore, Area 51 is where the government has hidden crashed flying saucers and alien bodies. The area played an important role in the famous 1996 blockbuster science fiction film *Independence Day*. One of the reasons for the belief that Area 51 has something to do with UFOs is that Area 51 and the surrounding area have generated a very large number of UFO reports. Starting in the 1950s, pilots and ground observers alike reported objects in the sky flying much higher and much faster than any known aircraft was capable of at the time.

The reason for the reports from Area 51 was simple. There really were things flying in the sky around Area 51 that really were flying much higher and faster than any known aircraft at the time could. They just weren't extraterrestrial craft. They were very secret United States military spy planes and, later, planes with then secret stealth technology. The planes included the U-2 spy plane and the SR-71, an elegant stealth spy plane produced by Lockheed. Such aircraft had capabilities unknown in any civilian or even military aircraft at the time. The SR-71 "Blackbird" was developed in the early 1960s. It could operate at an altitude of 85,000 feet at speeds of Mach 3.2, or about 2,100 miles per hour. In contrast, the Boeing 727, one of the top-of-the-line commercial jets of the 1960s, cruised at 570 miles per hour and at an altitude of 36,000 feet. No wonder an SR-71 flying, as they did, only at night over Area 51 would provide a most astonishing sight to anyone who saw it. And they wouldn't see the entire aircraft, which was black, but only patterns of lights moving across the sky.

Project Bluebook, mentioned earlier, investigated UFO sightings. It did investigate sightings in the region of Area 51 and "found that most reports in southern Nevada could be explained by spy planes" from Area 51 (Prothero and Callahan 2017, 57). The true explanations for these sightings could not be revealed to the public because of the need for security during the Cold War. So, ironically, there *were* mysterious and unknown craft flying around southern Nevada in the 1950s and 1960s. And there was a government cover-up of sorts to keep this secret. But it had nothing to do with aliens and flying saucers.

A feature of the UFO narrative since the earliest UFO reports is the lone whistleblower who has or had access to secret government information that not only are UFOs real but the government knows it and has alien technology or bodies. A constant characteristic of these claims is that the individuals making them have never produced actual evidence that their stories are true. These types of claims typically generate, for a brief time, a lot of publicity in the uncritical media. An early example was Air Force major Jesse Marcel. He was involved in the investigation of the crash at Roswell and later claimed that an alien spacecraft had crashed there. A most recent version is David Grusch, a former Air Force intelligence officer. Grusch testified before Congress in July 2023. He says that the government has a program that has collected alien spacecraft and bodies. Sounds impressive. But, as always, no actual evidence is provided. Grusch doesn't even claim that he has seen any alien bits and pieces, but someone else *told him* about them. Grusch will have his proverbial fifteen minutes of fame and will fade away like the others before him. Sooner or later someone else will appear with claims that they know the government is hiding UFO secrets, and the cycle will repeat itself.

Alien Autopsy

If flying saucers had crashed at Roswell, or anywhere else for that matter, and bodies had been recovered, the bodies would serve as incontrovertible proof of the extraterrestrial origin of UFOs. Moore and Berlitz (1979) claimed that bodies were discovered at Roswell and that autopsies were performed on the bodies. While no actual alien bodies have ever turned up, it appeared in 1995 that the next best thing had—a film showing an autopsy on an alien body recovered from a crashed saucer.

Before discussing the film *Alien Autopsy*, it is worthwhile to consider what a real autopsy on the first-discovered alien body would be like. The discovery of such a body would rank among the greatest scientific discoveries in the history of humanity. The autopsy would be done with great care. The procedure would be performed by the best scientists available, and every aspect would be very carefully recorded and each step documented on film. Unlike normal autopsies, the dissecting portion of which can be finished in a few hours, the dissection alone of an alien body would probably take days, if not weeks.

This is hardly what is shown in *Alien Autopsy*. What is shown in the black-and-white film is a careless, sloppily performed autopsy shot in so amateurish a way that it is impossible to see much of what is going on during the procedure. The two "pathologists" are constantly getting in the way of the camera and obscuring the body. When the opened body is in full view, the film is often out of focus so details are hard to see. One almost gets the impression that the film was intentionally shot so that it would be difficult to see details. This is just how a bad hoax film would be shot.

There are numerous other features of the film that show it to be a hoax (Ellis 1995; Nickell 1995a). For one thing, one of the "pathologists" holds his scissors in the wrong position for cutting flesh. In addition, when the body and skull are opened, the organs (which are never clearly shown) are simply lifted out, with no additional cutting. In reality, the organs in any body have to be connected to the inside of the relevant cavity. If this was not the case, they would simply slosh around and be very easily damaged. Thus, the often very tough connective tissue must be cut before the organs can be removed. That there is no sign of such tissue in the film reveals the hoaxers' ignorance of basic anatomy. In addition, the two "pathologists" are shown wearing white suits, presumably for protection. But for protection against what? It couldn't have been for protection against germs, bad smells, or radiation because the suits were not sturdy enough to guard against radiation and there was no obvious breathing device to protect against odors or germs. Finally, when the film first appeared, it bore a supposed military security classification of "Restricted access, AO 1 classification." After it was shown that no such classification ever existed, this disappeared from later copies of the film (Nickell 1995a). All in all, it is easy to conclude that the *Alien Autopsy* film is a crudely done hoax.

Crop Circles

One of the more bizarre offshoots of the UFO movement was the advent of crop circles. Initially largely confined to England, the phenomena spread to other countries such as France, Germany, Japan, and to a lesser extent the United States. Although crop circles had been noticed in the late 1970s, it wasn't until the early 1980s that they began to occur in southern England in large enough numbers to attract real attention. Crop circles were patterns of varying size and shape that were found in farmers' fields and were made by using various tools as simple as boards to bend over stalks of field grains. They were inevitably found in the morning, having somehow been produced overnight. Their creators were not to be found. A simple crop circle is shown in figure 8.7.

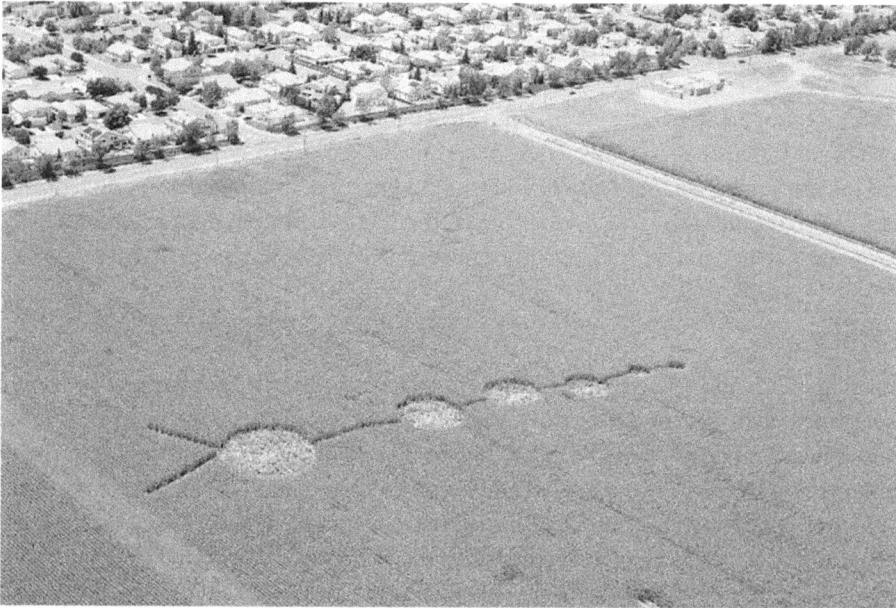

Figure 8.7. Aerial photo of crop circles in Vacaville, California. Photo by Steve M. Windham, LLM, www.windhamsolutions .com; piloted by Gene N. Windham, Esquire (https://en.wikipedia.org/wiki/File:VACAVILLE_CA_CROP_CIRCLE_ %28SMALL%29.jpg)

As is often the case with allegedly paranormal phenomenon, the more outlandish possible explanations generate much more attention and publicity than the more mundane explanations, at least at first. Such was the case with crop circles. There were several hypotheses as to their cause. One was that they were due to some type of small tornado or "whirlwind." Another camp held that they were created by UFOs, either directly when a UFO landed or hovered over the field, or indirectly by UFOs using some sort of energy from far above the atmosphere. A more amorphous theory looked to some new type of mysterious energy as the cause. As the fame of crop circles grew, dowsers flocked to the circles and swore that they could detect the presence of this mysterious energy inside the circles, but not outside the design. Finally, there was the boring old skeptical view that the circles were, in fact, created by an intelligence, but by a totally human intelligence. In other words, hoaxers.

As the 1980s progressed, the designs of the crop circles became more and more elaborate. Many were quite beautiful. One might think that as this complexity increased, and as messages like "WEAREИOTALOИE" (with the Ns reversed) began to appear, it would become clearer and clearer that the designs were of strictly human origin. Such was not the case. The continuing complexity was simply seen as further support for the proponents of each nonhuman origin story (Schnabel 1993). As the circles grew more complex and as the 1980s passed, UFO believers, new agers of various types, and mystics in general flocked to the circles.

The beginning of the end for crop circles came in September 1991 when two men from southern England, Doug Bower and Dave Chorley, admitted to the press that they had been making crop circles throughout the area around Southampton for years. They had used the simplest of tools—wooden boards attached to ropes—to knock down the grain. They left no footprints because they were careful and, when possible, walked in the tractor lines between the rows of grain. In many of their creations they left a sort of signature, two small half circles of bent-over grain stalks that looked like two filled-in letter *D*s. Of course, Doug and Dave were not the only hoaxers working, but they were the most prolific. Time and again their designs were certified as absolutely genuine by the dowsers as well as by the exponents of the various extraordinary theories of crop circle formation.

Following the revelations of Doug and Dave, interest in crop circles faded, and the number of circles seen each summer dropped (Nickell 1995b). Schnabel (1993), himself a creator of crop circles, has written the best account of the history of crop circles. As an insider for much of the time, he provides valuable insights into the movement. Nickell's (1996) entry in the *Encyclopedia of the Paranormal* provides a good short history and relevant references. Interest in crop circles was briefly rekindled in 2002 by the Mel Gibson movie *Signs*, which not-so-mysteriously vanished from theaters shortly after its release.

Face on Mars

When discussing UFOs and related phenomena, I'm sometimes asked, "What about the face on Mars?" The face first turned up in 1976 in a couple of photos of the surface of Mars taken by *Viking 1*. These rather low-resolution images (figure 8.8, left) seemed to show a gigantic face and attracted the attention of the UFO community. Proponents, chief among them Richard C. Hoagland (2001), who touted the face in his book *The Monuments of Mars: A City on the Edge of Forever*, argue that the face is evidence of an advanced Martian civilization. Much like George Leonard (page 3), who saw complicated structures in pictures of the moon's surface, Hoagland sees manufactured structures in photos of the Martian surface. He also sees all sorts of obscure pseudomathematical meanings in the arrangement of these Martian features. This is all little more than a high-tech version of Lowell's canals—with a bit more nonsense thrown in the pot.

Even if the initial images of the Mars face had turned out to be what the formation really looked like, so what? There are lots of geological formations that look meaningful in some way to the human brain. One of my favorites was the Old Man of the Mountains from my home state of New Hampshire. Figure 8.9 shows a U.S. postage stamp issued in 1955 to honor the Old Man. If the Mars face is a creation of one extraterrestrial civilization, then why is the Old Man not evidence of ancient civilizations visiting New

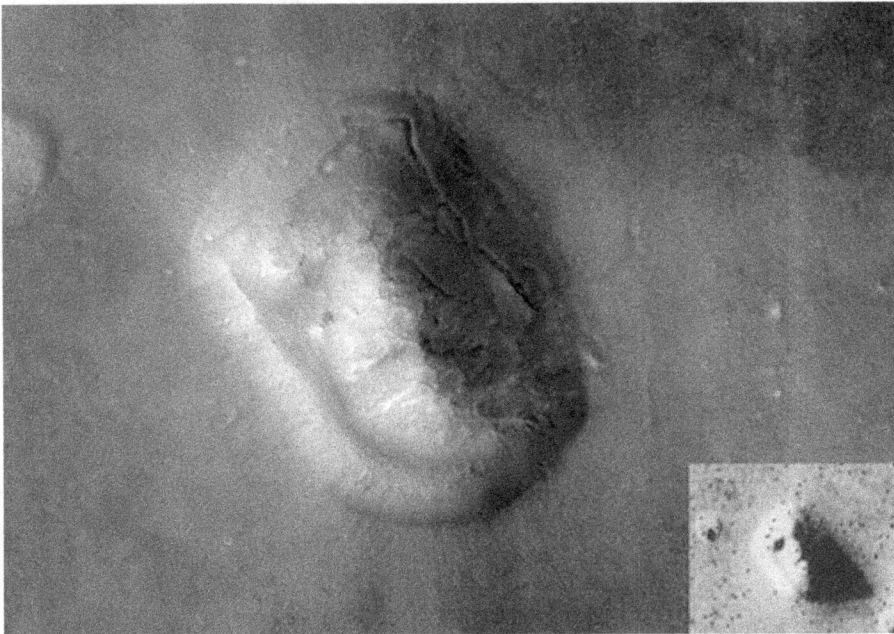

Figure 8.8. Photo from "Face on Mars with Inset." NASA/JPL/University of Arizona, 2007, via Wikipedia (https://en.wikipedia.org/wiki/File:Face_on_Mars_with_Inset.jpg). Cropping by User:Plumbago with Paint Shop Pro 9

Figure 8.9. 1955 Commemorative stamp showing New Hampshire's "Old Man of the Mountains." United States Scott Catalog #1068

Hampshire (perhaps to get a good view of the autumn foliage before all those annoying leaf-peepers arrived)? Sadly, the Old Man collapsed in May 2003. If the Old Man wasn't enough, there's also a Kermit the Frog on Mars (MacRobert 1982). Posner (2000) has published a review of the face-on-Mars claims. More detailed images from a 1998 survey of the red planet by the Mars Global Surveyor showed a much less dramatic picture. Of course, Hoagland (2001) can explain the lack of support for the reality of the face in the latest images. It's all a conspiracy, a cover-up. You see, the government really knows all about the Martian civilization and they (the big *they*) are doing everything they can to hide the truth. In reality, the Old Man, the Face on Mars, and Kermit are just more examples of pareidolia.

This and the preceding chapter have shown that the evidence for UFOs as extraterrestrial spacecraft "rests entirely on . . . uncorroborated human testimony" (Sheaffer 1978–1979, 67), the most unreliable type of evidence to be found. In more than seventy years of investigation, not one authentic photo of a UFO has been taken and not one piece of genuine debris or other physical evidence has been found. Impressive-sounding sightings are reported year after year, and, year after year, when carefully examined they disappear into the mists of misperceptions, misidentifications, and hoaxes. This has no effect on true believers; there is always another case to be sloppily investigated and trumpeted in the media as—finally—the conclusive proof that UFOs are "real." Upon investigation, this new case joins the multitude of others that were caused by misidentification of Venus, advertising aircraft, or hoaxes. Soon, however, there is *another* case that proves beyond a doubt . . .

ANCIENT ASTRONAUTS AND THE BERMUDA TRIANGLE

This chapter covers two pseudoscientific ideas that became popular in the 1970s, are related to the broader area of UFO beliefs, and are still widely accepted today. Both the ancient astronauts idea and, to a somewhat lesser extent, the Bermuda Triangle legend have been kept alive by popular TV shows like *Ancient Aliens* on the History Channel, which entered its twentieth season in 2024. Like the books that originally promoted these ideas, these so-called documentary programs consist of made-up stories, misinterpretations of basic facts, faked illustrations, and commentary from fake experts. It is typical History Channel and Syfy channel fare. Jason Colavito (2005), author of *The Cult of Ancient Aliens*, maintains a running review of the errors, frauds, and fallacies in each episode of "Ancient Aliens" at https://www.jasoncolavito.com/ancient -aliens-reviews.html.

ANCIENT ASTRONAUTS

The "ancient astronaut" theory was popularized during the 1970s and has adherents to this day. Its major promotor, Erich von Däniken, made an appearance, at age eighty-three, at AlienCon in Pasadena in June 2018. Von Däniken's basic ideas is that Earth was repeatedly visited in the historic past by intelligent beings from other worlds. The "ancient astronauts" helped ancient cultures create some of the great wonders of the ancient world, such as the Great Pyramid, the statues on Easter Island, and the huge markings on Peru's Nazca Desert. The idea is that these ancient humans could not have created these artifacts by themselves. Von Däniken claimed that there was clear evidence of these ancient astronauts (whom primitive humans viewed as gods) in the drawings, carvings, myths, and legends of ancient peoples and that the ancient astronaut theory solves many archeological mysteries.

Von Däniken was not the first promoter of this theory (Krupp 1981; Story 1976), but he is certainly the most successful. He made millions of dollars from his numerous books, movies, television shows, and lectures. Von Däniken was a master of that popular technique among proponents of pseudoscience, looking for mysteries (Radner and Radner 1982). He searched the archeological literature to find artifacts, objects, and phenomena that he, and most of his readers, could not explain even though the explanations were well known to anyone who had majored in archeology. He then attributed them to the ancient astronauts. His style of writing was such as to direct readers' thoughts away from other possible explanations for the phenomena in question. "How could such and such have been produced," he asks rhetorically, "if not by ancient astronauts?" The reader of ancient astronaut books or viewer of ancient astronaut TV shows, whose knowledge of archeology is probably limited, doesn't know how the object was actually produced and so accepts the ancient astronauts explanation. Von Däniken developed this technique further: he fabricates mysteries where one never existed in the first place. His comments about the Piri Re'is map, a map dated to 1513 showing the Mediterranean area, illustrate this technique. Von Däniken claimed that the map is "absolutely accurate" and that "the coasts of North and South America and even the contours of the Antarctic were also perfectly delineated" (von Däniken 1970, 30). What is his explanation for this great accuracy? "Comparisons with modern photographs of our globe taken from satellites showed that the original of the Piri Re'is maps [sic] must have been aerial photographs taken from a very great height. How can that be explained? A spaceship hovers high above Cairo and points its camera straight down" (31).

Even if the reader of the above scenario doesn't immediately accept von Däniken's explanation for the great accuracy of the Piri Re'is map (in spite of von Däniken's frequent use of the plural, there is only one map), the mystery of the map's great accuracy will certainly stay in mind. But there is no mystery that needs explaining in the first place. The Piri Re'is map is a very good map—but only in comparison with other maps of its day (Story 1976). There are numerous inaccuracies in the map, such as leaving off half of the island of Cuba (Hapgood 1966). This would hardly be expected from the advanced civilization von Däniken proposes. In this instance, as in so many others, von Däniken lies to his readers. He fabricates evidence and distorts the facts with the sole purpose of supporting his theories. Readers unaware of the detailed archeological research on the various pseudomysteries that von Däniken makes up are tricked into thinking that the evidence for the ancient astronaut theory is much stronger than it really is. Another nonmystery concerns an island in the Nile called Elephantine. Von Däniken (1970) says it is called Elephantine "even in the oldest texts" because the island is shaped "like an elephant." But how, he asks, "did the ancient Egyptians know that? This shape can be recognized only from an airplane at a great height" (84). The island is not shaped like an elephant. A glance at a map reveals it to be rather long and pointed at one end. The island bears the name it does because there may have been elephants on it at one time and because it was the site of ivory trading (Story 1976). Again, von Däniken simply lied to his readers.

Von Däniken was at his most creative when he discussed the alleged mysteries of ancient Egypt. The pyramids of Egypt fascinate him, as do the mummies. More than anything else, von Däniken's distorted and inaccurate writings on ancient Egypt were responsible for the belief in "pyramid power," the idea that the shape of the pyramid is itself magical and possesses preservative powers.

PYRAMID POWER, PYRAMIDS, AND MUMMIES

Influenced by Erich von Däniken's claims that Egyptian mummies had been preserved by some process unknown to science, pyramid power became quite a craze in the world of pseudoscience in the mid-1970s. The idea was that the pyramidal shape itself was magical and filled with a mysterious energy and power. In Toth and Nielsen's (1976) *Pyramid Power*, we are told that pyramid power is "the fuel of the future" (frontispiece). The back cover of King's (1977) *Pyramid Energy Handbook* hints that pyramids can "deepen your ESP" and "make your plants grow." MacRobert (1982) reports that it was not unusual to see people walking around with pyramid-shaped hats at new age gatherings. I recall seeing an advertisement in a Sunday newspaper supplement for a pyramid-shaped doghouse guaranteed to rid dogs of fleas.

Pyramid power claims have been tested. Alter (1973) and Simmons (1973) placed meat and flowers in pyramid-shaped containers. These were no more effective than any other shape at preserving the material placed in them. Nor did putting dull razor blades in a pyramid-shaped holder restore them to sharpness, contrary to a frequent claim of pyramid power promoters. Nonetheless, it was certainly possible to obtain testimonials from people who swore that putting a razor blade under a pyramid made it sharper. How could they believe that? As anyone who has used razor blades knows, even a dull blade can be used if it is needed badly enough. The pyramid power believer puts a dull blade under a pyramid at night and then shaves with it the next morning. Expecting it to be sharper, at least a little bit, he perceives it as sharper, but never bothers to make any real measurements of the sharpness. Thus, the belief is perpetuated. Pyramid power is still with us and has become part of the new age belief system. A Google search for "pyramid power" resulted in over 139 million hits.

Von Däniken (1970) tells us that the primitive Egyptians couldn't possibly have built the pyramids by themselves. The entire culture of ancient Egypt "appears suddenly and without transition with a fantastic ready-made civilization" (95). Certainly, the Egyptians couldn't have evolved such an advanced culture so rapidly; it must have been due to infusions of advanced knowledge from extraterrestrial visitors. As usual, von Däniken's facts are simply wrong, as any text on Egyptian history shows. The evolution of Egyptian culture is well known from the time of the region's unification, about 3100 BCE; through the Old Kingdom, about 2680 to 2180 BCE; to the New Kingdom, about 1600 to 1085 BCE. The New Kingdom was the period of the Great Pyramids.

Contrary to von Däniken's claims, the pyramids did not simply spring up out of the desert with no history of development. The history of the pyramids can be traced from their predecessors, called *mastabas*, which were small brick tombs. One famous pyramid shows that the pyramid builders occasionally made errors. This pyramid, at Meidum (figure 9.1), was originally built with its walls too steep to support its own weight. The top part of the structure collapsed into the rubble now found at the base of the pyramid. This is hardly the kind of accuracy one would expect from super advanced space-traveling beings. The Egyptian engineers, like any intelligent humans, learned from their mistakes, and later pyramids were built with less steep sides.

Von Däniken (1970) made other claims about the pyramids that simply aren't true. He asked, "Is it really a coincidence that the height of the pyramid of Cheops multiplied by a thousand million—98,000,000 miles—corresponds approximately to the distance between the earth and sun?" (98). The answer is clearly yes. And von Däniken even managed to get the distance between Earth and the sun wrong: it is 93 million, not 98 million miles. An error of 6 percent is hardly the accuracy to be expected from interstellar navigators. Such a numbers game is easy to play, even if one takes the effort to get one's numbers right. As was pointed out on an episode of National Educational Television's *Nova* program titled "The Case of the Ancient Astronauts," which was first broadcast in 1978, the height of the Washington Monument multiplied by forty gives the distance in light-years to the second nearest star, Proxima Centauri. In the far future, will some von Däniken–like charlatan claim that ancient Americans were much too dumb to have built such a

Figure 9.1. Meidum pyramid. Photo by Kurohito, 2010 (https://commons.wikimedia.org/wiki/File:Meidoum03.jpg). CC BY-SA 3.0

magnificent monument themselves and must, therefore, have had help from space travelers from a planet in the Proxima Centauri system?

Von Däniken (1970) also said that the building of the pyramids was impossible for the Egyptians because they lacked the necessary technology. He said that the method of building the pyramids is unknown and that conventional methods could not have been used since the Egyptians didn't have rope or trees to make rollers to move the stones. All this is false. The methods of building the pyramids are recorded in the pyramids themselves. Rope was available in great quantity, and examples are preserved in many museums. Logs for rollers were widely used. The methods of quarrying the stone and transporting it by barge from the quarries to the site of the pyramids are also known (Story 1976).

If pyramids baffle von Däniken, mummies pose even more of a puzzle for him. Their existence suggests to him that the Egyptians were given the secret of immortality by their extraterrestrial visitors. The extraterrestrials will be able to bring the mummies back to life when they return. In an interview broadcast on the *Nova* program mentioned above, von Däniken said the extraterrestrials might have told Pharaoh, "Listen, we come back let's say in 5,000 years, we are able to reconstruct your body, if you only take care that we find at least a few living cells of your body, but be careful, take your brain away into a separate pot because if we want to construct also the same memory as you had, we need your brain separately." In his 1970 book he says that mummies are "incomprehensible" (101) and that the techniques of mummification remain a mystery to modern science. This is all totally false.

Like the techniques used to build the pyramids, the techniques used in mummification developed gradually during the history of Egypt. Harris and Weeks (1973) described this development briefly and then discuss in more detail the thirteen separate steps involved in mummification during the New Kingdom. Examination of the steps shows the ridiculous nature of von Däniken's claims regarding the purpose of mummification. Advanced as they were, the ancient Egyptians had little knowledge of the brain's function. They viewed the brain as an organ of little importance (the understanding that the brain is the organ of the mind is a very modern one, dating only from the seventeenth and eighteenth centuries in Western thought). Thus, when the body was mummified, the brain was pulled out bit by bit through the nose, using long tweezers, and thrown away. Unlike the other internal organs, it was not saved in a separate jar. So much for bringing back Pharaoh, complete with his memories.

In fact, the elaborate mummification ritual was designed to aid the trip to the afterlife. The internal organs (except the brain) were preserved because the dead would still need them in the afterlife, just as in this one. Pets and servants were often killed and mummified so they could accompany the deceased. The Egyptians clearly did not believe that people came back from the dead. This is shown by the lovely "Song of the Harpers," found inscribed on the walls of several tombs from the Middle Kingdom period:

> What has been done with them? What are their places [now]?
> Their walls have crumbled and their places are not, As if they had never been
> No one has [ever] come back from [the dead]
> That he might describe their condition, And relate their needs;
> That he might calm our hearts
> Until we [too] pass into that place where they have gone [Let us] make holiday and never tire of it!
> [For] behold, no man can take his property with him, No man who has gone can return again. (Harris and Weeks 1973, 117)

In his later writings, von Däniken (1984) suggested that the famous curse on King Tutankhamen's tomb may have been the result of some sort of extraterrestrial protection given the tomb. According to the usual legend, many of the individuals who opened Tut's tomb when it first was found in 1922 died shortly thereafter under mysterious circumstances. The deaths are attributed to a curse allegedly placed on anyone who defiled the tomb. This curse was said to be inscribed on the door of the tomb when it was found. Randi (1978) analyzed the deaths supposedly due to the curse and found that the death rate was just what would be expected, given that many of the members of the expedition were quite elderly and that they were living in a country where modern sanitary facilities and health measures were lacking.

It was later revealed (Frazier 1980–1981) that the curse was a hoax in the first place. The security officer for the expedition, Richard Adamson, stated in 1980 that the curse story was dreamed up to keep would-be robbers away from the opened tomb. The news that the Curse of Tut had been a hoax did not stop an enterprising San Francisco policeman from suing the city for disability payments when he suffered a stroke while guarding the King Tut museum exhibit while it was in San Francisco in 1979. He claimed that Tut's spirit "lashed out at him," causing the stroke. The suit was dismissed (Frazier 1980–1981, 12).

VON DÄNIKEN IN PERU

Another favorite von Däniken pseudomystery is the set of large designs found in the Nazca Desert of Peru. Intricate patterns of lines, pictures of giant birds, monkeys, spiders, and other animals, cover an area of about sixty by ten miles. Von Däniken suggested that the lines are the remains of an ancient "spaceport" and landing field. He doubted that primitive peoples could have produced the lines and figures without some extraterrestrial help through "instructions from an aircraft" (von Däniken 1970, 33). (See figure 9.2.)

In reality, the lines in the Nazca plain represent a complex astronomical calendar and observatory, testifying to the astronomical sophistication of the peoples who created them (Story 1976; Kosok and Reiche 1949; Krupp 1978; Hadingham 1987). Von Däniken's contempt for "primitive" peoples is shown when he belittles their ability to create such large figures on their own. How, he asks, could they have created the nearly perfect circles found in some of the figures? Simple—dig a hole and place a stake in it. Tie a rope of a certain length to the stake. Stretch the rope to its full length and then walk in a circular

Figure 9.2. Nazca figure. Photo by Diego Delso, delso.photo, 2015 (https://commons.wikimedia.org/wiki/File:L%C3%ADneas_de_Nazca,_Nazca,_Per%C3%BA,_2015-07-29,_DD_54.JPG). CC BY-SA

pattern. The stake, moving freely around in the unfilled hole, will turn and the rope, maintaining its length, will allow one to trace out a nearly perfect circle. Certainly, the people who created the Nazca designs thought of this simple method. Nickell (1982–1983) showed that it is possible to produce a full-size duplicate of a Nazca drawing—440 feet long—using only "sticks and cord such as the Nazcas might have employed" (42). It took six people about a day and a half to complete the figure.

In his other six major books, von Däniken creates hundreds of other pseudomysteries. The books are masterpieces of distortion, evasion, and deceptive writing, all in support of his half-baked ideas. Like a true proponent of pseudoscience, von Däniken does not revise his theories or claims in light of new evidence. For example, in *Chariots of the Gods?* (1970) a picture appears with the legend, "This is very reminiscent of the aircraft parking bays on a modern airport." The picture shows part of the wing, with individual feathers, of one of the giant Nazca plain bird designs. What the reader is not told and cannot judge from the photograph is that the whole photo shows an area only twenty feet across—hardly enough to contain extraterrestrial aircraft. In his *Nova* interview, von Däniken acknowledged this, saying, "I fully admit that this explanation of being a parking place is simply ridiculous." But while the book went through numerous printings, the error was never corrected.

THE BERMUDA TRIANGLE

Von Däniken brought his ancient astronaut idea to popularity in the 1970s. Another modern myth was also fabricated in the 1970s: the Bermuda Triangle, where ships and planes allegedly disappear under the most mysterious of circumstances.

Stories of mysterious disappearances in the Bermuda Triangle area are alleged to date back to the 1800s. For years they appeared in books of miscellaneous "mysterious" events, such as Frank Edwards's *Stranger Than Science* (1959) and *Strangest of All* (1956). It was Charles Berlitz's 1974 *The Bermuda Triangle Mystery* that really brought to the public's attention the idea that strange events were taking place in the area. The book became a bestseller and, like von Däniken's books, spawned a series of films, television programs, and imitators. Berlitz, like von Däniken, made a fortune from royalties and the lecture circuit.

The Bermuda Triangle is a manufactured mystery from start to finish. The numerous articles and books touting the "mystery" are inaccurate, misleading, and often willfully deceptive in their descriptions of the alleged mysterious happenings in the triangle. Kusche (1981, 297) accurately characterizes the triangle mystery as "the epitome of false reporting; deletion of pertinent information; twisted values among writers, publishers and the media; mangling of scientific principles; and the often deliberate deception of a trusting public." For example, ships that are said to have vanished under mysterious and unexplainable circumstances turn out upon investigation to have sunk during hurricanes. Other reported disappearances never happened at all. In some cases, ships said to have disappeared never existed in the first place. Other sinkings and disappearances attributed to the triangle took place thousands of miles away.

There is not enough space here to detail what really happened to each of the ships and planes that, according to the mythmakers, vanished mysteriously in the triangle. I will describe several representative cases found in the sensational literature and contrast these fantasies with the results of careful investigations of the actual occurrences. These investigations were carried out by Kusche (1975) and are reported in his book *The Bermuda Triangle Mystery—Solved*. Other critical discussions of the Bermuda Triangle can be found in Kusche (1977–1978a) and Dennett (1981–1982).

Berlitz's (1974) best-selling *The Bermuda Triangle Mystery* describes the strange case of the *Marine Sulphur Queen*. She carried a cargo of fifteen thousand tons of molten sulfur and sailed from Beaumont, Texas, on February 2, 1963. According to Berlitz, "the weather was good" and "the large vessel disappeared in good weather" (56, caption on fourth page of plates). Berlitz further states that two life jackets were the only remains of the ship ever found and that the Coast Guard investigation offered "neither solution nor theory concerning this disaster" (57).

These statements are simply false. The weather may have been good on February 2, 1963, when the ship left harbor, but it certainly wasn't good when she sank. A routine radio message from the ship was sent at about 1:30 a.m. on February 4. This was the last radio contact. About twelve hours previously, according to the Coast Guard Board of Investigation report that Kusche (1975) examined, another ship in the area reported that there were "very rough seas and her decks were awash" (186). Winds gusted to just below hurricane strength, and the waves were more than thirty-five feet high. This is hardly the calm, peaceful ocean scene painted by Berlitz.

The claim that only two life jackets were ever found adds to the picture of a ship simply vanishing without a trace. The Coast Guard Board of Investigation report shows that the true story is quite different. A foghorn from the ship was found, and over the second phase of the search "additional debris were recovered and identified as coming from the *Marine Sulphur Queen*" (Kusche 1975, 188).

Contrary to Berlitz's claim, the Coast Guard did propose several theories and possible solutions for the sinking. Among these was the suggestion that the ship may have broken in two. During its conversion to a molten sulfur carrier, bulkheads that strengthened the hull had been removed. Another possible solution mentioned by the Coast Guard is that the ship capsized in the rough seas known to be running at the time. Also mentioned was the possibility of an explosion, either from steam or from the fumes of sulfur. The latter theory is given credence by the fact that tons of molten sulfur were known to have leaked into the ship's bilges during previous voyages.

The loss of the *Marine Sulphur Queen* was certainly tragic, and the exact cause of the sinking will probably never be known. However, it is far from a mysterious occurrence. The weather was very bad, and the ship suffered from at least two serious structural flaws (the removal of the bulkheads and the leaking of molten sulfur) that could have been responsible. The promoters of the triangle mystery, in their eagerness to sell sensational books, have failed to mention these facts.

Gaddis (1965), another triangle mystery proponent, described the loss of the *Sandra*, a freighter "350 feet in length," in June 1950: "She disappeared as completely as if she had never existed—in the tropic dusk, in peaceful weather—just off the Florida coast" (202). The length given by Gaddis is nearly double the ship's actual size. The weather was not peaceful. The ship left harbor on April 5, 1950, and the *Miami Herald* reported on April 8, 1950, that "a storm growing from the low pressure areas which caused thundershowers and strong winds in Florida during the past three days approached hurricane force and buffeted Atlantic shipping lanes Friday. . . . [Winds] reached a speed of 73 miles an hour off the Virginia Capes" (Kusche 1975, 163). The "Friday" mentioned was April 7, two days after the *Sandra* left port in Savannah, Georgia. Once again, the "calm sea" picture is false—there is no mystery about this disappearance. Berlitz (1974) even manages to place one ship in the wrong ocean. He reports the case of the *Freya*, which he says was found abandoned "in the Triangle area . . . sailing from Manzanillo, Cuba, to ports in Chile" (50). The *Freya* was found partially dismasted and floating on her side in the Pacific Ocean off the western coast of Mexico. In reporting the incident, the British science magazine *Nature* reported that severe earthquakes had occurred in western Mexico for two or three days after the ship's departure from a western Mexican port. Such quakes can cause tidal waves that "probably caused the damage to the Freya which led to its abandonment" (*Nature*, April 25, 1907, p. 610; cited in Kusche 1975, 48).

Kusche (1981) analyzed in detail the made-up mystery of the *Ellen Austin*. This is an example of an incident that almost certainly never occurred. Kusche's analysis shows how reports of triangle mysteries grow as they are copied and embellished by one careless writer after another. The end product is a tale full of such specific but made-up detail that most readers will accept it as fact.

The basic story of the *Ellen Austin* is best given in the first version of the story that Kusche (1981) could find. The following passage is from that version, which appeared in Gould (1944).

> Last, and queerest of all, comes the case of the abandoned derelict, in seaworthy condition, which the British ship *Ellen Austin* encountered, in mid-Atlantic, in the year 1881. She put a small prize-crew aboard the stranger, with instructions to make for St. John's, Newfoundland, where she was bound herself. The two ships parted company in foggy weather but a few days later they met again. And the strange derelict was once more deserted. Like their predecessors, the prize crew had vanished forever.

Even after extensive research, Kusche (1975, 1981) was never able to find any evidence that this ever occurred. Gould, as is typical of "mysterious events" writers, gave no source for his information on the *Ellen Austin*. Kusche checked the indexes of the *New York Times* and the *London Times*. They contained no references to stories describing such a ship. The *Boston Globe*, the *Boston Herald American*, and the *Boston Evening Transcript* were also devoid of stories on the incident. The ship was said to be bound for St. John's, Newfoundland. The public library there could find no references to such an event in its files. The two St. John's newspapers of the day, the *Evening Telegram* and the *Newfoundlander*, were also empty of any reports relevant to either the incident or the ship *Ellen Austin*. If such a strikingly unusual occurrence had taken place, it is inconceivable that it would not have been reported in at least one of the papers Kusche searched. That no such story even appeared strongly suggests that Gould made up the whole thing in the first place.

Gould's original report contained eighty-two words. The word count grows over the years as the story is copied from one Bermuda Triangle author to another, none ever bothering to check whether the event really occurred as described. Vincent Gaddis's (1965, 131) version of the story contains 188 words and is marked by much detail that was not present in Gould's (1944) original report. Thus, for example, when the *Ellen Austin*'s captain saw the derelict for the second time, it was "pursuing an erratic course. He ordered the helmsman to approach the derelict. When there was no response a boarding party was sent over. To a man the frightened remaining sailors refused to join another prize crew."

Where did these additional details come from? Gaddis references only Gould's original (1944) report, but since these details are not in Gould, Gaddis must simply have made them up to make the story sound better.

Sanderson (1970) reports the incident in 429 words, and much new detail emerges. He mentions a temporary log kept by the prize crew, for example. Sanderson's version is an embellishment of Gaddis's version, which in turn is an embellishment of Gould's version.

In his 1974 *The Bermuda Triangle Mystery*, Berlitz describes the *Ellen Austin* mystery in a spare 172 words. But an amazing thing happened between 1970 (Sanderson's version) and 1974. In Berlitz's version, a second prize crew is persuaded to go aboard, and they vanish along with the derelict. Berlitz cites as sources both Sanderson (1970) and Gaddis (1965). Obviously, the story of the second prize crew is pure fiction made up by Berlitz to enhance the mystery.

Ships are not the only things at risk in the Bermuda Triangle. Aircraft of all sorts, we are told by the myth mongers, run the risk of mysteriously winking out of existence if they dare fly in or near the triangle. The reports of aircraft disappearances in the triangle are of the same low reliability as reports of disappearing ships. Relevant facts are withheld from readers and fictional details are added. It is largely because of such fictional additions that one of the missing aircraft stories has become the most famous of all the Bermuda Triangle legends. This is the case of Flight 19.

Flight 19 consisted of five U.S. Army Air Corps Avenger aircraft. These were introduced in 1941 as carrier-based torpedo planes and carried a crew of three—pilot, gunner, and bombardier (figure 9.3). The flight was under the command of Lt. Charles C. Taylor. It left Fort Lauderdale, Florida, Naval Air Station on December 5, 1945, at about 2 p.m. The flight plan called for a course eastward, then a turn to the north, followed about seventy miles later by a turn to the southwest to bring the flight back to base.

Figure 9.3. Avenger aircraft. Photo by USN, from en.wikipedia, by uploader Felix c, 1942 (https://commons.wikimedia.org/wiki/File:TBF_mid1942.jpg)

The version of the Flight 19 story presented to the public by such unreliable writers as Gaddis and Berlitz has it that the pilots and crew were all "experienced airmen" (Berlitz 1974, 13). As the flight progressed, these experienced flyers became mysteriously lost, despite the "ideal flight conditions" (Gaddis 1965, 191). Radio communications between the pilots and the base revealed something strange going on: "Everything is wrong . . . strange. Even the ocean doesn't look as it should," Gaddis (1965, 191) and Berlitz (1974, 14) quote one of the pilots as reporting. Gaddis adds, "Apparently not only the sea looked strange, but *the sun was invisible*" (1965, 192, emphasis added). No trace was ever found of the planes or any of the crew. This, too, we are told, is a great mystery. How could five such aircraft vanish so completely, especially in the face of the massive search that was conducted? Berlitz suggests a shocking answer: The planes, crews and all, were kidnapped by UFOs. He says, "A mother of one of the lost pilots who attended the naval hearing stated at the time that she had received the impression that her son 'was still alive somewhere in space.'" He also quotes approvingly the view of a local "scientist" that "they are still here, but in a different dimension of a magnetic phenomenon that could have been set up by a UFO" (1974, 18). (Incidentally, the sharp-eyed movie viewer may recall that Flight 19 played a minor part in *Close Encounters of the Third Kind*. When the UFO finally lands at the secret government installation at Devil's Tower, who pops out of the UFO but the crew of Flight 19, all decked out in their original flight gear and not having aged a bit.)

Investigation of what actually happened to Flight 19 explodes the fictionalized stories that are foisted on the reading public as nonfiction. Kusche (1980) devoted an entire book, *The Disappearance of Flight 19*, to telling what really happened to this flight. The following information is taken from that book. Flight 19 was not manned by a group of experienced aviators. It was a navigational training flight. With the exception of Taylor, the leader, the other pilots were not experienced. They were students. The "excellent flight conditions" are another fiction. The weather was only "average to undesirable for a training flight" (Kusche 1980, 7), with gusty winds up to thirty-one knots and moderate to rough sea. The forecast called for scattered showers until about 6 p.m. On December 5, 1945, the sun set at 5:29 p.m. It is important to understand that aircraft in 1945 had none of the sophisticated navigational equipment that is now carried even by light private aircraft. The pilots of Flight 19 were navigating with compasses, air speed indicators, and turn-and-bank indicators. To make matters worse, air speed is not equal to ground speed. It can be greater than, equal to, or less than ground speed, depending on the strength and direction of the wind. Further, the compasses of the only experienced pilot in the flight, Lt. Taylor, were broken, so he couldn't navigate. He had to depend on the students for correct navigation. The flight was over water, which obviously has very few landmarks. These factors alone would lead any experienced pilot to predict trouble of some sort, but another factor is important: Taylor had been flying out of Fort Lauderdale, Florida, for only two weeks. His previous flying assignment in Florida, after transferring stateside from the Pacific Theater, had consisted of eight months of flying from a base in Miami, well south of Fort Lauderdale. Thus, when he led Flight 19, he was unfamiliar with the area into which he was flying. If he was flying out of Miami, he would be nearer to the Florida Keys than when flying from Fort Lauderdale.

As could be predicted based on the poor conditions—meteorological, instrumentational, and experiential—about one hour and twenty minutes after takeoff, Taylor was unsure of his location. The Naval Board of Investigation quoted him as asking for directions and saying, "I'm sure I'm in the Keys" (Kusche 1980, 4). As the afternoon wore on, the flight became more lost and confused. Radio messages among the five pilots that were monitored on shore and printed in the transcript of the Naval Board of Investigation report or associated documents reveal considerable confusion as to their location. Taylor ordered several changes of direction during the next few hours, including 180-degree changes. Importantly, the statements attributed to the flight that appear in the Gaddis and Berlitz volumes, and that were noted above, do not appear in the official record. They, like so much else in this manufactured mystery, were made up after the fact to spice up the story.

By the time the sun set at 5:29 p.m., Flight 19 had been flying around lost for about two hours. Being lost, especially over the ocean with no landmarks (and no airports!), is a terrifying experience for any pilot, especially a student pilot. Fear does not lead to clearheaded, rational behavior, and even experienced individuals' decision-making abilities are severely impaired in stressful situations. This fear probably contributed to the several unhelpful course changes ordered by Taylor that must have badly disoriented all five pilots.

All during this time, radio communication between the planes and shore bases had been weak. Taylor did not switch from the static-filled training frequency to another frequency, perhaps, Kusche (1980) speculates, out of fear that switching radio frequency would put the five planes out of radio contact if it were not carried out correctly by all the students. As sunset approached, and as the planes flew farther and farther away from Fort Lauderdale, communication became even worse.

Where were the planes going? Contrary to the usual report of the incident, an approximate position for the lost flight was calculated from different directional bearings. These bearings revealed that the flight was much farther north than had been suspected, about three hundred miles north of Fort Lauderdale and about two hundred miles east of the Florida coast. At 6:04 p.m., thirty-five minutes after sundown, when the flight was flying in the dark, Taylor was heard to order the flight, "Holding west course. Didn't go far enough east. Turn around again. We may just as well turn around and go east" (Kusche 1980, 36). Of course, flying east would take them away from land, not toward it. Taylor was obviously very confused about his position. At 6:06 p.m. Taylor ordered, "Turn around and fly east until we run out of gas" (36). Unfortunately, the flight's position as calculated by the radio bearings was never radioed to the flight due to failure of the teletype communication system used and radio problems.

The flight had fuel to last until about 7:00 p.m. Then they would have to ditch their aircraft in the sea. While Taylor had ditched twice before in the Pacific, the conditions there were quite different from those he now faced. His previous two ditches had been in daylight with rescue ships standing by. Now he had to ditch at night in rough seas. None of the students had ever ditched before. Landing an aircraft on the water is never an easy task, even in the best of conditions. When an Avenger ditched, it usually hit the water at about eighty miles an hour. Such an impact can produce everything from a dazed state to unconsciousness. The best "ditch" is one where the plane's tail hits the water first and pulls the rest of the plane down. Flying headfirst into the water will cause much greater injury to the crew. To be able to land tail down in the water, one needs first to be able to see the water, which is difficult at night, and needs experience, which only Taylor had. Rough seas, like those running that night, make ditching even more dangerous.

Contrary to the usual version of the story, the Avenger is a very unseaworthy craft. It sinks like a "lead banana" (Kusche 1980, 28) within thirty seconds to a minute and a half. Nor is it easy to climb out of the aircraft and get out the emergency life raft. The pilot and the two crew members must get out of the plane, stand on the wing (in this case at night in rough seas), pull out and inflate the life raft, and get in it. On top of this, many of the crew were probably stunned and relatively helpless due to the impact of the crash. All this had to be accomplished by frightened men who had never had any such experience before. And it had to be done in the rolling seas in the dark in the ninety seconds before the planes sank. Tragically, the task was not accomplished. That no bodies and no trace of life rafts or the aircraft themselves were ever found shows that no one was successful in freeing the rafts from the planes. Perhaps a few crew members got out of the planes and in panic jumped into the sea and drowned. In that vast expanse of ocean there would be almost no chance of finding a body. Probably most of the crew members, stunned by the impact and unsure of what to do, drowned when their planes sank. Their deaths, although tragic and unnecessary, are not mysterious.

The legend of Flight 19 is enhanced by the fact that one of the planes sent to search for the five Avengers was also lost. The plane, a Mariner, took off about 7:30 p.m. and not, as is often claimed, during the late afternoon. Mariners were called "flying gas tanks" by flight crews "because of the fumes that were often present, and a crewman sneaking a cigarette, or a spark from any source could have caused [an] explosion" (Kusche 1980, 119). An explosion was seen in the air just where the Mariner would have been about twenty minutes after takeoff. Clearly, the Mariner had blown up. Another tragic, but not mysterious, loss of life. The loss of Flight 19 turns out to be no less a manufactured mystery than any of the other nonmysteries described by the likes of Berlitz and Gaddis.

It is amusing and instructive to examine the explanations that Berlitz puts forward for the nonevents he made up for his book. The Bermuda Triangle is a popular topic with UFO proponents, the idea being that the triangle is some type of prime hunting ground for the saucer people. As noted above, Berlitz described the UFO kidnapping hypothesis as a reasonable one. In fact, over half of *The Bermuda Triangle Mystery* is devoted to UFOs, ancient astronauts, and even the tale of Atlantis. Berlitz, it turns out, has found out about a well-known structure called the Bimini Road or Wall. Of it he says, "Shape and placement of these monoliths, rightangled corners, and pillars underneath some of the stones are conclusive, although not yet universally accepted, proof that they are man-made" (Berlitz 1974, figure caption following p. 134). He goes on to speculate that the builders were the Atlanteans, who had an advanced civilization. The "columns" Berlitz refers to are actually a mile or so from the "road" and are of recent origin—they are cement that was stored in barrels and tossed into the sea. The barrels rotted away, leaving the "columns." The actual rocks in the Bimini Road are known to be natural formations. They are just a little over two thousand years old (Shinn 1978).

Berlitz (1977) claimed in *Without a Trace* that he found a giant pyramid, like the ones in Egypt, in the triangle and that somehow it is responsible for all the disappearances in the triangle. No one else, including the U.S. Navy, has been able to locate this giant object, and the book contains Berlitz's usual false statements, errors, and deceptions (Kusche 1977–1978b; Klass 1977–1978).

In 1979, Berlitz (Moore and Berlitz 1979) turned his attention away from the Bermuda Triangle and toward a most amazing navy experiment. It seems that in the 1950s the navy managed to make an entire battleship invisible and transport it instantly from Newport News, Virginia, to a navy yard on the West

Coast. Of course, only Berlitz has managed to ferret out the truth about this. It's interesting that the navy seems utterly unconcerned about having the most spectacular defense secret of the century revealed.

In the end, the Bermuda Triangle mystery turns out to be one of the longest-running hoaxes of the twentieth and twenty-first centuries. Yet many people are surprised to hear this. They have heard so much about it that they assume there must be something to it. There isn't, but the continued existence of the triangle hoax is another example of the power of irresponsible writers and the media to deceive the public.

FAITH HEALING

You are at a "miracle service" given by famed faith healer Kathryn Kuhlman (1907–1976). There are thousands of people in the audience. You have seen several seemingly amazing cures, but the most dramatic is about to occur. Kuhlman shouts out, "Someone here is being cured of cancer!" Then you see a fifty-year-old woman, a Mrs. Helen Sullivan (not her real name), arise from a wheelchair and hobble painfully up onto the stage. She has stomach cancer that has metastasized to her liver and the bones of her spinal column, making walking extremely painful. She can walk, but only with the aid of a back brace. William A. Nolen (1974), MD, in his book *Healing: A Doctor in Search of a Miracle* describes what happened next: "Mrs. Sullivan had, at Kathryn Kuhlman's suggestion, taken off her back brace and run back and forth across the stage several times. Finally, she walked back down the aisle to her wheelchair, waving her brace as she went, while the audience applauded and Kathryn Kuhlman gave thanks to the Lord" (87).

The effect of this miracle cure on the audience must have been immense. How could anyone, no matter how skeptical, doubt what they had seen with their own eyes: a woman devoured by cancer (and she really did have cancer—she was not a shill or a plant) had been cured by God. Now she could not only walk but run without assistance of any sort.

The above example is just one of tens of thousands of miracle cures claimed by faith healers worldwide. Faith healers, whether called that or witch doctors or shamans, have been around since the dawn of civilization. In the twentieth century, at least among Western cultures, belief in faith healing had declined until the last few decades. With the rise of religious fundamentalism in the 1980s, faith healing again became popular. It is still practiced to some extent by traveling healers, who move from town to town, but also by "prime-time preachers" who have their own television shows.

Several factors are extremely powerful in convincing people that faith healers are able to cure the sick. One is witnessing a "cure" such as the one described above, or seeing it on television, or hearing about it from someone who saw it. How can one explain a cure such as Mrs. Sullivan's? In fact, no cure took place. Nolen followed up the case and interviewed Mrs. Sullivan two months after her miracle cure. She had gone to the "miracle service" expecting a cure, she said.

> At the service, as soon as she [Kathryn Kuhlman] said, "Someone with cancer is being cured," I knew she meant me. I could just feel this burning sensation all over my body and I was convinced the Holy Spirit was at work. I went right up on the stage and when she asked me about the brace I just took it right off, though I hadn't had it off for over four months, I had so much back pain. I was sure I was cured. That night I said a prayer of thanksgiving to the Lord and Kathryn Kuhlman and went to bed, happier than I'd been in a long time. At four o'clock the next morning I woke up with a horrible pain in my back. It was so bad I broke out in a cold sweat. I didn't dare move. (Nolen 1974, 98–99)

X-rays revealed that one of the bones in her spinal column, a vertebra already weakened by the cancer, had collapsed. It had collapsed due to the strain that had been put on it when she had run back and forth across the stage. She died two months later, in great pain, of the cancer that Kathryn Kuhlman had "cured" her of before an audience of thousands.

What explains Mrs. Sullivan's surprising freedom from pain during and immediately after the service? The body has its own physiological and biochemical systems for dealing with pain. One way to control pain is by causing the release of endogenous substances that are naturally occurring analogues of opioid drugs like morphine and its biochemical relative, heroin. These endogenous substances, called *endorphins*, are released at times of stress. A high level of excitement, such as that clearly felt by Mrs. Sullivan, is a stressful event, in the physiological sense. Thus, her pain was temporarily eliminated, not because of any miracle cure but because the excitement brought on by the environment caused a release of endorphins. A few hours later, when these endorphins were no longer present, her pain returned, much magnified by the new damage to her spinal column.

But Kathryn Kuhlman didn't see Mrs. Sullivan as she lay in her bed, crippled and dying. Nor did the thousands of people who "saw with their own eyes" that Mrs. Sullivan had been blessed with what appeared to be a miraculous cancer cure. Since faith healers almost never follow up on the cases they claim to have cured, it is easy to understand why both members of the audience and the healers themselves can become convinced that their cures are real. Psychologically, the situation is little different from that of cold readers convinced they can foretell the future (see chapter 2). Their failures don't return, so they see only their apparent successes. Nolen (1974) followed up many cases of "cures" by faith healers and found no miracles. This has been the universal result when faith healers' "cures" are carefully investigated. Many people, if asked during or immediately after a healing session, will report that their pain has gone away or at least lessened. When asked about it again later, they will report that their pain has returned.

FAITH HEALERS' TECHNIQUES

Outright fraud and trickery are tools of the faith healer. Healers use a variety of tricks to con their audiences into believing that miracle cures are taking place right before the audience's eyes and that the healer is in direct contact with God or Jesus.

Two notorious practitioners of this cruel con game were the Rev. W. V. Grant and the Rev. Peter Popoff. Both have been exposed as frauds (see Randi 1986a, 1986b, 1986c; Kurtz 1986, for details). Randi's (1987) book *The Faith Healers* is highly recommended for a detailed treatment of all aspects of faith healing.

Both Grant and Popoff, and other such healers, made use of a combination of cold reading, sleight of hand, and fraud in their performances. In May 1986 I played a small part in an undercover investigation of faith healer W. V. Grant, spearheaded by magician James Randi. Grant gave a "service" at the Brooklyn Academy of Music in New York. Randi, along with several others including myself, went to see what we could find out. Randi had suggested that I volunteer when the call was made for volunteer ushers from the audience. I did so and, as an usher, had access to the backstage area and was able to wander about with considerable freedom during the performance. We arrived at the Brooklyn Academy of Music well before the service was scheduled to start. During the healing portion of his services, Grant typically walked up to people in the audience, asked them to stand if they were able, and announced their name, perhaps the name of their doctor, and what they were suffering from. How did Grant get this information? Our investigation confirmed what Randi (1986b) reported. Before the service started, members of Grant's staff, who posed as just other audience members, walked through the hall and chatted with those who arrived early. These people were being pumped for information, which was then reported to Grant. We saw, as did investigators at other Grant performances, that those who chatted with staff before the service started were quite likely to be called on to be "cured" later, during the service. When Grant was curing someone, he made a point of asking whether the person had ever spoken to him or to the individuals who assisted him during this part of the service. The person quite truthfully replied no. The response, although truthful, was misleading, as Grant knew, since the members of Grant's staff that the person talked with were different from the assistants onstage with Grant when he did his healing. After attending one of Grant's services in Florida, Randi found crib sheets listing information about people who were "cured" in the trash. It was also seen that one of Grant's staff was using hand signals to let the reverend know what part of his victim's body was afflicted.

Peter Popoff used a much more sophisticated method for obtaining information about people in his audience. Like Grant, his staff pumped people for information before the show. That information was given to his wife, who sat in a truck outside the auditorium. She relayed the information to him during the show by radio. He had a tiny radio receiver in his ear through which he received messages via a transmitter in the truck. All the while, Popoff was claiming that he got his information from God. Alec Jason, a communications specialist working with Randi, managed to pick up and record these broadcasts to Popoff during a California service in 1986 (see Randi 1986c, 1987, for details).

Popoff's use of fraud was dramatically revealed on Johnny Carson's *The Tonight Show* in May 1986, when Randi showed videotapes of Popoff performing a healing and simultaneously played a tape of the messages from Popoff's wife. Popoff's reaction was to deny everything and ask his followers to pray for him. His ministry then charged that NBC had hired an actress to imitate his wife's voice and that the videotape shown on the program had been faked. Finally, Popoff admitted that he "occasionally" was given names over the radio. During the service when the radio messages to Popoff were recorded, the names of all the people he called out were passed to him via radio (Randi 1986a, 1986c).

At the Grant service I attended, I was surprised to see how unsophisticated the healings were. Grant would frequently approach older people and announce that they had "the arthritis." Since many of the older people had canes, this was not a bad guess, and even if it was wrong, Grant didn't give people a chance to correct him. In one particularly sad case, Grant asked an old man with a cane to hobble out to the aisle. Grant performed his usual healing routine. This included asking the audience if they believed that "Dr. Jesus" could cure the man, which was followed by a thunderous yes. Grant then laid his hands on the man's shoulders and cursed the arthritis out of his body. In some cases, the healer will push the individual back to make it seem as if the affliction has been "struck by Dr. Jesus," as Grant did. He then declared the man cured, dramatically grabbed the man's cane, broke it in two, and tossed it down onto the stage. A great cheer rose up. Another miracle had taken place; the old man no longer needed his cane. Grant immediately dashed off to another part of the theater, with all eyes, and the house lights, following him. Except mine. I watched as the old man, now without his cane, hobbled back to his seat, walking no better than he had before.

For another cure, a man in a back brace was brought to the stage. He walked onto the stage perfectly normally. Grant asked the rather overweight fellow how long it had been since he had been able to touch his toes. "Years," came the reply. Grant then directed the fellow to bend over and touch his toes. He promptly squatted down and did so. This was no miracle since there was nothing wrong with this man's knees, but the audience let out another cheer and praised the Lord again for showing another miracle.

At one point an old man in a wheelchair at the front of the hall was made to walk again—or so it seemed to the audience. Other members of our group had noticed that this man had walked into the hall under his own power before the performance and had been seated in the wheelchair by Grant's staff. I doubt if anyone else noticed this. So, when Grant had the man stand up and walk, the natural, if incorrect, assumption the audience made was that he had been miraculously cured. This is an example of a common trick used by Grant, Popoff, and other faith healers. Wheelchairs are placed at the front of the theater. Before the service, when frail-looking older people enter, they are escorted to the wheelchairs. Then, when they stand up and walk during the service, the healer takes credit for a miracle. The supposedly healed person is never given the chance to say, "Hey, I could walk before."

Grant could be fast on his feet when the occasion demanded. He approached one woman and asked how long she had been blind and held his microphone out to her. She replied, "Partially," but Grant ignored her and asked the audience if they believed that Jesus could cure her. "Yes," they shouted. With that, Grant held up several fingers and asked the woman, "How many?" She promptly gave the correct answer—not surprising, since she was only partially blind. But Grant was given credit for yet another miraculous cure.

The final "cure" before the "offering," when money was to be collected, was designed to impress the audience. Grant announced that one of the volunteer ushers had one leg shorter than the other and that this would be cured. When this "volunteer usher" was brought onto the stage, he turned out to be a member of Grant's staff whom I had seen backstage when I first went there for my instructions on what to do as an usher. After a laying on of hands, Grant made a great show of removing the man's orthopedic shoes and tossing them to the corner of the theater, as if to say, "You're healed, no need for these anymore." Another huge cheer went up, and Grant's latest miracle cure walked, without limping, offstage. Of course, he hadn't limped when he came onstage, but I suspect this was not widely noticed. He also walked offstage barefoot, but that was quickly remedied as another Grant staff member scurried around, collected his shoes, and returned them to him. It appears that Grant does not always use a shill when he does this leg-lengthening trick. Randi (1986b) described how, by pulling a person's shoes and making his or her leg move slightly, Grant can make it appear to the audience that the person's leg is being lengthened by an inch or so.

At this point the reader may be wondering how the audience could have fallen for what was, to me at least, such obvious trickery. This is an important question, and there are a number of factors involved. First, I did not go expecting to see miracles. I went prepared and knowing what sort of tricks to look for. The audience, unprepared and expecting miracles, was easily taken in. Second, before the healing portion of the service started, there had been about an hour of preaching and singing, which had roused the audience's emotions. At least one woman fainted. When people are in such a state, their critical faculties are impaired. The combination of the audience's high level of emotional arousal and their initial uncritical acceptance of the claim that miracle cures would happen was all Grant needed to allow him to succeed in what was, to those of us who were there to investigate him, such obvious trickery.

This is not to say, and this is a vital point, that the members of the audience were in any way "dumb" or less intelligent than the investigators. This was clearly not the case. Like the great majority of people, they simply didn't have the background information necessary to prepare them to spot tricks like those Grant and other healers use. Thus, they were taken in.

After the leg lengthening, it was time for the offering. Grant spent about fifteen minutes reiterating that no one was obligated to give (admission had been free), but he also spent time detailing the great expenses of his church's good works. He said his television program was seen in more than three hundred cities. (In fact, he was then on television in only about ninety cities [Randi 1986b].) He told of the great expense of his missions in Haiti. He also said that if people gave money, Jesus would return it to them one hundred times over by the end of the year.

Then it was time for the actual offering, and one of the jobs of the ushers was to pass the collection buckets. That's right, collection *buckets*, not collection plates. I was dumbfounded at the amount of money we collected. I had been assigned to a rather small part of the theater, yet I estimated that I collected at least six thousand dollars in my bucket. The donations were almost wholly in cash—twenty-, fifty-, one-hundred-dollar bills. There were at least twelve ushers to start with, although a few more appeared in time for the offering, so a conservative estimate of the amount of money collected during the offering alone was seventy-two thousand dollars.

Grant had other ways to relieve people of their money. Earlier in the program there had been an opportunity for anyone who wished to do so to make a personal offering to Grant. The offering was to be placed in an envelope and handed to Grant, who stood onstage taking the envelopes one by one. You were supposed to write on a form that went with the envelope what your problem was and what or who you wanted healed. Those who made a personal offering were carefully instructed not to speak to Grant as they passed him their envelope, presumably so that no one could later claim they had given him personal information. But Randi (1986b) found that Grant uses this period to commit to memory the faces of at least some of the people who make a personal offering so they can later be picked out of the audience and "cured." In any event, between four hundred and five hundred people stood in line to give Grant their personal offering. There is no way to know how much money was in the envelopes, but since it was implied that those who gave personal offerings would receive special healing, it seems safe to assume that these were larger than the average contribution given during the later offering.

Grant also had books, pamphlets, tape-recorded Bible study courses, and similar merchandise for sale. I would conservatively estimate that he took in $100,000 cash that night. If he staged this sort of show five days a week, forty weeks a year, his income would be twenty million dollars a year. This does not count income from his huge direct-mail solicitations and money he receives in response to appeals made on his television program. Further, note that since Grant is running a "religious charity," he pays no taxes on any of this money. He doesn't even have to file an informational tax return. Grant and his fellow faith healers have literally found a license to steal. And they steal from those who can least afford it—the poor, the old, the sick, and the hopeless.

The saddest aspect of Grant's "service" was the truly lame and seriously ill people who were carefully herded by Grant's staff to the rear of the theater. There were several children with cerebral palsy, or some other crippling disease. There was an old woman, strapped into a wheelchair, who would thrash around, moan, and call out. Her caregiver had put a handkerchief in her mouth to keep her quiet. These people, and their parents or guardians, had come to Grant hoping for a miracle cure. They gave donations, like nearly everyone else. They would go home disappointed. And what was Grant's explanation to those who weren't cured? (He claimed that 90 percent of the people present would be cured.) He said that Jesus would only heal those who were pure in heart and without bitterness. If anyone wasn't cured, his or her heart still had some bitterness. It might not be much, it might be unconscious, but still it was there and would prevent the cure. So people who weren't cured would have only themselves to blame.

Grant did have a run-in with the Internal Revenue Service and was convicted of tax evasion in 1996, for which he received a sixteen-month prison sentence. But he got out after sixteen months and continued to practice faith healing (Shaffer 2010). His Eagle's Nest Cathedral is currently located in Dallas, Texas.

Pat Robertson, moderator of the popular *700 Club* television program, broadcast nationwide by his Christian Broadcasting Network, does faith healing during the program. He makes use of the "multiple out" (described in chapter 2) to make it appear that his cures are real. He typically "sees" some disease or problem and, after describing it, announces that it is being cured. For example, he might say, "I see a man with a hip problem. The Lord is curing you. There is a woman with a kidney illness. Jesus will cure you." Days, weeks, or months later, a woman may write and report that, after she watched the broadcast, her kidney infection cleared up. A man may write to say that his sprained hip was much less painful after he had seen the program. These reports are then taken as evidence of specific, predicted cures.

It's easy to see what is really going on here. The initial cure predictions are extremely vague. Robertson's audience is huge, and there will certainly be many in it with problems resembling the type he vaguely describes. Like most illnesses, most of these problems will go away, either spontaneously or under medical treatment. However, Robertson will be given credit for the "cure," even if the cured person was under a doctor's care. If the problem disappears spontaneously, it is even more likely that the "cure" will be attributed to Robertson and not to the body's natural, and considerable, ability to heal itself. Further, there is no medical verification that people claiming cures really had what they say they had. People with problems who listened to the program but weren't cured are hardly likely to write in and say so. If they do, their reports certainly won't be mentioned on the program. Thus, Robertson and his staff are selectively exposed to reports of cures and, like cold readers who become convinced of their power to foretell the future because their victims keep telling them they can, become convinced that true cures are taking place.

Sister Grace, also known as "Amazing Grace," was another popular faith healer in the 1980s. She made impressive claims about the people she cured and the miracles God has brought about through her. However, when actual evidence is requested to back up these claims, there is total silence. I had an interesting interaction with Grace on WCBS-TV in New York City in the spring of 1984. We briefly debated the issue of faith healing. Grace brought with her a man who said that she had cured him of lung cancer and of emphysema. He produced X-rays and a medical record to support the claim. These were shown with great flourish on the air. I have no doubt that they impressed the viewing audience. After the debate, I asked if I could obtain a copy of the medical record and the X-rays for further study and verification. Not only was the request flatly refused, but the name of the doctor who supposedly treated the patient was kept secret.

At her services, Grace tells the audience that God tells her the names of audience members and what diseases they have. She then does the laying on of hands and "cures" the disease. In one particularly interesting case, Grace "cured" a man of a disease he didn't have (Steiner 1986–1987). Steiner had planted a "stinger" in Grace's audience at one performance; she not only "cured" him of a disease he didn't have but also called him by the pseudonym he had used to get into the performance, not his real name. Steiner commented, "This is not religion. This is a con game" (31).

Faith healing, with all its tricks, is still with us in the twenty-first century. One up-to-date healer is Benny Hinn, who holds "miracle crusade" services around the world where thousands of the ill are promised healing, both physical and spiritual. Hinn says he was inspired by attending a service of Kathryn Kuhlman. Nickell (2002) attended one of Hinn's services and found the usual tricks of the faith healing trade in play. But in addition, Hinn reverses one of the usual ploys of the faith healer by "instead of the afflicted being invited up [onstage] to *be* healed," Hinn "encourages receptive, emotional individuals to believe they *are* healed. Only that self-selected group is invited to come forward and testify to their supposedly miraculous transformation" (emphasis in original). Further, only those "who tell the most interesting stories and show the greatest enthusiasm are the ones likely to be chosen" (Nickell 2002, 15). With the COVID-19 crisis of 2020, Hinn really brought faith healing into the online age using Zoom to conduct online healing services. The promotion on his official website for a July 17, 2020, healing service asked, "Do you need a touch from God or a healing in your body, mind or soul?" The website also has various healing products for sale, including digital downloads titled "God's Word Speaks Healing" ($8.00) and "Diving Healing" ($25.00).

Another twenty-first-century globe-trotting faith healer, medium, and psychic surgeon was John of God, a Brazilian who, as a medium, said he could speak to the spirits of the dead, including but not limited to King Solomon. He had a retreat or "clinic" in Abadiania, Brazil, where many miracle healings were said to have taken place. He used his mediumistic powers to contact the spirits of dead doctors while he did his psychic surgery. In reality, he used various sleight-of-hand techniques commonly used by psychic surgeons (see below) as well as common carnival tricks, as revealed by Joe Nickell (2007a), who went undercover to one of his performances. Nickell, who wrote an excellent book describing the tricks of the carnival and sideshow (2005), later recreated many of the tricks using carnival performers.

John would probably have been little known in the United States had he not been featured twice by Oprah Winfrey on her television programs. He first appeared on the *Oprah Winfrey Show* in November 2010 and then in March 2013 on *Oprah's Next Chapter*. These appearances gained him great recognition and prestige, as there was almost no skeptical appraisal of his claims on either show. In 2018 accusations began to appear that John had sexually abused hundreds of women in Brazil. In 2019 he was tried, found guilty, and sentenced to nineteen years in prison (Nogueira 2019).

While faith healers are still around, the con artists have, in the second decade of the twenty-first century, moved on to another lucrative scam known as the "prosperity gospel." The idea is based on the biblical injunction to "cast your bread upon the waters" (Ecclesiastes 11:1), with the common misinterpretation that the rest of the phrase is something like "and it shall be returned to you ten (or a hundred, or a thousand) times." That's a lot of soggy bread! The actual rest of the phrase reads "for after many days you will find it again." In any event, the prosperity gospel preachers use the misrepresentation of Ecclesiastes 11:1 to con people into sending them money, the idea being that if you send them one dollar, you'll get ten dollars, or a hundred or even a thousand back. Oh, not from them! No, no. But from . . . well, you'll get your reward from someone, somewhere, somehow. These religious con artists are fabulously wealthy. They own private jets and huge mansions and even boast about it. And, since they are pastors in a church, not a penny of the money they con out of people is taxable.

Peter Popoff has transformed himself into a fabulously wealthy prosperity gospel preacher (Oppenheimer 2017). His history of exposed fraud has not prevented this. He mixes healing with his prosperity message, uses the tricks of the healing trade and mixes them in with his prosperity gospel message. At a service in England, he healed a woman who claimed to be suffering from great pain. But that same woman had been distributing questionnaires and writing implements outside the hall before the performance, very likely a shill working for Popoff (Penman 2015).

John Oliver, on his *This Week Tonight* program on August 16, 2015, did a scathing, hilarious, and very sad exposé of the prosperity gospel movement, including setting up his own tax-free church, Our Lady of Perpetual Exemption. It is well worth watching. The program highlights the fact that prosperity gospel theology preys on the ill, the desperate, and the poorly educated. It only increases the prosperity of prosperity gospel preachers. For example, one preacher, Mike Murdock, bragged about buying one Cessna Citation jet "for cash" and then buying another, more expensive one, also "for cash." The base price of the cheapest Cessna Citation private jet is about $4.5 million.

PSYCHIC SURGERY

Psychic surgery, most popular from the mid-1960s through the mid-1970s, is one brand of faith healing where sleight of hand is relied on to achieve the "miracle." Psychic surgeons usually claim to be able to insert their hands inside the patient's body without making an incision and to remove dead and diseased tissue. More recently some say that they can use their powers, obtained from God, to liquify or otherwise destroy the tumors or diseased tissue from outside the body with no need of an incision. As the psychic surgeon performs "surgery," his hand is seen to disappear into the patient's belly and a pool of blood appears. After groping around, apparently inside the body cavity, the psychic surgeon dramatically pulls his hand "out" of the body, clutching what is said to be the tumor or diseased tissue that was causing the patient's problem. The offending tissue is promptly tossed in a handy nearby fire to be purified. When the patient's belly is wiped clean of the blood, no incision is found.

Testimonials to and eyewitness reports of such miracle operations were common when psychic surgery was popular and still turn up from time to time. In 1974 John Fuller wrote a glowing, credulous book on Brazilian psychic surgeon Arigo titled *Arigo: Surgeon of the Rusty Knife*. (This is the same author who wrote the "true" account of Betty and Barney Hill's abduction by a UFO, discussed in chapter 8.) Actor Andy Kaufman, who was in the television series *Taxi*, visited a psychic surgeon in the Philippines in hopes of curing his terminal cancer. Kaufman's girlfriend was convinced that sleight of hand was not used because she stood "not a foot away" (Gardner 1984, 8). Kaufman died in 1984 of his lung cancer after his "cure." The Philippines was home for most of the psychic surgeons during the time of their great popularity, and tens of thousands of often desperately ill Americans and Europeans trekked there in hopes of a miracle cure. Unscrupulous travel agencies were set up specifically to book flights to the Philippines for seriously ill individuals to get treatment from psychic surgeons there. In 1975 the Federal Trade Commission shut down one such travel agency (Anonymous 1990), but the Philippines continued to be a haven for psychic surgeons. Tony Agpaoa, who worked his psychic surgery con in Detroit in the 1960s, was arrested for fraud there in 1967. He skipped on twenty-five thousand dollars in bail that his supporters had donated and flew to the Philippines, where he continued to take advantage of the seriously ill.

Both Nolen (1974) and Randi (1982a) exposed the methods the psychic surgeons used. Nolen went to the Philippines and was "operated on" by one. The "operation" starts as the hand appears to enter the patient's belly. This is accomplished by creating an impression in the belly by pushing down and flexing the fingers slowly into a fist. The fingers thus appear to be moving into the belly, but are really simply hidden behind the hand. The blood that further disguises the true movement of the fingers and adds drama to the proceedings can come from at least two sources. One is a fake thumb, worn over the real thumb and filled with a red liquid. Such a fake thumb is a common magician's implement. Blood, animal blood or blood-colored liquid, can also be passed to the surgeon by an assistant using red balloons hidden in cotton the psychic surgeon needs. The bits of "tumor" can also be passed to the psychic surgeon this way or hidden in the false thumb. What is the "tumor" that is removed from the body, and what is the blood? Psychic surgeons are unwilling to give up samples of material for analysis. When samples have been obtained, usually by grabbing the material before the surgeon can destroy it, the material turns out to be chicken innards or similar animal remains.

As if psychic surgery wasn't enough, there was even at least one psychic dentist—Willard Fuller (1915–2009)—who helped God fill teeth and reshape maloccluded jaws for nearly twenty years. In spite of the usual testimonials, Fuller was nothing more than a practitioner of sleight of hand. One dentist examined twenty-eight people before they were "healed" by Fuller. Those claiming to be healed were reexamined after the healing. In one case "gold fillings miraculously bestowed turned out instead to be tobacco stains" (Radke, quoted in Hegstad 1974, 252). In another case, a woman reported a new silver filling where only a cavity had existed before the healing service. Dentist Radke had taken pictures of this woman's teeth before the service and found that the filling was indeed there when the pictures were taken. The woman then "readily admitted that she had forgotten that the filling was there" (Radke, quoted in Hegstad 1974, 253). In May 1986 Fuller went on a tour through Australia, where he was arrested, tried, and found guilty of practicing dentistry without a license and of fraud (Plummer 1986). This did not in any way impede a coast-to-coast tour of the United States upon his return from Australia.

THE DANGERS OF FAITH HEALING

One point about faith healers cannot be overemphasized: they kill people. Convinced that they are cured when they are not, patients may be dissuaded from seeking legitimate medical help that could save their lives. For example, many kinds of cancer are quite treatable, if treatment begins early enough. However, the diagnosis of cancer still carries enormous emotional power and drives people to seek out faith healers. Since cancer of many types can be detected very early, well before patients suffer any serious symptoms, it is likely that they will come back from the faith healer relieved and "feeling better" since they have received the assurance that they are cured. Since the cancer has been "cured," there is no need to go back to the physician—until the cancer, unaffected by the blandishments of the faith healer, grows to a point where it can no longer be ignored. A return to a doctor at this point will frequently bring a diagnosis of a now-untreatable disease that could have been cured if treatment had been begun when the initial diagnosis was made. In an especially callous display of showmanship, faith healer Peter Popoff at the end of some of his services urges the audience to throw away their medicines because everyone has been cured by "Doctor Jesus." A shower of prescription and nonprescription bottles follows. How many of the largely elderly and poor members of Popoff's audience go home to great pain, or even to die, because they have thrown away the medicine that is really treating their health problems?

Devout members of one well-known religious sect, the Church of Christ, Scientist, depend entirely on faith healers called "practitioners" for treatment of their illnesses. The core belief of the church is that pain, disease, and illnesses are illusions caused by bad thoughts and that prayer and mental effort will remove these thoughts and thus cure the illness. Christian Science was founded in the 1870s by Mary Baker Eddy (1821–1910). In 1898 Eddy, writing in the December 16 issue of the *New York Sun* newspaper, claimed that, using the principles of Christian Science, she had "physically restored sight to the blind, hearing to the deaf, speech to the dumb and made the lame walk." However, Eddy used glasses herself at times, and church doctrine allowed members to seek medical help in the case of broken bones.

Members of the Christian Science church are not allowed to seek medical help for any sort of pain, illness, or disease. The only treatment is through so-called Christian Science practitioners. The practitioners' training consists of a few weeks of religious instruction. The practitioner is not permitted to engage in any sort of assistance to patients other than praying for them. Thus, the use of drugs, thermometers, and "even the simplest human measures for relieving suffering or discomfort, such as hot packs, ice packs, enemas, and back rubs" are forbidden (Swan 1983, 1640). The practitioner's praying may even be done over the telephone. Practitioners charge for their "services," and the Internal Revenue Service has been persuaded that such charges can be deducted as medical expenses. Even more astonishingly, Blue Cross Blue Shield in many states will reimburse such expenses.

The bizarre and deadly practices of the Church of Christ, Scientist are also applied to children. Parents are forbidden to take their children, no matter how sick, to legitimate physicians, but must rely on Christian Scientist practitioners. As might be expected, this has resulted in the deaths of Christian Scientist children from diseases that could have been treated, and the child's life saved, had medical attention been provided. The Church of Christ, Scientist, along with many other fundamentalist sects and cults that believe in faith healing, argues that it is parents' right to withhold legitimate medical treatment from their children and that they should not be prosecuted for child abuse when children die from the lack of such treatment. The laws of thirty-five states (as of 2023) covering child abuse and neglect contain specific religious exemptions. These permit a parent to withhold medical treatment from a child if the parent is a member of a religious group that believes in the power of faith healing or in the power of prayer to heal. Such exemptions have resulted in the deaths of numerous children whose lives could have been saved by legitimate medical treatment. The Church of Christ, Scientist lobbies vigorously when attempts are made to eliminate such exemptions.

Responding to the serious issues raised by Rita Swan (1983), who was a Christian Scientist herself until one of her children died of a treatable meningitis at the hands of a Christian Science practitioner, Nathan Talbot, a church official, attempted to justify the church's reliance on prayer. He stated that "the most important body of evidence concerning Christian Science healing is the ongoing published testimonies of healing in the denomination's periodicals" (Talbot 1983, 1642). Talbot argued that a few of these cures have been medically verified but gave no specific examples.

In the 2010s the church softened somewhat its stance on the use of real medicine to treat disease. This probably came about because of the terrible publicity from several cases where children died, often in great pain, from disorders that could have been easily treated by legitimate medical therapies. The church still required the use of practitioners.

The Christian Scientists are, of course, not the only religious sect that relies heavily on faith healing and objects to having their children treated by modern medicine. It is only the largest. Numerous other fundamentalist groups do the same, and one result is the deaths of many children who could have been cured had they been taken to a real doctor.

THE ROLE OF SHRINES

Not only people but places have been alleged to produce miracle cures. The most famous is probably the shrine at Lourdes, France, where, according to popular legend, thousands of cures have taken place since 1858, when a teenage girl had a vision of the Virgin Mary at the site of the shrine. Alleged miracle cures at Lourdes are now investigated by the Lourdes Medical Bureau. If the case warrants, it is then taken up by the International Medical Committee of Lourdes (IMCL), composed of Catholic doctors from each of the European countries that sends large numbers of pilgrims to Lourdes. If the IMCL decides that the case is medically inexplicable, it is up to the Roman Catholic Church to make the final judgment as to whether a miracle has taken place (Bernstein 1982; Dowling 1984). Out of the estimated two million sick who have traveled to Lourdes since 1858, the church has accepted seventy cures as miraculous as of 2022. Nearly six thousand other cases in which individuals claimed to have been miraculously cured have been rejected.

A careful examination of the cases certified by the church in 1978 as miracle cures suggests that the medical evaluations of even the certified miracles leave much to be desired. Serge Perrin was diagnosed as suffering from "recurring organic hemiplegia with ocular lesions, due to cerebral circulatory defects." Bernstein (1982) concluded that "U.S. specialists agreed that if there were an organic illness at all, multiple sclerosis was a more likely possibility" (134). Perrin's symptoms were also consistent with a hysterical disorder, in which seemingly physical symptoms are due to psychological problems. Such disorders are frequently "cured" when the patient believes a treatment will be effective, an example of the placebo effect. The belief is the key; it does not matter whether the treatment is a real one or not.

That Perrin may have had multiple sclerosis is an important point. Three other certified miracle cures have been of multiple sclerosis. One of the criteria for acceptance of a case by the IMCL for further study, even before it has been decided whether to recommend the case to the church for final judgment, is "that the natural history of the disease precludes the possibility of spontaneous remission" (Dowling 1984, 635). But it has long been known that multiple sclerosis shows just such periodic remissions.

Another case touted as proof occurred in 1963. A young woman was certified as having had a miraculous cure of Budd-Chiari syndrome, in which the veins of the liver become blocked. In 1970 she died of Budd-Chiari syndrome. The IMCL "concluded that when they reached their decision [that the woman had had a miracle cure] they were insufficiently aware of the natural history of Budd-Chiari syndrome and the possibility of natural remission" (Dowling 1984, 637). This shows admirable candor on the committee's part, but this case, as well as that of Perrin and the other three "miraculous" multiple sclerosis cures, points to very poor investigations. Starting in 2006 the bishop of Lourdes made miracles "a little easier" to get (Burke 2006). Three new categories of semi-miracles are now accepted: unexpected healings, confirmed healings, and exceptional healings.

A major source of the fame of Lourdes is not the certified miracle cures but the thousands of personal reports, or testimonials, of people who went there and "got better." The shrine is lined with the discarded canes and crutches of those who could walk without them after their visit. However, the trip to Lourdes and the ceremonies performed there serve to build great excitement and hope in the pilgrims. Bernstein (1982) described the "electricity in the air as the huge crowd [of pilgrims] moves from the bank of the river to the grand upper basilica, singing in unison" (146). In such a situation, there is obviously a great deal of motivation to try harder to walk and ignore whatever pain one usually feels while doing so. This is also the type of exciting but stressful situation that causes release of pain-reducing endorphins, as described earlier. Those who come to Lourdes finding it difficult, but not impossible, to walk with crutches or a cane will thus experience a reduction in their level of pain, perhaps enough to allow them to walk unaided, at least for a while. When the pain returns, the period of relative freedom from pain will be accepted as a miracle. After all, the biochemistry of pain reduction via endorphin release is far from common knowledge. The pain's return will be explained as due to failure to pray enough or to some other mystical cause. The French writer Anatole France made a telling and pungent comment upon visiting Lourdes in the late nineteenth century and seeing all the abandoned crutches and canes: "What, what, no wooden legs???"

There is apparently a brisk market in the United States for water from Lourdes. It is imported by the Lourdes Center in Boston. The center sells a one-ounce bottle for a three-dollar "offering." The center's newsletter is filled with testimonials to the wonderful curative powers of the water: "For the past six years I was handicapped with a sore toenail; each spring I was obliged to have it lanced by the doctors. I applied Lourdes water constantly [and] I now have a normal white nail and no infection," or "My mother was delivered from cancer pain" (quoted in Bernstein 1982, 141).

Healing Effects of Intercessory Prayer

Does prayer of one person for the health of another (*intercessory prayer*) result in any improvement in the condition of the prayed-for person? Somewhat surprisingly, empirical research on this question dates back more than 140 years. What was apparently the first study of this question was conducted by Sir Francis Galton, one of the founders of modern statistical analysis (Tankard 1984). Galton (1872) reasoned that members of the clergy prayed more (and were probably prayed for more) than those in medical and legal professions. To the extent that prayer was effective, clergymen should live longer than doctors or lawyers. He found no difference in the life spans of members of these three professions. More modern studies have provided little additional support for the positive effects of prayer. In their review of the twentieth-century research in this area, Matthews, Conti, and Christ (2000) discussed eight empirical studies of prayer effects. Six found no effects of prayer. One (Green 1993) found that for subjects who had a strong belief that prayer would reduce anxiety, being prayed for reduced their anxiety. The eighth study (Byrd 1988) is often cited as providing supportive evidence for real effects of prayer. In this study, patients suffering from cardiac disease were prayed for. This study suffers from two serious flaws. First, in the original publication it was claimed that the study was done in a double-blind fashion. It wasn't. Tessman and Tessman (2000) pointed out that Byrd assessed the degree to which patients had improved after he became aware of whether or not they had been prayed for. Second, Byrd examined thirty-two different variables for prayer effects and found such effects on only six variables. The pattern of results can best be interpreted as a statistical fluke. The more variables one examines, the more likely it is that, just by chance, some type of significant effect will be found. And the multiple comparison fallacy appears yet again!

Conti and Matthews (reported in Matthews, Conti, and Christ 2000) performed a clever study to tease apart the effects of patients' expectations about prayer effects from any actual prayer effects. They used as subjects patients with renal disease. Two groups of patients were told that they would be prayed for. One group was, in fact, prayed for, while the other was not. Two more groups were told that they would not be prayed for. One was prayed for and the other was not. The results showed that whether or not patients were actually prayed for had no effect on outcome measures. However, patients who thought that they were being prayed for improved more than those who did not think they were being prayed for, regardless of whether or not they really were being prayed for.

Another study of prayer effects was that of Harris and colleagues (1999). These authors used as subjects more than one thousand patients admitted to a coronary care unit (CCU). The prayers for the prayed-for group asked specifically for a fast recovery and a lack of complications. There was no difference between the prayed-for and not-prayed-for groups in terms of either the time spent in the CCU or the total time spent in the hospital. Two other, more general measures of recovery were also examined. On one there was a slightly significant difference favoring the prayed-for group. There was no difference on the second general measure, which, interestingly, was one of the same measures on which Byrd (1988) claimed to find a benefit for his prayed-for group.

Even if this was all there was to this study, the finding of one barely significant difference out of three would not be a very impressive result. But there is another interesting feature of this study. Humphrey (2000) pointed out that the Harris and colleagues (1999) study started with a total of 1,013 patients, of which 484 were assigned to be prayed for and 529 were assigned not to be prayed for. However, because it took a day to begin prayer after a patient was assigned to a group, twenty-three patients who stayed in the CCU for less than twenty-four hours were eliminated from the study. But these eliminations were far from random. Of the twenty-three, eighteen had been assigned to the prayer group and five to the nonprayer group. This is a highly significant difference. Humphrey described three possible explanations for this effect. The first is that prayer shows "backward causation," working on patients assigned to the prayer group before anyone actually starts praying for them. A second, more mundane possibility is that assignment to the two groups was not random, with the less severe cases being placed in the prayer group. But there is another reason that patients can leave the CCU rapidly: they can die. So it is possible that there was a higher immediate death rate among the to-be-prayed-for patients. Humphrey asked Harris about this possibility, but Harris did not perform this analysis (Humphrey, personal communication, November 28, 2000).

Cha, Wirth, and Lopo (2001) reported that prayer had a highly significant effect on the success of in vitro fertilization. The success rate was 50 percent in a group that was (sort of; see below) prayed for, compared to 26 percent in a control group. However, the prayer used was extraordinarily vague—that God's will be done. These prayers weren't even for the success of the fertilization (Flamm 2002). With that as the prayer, even a finding in which there were no differences between the groups could be described as supporting the effectiveness of prayer—it just happened that God's will was for there to be no difference between the groups. And if the sort-of-prayed-for group had had a lower success rate, that could have been seen as God's will as well. The highly complex, even bizarre, experimental design had successive groups of people praying for the success of the prayers of the previous groups of people praying. The obvious way of designing the study would have been to have one group prayed for with an obvious prayer for successful fertilization, and the other not.

Several years after the Cha, Wirth, and Lopo (2001) study was published it became clear that the entire study was a fraud and may never have actually taken place (Flamm 2004, 2005). Three years after its publication Dr. Rogerio Lopo of Columbia University requested that his name be removed from the study because he had nothing to do with the actual research and only edited the final manuscript for proper English grammar. The second author, Daniel Wirth, has no medical degrees. In 2004 he was charged with multiple counts of mail fraud, moving stolen money across state lines, and other fraud-related offenses. He pleaded guilty and was sentenced to a prison term of five years. It was Wirth who was said to have actually arranged and carried out the study, which took place in Korea, at the same time he was committing his frauds on a TV cable company in the United States.

In 2001 Leibovici published a study that examined, I kid you not, the retroactive effects of prayer. People either prayed for or didn't pray for patients who had been hospitalized several years earlier for blood infections. The prayed-for group had a one-day shorter median hospital stay and a very slight reduction in the duration of their fevers. But there was no difference in death rates.

Two other studies failed to find any evidence of prayer effects. Krucoff and colleagues (2005) found no better clinical results in cardiac patients as a function of prayer. They also examined the effects of music, touch, and imagery therapy and found no effects of these either. Benson and colleagues (2006) divided their cardiac bypass patients into three groups. Those in groups one were prayed for but didn't know it. Those in group two were not prayed for and also didn't know it. Group three patients were prayed for and were informed that this was taking place. There was no difference between the first two groups in the number of medical complications suffered. But those patients who were prayed for and knew about it had significantly more complications than those in groups one and two.

There have been three reviews of the literature on the effects of intercessory prayer. Masters, Spielmans, and Goodson (2006) concluded that the studies had "failed to produce significant findings" (21) and recommended that research on the topic be discontinued. In an updated meta-analysis, Masters and Spielmans (2007) "concluded that no discernable effects [of prayer] can be found" (329). Hodge (2007) found the results of the studies he reviewed "inconclusive" (174). Interestingly, Hodge included the Cha, Wirth, and Lopo (2001) study in his list of studies with a positive outcome and makes no mention of the fatal problems with this study revealed by Flamm (2004, 2005) a few years previously. Ernst (2006, 393) concluded that "there is no good evidence to show that these methods work therapeutically and plenty to demonstrate that they do not."

ALTERNATIVE MEDICINE

Health and nutrition quackery, relabeled in the past decades as *complementary medicine, alternative medicine,* or *integrative medicine,* is a serious problem for modern consumers of medical services. As early as 1984, a congressional committee reported that the "promotion and sale of useless remedies promising relief from chronic and critical health conditions" cost the American public at least ten billion dollars a year (Pepper 1984, v). Since that report forty years ago, health quackery in numerous forms has become much more common. This is indicated by scads of websites, social media ads, and best-selling books touting all sorts of absurd treatments. Insurance reimbursement for "alternative" treatments and even the introduction of courses and programs in complementary and alternative medicine (CAM) at otherwise respectable medical schools have become common. There is even a federally funded National Center for Complementary and Alternative Medicine that supports research on CAM practices. The research thus supported is of highly dubious quality and utility (Mielczarek and Engler 2013). The use of the quack treatments marketed under the rubrics of CAM is deadly. In a study of patients with *curable* cancers, those who resorted to CAM treatments were twice as likely to die (Johnson et al. 2018). There can be little doubt about the real dangers of turning to quack cures instead of validated, scientific practices.

Several traits of CAM (textbox 11.1) mark it as pseudoscientific and distinguish it from scientific medicine. A common characteristic is the acceptance on the part of alternative medicine practitioners of patient testimonials as proof of therapeutic effectiveness. Related to this has been the tendency of alternative medicine practitioners to ignore the importance of, or actually denigrate the usefulness of, nonbiased, empirical studies of whether therapies actually work. For example, Mehl-Madrona (1997) objected to rationality in general, saying that "rational explanations are destroying medicine today" (143). CAM proponents have come to realize the importance of at least sounding like they have scientific support for their practices. Their advertising and websites are now filled with claims that whatever they're selling is "scientifically proven" or "backed by science." When one looks at the so-called science said to support these claims, there is very little real science present. CAM has spawned numbers of what appear to be scientific journals publishing studies that, amazingly, almost always find support for whatever CAM treatment is being tested. These journals are typically not peer reviewed so that the published papers have not been exposed to criticisms from the scientific community. The papers are frequently filled with egregious methodological, statistical, and logical errors. This is fake science trying to dress itself up and pass itself off as real science.

TEXTBOX 11.1. CHARACTERISTICS OF QUACK OR ALTERNATIVE MEDICINE

1. Reliance on testimonials as proof.
2. Claims that the treatment removes "toxins" from the body.
3. Use of sciencey-sounding terminology such as *energy fields*, *vibrations*, *quantum theory*, and the like.
4. Citing bogus, irrelevant, or out-of-date articles as support.
5. Ads use weasel words like *supports* or *maintains*.
6. Reluctance to use verified methods such as double-blind placebo studies to prove the claim.
7. Uses terms like *breakthrough* or *revolutionary* or refers to a secret ingredient or procedure of some sort.
8. One simple product or procedure can treat many different conditions.
9. Money-back guarantees. Because only a few people will ask for money back when the treatment does not work.

The writings of CAM proponents are often filled with scientific-sounding jargon that, on examination, turns out to be little more than gibberish without much meaning. An important difference between CAM and scientific medicine is that alternative medicine relies in large part on testimonials and subjective reports and "feelings" of patients and therapists to validate therapeutic effectiveness. In other words, if a patient simply reports that therapy X has really made them better, this is accepted as proof that therapy X really has made the patient better. Testimonials are extraordinarily unreliable sources of evidence for the effectiveness of a treatment or cure but are a stock-in-trade of alternative medicine scammers. Testimonials can be honestly given and heartfelt and still not be evidence of effectiveness. A chilling example of this phenomenon is seen in figure 11.1. It shows a late nineteenth-century poster reprinting the testimonials of five people who believed that taking quack medicines cured their tuberculosis. All died of tuberculosis.

Figure 11.1. Good-faith testimonials for tuberculosis cures by individuals who later died of tuberculosis. From *Nostrums and Quackery*, vol. 1, 2nd ed. (Chicago: American Medical Association Press, 1912), 139 (https://archive.org/details/nostrumsquackery01ameruoft/page/139/mode/1up?view=theater)

A proponent of CAM who became popular in the late twentieth century is Dr. Andrew Weil, author of several books on the topic (Weil 1995a, 1995b, 1997, 1998) that, among other things, exemplify the importance that unsupported testimonials and anecdotes have in alternative medicine. Relman's (1998, 2000) thorough critiques of Weil's views illustrate how credulous he is. Weil accepts as evidence reports of cures where not only is there no documentation that the patient was cured, but there is no documentation that the patient was even sick in the first place! In one case, reported in Weil (1997), an individual wrote Weil and said he had been diagnosed with "bone cancer." He went on to say that he cured himself by riding a bicycle and eating healthy foods. Nowhere did he provide Weil with the slightest evidence for his illness, and yet Weil reports this "case" as proof that a good diet can cure cancer!

Another highly visible alternative medicine guru is Dr. Mehmet Oz, who was heavily promoted by Oprah Winfrey and had his own show from 2009 to 2022. Oz is actually a medical doctor, specifically a heart surgeon at Columbia University. He ran, unsuccessfully, for the U.S. Senate from Pennsylvania in 2022. On his program he endorsed several quack treatments and allows therapeutic touch (see below) to be performed in his operating room. He endorsed an extract of green coffee beans as a surefire obesity treatment. Trouble was that the beans didn't do anything. In 2015 the Federal Trade Commission fined the company selling this nontreatment 9 million dollars for false advertising. Representatives of the company pushing the product as a dietary supplement had appeared on *The Dr. Oz Show*. The green coffee bean nonsense was only one of Dr. Oz's quack treatments. Before he promoted green coffee beans, Oz had hyped "raspberry ketones, acai berries, and African mango . . . as amazing 'fat burners'" (Schwarcz 2013, 28). He has also promoted homeopathy, reiki, and energy healing and even contacting the dead to relieve stress, having fraudulent medium John Edward on his show in March 2011. Korowynk and colleagues (2014) examined the evidence behind medical recommendations on two television medical talk shows—*The Dr. Oz Show* and *The Doctors*. They found that "approximately half of the recommendations have either no supporting evidence or are contradicted by the best available evidence" (1).

Yet another CAM guru who became popular on Winfrey's program is Deepak Chopra. Chopra advocates for all sorts of "energy medicine" and speaks of how quantum mechanics explains how much of alternative medicine works. The use of quantum mechanical terminology is very popular in CAM and is a large red flag indicating that the claims are bogus. Chopra is very well known for his profound-sounding sound bites. Here is an example, cited in Pennycook and colleagues (2015): "Attention and intention are the mechanics of manifestation."

I know what each and every one of those words mean, but I have no clue what the sentence is supposed to mean. Chopra's tendency to produce such grammatical, but meaningless, phrases has resulted in a website, http://wisdomofchopra.com/. This site will generate endless similarly new-age-sounding grammatical sentences devoid of any meaning. Some examples:

Each of us relies on the light of chaos.
The universe inspires the progressive expansion of external reality.
Interdependence differentiates into the door of life.

The site http://sebpearce.com/bullshit/ does much the same thing with a somewhat more, to my eye, new age flavor: "By redefining we self-actualize. To transverse the circuit is to become one with it." The Seb Pearce site generates multiple gibberish sentences and, if you want, entire pages of this stuff. For readers of a certain age, the above statements will call to mind the character Rabbi Shankar, played so brilliantly by the late Arte Johnson (1929–2019) on the 1968–1973 NBC TV program *Rowan & Martin's Laugh-In*.

Interesting research has been done on the characteristics of people who find such statements meaningful, and presumably are more likely to accept the claims of alternative medicine practitioners. In a very clever study provocatively titled "On the Reception and Detection of Pseudo-Profound Bullshit," Pennycook and colleagues (2015) studied the personality variables that were found in people who find such gibberish profound. In four studies people read statements by Chopra himself (i.e., "Nature is a self-regulating ecosystem of awareness"), Chopra-like statements, and statements that were actually meaningful (i.e., "Most people enjoy some sort of music"). Each statement was rated on how profound it was. Several questionnaires on personality were given. The results showed that "those more receptive to bullshit are less reflective, lower in cognitive ability (i.e., verbal and fluid intelligence, numeracy), are more prone to ontological confusions and conspiratorial ideation, are more likely to hold religious and paranormal beliefs, and are more likely to endorse complementary and alternative medicine" (559). Along the same line, Walker and colleagues (2019) showed that those more likely to perceive visual patterns where there were none were also more likely to interpret pseudo-profound bullshit statements as truly profound.

There is a relationship between acceptance of alternative medicine beliefs and practices and other pseudoscientific phenomena. Abheiden, Teut, and Berghofer (2020), studying a large sample in Germany, found that acceptance of alternative medicine and its use was strongly correlated with "lifetime use and approval of paranormal practices such as fortune-telling, dowsing or spiritualism" (5).

Scientists in all fields of investigation have long known that the world is much too complex to be understood on the basis of subjective impressions, beliefs, and feelings. Rather, careful and sometimes tedious procedures have to be followed to tease apart the welter of interrelationships that lead to cause-and-effect understanding. This is especially true when dealing with issues of therapeutic effectiveness, where the subjective result of the therapy may be very different from the actual result.

There are several factors that work to convince both patients and therapists alike that an ineffective therapy has worked. The best known of these is the *placebo effect*, which was mentioned earlier in the context of psychotherapy and faith healing. But placebo effects also occur in medical therapies—including drug therapies and even surgical therapies. A therapy can be considered to be truly effective only if it produces greater improvement than a placebo therapy. In order to determine this, is it vital to carry out what is known as a *double-blind, placebo-controlled study*. In such a study, at its simplest, one group of patients gets a placebo, and the other group gets the actual treatment or therapy being tested. The patients in the two groups do not know whether they are receiving the actual treatment or the placebo, nor do the individuals administering the treatment or the individuals evaluating the patients during and following treatment. If done properly, such a study will eliminate effects of bias (often unconscious) on the part of patients, therapists, and evaluators and reveal a truer picture of the effectiveness of the treatment.

Spontaneous remission is another factor that can, incorrectly, lead to the belief that an ineffective therapy is effective. Many disorders will go away even if no specific therapeutic intervention is undertaken. Our immune system and other physiological processes act to protect us against disease and fight off disease once we become ill. This is different from the placebo effect because these are real processes that act in the absence of therapy to restore health. I first learned about spontaneous remission from an episode of that well-known educational television program from the 1960s, the *Beverly Hillbillies*. In one episode ("The Common Cold," season 4, episode 15, aired December 29, 1965) Jethro gets a bad cold. Granny sets out to cure him using one of her backwoods potions. She mentions this to their greedy neighbor, the banker Drysdale, who is always looking out to make money off the hillbillies. Granny tells him that her potion always cures the common cold. Wow! Drysdale gets very excited, convinced he's stumbled across a wonder cure that will make him a fortune. He gets a business partner, who is president of a large pharmaceutical company, interested, and together they plot to get the "secret" formula from Granny. It's not really a secret—she ends up telling them what's in it. Somewhat taken aback at the ingredients, they ask her how the potion is given and how she knows it works. Granny happily cackles in reply that you just give the tonic every day for two weeks and at the end of the two weeks, the cold will be gone! When an illness goes away on its own, but the patient is engaging in some form of therapy, it is natural, but incorrect, for both the patient and the therapist to credit the therapy with the effect.

A less well-known effect that can lead to unwarranted beliefs in therapeutic effectiveness and thus testimonials is a statistical artifact called *regression to the mean* or average. Regression to the mean is the fact that an extreme score (either well above or well below the mean) will tend to be less extreme at some time in the future. Take a simple example of students taking the Scholastic Aptitude Test (SAT). Let us consider only the verbal test, in which scores range from 200 to 800, with a mean score of 500. Two students take the test for the first time. Student 1 scores 225. Student 2 scores 775. Six months later both students take the test again. Assume that neither takes any kind of SAT preparation or tutoring courses during this six-month period. What would one expect about their scores the second time around? First, it would be surprising if both students got exactly the same scores the second time, so we can be pretty sure that there will be some change. The question is, in what direction will the changes be? It would certainly be surprising if Student 1 did any worse. There is much more room for improvement than there is to get worse. So the student's score will be, in all likelihood, greater than 225 and thus closer to the mean of 500. What about student 2? This student doesn't have very much room to improve, so it is most likely that, on the second test, the score will go down, moving closer to the mean score of 500.

Regression to the mean is a nasty little statistical gremlin that can seriously cloud the interpretation of many scientific studies. But, in the present context, it can also lead to incorrect beliefs about whether or not a treatment works. A good example is using copper bracelets or "energy bands" to treat arthritis pain. The pain in arthritis, like the pain in many other pain-causing disorders, waxes and wanes. Sometimes it's worse; sometimes it's better. When is it most likely that one will resort to some sort of treatment for arthritis pain? When the pain is greater or above average. People are much more likely to get a copper bracelet when they are in greater pain than when they have little pain at all. Thus, in the few days after starting to wear the bracelet, by regression to the mean, the arthritis pain is very likely to reduce, for reasons having nothing to do with the bracelet. But the bracelet will almost certainly get credit for the change. Of course, the placebo effect is also involved in situations like this, as there is a well-known placebo effect for pain. Two placebo-controlled studies of copper bracelets for arthritis found no effect other than a placebo effect (Richmond et al. 2009; Richmond et al. 2013).

People will, of course, selectively take legitimate treatments for arthritis and pain in general, such as aspirin, when the pain is greatest. Does this mean that aspirin effects are just due to regression to the mean? No. Certainly, part of the aspirin effect is due to regression, and part is due to placebo effects—but properly controlled studies have shown that aspirin does reduce pain (for example, Berde and Sethna 2002).

In a classic paper, Berry Beyerstein (1997) described several more factors that lead to false beliefs in the efficacy of quack treatments. These include false diagnoses in which either the individual or the physician gets it wrong and what was thought to be a serious problem or disease isn't. Patients who use quack treatments will very often also use proven treatments. But when these cure the ailment, they give credit to the quack treatment, often not even mentioning the use of real medicine. When one hears something like "my brother's wife's assistant's son had his cancer cured because he was given fresh goat urine every day," it's often revealing to follow up and ask if conventional medicines were also being used. One will often hear, "Oh, yeah, well, uh, he did have chemo and some radiation therapy. But I just know it was the urine therapy that cured him." And I'm not joking—drinking one's own urine as a therapy or preventive measure is discussed below.

Another important factor that Beyerstein described is that many of the ailments that are "cured" by quack treatments have very large psychosomatic/subjective components. Minor aches and pains are among these. Symptoms of such disorders are extremely responsive to placebo effects. The placebo effect has permitted some truly crazy therapies to claim successful cures of such symptoms, as noted earlier in chapter 5 in the description of Perkins's "tractors." Another such testimonial-generating therapy was blue light therapy, the brainchild of U.S. Civil War general A. J. Pleasonton. In his 1876 book Pleasonton claimed that simply being exposed to blue light could cure all sorts of maladies. And, of course, he had testimonials aplenty to prove it. Even better, not only could blue light cure diseases, but it made flowers bloom and fruit trees more productive. Collins (2001, chapt. 11) gives a more detailed, and amusing, account of the history of Pleasonton's blue glass cure-all and the craze it caused in the United States and Europe in the late 1870s.

Even more bizarre and revealing of the nature of placebo effects is the story of "Dr." John R. Brinkley. The good doctor made a fortune reviving the sexual drives of elderly men in the early twentieth century, long before Viagra. He did so by transplanting the testes of goats into the testicles of his, obviously male, patients. Testimonials, and money, poured in. Men were delighted to have regained their libido, and some even fathered children after the operation. Both Lee (2002) and Brock (2008) have written excellent books about this little-remembered bit of the history of quackery. Brinkley was so popular that he ran for governor of Kansas in 1930 and nearly won. At about the same time, Serge Voronoff was transplanting monkey testes into humans, also with positive placebo results (Hamilton 1986). Of course, in both cases, the transplants had absolutely no actual effect, being rejected and walled off or destroyed by the recipient's immune system. But the actions of the immune system weren't known at the time.

Yet another factor responsible, in part, for the false belief in useless treatments is selective dropout. Those who are least satisfied with a therapy, or who are receiving the least benefit, are much more likely to drop out during the course of therapy. Conversely, those who like the therapy/therapist and feel that they are benefiting are more likely to stick it out. Thus, at the end of a study that does not take into account dropout effects, and many don't, it will falsely appear that the therapy is effective.

All the factors noted above combine to make it very difficult—I would say impossible—for even the brightest, best-intentioned therapist to determine, without the aid of procedures like double-blind, placebo-controlled studies, whether a therapy really works. There are other factors as well, and for a fine discussion of them, as well as a lengthier consideration of those mentioned here, Beyerstein (1999) is an excellent source. The complexity of the task of evaluating therapeutic effectiveness should put the lie to the alternative medicine claim that one can simply rely on subjective judgments to do the job. My own view is that it is highly unethical to rely on such judgments. In any area of therapy, one is dealing with very important, sometimes life-and-death, personal issues. To promote a therapy as effective without being as certain as one can be that it *is* effective risks the well-being and maybe even the life of the patient. We will see examples of this in the sections below.

In evaluating claims for alternative medicine treatments, or the possible harmful effects of some alleged environmental agent (see chapter 12), it is always important to look out for a statistical flaw called the multiple comparison fallacy, previously mentioned briefly in chapter 4. The basic idea is that if one does enough statistical tests on a dataset, or on multiple different datasets, one will almost certainly find a result that supports one's claims. The comparisons that do not support those claims are simply not reported and are ignored. The technical term for this is "p-hacking" where the p stands for "probability."

Alternative medicine promoters make heavy use of scientific-sounding terms and language, usually involving "energy fields," "human auras," "frequencies," and the like. An excellent example is given by Raskin (2000) in his discussion of the nursing theory of Martha Rogers. In Rogers's theory, "a unitary human being is an irreducible, indivisible energy field and a unitary one. . . . In fact human beings do not have energy fields; they *are* energy fields. They are open for exchange and extend to infinity" (32, emphasis in original). Further, "energy fields are identifiable through dynamic-nonstatic wave patterns and organization that changes from 'lower frequency, longer wave pattern to high frequency shorter wave pattern' based on the principle of resonancy." Sounds pretty scientific, right? From that description, a reader would naturally think that someone, perhaps Rogers herself as the main proponent of the theory, would have gone out and measured some of the physical characteristics of these energy fields. She could not have measured the fields' amplitude or frequency because these properties describe waves, not fields. To find out if this was the case, Raskin sent inquiries to several Rogerian nursing theorists and asked simply what the frequencies were and how the frequency measurements had been done. None of the theorists was able to say. In contrast, inquiries to physics teachers about the well-known Millikan experiment showing that charge is quantized were all answered by a description of the famous oil drop experiment.

Andrew Weil, the alternative medicine guru mentioned earlier, is right in the mainstream of alternative medicine in his use of scientific-sounding jargon. He even invokes quantum physics, one of the sure signs of an alternative medicine quack, in the support of his view that the mind can, by itself, cure diseases. To be sure, there are a number of phenomena in quantum physics that are very strange and, to say the least, counterintuitive. This weirdness has allowed writers in a number of fringe areas to invoke quantum mechanics as a way of providing a seeming explanation and seeming scientific support for the reality of phenomena they have been otherwise unable to demonstrate. The general argument seems to be, "Well, there's all this really weird stuff going on in quantum mechanics, so why can't the really weird stuff that I'm pushing [ESP, mind cures for cancer, etc.] be real as well?" The fundamental difference is that the admittedly really weird stuff that goes on at the quantum level goes on in highly predictable and reproducible ways. These phenomena are produced regularly and predicted with high precision every day in physics laboratories around the world. The basic principles of quantum mechanics play vital roles in many aspects of modern everyday life, from cell phones with GPS capabilities to CDs, DVDs, and medical imaging (Kakalios 2016). The precision and reliability of quantum-mechanical effects are certainly not found in psychic phenomena and mind cures for cancer. In the absence of actual supporting evidence, the existence of weirdness at the quantum level does not, in any way, support the claims of alternative medicine.

The scope of alternative medicine is huge and contains far too many different claims and products for all of them to be considered here. So rather than attempt the impossible task of examining each and every claim, the remainder of this chapter will examine some of the most common and popular major alternative medicine practices. Those specifically related to brain pseudoscience and autism will be discussed separately in chapter 13.

HOMEOPATHY

Until the 1970s, *homeopathy* or *homeopathic medicine* was essentially a European phenomenon very little seen on this side of the Atlantic. But with the explosion of interest in alternative medicine, homeopathy has gained a strong following in the United States. Homeopathy was developed in the eighteenth century by German physician Samuel Hahnemann (1755–1843). It became popular in the eighteenth and nineteenth centuries as an alternative to what was then considered traditional medicine. The basic idea behind homeopathic medicine is straightforward: patients can be cured of what ails them by giving them extraordinarily diluted solutions of a drug or substance that would, if given in higher doses, cause the symptoms from which the patient is suffering. Thus, if a patient is having seizures, the homeopathic treatment would be to give a very, very, very diluted solution of a substance that induces seizures. If this seems implausible, it is. But when homeopathy was developed, such treatments had a great advantage over the treatments administered by nonhomeopathic physicians: they didn't do any real harm. Such could not be said of some of the most common nonhomeopathic treatments of the time, which included bleeding, in which varying quantities of blood were removed from the patient, and the administration of drugs that contained high levels of the poison arsenic. Homeopathically treated patients were basically given water to drink and otherwise left alone so that their immune systems and other natural restorative mechanisms could fight off their maladies. Had anyone at the time thought to do a controlled study of the survival rates of patients treated homeopathically versus those treated with nonhomeopathic methods, it is likely that the patients treated homeopathically would have shown a higher survival rate.

As scientific medicine progressed in the twentieth century, it became possible to do more than simply leave patients alone to heal themselves. One could directly target the disease progress, thus greatly increasing the rate of cure of hundreds of diseases. In this context, the "do-nothing" approach of homeopathy made less and less sense. And yet, as noted, homeopathy has become more and more popular recently. This is certainly due to the factors noted above that convince people that ineffective treatments really work.

Proponents of homeopathy argue that their approach really does work. The active substance is diluted, usually in water. It is often diluted to such an extent that there is not a single molecule of the original substance left in the solution that the patient takes. How, then, is the original substance supposed to have any effect? According to homeopaths, as the dilution process progresses, the water "remembers" the properties of the original substance being diluted. It is this "memory" that accounts for the curative properties of the homeopathic medicine.

The idea that water could remember substances that it used to contain received much publicity in 1988. Researchers (Davenas et al. 1988) at a French laboratory reported in the prestigious scientific journal *Nature* experiments that they said proved that water that used to have particular antibodies in it still had a strong immunological effect even after the original solution had been diluted so that only one part in 1,020 of the original remained. In practice, this meant that not a single molecule of the original substance remained in the solution. *Nature* published the paper, in spite of serious reservations about its scientific merit, because the journal's editors considered the topic of such great interest. However, they took the extraordinary step of publishing along with the paper a critique based on the findings of a team of investigators sent to the laboratory to check the methods used. This is very reminiscent of Wood visiting Blondlot's laboratory to check on N-rays back in 1904 (chapter 1). And, like Wood, the *Nature* investigating team, which included *Nature* editor John Maddox and magician and psychic investigator James Randi, found serious problems in the lab. To assess the immunological effect of the diluted antibodies (of which, it will be recalled, none in fact remained due to the degree of dilution), a visual judgment, made by looking through a microscope, about the color of portions of cells called basophils was made. This subjective judgment, much like Blondlot's judgment of brightness in his N-ray experiments, was apparently done by one scientist who performed all the assessments in an unblinded fashion. The team found that, as Randi (1988–1989) puts it, the laboratory "had omitted much negative data from their lab records because some mitigating circumstance had suddenly become apparent after it was discovered that a particular experiment gave negative results" (144). In other words, negative results were explained away, after the fact, by one excuse or another, but positive results were retained. The *Nature* team tried to replicate the original findings. Working in the same laboratory and using the same equipment, but putting in place proper experimental controls, no positive results were found. Gardner (1988–1989) provided a lengthier discussion of this matter.

The director of the laboratory in which the experiments discussed above were carried out was Jacques Benveniste, who reacted strongly to the criticism of his laboratory's methods (Benveniste 1988). But his reply did not really address the specific issues of shoddy methodology that were raised by the critique; rather, it consisted largely of insults aimed at the *Nature* investigating team. Benveniste continued his interest in homeopathic treatments and in 1997 announced a finding even more momentous than his 1988 claim. He had discovered, he said, that homeopathic treatment effects could be transmitted over telephone lines and even sent by email (Sheaffer 1998a)!

Regardless of how weird the proposed mechanism of a treatment is, the treatment should be subjected to objective tests to see whether or not it is effective. Even if there is very little a priori chance that a treatment will be effective, tests demonstrating that it does not work can be valuable in showing the public that money, time, and effort should not be wasted using it. Homeopathy has been subjected to numerous tests of its effectiveness and has consistently been found to be wanting in this regard. Two early reviews (Hill and Doyon 1990; Kleijnen, Knipschild, and ter Riet 1991) covered more than one hundred different studies of homeopathic treatments for numerous different conditions ranging from stroke and hypertension to arthritis and bowel problems after surgery.

Hill and Doyon (1990) limited their review to studies that used randomized clinical trials to compare homeopathic treatments to either no treatment, a placebo, or standard treatment. They concluded that "the results do not provide acceptable evidence that homeopathic treatments are effective" (139). Kleijnen, Knipschild, and ter Riet (1991) reviewed 107 studies of homeopathic effectiveness. Their conclusion was a cautious one, to the effect that the results of the studies reviewed were "positive but not sufficient to draw definitive conclusions because most trials are of low methodological quality and because of the unknown role of publication bias" (316). In effect, this is a nice way of restating the maxim that extraordinary claims demand extraordinary proof. And homeopathy, at the time of the review, had not met that requirement. The authors did make an important point toward the end of their paper. They noted that several earlier studies had suggested that homeopathic treatments did have a positive effect on bowel movements after surgery to the abdomen. But a later, well-controlled study using a large number of subjects failed to find any such effect. This is a common pattern in the study of any therapeutic approach. Early studies, often done with fewer subjects than should have been used and suffering from various methodological problems, turn up what looks like positive evidence for the treatment. Later, better-controlled studies do not.

I should also mention one interesting aspect of homeopathy that I was unaware of until I read Kleijnen, Knipschild, and ter Riet (1991). Homeopathic treatments are, at least in Europe, used in agriculture. The authors cite a review (Scofield 1984) of this field that concluded that "despite the great deal of experimental and clinical work there is only little evidence to suggest that homeopathy is effective. This is because of bad design, execution, reporting or failure to repeat experimental work" (Kleijnen et al. 1991, 321).

Wagner (1997) reviewed studies published since the two previously mentioned reviews. Once again, the results were not supportive of any effectiveness of homeopathic treatments. Wagner discusses one study of homeopathic treatment of diarrhea (Jacobs et al. 1994) that is often touted as proving that homeopathic treatment works. Children in Nicaragua suffering from diarrhea were given either a homeopathic treatment or a placebo. It is important to note that the children with the worst cases of diarrhea were not included in the study, a serious biasing problem. In addition, there was not a third group that got a diarrhea treatment known to be effective. These problems aside, the results were far from impressive. The children in the two groups were evaluated each day for a five-day period. There was a significant difference favoring the homeopathically treated group only for the third day. The two groups were the same on the other four days. This is not, to say the least, terribly impressive evidence for homeopathy. A more detailed critique of this study has been published by Sampson and London (1995).

Taylor and colleagues (2000) published a study in which homeopathy was compared to a placebo for treatment of "allergic rhinitis," a nasal congestion caused by allergic reactions to pollen, dust, and the like. On a measure of the amount of relief provided, the homeopathic treatment and the placebo were rated as equally effective by the subjects. The homeopathic treatment group did show a greater change in a measure called nasal inspiratory peak flow. However, this is an unreliable measure and is no longer in clinical use.

There are even homeopathic vaccines that are "licensed in many countries, including Canada" (Loeb et al. 2018, 7423). These authors tested whether such vaccines produced an antibody response as a real vaccine would. In a blind, placebo-controlled study, individuals were given either a real vaccine, a homeopathic vaccine, or a placebo vaccine. The real vaccine generated the expected antibody response. Neither the placebo vaccine nor the homeopathic vaccine did so. The existence of homeopathic vaccines poses a real threat to the health of those who get them and believe that they are now protected from whatever disease the vaccines are claimed to prevent.

Organizations in both Britain and Australia have compiled lengthy reviews of the literature on homeopathic effectiveness. In 2010, the United Kingdom's House of Commons Science and Technology Committee published an exhaustive report that concluded that there was no evidence at all that homeopathy was any more effective than a placebo and that the National Health Service should stop reimbursement for homeopathic treatments. In 2017 the NHS did end payment for such treatments. In 2015 the Australian National Health and Medical Research Council reached the same conclusions.

Years of testing of homeopathic claims have made it clear that there's nothing to homeopathy (Ernst 2017). And yet people continue to buy homeopathic products and give heartfelt testimonials for their powers. Patients often use them while not taking medication that could help with whatever condition they suffer from. Why the continued use? The title of a paper by Brien and colleagues (2011) answers that important question—"Homeopathy Has Clinical Benefits in Rheumatoid Arthritis Patients That Are Attributable to the Consultation Process but Not to the Homeopathic Remedy."

Any store that continues to sell homeopathic products is engaging in consumer fraud. It is high time that local, state, and federal consumer protection officials began prosecuting sellers of such quack remedies. To this end, in June 2018 the Center for Inquiry, a consumer advocacy group, sued CVS Pharmacies in Washington, DC, for fraud for marketing homeopathic products as effective. The case is still in the courts.

The British comedy team of David Mitchell and Robert Webb had a television program called *That Mitchell and Webb Look*, made up of comedy sketches. One of their sketches from 2009 was titled "Homeopathic A&E," which imagines what an emergency room ("accident and emergency" [A&E] in British usage) would look like if homeopathy were real. It's hilarious and on YouTube.

ENERGY MEDICINE: THERAPEUTIC TOUCH, REIKI, AND AURA READING

One characteristic of energy medicine that is so common that it is almost definitional of the techniques in this area is the use of impressive sounding science terms that mean nothing in the context in which they are used by energy medicine quacks. Terms like *frequency*, *vibration*, *quantum*, *energy*, *harmonic*, and *oscillations* can be combined with terms like *healing* and *balance* to produce such vacuous phrases as "quantum frequency vibrational healing." Of course, the quacks who use these terms have no idea about their real, scientific meaning, as the example above of Martha Rogers's use of such terms showed.

Energy medicine quacks use the idea of a form of energy unknown to science called "chi" or "qi," allegedly from ancient Chinese medicine, to explain their practices. As noted previously, instruments widely available in any quality modern physics laboratory are able to detect incredibly small amounts of energy or force. And yet, with all this precision available, physicists have somehow managed to miss a previously unknown type of energy that is so obvious that energy medicine practitioners can detect it and manipulate it by merely waving their hands around. This seems unlikely.

To get around the problem of measurement, energy medicine practitioners argue that chi, or whatever term they use, can't be detected or measured by science. But if they say they can detect it and determine that it is out of kilter in people who are ill, then they are obviously measuring it in some way. They can't have it both ways. If they're measuring something using their hands as sensors, then there would be a way for anyone to measure it, just like anyone, with the right equipment, can measure the tiny energies known to physics. The response to this type of argument is to fall back on the usual special pleading that crops up so frequently in alternative medicine—science just isn't sensitive enough to detect the effects of the mystic energy fields.

Unfortunately, nonsense like energy medicine and other forms of quackery have been making their way into previously reputable medical schools and clinics (Li, Forbes, and Byrne 2018). For these clinics, it's a cheap way to make money. It costs very little to have someone wave their hands around a patient, but such "services" can and are billed at high rates. For example, the Cleveland Clinic on its website (www.myclevelandclinic.org) offers abundant quack options to patients, including energy medicine (Summers 2017), which the clinic defines in the usual vague terms as "balancing and restoring the body's natural energies." Through its Center for Integrative and Lifestyle Medicine, the Cleveland Clinic has a partnership with Jeffrey Bland's Institute for Functional Medicine. Bland was fined forty-five thousand dollars in 1998 for the false claims made for his health-care companies (Li, Forbes, and Byrne 2018). Quack medicine has infiltrated many other such institutions that seem to care more about profit than patient care.

The idea that "laying on of hands" can treat disease dates back thousands of years. As was seen in chapter 10, it plays a major role in religious faith healing. This section will discuss a more secular version of the laying on of hands, one that has come to be known as *therapeutic touch* and since the mid-1970s has become more and more popular in the nursing profession. The term *therapeutic touch* is a misnomer since the *practitioner*, as he or she is called, does not actually touch the patient, but moves the hands over the patient's body, keeping a space between them. This version of the laying on of hands was developed in the 1960s and 1970s mostly by Dolores Krieger, a nurse on the faculty at New York University in New York City, and Dora van Gelder Kunz, an Indonesian-born mystic and self-claimed clairvoyant. Stahlman (2000) provides details of the history of therapeutic touch.

The idea behind therapeutic touch is that by passing their hands over a person's body, a therapeutic touch practitioner can detect the aura or *human energy field*. Further, in individuals who are ill, the practitioner can, through some mechanism that is never specified, detect disturbances in the field and "realign" the field, helping to restore health. This set of claims raises three specific issues that are, at least theoretically, separate. The first is whether the human energy field, as postulated by supporters of therapeutic touch, exists at all. The second centers around the question of whether practitioners can, in fact, detect any energy field that may exist. The third is the empirical question of whether therapeutic touch results in demonstrable improvement over and above placebo and other effects. These three issues will be considered in order.

The question of whether a human energy field exists is really a question of physics. Does the human body generate some kind of field that might be detected by human hands? The answer is yes. The human body does constantly put out an electromagnetic field of sorts—we radiate heat, at least when we are alive, and sometimes—as during decomposition—when we aren't. Heat is just one type of energy, one that happens to lie in the infrared range. Devices such as infrared sensors and cameras with special film can easily detect the electromagnetic energy in this range. Our infrared radiation will be important in the discussion below of just what it might be that therapeutic touch practitioners are detecting when they claim to be sensing a human energy field. Such practitioners, of course, are not claiming that they are detecting something as mundane as body heat. The human energy field is, they argue, something previously unknown to science: a new type of force, previously undetected by physicists. But as discussed previously, it is extremely unlikely that physics has missed any such type of energy.

If the claim made by therapeutic touch supporters is true, the discovery of a previously unknown type of force would be a major scientific breakthrough, worthy of a Nobel Prize. Given the potential importance of such a discovery, both theoretically and practically, one would expect that the developers of therapeutic touch would have spared no expense in doing elegant experiments clearly demonstrating that this new force really exists and outlining its characteristics. Such an expectation would meet great disappointment. Consistent with the pseudoscientific characteristic of not looking closely at the phenomenon in question, therapeutic touch proponents have done no well-controlled studies to try to conclusively show that this force exists or what its characteristics are. Nor have they ever done studies aimed at determining whether practitioners could really detect the alleged force. Others have done such studies, as described below.

The concept of the human energy field or some sort of vital life force predates the rise of therapeutic touch by many years (Perez and Hines 2011). That the human energy field or aura could be photographed was first claimed by Semyon Davidovich Kirlian (1898–1978) in 1937 (Singer 1981), and thus Kirlian photography of the aura was born. In Kirlian photography the photographic plate is connected to a source of electricity. This type of photography has been popular with proponents of the paranormal and the human energy field ever since. Kirlian photographs do show impressive, colorful fringes around the borders of living things. The question is what causes such images. Pehek, Kyler, and Faust (1976) showed that the effect was due to moisture present on the objects being photographed. The electricity produces a fringe of ionized gas around the photographed object, if moisture is present. If the photograph is taken in a vacuum, where no ionized gas is present, no Kirlian image appears (Cooper and Alt, cited in Singer 1981). If the Kirlian image were due to some paranormal fundamental living energy field, a mere vacuum should not eliminate it. That the Kirlian effect is enhanced by emotional arousal is easily explained by the sweating, and thus increased moisture, that accompanies such arousal.

Careful investigations have revealed that physical variables affect the nature of the Kirlian image. These include the type of film, the type of electrode used, and the characteristics of the electric input. In all, around twenty-five variables affect the image (Watkins and Bickel 1988–1989). As Singer (1981, 208-9) concludes, "No mysterious process has been discovered by mainstream scientists investigating the Kirlian process. The paranormal claims about the photographs seem to have resulted from misunderstandings about the physical processes involved, and lack of expertise in conducting rigorous technical measurements."

For more than a hundred years, psychics and related mystics have claimed to be able to see the human aura and sense a human energy field. They seem to be dead on at detecting the presence of these phenomena when there is a human being directly in front of them. Since the aura is said to extend a few inches outward from the body, it ought to be possible to detect the presence or absence of a human hidden behind, but very close to the edge of, an object that blocks the actual person from view.

Therapeutic touch practitioners never bothered to test the reality of their claimed powers to detect auras. They have simply asserted that they have this power. Loftin (1989–1990) performed a test on one psychic who claimed to be able to see auras. This person did not score above chance at detecting whether or not a person was actually hidden behind a partition. In a larger study, Gissurarsson and Gunnarsson (1997) had aura readers and people who were not aura readers try to determine which barriers people were standing behind. Neither the self-proclaimed aura readers nor the non–aura readers were any better than chance.

The first properly controlled test of whether therapeutic touch practitioners could detect the human energy field was published by Rosa and colleagues in 1998. In this study, twenty-one different practitioners took part in a very simple test of their ability to detect the energy field. The practitioners sat on one side of a table. On the other side of the table was the experimenter. The table was divided by an opaque screen with two holes cut at the bottom through which, on each trial, the practitioner would put their hands. Once the hands were placed through the holes, a cloth was placed over the practitioner's arms to prevent any cues from the experimenter's side of the screen from being visible through the holes. On each trial, the experimenter would place one of her hands about four inches above either the left or right hand of the practitioner. Whether the left or right hand was the "target" was determined at random. The practitioner's task was to simply indicate whether the experimenter's hand was above their left or right hand. If practitioners can detect a human energy field, as they claim, then they should score well above the 50 percent chance figure in this situation. They did not. The overall score was 44 percent correct, which is below but not significantly different from chance.

The publication of the Rosa and colleagues (1998) study generated a great deal of attention in the media. One reason was that the study was such a simple and elegant test of a controversial theory. Another reason was that the experiment was designed and carried out by a nine-year-old girl, Emily Rosa, who was also the second author on the paper. Emily's mother, Linda Rosa, was the first author. With this publication, Emily became the youngest person to author a scientific paper published in a professional scientific journal. Linda Rosa was a registered nurse who had serious doubts about therapeutic touch. Overhearing her mother discuss the issue, Emily came up with her experiment for a school science fair. This combination of an interesting and easily understood experiment with the human-interest aspect of a nine-year-old carrying it out was irresistible to the media. The story was featured on the evening news programs of all the major networks on March 31, 1998, and on the front page of the *New York Times* on April 1, as well as in hundreds of other newspapers and local television stations around the country and the world.

The reaction of the therapeutic touch community to the publicity was the expected outrage and a considerable amount of hand waving and unintentionally humorous attempts to discredit the results of Rosa and colleagues (1998). It was argued that the results weren't valid since Emily Rosa, whose energy field was to be detected in the study, wasn't ill, and therapeutic touch practitioners could only work with the energy fields of sick people. Oddly, nowhere in the therapeutic touch literature had this fact ever been mentioned—it was only trotted out as an excuse after the study's findings were published. There was much new age–type babble about the inability of science to deal with something as mysterious as therapeutic touch. Schuller and Pennachio (1998), two RNs at Yonkers (New York) General Hospital, said that there is a "problem inherent in using standard research methodologies to research holistic practices" such as therapeutic touch. They never said just what this "inherent" problem was. Therapeutic touch founder Dolores Krieger gave a response to the Rosa and colleagues study that shows her own serious lack of understanding of how scientific research is done. She stated that Emily Rosa "completely misunderstood what the nature of basic research is" (Kolata 1998, A20).

The idea that the effects of therapeutic touch can't be tested scientifically is nonsense. Practitioners of therapeutic touch claim that they can perceive certain things and that certain procedures have effects on the patient. Either they do or they don't. The only way to really find out is to do properly controlled studies that rule out placebo effects and other biasing phenomenon. Those who argue, when such studies fail to vindicate a particular cherished belief, "My claims can't be evaluated by mere science," are engaged in special pleading—that their claims be subjected to a much less rigorous standard of proof than everyone else's. Just the opposite should be the case. Extraordinary claims demand *extraordinary* proof, not *less* proof.

Given the simplicity of the method used in Rosa and colleagues (1998), one might wonder why no one had thought to do such a study before. This is yet another example of pseudoscientists not looking closely at the phenomena they claim to be real. They prefer to rely on intuition and the fact that they just "know" that the effect is real or the treatment works—no need to waste time doing boring old science! Schuller and Pennachio (1998) again provide a great example of this type of magical thinking. How do they know therapeutic touch works? "We have had very good experiences with therapeutic touch. We have had it done to ourselves, have learned how to do it, and use it with staff and patients" (14A). I wonder if they would accept the same standard of proof for, say, a new drug therapy. Personal experience with a new therapy of whatever type can only be a vague guide as to what might or might not be effective, but such experience should *never* be taken as the end point of an evaluation of a therapy's effectiveness. Such experience can serve only as a starting point for further objective testing of effectiveness.

While the therapeutic touch community may have thought about a study like Rosa and colleagues (1998), they never carried one out. However, other, more skeptical investigators had thought of doing such a study. Specifically, James Randi tried to do a very similar study but was unable to get any therapeutic touch practitioners to agree to take part (Kolata 1998). Randi felt that practitioners stayed away from his study because they knew it would be a careful, rigorous examination that would be very likely to show that their beliefs were wrong.

Ironically, a later report (Long, Bernhardt, and Evans 1999) showed that a human energy field can be detected by one's hands alone—but it's not the human energy field therapeutic touch practitioners claim to be detecting. Long, Bernhardt, and Evans performed an experiment using apparatus much like that used by Rosa and colleagues (1998). Subjects, who were not therapeutic touch practitioners, placed their hands through a hole in a screen and tried to detect the presence or absence of the experimenter's hand held over theirs. The experimenter's hand was held at varying distances (three, four, or six inches) above the subject's hand. In one condition, subjects responded at a rate significantly above chance when the experimenter's hand was three or four inches above theirs. Is this proof of the existence of the human energy field as postulated by therapeutic touch proponents? Not in the least: it's proof that living human hands emit body heat, and other hands can detect that heat. This was shown in another condition in the experiment in which a piece of glass, which blocks heat, was placed between the hands of the subject and the experimenter. In this condition, even at the closest (three-inch) distance, subjects scored at chance. In another study of a single therapeutic touch practitioner, Glickman and Gracely (1998) used a slightly different methodology. The practitioner tried to detect the presence of a hand inside a mold made of cardboard and fiberglass. This mold effectively blocked the heat from the hand when it was present. The practitioner scored at chance on this test.

The issue still remains as to whether therapeutic touch actually has any effect on patients. Does it make people better, compared to a placebo treatment? Therapeutic touch proponents certainly think so. Proponents claim that much research has proven that therapeutic touch really works. Scheiber (1997) quoted an article in the popular press that "more than 200 studies have tested the technique's effectiveness on conditions including wound healing, chronic anxiety, tension headaches and post-chemotherapy nausea and vomiting" (13). Somewhat more vaguely, Schuller and Pennachio (1998) referred to twenty-five years of research on therapeutic touch. Does such research really exist? What does it show? Scheiber (1997) set out to examine the research on the effectiveness of therapeutic touch. One listing (Scheiber 1997) contained references to two hundred publications on therapeutic touch. Of these, only thirty were reports of actual outcome research on the technique; the rest were general articles in the popular press, books, and articles about the technique in the nursing literature that did not report the results of research. Of the thirty that reported research results, fifteen reported results that *did not* support therapeutic touch. Five more could not be found from the citations given. The remaining ten purported to show that therapeutic touch was effective. Even if these ten studies were flawless in terms of methodology, which they certainly were not, in light of the fifteen critical studies, the overall results were not particularly favorable for the technique. In fact, these ten studies suffered from numerous methodological flaws, as detailed in Scheiber and Selby (2000) and Bullough and Bullough (1998).

Additional studies alleging that therapeutic touch is effective fare little better when examined. Often cited in this regard is a study by Wirth (1990) that found that skin wounds treated with therapeutic touch healed faster than wounds not so treated. Proponents fail to cite other studies by Wirth that showed different results. Wirth performed five different studies of the effects of therapeutic touch on wound healing (Beyerstein 1999; Wirth 2000). In two of these studies, wounds treated by therapeutic touch healed significantly faster than control wounds. In one study there was no difference. In two other studies, the control wounds healed significantly faster than the treated wounds. Across the group, then, there was no effect.

Turner and colleagues (1998), in a study funded by a $355,000 grant from the Defense Department, examined whether therapeutic touch reduced pain and anxiety in patients who had been burned, using six measures of pain and one measure of anxiety. In their published report, the authors state that three of these seven measures showed a significant advantage for the group treated with therapeutic touch. However, they adopted a very lax criterion for judging statistical significance (called a *one-tailed test*) that was inappropriate. In addition, the two pain measures that were significant were very highly correlated ($r = .89$) and so were really measures of the same thing. Taking these factors into account, Turner and colleagues actually found that only one out of six of their measures showed an advantage for the therapeutic touch group. This is not a very strong showing. Gordon and colleagues (1998) used subjects suffering from osteoarthritis in the knee to test the effectiveness of therapeutic touch. One group ($n = 8$) received therapeutic touch; a second group ($n = 11$), a placebo; and a final group ($n = 8$), standard treatment. A major problem with this study is the tiny number of subjects used in each group. Further, the authors performed a welter of statistical tests on the data. It is often difficult, if not impossible, to tell from the published paper just how many analyses were actually performed and which showed significant effects. Those fascinated by detailed discussions of statistical problems can find such a discussion of both the Turner and colleagues and Gordon and colleagues studies in Wagner (2000).

James and colleagues (2019) studied whether therapeutic touch had any effects on measures of sleep, peri-operative pain, how long it took to come out from anesthesia, and anxiety in patients who had an "elective operation at a pediatric burns hospital" (265). On none of those measures was there an effect of therapeutic touch. Nor did the procedure have any effects on a number of clinical chemistry measures, including blood glucose and cortisol levels.

The most reasonable conclusion that can be drawn from the extant literature on the effectiveness of therapeutic touch is that no one has even come close to showing that the technique is effective. Given this, it is unethical for the treatment to continue to be used (and billed for!).

A bizarre combination of therapeutic touch and acupuncture is thought field therapy (Pignotti and Thyer 2015). This is a new age therapy in which the therapist just taps acupuncture points rather than sticking needles in their patients. This is supposed to somehow remove disturbances in the patient's energy fields, or some such. Sadly, the American Psychological Association, the largest professional organization of psychologists in the United States, gives continuing education credits for this quack therapy.

Reiki and Reflexology

Reiki practitioners claim that by moving their hands about they can alter, for the better, imbalances in the qi energy fields that are supposed to cause diseases and other medical disorders. It is slightly different from therapeutic touch, which doesn't involve actual touching, since a reiki session will include message-like touching. The findings on reiki are as negative as those on therapeutic touch. It's just a placebo and fails in controlled studies (Lee, Pittler, and Ernst 2009). For whatever reason, however, perhaps because of the message component, reiki is gaining wide popularity, and, sadly, courses in it are offered by some medical schools. In what is almost a parody of a well-controlled trial of a treatment, Dyer, Baldwin, and Rand (2019) published a "large scale effectiveness trial of reiki for physical and psychological health." The authors concluded that reiki is effective for almost any variable you'd care to name. But a close look at the study reveals several fundamental problems. The subjects were people already paying the reiki "masters," who specifically recruited the subjects from among their own patients. Each individual subject was given questionnaires before and after a single reiki session. These measured many different physical and psychological variables. Guess what? The subjects felt better after their sessions. There was no placebo control group and, obviously, the subjects were preselected to be those most favorable to reiki. Further, it is absurd to claim that any intervention is effective after only one session lasting at most an hour and a half.

The Dyer, Baldwin, and Rand (2019) study would receive a grade of "F" in any college research methods course. That the study was published in the *Journal of Alternative and Complementary Medicine*, the "flagship" journal of the "alternative medicine is really scientific" movement, speaks volumes about the low quality not only of that journal but of the nature of research done by proponents of quackery.

Reflexology is based on the false concept that different parts and organs of the body are "represented," whatever that means, on the hands and soles of the feet. By manipulating these areas, practitioners say that they can treat afflictions of different types. Two reviews of the literature (Ernst, Posadzki, and Lee 2011; Baggoley 2015) found no evidence that reflexology is effective for any type of disorder. Like so many quack and alternative practices, it engenders placebo effects.

Feng Shui

While feng shui isn't an actual alternative medical treatment, it is based on the same nonexistent energy "chi" that is used to justify energy medicine claims such as found in traditional Chinese medicine, as noted by Matthews (2019), whose book provides an excellent and detailed historical analysis of feng shui. The belief in chi is so powerful that in Hong Kong buildings have been built with immense holes in them to allow the chi to flow freely. The idea is that by tapping into the chi the feng shui practitioner will be able to arrange furniture, parts of buildings, and even entire buildings in ways that are more "harmonious." Just what "harmonious" means and just how it is measured in feng shui is never made clear. There is no doubt that some arrangements of furniture and buildings are going to be more aesthetically pleasing than others. One doesn't have to tap into some nonexistent force to be able to avoid hideous room and building designs. But feng shui practitioners claim that feng shui is a "science" and that their design recommendations are not just personal judgments. Given this, how might one test feng shui scientifically? Perhaps feng shui practitioners simply have a better aesthetic sense that has nothing to do with energy fields. In the seventh episode of the first season (2003) of their wonderful HBO TV series *Bullshit*, Penn and Teller devised a way to test the principles of feng shui. They hired three different feng shui consultants to arrange the furniture in a home. None of the consultants (whose fees were considerable) knew about the others. If there was anything to the "science" of feng shui, then all three of the practitioners would arrange the furniture in the house in at least approximately the same way. Nothing of the sort happened. Each of the three arranged the house in very different ways, each accompanied by colorful feng shui babble justifying the practitioner's particular arrangement.

Crystal Power

Crystals are attractive and interesting. It is their very attractiveness that has probably made them so popular among energy medicine proponents who claim that crystals of numerous types and colors have all sorts of wonderful, magic healing powers. The claims for crystals are usually dressed up with the usual sciencey-sounding babble so common in energy medicine. However, there is no evidence that crystals have any healing powers whatsoever. The proponents of the powers of crystals have never put forth any attempt to provide a double-blind placebo study that would show that crystals actually can promote healing. The testimonials for crystals are, as usual, due to factors such as placebo effects, spontaneous remission, and selective memory. Two studies (French and Williams 1999; French, O'Donnell, and Williams 2001) demonstrated the power of belief in crystal effects. In both studies people were given either a real quartz crystal or a matching piece of glass, the two being indistinguishable. They were asked to report any bodily sensations, sensations associated with crystal power according to proponents, during a five-minute meditation session. In both studies such sensations were reported frequently. But there was no difference in the frequency of these reports between the real crystal and piece of glass conditions. This lack of difference, which would not be expected if crystals had the powers claimed for them, shows that the effects were due to the power of suggestion and not to any mystical crystal powers. The results "provide no support whatsoever" for claims relating to the alleged mysterious powers of crystals (French and Williams 1999, 4). Using very different measures of crystal power, Jerome (1989) found that crystals do not increase gas mileage, make plants grow more, or purify water.

NATUROPATHY

Naturopathy is an increasingly popular form of alternative medicine that claims to be able to treat diseases without the bother of actual medicines and the procedures of modern medical knowledge. According to naturopathy, disease is caused by such things as "toxins," allergies to various foods, lowered immune system response, and other vague causes. It emphasizes a welter of so-called treatments, including herbs and supplements that are said to "boost" the immune system, acupuncture, aromatherapy, homeopathy, breathing exercises, wrapping wet towels around the afflicted body part, use of ozone and hydrogen peroxide baths (to increase oxygen levels in the blood of asthma patients), and the like. In his comprehensive review of naturopathy, Atwood (2003) described one especially troubling aspect of naturopathic treatment procedures. To treat an acute stroke, the patient should have an ice bag pressed on the neck (over the carotid artery) for twenty minutes or so. This is mind-numbingly stupid advice. This approach will kill people if used. An acute stroke is a medical emergency that requires immediate attention by a trained neurologist.

An even more bizarre, if less immediately harmful, treatment is the, I kid you not, endonasal balloon. Yup—they stick a balloon up your nose and pump it up to, as Atwood (2003, 3) quotes, "release tensions stored in the connective tissue and return the body to its original design." This is said to treat learning problems. You know, whenever I feel tensions and have difficulty learning, I get this uncontrollable urge to shove a balloon up my nose and inflate it. Maybe there is something to this naturopathy after all! (Just kidding.)

Atwood (2003) documented several of the invalid and fraudulent procedures naturopaths use to make their diagnoses. Hair analyses is said to be able to detect damaging "toxins," nutritional deficiencies, and other problems. Talk of toxins is a sure sign of a quack. Although people can clearly be poisoned, mysterious toxins are not running around in the blood—the liver is quite efficient at removing unwanted and harmful materials from the blood. In otherwise healthy people, it doesn't need any help. Naturopaths take hair samples and send them to private laboratories for analysis. How accurate are these reports? Not very. In an early study Barrett (1985) sent bits of hair from two healthy teenagers to thirteen different hair analysis laboratories. If there was anything to hair analysis, the reports from the different labs should have agreed. They didn't. The reports "were voluminous, bizarre, and potentially frightening to patients" (1041), and different labs recommended very different types of nutritional supplements. In 2001 Seidel and colleagues found exactly the same thing when they sent hair samples from one healthy person to six different labs. Finally, Kempson and Lombi (2011) in a longer review found hair analysis to be of no value in diagnosis.

Jones, Campbell, and Hart (2019) reviewed the use of numerous laboratory tests used by naturopaths and alternative medicine practitioners in general. They found that there is a "lack of evidence for clinical validity and utility" (319) of the tests used in alternative medicine. The tests included hair analysis, antioxidant status, mitochondrial function, food intolerance testing, and adrenal stress test, among others.

Parasites are another big deal in naturopathy and, it is said, can be detected by running a tiny jolt of electric current through the skin and measuring how much electrical resistance the electricity encounters. Parasites may infect some people, but running a small shock through the skin isn't going to detect them. But one could certainly design a study to test whether the naturopaths' procedure works. Think for a moment of how you would design a study to test this before you continue reading. Okay, here's how I'd design such a study: We'd have two groups of, say, twenty-five people, one group with some type of verified parasitic infestation and one group verified parasite free. The people in the two groups would be matched for the usual variables—sex, age, education, favorite flavor of ice cream (okay, I made that last one up, but you get the idea). Then all the people in both groups would have "electrodiagnosis" done by someone who did not know which group they were in. The results of each electrodiagnosis would then be randomized and presented to a panel of naturopaths who had previously agreed that they would be able to distinguish the electrodiagnosis results of the infected from the noninfected people. If they could do so, their accuracy should be well over chance. If electrodiagnosis is a crock, their accuracy rate should be about chance—50 percent. As far as I can tell, no such study has ever been done. I wonder why. In ethical medicine, one carefully tests a diagnostic procedure to see if it is really valid before using it. Not so in naturopathy.

Another naturopath scam diagnostic procedure is known as applied kinesiology. It's also used in shopping malls around the world to con people into buying copper bracelets, "holographic energy bands," and other gimmicks that are touted to increase energy levels, balance, strength, vitality, rid the body of toxins—the usual alternative medicine new age babble. Here's how it works. The victim is asked to stand on one foot with the other leg braced against the leg on which they are standing and then extend the arm on the side of the body opposite the standing leg straight out. The con artist then shows how easy it is to push on the extended arm and make the person fall over. But wait, there's more! Then our con artist places the magic whatsit in the hand of the extended arm and shows that now no matter how hard the arm is pushed on, the person doesn't fall over. Wow—incredible proof of the amazing quantum energy vibrational balancing power of the expensive whatsit. *Wrong*. It's a scam. It's much easier, and convincing, to see how the con is done than for me to write about it. So google "applied kinesiology—how it's done," which is the title of the *Skeptic Zone Podcast* episode of May 12, 2010, and see for yourself.

Naturopaths say they are as well trained as real doctors. This is absurd. They do have residency programs, go to school, and have textbooks, but these are mere shadows of what real doctors have (Atwood 2003). Unfortunately, many states now license this form of quackery, and in California naturopaths are trying to get the right to prescribe medicines. This is a serious danger. Make no mistake, naturopaths kill people. By convincing people with serious or even life-threatening illnesses, that could be treated successfully by real medicine, to forgo real treatment, naturopaths, like faith healers, are directly responsible for patients dying unnecessarily. Naturopaths and similar quacks will retort that real doctors sometimes kill their patients. This is, sadly, true. But the difference is that real doctors can treat disease, cure people, and save lives. Quacks never can. They only make things worse.

HERBAL REMEDIES, VITAMINS, AND SUPPLEMENTS

Of all the areas of alternative medicine, the one that is probably best known and most used by the public is that of herbal remedies. The impression one gets from the "alternative" medicine literature is that herbal medicines are something new and the idea of using natural substances to treat disease originated with the "alternative" medicine movement. This is incorrect. Many widely used conventional medicines have plant origins. For example, digitalis, which is used to treat certain heart conditions, is found naturally in deadly nightshade berries. Even the active ingredient in aspirin, salicylic acid, is found in many plants. The difference between established medicines with herbal origins and the numerous herbal substances promoted by "alternative" medicine is that the former have had their effectiveness proven by scientific methods. The latter have generally not been subjected to any such analysis.

Since many established drugs have herbal origins, it is possible that at least some of the "new" herbal compounds may have real, beneficial effects. One of the most popular in this context is ginkgo biloba, which is marketed as enhancing memory function. The results of studies on ginkgo are mixed at best. Laws, Sweetnam, and Kondel (2012) reviewed the literature and found no beneficial effects in normal individuals with no cognitive impairment. Nor does ginkgo help cognitive function in those with cognitive impairment (Cooper, Lyketsos, and Livingston 2013). One review (Charemboon and Jaisin, 2015) found that ginkgo may reduce dementia in the aged. Yuan and colleagues (2017) concluded that ginkgo *may* have beneficial effects on cognition. However, the quality of evidence in the papers they reviewed was only "low to moderate" (1). More seriously, the sort-of-positive effects appeared only on some measures and only for some dosages of ginkgo. These potential benefits are most likely due to false positives due to multiple statistical comparisons. Ginkgo does have anticoagulant effects that could be potentially serious in patients having surgery, those taking other drugs that affect coagulation, or women giving birth.

Faring better when properly controlled studies are done is St. John's wort. Two large reviews have both concluded that it may be somewhat effective in the treatment of depression. Linde and colleagues (2015,

69) concluded that St. John's wort "showed some positive results, but limitations of the currently available evidence makes [*sic*] a clear recommendation on their place in clinical practice difficult." Apaydin and colleagues (2016) found that St. John's wort was "superior to placebo in improving depression symptoms and not significantly different from antidepressant medication. However, evidence of heterogeneity and a lack of evidence on severe depression reduce the quality of the evidence" (1). It is important to know that the studies reviewed in these papers used verified doses of the active ingredient in St. John's wort, hypericum. Because of the Dietary Supplement Act (see below), there is no guarantee that pills in a bottle labeled "St. John's wort" bought over the counter will have any hypericum in them at all or will be free of contaminants. The same can be said for over-the-counter ginkgo.

Another well-known herbal that may have beneficial effects is garlic. It can be beneficial for reducing high cholesterol levels in the blood and has several other small but positive effects. However, as Ernst (2019, 105) puts it, "the effects of garlic are small and cannot measure up to those of prescribed synthetic drugs. However, the multitude of its different effects might work in concert and add up to a significant cardiovascular benefit." Future careful research is the only way to know. But at least garlic keeps vampires away (van Helsing 1863).

The marketing of herbal remedies highlights a huge difference between real medicine and fake alternative medicine. If there is a hint that some herb has actual beneficial properties, real scientists will study that herb to find the active ingredient responsible for the benefits. If the benefits are real, such studies will lead to a purified preparation of the chemical, or chemicals, which can then be used to help the sick. Alternative medicine practitioners will not do any such research. They'll just continue to insist that the herb is beneficial, without seeking out evidence that this is true, and continue to sell weak or impure products often laced with unknown and potentially dangerous contaminants.

The common cold is one of those minor miseries that everyone has to endure. So it's no surprise that it has been the target of quack cures. The Nobel Prize–winning chemist Linus Pauling (1901–1994) promoted vitamin C as a common cold cure. While vitamin C may have a small beneficial effect for individuals subject to extreme physical stress, it does not have any beneficial effects on colds for the likes of you and me (Hemila and Chalker 2013). More recently the herbal echinacea has been sold as being effective for both preventing and reducing the symptoms of the common cold. A major review by Karsch-Volk and colleagues (2014) concluded that the herbal does not "provide benefits for treating colds, although, it is possible there is a weak benefit" in prevention, which, however, is "of questionable clinical relevance." The great number of personal testimonials for the effects of both vitamin C and echinacea are due to placebo effects, selective memory, and the other variables that lead people to accept as effective treatments that are not.

Pauling also promoted vitamin C as a cure for dozens of other diseases, including AIDS and cancer. His enthusiasm for the substance as a cancer cure came from a study (Cameron and Pauling 1976) in which it appeared that terminal cancer patients who got doses of vitamin C lived longer than a control group that did not. Major differences between the control and treatment group render this study worthless. Specifically, the patients in the vitamin C group were defined as terminal sooner than those in the control group. That is why they lived longer. The study only served to convince those unaware of the characteristics that define good clinical trials. Since then other studies have failed to find any effect of vitamin C on cancer (Cabanillas 2010; Offit 2013, chap. 2), although Cabanillas tried to put a brave face on the negative results by saying "we still do not know whether Vitamin C has any clinically significant antitumor activity" (215). After over thirty years of study, if an effect hasn't been found in well-designed studies, it very likely isn't there and further studies would be a waste of money and unethical since they would subject patients to a worthless treatment.

Supplements and herbal remedies are almost always marketed as "dietary supplements." The herbal, vitamin, and supplement industry is a thirty-plus-billion-dollar-a-year business in the United States.

Millions of Americans take numerous vitamins and supplements every day. Consumers probably expect that the substances they buy are required by law to have been tested for effectiveness and safety, to contain the ingredients that are listed on the packages, and to be free of contamination. In fact, none of these things is true. The 1994 Dietary Supplement Health and Education Act specifically exempts the supplement industry from any type of regulation regarding product safety, purity, or truth in labeling. In other words, there is no legal requirement that these substances be proven (1) effective, (2) safe, or (3) even that the ingredients claimed to be in the product are actually included. The Dietary Supplement Act was heavily supported by the alternative medicine community and especially the diet supplement, herbal, and vitamin industry. Think about that—the law turned the clock back, in America, to the nineteenth century, when manufacturers could put any kind of harmful substances into the products they sold. Not surprisingly, the nutritional and supplement industries have powerful lobbies in Congress and give huge contributions to members of both the Senate and House.

The results of the lack of regulation have been clear. Studies of herbal ginseng found that the actual amount of the active compounds in each pill sold over the counter "varied by as much as a factor of 10 among brands that were labeled as containing the same amount." To make matters worse, "some brands contained none at all" (Angel and Kassirer 1998, 840). It is worth noting that homeopathic remedies have been exempt from any sort of regulation since 1938 (Wagner 1997).

In February 2015 New York State attorney general Eric Scheiderman's office issued a cease-and-desist order to General Nutrition Centers, Target, Walgreens, and Walmart, requiring them to stop selling supplements that had been fraudulently labeled. DNA tests showed that supplements labeled as echinacea, gingko biloba, ginseng, and St. John's wort did not contain any of these substances. Only six of twenty products claiming to be saw palmetto contained any saw palmetto. The mislabeled products did contain fillers such as rice and alum. Overall, only 21 percent of the tested supplements contained *any* of the ingredients listed on the label. A full 33 percent contained ingredients not listed on the labels.

Supplements have a good chance of containing none of the ingredients listed on the packaging. And the manufacturers of such fraudulent products are allowed to do so with no penalties at the federal level, except when the ingredients are harmful. Which they sometimes are. Offit (2013, 91) reports that nearly a quarter of supplements purchased in Boston were found to contain "potentially harmful levels of lead, mercury and arsenic." The bottom line is simple. Supplements are often mislabeled and can contain either inert fillers or, sometimes, harmful substances. Even if the packages contained what they say they contained, there is almost no evidence that they would be beneficial in any way. The popularity of otherwise useless supplements is yet another beautiful demonstration of the power of cognitive illusions, such as the placebo effect and selective memory, to convince people that inert substances have effects that, in reality, they do not have. As Offit and Erush advised, in an op-ed piece in the December 15, 2013, *New York Times*, "skip the supplements."

Coghlan and colleagues (2015) reported the results of their extensive DNA and toxicological analyses of a wide range of popular herbal and traditional Chinese medicines. They found an extremely high percentage of these were contaminated in one way or another or did not contain the ingredients as advertised. Some of the findings are especially troublesome. In half of the samples an "undeclared pharmaceutical agent was detected including warfarin, dexamethasone, diclofenac, cyproheptadine and paracetamol" (1). Very disturbingly, half of the tested compounds had DNA from the rare and endangered snow leopard. Traditional Chinese medicines often contain animal by-products (i.e., bear bile) that are obtained by killing or torturing animals of various species, including endangered species. The study also found highly toxic "heavy metals including arsenic, lead and cadmium, one with a level of arsenic > 10 times the acceptable limit" (1). Overall, 92 percent of the samples were found to be adulterated in some way. These are all potentially dangerous contaminants.

Kabat (2017) recounts a medical detective story that started when women in Belgium were found to be suffering from serious, potentially fatal kidney disease. After much detective work, it was discovered that the afflicted women had all been going to a workout and weight-loss clinic that had been giving them a traditional Chinese medicine. Unfortunately, this medicine contained a substance that was very toxic to the kidneys and causes cancer in genetically susceptible individuals. In another case, the popular Chinese herbal *ma huang* (aka ephedra) turned out also to be toxic (Marcus and Grollman 2003).

The profound lack of effectiveness of traditional Chinese medicine is not the only problem with the continued practice of this brand of quackery. Many ingredients other than plant products used in traditional Chinese medicines come from animals. This has fueled a large and extremely cruel trade in such things as bear bile, taken from living bears kept in cages with a tube in their gall bladders to extract the bile. The bones, skin, and other body parts of big cats are prized for their nonexistent medicinal properties. These magnificent animals are kept in captivity and killed to supply this market (World Animal Protection US 2019). Rhino horn has been promoted as a cure for cancer, hangovers, and various other maladies. This, and its value as a luxury item, has led to destructive rhino poaching (Ladendorf and Ladendorf 2018).

One herbal supplement that has been long hyped as a natural, effective, and safe treatment for many diseases and disorders is turmeric. The main ingredient said to be responsible for its beneficial effects is curcumin. The problem is that this substance isn't chemically stable and has low bioavailability. Low bioavailability means that it has little, if any, effect on the body—it is simply passed through. Nelson and colleagues (2017) reviewed the biochemistry of curcumin and showed that it can have little or no effect on biological systems. They further note that after over 120 clinical trials, "no double-blind placebo controlled clinical trial of curcumin has been successful" (1620). Turmeric continues to be popular because of testimonials and successful marketing.

A fad for taking supplemental vitamin D was jump-started in part by a claim that deficiency in vitamin D was a very common problem in otherwise well-nourished people and that up to half of the population of the United States needed vitamin D supplementation and that huge numbers of otherwise normal individuals should be tested for their vitamin D levels. That recommendation was put out by the Endocrine Society, a medical group "whose guidelines are widely used by hospitals, physicians and commercial labs nationwide" (Szabo 2018, 6). However, the ultimate source of the recommendations was a Dr. Michael Holick. Dr. Holick just happened to have been employed by Quest Diagnostics, a company that does vitamin D testing. Szabo summarizes the evidence that shows that there is "no evidence that vitamin D reduces the risk of cancer, heart disease or falls in the elderly." Manson and colleagues (2019b) in a study of nearly twenty-six thousand people found that vitamin D supplements did not lower rates of cancer or heart disease. Studying the same individuals, Manson and colleagues (2019a) found no beneficial effects of fish oil on cancer or heart disease. Bolland, Grey, and Avenell (2018) analyzed the results of studies of the effects of vitamin D in over fifty-three thousand individuals and found no beneficial effects on bone fractures, number of falls, or the density of bone. Barbarawi and colleagues (2019) published a review of studies examining whether vitamin D supplements had any effect in decreasing the risks of heart disease. In the reviewed studies over forty thousand patients were given vitamin D and over forty thousand others received a placebo. There was no difference between the two groups in the rate of cardiac disease.

The massive VITAL study enrolled over twenty-five thousand individuals over fifty years old in a double-blind, placebo-controlled study of vitamin D's protective effects. The results of this study showed that "vitamin D supplementation did not prevent cancer or cardiovascular disease, prevent falls, improve cognitive function, reduce atrial fibrillation, change body composition, reduce migraine frequency, improve stroke outcomes, decrease age-related macular degeneration, or reduce knee pain" (Cummings and Rosen 2022, 369). These results show that screening for vitamin D levels is unnecessary. On a more positive note, Ghahremani and colleagues (2023) reported that vitamin D supplementation decreased the likelihood of dementia. This is a surprising result and needs independent replication.

The best advice for people with normal diets and nutritional needs is summed up in an editorial in the *Annals of Internal Medicine* titled "Enough Is Enough: Stop Wasting Money on Vitamin and Mineral Supplements" (Guallar et al. 2013). The article summarized several papers showing that supplementation with vitamins and minerals had no beneficial effects on a range of variables from overall death rates to heart disease and cancer and cognitive performance in elderly men. However, "B-carotene, vitamin E, and possibly high doses of vitamin A supplements *increase* mortality" (850, emphasis added). These substances are well-known antioxidants, which are heavily promoted by the supplement industry as healthy and without risk. Loftfield and colleagues (2024) reported the results of studies of almost 350,000 people and found no benefits on mortality of taking multivitamins. Taking such vitamins produces only expensive urine and profits for the scammers selling them.

Yet another supplement promoted to treat numerous problems from Parkinson's disease to heart conditions is coenzyme Q10, usually marketed as CoQ10. It has been shown to be ineffective for Parkinson's disease (Negida et al. 2016), for patients suffering from problems with their statin drugs (Taylor et al. 2015), and for several other disorders, including heart disease and Huntington's disease (Klasco 2018). Recall that one sign of a quack treatment is the claim that it is effective for numerous different disorders, all caused by different basic pathologies. Coenzyme Q10 is a perfect example. Studies that failed to show positive effects of CoQ10 have been criticized by proponents because the studies "were not large enough, or were not long enough, or used various preparations and doses" (Klasco 2018, D4) of the enzyme that weren't just right. This is the standard fallback position of quacks—"Oh, you did the study on Tuesday!? Well, that explains it, the effect is weak on Tuesdays."

To the extent that some of the newer herbal remedies really do turn out to be effective, another problem arises. Any truly effective drug will have some side effects in some patients. Just because something is natural does not guarantee that it is safe. Digitalis, which occurs naturally in plants called foxgloves, can be fatal under certain conditions. Nonetheless, it is an extremely useful drug for treating several heart conditions. The presence of side effects is another reason that it is so important to carefully study the effects of any new substance touted as a remedy. The issue of side effects of the newer herbal remedies is not a simply theoretical one. Nortier and colleagues (2000) reported that an ingredient in a Chinese herbal plant can cause renal (kidney) failure and cancerous tumors in the urinary tract. Gingko biloba (as well as garlic and vitamin E) has been shown (Cupp 1999) to decrease the ability of the blood to clot. This can increase the risk of serious complications during surgery, especially if the surgeon is unaware that the patient has been taking gingko.

A frequent claim for herbal supplements is that they help "detox" or "cleanse" the body, or especially the liver. Claims for detox are one of the greatest frauds of alternative medicine. Detox products are often endorsed, and sold, by celebrities who know nothing about health or medicine. A healthy person's body already does a fine job of removing harmful substances—that's what the liver and kidneys are for. To be taken seriously, a claim that a product "detoxifies" anything would have to provide proof. Such proof would have to include specific statements about (1) what substances the product removes from the body, (2) evidence that the substances are found in harmful levels in healthy people, (3) details about the chemistry that accomplishes that removal, and (4) evidence that the product in question really removes the substances referred to. Marketers of herbal supplements never provide anything even close to this level of evidence for their products. This being the case, claims about detoxification are a major warning sign of health fraud.

Another common tactic used by promoters of alternative medicine is to make claims for the effectiveness of their product based on very preliminary published studies. Such studies are very often riddled with the most egregious methodological and statistical errors. Lie and colleagues (2019) studied the effects of probiotic *Lactobacillus plantarum* on behavior of children with autism. They examined children in six age groups from seven to fifteen years on twenty-six different measures and compared their scores on these tests from a baseline period with no treatment to their scores after treatment. This yielded a staggering 156 different statistical tests. The authors did not correct for this huge number of multiple comparisons and reported thirteen significant differences. Correcting for the multiple comparisons results in no significant differences. Nonetheless, promoters of probiotic treatment for autism cite this study as evidence.

Ads for supplements often use a particular "sleight of mind" trick to make it appear that their products are beneficial to normal healthy individuals. This consists of claiming that the product "supports" some process like anti-inflammation. Now, it's clear that abnormal levels of inflammation are not good for you. But the word *supports* is extremely vague. Because drinking water is necessary for good health, one could say, correctly, that water "supports anti-inflammation." The verb *supports* is not saying that the product enhances anti-inflammatory processes in the body. These products almost certainly have no such effect. But even if they did have anti-inflammatory effects, normal healthy individuals wouldn't need them because such individuals aren't suffering from any inflammatory disorders. Like so much of alternative medicine, the multibillion-dollar supplement and vitamin industry is marketing largely to the well-to-do worried well.

As will be discussed in detail in the next chapter, bogus treatments for Alzheimer's disease (AD) and improving "brain health" have become common (Hellmuth, Rabinovici, and Miller 2019). These are especially cruel as they prey on vulnerable and desperate patients and their families. One substance that has attracted attention as a supplement supposedly able to treat AD is a substance found in the eye, macular carotenoid. Nolan and colleagues (2015) concluded that supplementation with this substance improved visual function in AD patients. But their sample included only patients and they performed multiple statistical tests without proper correction. The same research group also claimed that macular carotenoid improved memory in nondemented individuals (Power et al. 2018). Of twenty tests of memory (their table 2), only one was significant. A further fourteen tests (their table 3) yielded only two that were significant when the number of comparisons was accounted for, which was not done in the published report. This is far too little evidence on which to base marketing claims that macular carotenoid may be useful in treating AD.

The advice given in Guallar and colleagues (2013) to just stop wasting money on vitamins and supplements is just as valid now as the day it was written. What has changed somewhat is the menu of substances marketed as supplements and claimed to be beneficial. There are literally hundreds of such substances, and it would take a separate book to evaluate them. Happily, such a book exists. Ernst (2019) provides a review of 150 different alternative medicine claims, including supplements, physical therapies, and diagnostic techniques. The section on each therapy or practice has references to the relevant scientific studies evaluating the claims. Ernst does not always find that the claims are wrong. For example, he concludes from the research on garlic that, as noted earlier, it can be effective in some conditions, but not in others, such as preventing cancer.

The COVID-19 pandemic brought out claims for the usual quack treatments, from homeopathy, herbals, crystals, and of course vitamins. Vitamin D was the one most commonly touted as a wonder drug for COVID. While it may have some beneficial effects in individuals who are vitamin D deficient, it has little effect otherwise. Muri and colleagues (2021) gave 118 hospitalized COVID-19 patients a placebo and 117 patients 200,000 units of vitamin D. The form they used, 25 hydroxyvitamin D, has a half-life of fifteen days in blood. They found no differences between the placebo and vitamin D treatment groups on any outcome measure.

Other nostrums including various herbals, and even crystals, were said to "boost" or otherwise enhance the immune system. All such claims are health fraud. Over-the-counter products do not improve immune system function. The immune system is an extremely complex set of subsystems operating in delicate balance. Any overall "boost" would destroy this balance and lead to unfortunate health effects. Drinking a glass of water or getting a good night's sleep would benefit the immune system more than wasting money on any product claiming to increase immune system function.

Many of the worried well have pets. The alternative medicine industry has not overlooked this lucrative market. Many of the same useless treatments aimed at the human market can be found marketed at our pets. There are even alternative medicine veterinarians. McKenzie (2019), a veterinarian himself, has published a book-length review of alternative veterinary medicine practices. They don't work for animals either.

Even veterinary supplements are often contaminated or mislabeled as to the quantity of the ingredients. With the legalization of sales of products with hemp as a component, such products have appeared in large numbers for both the human and animal markets. Hemp-based products may have some legitimate uses in the hands of veterinary professionals (Ukai, McGrath, and Wakshlag 2023). However, the hemp products sold over the counter as veterinary supplements are as likely to be misrepresented on their labels as the supplements sold for human use. Wakshlag and colleagues (2020) analyzed twenty-nine different veterinary hemp products and found that almost 14 percent were contaminated with heavy metals. Further, the concentration of hemp in the products was incorrectly specified on the labels in 41 percent of the products. These results are just another example of the widespread consumer fraud in supplement products and emphasize the need for tighter regulation of such products. The repeal of the 1994 Dietary Supplement Health and Education Act that protects manufacturers and retailers of supplements from legal action for fraud and misrepresentation would be an excellent start. The supplement industry has turned a huge segment of the nation into a bunch of worried-well pill-popping quasi-hypochondriacs who can't get through the day without taking their useless supplements and vitamins. If such products were removed from drug store shelves, the stores could probably reduce their floor space by about a third.

OTHER ALTERNATIVE TREATMENTS

The number of different types and varieties of treatments within the broad category of alternative medicine is far too great to allow all to be discussed here. This section will cover several from this group that are either especially interesting or especially popular.

Urine Therapy

Yes, you read that right—urine therapy. This is the practice of drinking your own urine, which, it is claimed, can treat and cure numerous illnesses. By the turn of the twenty-first century, urine therapy had become, if not a major one, certainly not a trivial star in the alternative medicine sky. A Google search results in around 102 million hits. The first World Conference on Urine Therapy was held in India in 1996. The eighth was held in London in 2018. Several books on urine therapy have been published, including Christy's (1994) *Your Own Perfect Medicine*. Gardner (1999) described the interesting history of urine therapy. Some urine therapists have combined urine therapy and homeopathy by recommending that one dilute the urine in water to such an extent that essentially no urine is left. (No doubt this helps to dilute the "yuck" factor as well!) Since urine consists of the body's liquid waste products suspended in water, drinking it simply amounts to running the waste back through the system.

Magnetic Therapy

The idea that magnets in one form or another can influence human behavior or have beneficial medical effects dates back to the sixteenth century (Ramey 1998). The current claim is that real magnetic fields can take away pain, make wounds heal faster, and improve sleep, among other things. Pillows, bed pads, insole pads, and wraps for various body parts that have magnets sewn into them can all be purchased. The promotional literature for these products is filled largely with testimonials, and we have already seen how unreliable testimonials are.

Magnetic treatments are quite recent as compared to, say, homeopathic treatments, so there are fewer studies of the effectiveness of magnetic therapy. The first review of studies of the outcome of magnetic therapy was published by Ramey in 1998. Ramey divided magnetic treatments into two types: those using *pulsating magnetic fields* and those using *static magnetic fields*. The magnetic fields produced by magnets in beds, shoes, wraps, and the like are static fields because the position of the magnets is constant with regard to the person using them. Somewhat surprisingly, Ramey found more studies on the effects of magnetic therapy in veterinary practice (exclusively with horses) than in human medicine. It is not clear why this is the case, but perhaps animals simply make more placid subjects. In any event, Ramey summarizes these studies thusly: "there appear to be no scientific studies available that demonstrate that any form of magnetic field therapy is valuable in the treatment of disease conditions of the horse" (1998, 17). These conditions, as would be expected given the species of the patient population, concerned bone and related tissues.

In humans, the few early studies of the effects of static magnetic fields that have been published have examined pain relief. Ramey (1998) found two studies from Japan that reported positive effects of static magnets on pain, but both were "poorly controlled." Of three studies that were better controlled, one showed some beneficial effects and two showed no effect. Since Ramey's review, two more reviews have been published. Neither Pittler, Brown, and Ernst (2007) nor Macfarlane and colleagues (2012) found evidence for the effectiveness of magnet therapy.

Acupuncture

Imagine some treatment that is totally ineffective that is said to help numerous different disorders and conditions. Tens of thousands of studies are done on this treatment. Because of placebo effects, regression to the mean, multiple comparisons, and spontaneous remission, some percent of these studies will seem to show that the treatment works. Even among studies with no methodological or statistical flaws, some will, simply by chance, show a statistically significant improvement following the treatment. This is essentially the case with acupuncture, a massive case of *p*-hacking. Of all the varieties of alternative medicine, acupuncture is probably the most popular treatment used and certainly the most studied. High methodological and statistical quality are not always found in acupuncture studies, as noted below in the discussion of the study design that almost guarantees a false positive result.

In the popular literature acupuncture is promoted as a part of traditional Chinese medicine that has been practiced since ancient times with great success. Although the practice dates back centuries, it was rejected in the very early nineteenth century when Emperor Dao Guang banned it from the Imperial Medical Academy (Colquhoun and Novella 2013). Chairman Mao revived the practice in the 1960s. It came to popularity in the United States in the 1970s following President Richard Nixon's trip to the People's Republic of China that opened relations between the United States and China. Much was made of a report that a single individual had gone through open heart surgery with only acupuncture as an analgesic. Media reports at the time were uncritical about this claim. But later investigation revealed that "the patient had been given a combination of 3 very powerful sedatives . . . and large volumes of local anesthetic injected into the chest. The acupuncture needles were purely cosmetic" (Colquhoun and Novella 2013, 1360).

Acupuncture comes in different varieties. One can use needles on different parts of the body, corresponding to special acupuncture points or specific "meridians." Some believe in auricular acupuncture, where needles are inserted into specific places in the ear to treat such things as drug addiction. It has never been made clear why sticking needles into the rather inert structures of the outer ear should have any effect on something as serious as drug addiction in the first place. Articular acupuncture is much like reflexology in that it assumes that by fiddling with one part of the body one can influence a totally different part—two parts that have no functional relationship at all. Then there is electroacupuncture, in which electric current is sent through the acupuncture needles. This is not really acupuncture at all since the electricity can easily produce real effects. To pass off studies showing effects of such electrical stimulation as supportive of acupuncture is deceptive.

Colquhoun and Novella (2013) reviewed studies on the effectiveness of acupuncture in relieving real pain in suffering patients. They conclude that "acupuncture and sham acupuncture treatments are no different in decreasing pain levels across multiple chronic pain disorders: migraine, tension headache, low back pain, and osteoarthritis of the knee" (1361). Sham acupuncture involves inserting the needles at points on the body where they are not supposed to work, according to traditional teaching, or using sham needles that don't penetrate the skin at all.

Such a placebo needle was developed by Streitberger and Kleinhenz (1998). This placebo needle does not penetrate the skin, but 78 percent of the individuals in their study perceived penetration, as opposed to 90 percent in the real needle condition. These results show that this device would be an effective placebo control in acupuncture studies. However, such a placebo has almost never been used in the thousands of studies claiming to show positive effects of acupuncture. By failing to use proper placebos, acupuncture studies are not looking closely to see if there is a real effect, showing the pseudoscientific nature of acupuncture.

As is the case in so many pseudoscientific claims, the better a study is in terms of methodology, experimental controls, and statistical analyses, the less evidence is found for the claim. This is the case with acupuncture. Colquhoun and Novella (2013, 1362) conclude that "the best controlled studies show a clear pattern, with acupuncture the outcome does not depend on needle location or even needle insertion. Since these variables are those that define acupuncture, the only sensible conclusion is that acupuncture does not work." In other words, it's a placebo effect; Colquhoun and Novella termed it "theatrical acupuncture" to emphasize the ritualistic nature of the procedure.

Lee (2008) described a common type of study design used in acupuncture research, as well as in other areas, that "generates only 'positive' results" (214). Two groups of patients are used. Group A (the experimental group) receives a verified treatment as well as the treatment being tested. Group B (the control group) receives only the verified treatment. Even if the new treatment being tested is nothing but a pure placebo, the placebo effect will lead to a better outcome for the experimental group compared to the control group. Lee examined studies of acupuncture and found that such experimental designs were very common and that the results were always interpreted, incorrectly, as showing that acupuncture was an effective treatment.

As might be expected given its origins, a large number of studies of the effectiveness of acupuncture come out of China. Of these Chinese studies, almost 100 percent report positive results (Ernst 2019). This is highly suspicious for several reasons. First, even if the non-Chinese studies favorable to acupuncture are taken at face value, the percentage of positive studies is far, far less than 100 percent. Second, in 2015 investigations by the Chinese government revealed a staggering amount of fraud in clinical drug trials. Over 75 percent of such trials were found to have been fraudulent, with faked data and other manipulations (Woodhead 2016). Given this, it is highly likely that a similarly huge percentage of the supposedly positive Chinese acupuncture studies are false.

In 2022 Allen and colleagues reviewed not the primary literature on acupuncture for the years 2013 to 2021 but the literature reviews of primary reports on acupuncture for those years. The literature on acupuncture has become so massive that it seems that as many literature reviews are being published as reports of new research. Allen and colleagues (2022, 10) concluded that these reviews "generally conclude that the certainty of evidence [for acupuncture effectiveness] is low or very low." The authors reached a similar conclusion from their review of reviews, specifically that "the number of clinical conditions for which there is high- or moderate-certainty of evidence is small compared with the number of conditions with low- or very low-certainty evidence" (10).

Even such equivocal conclusions probably way overstate the effectiveness of acupuncture because the reviews include the numerous fraudulent studies that were referred to above. If these were removed from the literature that was reviewed, the conclusions would be even more negative than they are. Another problem that crops up here is the so-called file drawer problem. This occurs when studies that don't result in positive results are relegated to the "file drawer" and never see the light of publication and so are not counted in published reviews. So the acupuncture juggernaut rumbles on, fueled by placebo effects, poorly designed studies, and outright fraudulent reports.

Although it was not their intention, Yoon and colleagues (2023) did a clever study that reinforces the argument that acupuncture is a placebo. The subjects in their study were pain free, so pain reduction was not the dependent measure. Rather, the researchers had subjects self-rate the strength of the acupuncture feeling called *deqi* following two very different types of acupuncture. In the normal acupuncture condition, a needle was inserted into the skin. In the visual condition, subjects watched "a prerecorded video of acupuncture stimulation (VA) of another person" (11270) receiving actual acupuncture in the same part of the body. Both the normal and the visual (I'd call it virtual) acupuncture condition resulted in feelings of the *deqi* sensation, which was greater in the actual acupuncture condition. But, most importantly, it was still there in the visual condition. In both conditions the magnitude of the sensation increased with the "dose" of acupuncture. Dose was varied by changing the vigor of either the actual or the viewed acupuncture needling. This study shows that, for at least one acupuncture effect, not even sham acupuncture is needed to generate the phenomenon. It would be interesting to use the visual acupuncture method to see if just watching someone get acupuncture would reduce pain reports. I suspect that it would further show the placebo origins of acupuncture effects.

Acupuncture reminds me very much of Elisha Perkins and the miracle cures his metallic tractors caused. The only thing the tractors caused was a placebo effect. Once that was clear, the popularity of the tractors faded and died out. Sadly, the multiple demonstrations that acupuncture effects are placebos have not had the same effect on the popularity of acupuncture.

The above discussion obviously does not cover the thousands of papers on acupuncture in the literature. But the message is still clear. When well-controlled studies are done, there is no evidence that acupuncture is anything more than a placebo effect—Perkins tractors of the twentieth and twenty-first centuries.

The field of quack and alternative and complementary medicine is far too vast to be covered in a single chapter. Several excellent book-length treatments are Offit's (2013) *Do You Believe in Magic?*, Ernst and Smith's (2018) *More Harm Than Good*, and Ernst's (2018) *SCAM: So-Called Alternative Medicine*. Ernst's (2019) *Alternative Medicine: A Critical Assessment of 150 Modalities* provides short descriptions of 150 different alternative approaches along with short but well-referenced evaluations of the literature relative to the effectiveness of each. Those with an interest in a historical approach will find Boyle's (2013) *Quack Medicine: A History of Combating Health Fraud in Twentieth-Century America* very informative.

CHIROPRACTIC

According to the principles of chiropractic, a major cause of human disease and even mental disorders is something called a subluxation of the spine. This supposedly occurs when the spinal nerves that travel through openings between the bony vertebrae of the spinal column are compressed. Chiropractors believe that the way to treat the diseases caused by subluxation is to manipulate the spinal column so that the subluxation is removed. The whole idea of subluxations causing disease was simply made up in the nineteenth century by D. D. Palmer, a believer in spiritualism who claimed that he got the basic tenants of chiropractic from the spirit of a dead doctor.

How do subluxations cause disease? The theory holds that when a spinal nerve going to, say, the liver is subluxed, this will cause liver disease. To treat liver disease, the chiropractor would manipulate the spine to remove the problem with that specific nerve. Chiropractic was developed at a time when there was very little knowledge of what caused diseases. When Palmer invented chiropractic, the fact that germs caused many diseases was still a new theory. And nothing was known about the genetic or environmental causes of cancer. So chiropractic claims that spinal manipulations can cure organic disease is a holdover from the days of prescientific medicine.

A study by Crelin (1985) showed that subluxation, the fundamental concept in chiropractic, does not exist. Crelin subjected dissected human spinal columns to mechanical stress. He found that no amount of stress, no matter how it was applied to the spinal column, resulted in pinching of the spinal nerves. The spinal column broke first. The chiropractors' only response to this study was to charge that it wasn't valid because it was done on dead tissue. In fact, the physical characteristics of a freshly dissected spinal column are the same as those of a column still fully attached to its owner.

It is important to note that subluxation is different from a real disorder such as a slipped disk, where a vertebral disk is rubbing on a spinal nerve. This can result in extremely painful symptoms. Chiropractic manipulation, which includes a good bit of massage, can be helpful for the sorts of aches and pains, like lower back pain, that any massage or physical therapy would be helpful for. Cherkin and colleagues (1998) found that chiropractic manipulation was as effective as physical therapy for lower back pain, a very common complaint.

An important study by Balon and colleagues (1998) examined the effects of actual chiropractic manipulation and sham (placebo) manipulation on asthma in children, a condition that chiropractors claim to be able to treat. Both the real manipulation and sham manipulation groups showed equal amounts of subjective improvement during treatment. But neither group showed any objective changes one way or the other in their symptoms. Similarly, Chaibi and colleagues (2016) found that relief from migraine headaches following chiropractic manipulation was due to placebo effects.

A bizarre and dangerous offshoot of chiropractic is called craniosacral therapy. This is based on the belief that disorders in the rhythmic flow of the cerebrospinal fluid (CSF) around the brain and spinal cord cause various maladies. The therapist can, it is claimed, detect problems with this rhythm by touch. By manipulating the bones of the skull, a proper rhythm can be restored, treating whatever malady the patient has. This is all pure nonsense. It's impossible to detect any rhythmic flow of the CSF from outside the head. In adults the bones of the skull are fused and don't move when fiddled with. This is not the case with young children. It is a very bad idea to push and pull on the unfused bones of a child's skull. Not surprisingly, reviews of studies of this particular brand of quackery shows that it doesn't work (Green et al. 1999; Ernst 2012). Therapists claim it works and can produce the usual testimonials from their patients. These are due to nothing more than placebo and other effects that cause therapists and patients to believe that worthless treatments work.

BIG PHARMA

The fact that the alternative medicine industry is filled with quacks, frauds, and charlatans does not mean that the legitimate pharmaceutical industry is without its own faults. Indeed, "Big Pharma," while it unquestionably produces numerous medicines that are truly effective, is well known for highly unethical practices in the evaluation of new compounds. Ben Goldacre's (2013) book *Bad Pharma: How Drug Companies Mislead Doctors and Harm Patients* describes many of the unethical practices of the modern pharmaceutical industry. Goldacre (2010) also wrote an excellent book, *Bad Science*, highly critical of alternative medicine. An example of the results of unethical practices of Big Pharma is the epidemic of opioid addiction and resultant deaths in the United States that can be traced, at least in large part, to the deceptive marketing tactics of the pharmaceutical companies that sold opioid pain killers, especially the Purdue companies run by the Sackler family (Posner 2020).

As I've said before, the double-blind, placebo-controlled study is the only way to really determine whether a treatment is effective. And Big Pharma does these. Lots of them. But, until recently, the companies were not required to report a study if they chose not to. So the companies engaged in a conscious use of the multiple comparison fallacy. They would perform multiple trials of a new drug and report only those trials in which the drug outperformed a placebo. Another trick was outsourcing the studies to third world countries where standards are not as high as they are in the Western nations. This allowed very sloppy studies to be done. Often the companies that performed the studies for Western pharmaceutical firms lacked the skill and understanding to do the studies properly. It was also the case that the companies were sometimes paid depending on whether or not the study's outcome showed that the new drug was effective.

The problems that are endemic in the studies supposedly supporting alternative medicine practices can also be found in studies of real medicine. Ioannidis (2005) published a provocative paper arguing that a high percentage of the papers published in the medical literature reach incorrect conclusions. Ioannidis was especially critical of the ease with which even prestigious medical journals publish sloppy research. One problem with such research is small sample size. A small sample may yield what appears to be a significant effect, but when the effect is studied with a larger sample, it turns out to have been a false alarm. But small samples are cheap and easy to study, so such false-positive studies are more likely to end up being published. Another problem is the use of multiple end points, where the study assesses several different variables. Even if only one or two of the several variables studied shows the desired effect, the study's authors will conclude that the treatment studied worked or that some alleged environmental pollutant did have a harmful effect when it did not.

Jureidini and McHenry (2020) discovered a different version of the multiple end point trick in studies of the effectiveness of drugs. If the initial end points show no effects, the data will be manipulated until a few, of many, comparisons show beneficial effects. It will then be concluded that the drug works. This is the multiple comparison fallacy again, and its use is not limited to pseudoscience. Examples of this will be seen in the next chapter. Finally, there are financial incentives to find effects. When it comes to studies of therapy, pharmacological, psychological, or otherwise, all these factors are likely to play a role. One would like to think that only studies that are methodologically and statistically sound would be published, but that is not the case. It is important to be aware of the characteristics of both good and bad studies when reading research reports to be able to evaluate them. Both quacks promoting bogus remedies and pharmaceutical companies promoting new drugs should be held to the same exacting and strict standards of proof and evidence.

The pharmaceutical industry also corrupts scientific publication at academic institutions (Jureidini and McHenry 2020). An example is the use of ghost writers. These are professional writers paid by the pharmaceutical company to write papers reporting the results of clinical trials of new drugs. These papers, which often end up being published in supposedly reputable scientific journals, are specifically designed to distort the results of drug trials to make it appear that the drugs are safe and effective when they may not be either. The ghost writers' names do not appear on the published paper. The official academic "authors" of the papers may never have written a word of the text or have had much, if any, involvement in the analysis of the data reported in the paper.

As Jureidini and McHenry (2020) show, research funding from the industry often comes with onerous strings attached that would be unacceptable in any ethical research program. For example, academic researchers who get such research funds to study drug effects may not be given access to the actual data on the drug the company is investigating. Rather, they receive summaries provided by the company, summaries that may hide results the companies do not want publicized. Further, researchers may be pressured or required to sign confidentiality agreements that forbid them from revealing results that show the drugs under investigation are neither effective nor safe. Such agreements are "gag order[s] against physicians' moral duties to warn patients" of ineffective or dangerous drugs (Jureidini and McHenry 2020, 150).

Stakeholders such as drug companies financing research has long been a problem. There are numerous ways the funder can influence the outcome of the research. But there are also ways this perennial problem could be dealt with. Robertson and Rodwin (2016) proposed what they term "money blinding" as a way to separate the funder from the funded and thus give more credence to whatever results emerge from the research. The basic idea is simple. Any company or organization wishing to fund a study of a particular topic would deposit funds for that research with an agency whose function would be to distribute the funds. Any person or organization receiving the funds would be totally unaware of the source of the funding, and the funder would be totally unaware of who received the funds. One doubts, however, whether drug companies would agree to such a procedure, knowing that they would not be able to control the outcome.

MASS HYSTERIA, SICK BUILDINGS, AND ENVIRONMENTAL HEALTH SCARES

The term *collective delusion*, also known as *mass hysteria*, describes a situation in which a significant part of the population of an area, which can be as small as a single building or as large as a nation, becomes convinced that some strange illness or danger is taking place for which there is no immediately obvious explanation. The event—sometimes an outbreak of illness occurring in rapid succession among people living or working in the same environment—can be attributed to a wide range of causes. Sometimes paranormal or pseudoscientific causes are proposed and accepted. In many cases of collective delusion, the media play an important role in spreading the delusion. (See Bartholomew 2001 for an excellent book-length treatment of this topic.) In addition, there is usually a fairly specific "trigger" for these events. It may be something like a single child getting sick. Or an adult complaining about a set of symptoms.

A prototypical case of collective delusion, described by Medalia and Larsen (1958), took place in Seattle, Washington, in March and April 1954. At first a few people noticed mysterious tiny pits in their car windshields. This was the trigger. Then more and more people reported finding such pits. Anything that could pit glass, it was reasoned with some justification, could certainly do damage to frail human flesh. Concern grew, as did the number of reports. Explanations for the pits were varied and creative. One held that acid pollution was responsible. Another was that fallout from atomic bomb tests in the Pacific, blown east and falling on Seattle, was causing the damage. On April 15 the mayor of Seattle asked for the assistance of the governor of Washington and the president of the United States. Clearly, Seattle was facing a dangerous situation. Or was it? The pits turned out to have a prosaic explanation: they had been caused by pebbles thrown up by the rear tires of cars on the unpaved roads that then struck the windshield of any car behind. The pits had simply not been noticed before. Yet when one person noticed them and pointed them out to someone else—who also had not noticed them, but now found them on their car and assumed, incorrectly, that they had never been there before—the stage was set for the collective delusion to appear. Medalia and Larsen (1958, 180) note that people in this particular episode came up with "evidence" to support what turned out to be clearly incorrect explanations. In the case of the atomic fallout theory, "many drivers claimed that they found tiny, metallic-looking particles about the size of a pinhead on their windows." These were nothing more than common dirt and dust.

The "Mad Gasser of Mattoon" is another classic case of mass hysteria. In September 1944 residents of Mattoon, Illinois, a town of fifteen thousand people, were terrorized by person or persons unknown sneaking around at night "gassing" residents in their homes. At least twenty-four people reported various vague symptoms, and a public health official fanned the flames of panic by stating that a "gas maniac" was on the loose and had caused several of the incidents. Reports of night prowlers skyrocketed. Local newspapers carried numerous stories on the attacks. But there probably never was any "gas maniac" in the first place. Bartholomew and Victor (2004) have analyzed this incident in some depth. They conclude it was a case of rumors getting started and then exaggerated both by the press and word of mouth. Taking a social-psychological (Colligan, Pennebaker, and Murphy 1982), rather than a psychiatric, approach Bartholomew and Victor (2004) suggest that those who reported being gassed were in no way mentally ill but rather had normal stress responses to a believed threat, even though the threat wasn't real. This is a valuable contribution to the understanding of the very real symptoms people experience in cases of mass hysteria.

A far more recent example of mass hysteria began as a small occurrence at the American Embassy in Havana, Cuba, in late 2016. What became known as the Havana syndrome then spread to become an international incident involving personnel from several nations and locations around the world. The first reports from embassy personnel in Havana were of extremely annoying high-pitched sounds. These were heard both in the embassy and at home. These would be credited with causing a wide range of psychological and behavioral disorders and even objective neurological damage, this latter being similar to the damage caused by a concussion. But the actual symptoms that embassy personnel reported were vague and wide ranging—headaches, memory problems, fatigue, anxiety, sleep disturbances, aches, and pains. These are all the "slings and arrows of outrageous fortune" that every one of us feels from time to time.

Later similar reports came in from U.S. embassies across the world as well as other embassies in Cuba, notably the Canadian Embassy. The Havana syndrome has been the subject of so much investigation and research that an entire book could be written about it. And indeed an excellent book has been, Baloh and Bartholomew's (2022) *Havana Syndrome*.

The State Department believed that the noises were due to some sort of previously unknown sonic or microwave weapon that could project sounds or microwaves through solid walls. The noises were seen as an attack on American Embassy personnel by the Cuban government, which remained hostile to the United States. Concerned, the United States government commissioned a scientific study of the noises by JASON, a think tank that consisted of highly trained scientists and experts that regularly advises the government on important technological and scientific issues. The JASON report was initially classified by the State Department and required a freedom-of-information request by BuzzFeed, an Internet news and media company, to obtain. One major conclusion of the JASON investigation ruled out any sort of sonic or microwave weapon as scientifically impossible (see also Roth 2022, chap. 8). In spite of this, the State Department continued to believe that a mysterious attack had occurred.

The JASON investigation compared recordings of the sounds that embassy personnel heard and recorded with the actual sounds made by a local species of cricket, the Indian short-tailed cricket (*Anurogryllis celerinictus*). The result of the comparison was that the sound of the cricket "matched in nuanced detail, the spectral properties of the recordings from Cuba" made at the embassy (JASON 2018, 8). In another analysis Stubbs and Montealegre (2019) came to the same conclusion. The sound, which can be easily found by searching online, is very high pitched and highly annoying when listened to even for only a few seconds. Prolonged exposure would certainly be distressing, especially if the source was unknown and therefore mysterious.

In the past the Cuban government had harassed embassy personnel in various physical and psychological ways and kept them under observation. Add to this the anxiety caused by claims from respected government officials that the sound was probably some sort of malicious attack, and it is easy to understand why some employees began to show psychological symptoms. The "US Embassy staff in Cuba were a close-knit group sharing a common work environment in an atmosphere of high stress in a foreign country where they knew they were being constantly watched" (Baloh and Bartholomew 2022, 38). This is exactly the type of environment conducive to mass psychogenic illness.

The claims that the noises caused cognitive impairments similar to those seen in concussions and even observable brain damage were especially anxiety provoking. The claims regarding cognitive impairment stemmed from a paper by Swanson and colleagues (2018) that was rapidly shown to be so deeply flawed that its conclusions could not be accepted (Cortex Editorial Board 2018). Two papers (Swanson et al. 2018; Verma et al. 2019) reported finding evidence of structural changes using MRI in the brains of embassy personnel exposed to the mysterious noises. However, both these studies found only vague and nonspecific changes that were probably incidental findings that can pop up in any examination of people in the age range of the individuals studied. Several other published studies claim to have found evidence of injury presumably cause by some sort of attack, but all suffer from extremely serious methodological flaws and gross overinterpretation of the results (references and more discussion in Baloh and Bartholomew 2022). On March 1, 2023, the National Intelligence Council released a brief report titled *Updated Assessment of Anomalous Health Incidents* (ICA 2023-02286-B) regarding the "incidents" in Havana and elsewhere. The council concluded that "there is no credible evidence that a foreign adversary has a weapon or collection device that is causing the AHIs" (2).

Using a more powerful MRI scanner than Verma and colleagues (2019), Pierpaoli and colleagues (2024) found no evidence of any brain injuries in a group of eighty-one government employees and family members claiming a history of AHI. Chan and colleagues (2024) examined eighty-six employees with a history of claimed AHIs using "extensive clinical, auditory, vestibular, balance, visual, neuropsychological, and blood biomarkers" (1109) as measures. No significant differences were found between the AHI group and a matched group with no AHI claims on any of these measures except for one measure of balance. Subjectively, the AHI group reported more psychological symptoms such as depression and anxiety, as would be expected. It's unfortunate that no tests of fantasy proneness or related variables were given. The results of such tests might have helped to understand these symptoms in spite of the lack of any real injuries.

An even more recent case of mass hysteria was the wave of sightings of unknown objects in the night sky, often labeled "drones," at the end of 2024. Some were drones, some normal aircraft, with full wing lights visible, and some were stars. This is another excellent example, made previously in the chapters on UFOs, of how liable perception is to misinterpretation when the sensory input is minimal.

Other examples of mass hysteria can occur on a smaller scale, limited to a single building, and involve the sudden outbreak of a mysterious illness, the symptoms of which are nonspecific, such as vomiting, headache, shortness of breath, or fainting. Small and Borus (1983) reported a detailed study of one such case, in which the victims of a mysterious illness were schoolchildren in a small Massachusetts town. At a rehearsal for a concert, children grew ill. Later, during the actual concert, more children became ill. The illness was at first attributed to environmental pollution, but no environmental cause was found. The very observable symptoms convinced people that some sort of toxic chemical was to blame. But it is generally not appreciated the extent to which anxiety can build up in such a situation and cause the observed symptoms. Jones and colleagues (2000) reported a similar case that sent one hundred people to a hospital emergency room. No physical cause for their symptoms, which included "headache, nausea, shortness of breath, and dizziness" (98), was found. Such events have been occurring for hundreds of years in schools (Bartholomew and Rickard 2014) and are often linked to stress and anxieties existing in the environment at the time. When some usually innocuous stimulus occurs, such as a strange smell, it is interpreted by some as a threat and then through psychological contagion causes others to panic and display the usual symptoms of such events.

Situations in which people working in a building report, over a period of time, various vague symptoms such as headaches, upset stomachs, slight feelings of fever, stuffy noses, and the like have become so common that the term *sick building syndrome* (SBS) has been coined to refer to such incidents. The term is unfortunate in that it implies that there really is something wrong with the buildings involved, when what is usually going on is a sort of temporary mass hypochondria (TMH). What probably triggers the event is one or two individuals becoming consciously aware of minor discomforts that we all have almost all the time but are usually unconcerned about. For example, as I sit here typing at my computer, I notice that I have a minor tummy ache, and also a very slight sore throat. At any given time, if you search through your body, as it were, you can find minor aches, pains, tickles, and the like that, quite properly, are usually simply ignored and dismissed as unimportant, if they are noticed at all. Some people will focus on these little aches and pains and start to worry about them: "My God, maybe that sore throat is a sign of cancer!" These thoughts create considerable anxiety, which in and of itself creates other symptoms such as a racing heart, upset stomach, sweating, and perhaps a feeling of a slight fever. Off to the doctor runs our anxious individual, convinced now that they actually feel the cancerous tumor growing in their throat. The physician does the appropriate tests and finds nothing. Is the hypochondriac relieved? Not in the slightest! The "symptoms" are still present, so the tests must have missed the cancer. The anxiety continues, as does the belief that the person really does have cancer or some other awful disease. Further testing that reveals nothing does not relieve the anxiety or change the belief that something terrible is wrong. The hypochondriac can always argue that the tumor (or whatever) is too small to show up on any test, or that it is some new, dreadful type of disorder that modern medicine cannot identify. Note that such an argument is nonfalsifiable. In a review of the cognition of what they term "illness-anxious individuals," Leonidou and Panayiotou (2018, 109) conclude that such individuals "interpret harmless health-related information and bodily sensations as dangerous and catastrophic and encode these biased interpretations in memory accompanied by negative emotional evaluations," thus leading to anxiety and its physiological effects.

An interesting study by Corn (1991, cited in Barrett and Gots 1998) supports the above analysis of the cause of TMH. Two groups of workers in two different buildings were compared using a questionnaire regarding physical symptoms they experienced while at work. Workers in one building had complained about health problems, while those in the other building had not. Yet workers in both groups reported the same symptoms on the questionnaire. As would be expected if workers in the building who had complained about health problems were simply more aware of their minor symptoms, more of them complained than did those in the other building. Similarly, Nelson and colleagues (1995) found that nearly half of the workers in buildings in no way thought to suffer from sick building syndrome reported some sort of minor symptom or symptoms when asked. Barrett and Gots (1998) conclude that "the symptoms associated with SBS are common complaints found in the population-at-large" (77).

Some research has been done to show that individuals who are more susceptible to TMH differ from those who are less susceptible. Small and Nicholi (1982) found that elementary schoolchildren who were admitted to a hospital following an episode of TMH were more likely than nonhospitalized children to have divorced parents or to have had a family member die. Small and colleagues (1991) examined sixth to twelfth graders and found that a history of "previous grief" predicted, to some extent, the severity of symptoms evidenced during an outbreak of TMH. However, the variable that best predicted whether a child would have symptoms was observing a friend with symptoms.

Marmot and colleagues (2006) studied over four thousand workers spread over forty-four buildings. They found that the largest determinant of sick building effects was psychological. Specifically, the "physical environment of office buildings appears to be less important than features of the psychosocial work environment in explaining differences in the prevalence of symptoms" (283) in different buildings.

None of the above is to say that buildings never cause real sickness. The classic case is that of the hotel in Philadelphia in which Legionnaires' disease first broke out in 1976. Many people attending a convention of the American Legion there fell ill and more than twenty-five died. But these individuals obviously had more serious symptoms than the usual runny nose and irritated eyes found in sick building syndrome.

In the cases described above, the hysteria was usually limited to a rather circumscribed geographical area or a rather small group of people. But in a somewhat different type of mass hysteria, millions of people across the country become convinced that some agent, usually found in the environment, is causing or has the potential to cause, various sorts of dire health problems. These beliefs are unfounded, but considerable effort is often wasted in doing further research on the topic. Several factors work to inflame and maintain the public's fear in these cases. The media, realizing that a good scare story is an excellent way to increase sales and boost ratings, highlights the most extreme and anxiety-provoking claims. There can be little doubt that had the Seattle window-pitting episode taken place today traditional and social media coverage would have ensured that the panic spread nationwide. Special interest groups, such as lawyers seeing profits from liability suits, work to highlight and keep alive public anxiety. The end result is a great deal of wasted time and money and a needlessly anxious public. In the following sections, several classic examples of this type of mass hysteria will be discussed. Included are claims that asbestos causes lung cancer in the general population, that microwave radiation and power lines cause cancer, that silicone breast implants cause immunological disease, that polychlorinated biphenyls (PCBs) in the environment are an important risk factor for cognitive impairment and birth defects, and that cell phones cause brain cancer.

As an example of how unwarranted health scares can arise, consider the claim that stamp collecting causes cancer (as a long-time collector, I hope that's not true!). Suppose a single individual who collected stamps and had cancer got a lot of publicity claiming that there was a causal link between the two. That might stimulate much research on the topic. Imagine that 120 studies of the possibility that there was a link were done. Even if there was no causal relationship between philately and cancer, out of those 120 studies it would be expected that, totally by chance alone, six of them would show a significant relationship. That is because the standard (if arbitrary) way of defining statistical significance is to say that a result is significant if it would occur *by chance alone* 5 percent of the time or less. So 5 percent of 120 studies is six. In other words, just by chance alone, and with no effect of collecting on cancer rates, six of the 120 studies would suggest just such a relationship. However, of those six, on average three would find that stamp collectors got cancer *less frequently* than noncollectors and three would find the opposite—that collectors were more likely to get cancer. It would be these latter three that would be much more likely to get published and to generate much more media attention. This is obviously an example of the multiple comparison fallacy. One single finding, or even a group of findings, is never enough to allow the conclusion that X is harmful. Or that X cures cancer (see chapter 11). The specific results must be looked at in comparison with other findings. One should worry if all, or the great majority, of studies show that X is linked to some disease. This is what one finds in the studies of cigarette smoking—all the studies show that smokers are about ten times more likely to get lung cancer than nonsmokers. But if the results of epidemiological studies are vague, with some showing a greater risk of X and some showing no risk, or even that X improves some dependent measure, one can be confident that X is harmless.

ASBESTOS

Probably the first example of a nationwide panic or national mass hysteria concerned the alleged ability of very low levels of exposure to asbestos to cause lung cancer. Asbestos is not man-made but a group of slightly different naturally occurring minerals that have the highly desirable properties of being heat resistant, unable to burn, and strong. In the past asbestos was widely used in construction as insulation, among other uses. In the 1970s it became clear that workers (i.e., asbestos miners) whose jobs had exposed them years earlier to high levels of asbestos were at a greatly increased risk for lung cancer (Whelan 1993). At about the same time houses, schools, and other buildings in which asbestos materials had been used were starting to deteriorate. This coincidence led to fear that exposure to tiny nonoccupational levels of asbestos might also cause lung cancer. The level of such exposure was thousands of times less than that seen in occupational exposure. This fear led to the development of an asbestos abatement industry, which offered to remove asbestos-laden materials from buildings and replace them with "clean" building materials. The industry made outlandish claims, including that "a single asbestos fiber can kill you" (Whelan 1993, 263). Such claims were certainly not based on any scientific evidence and were designed to induce anxiety and increase profits. The panic was further fueled by the Asbestos Hazard Emergency Response Act. This act required that schools be inspected for asbestos and, if any was found, no matter how little, students' parents had to be notified. Mossman and colleagues (1990) put the estimated cost of asbestos abatement at between $53 and $150 billion.

Ironically the cure here was worse than the disease. A major principle of toxicology is "the dose makes the poison," a concept that comes into play in the case of asbestos and many other substances that have, or will in the future, cause worry, anxiety, and even panics. The idea is simple—a substance that is highly toxic at high levels of exposure can be totally harmless at very low levels. A common reaction of those not familiar with this basic concept is to read that substance X has been shown to be damaging, even fatal, at extreme doses, doses that would almost never be encountered in one's normal daily life, and jump to the conclusion that very low levels of exposure are really scary and dangerous.

In the case of asbestos, there really wasn't any disease to worry about in the first place. While very high levels of exposure to asbestos in individuals working with it in their occupations can lead to lung cancer, the level of exposure in buildings that have been constructed with asbestos materials is trivial. Mossman and colleagues (1990) reviewed the epidemiological studies on such exposure and conclude that the risk from such exposure is "minuscule" (299). For example, playing football in high school carries a risk of death that is, minimally, 107 times greater than exposure to asbestos in school. The risk of dying from an accident at home while between one and fourteen years of age is 645 times greater. Finally, the risk of dying from lung cancer caused by the best-known cause of lung cancer, prolonged cigarette smoking, is almost thirteen thousand times greater than that from asbestos exposure. To make matters worse, the very removal of asbestos from buildings created a new group of at-risk workers—the abatement workers who had to actually remove the asbestos.

The asbestos panic shows several characteristics of the cases of national mass hysteria that followed it. A real disease (lung cancer) came to be linked—not through any scientific evaluation but by a sort of "guilt by association" mechanism—with a fairly common and previously accepted environmental agent. Once this association was made, the media hyped the story, feeding the panic, much like throwing gasoline on a fire while claiming to be trying to put it out. Unique to the asbestos case, an industry sprang up to remove the nonproblem material. As will be seen, this was generally not a possibility with several subsequent panics. Certainly not unique to the asbestos case, lawyers appeared and filed liability actions left and right. But here they were not as well organized as they would become in later cases. Panics grow rapidly, while good science takes years to sort out whether tiny levels of some agent is really causing disease. Thus, by the time it became clear from epidemiological studies that exposure to low levels of asbestos was basically harmless, billions of dollars had been wasted on abatement procedures, and who knows how many hours of research had been squandered that would have been much more productively used to examine more important medical questions.

MICROWAVES AND ELECTROMAGNETIC FIELDS

The alleged health risks of microwave radiation formed the prelude to the next major incident of mass hysteria. The fear here was that the electromagnetic fields (EMFs) from power lines caused, among other things, cancer, especially in children who grew up near power lines. The fear about the dangers of microwaves first surfaced in the mid-1970s with the publication of two articles in the popular *New Yorker* magazine that were later published in book form (Brodeur 1977). According to Brodeur, exposure to microwaves produced numerous unpleasant health effects, up to and including cancer. During the mid- to late 1970s, microwave ovens were introduced and becoming popular, so there was fertile soil for the seeds of fear to fall on.

The most serious claim was, of course, that microwaves caused cancer. But, as Park (2000) noted, there is no mechanism by which microwaves *could* cause cancer. When cancer is caused by some external agent (as opposed to cancer caused by genetic problems within the individual's genome), the mechanism is the breaking of chemical bonds in the DNA. Microwave radiation simply doesn't have enough energy to break these bonds. Park (2000) used an excellent analogy to clarify this point: Imagine trying to throw stones across a river to break a target on the other side. If you're not strong enough to get the stones across the river, it doesn't matter how many you throw, the target will remain undamaged.

Throwing more stones in this analogy is equivalent to increasing the intensity of the microwaves. This does have a result—heat. That is why microwave ovens work. But by the time this increased heat had broken any DNA bonds, the target tissue would have been cooked and cancer would be the least of its worries (Adair 1991, 2003). The anxiety over the would-be dangers of microwaves faded out over the next several years, probably because of the realization that microwave ovens were extremely handy things to have around the kitchen.

But if the microwave portion of the electromagnetic spectrum had ceased to inspire fear and dread, another portion was just becoming a target for even more panic. And once again, Paul Brodeur was in the lead. It was Brodeur who sounded the alarm, again in a series of articles in the *New Yorker*, which were also later published as a book (Brodeur 1989). The subtitle of Brodeur's book indicates that he had climbed on the conspiracy theory bandwagon: "Power Lines, Computer Terminals, and the Attempts to Cover Up Their Threat to Your Health." In a later book, subtitled "How the Utilities and the Government Are Trying to Hide the Cancer Hazard Posed by Electromagnetic Fields," Brodeur (1993) continued the conspiracy theme. Brodeur's writings brought to the attention of a wide public audience the claims and rumors that power lines caused cancer, which had been circulating for about ten years. Some of the claims were based on published epidemiological studies (i.e., Wertheimer and Leeper 1979), and others were based on what can best be called amateur epidemiology. In this case, individuals or groups with little or no training in data collection and analysis sought out evidence for a power line–cancer relationship. Evidence generated in this way was both the least reliable and the most emotionally compelling—a dangerous combination. Amateur epidemiology often starts when tragedy strikes a family, usually in the form of childhood cancer. One common type of cancer in childhood is acute lymphoblastic leukemia (ALL). The cause of this type of cancer is unknown, which is obviously extremely frustrating to the parents of diagnosed children and in some cases starts a search for some environmental cause of the cancer. As rumors about power lines began to spread, these lines became a handy and common target. After all, it was almost always easy to find a group of power lines somewhere near the affected child's home, school, or playground. Equally, it was often possible to find groups of affected patients, a so-called cancer cluster, scattered over the landscape in space and time. And, of course, sometimes the cancer cluster seemed to coincide with areas with high concentrations of power lines. To the amateur epidemiologist, such coincidences of cancer clusters and power lines were all that was needed to prove that the power lines were causing the cancer. Some individuals believed that the mere existence of cancer clusters by themselves proved that *some* environmental factor was responsible for cancer.

A causal association between an environmental factor such as power lines and a disease such as ALL requires a much higher standard of proof than just noting the presence of occasional coincidences. Clearly *something* is causing cancer in affected individuals. But even if causation was totally random over time and space, there would still be cancer clusters, due simply to the laws of chance. As an analogy, imagine a flat, bare room twenty feet square divided into four hundred individual one-foot-square sections. Into this room we throw four thousand marbles that come to rest at random throughout the room. On average, there will be ten marbles per square. Obviously, not every single one of the four hundred one-foot squares will end up containing exactly ten marbles. There will be some squares with lots of marbles and some with none. And yet there is no special "marble attractor" that causes more marbles to come to rest in certain squares. The laws of chance simply dictate there will be "marble clusters," even in the absence of any nonchance factors.

Let us repeat the marble demonstration—but this time the floor has patterns of lines drawn on it that represent power lines. Again, four thousand marbles are thrown into the room and scatter at random. Will it be possible to find squares in which there is a concentration of both "power lines" and marbles? Certainly. And, again, the coincidence will be due purely to chance factors, not to any ability of the drawn lines to attract marbles to them. To determine if the relationship between power lines (or any other variable) and disease is real, it is necessary to show that the association occurs more frequently than would be predicted by chance alone.

By 1997, after eighteen years of research on the issue, it was clear that there was no association between power lines and cancer. Studies claiming to show such an association suffered from various serious flaws in methodology and statistical procedures (see National Research Council 1997; Linet et al. 1997; Lacy-Hulbert, Metcalf, and Hesketh 1998, for highly detailed reviews). One study (Feychting and Ahlbom 1993), done in Sweden, at first looked like truly strong evidence that power line exposure was causal in childhood leukemia. The results looked so powerful, in fact, that the Swedish government was planning to switch children from schools near power lines to schools farther from such lines.

In the Swedish study sixty-six risk ratios were reported. A risk ratio (RR) is a number giving the relative risk of some outcome (e.g., disease, accident, etc.) in a group exposed to some condition relative to a control group that is not exposed. If the RR is 1, there is no difference between the risk of the outcome in the exposed and nonexposed groups. RRs of less than 1 indicate that the exposed group is less likely to suffer the outcome. (Lest this seem implausible, note that the RR for dying in a traffic accident is less than 1 for a group "exposed" to wearing seat belts.) RRs of greater than 1 indicate that the risk of the outcome is greater in the exposed group. An RR of 2 indicates a doubled risk. RRs can't be negative, so there is much more "room" to find RRs of greater than 1 than those of less than 1. Generally, RRs of 2 and above, if found consistently, are considered good evidence that exposure to whatever is being studied does have a real effect on the probability of suffering the outcome. For example, the RR for contracting lung cancer in smokers is about 10 to 15 compared to nonsmokers; that is, smokers are about ten to fifteen times more likely to get lung cancer than nonsmokers.

With that background in mind, the Swedish study (Feychting and Ahlbom 1993) seemed rather impressive. One of the RRs it reported was 3.8 for leukemia in children. In other words, children exposed to power line radiation were almost four times more likely than nonexposed children to develop leukemia. But even in the context of the published paper, that single result loses some of its terror-inducing properties when one notes that the paper reported sixty-five other RRs for different types of cancer and different measures of exposure to EMFs. Of the total of sixty-six RRs, twenty-three were 1 or less. Still, it was the 3.8 RR that was the focus of attention. It turned out, however, that the published paper didn't tell the whole story. When the results of all the comparisons that the investigators made were released in the mid-1990s, that single RR of 3.8 turned out to be much less impressive. The investigators had in fact calculated a total of nearly eight hundred different RRs (*Frontline* 1995). Of this huge number, the RR of 3.8 for leukemia was simply the one that happened to be the largest. If one calculated eight hundred RRs for such things as collecting coins, using pens with red ink, or listening to National Public Radio, it would be extremely surprising if, just by chance, you didn't turn up one or two RRs of 3.5 to 4. When the real nature of the results of this study became clear, the Swedish government abandoned its plans to bus children to new schools.

It has also been claimed that studies of animals and of individual cells in culture have shown harmful effects of exposure to EMFs. As is so often the case, a few initial and preliminary studies seemed to show positive results. Later, more carefully controlled studies showed nothing. Lacy-Hulbert, Metcalf, and Hesketh (1998) provided a comprehensive review of this aspect of the EMF research.

In the United States in 1997, the National Research Council published a report that concluded that there was no evidence of any harmful health effects of EMFs. The same year Linet and colleagues (1997) published a major study in the *New England Journal of Medicine* of 638 children who had ALL and found that these children had had no greater exposure to EMFs than control children without ALL. In an accompanying editorial Campion (1997) noted that "it is sad that hundreds of millions of dollars have gone into studies that never had much promise of finding a way to prevent the tragedy of cancer in children" (46).

A recent instantiation of the "EMFs cause cancer" claim is that the radiation from cell phones causes brain cancer, especially in the brain tissue in the part of the brain closest to the phone itself. In 1992 a tragic case in which a woman died of brain cancer was highlighted in the media when her husband became convinced that her use of a cell phone had caused her cancer. He went on a crusade against cell phones that included suing the major cell phone manufacturers. Keller (1993) provided a good history of the early stages of this controversy. One result was that the stock of cell phone manufacturers plummeted in value. It also led to widespread worry among cell phone users.

At the time, no epidemiological studies had been done of cell phones. The publicity over this case, however, led to the initiation of several studies of the risks of cell phones. Muscat and colleagues (2000) studied 469 patients with primary cancerous brain tumors. These patients had not used cell phones at a greater frequency or for a greater time than a control group that did not have any brain cancer. Inskip and colleagues (2001) reported a similar study of 782 patients and found that cell phone use was not related to brain cancer, nor was there any association between the side of the brain in which the tumor was located and the side of the head to which the phone had been held, if the patient had been a cell phone user. Johansen and colleagues (2001) examined cancer rates in 420,095 cell phone users in Denmark between the years 1982 and 1995. Within this huge sample, there was no greater incidence of brain tumors than would be expected. In addition to examining brain tumors, this study examined the incidence of cancer in all organs of the body. Overall, cell phone users had a significantly lower rate of cancer than expected. This was due to reduced rates of "lung cancer and other smoking related cancers" (203). This effect, in turn, was probably because at the time cell phone users were somewhat more affluent than nonusers and thus more aware of real health risks such as smoking.

Cell phone risks continued to be researched into the twenty-first century and the object of much interest on the part of the public since cell phone use has become ubiquitous worldwide. This research has not shown any good evidence that cell phones cause cancer. Repacholi and colleagues (2012, 187) concluded that "epidemiology studies showed no statistically significant increase in risk (defined as $p < 0.05$) for adult brain cancer or other head tumors from wireless phone use." Nor did studies examining "in vivo oncogenicity, tumor promotion, and genotoxicity" reveal any effects of exposure and brain cell damage. Kabat (2008) reviewed studies on electromagnetic fields in general and concluded that there was no relationship between exposure and cancer or other diseases. He also made the cogent point that epidemiological researchers studying the purported relationship between EMFs and disease "rarely made use of the criteria for judging the causality of an association" (107) that are so important for establishing such a relationship. Ignoring such criteria easily leads to incorrect conclusions that a variable may cause cancer, or some other disease, when it does not. Kabat (2017, chap. 4) reviewed the research on cell phones and cancer again and, again, found no evidence of a link between their use and cancer.

None of this should surprise anyone with any knowledge of basic physics. Cancer is caused by the breaking of bonds in DNA. But the energy in the radiation emitted by cell phones is many orders of magnitude less than that required to break these bonds. The same is true of the EMFs produced by power lines and cell phone towers. More recently some have claimed that the danger in cell phones comes not from the breaking of bonds causing cancer but from the increased temperature that results from having the phone next to the head. But if temperature were the causative factor, there should be an association with environmental temperature in brain cancer that such cancers should be more common closer to the equator. But there is no such geographical effect.

It has always puzzled me why it was brain cancer that was supposed to be caused by cell phones. After all, the brain is encased in the thick boney skull, which is covered by skin. So any cancer-causing radiation would hit the skin and skull before getting to the brain. And skin and bone cancers are much more common than brain cancer. And skin cancer is easy to get—merely staying in the sun too long is a risk. But no one, as far as I know, has claimed that cell phone use results in increased rates of skin or bone cancer.

In 2016 a study by the National Toxicology Program (NTP) appeared that, according to the media, showed that cell phones did cause cancer. This study was done on rats. Over one thousand rats were exposed to various levels of cell phone radiation for nine hours a day, a level that even the most self-absorbed cell phone user is unlikely to experience. Further, the exposure was "whole body," meaning that, as you probably guessed, the entire body was exposed. They didn't make up little cell phones and glue them to the rats' heads! The results were, as expected, hyped in the media as showing that there really was a link between cell phone use and cancer. Two types of tumors were investigated, malignant tumors of the brain and a nonmalignant type of tumor called a schwannoma. This latter comes from cells called, as you might expect, Schwann cells. These are found in many places throughout the body. Overall, there were some positive associations between exposure and tumors. But this was the case only for the male rats, not the females. Exposed male rats had more malignant brain tumors, but these were still very rare. They also had more schwannomas but only in the heart, nowhere else. But, adding to the suspicion that this study was badly flawed from the start, the exposed rats actually *lived longer* than the nonexposed group. So the scare headlines touting the study as evidence that cell phone radiation causes cancer could as easily (and, to be fair, as misleadingly) have read, "New study shows cell phone radiation prolongs life." But that nonscare headline wouldn't have sold papers or magazines. Gorski (2016) has reviewed in detail the other problems with the NTP report. These include the fact that it was not peer reviewed by any legitimate medical or scientific journal.

My take on the risks of cell phone use? Cell phones can, and are, deadly when they are used while driving, operating heavy machinery, or even walking across the street. This very clear risk doesn't result in anything close to the level of hand ringing and angst as does the nonexistent cancer risk. This is an example of how people are much, much more frightened by things they don't understand and think they have little or no control over compared to things they think they can control. But in terms of getting cancer from cell phone use? Be unafraid. Be very unafraid.

ELECTROMAGNETIC AND CHEMICAL HYPERSENSITIVITY

Related to the fear that cell phones and other sources of electromagnetic radiation (EMR) can cause disease is the claim that some people are made sick simply by being exposed to electromagnetic fields. Their symptoms include a wide range of subjective disturbances, including nausea, sleep problems, ringing in the ears, and even dry and itchy skin. These people try to shield themselves from the radiation produced by such common devices as TVs, radios, computers, and the like. They say they feel much better when such radiation is blocked or absent. Or when the offending device is turned off. The crucial test of whether electromagnetic sensitivity is real or some type of psychological/hypochondriacal condition is whether sufferers can distinguish the presence or absence of EMR. They claim that as soon as a device is present, it makes them feel worse. Since it's obviously impossible to see EMR, it's easy to test whether sufferers can distinguish between its presence and absence. They can't. Tests in which sufferers are placed in conditions where EMRs are either present or not, but there are no visual (or other) cues such as a small light indicating that a device is on, show sufferers cannot distinguish between the presence and absence of EMR (Röösli 2008; Rubin, Nieto-Hernandez, and Wessely 2010). The condition is a psychological one and not caused by EMR. It is not a coincidence that the symptoms of electromagnetic sensitivity are quite like those suffered by people with sick building syndrome, described earlier. These can be thought of as nocebo (the opposite of a placebo) effects where belief that an inert, or imaginary, substance is dangerous induces a person to experience unpleasant effects.

Domotor, Doering, and Koteles (2016) studied the personality characteristics of those who suffer from electromagnetic hypersensitivity. They administered a battery of personality tests to sufferers and nonsufferers. Their major finding was that a variable called somatosensory amplification was stronger in the sufferers. Somatosensory amplification is "the tendency to experience somatic sensations as intense, noxious, and disturbing" (137). Thus, when a sufferer believes that they are being exposed to electromagnetic fields, they interpret normal body sensations as evidence of harmful effects. These authors also measured the number of somatic symptoms sufferers and nonsufferers reported in two different conditions. In the baseline condition neither group believed that they were being exposed to electromagnetic fields. In the "sham" condition both groups believed that they were being exposed but were not. Sufferers reported more symptoms in both conditions than no-sufferers. Sufferers also reported a significant increase in the number of symptoms when they believed that they were being exposed. Nonsufferers did not.

The fad of EMR hypersensitivity has resulted in some revealing, and bizarre, situations. In 2010 a man in Santa Fe, New Mexico, went to court to try to forbid his neighbor from using Wi-Fi because he said the radiation made him sick. In 2009 in Craigavon, South Africa, a group of local residents said that a nearby microwave tower was making them ill, with symptoms as described above. They protested loudly about the tower. The trouble was that at the time they were suffering, the tower was turned off (Doctorow 2010). In California people protested the installation of "smart" electrical power meters that report individual homes' power use directly to the power company because they fear the EMR involved in sending the signal. This irrational fear of EMR is yet another example of how people are much more likely to be afraid of things they don't understand and don't think they can control.

Multiple chemical sensitivity is a condition similar to EMF sensitivity, but in this case the villain is unspecified "chemicals." Those who suffer from this condition believe that all sorts of toxic chemicals present in the everyday environment, even in tiny, trace amounts, cause them to have all sorts of symptoms. These can include headaches, skin rashes, dizziness, nausea, fatigue, and cognitive problems, often referred to as "brain fog," among others. These symptoms, while real for the individual, are vague and not traceable to any specific pathological process. As noted above, EMF sensitivity sufferers cannot distinguish between the presence or absence of EMFs under blinded conditions. The same is true for sufferers of chemical sensitivity. Bornschein and colleagues (2008) performed a double-blind study in which individuals with chemical sensitivity were tasked with distinguishing between a condition were chemicals were present in the air and when they were not when they were blinded to the presence or absence of chemicals. They were unable to make the distinction.

Wind turbines too have engendered claims that they cause various physical and mental symptoms. Rubin, Burns, and Wessely (2017) reviewed the studies on "wind turbine syndrome" and found that there is a great deal of similarity between this syndrome and that of EMR sensitivity. Any new technology, the authors note, will be blamed for numerous symptoms. Even the first telephones were not exempt. There was a "fear in the late 1880s that early telephones produced 'aural overpressure' causing 'nervous excitability'" (116). The authors list four psychological effects that can cause wind turbine syndrome. The first is the "nocebo" effect. Second, some people will blame the new technology for already existing conditions or symptoms that appear due to other factors than the new technology. Third, "worry about modern technology increases the chances of someone attributing symptoms to it" (116). Finally, media coverage, often uncritically alarmist, and the action of protest groups enhances the belief that the new technology is the cause of the experienced symptoms.

Media coverage has been shown to influence, for the worse, public attitudes toward health risks and even the perception of personal symptoms. Petrie and colleagues (2001) found a positive relationship between a variety of what they term "modern health worries," including several with no evidential basis (e.g., microwave ovens, power lines, cell phone towers), and subjective health complaints. The more worried were more likely to seek out alternative medicine treatments. Witthoft and Rubin (2013) answered yes to the question in the title of their paper: "Are media warnings about adverse health effects of modern life self-fulfilling?" Individuals saw a television program claiming that Wi-Fi exposure was harmful or a neutral program. All subjects were then told they had been exposed to Wi-Fi radiation when they had not. Fake exposure resulted in more frequent reports of vague "symptoms" in those who had seen the scare program than in those who had seen the control program. The scare program also increased the chances that the symptoms were believed to have been caused by the (fake) EMF exposure in those who scored higher on a scale of anxiety. Brascher and colleagues (2017) also answered yes to the question in the title of their paper "Are media reports able to cause somatic symptoms attributed to WiFi radiation?" They studied individuals with no history of self-reported sensitivity to electromagnetic fields. After watching a television program touting the dangers of EMF exposure, subjects had a lower threshold for reporting a tactile stimulus when they believed that they had been exposed to EMFs than did a control group that watched a neutral program. They were also more anxious about exposure.

Witthoft and colleagues (2018) replicated the finding of Witthoft and Rubin (2013) regarding the effects of media exposure to scare stories about EMF exposure and also found a similar effect for exposure to scare stories about chemical sensitivity.

Winters and colleagues (2003) studied the effects of media warnings about pollution on somatic symptoms following exposure to odors. They found that reading a pamphlet about pollution as a possible cause of multiple chemical sensitivity increased the reporting of "subjective health symptoms" (332) such as tingling, chest tightness, sweating, and heart pounding. This report, and those on sham Wi-Fi exposure, show the power of misleading media information to induce irrational fears, probably especially among those who are more anxious to begin with, and possibly to induce full-blown anxiety disorders such as multiple chemical sensitivity and EMR hypersensitivity.

PCBs

Polychlorinated biphenyls (PCBs) are a class of chemicals that were used in numerous industrial processes until the 1970s. Through various routes, they entered the environment in small concentrations. The cause of most of the worry over PCBs is the fact that they are found in freshwater fish that are often eaten by humans. Specifically, it is claimed that the children of women who ate fish contaminated with PCBs show various physical and mental abnormalities. It is this possibility that has caused the worry over PCBs because, while they are no longer found in the workplace, they are still present in the environment and, as noted, in fish. In the Hudson River Valley in New York State, worry about the effects of lingering PCBs was so great that in 2002 the Environmental Protection Agency ordered the General Electric Company to spend hundreds of millions of dollars dredging the river bottom to remove PCB-contaminated soil. In 2019 the EPA concluded that GE had completed the removal of the contaminated soil. However, the State of New York challenged that decision and contends that there is still more dangerous PCB pollution in the river bottom soil. The important question thus becomes whether exposure to PCBs by eating PCB-contaminated fish really poses a hazard to human health.

Before discussing the research on the possible effects of PCBs on infants, it is appropriate to discuss the relationship between PCB exposure and cancer. While it *is* the case that giving massive doses of PCBs to animals can cause cancer, these doses are vastly greater than those to which any human would ever be exposed (Kimbrough 1993). Kimbrough, Doemland, and LeVois (1999) addressed the hypothesis that occupational levels of exposure to PCBs resulted in a greater incidence of cancer and other health problems. This study examined the causes of death of 1,157 industrial workers who had been exposed to high levels of PCBs because of their work. This sample is the largest ever studied in this regard. There was no increase in the rate of cancer among these workers.

The possible effects of PCBs on the children of women who ate fish with PCBs have been extensively studied. The results show a very minimal risk, if any. An early study to examine this issue was that of Fein and colleagues (1984), who found that, compared to infants of mothers who had not eaten PCB-contaminated fish, the infants of mothers who had showed a smaller birth weight, a smaller head circumference, and had lower "neuromuscular maturity." These differences, while statistically significant, were very small. For example, the actual difference in head circumference was only 1.6 percent. Using the same group of infants, Jacobson and colleagues (1984) reported that the exposed children showed "worrisome" results on three out of seven measures of neonatal behavior at three days of age. The authors noted that their results "must be interpreted with caution" because such behavioral differences "are frequently transitory [and] their long-term developmental implications are uncertain" (530). In a 1996 study Jacobson and Jacobson reported that greater prenatal exposure to PCBs was associated with significantly lower scores on five out of eleven measures of intelligence. Even on the five measures where the differences were statistically significant, they were tiny. The largest association had a correlation with an absolute value of .18. This means that only a little over 3 percent of differences among the children on this measure was due to PCB exposure.

Contrary to the findings noted above, Rogan and colleagues (1987) did not find any effect of exposure to PCBs or another chemical pollutant—dichlorodiphenyldichloroethylene (DDE)—on infant weight, head circumference, or how often the children suffered from various childhood illnesses. A later study (Gladen et al. 1988) examined various behavioral and intelligence variables in PCB- and DDE-exposed infants. Out of sixteen comparisons made, only two showed any effects of PCB exposure. In both cases, exposure was related to lower psychomotor development scores. As would be expected based on the quote from Jacobson and colleagues (1984) above that such findings are "transitory," Gladen and Rogan (1991) found that, when tested at ages three to five, exposed children showed no effects of exposure. The small effects seen earlier had vanished.

Jacobson and colleagues (1985) reported an effect of PCB exposure in utero on a measure of visual recognition memory in infants. Gladen and colleagues (1988), however, found no effect of PCB exposure on several measures of infant cognitive function.

Lonky and colleagues (1996) examined the relationship between prenatal PCB exposure and several measures of infant behavior. Infants were tested one and two days after birth. It is not at all clear from the published report just how many statistical comparisons were done, but in their table 8 (p. 208) twenty-four are reported. Of these, only five were significant, the definition of significance being adjusted to take into account the number of tests performed. Nonetheless, if there really was an effect of PCBs, one would expect it to be more pervasive and show up in more than five out of twenty-four results. Making the interpretation of these results even more problematic is the fact that Lonky and colleagues did not analyze the actual scores on the tests from day one and day two; rather, they took the difference between day one and day two scores and analyzed these *difference scores*. This is a serious problem. For one thing, using difference scores throws away a great deal of actual data. For another, difference scores are much less reliable than using the original scores. Consider baby A and baby B. Both are given a test of behavior on which the lowest possible score is 0 and the highest is 10. Baby A scores .5 on day one and 2.3 on day two. Baby B scores 7.7 on day one and 9.5 on day two. Both babies have a difference score of 1.8, but obviously there is a huge difference between the two babies on whatever aspect of behavior the test measures. Using only difference scores obliterates this information.

Stewart and colleagues (2000) reported a slightly different analysis of what appears to be basically the same data reported by Lonky and colleagues (1996). While Lonky and colleagues found PCB exposure to be associated with poorer performance on three out of seven measures of infant behavior, Stewart and colleagues found it associated with poorer performance on only two of seven measures. Publishing repeated analyses of the same data results in a spurious impression of replication.

Using older infants (between six and twelve months of age), Darvill and colleagues (2000) reported that PCB exposure impairs performance on a test of infant intelligence. But, as usual, the effects were inconsistent and very small, such that exposure to PCBs accounted for only about 2 percent of differences on test scores.

The Gladen and colleagues (1988) study was mentioned above, but I did not describe one of their most interesting results. This was not an effect of PCB exposure but an effect of exposure to DDE—and the effect was not a deleterious one. At six months of age, children exposed prenatally to DDE scored significantly higher than nonexposed children on a test of intelligence. Now it seems to me highly unlikely that prenatal exposure to DDE really makes kids smarter. Rather, this finding is yet another example of the fact that if one does many statistical comparisons, just by chance alone, some are going to turn out to be "significant," much as if one calculates enough risk ratios some will look frighteningly high just by chance. Similarly, the scattered findings of small deleterious effects of PCBs are most likely due to chance. The observed effects are small, as noted above, and inconsistent. This is just what would be expected if PCBs have no real effect but hundreds of statistical tests are performed looking for such effects. To be consistent, those who believe that PCBs are really dangerous should recommend that pregnant women take small doses of DDE during pregnancy to increase the intelligence of their children!

Schantz and colleagues (2001) argued that exposure to PCBs via eating fish caused memory problems in older adults. When this study was reported on by the media in the summer of 2001, it was usually simply stated that the study proved that PCBs caused such impairments in adults—but reading the study shows something quite different and far less alarming. In this study, the effect of exposure to PCBs and DDE was examined using twenty-four different tests of memory and cognitive function. This resulted in forty-eight different statistical tests, of which only three showed an effect of PCB exposure and two an effect of DDE exposure. Of these latter two, in one case the effect was deleterious. But the other was in the opposite direction—greater exposure to DDEs was associated with *better* performance. At least three other tests were also carried out that showed no effect of exposure to either chemical. This is a great example of the shotgun approach to this sort of problem: take a whole bunch of tests, give them to a whole bunch of people, and then highlight the few significant effects that were obtained and downplay the much greater number of tests that showed no effect. If PCBs or DDEs really had a detrimental effect on memory, one would expect that more than just a small fraction of the tests would have picked it up.

Walkowlak and colleagues (2001) studied the effects of PCB exposure on "psychodevelopment in early childhood." Out of eleven tests, only three showed significant deleterious effects of PCB exposure. In arriving at this number, I am using the more conservative—and appropriate—two-tailed probability levels. The authors used one-tailed probabilities and argued that eight of the comparisons achieved significance.

In 2019 Pessah and colleagues published a comprehensive review of the research on PCB toxicity. The review covered studies of PCB effects in animal studies, tissue culture, and in vitro studies as well as epidemiological studies of the effects of PCB exposure on the developing human brain. It is clear from this review that PCBs are extremely toxic when a person, animal, or group of cells is exposed to them at very high concentrations.

It is not at all clear from the epidemiological studies reviewed by Pessah and colleagues (2019) that prenatal exposure to PCBs is harmful, although the authors conclude that it is. They do include in their review the studies that have shown no harmful effects of PCB exposure—one even showed a beneficial effect of reducing the frequency of autistic behaviors (Nowack et al. 2015; see the review for the other specific references). It is important to keep in mind that "the dose makes the poison" and that the level of prenatal exposures in the reviewed studies was very low. The problems with the epidemiological studies cited in the review as showing harmful effects are the same as the problems seen in studies claiming that power lines or cell phones are harmful. The most serious is the use of multiple comparisons and then emphasizing only those few comparisons that show deleterious effects. For example, Pessah and colleagues (2019) classify a study by Grandjean and colleagues (2001) as showing negative effects on "language development" (Pessah 2019, 372). Reading the actual study shows that Grandjean and colleagues measured at least twenty-seven different variables and performed at least eighty-one different statistical tests. Of these eighty-one, only fifteen met the $p < .05$ criteria for statistical significance. The children studied by Grandjean and colleagues had also been exposed to methylmercury in utero. The authors conclude that the "limited PCB-related neurotoxicity" (Grandjean et al. 2001, 305) found in the children they studied was influenced by the additional mercury exposure. The Pessah and colleagues (2019) review does not include the study by Lonky and colleagues (1996) described above, which, when read with care, does not show a harmful effect of PCB exposure. It appears, then, from the most recent review of the literature, that prenatal PCB exposure falls into the same category of risks as those of power lines and cell phones—much less to be worried about than it seems at first.

ROUNDUP—GLYPHOSATE

Roundup, the trade name under which the pesticide glyphosate was marketed by Monsanto, first came on the market in 1973. Roundup quickly became an extremely popular pesticide with hundreds of thousands, if not millions, of people using it or exposed to it. Monsanto's patent expired in 2000, but the company continues to sell Roundup, and other manufacturers produce and sell their own brands of glyphosate. Roundup especially has been the target of lawsuits alleging that exposure causes cancer, especially non-Hodgkin's lymphoma (NHL). These have resulted in several multimillion-dollar judgments against Monsanto, which was acquired by Bayer in 2018.

The question, of course, is whether glyphosate does cause cancer. Tarazona and colleagues (2017) reviewed the research done to that date on the dangers of glyphosate and concluded that the levels humans are exposed to, either through food consumption or occupational use, are so low that they "do not represent a public concern" (2723). In 2018 Andreotti and colleagues published a study of almost forty-five thousand professional pesticide workers who had used glyphosate. They found that "no association was apparent between glyphosate and any solid tumor or lymphoid malignancies overall, including NHL and its subtypes" (509). A small association was found for acute myeloid leukemia. This, however, is not surprising. A very large number of risk ratios, 221 to be exact, were calculated and reported by Andreotti and colleagues. Out of so many risk ratios, some will show some type of relationship just by chance.

Another study that looked at a huge number of individuals found only a very small risk ratio (1.36) for NHL. This was the study by Leon and colleagues (2019), which used data from over 316,000 American and European farmers. The risk ratio of 1.36 was one of 231 calculated and thus provides no support for the claim that glyphosate is a risk for developing NHL.

Zhang and colleagues (2019) performed a meta-analysis on previously published studies of glyphosate exposure and NHL. A meta-analysis is a type of statistical analysis of the findings reported in already-published studies. The authors argued that there was an increased risk but only for high levels of exposure and then only if the individuals were followed for twenty years to see if they developed NHL. There are two problems with this analysis, as Kabat, Price, and Tarone (2021) point out. First, some of the studies included in the meta-analysis were likely contaminated by recall bias such that individuals suffering from NHL knew that there was the claim that exposure to glyphosate caused NHL and could have recalled more exposure than occurred. Second, NHL has a shorter lag time (time to appear) than twenty years. If one waits that long, cases of NHL will appear spontaneously and will be incorrectly blamed on glyphosate exposure.

Numerous national and international regulatory organizations have evaluated the data on the relationship between glyphosate and cancer and concluded that the substance is safe for use. These agencies include the U.S. Environmental Protection Agency, the European Food Safety Authority, and the World Health Organization, among others. But one organization reached a different conclusion. The International Agency for Cancer Research (IACR) decided in 2015 that glyphosate exposure was a risk factor for cancer. Why did this one group come to a different conclusion? IACR based its decision on animal, not human, research findings and reasoned that if glyphosate caused cancer in animals, it must be a risk factor for humans as well. That is a faulty conclusion. Things that cause cancer in animals may or may not cause cancer in humans. But there was a more serious problem behind the IACR decision. One of the studies that led IACR to its conclusion seemed to show that glyphosate exposure caused an increase in the number of tumors in rats. But IACR did not include in its final report the results of two other rat studies that found no such effect (Tarone 2018). Tarone summarized the animal research and concluded that the claim that glyphosate can cause cancer in animals "is not supported empirically" (84). While the final IACR report did not include these negative studies, earlier drafts of the report did (Kabat 2017). Thus the final report was unnecessarily alarmist and helped stoke the fires of anxiety and worry about glyphosate exposure.

Given that there is so little evidence that glyphosate exposure causes cancer in humans, why have there been so many, often successful, lawsuits against the manufacturers of products that contain it? This is a result of the legal system discounting scientific evidence when assessing causality. Clients with real cancer make very sympathetic witnesses in the courtroom. Juries are much more likely to be swayed by their emotional testimony than by the often-tedious recitation of the scientific evidence. It is very difficult to make descriptions of the results of often complex and technical medical and statistical analyses interesting, exciting, and emotional. Kabat (2021, 5) has cogently compared what goes on in a courtroom in cases like those involving glyphosate to "a drama in which an unfortunate person suffering from a terrible cancer, about which little is known, is portrayed as the victim of a heartless multinational corporation."

CHEMICAL PHOBIA

Many chemicals have engendered unwarranted fears. A widespread fear of anything chemical seems to be quite common in modern society. The fears aren't specific at all—the basic idea seems to be that anything with a chemical-sounding name might be, maybe is, sort of dangerous, especially if the substance is artificial. The classic example of chemophobia is how easy it is to get people to condemn the use of the chemical DHMO, dihydrogen monoxide, which has the following terrifying properties, as noted on the website www.DHMO.org:

1. It can be used as a paint thinner.
2. It is used in the tanning of leather.
3. In high enough doses, it can cause death.
4. It is found in cancerous tumors.
5. It corrodes some metals.
6. It erodes the soil in the environment.
7. It can liquify some solid materials.

What is this awful chemical you ask? Dihydrogen monoxide is otherwise known as H_2O—water. The list above shows that the description of any chemical, natural or otherwise, can be made to sound frightening with selective reporting.

The average chemophobe would probably not want to eat anything with food colorings called yellow-orange E101 and yellow-brown E160a, flavoring compounds like 3-methylbut-a-ylethanoate, and a ripening agent of ethene gas. But these are only some of the naturally occurring chemicals found in natural, healthy bananas (Kennedy 2018). Whether a substance is harmful or not has little to do with whether it's natural or artificial. The element selenium (#34) is quite toxic at high doses. But it is an essential trace element for normal physiological function. And many deadly poisons are perfectly natural.

One longtime target of chemophobes has been fluoride in drinking water. Fluoridation of public water supplies in the United States became common by the 1950s and has been a major cause of reduction in tooth decay. In 2012 Choi and colleagues published a paper that is widely cited online as evidence that fluoride is a poison that is neurotoxic and reduces the IQ of children who drink fluoridated water. Choi and colleagues reviewed over twenty-five papers that examined the effects of fluoride in drinking water on children's IQ. The great majority of the papers were from China. The problem with this is that these papers studied children who lived in areas where the fluoride levels in drinking water were very, very high—up to twenty times higher than levels found in water fluoridated by local governments to prevent tooth decay. In these Chinese studies the very high levels of fluoride in the water were due to environmental contamination. It is intellectually dishonest to argue from this study that the levels of fluoride in municipal drinking water is harmful. Broadbent and colleagues (2015) studied the specific question of whether fluoride in municipal drinking water had any deleterious effect on children's cognition. There was not a hint of any such effect.

A much more extensive study by Aggeborn and Ohman (2016) used data on all Swedes born between 1985 and 1992. They examined local differences in water fluoridation and found no effects at all on cognitive abilities, although the well-known beneficial effects of fluoridation on dental health were replicated.

Hall (2021) reviewed the research on dangers of fluoride in drinking water. The research shows that the level of fluoride in public drinking water "is not harmful or toxic" (20). Once again, "the dose makes the poison"—very high levels of fluoride can be harmful. But much lower levels have clear beneficial effects.

SILICONE BREAST IMPLANTS AND CONNECTIVE TISSUE DISEASE

A slightly different type of mass hysteria erupted in the early 1990s over the fear that silicone in breast implants caused connective tissue disease. Here, the agent allegedly causing the problem wasn't one out there in the environment but one that women had had put inside their own bodies. The history of this major medical and legal controversy is covered in detail in Marcia Angel's excellent *Science on Trial* (1997), which has served as my source for much of this section.

While the dispute over breast implants causing connective tissue disease had been going on for some years previously, it really came to the general public's attention in April 1992, when the Food and Drug Administration (FDA) banned the use of silicone breast implants for both reconstructive and cosmetic surgery. In the early 1980s a few individual women who had had implants and also suffered from various diseases, especially connective tissue disease, claimed that the implants were the cause of their diseases. They went to court and sued implant manufacturers. At the time, there was no scientific evidence one way or the other on whether silicone in implants could cause such diseases. No one had bothered to undertake the time-consuming and expensive studies needed to address this question because such a link didn't seem very likely based on what was known about silicone, on the one hand, and connective tissue disease, on the other. In the absence of convincing evidence one way or the other, juries in these cases tended to decide in favor of the women, often awarding huge sums in damages.

It was into this legal context that the FDA's 1992 ban fell. While the FDA may have intended the ban to be a response simply to the lack of evidence of safety, women who had implants, as well as others, took the ban "as proof that the implants were extremely dangerous" (Angell 1997, 20). The legal floodgates were now opened, and thousands and thousands of women filed suits against implant manufacturers. In a feeding frenzy never before seen in U.S. legal history, lawyers of dubious ethical standards essentially "farmed" breast implant cases by convincing women, first, that implants were truly dangerous and, second, that they should sue. The end result was that the Dow Corning Company, the manufacturer of silicone (but not the actual implants), was forced into bankruptcy by the judgments against it. It may seem odd that a company that didn't manufacture the allegedly harmful product, the implants, should be held liable. But Dow Corning had the deepest pockets around and was thus a prime target.

All the legal goings-on took place, as noted, in the absence of any real evidence that breast implants caused disease. As soon as the question was raised, epidemiological studies got underway. But such studies take years to complete and were not finished as the thousands of legal cases moved through the courts. In this case the legal system got way ahead of the scientific evidence. By the time Angel's (1997) book was published, it was clear from many studies (references in Angel 1997) that there was no relationship between silicone breast implants and connective tissue disease. Like the alleged association between power lines and cancer, the association between implants and disease was spurious. With hundreds of thousands of women having breast implants, some will also have connective tissue disease—and some will win the lottery—just by chance. But when these coincidences are focused on by uncritical media sources and exploited by lawyers, a panic results.

The breast implant story highlights the role of scientific evidence in the American legal system. This is an important and fascinating question, especially when the issue of junk science is involved. *Junk science* is a term used to describe testimony that is presented by someone who claims to be a scientific expert but who is really putting forth pseudoscientific types of arguments and claims. The legal issues involved are well beyond the scope of this book, but Huber's (1993) *Galileo's Revenge: Junk Science in the Courtroom*, while somewhat dated, is still an informative and enjoyable introduction.

The fears induced by uncritical media hype and groups with a vested interest in heightening the hysteria in the cases discussed above were unjustified. Fears are easiest to whip up over new possible dangers coming in the form of agents most people don't understand and over which they have little control. An incident I witnessed during the Alar panic in 1989 brings this point home. Alar was a chemical used on apples that was charged with causing cancer in humans. It didn't (Whelan 1993), but it took a year or so for the furor to die down. During the controversy, I was shopping at a small local fruit stand. One customer was engaged in a very vocal discussion with another about the great dangers of Alar and how glad she was that the fruit at this market wasn't polluted by that dangerous, unnatural, cancer-causing chemical. All the while she was puffing away on her cigarette!

There are numerous other stimuli that now cause irrational fears but which there is not space to cover here. Jorgensen's (2016) book *Strange Glow: The Story of Radiation* provides an excellent discussion of both the real risks of some radiation exposure and why people are much too afraid of other exposure, such as environmental radon. The book is also a fascinating history of the early discovery and research on radiation. Kabat (2008) also discussed fear of radon in the home as well as secondhand smoke as a carcinogen for adults in this regard. Of special interest is his first chapter, "Toward a Sociology of Health Hazards in Daily Life," which covers research on the causes of irrational fears in more detail than I have. Not all modern fears are of chemicals or other things in the environment. Glassner (1999) has written cogently on the "culture of fear" that leads so many Americans to fear things that should not, in fact, cause much fear at all. He discusses fears of marijuana, minorities, and juvenile crime, among others. New fears spread much faster in the twenty-first century than they did years ago for several reasons. The media is obsessed with the "fear of the week" and dwells on the latest scare, rarely pointing out later that the scare was unfounded. In addition, the Internet allows rumors to move vastly faster than they would have previously. But the Internet can also help put unfounded fears to rest. At least two organizations have devoted portions of their websites to debunking the latest fears: the American Cancer Society (www.cancer.org) and the Centers for Disease Control (www.cdc.gov).

SPECIAL TOPICS IN PSEUDOSCIENCE

BRAIN PSEUDOSCIENCE
Hemispheric Differences

The most common myth about the human brain is that there are large functional differences between the left and right hemispheres. The myth holds that the left hemisphere controls rational, logical, and scientific types of cognition. The right hemisphere is said to be musical, artistic, and creative. It is certainly the case that the two hemispheres of the brain control different types of cognitive processing. But the differences are nothing like those put forth by the myth. The reality is that in most people, whether they are right or left handed, the left hemisphere is much more involved in both producing and understanding languages. The right hemisphere is better at what have been called visual-spatial tasks, which includes such things as recognizing faces and shapes as well as maintaining attention to locations in space. The right hemisphere is also more involved in the social aspects of cognition.

Important as these differences are, however, they are nothing like the strict dichotomy proposed by the left brain/right brain mythology. It is a basic misunderstanding of what constitutes science and creativity to separate these two and say that one is located in the left and the other in the right hemisphere. Good art, just like good science, requires both logical and rational cognitive processes.

Studies of brain-damaged patients show that musical abilities and creativity are impaired, albeit in different ways, by damage to either side of the brain. The same is true of creative abilities in the graphic arts, while creativity in writing is much more impaired by damage to the left rather than the right hemisphere (Gardner 1983). This is directly contrary to the "right hemisphere creativity" myth and is due to the much greater linguistic content of writing. Studies of normal brain-intact individuals do not support the left brain scientific, right brain creative myth. Rather, both sides of the brain are active during creative cognition (Corballis 2007; Ellamil et al. 2012).

Left brain/right brain mythology is now almost part of Western culture. Sadly, it is widely accepted in the educational community (Howard-Jones 2014), where expensive, if useless, right brain training programs are touted as a way to increase artistic abilities in children and even managerial skills in executives.

Directly related to the left brain/right brain myth is the idea that individuals are either left- or right-brain dominant. This is known as "hemisphericity." As long ago as 1984 Beaumont, Young, and McManus reviewed this concept and the tests that were supposed to be able to determine whether one is left- or right-brain dominant. They concluded that the concept of hemisphericity "is a misleading one which should be abandoned" (191). Further, claims for hemisphericity "cannot be supported by current scientific studies of cognitive functions of the cerebral hemispheres, and it is most unlikely that more thorough understanding of the relation between cognitive function and cerebral structural systems will lead to any change in this state of affairs" (206). Those prophetic words were written before the development of modern neuroimaging technologies that have led to an explosion of knowledge about human brain function. None of this new research supports any aspect of the left brain/right brain mythology, let alone the idea of hemisphericity. Nielsen and colleagues (2013) examined the brain scans of over one thousand individuals. They found no evidence at all for any type of left-brain or right-brain dominance.

Brain and Memory Training

It would be great if we could prevent, or even overcome, the cognitive declines that come with normal aging, the worse declines seen in dementia, or even just improve the memory and cognition of normal people by simple mental exercises. Well, the brain or memory training industry is ready and willing to take your money and promise just such results. This is big business, as the industry was projected in 2019 to be worth about eight billion dollars by 2021 (Ahuja 2019). It seems a reasonable idea—practice on different video games or working memory exercises and improve your working memory or slow your cognitive decline. So the obvious question is whether or not such brain training games and programs actually work. It is the case that playing a particular video game repeatedly makes you better at the specific task in the game. The same is true for practicing specific working memory tasks. That's not very interesting or useful. The more important question is whether playing a game or practicing memory tasks causes improvement in real life, away from the video screen. One literature review (Melby-Lervag, Redick, and Hulme 2016) found that training on working memory tasks, a common target of brain training programs, produced temporary improvements. But the training does not generalize to real-world memory situations or other cognitive measures. Another very comprehensive review (Simmons et al. 2016) of the brain training literature covering essentially all the studies published to that point on the topic concluded that there was very little evidence that brain training programs had any effects other than improvement on the specific tasks being trained or very similar tasks. In other words, if you spent a lot of time playing a game that sought to improve a specific aspect of memory performance, you did get better on that very specific task. No real surprise there. But that improvement didn't transfer to real-world situations, just the type of transfer the brain training industry claims that their products provide. Sala, Tatlidil, and Gobet (2017) reached a similar conclusion that playing video games did not enhance cognitive abilities. However, Bediou and colleagues (2018) argued that there was some evidence for improvement in attention and spatial abilities due to playing action video games. However, Hilgard and colleagues (2019) argued that Bediou and colleagues had not taken into account publication bias, "the exclusion of non-significant results from the published literature" (1), also known as the file drawer effect, in the data they analyzed. When this was done, beneficial effects of game playing were not found. As with other ineffective treatments, brain training programs can appear to be effective because of placebo effects (Foroughi et al. 2016) and the other factors such as confirmation bias that result in the false acceptance of useless treatments.

Redick (2019, 424) highlights another problem with memory/brain training research. Specifically, "the strongest claims that working memory training 'works' often come from studies with the most problematic design and data issues." In this regard this research is similar to parapsychological research, where the methodologically weakest studies yield better evidence for paranormal effects than more tightly controlled studies.

In a major review of the outcomes of commercial brain training programs for healthy and cognitively impaired older persons, Nguyen, Murphy, and Andrews (2022) found that while such programs "may be suitable for enjoyment and entertainment purposes," there is no evidence that they "can improve memory, general cognition, or everyday functioning" (601). One of their results helps explain the popularity of such ineffective programs—there was a significant effect such that brain training programs were perceived as improving cognitive function, even though they did not—a classic placebo effect.

In spite of the evidence of the lack of effectiveness of brain training programs, there are a great number of unethical companies making claims about their brain training programs that are clearly not supported by the evidence. Lumosity, one of the major brain training companies, paid a two-million-dollar fine in 2006 when it was found by the Federal Trade Commission to have engaged in deceptive advertising to the effect that its games could improve cognition not only in normally functioning individuals but in the elderly, those with dementing diseases like Alzheimer's, as well as those with other diseases that cause cognitive impairment. Lumosity used testimonials in their ads, and testimonials are a sure sign of an unethical advertiser making a false claim. The testimonials were, of course, based on subjective judgments and, worse, were bought and paid for by Lumosity.

A common ploy used by unethical brain training companies is to claim that their products will improve the balance between the left and right hemispheres, thereby increasing creativity, intelligence, school performance in children, and the like. Such claims are a sure sign of fraud.

In an excellent example of thinking outside the usual experimental box, Stojanoski and colleagues (2020) studied the effects of brain training on actual brain training users, not individuals recruited for a laboratory experiment. Over one thousand self-reported brain training users provided demographic data as well as data on how long they had used brain training programs and what particular programs they had used. All participants completed a battery of twelve cognitive tests. This huge dataset allowed for testing several hypotheses regarding possible "real-world benefits of brain training" (730). The results "consistently failed to find evidence that self-reported brain training benefitted any aspect of cognitive functioning" (735). The authors examined three hypotheses regarding the benefits of brain training. The findings again were totally negative. First, the time spent using brain training programs, which varied from two weeks to five years, did not show any correlation with cognitive functions. Second, dividing the study sample into subgroups based on age showed that brain training benefited neither the younger nor the older subsamples. Third, examining the effects of the three most popular programs (Elevate, Lumosity, and Peak) failed to show that any one of these, when considered in isolation, had any beneficial effects on cognition. *Real world* is the key word here. This was not a laboratory study but an examination of the effects of brain training programs on people motivated to use them. Brain training clearly failed.

The numerous over-the-counter drugs marketed as "nootropics," said to improve memory, cognition, or, more generally, "brain health," are another major source of brain-and-memory-related health fraud. These are widely advertised on television and online in social media. A typical example is Prevagen, a substance manufactured by a company called Quincy Bioscience, which is advertised on television and online as an effective memory supplement for the aged. The major component of this stuff is a protein. The trouble is that any protein you swallow is destroyed in the stomach—broken down into its constituent amino acids. So any of the amino acids from Prevagen you'd take would be completely lost in the masses of amino acids we all ingest every day. The firm's advertising claimed that "clinical trials" had proven that Prevagen works. Claims of "clinical trials" or "clinical tests" as proof in an ad are a major red flag. In the case of Prevagen the tests were performed by the company and never published. In 2012 the FDA warned Prevagen's manufacturer about its claims of "miraculous" cures for memory problems in the elderly and demented. The company had also not let the FDA know about nearly one thousand incidents of negative side effects of the substance. Several people were hospitalized. By 2014 the company had, to some extent, cleaned up its act but still sold the useless substance.

Prevagen is probably no better or worse than the numerous other products claiming to improve brain health. All should be avoided. In 2019 the Food and Drug Administration cited seventeen other companies for fraudulently claiming that their products were effective against Alzheimer's disease. A commentary in the journal of the American Medical Association warned of the "rise of pseudomedicine for dementia and brain health," including dietary supplements, that can cause actual harm. Increased vitamin E, for example, can increase the chances of a hemorrhagic stroke. Even if the product is not directly harmful, these products are "not ethically, medically or financially benign for patients or their families" (Hellmuth, Rabinovici, and Miller 2019, 543).

The claims for the effectiveness of brain/memory boost products are sometimes backed up by extremely poorly done studies that do not include control or placebo groups, make fundamental statistical errors, or use very small numbers of subjects. Such studies are passed off to the public, unaware of the shortcomings, as proof of the products' effectiveness. A prime example is Saitsu and colleagues (2019), who tested whether doses of the mushroom *Hericium erinaceus* (HE) had beneficial effects on cognitive functions. This mushroom is widely said to have such beneficial effects by supplement promoters. The authors claimed that their results showed that HE improved cognition and was a "safe and convenient method for dementia prevention" (125). Examination of the article shows that the authors performed forty-four different statistical tests comparing performance of the placebo group and the treatment group. Of those forty-four tests, one—just one—showed a significant difference between the two groups with the treatment group being better. Especially egregious was the claim that HE was a "safe and convenient" way to prevent dementia since the participants in their study did not suffer from dementia.

A 2023 study by Abbott-Imboden, Gonzalez, and Utley examined the effects of taking the supplement Mind Lab Pro for four weeks on several measures of memory. The authors claimed that their results showed that the supplement improved memory. But close examination of the results showed that what improvements were found were very small.

In addition to the problems with the simple lack of effectiveness of the welter of, usually very expensive, nootropics, there is the problem of the contents of these compounds. Supplements are not regulated, and so the labels on the containers may not reflect what is contained in the products. Cohen and colleagues (2021) analyzed ten over-the-counter nootropics and found high levels of unapproved drugs in all ten. In a later study Cohen and colleagues (2023) found that the labels on containers of supplements claiming to enhance sports performance were also misleading.

AUTISM AND VACCINES

The claim that vaccines, specifically the measles, mumps, and rubella (MMR) vaccine or the mercury that used to be in it, cause autism isn't so much an example of alternative medicine, where some ineffective remedy is advocated, as it is what might be called alternative antimedicine. This is because those who believe that vaccines cause autism are saying that one of the most effective and proven ways of preventing disease not only doesn't but causes disease itself. The antivaccine movement has spawned a number of quack treatments for autism, to be discussed below. The antivaccine belief is at once one of the most bizarre and troubling of the modern misunderstandings of science because it puts real people at real risk of getting preventable diseases that, before vaccines, ravaged children across the world. In large part because of antivaccine pseudoscience, there have been serious outbreaks of measles, especially in 2019 in several areas in the United States. The topic has generated a large literature, to say the least. It deserves an excellent book-length treatment, and happily there are two: Paul Offit's (2008) *Autism's False Prophets* and Seth Mnookin's (2011) *The Panic Virus*.

The whole thing started with an outrageous medical fraud. Andrew Wakefield, a British doctor, published an article, along with twelve other authors, in 1998 in the prestigious British medical journal the *Lancet* in which he alleged that MMR shots caused autism. This argument was based on the study of twelve children who, according to the article, had developed signs of autism following getting their MMR shots. In addition the children were reported to have suffered from gastrointestinal problems. There was a connection, Wakefield believed, such that the measles from the MMR vaccinations caused infections in the gut that, in turn, caused toxic proteins to travel to the brain and cause damage there. The trouble was that much of the data in Wakefield's article was fabricated. British investigative journalist Brian Deer published a three-part article in 2011 exposing the multiple problems with Wakefield's article. Deer expanded these articles into a full-length book published in 2020. Both the original articles and the book are important sources for the story. Wakefield was later charged with scientific misconduct in regard to the article. The hearing, lasting over a year, allowed Deer to examine the medical records of the children reported in the study. It was found that "no case was free of misrepresentation or alteration" (Deer 2011, 81) of the actual medical records of the children. In addition, the children were subjected to the serious and highly unpleasant medical procedures of colonoscopy and lumbar puncture (spinal tap).

One of the two major claims in the Wakefield and colleagues (1998) article was that the children's autistic symptoms emerged shortly after they had received their MMR shots. Examination of the actual medical records showed that this was not true in many cases. The children had exhibited abnormal behavior before receiving the shots. Some children also didn't even have autism. Rather than being from an unselected sample, the parents were encouraged to submit their children for the study. The second major claim was that the MMR vaccine caused autism by first causing problems in the gut. The article reported that all twelve children had some type of pathology in their colons, termed "non-specific colitis." This claim was contradicted by the medical records. Only three of the twelve children had any such pathology.

The result of the hearing by the United Kingdom General Medical Council (2010) was that Wakefield was stripped of his medical license, "struck off" in British terminology. The council found Wakefield guilty on four charges of dishonesty and twelve charges of abusing children with developmental disabilities. Earlier, in 2004, ten of the authors (Murch et al.) of the original article published a retraction. Wakefield was not among them. After much evasion, the *Lancet* finally entirely retracted the article in 2010.

Wakefield had a serious conflict of interest regarding the research he published (Deer 2011, 2020). It turned out that nearly two years before the article was published Wakefield was employed by lawyers bringing a lawsuit against manufacturers of the MMR vaccine and was planning to develop his own vaccine. His compensation for this was 435,643 British pounds, over seven hundred thousand dollars.

The discrediting of Wakefield and his research has not put a stop to hysteria over the effects of vaccines. Since it all started in 1998, there have been two major claims about the dangers of vaccines causing autism. The first is that the vaccines themselves are responsible for the autism. As will be seen below, the research clearly shows that this isn't true. The second claim is that it is, or was, the mercury-based preservative thimerosal that was responsible for autism. That turned out to be false as well.

The Wakefield and colleagues (1998) article started a spate of research on the possibility that the MMR vaccines caused autism. The hypothesis regarding the vaccines causing changes in the gut didn't last long. The new villain in the picture quickly became the mercury compound thimerosal that was used as a preservative in many vaccines. The story of mercury and its link to autism is a complex one that can only be summarized here. Offit's (2008) *Autism's False Prophets* goes into more detail.

An important distinction is between ethyl mercury, used in vaccines, and methylmercury, which was never used in vaccines. This is because methylmercury is vastly more toxic than its ethyl relative. Offit (2008) draws an important analogy between ethyl alcohol, which I ingested a bit of the day before yesterday (in the form of a nice white wine) with no harmful effects and methyl alcohol, which if taken can cause blindness, brain damage, and death.

There were several types of evidence that proponents of the vaccine/autism link pointed to in support of the reality of the link. First was the idea that the symptoms of mercury poisoning and those of autism were almost the same. Second, studies were said to show that mercury caused autism in animals. Third, it was said that epidemiological studies showed a powerful relationship between vaccinations and autism. Fourth, therapies that removed mercury were said to treat and cure autism. Finally, and probably most persuasive from an emotional point of view for parents of autistic children, the major symptoms of autism emerged at just about the same time that children received their early vaccinations.

None of the claims about autism and mercury panned out. The effects of real mercury poisoning include problems with vision, somatosensory abnormalities, weakness, and psychotic behaviors. These symptoms were dramatically shown in the 1950s and 1960s by people who had eaten fish from Minamata Bay on the island of Kyushu Japan, where industrial pollution resulted in very high mercury levels in fish. These symptoms of real mercury poisoning are not found in autism (Nelson and Bauman 2003; Davidson, Myers, and Weiss 2004).

Animal studies also failed to show any causal relationship between mercury exposure and autism. Gadad and colleagues (2015) gave vaccines with thimerosal to baby rhesus macaques. A total of seventy-nine animals were used in the study, sixteen controls who received no vaccines and sixty-two who were given vaccines with thimerosal according to several different widely used vaccination schedules by which vaccines are or were administered to human children. This extensive study found no effects of thimerosal on any measure of social or cognitive behavior. Studies of the brains of the animals exposed to the highest levels of mercury showed none of the neuropathological changes seen in autistic humans.

Offit (2008, chap. 6) reviewed the evidence from epidemiological studies on the effects of immunizations on autism. The results are clear. There is no relationship. That is, vaccinations do not cause autism. A 2019 study by Hvidd and colleagues looked at over 6,500 Danish children diagnosed with autism. Children who did not receive the MMR vaccine were at no lower risk for autism than those who were vaccinated. What happened after thimerosal was removed from vaccines, due to public pressure, reinforces the conclusion that vaccination does not cause autism. If the mercury-containing thimerosal was the culprit in causing autism, it's removal should result in a decrease in the incidence of autism. This has not happened. An editorial in the *Archives of General Psychiatry* (Fombonne 2008) was aptly titled "Thimerosal Disappears but Autism Remains."

If mercury was causing autism, then therapies that removed mercury should at least improve the symptoms of autism, if not cure it entirely. Autism has probably led to more quack, and downright dangerous, therapies than any other disease or disorder I can think of. One, chelation, was aimed directly at removing mercury from the bodies of autistics. Chelating agents can remove heavy metals from biological systems. But simply removing those metals, which can cause real damage, does not result in fast repair of any damaged cells. Nonetheless, parents who gave chelating agents to their children sometimes reported dramatic improvements in their behavior. This is just a placebo effect. Since mercury has been shown not to cause autism, reports of the supposed removal of mercury improving autism are due to the various reasons that patients, their parents, and therapists accept as effective treatments that, at best, are not effective and at worst are actively harmful. In the case of chelation, proponents reported that these chemicals did remove mercury from the bodies of autistic individuals. Of course this happened—we all have small amounts of mercury in our bodies, amounts that cause no harm at all. Methylmercury, in tiny amounts, is a natural component of the earth, and by living on the earth we are all exposed to, biologically insignificant, amounts. Specifically, a "typical breast-fed child will ingest almost 400 micrograms of methylmercury during the first six months of life. That's more than twice the amount of mercury that was ever contained in all vaccines combined" (Offit 2008, 114). So when chelation is done, a tiny bit of mercury is found. The same would be found if nonautistic children were subjected to chelation. At least one child has died from chelation therapy for autism. The chemical used (EDTA—ethylenediaminetetraacetic acid) had removed vital calcium from the child's blood stream, resulting in a heart attack (Offit 2008, 146).

What started, and continues to fuel, the belief that vaccinations cause autism? It is easy to understand that desperate parents will have a strong desire to seek out the cause of their child's autism and to try to remove it. The obvious symptoms of autism appear at just about the same time as children receive their vaccinations. The fact of this co-occurrence leads people to conclude that the vaccinations caused autism. This is a fundamental logical error. Both things could, and in this case do, happen around the same time but for totally different reasons. One is reminded of the story of the little boy walking home from school in New York City on the evening of the great northeast blackout on Tuesday, November 9, 1965. He playfully hit each power pole he passed with a stick as he walked home. Just after he hit one, the entire city went dark. Panicked, he ran home terrified that he had caused the blackout. Our brains are wired to draw causal inferences between events happening close together in time. Sometimes, especially in the natural environment where we evolved, that tendency can be very adaptive. I walk by a particular bit of forest and am attacked by a lion. It's a good idea to remember that co-occurrence and avoid the area in the future. So parents of autistic children note the co-occurrence of the onset of symptoms and vaccinations and draw the wrong conclusions. The belief that autism is caused by vaccinations is caused by faulty reasoning very similar to the belief that living near power lines causes childhood cancer.

Another serious problem for the idea that vaccinations cause autism is found in research that shows that there are differences between the behavior of autistic and nonautistic children well before the vaccinations thought to cause autism are given. Yirmiya and Charman (2010) reviewed this interesting research. One type of study uses films and videos of very young children. These studies show that as early as six months of age independent judges viewing the behavior of these children can discriminate between those who will and those who will not develop the classical signs of autism over a year later. The behaviors that differ this early are various social and motor behaviors such as eye contact and gaze direction (Shic, Macari, and Chawarska 2014).

Nair and colleagues (2021) studied the pattern of connections in the brains of six-week-old infants who were or were not at risk for developing autism spectrum disorders. There were differences in both the structural and functional aspects of the brains between these two groups. Specifically, the connections between the thalamus and the prefrontal cortex were reduced in the at-risk group. These results show an anatomical difference in the brains well before vaccination.

It has been suggested that vaccines "overwhelm" the child's immune system, thus putting vaccinated children at risk for other diseases. The quantity of antigens in vaccines is negligible compared to the bacteria and viruses that children are exposed to every day. The child's immune system is more than capable of dealing with a few new antigens (Offit et al. 2002).

The nomination of anti-vaxxer Robert F. Kennedy Jr. to be secretary of the Health and Human Services Department will, if confirmed, only prolong the erroneous belief that vaccines cause autism and are ineffective or harmful when aimed at serious diseases.

The reaction of a small group of autism parents to the overwhelming evidence that vaccinations do not cause autism has been extremely vitriolic and even physically threatening to the scientists who have investigated the hypothetical link between autism and vaccinations and concluded that the link is illusory. Rather than debate the science factually, for example, the autism support group Generation Rescue hired a public relations firm and placed full-page ads in newspapers attacking the research they didn't agree with. Some zealots send harassing and threatening calls or emails to researchers and writers who disagree with the autism vaccination link (Offit 2008, 117–18). In no other case that I am aware of has the reaction to good science been so extreme that it verges on terrorism against the scientists involved.

There have been two federal legal responses to antivaccine pseudoscience. In the 1980s a "special master" at the U.S. Federal Court of Claims was established to hear cases regarding damage caused by vaccinations, the so-called vaccine court. The establishment of this nonjury hearing system was in response to large jury awards against companies producing vaccines. In 2010 the court ruled in three cases that there was no link between autism and vaccinations. In a bizarre twist, in 2017 the highest court of the European Union ruled that scientific proof that vaccinations were harmful was not—yes, *not*—necessary for cases against vaccine manufacturers to proceed. It was enough, the court ruled, to proceed with a case for the plaintiff to show that a vaccination had occurred at some unspecified time before the onset of the disease, multiple sclerosis in the case at issue. This sets an extremely low bar for "proof." Just because two events occur close to each other in time does not mean that the first caused the second.

In 1990 the federal Vaccine Adverse Events Reporting System was created to track problems caused by vaccinations. It is often used as a source of claims that vaccines cause autism. However, anyone can report anything to the system; there are no checks to ensure that the reports are accurate. So parents who believe that vaccinations caused their child to develop anything from autism to a stubbed toe can enter an "adverse event" report. It transpired that personal injury lawyers were entering adverse reports themselves. These lawyers then used the existence of such reports to "prove" that their clients had been harmed by vaccination (Offit 2008, 137; Goodman and Nordin 2006).

The COVID-19 crisis brought the antivaccine movement back into the public eye with greater force than ever before. Previously the movement had focused on vaccines as a cause of autism. Now the movement enlarged its scope to argue that the COVID-19 vaccines caused any number of horrible side effects. These included permanent changes in your RNA that could be "shed" and thus passed to others, infertility, bleeding, strokes, and heart attacks. None of these, of course, are actual side effects of the vaccines. Another fearmongering technique was to claim that people died following the vaccinations and the vaccinations caused the deaths. This is exactly the same illogic used to claim that, because the symptoms of autism become most obvious around the time children are vaccinated, therefore the vaccination caused the autism. When millions of people are vaccinated, some will die of unrelated medical conditions in the following hours or days. These are the cases that get trotted out to try to frighten people about the COVID vaccines. If one looked closely, undoubtedly one would find cases where individuals were killed in traffic accidents in the hours or days following their COVID-19 vaccination. Presumably (I hope!) no one would be foolish enough to believe that grandpa getting hit by a cement truck in the afternoon was caused by him receiving a COVID vaccination that morning.

According to a report from the Center for Countering Digital Hate, "the global scientific consensus on vaccines is being undermined by a small but determined and sophisticated network of individuals and groups spreading misinformation online" (2020, 4). Prominent among these groups is the National Vaccine Information Center. In 2020 this group organized a large anti–COVID-19 vaccine conference that featured as speakers Andrew Wakefield and Joseph Mercola. The latter is a well-known promotor of alternative medicine who advocates homeopathy, among other quack treatments. It is this type of organized disinformation that is responsible in large part for the high degree of vaccine hesitancy seen in the COVID-19 pandemic. In the years following COVID, preventable outbreaks of measles in the United States and around the world have dramatically increased.

Combine the fact that there are no effective treatments or cures for autism at present, the unclear cause(s) of autism, and the understandable concern on the part of parents, and it is not surprising that autism has attracted the most varied group of quack treatments, some quite dangerous, that I am aware of for any disease or disorder. Chelation therapy was mentioned above. But other treatments are as bad. Some autism quacks advocate using a drug called Lupron that reduces testosterone levels in the body. The drug is used by some states to chemically castrate male sex offenders. Some even advocate using Lupron at the same time as chelation, arguing that since mercury and testosterone bind together, chelation would then be better able to remove the toxic mercury (which, recall, does not exist at toxic levels in autistics). The trouble is that testosterone and mercury only bind "in a test tube at very high temperatures and with the use of benzene, a toxic chemical not found in the body" (Offit 2008, 141). Proponents of the combined Lupron-chelation therapy just sort of ignore that little detail.

Another quack treatment that became popular in the 2010s was called the Miracle Mineral Solution (or Supplement), abbreviated MMS. One can find dozens of testimonials online where parents state that they used this stuff and their autistic children were cured or much improved. The MMS is given anally or by mouth. Or even injected. What is in MMS? Industrial strength bleach. It is a highly toxic substance that has absolutely no therapeutic uses. Louise Daniel Smith was a major proponent of the use of MMS, and, what a surprise, also a major dealer who created phony testimonials to market his MMS concoctions. In May 2015 he was convicted in federal court on charges of fraud and smuggling after several associates pled guilty to similar charges related to their marketing of MMS. In the summer of 2019, the continued marketing of MMS caused the Food and Drug Administration to issue a warning that this was a dangerous and ineffective treatment. Not only was it being promoted as a cure for autism but as a cure for cancer, AIDS, and other diseases as well. Another proponent of MMS as a cure for COVID, autism, Alzheimer's disease, and other illnesses was Mark Grenon. In July 2023 he and his sons were convicted of fraud for selling MMS. In October 2023 they received sentences ranging from five to over twelve years in federal prison.

Offit (2008, 122–23) described other quack treatments for autism that are "expensive and unproven" that can cost "thousands and sometimes tens of thousands of dollars." Some are potentially dangerous. These include injections of high doses of various vitamins and other chemicals or taking various bacteria orally to repopulate their stomach and intestines with the bacteria. Perhaps the most widely known treatments for autism are the various special gluten-free and casein-free (GFCF) diets touted as improving the behavior of autistic individuals. Like so many ineffective treatments, the support for these comes from honestly given testimonials. But, as is known, seeming improvements can be produced by all sorts of biases, and testimonials cannot be taken seriously if that is the only evidence available, no matter how heartfelt they are. The best way to evaluate the effectiveness of such claims is not only to do a double-blind placebo study but to do what is termed a challenge study. If substance X really causes some sort of observable behavior, then giving an individual substance X should result in that behavior whether or not the person or persons observing the individual know whether the individual was given substance X or an inert placebo.

Hyman and colleagues (2016) conducted a double-blind challenge study of GFCF diets. Previous studies that had not been conducted using a double-blind method found some evidence in favor of such diets, but in these studies the "caregivers . . . were aware of whether or not their child was on the GFCF diet" (206) or not. These studies suffered from other serious problems. Such sloppy studies should never have been published. Hyman and colleagues found that challenge with the dreaded gluten and casein had no effect on any measure of "physiologic functions, behavior problems, or autism symptoms" (205). In other words, giving autistic children doses of gluten or casein, when neither their parents nor the children knew that was what they were being given, had no effect on their behavior. To my knowledge, this is the only well-controlled challenge study currently in print. The sample size (fourteen) was small, and the issue needs to be addressed further with larger samples. But it would be surprising if studies using larger samples found positive results. Reilly (2016) and Mari-Bauset and colleagues (2014) have reviewed the literature on diet and autism. Both reviews concluded that there is no good evidence to support the benefits of GFCF diets in autistic children. In an earlier review Buie (2013) found no evidence for gluten as a causative factor in autism. Buie found that some studies "did report benefit from gluten-free diet." However, "controlling for observer bias and what may have represented unrelated progress over time in these studies is not possible" (578). This is yet another example of where poorly performed studies are much more likely to report, falsely, that some variable has an effect when it does not.

Gluten sensitivity in nonautistic individuals is all the rage these days. Some percentage of the population is trying to go gluten free. Gluten-free foods are everywhere, and marketers are advertising as gluten free products that never had any gluten in them in the first place. A cartoon in the *New Yorker* magazine of April 28, 2014, shows one woman saying to another, "I've only been gluten free for a week, but I'm already really annoying." However, there is some doubt whether gluten has anything other than a nocebo effect in people without real celiac disease who believe they are gluten sensitive. Placebo effects result in an improvement of symptoms when an inert treatment is given. Nocebo effects are a worsening of symptoms when patients think they are getting a real treatment but are only getting an inert substance. Biesiekierski and colleagues (2013) studied patients who reported gluten sensitivity but who were confirmed not to have celiac disease. When given a diet with gluten, compared to one without, their gastrointestinal symptoms worsened, although this was not dose dependent. If gluten was having a real effect, higher doses should result in worse symptoms. When patients were put on a diet they thought included gluten, but in reality did not, they also got worse.

Lionetti and colleagues (2017) reviewed studies that used a "rechallenge" paradigm to test whether people without celiac disease exhibited more symptoms when they were on a diet that included gluten compared to one in which they were not—a sort of placebo diet. The subjects of these studies did not know which type of diet they were on. The results of the reviewed studies showed that between 30 and 40 percent of individuals reporting adverse reactions to gluten did show more such reactions when on the gluten-including diet compared to the gluten-free diet. This means that between 60 and 70 percent of those reporting that gluten made them sick showed no differences between the two types of diet.

Another dietary substance that has a bad reputation is sugar. While sugar certainly contributes to obesity, it is also widely believed that ingesting sugar causes hyperactivity in children. As long ago as 1995 Wolraich, Wilson, and White reviewed the literature on this idea. They found no evidence that sugar had any such effect. Why, then, is this nutritional myth so widely believed? One major factor is confirmation bias. When parents know that their children have just had some surgery snack, they selectively remember more active behavior. This effect was beautifully shown by Hoover and Milich (1994). They studied boys between the ages of five and seven whose parents believed they were "sugar sensitive," that is, that they became hyperactive when given sugar. The boys were divided into two groups, both given a nonsugar placebo. The mothers of the boys in the experimental group were told that the boys had been given a "large dose of sugar" (501). Mothers in the control condition were told, correctly, that their boys had received the nonsugar placebo. The results were clear. Although there were no objective differences in activity between the boys in the two groups, the mothers who *thought* that their boys had been given sugar reported that the boys were much more active.

Autism and Facilitated Communication and Other Bogus Treatments

In the mid-1980s a new "miracle cure" for autism roared into the popular media. This was *facilitated communication* (FC). The technique was developed in Australia by a nurse named Rosemary Crossley. It was brought to the United States by Douglas Bikien, a special education professor at Syracuse University in Syracuse, New York, who opened the Facilitated Communication Institute at Syracuse in the early 1990s. In 2010 the institute was renamed the Institute for Communication and Inclusion, in part to distance it from the extremely bad reputation of facilitated communication.

According to the proponents of FC, autistic individuals' only real problem is an inability to communicate verbally. They are, it was held, just as intelligent, if not more intelligent, than normal individuals. To tap into this intelligence, all that was needed was some sort of device that would allow them to communicate in a nonverbal manner. The device of choice was a standard keyboard or letter board. But the autistic individual couldn't use the board unaided. When simply given a letter board, no communication resulted. Rather, the facilitator had to hold the individual's hand and give support for the movements pointing to individual letters and numbers. It was via such pointing that communication happened. And it was via such pointing that report after report of miracles appeared, many of them uncritically ballyhooed in the media. Parents of children who had been uncommunicative for years reported that their children were producing completely grammatical, perfectly worded answers to all sorts of questions. Children who had never even been given any reading instruction were said to be able to read perfectly. The evidence for this was that they could, through FC, answer questions about material they had supposedly just read. Other, sometimes profoundly intellectually challenged children were said to have produced stories, songs, and poems that were properly spelled, grammatical, and eloquent. Others took, and got very high grades in, classes in literature and mathematics—subjects they had never studied. Truly, this seemed a miracle cure for autism, and the parents' totally understandable enthusiasm fueled an almost religious movement that promoted FC. Unfortunately, these "miracle" reports so widely touted by FC proponents as proof that FC was effective were nothing more than anecdotes told by parents or FC facilitators themselves. Like the proponents of so many other failed treatments, they let the anecdotes, testimonials, and general excitement of being at the spearhead of a wonderful new treatment get ahead of any careful scientific research to determine whether the treatment worked. This was a classic case of putting the cart before the horse. It was not just excited parents and trainers who jumped on the FC bandwagon prior to any objective evidence. In their comprehensive article on the history and scientific status of FC, Jacobson, Mulick, and Schwartz (1995) note that those uncritically accepting FC included "some communications disorders and special education professionals" (754), who presumably should have known better.

In the early 1990s, research began to appear that carefully evaluated the effects of FC. The major question was whether it was the patient who was producing the impressive responses spelled out on the letter boards or that these responses were actually being made—albeit unconsciously—by the facilitators. Facilitators swore up and down that they were not the source of the answers, but it had been noticed that FC tended not to work well at all when the patient knew (or should have known) the answer to the question but the facilitator did not know. It was an easy matter to set up experimental situations in which patients were shown the correct answer to spell out but the facilitator was not. A common paradigm was to use a task in which the patient was shown a picture of a common object and the task was to spell out the object's name. This was something that the patients could almost always do under uncontrolled conditions. But the crucial test was when a picture of one object was shown to the patient and the facilitator was shown a picture of a different object. Of course, if FC had been real, the patients should have easily typed (or pointed to) the letters spelling out the name of the object they had been shown. This never happened. Time after time after time, the patients easily typed out the name of the picture they had not seen but that the facilitator had seen (Jacobson, Mulick, and Schwartz 1995). From a scientific point of view, this should have been the end of FC. The proponents could have written it all off as a noble effort, but one that happened to be wrong. This happens all the time in science. You get an idea, which seems at the time like a brilliant one that just *has* to be right. You talk to others about it and they agree. Then you go and test it. Damn! Another beautiful theory, as someone once said, killed deader than . . . well, killed dead by cold, ugly data. So you move on.

But FC would not die so easy a death. Soon after the negative results began to appear, FC proponents began to argue that FC was, somehow, immune to normal scientific investigation techniques. Several instances of such "special pleading" are given by Jacobson, Mulick, and Schwartz (1995, 759). Basically, the argument was that FC should not be held up to the same scientific standards as other therapies because some consider it a postmodern idea (Jacobson, Mulick, and Schwartz 1995).

There was another defense of FC mounted by its proponents. They argued that FC patients failed to provide evidence of real reading, understanding, or whatever when carefully tested because such testing was "confrontational," and the testing so disrupted and disturbed the patient that performance dropped to zero. This argument suggests the image of some cruel researcher shouting at the poor, terrified patient. Perhaps this was the image this defense was intended to send. In fact, the testing was done in very low-key situations, sometimes by the very same facilitators who had facilitated successfully with the patients and who had the patient's full trust just moments before. The argument is a red herring—what I call the "Oh, didn't I tell you? It doesn't work on Tuesdays" defense. As soon as disconfirming research appears, the proponents suddenly discover that the research couldn't possibly have worked because of some factor that they never bothered to mention to anyone as having the slightest relevance before. This defense was also used, it will be recalled, by the proponents of therapeutic touch when research showed that practitioners could not detect a human energy field.

Even if it didn't really work, FC might seem a fairly benign procedure—one that couldn't do any real harm. If it made the patient happy (but how would you really know that?) and made the parents or caregivers happy to think that they really were communicating with a bright, intelligent individual, what was the harm? The research showed that the answers in FC were coming from the facilitator, not the patient. So those who continued to believe in FC were living a delusion. They were also creating in their own mind a human being who did not exist and ignoring the very real human being who did exist and very likely had very different needs and wants from the one they interacted with in their delusion. By effectively eliminating the human being as he or she really was and substituting a fantasy, FC deprived the individual of their basic human identity.

There was a much more sinister problem with FC. Before it was widely accepted that FC was invalid, a number of children reported, through facilitated typing or pointing, that they had been physically or sexually abused by parents or caregivers. According to Jacobson, Mulick, and Schwartz (1995), these sorts of charges occurred "at an undetermined, although socially significant frequency (Levine, Shane, and Wharton 1994)" (756). As of 1994, there were at least sixty such cases (Margolin 1994, cited in Jacobson, Mulick, and Schwartz 1995). Happily, all but two were dropped early in the proceedings. But this does not mean that the accused did not suffer great torment from simply being accused.

In extreme cases FC led to the sexual abuse of the disabled. The worst such case that I know of is that of facilitator Anna Stubblefield, at the time a forty-one-year-old professor of ethics(!) at Rutgers University in New Jersey, who was facilitating with D.J., a thirty-year-old mute intellectually challenged man with cerebral palsy (Engber 2015). Stubblefield became convinced, through facilitation, that D.J. was in love with her. She reciprocated this supposed feeling and ended up having sex with him during their "therapy" sessions. In 2015 she was convicted of two counts of aggravated sexual assault and, in January 2016, sentenced to twelve years in state prison. However, her conviction was overturned on appeal. In March 2018, she pleaded guilty to the lesser offense of "aggravated criminal sexual contact" and was sentenced in May to time served, about two years.

The Stubblefield case is sadly not unique. Chan and Nankervis (2015) report five other cases in which severely mentally handicapped individuals were sexually or financially abused by their facilitators. The facilitators claimed that the abuse was consensual and that the consent had been communicated through FC. Most facilitators were almost certainly not aware that they were the source of the messages. This finding adds FC to a list of other "nonconscious movements" (Spitz 1997) such as table turning and the Ouija board as well as dowsing.

In their review of FC, Jacobson, Mulick, and Schwartz (1995) attributed the sudden rise in FC to, in part, a distrust of science and a strong antiscience attitude on the part of many in the educational community from which FC gained so much support. Proponents of any new therapy have an ethical obligation to see that the therapy works—that it really works, not just that they think it works—before subjecting patients to what may be, at best, a waste of time and money and, at worst, a therapy that can cause real damage.

By the end of the 1990s it appeared that FC was a thing of the past. But, like the zombies on the *Walking Dead*, it has sprung to life once again. This is in spite of Mostert's (2001) review of studies of FC done since 1995 that showed, once again, no evidence whatsoever of anything other than the facilitator unconsciously moving the hand of the person they are facilitating. In their important book *The Horse That Won't Go Away*, Heinzen, Lilienfeld, and Nolan (2015) describe yet another resurgence of FC. This was based not on any new evidence that FC actually worked but on credulous media reports and documentaries. Hemsley and colleagues (2018) reviewed the research done during the years 2014 to 2018 and found "no new evidence that messages delivered using facilitated communication are authored by the person with disability" (1). So, despite continued use of the technique, its proponents have continued to fail to present any evidence that it works. Worse, during the period studied, proponents did not publish a single article that even attempted to empirically evaluate the effectiveness of FC. Like pseudoscientists always, they choose not to look closely, or at all, at the reality of their claims.

As might be expected, the use of FC has continued to result in false accusations of child abuse against parents. A case in point took place on Prince Edward Island in Canada, where in February 2015 the parents of a thirty-five year-old woman with severe autism and mental impairment living in a group home were accused of sexually abusing her. The staff at the home had used FC to generate the abuse claims. A provincial court later termed the behavior of the group home "deplorable," and careful testing showed that the woman was not the author of the claims. As is always the case, the claims came from the facilitators. It took over a year for the situation to be clarified (Canadian Press 2016).

Proponents of FC have engaged in an effort to sneak FC back into acceptability. Some have dropped the term *facilitated communication* in favor of *supported typing* or *rapid prompting method* (RPM). Another approach to rehabilitate FC is to accuse those who demand scientific evidence that something actually works of engaging in "hate speech" regarding the disabled. The continued acceptance and promotion of FC/RPM by a large part of the special education community in the face of overwhelming evidence that FC is bogus demonstrates the continued hostility of that community to real science and critical thinking. FC and RPM share many traits of a pseudoscience, and "proponents of RPM denounce the scientific method and avoid peer review" (Tostanoski et al. 2014, 222).

FC and related techniques substitute the thoughts and feelings of the facilitator for the thoughts and feelings of the individual being facilitated, often against their will. As such, these techniques are coercive toward the person being facilitated. It is a fundamental human right to be free to express one's own thoughts and feelings. The United Nations Convention on the Rights of Persons with Disabilities makes it clear that these rights extend to those with disabilities. By making it seem that facilitated individuals are expressing thoughts and feelings that, in reality, are not their own, FC techniques grossly violate the basic human rights of those individuals (Chan and Nankervis 2015; Simmons, Boynton, and Landman 2021). Because of this, the use of these techniques is abuse of the disabled.

The acceptance of bogus techniques such as FC, and its variants, raises the important question of why such acceptance occurs in the face of overwhelming evidence that the techniques just don't work. Lilienfeld and colleagues (2015) list three reasons for this. First is what they term "naive realism." This is the belief that one's personal, subjective experiences trump actual scientific data. The world is much too complex to be understood simply through such personal experiences when dealing with complex issues of whether a particular therapy works or not. For all the reasons outlined earlier in chapter 12, people can become convinced that useless, even harmful, therapies work if they ignore the scientific data. Second, such naive realism is reinforced by confirmation biases—the tendency to selectively remember those events that seem to support one's preconceived beliefs while ignoring those that don't. Finally, there is a familiarity effect in which repeated exposure to claims that "therapy X works, I saw it myself" engender belief and acceptance.

Facilitated communication is certainly not the only quack therapy promoted for autism and other developmental disabilities. Another is the Doman-Delacato patterning method. This treatment subjects the child to repeated sessions of "patterning" in which the limbs are moved in rhythmic ways or in which the child is exposed to repeated, often aversive, sensory stimulation. Take the case of Mary, a ten-month-old baby who is, according to Doman (2003, 154), "for all practical purposes deaf" although she has a normal startle reflex to sounds which means that she is not, in reality, deaf. The treatment? "Mother will stimulate her [Mary] auditorily every waking half hour. . . . Mother will do so by unexpectedly banging two blocks of wood just behind Mary's head. She does so ten times at three-second intervals in each of twenty-four sessions" (Doman 2003, 156). What a cruel and reckless "treatment." As might be expected, studies of this sort of treatment show that it has no beneficial effects (Hines 2001). But, as the case of Mary shows, such quack therapies have the potential for real harm. Berneen Bratt's son had cerebral palsy. Her 1989 book *No Time for Jello* recounts the horrible experience he and the family were subjected to using the Doman-Delacato patterning therapy.

This method provides a clear example of the fact that any therapy that claims to be able to treat or cure multiple different disorders with multiple different causes should be regarded with great suspicion. The full title of the 1994 edition of the book by Doman promoting this therapy is *What to Do about Your Brain-*

Injured Child, or Your Brain-Damaged, Mentally Retarded, Mentally Deficient, Cerebral-Palsied, Emotionally Disturbed, Spastic, Flaccid, Rigid, Epileptic, Autistic, Athetoid, Hyperactive, Down's Child. The original 1974 edition did not include "Down's Child." By the 2003 "30th Anniversary Edition," the categories of "Attention Deficit Disordered" and "Developmentally Delayed" had been added to the title.

The book is an excellent example of ignorance of relevant basic science. One would expect the author of a book on treating brain damage to have at least a passing knowledge of brain anatomy. But a diagram in the book contains so many fundamental errors in basic brain anatomy that I use it in a question when I teach classes including neuroanatomy. Students get one point for each error they spot. There are a lot of them! For example, visual outline perception is attributed to the brain stem, which has no such function.

Another unsupported therapy that involves moving the body is the Anat Baniel Method, also called "neuromovement," according to which "movement is the language of the brain." Movement is defined so broadly by practitioners of this quack therapy that the term becomes almost meaningless—language, thinking, and emotions are all considered to be "movement." A clear sign that this is a quack treatment is the claim that it, like the Doman-Delacato method, can help almost any type of disorder, including chronic pain, special needs children with autism, cerebral palsy, Down syndrome, attentional disorders, and adults with brain trauma caused by injury or stroke. It can increase one's joy and enthusiasm and is good for "people who want to experience a higher quality of life." And it is very expensive. I could find not a single study that even attempted to validate any of these claims. But the website and the Web are filled with glowing testimonials.

On the sensory side of things, sensory integration training, and auditory integration training are also highly suspect. A book edited by Foxx and Mulick (2016) includes chapters reviewing the research on these and many other fraudulent treatments. Such treatments can thrive due to several factors. The first is desperation on the part of parents. Combine this with practitioners of questionable ethics and gullible media reports, and the stage is set. Of course, not all practitioners of such therapies are mendacious; often they are just naive and uninformed. However, as noted above, there is a pervasive hostility to scientific investigation of the actual effectiveness and safety of therapies by many in the disability community. Such investigation too often crashes the fantasy world such therapists, and their clients, live in.

CREATIONISM AND INTELLIGENT DESIGN

Creationism is the belief that the biblical story of God's creation of the earth only some six thousand years ago, with all the different species distinct and in place, including modern humans, is literally true. This was the standard Judeo-Christian belief in Western culture until in the nineteenth century scientific advances and Darwin's theory of evolution began to challenge this belief system. In spite of well over one hundred years of scientific advances in the understanding of the origins of the universe, the planet Earth, and human beings, a creationist view is still widely held in the United States. Gallup polls have shown consistently from the 1980s that just over 40 percent of Americans believe in creationism, specifically that "God created humans in present form" (Newport 2014).

The first major public conflict between creationism and evolution came in 1925 in Dayton, Tennessee. In that year the Tennessee legislature had made it illegal to teach any form of evolution. John Scopes, a substitute high school teacher, defied the law. He was arrested and came to trial in July. The trial led to the famous confrontation between fundamentalist William Jennings Bryan, who ran for president three times on the Democratic ticket (1896, 1900, and 1908), acting for the prosecution and Clarence Darrow for the defense. The trial has been dramatized in the play and movie *Inherit the Wind*. Scopes was found guilty—he did violate the law—and fined one hundred dollars. A technicality led to the verdict being thrown out, but the trial received a huge amount of publicity and brought the creationism-versus-evolution debate to the public eye.

The issue of teaching creationism in the public schools came to the attention of the United States Supreme Court in 1987 in the case of *Edwards v. Aguillard* (482 U.S. 578). A Louisiana law required that creationism be taught alongside evolutionary theory. High school teacher Don Aguillard, among others, challenged the law. Edwin Edwards was Louisiana's governor at the time. The court held, by a seven-to-two vote, that teaching of creationism, or creation science as it was then starting to be called, was unconstitutional.

In 2005 a similar issue came before the Federal District Court for the Middle District of Pennsylvania, *Kitzmiller v. Dover Area School District* (400 F. Supp. 2d 707). Tammy Kitzmiller was one of several parents who objected to the use by the school district of a biology textbook that claimed that creationism was scientifically supported. But the wording in the book had been changed to replace "creationism" with "intelligent design." This was an attempt to remove the religious connotations of the term *creationism* and thus to try to slip the concept into the schools without violating the separation of church and state required by the Establishment Clause of the First Amendment of the United States Constitution. The court didn't buy this argument and held that intelligent design was nothing more than a religious doctrine renamed.

Whether it is called creationism, creation science, or intelligent design, the basic idea is that there is scientific evidence to support the biblical story of creation and to show that theories of evolution (whether strictly Darwinian or not) are wrong. One piece of so-called evidence cited for years in this regard was the claimed co-occurrence of human and dinosaur tracks in limestone along the Paluxy River in Texas. The coexistence of humans and dinosaurs was said to be proven by these tracks, thereby showing that both were created at the same time and, further, that evolution of humankind never occurred but rather that humankind was created and did not evolve. The supposedly human tracks are actually those of a small dinosaur (Kuban 1986; Godfrey and Cole 1986; Wilford 1986). The tracks in the limestone along the river did resemble, to the untrained eye, crude human footprints. After years of exposure, the softer rock inside the tracks has weathered away, leaving an imprint that sort of resembles a human foot but is that of a small three-toed dinosaur. The change in definition of a fossilized impression due to weathering is a well-known phenomenon in paleontology (Thulborn 1986). Other "man tracks" are the result of the overactive imagination of creationists, who see a human footprint in nearly every small depression in the rocks caused by natural processes of erosion. Finally, blatantly fake human footprints, actually carved in rock, are displayed in creationist museums and offered for sale in the Paluxy River area (Godfrey and Cole 1986).

A common tack of creationists is to point to the complexity of some feature of some species and state that such a specialized feature could not have come about through evolution; thus, evolution is false and creationism is true. A classic example of this tactic concerns the bombardier beetle. Weber (1980) "exploded" the creationists' use of this interesting beetle as support for creationism. The beetle protects itself from predators in an unusual way: it expels an extremely hot liquid from sacs in its abdomen at any attacker. According to Duane Gish (1977) of the Institute for Creation Research in Dallas, Texas, the chemicals that make up the active ingredients of the beetles' defensive fluid, hydrogen peroxide and hydroquinone, are explosive when mixed together. To prevent itself from being blown up, the beetle adds another chemical, a so-called inhibitor, to the mixture to prevent an explosion. When the beetle needs to use its defensive weapon, a fourth chemical, an anti-inhibitor, is added, and the explosive mixture is immediately squirted at the attacker. Gish's point is that this complex system could not have evolved through any intermediate steps because the apparatus to make hydrogen peroxide and hydroquinone would have had to evolve before the ability to produce the inhibitor and anti-inhibitor. But if the ability to produce hydrogen peroxide and hydroquinone evolved first, then the beetle would have blown itself up when the two mixed, so the inhibitor and anti-inhibitor would never have had the chance to evolve. Therefore, Gish and other creationists conclude, the whole system must have been created at the same time.

Gish's (1977) argument might be impressive if it were based on the actual physiology of the bombardier beetle. But he, like many other creationists, gets his facts wrong when discussing scientific evidence. First, hydrogen peroxide and hydroquinone do not explode when mixed. Second, Gish's description of the biochemistry of the production of the fluid that the beetle emits is wrong. Since the two chemicals that make up most of the fluid do not explode when mixed, there is no need for any "inhibitor" and, not surprisingly, the beetle produces no such chemical. What does happen is that the beetle adds an enzyme to the mixture that produces an "explosive" transformation of the chemicals into oxygen, quinone, and water (Weber 1980). Thus, Gish mistakes the details of the actual physiological process that underlies the beetles' defense mechanism. Where did the hydrogen peroxide and hydroquinone come from in the first place? The former is found in insects as a normal product of physiological reactions. The latter helps to make insects' cuticle hard and, further, "tastes bad to predators and is the chemical that makes stink bugs stink" (Weber 1980, 5). Given this, it is easy to understand why these two chemicals would evolve separately in an insect. Although Gish was informed in 1978 of the errors in his presentation of the bombardier beetle, he continued to use it two years later (Weber 1980). Creationists often don't let truth stand in the way of a good argument against evolution.

A creationist technique related to that used by Gish is to present some specific feature of some creature and demand an explanation of how that feature evolved. If no such explanation is immediately forthcoming, it is assumed that the feature must have been created and, therefore, that creationism is correct. On logical grounds this is the same as the argument of the proponents of UFOs as extraterrestrial craft: if skeptics can't explain away every single UFO sighting, then UFOs must be extraterrestrial in nature. This is a fundamental logical error. In the case of evolution, it will probably never be possible to explain how every feature of every species evolved. We will never have a time machine with which to go back and observe the selection pressures that brought about each feature. The fact that evolutionary theory can explain so many features across numerous species is extremely powerful evidence in its favor.

A very common charge against evolutionary theory is that it is "only a theory." In science the term *theory* has a specific meaning that is different from that used in everyday language. In science a theory is "a well-substantiated explanation of some aspect of the natural world" (National Academy of Sciences 1999, 2). The substantiation comes through rigorous experiments and scientific investigations. In this sense a scientific theory is not just some sort of guess but the result of often decades of careful study.

If creationists object to the teaching of evolution because it is "just a theory," they should also object to teaching the "theory" of gravity. But I have never seen any creationist claim that gravity isn't real because it's only a theory. However, on August 17, 2005, the satirical newspaper the *Onion* published a hilarious parody of creationist thinking titled "Evangelical Scientists Refute Gravity with New 'Intelligent Falling' Theory." You see, there is no such thing as gravity. In reality God is pushing things down. The piece was so well done, and creationist thought so absurd, that when a friend emailed me a link to the *Onion* piece I thought it was real until I saw where it had come from.

Creationists point out that there is disagreement among evolutionary biologists about the details of how evolution works. This is perfectly correct. The details of evolutionary theory are an active area of continuing research. But this does not detract in the slightest from the fact that evolution is a real process. It is useful here to again compare the theory of evolution to the theory of gravity. The details of how gravity works are far from well established (see, e.g., Will 2018; Rothleitner 2021). It may be fair to say that we understand evolution better than we understand gravity. But, again, no sane person would argue that because of this gravity isn't real.

Creationists believe that all species were specially created by God during creation, as related in the biblical Book of Genesis. If they were specially created, one would expect that the creator would have produced physiological structures that are perfectly suited to each species' environmental requirements. This is often not the case, as Gould (1980) discussed in his essay "The Panda's Thumb." Although the panda's thumb performs the role of a thumb in primates, allowing the panda to skillfully manipulate objects—especially the bamboo it feeds on—it's really not a thumb at all. Rather, it is a highly modified sesamoid bone, a bone usually found in the wrist. The panda's thumb "wins no prize in an engineer's derby. It is, to use Michael Ghiselin's phrase, a contraption" (24). Another example of poor engineering is found in the human spinal column. The spinal column gives so many people so much trouble because it is poorly constructed for the bipedal, upright posture of humans. The human spinal column still shows signs of having evolved in an organism that walked on all fours. One would not expect an intelligent designer or creator to have come up with such slapdash contraptions—unless it was a particularly inept designer or one that was just having a really bad day. But this kind of device is exactly what would be expected from a process of evolution that operates in the way Darwin and his successors have described.

Often touted as an example of perfect creation, the human eye is quite badly designed. The retina contains the light-sensitive rod and cone cells that transform light energy into neural signals. In any reasonably well-designed optical instrument, the mechanisms (cells in this case) that first respond to light would be placed in a position where they would be directly exposed to the light, not buried under layers of interfering structure. But human eyes (and vertebrate eyes in general) have evolved in a way such that the photoreceptors, the rods and cones, are located under much interfering material. The retina itself is organized precisely backward. The rods and cones are at the very back of the retina. Between these cells and the light are two layers of other cells, the bipolar and ganglion cells. There are also horizontal and amacrine cells interspersed between the bipolar and ganglion cells that further distort the light that strikes the retina. And to top it all off, the eyeball itself is filled with a Jell-O-like substance, the vitreous humor, that also scatters the light. That we see as well as we do is due to the fact that numerous rather clunky bells and whistles have evolved to overcome the basic crappy design of the eye. Schwab (2012) discusses the evolution of eyes in much more detail.

Moving away from the eye, there is a nerve in the neck called the recurrent laryngeal nerve (RLN). This nerve is a branch of the tenth cranial nerve, the vagus. It provides innervation for parts of the larynx, esophagus, and trachea, among body parts. The place this nerve branches off from the vagus is very close, laterally, to the structures it innervates. But does it take the direct route, as any competent designer would have it do? No, it does not. The right RLN dips down into the chest and loops around the right subclavian artery before going back up to its targets. On the left side, the "design" is even worse. The left RCN drops all the way down and has to go under the aortic arch before it trundles all the way back up into the neck.

The situation becomes rather comical in the case of the giraffe (figure 13.1), where the left nerve makes the same trip as it does in humans, but because of the giraffe's very long neck, the nerve must travel something like fifteen feet out of its way to get where it's going. Imagine a plumber who installed a toilet on the second floor of a building but hitched up the pipes so water from the toilet tank had to go all the way down to the ground floor and then back up to get to the toilet bowl. I doubt such a plumber would be in business very long or that such a plumber would be given any awards for intelligent plumbing design.

One final example will suffice, although Hafer (2015) and Olshansky, Carnes, and Butler (2001) provide many more. Consider vitamin C. It's an important chemical for survival. Lack of this substance causes scurvy, a serious disease that can be fatal. Humans (and some other primates) must obtain all our vitamin C through our diet. We cannot produce it. Other species, cats, dogs, and rats included, have the biochemical pathway to produce vitamin C. This is because they do not get sufficient quantities of vitamin C in their diet—they have to make it themselves. There is a specific biochemical pathway that other species use to synthesize vitamin C. We humans have almost every step in that pathway. Except for the very last one, the one in which l-gulonolactone (l-GA) is changed to l-ascorbic acid by the enzyme l-GA oxidase. This is due to a specific mutation that occurred long ago that eliminated humans' ability to perform this final synthetic step. The mutation wasn't fatal because the early primates ate fruits and other materials that contained sufficient vitamin C for survival, so the mutation wasn't selected against. Evolutionary theory nicely explains why some species can produce their own vitamin C and others can't. The idea of an intelligent designer can't explain this—unless one suggests that the designer just forgot to add that last

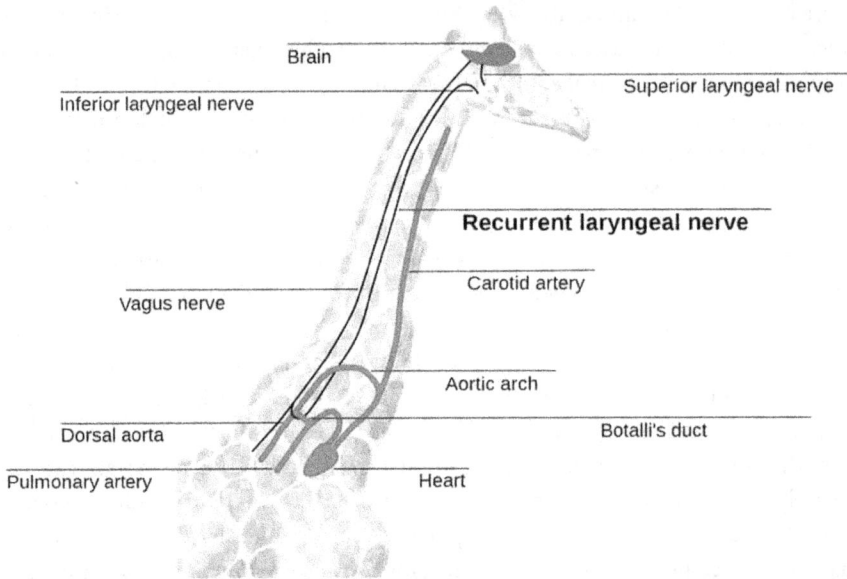

Figure 13.1. Recurrent laryngeal nerve in giraffe. Figure by Dr Bug (Vladimir V. Medeyko), 2010, Wikimedia Commons (https://commons.wikimedia.org/wiki/File:GiraffaRecurrRu.svg); derivative of "Oakland_Zoo_dsc_2658.jpg" by Eugenia and Julian, San Jose–Bay Area, California, 2008. CC BY-SA 2.0

important step in what creationists claim is the creator's most magnificent creation. Evolution has produced in the human, and other species, rather slapdash contraptions that, usually, work pretty well. But as these examples show, they are hardly the work of some all-knowing omniscient superbeing.

A criticism that is often leveled at evolutionary theory by creationists is that it is, itself, nonfalsifiable. This is simply not the case. It would be simple to refute evolution—find a fossil far out of place in the geological strata. One could also find an organism with a feature that could not have evolved. An example would be a newly discovered species with an eye in which there was a previously totally unknown form of organic plastic or bones strengthened with metal.

If one is going to contend that the universe was created only some six thousand years ago, as many creationists do, one must argue against much more than evolutionary biology. One must argue against much of modern science, including geology, astronomy, and physics, because fundamental findings in all these disciplines point to the great age of the universe. It is therefore not surprising that some of these sciences have come under creationist attack. Sheaffer (1982–1983) quoted one group of creationists as stating that the idea that Earth revolves around the sun "is an anti-Biblical notion and is the precursor of Darwinism" (7). Another problem exists for creationists. If the universe is only six thousand or so years old and as vast as it is, which most creationists accept, then how could the light of stars billions of light-years away have reached Earth in the mere six thousand years the universe has been in existence? The obvious answer is that it couldn't. Another answer given by creationists is that the speed of light has been slowing down since creation. This is but one example of how far the creationists will go to twist the facts to support their pseudoscientific theory.

When pressed by detailed refutations of their arguments, creationists often resort to that ultimate defense of the proponents of pseudoscience, the nonfalsifiable hypothesis. One form of this defense of creationism is that the evidence for evolution, the age of the earth, the age of the universe, and so on was put there by God to test our faith. A closely related version holds that the evidence was put there by Satan to lead us astray. Note that there is no conceivable piece of evidence that could disprove these hypotheses.

No matter what new evidence turned up to support evolution, it could always be explained away using either of these nonfalsifiable hypotheses. As has been noted, such hypotheses can be very seductive because of their seeming power. Their use demonstrates only the intellectual bankruptcy of the belief system they are used to support.

Then there is the argument about "missing links." The fossil record is not complete. There may be fossils of one species (call it A) that evolved into another species (call it B), but there is no fossil of an intermediate species between the two. There is a missing link. Creationists like to point this out and say that the lack of the missing link invalidates evolution. Somehow. Now imagine that a fossil is found that is intermediate between A and B. Call it A'. Now creationists will argue that there are *two* missing links. One is between A and A' and the other between A' and B.

It is also argued that evolution violates the second law of thermodynamics. This law can be stated in many ways, but for the purposes of the present discussion, it basically states that a system will not spontaneously become more organized or complex. So, opponents of evolution argue, evolution can't be right because the theory requires that organisms do become more complex as they evolve. In the first place, it isn't always the case that evolution increases the complexity of organisms. Sometimes they get simpler. This seems to be especially the case with parasites that, in the course of evolving from a nonparasitic to a parasitic form, may lose certain features (see Zimmer 2000 for a fascinating discussion of parasites and their evolution). Nonetheless, it is the case that for most species, evolution has resulted in more complex forms. But this does not violate the second law because that law pertains only to closed systems with no net energy input. Earth is not such a system—there is constant energy input from the sun. It is this energy that ultimately allows evolution to proceed (Patterson 1983).

This brief discussion has by no means covered all the fallacies of the creationists' arguments. Further such discussions can be found in Miller (1999), Pennock (1999), and Eldredge (2000). Rennie's article "15 Answers to Creationist Nonsense" (2002) is an especially nice summary of the refutations of the most common creationist arguments. Prothero (2007) covers the evidence for evolution in the fossil record.

CRIMINAL PROFILING AND OTHER FORENSIC JUNK SCIENCES

Of all the forensic techniques that are highly questionable and based on junk science, criminal profiling is the best known. Profilers claim to be able to determine important characteristics of criminals from the crime scene and the nature of the crime itself. Much of profiling is common sense. It is well known that murderers are very likely to be of the same racial or ethnic group as their victims. If one is profiling the killer of a young white female, it's a good guess that the killer will also be white. And male. Killers are overwhelmingly male. And young. So it is not hard to figure out that the killer of this hypothetical woman is a white male between around sixteen to thirty years of age. Knowledge of this information, known as base rate information, can make a profile look impressive when it really isn't the result of anything more than knowledge about what characteristics of a perpetrator are most common. It would be the foolish profiler indeed who would predict that the killer of the young woman was a seventy-four-year-old African woman in a wheelchair!

Research has been done on profile accuracy. It is not positive, as a review by Snook and colleagues (2007) showed. These authors concluded that profiling "relies on weak standards of proof and that profilers do not decisively outperform other groups when predicting the characteristics of an unknown criminal" and that profiling "appears to be an extraneous and redundant technique for use in criminal investigations." Further, profiling will "persist as a pseudoscientific technique until such time as empirical and reproducible studies are conducted" (448). Fox and Farrington (2018) reviewed research on profiling done since the Snook and colleagues review. They found that profiling research has matured in some respect to using more sophisticated analytical and statistical methods. They also found a hint of greater-than-chance accuracy in some profiling techniques, but nothing to substantiate the great confidence that many in the law enforcement community place in profiling.

There is a great similarity between profiling and cold reading (Lilienfeld et al. 2010, chap. 10). Like cold readers, profilers produce a plethora of predictions about the criminal, some of which will be correct simply by chance. It is those correct predictions that are reported in the media and stick in the minds of both the profilers and those who employ them. In television depictions of profilers and profiling, the profilers' predictions are inevitably amazingly accurate, leading to public belief in the validity of profiling.

Profiling is far from the only pseudoscientific method used in law enforcement. Lilienfeld and Landfield (2008) describe others, including graphology, lie detectors, hypnosis, anatomical dolls, the use of truth serum, and even fingerprinting. Techniques that are staples of crime dramas like CSI include bite mark analysis, hair analysis, ballistics, and blood spatter analysis. All suffer from serious problems, and their use has resulted in serious miscarriages of justice (Koen and Bowers 2017). If they continue to be used, and relied on by the courts, further such miscarriages are guaranteed to occur.

The idea behind bite mark analysis is that a bite mark on a body can be matched to the pattern of teeth in the perpetrator. Unfortunately, this is simply not the case. Bowers (2017, 154) stated, "Forensic dentists cannot reliably associate dentition [of a suspect] with a bite mark." The flesh of a body is far from solid, and the pattern left by a bite may differ from that of the teeth that left it. Especially if the victim is moving, as is highly likely, the bite mark will appear to be much different from that of the teeth that inflicted it. Another problem is that tooth patterns are not nearly as individual as fingerprints. Because of this, even if bite marks left on a body were perfect and not distorted by movement, the passage of time, and other factors, it would be impossible in the great majority of cases to be certain that a specific pattern had been left by a specific person.

While bite mark analysis is completely invalid, the validity of various types of blood analyses is mixed. Of all the blood analyses, blood pattern analysis is the worst. The basic idea is that inferences can be drawn about the type and nature of the weapon(s) used and nature of the attack from the pattern of blood found at a crime scene. While sometimes true, blood pattern analysis is fraught with interpretative problems (Goetz 2017) that have led to the conviction of innocent people. One obvious problem is the use of "old cops' tales" in place of scientifically verified techniques when analyzing blood patterns. Goetz (2017, 282) nicely describes this problem as "what one officer believes and teaches becomes folklore for an entire community of officers." There is also a large element of pareidolia involved as blood patterns are almost always highly irregular, thus giving an opportunity to see incriminating patterns where none may exist. A similar problem of "crime scene pareidolia" exists with arson analysis, where investigators have little or no scientific training and rely instead on techniques of investigation that have not been validated but have been passed down across generations of arson investigators (Lentini 2017).

Unlike blood pattern analysis, chemical analysis of blood and presumed blood stains first to determine whether the questioned substance is blood at all and then whether it is human blood can be more probative. Some techniques, still often seen on CSI-type TV shows and unfortunately still sometimes used in real life, have problems with high false alarm rates. Luminol, which reacts with blood to produce a bright light under fluorescence illumination, will produce false positive reactions to "bleach, plant peroxidases, chemical oxidants such as potassium permanganate ($KMnO_4$), copper, brass, lead, zinc, bronze, iron or cobalt" (Halkides and Lott 2017, 250). Luminol cannot distinguish between human and nonhuman blood. Other tests for blood also produce unacceptably high false positive rates to nonblood substances. It was just such false positive results that sent Australian mother Lindy Chamberlain to prison for four years for murdering her nine-month-old daughter Azaria in 1980 while the family was camping near Ayers Rock. The baby had actually been taken by a dingo, a wild Australian dog. Blood tests on the family's car convinced the authorities that Lindy had slit the baby's throat. But the tests used give false positive responses to a number of nonblood substances such as chocolate milk, paint containing bitumen (which was used in the car), mucus from the nose, and copper oxide, "a material prevalent where the Chamberlains lived in Mt. Isa, Queensland" (Halkides and Lott 2017, 243). Mrs. Chamberlain was finally exonerated when Azaria's badly torn jacket was found in the wild, confirming the attack by dingoes.

A problem with many tests for the presence of blood is that whether a result is classified as a true positive or a false positive depends almost entirely on subjective judgments of characteristics such as the color or brightness of the chemical result. More recent tests use antibody techniques and are less problematic.

It will probably come as a surprise to most readers that even fingerprint analysis is not free of problems that, under certain circumstances, render it little more than junk science. Even if no two individuals have identical fingerprints, this does not mean that junk science problems do not insinuate themselves into fingerprint analysis. Imagine yourself as a trained fingerprint examiner. Your superior hands you a bloody knife and tells you that there are partial fingerprints on the knife. If, she says, those prints match the clear prints of a suspect taken when he was arrested, a suspect who, you are told, is known to have committed several other murders for which he could not be convicted, this serial murderer will be put away. The pressure on you, the examiner, to see a match in such a situation is obvious. Since the fingerprints taken from objects at a crime scene are almost never the sharp, clear prints taken when a suspect is fingerprinted in police custody, there will always be room for the examiner to interpret the partial prints found at the crime scene. Again, pareidolia raises its ugly head.

The proper way to evaluate fingerprints would be for the examiner to do so without any prior knowledge of whose prints she is "supposed" to identify (Robertson and Kesselheim 2016). In other words, keep the examiner blinded as to which print comes from the suspect. Sadly, such procedures are, so far, essentially never used. Useful as it is, fingerprint analysis must be approached with great care, especially because of the widespread belief that it is infallible. Bright-Birnbaum (2017) has discussed the problems with fingerprint analysis in more detail.

Even DNA analysis is not without its problems. While such analyses have been responsible for exonerating over one hundred innocent people convicted of serious crimes such as murder and rape, it, like any tool, can be misused. The laboratory analyses needed are complex and require that the technicians be well trained. As with any test, the initial laboratory results must be interpreted. Krane and Ford (2017, 215) in their review of the problems with DNA analysis also note the lack of blinding, saying, "We often see indications in the laboratory notes themselves that the analysts are familiar with facts of their cases, including information that has nothing to do with genetic testing, and that they are acutely aware of which results will help or hurt the prosecution team." Again, blinding the analysts is an important, but seldom taken, step to ensure valid results (Koppl and Krane 2016).

The forensic techniques discussed above are not the only ones that have serious problems with reliability and validity and thus verge on junk science. Others include crime scene reconstruction, bullet lead analysis, firearms identification, and hair analysis. Details of the problems with these techniques can be found in the excellent volume *Forensic Science Reform: Protecting the Innocent* by Koen and Bowers (2017).

The use of junk science and pseudoscience in the criminal justice system is especially disturbing because the use of these bogus techniques has real life-and-death consequences. I can think of no other area except in that of alternative medicine quackery where it is so important to recognize the bogus nature of such too commonly accepted practices and root them out.

CRYPTOZOOLOGY

Cryptozoology is the pursuit, usually by interested amateurs with little training in zoology, of large creatures said to exist but unknown to science and for which there is little or no real evidence other than vague eyewitness reports. The highly questionable nature of eyewitness reports has been noted repeatedly previously in this book. As early as about 50 BCE the Roman poet Lucretius implicitly recognized the difficulties with eyewitness accounts of monsters, the then-current term for what would now be called cryptozoological creatures. In his poem *De rerum natura* (On the Nature of Things) he attributed monster reports to "optical illusions and tricks of the mind" (Dendle 2006, 193). The most famous targets of cryptozoological investigation are the Loch Ness monster in Scotland, followed by Bigfoot in the United States (or the yeti in the Himalayas) and more recently the chupacabra, first in Puerto Rico and then in other Latin American nations. A host of lesser-known creatures follows behind as described by Loxton and Prothero (2013).

Reports of creatures such as the Loch Ness monster, the yeti or abominable snowman, and Bigfoot have a great deal in common with reports of UFOs. First, monster reports are common. Second, monsters are reported by sane, reliable witnesses who frequently truly believe that they have seen something huge, mysterious, and frightening. As it does for UFO reports, the honesty of such reports leads many to accept them at face value. Third, the case for the existence of monsters relies almost entirely on eyewitness reports, as genuine physical and photographic evidence for their existence is lacking. Some individuals in the UFO movement even contend that there is some sort of relationship between UFOs and monsters, as the latter are allegedly seen more commonly after UFO sightings (Clark and Coleman 1978). Given the similarity between UFO and monster reports, what was said in previous chapters regarding the constructive nature of perception and memory applies with full force to reports of monsters.

The Loch Ness monster of Scotland is probably the world's best-known monster, second only to Bigfoot in the United States. Binns (1984), Campbell (1997), and Loxton and Prothero (2013, chap. 4) have carefully examined the Loch Ness monster story. That Loxton and Prothero chapter is the best source for additional information. It is widely believed that sightings of the monster date back more than a thousand years to one by Saint Columba, and that sightings have continued on a more or less regular basis since then. This is incorrect. The Saint Columba sighting report is an example of the poor scholarship that plagues the Loch Ness mystery. The sighting is taken from a biography of the saint written in 565 CE, a time when the biographer of a saint was expected to prove his saintliness by telling marvelous stories about strange and miraculous occurrences associated with the saint. Such stories can hardly be taken as reliable. Furthermore, Saint Columba's "monster" wasn't even seen in Loch Ness but in the River Ness, a different body of water so shallow that it cannot support navigation, let alone a resident monster.

Reports of sightings made in 1520, 1771, and 1885 first came to light in a letter published in the October 20, 1933, issue of the Edinburgh newspaper the *Scotsman*. The letter was from a D. Murray Rose, who "failed to supply either his address or any specific references to the chronicles or publications wherein his weird and wonderful stories could be found" (Binns 1984, 51). No one has ever been able to find any other reference to these alleged sightings than Rose's letter, but the supposed sightings have become part of the Loch Ness monster legend.

The city of Inverness lies a few miles northeast of Loch Ness, and the first recorded report of the monster appeared in the *Inverness Courier* of May 2, 1933, written by Alex Campbell. The witnesses were Mr. and Mrs. John Mackay, a local couple who were driving along the lake. Campbell's report of what the Mackays saw is greatly exaggerated. He states, for example, that "the creature disported itself, rolling and plunging for fully a minute, its body resembling that of a whale" (quoted in Binns 1984, 10). In fact, Mr. Mackay, the driver, saw nothing and Mrs. Mackay saw "a violent commotion in the water which seemed to be caused 'by two ducks fighting'" (12).

It turns out that this classic first sighting of the monster was a hoax. It was dreamed up by a couple of publicity agents who had taken on the job of drumming up publicity for several local hotels. This was revealed by Bauer (1986) in a book that is generally favorable to the idea that there is something truly unusual in Loch Ness. Bauer argues, rather unconvincingly it seems to me, that sometimes a hoax such as this is necessary for a true mysterious phenomenon to be noticed. Nonetheless, Bauer's book is very valuable for its detailed listing of sightings and reports of the monster and an extremely detailed bibliography.

Since 1933 numerous reports of the monster have been made. What prompts them? Loch Ness is a large, long, and deep lake where natural phenomena can provide the stimulus for perception to construct a monster where none exists. For example, the lake contains numerous salmon. On rare occasions, they come to the surface in groups, causing a considerable disturbance. Captain John Macdonald, who had sailed the lake for more than fifty years without ever seeing anything resembling a monster, suggested this type of event as an explanation for the Mackay sighting a few days after Campbell's story was published (Binns 1984). There are also otters in the lake, which run an average of about four feet in length. When playing together, with several swimming in line, one diving, the next surfacing, and so forth, a group of otters would easily simulate the snakelike aspect that the monster is sometimes said to have. Further, otters are rather rare and so unfamiliar to most people. Otters have been mistaken for monsters in other Scottish lakes, as Binns notes. Deer are common around the lake and have been known to swim across it. A deer swimming in a lake is not something most people expect to see and so, if the lake happens to have the reputation of housing a monster, a monster will likely be perceived. Binns reports one case in which enlargement of a photograph of the monster revealed a swimming deer. Floating logs and bizarrely shaped pieces of driftwood can also be mistaken for a monster, if that is what one is half expecting to see. And who could go to Loch Ness without at least half hoping to get a good view of the monster? Lehn (1979) demonstrated that atmospheric refraction, associated with a temperature inversion layer (cold air near the surface of the lake, warmer air above), can produce striking illusions in which otherwise well-known objects are visually distorted, both in shape and size. The perfect conditions for such illusion-creating temperature inversions exist at Loch Ness and many other lakes where monsters are occasionally reported. Keeping in mind the constructive nature of perception, it is easy to understand how witnesses, very often expecting to see something monstrous, misperceive ordinary objects as, well, something monstrous.

Photographs exist that are said to show the monster, and here again the parallel between monsters and UFOs is striking. Many of the photographs show nothing other than indistinct shapes in the water. They could be anything, and probably are. Further, some of the photos don't include any shoreline in the image and could have been taken anywhere—in a pond in the photographer's backyard, for instance. Given that almost everyone now has a cell phone complete with camera and video recorder, it is astonishing that more and better monster photos don't exist, if the monster does. Fraud has also played a role in monster photographs. Photos taken in 1934 by R. A. Wilson that show a reasonably clear dinosaur-like shape are now known to be fakes (Binns 1984).

A set of famous Loch Ness photographs—actually a film—was taken by Tim Dinsdale in the spring of 1960. The film was analyzed by the Royal Air Force Joint Air Reconnaissance Intelligence Center in 1966. The center reported that the moving object in the film was "probably an animate object" (quoted in Binns 1984, 109). This report has received much publicity, but Binns shows that it faces real problems as proof of the existence of the monster. A careful reading of the report shows that the object's appearance is equivalent to that of a fast motorboat. This explanation was rejected because such boats are "normally painted in such a way as to be photo visible at any time" (quoted in Binns 1984, 123), and Dinsdale said it wasn't a motorboat. On the day the film was taken, Dinsdale, an ardent believer in the existence of the monster, was greatly fatigued and had already mistaken a floating tree trunk for the monster. The report, then, actually shows that the object could have been a motorboat that was painted an unusual (e.g., dull as opposed to bright) color.

On geological and ecological grounds, the existence of a large monster of some sort in the loch is, to put it mildly, highly unlikely. Some say the beast is a surviving dinosaur or perhaps a plesiosaur. But the dinosaurs and plesiosaurs died out about sixty million years ago. Loch Ness was created 2.5 million years ago, and all of Scotland was covered by an ice sheet about a half mile deep "as recently as 18,000 years ago"

(Loxton and Prothero 2013, 121). In terms of ecology, if the monster exists, there have to be quite a few of them to maintain a population. What do they eat? There just aren't enough fish, or other prey, in the loch to support a group of such large creatures.

Over the last nearly fifty years Loch Ness has been the site of enormous efforts to obtain, once and for all, proof positive of the monster's existence. In the 1970s, round-the-clock surveillance was maintained for months. Sensitive sonar scanned the lake, and sensitive cameras were lowered into it. (One of the problems facing underwater photography in the lake is that the water is extremely murky.) A small underwater submarine spent 250 hours in the lake. In 1987 a fleet of at least eighteen boats was used in another sonar scanning expedition. The results of all this? Nothing: no surface sightings, no surface photographs, no sonar tracings of a monster, no monster skeletons found on the bottom of the loch, and only one photograph, obtained from an underwater camera in the summer of 1972, that showed a clear image of what appeared to be the large flipper of an unknown species. Was this proof at last? Robert Rines, who set up the camera that took the photograph, felt that it did establish the existence of the monster (Rines et al. 1975–1976). The original photograph was sent to NASA's Jet Propulsion Laboratory in California for computer enhancement, a technique used to clarify photographs such as those beamed back to Earth from space by interplanetary probes. It was allegedly the computer-enhanced photo that was published in the article by Rines and colleagues (1975–1976) and reproduced widely throughout the world. But the published photo was not the computer-enhanced photo. The published photo had been greatly retouched and appears much more obviously to show a flipper, while the actual computer-enhanced photograph could be of almost anything (Razdan and Kielar 1984–1985). Razdan and Kielar also point to serious shortcomings in the sonar evidence that Rines and colleagues argued supports their interpretation of the photograph.

The Loch Ness monster has been the object of great interest for almost ninety years. Although the loch has a heavily traveled highway along one side, and an important city, Inverness, at one end, Nessie has never put in a close personal appearance that would have resulted in hundreds of confirmed reports and photographs. In all that time and with all that effort using some of the most technologically sophisticated devices available, no trace of conclusive evidence has been uncovered that the monster exists. It is most instructive to compare this situation to another where a creature, if by no means a monster, was found alive, although the scientific world believed that it had been extinct for two hundred million years. The creature is a fish called a coelacanth, which runs to about five feet in length and lives in the Indian Ocean. In 1938 a single specimen was caught, arousing considerable interest among scientists (Smith 1956). The story of the discovery of the coelacanth has been very well told by Thomson (1991) and Weinberg (2000). In the few years following 1938, scientists turned up some additional specimens of this "living fossil." Compare the Loch Ness monster and the coelacanth. The monster is said to be a very large creature living in a lake in a rather heavily populated and traveled area, which is a favorite summer vacation spot with a highway running along it. In all the years that people have so diligently looked for the monster, no satisfactory evidence for its existence has ever been found. The coelacanth, on the other hand, is a relatively small fish living in a vast ocean. When it was discovered in 1938, the countries bordering on the Indian Ocean were largely nontechnological colonial states. And yet in just a few years several more examples of the fish were found. It strains credulity to argue that if the coelacanth was found so rapidly and under such unfavorable conditions, the Loch Ness monster has somehow managed to evade its much more persistent and sophisticated searchers for so long. Of course, the same can be said for any of the other cryptozoological creatures described here.

Loch Ness is certainly not the only large body of water said to be inhabited by some sort of mysterious monster. In the United States and Canada it seems that almost every large lake has one, often happily promoted by the local chamber of commerce. In the United States the most famous is Champ, the happy monster said to be found in Lake Champlain on the northern Vermont/New York/Quebec border.

Bartholomew (2012) described the search for Champ in an excellent book. Like Nessie, Champ is an elusive creature. Its existence is based on the usual eyewitness reports and a few grainy photographs. As usual the eyewitness reports are of "something" seen that, because it can't be immediately identified, is assumed, by default, to be the monster. As with Loch Ness, there are things in Lake Champlain that are unfamiliar to many people. Otters and deer are found there. The lake is home to large fish such as carp that can reach a weight of almost fifty pounds. Spawning carp gather in large groups and thrash around in shallow water and release sperm and eggs. This is an impressive sight that I once saw in a lake in Michigan. If one was not aware of what was happening, it would be easy to mistake this fishy orgy for one large serpentlike creature.

There are, of course, pictures of Champ (Bartholomew 2012). They are of the same poor quality as those of Nessie. The most famous picture was taken in 1977 but not brought to light by the photographer until 1981. It shows, you guessed it, a dinosaur-like creature. Unlike so many Loch Ness photos, however, this picture shows a shoreline in the distance and a bit of vegetation in the foreground. Several things about this picture, or rather, the behavior of the photographer, raise serious suspicions that it's a hoax. First, the photographer didn't reveal the existence of the photograph for four years. If you had a pretty clear picture of what you really believed was a lake monster, wouldn't you have revealed it immediately? I certainly would have. Second, there is only one picture. Again, if I had a swimming lake monster in my sights, I'd squeeze off as many photos as I could. Finally, the photographer claims not to remember where along the lake the photo was taken. Again, I'm pretty sure that if I had a good photo of a real lake monster, the first ever, I'd be damn sure to remember where I took it. Attempts have been made to match the shorelines seen in the photograph to any place along the shore of Lake Champlain but without success.

Other lakes have their monsters as well. For those with an interest in these somewhat more obscure monsters, Radford and Nickell's (2006) book is an informative discussion of many of these. It is also an excellent guide on how to investigate such mysteries.

Bigfoot and Yeti

In the United States the most famous cryptozoological creature is Bigfoot, also known as Sasquatch. Bigfoot is said to be a very large, eight- to twelve-foot-tall humanlike creature unknown to science. Proponents of the reality of Bigfoot say that the creature is described in the myths and legends of Native Americans, especially those from the Pacific Northwest. However, the creatures of Native American legends are very different from modern-day Bigfoots (yes, that's the correct plural) (Loxton and Prothero 2013).

Like so many other cryptozoological creatures, the evidence for Bigfoot is amazingly sparse considering that believers contend that an entire population of humanoid giants is wandering around in all the forests of North America. A film taken by Roger Patterson and Bob Gimlin in 1967 is the clearest film evidence for Bigfoot. It shows a large humanoid creature covered in black fur ambling across the forest landscape. I agree with Loxton and Prothero (2013), who discuss the film at some length, that it may never be possible to determine whether for certain this film is a fake or not. However, the fact that Patterson was a known con artist and Bigfoot enthusiast suggests that skepticism is in order here. This is especially true since other than the Patterson-Gimlin film, the evidence for Bigfoot consists of nothing more than the usual poor photos, vague moving blobs on film or video, and eyewitness and "ear-witness" reports. These latter consist of people hearing things in the woods, almost always at night and, not being able to immediately identify what the sound source is, jumping to the conclusion that "it must be Bigfoot." And footprints. Oh yes, there are lots of Bigfoot footprints. Or casts thereof. They're easy to fake.

It's revealing to consider what sort of evidence would exist if there really were tens or hundreds of thousands of giant apelike creatures running around in the woods of North America compared to the sort of evidence that *doesn't* exist. There are no Bigfoot bodies, but quite a few Bigfoot body hoaxes. There are no Bigfoot skeletons. There are no Bigfoot fossils. Bigfoot never shows up on wildlife trail cameras, even though trail camera pictures regularly show rare animals. Modern hunters have never killed one. Bigfoot is never hit by a car or truck. There are no Bigfoot droppings. In other words, every single type of evidence that would exist, and exist in quantities, if Bigfoot was real, does not exist.

Proponents argue that, on the one hand, Bigfoot is pretty much everywhere. But, when confronted with the lack of evidence, they claim that the creature stays only in the deepest unexplored woods where humans (almost) never go. Unfortunately for the proponents, such unexplored woods just do not exist in North America anymore. Hunters, hikers, and wildlife biologists get essentially everywhere. And professional woods people don't report seeing Bigfoot. Or finding bodies or any other physical evidence. Given this total lack of physical evidence, the personal reports, no doubt recounted with great sincerity, count for nothing, other than as yet more examples of how peoples' perceptions can be misled by their beliefs and expectations.

Bears are the animals that most resemble Bigfoots, especially when they stand on their hind legs, as they often do. Given this, it might be expected that Bigfoot sightings would be more common in areas where bears are more common. Foxon (2024) found exactly this relationship.

Bigfoot has enjoyed a surge in fame and popularity in recent years thanks to one of the silliest "reality" programs on TV—*Finding Bigfoot* on the Animal Planet channel since 2011. The program ended in 2017 with episode number 100. It was a fun program to watch one or two times. When the *Finding Bigfoot* team goes to some small town, they do not find Bigfoot but people who claim to have seen or heard Bigfoot in the local woods. Then, at night, they trek into the local woods to, well, find Bigfoot. They never find Bigfoot. What they find are odd noises in the night forest. Odd sights—a funny shadow here, or a seemingly moving something over there. Must be Bigfoot. These intrepid explorers of the nocturnal forest act as if there's nothing else in the forest at night that would move around and make noises like those they hear. No deer, racoons, foxes, skunks, possums, coyotes, or bear and owls. So after years of stomping around in the woods at night, perhaps it's time to admit that Bigfoot doesn't exist.

Bigfoot believers will find "evidence" for Bigfoot everywhere. In her book *Backyard Bigfoot* Lisa Shiel (2006) takes as evidence of the reality of Bigfoot sticks in mysterious patterns that she has found in the woods. Like sticks laying parallel to each other. Or sticks in an *X* pattern. Then there are the sticks in a sort of arrow shape. She even has pictures proving that these are real. There must be dozens of Bigfoots in the woods behind my house because every time I take the dog for a walk in those woods I can find sticks in exactly these same patterns. And many more patterns as well!

It is instructive to compare the lack of physical evidence for Bigfoot with the physical evidence for an actual large bipedal creature. The creature in question was a huge flightless bird, the moa, native to the wilds of New Zealand. There were several species of moa, some larger than a human. Despite being extinct for over five hundred years, there are copious amounts of moa bones, fossils, and other physical evidence (Berentson 2012) testifying to the existence of these impressive birds. Given this, the lack of any Bigfoot remains at all makes it abundantly clear that Bigfoot does not exist now and never has.

In the fall of 2012, the Bigfoot believers were ecstatic—finally, the real, undeniable scientific proof they had so long waited for was at hand. A reputable veterinarian had obtained multiple tissue samples from real Bigfoots, and scientific DNA analysis proved that the tissue was from an unknown humanoid species. Thus started the saga of Dr. Melba S. Ketchum. The full story is told by Sharon Hill (2013a) in much more detail than I have room for here. Major scientific breakthroughs are properly published in peer-reviewed scientific journals. Peer review is not perfect, but it is one way to screen out unfounded claims and sloppy research. But Ketchum didn't submit her findings to any journal. She issued a press release. This is a Bad Sign. No reputable scientist would issue a press release before submitting their research to peer review. The classic example in this regard is cold fusion, where Pons and Fleishman announced their "discovery" of cold fusion at a press conference.

For several years before Ketchum's press release, rumors and speculation had been swirling through the Bigfoot community. After the release, things went from bad to worse. Ketchum claimed to have submitted her article to one or more reputable scientific journals that would not publish it. Finally, in 2013 the article appeared in a brand-new journal called *DeNovo: Journal of Science*. However, as Hill (2013a) revealed, this was a made-up journal owned and operated by Ketchum herself. The article itself was little more than a joke. Independent scientists who read the article "reported a dismal opinion of it noting it made little sense" (Hill 2013a, 5). One of the references Ketchum cited as serious support for Bigfoot turned out to have been an April Fool's joke that Ketchum just didn't get. Ketchum also claimed that she had seen Bigfoots and that they braid the hair in horses' manes.

As of this writing (January 2024), no more has been heard from Ketchum in terms of her claimed DNA evidence. But it is clear that Bigfoot will continue to roam the forests of North America, at least in the imaginations of those determined to continue to believe despite the stunning lack of evidence.

Yeti, aka the abominable snowman, is the Himalayan version of Bigfoot. The quality of the evidence for the yeti is the same as that for Bigfoot. A few blurred photographs, the occasional bit of skin or hair, footprints in the snow, and the usual eyewitness reports. Again, no bodies and no good photographs. Loxton and Prothero (2013, 116) conclude that "many peoples of the Himalayas *know* and *admit* that Yeti is a myth, built on the foundation of the terrors of the Himalayan brown bear and then transmuted into their religious symbol" (emphasis in original).

Chupacabra

The chupacabra is a very recent addition to the pantheon of mysterious creatures. It is seen mostly in Central and South America. The first sighting was in 1995. Over the years the number of sightings increased, which resulted in, if not panic, certainly concern in various areas, especially Puerto Rico. One thing that led to the concern was the name of the creature, which translated from the Spanish means "goat sucker." The idea was that this was a sort of animal vampire. In addition to eyewitness reports, farmers reported finding dead animals with all the blood drained from their bodies. Further, bodies of mysterious dead animals that could not be identified, at least at first, were said to be proof of the reality of the chupacabra.

Paranormal investigator Benjamin Radford set out to determine whether the chupacabra was real. He reported the results of the research in his 2011 book *Tracking the Chupacabra*. Despite all the hoopla about the chupacabra, Redford found no evidence that there really was such a beast. The first sighting in 1995 was made by a Ms. Tolentino in Puerto Rico, whose description set the pattern for later reports. Radford found something very interesting regarding this first report. Ms. Tolentino's description of the creature that she had seen was nearly identical to the creature Sil in the science fiction/horror movie *Species*, which appeared in theaters a few weeks before the first sighting. And Ms. Tolentino had seen *Species* a few weeks before her chupacabra report. So either Ms. Tolentino had seen something that night she couldn't make out and misperceived it as Sil from *Species* or, by some incredible coincidence, a previously unknown creature that just happened to look very much like the movie creature (figure 13.2) was first spotted just a few weeks after the first witness saw the movie. Following the release of *Species*, eyewitness reports of chupacabra took off.

What about the alleged physical evidence such as the bloodless bodies of animals? How would you know that the body of a dead animal had been drained of all its blood? After a period of bloating, the body of a dead animal will tend to appear shrunken even though no blood has been drained. To determine whether the blood has actually been drained, it is necessary to perform at least a minimal autopsy—cut the body open to see if there is any blood left. In no case that Radford (2011) could find was any such investigation undertaken. It was merely assumed that the bodies found were bloodless. Radford also investigated the claims that chupacabra bodies had been found. What he found was misidentification of

Figure 13.2. Chupacabra. From Benjamin Radford, "Slaying the Vampire: Solving the Chupacabra Mystery," *Skeptical Inquirer* May/June 2011, figure 4 (https://skepticalinquirer.org/wp-content/uploads/sites/29/2011/05/p45.pdf)

dead dogs and coyotes. When an animal dies, the process of decomposition includes the hair sloughing off. This results in a very weird-looking body that can easily be misidentified as something unknown.

Radford's (2011) investigation of the chupacabra phenomenon represents the best analysis of any cryptozoological creature. He traced the early reports to a known source, the movie *Species*, showed that the claims of bloodless animal bodies were unfounded and that the dead chupacabras, when analyzed, sometimes using DNA, were just bodies of known animals. Like all good horror legends, reports of chupacabras will undoubtedly continue. But Radford's investigations have shown that these future reports will be traceable to similar errors of perception and interpretation.

There are, of course, other cryptozoological creatures out there other than those discussed above. There is the dinosaur that is said to live in the Congo River basin in Africa. And sea serpents, the Loch Ness monsters of the oceans. The interested reader can do no better than to consult the best analysis of cryptozoological creatures and why people continue to believe in them yet written, Loxton and Prothero's (2013) *Abominable Science*, which covers all the creatures described here and more. New Jersians will be especially interested to learn the nonparanormal origins of their own "Jersey devil" (Regal and Esposito 2018).

DOWSING AND THE MAGIC PENDULUM

Dowsers claim to be able to find underground water—and sometimes other substances such as oil or gold—by walking over the ground holding a forked stick, known as a *dowsing rod*. When the rod is felt to make sudden movements, seemingly on its own, that is an indication that the dowser is above a source of water or whatever is being sought. Dowsing is another excellent example of the ideomotor effect (Spitz 1997), which accounts for the movements of the Ouija board as described in chapter 3. Dowsing is an old and venerated folk tradition, especially in northern New England. In addition to predicting where water is, the dowser frequently also predicts the depth at which it will be found and the amount, or flow, to be found. The actions of the rod are vaguely ascribed to some sort of magnetic influence of the water, the psychic abilities of the dowser, or some combination of these. Some more modern dowsers have dispensed altogether with the need to actually walk over the land being dowsed and, instead, dowse over a map of the land in question.

A major factor in convincing people that dowsing works is the seemingly autonomous movements of the rod. As Vogt and Hyman (1979) describe, dowsing requires considerable physical effort: "The muscles and body of the diviner are under considerable tension. The rod is compressed with great force and this compression is maintained over a considerable period of time" (130). Even under normal conditions of muscle tension, the feedback from the muscles that tells the brain about the degree of muscular movement is far from perfect (Matthews 1982). The tension placed on the muscles during dowsing aggravates this situation, so the dowser is unable to feel the small muscle twitches that are responsible for the sudden movements of the rod. It is thus natural, although incorrect, to attribute these sudden movements to the rod itself and to feel that they occur without any intention on the part of the dowser.

Anecdotal eyewitness reports of the success of dowsers are a major source of supposed evidence that dowsing really works. Such reports should be viewed with considerable skepticism because, as has been pointed out many times previously, eyewitness reports are frequently extremely unreliable. There is an additional factor working to enhance dowsers' "successes" in anecdotal reports: selective memory. To quote Vogt and Hyman (1979, 41) again:

> We know a well-driller in Massachusetts who divines all the wells that he drills. This diviner, in an interview, recounted one success after another in his water witching career; he had not one failure to report. The driller's assistant, however, was skeptical about the value of water witching. He explained it away as "just imagination." In a separate interview, he told one story after another of failures that followed upon a diviner's advice. We had no reason to doubt the honesty or sincerity of either of these men. One was a believer, and, if we accepted his testimony at face value, water witching was invariably successful. From the skeptic's accounts, however, we would gather that water witching was very unreliable, and successes with it were matters of luck. Both these men were illustrating the tendency to recall only those incidents that are in accord with what we believe or would like to believe.

In addition, there is a large element of the multiple out in dowsers' predictions. A dowser may predict that water will be found at several locations. When water is found at any one of these, dowsing seems to have been successful. Since well drilling is likely to stop with the first successful well, later predictions that might well have turned out to be wrong won't be tested. In addition, multiple depths may be predicted, or the predicted depth may be very vague, as in "water will be found at a medium depth." In some areas of the country, one will almost invariably find water if one drills deep enough. In these areas, the dowser will almost always be right if the well goes down far enough. And, of course, vague depth predictions may be forgotten or "adjusted" to become more accurate after the fact. Finally, geological clues in the land help indicate where underground water may be found. Trained geologists can use these clues to increase their accuracy at predicting where to drill to a level above chance. The dowser may often have picked up these same clues and may use them while dowsing, consciously or unconsciously.

What is needed to properly evaluate the claims of dowsers are controlled studies done either in the laboratory or in the field. Vogt and Hyman (1979) reviewed many such studies. None of them showed any evidence that dowsers could find water. One study (Ongley 1948) examined a total of fifty-eight dowsers who claimed to be able to find water. None of them performed at a level better than chance. Other studies have had the same result. Vogt (1952) recorded the comparative numbers of dry and successful wells that had been drilled with and without the advice of dowsers. Of the twenty-nine wells drilled with dowsers' advice, twenty-four were successful. That sounds good, until one realizes that of the thirty-two wells drilled without dowsers' advice, twenty-five were successful. There is no statistically significant difference in the relative success rates of wells that were and were not drilled with input from dowsers. Randi (1979–1980) tested four Italian dowsers. A pattern of three underground pipes was buried (figure 13.3). Any one of the pipes could have water flowing through it. The dowsers' task was to trace the route of the one pipe that did have water flowing through it. The dowsers, who didn't know the route of any of the pipes, were totally unable to divine the route of the one with water in it.

A very large study carried out in Munich in the late 1980s (Wagner, Betz, and Konig 1990) examined the dowsing abilities of approximately five hundred self-proclaimed dowsers. The task was to locate pipes filled with water inside a building, a task all the dowsers agreed beforehand that they could do. The initial

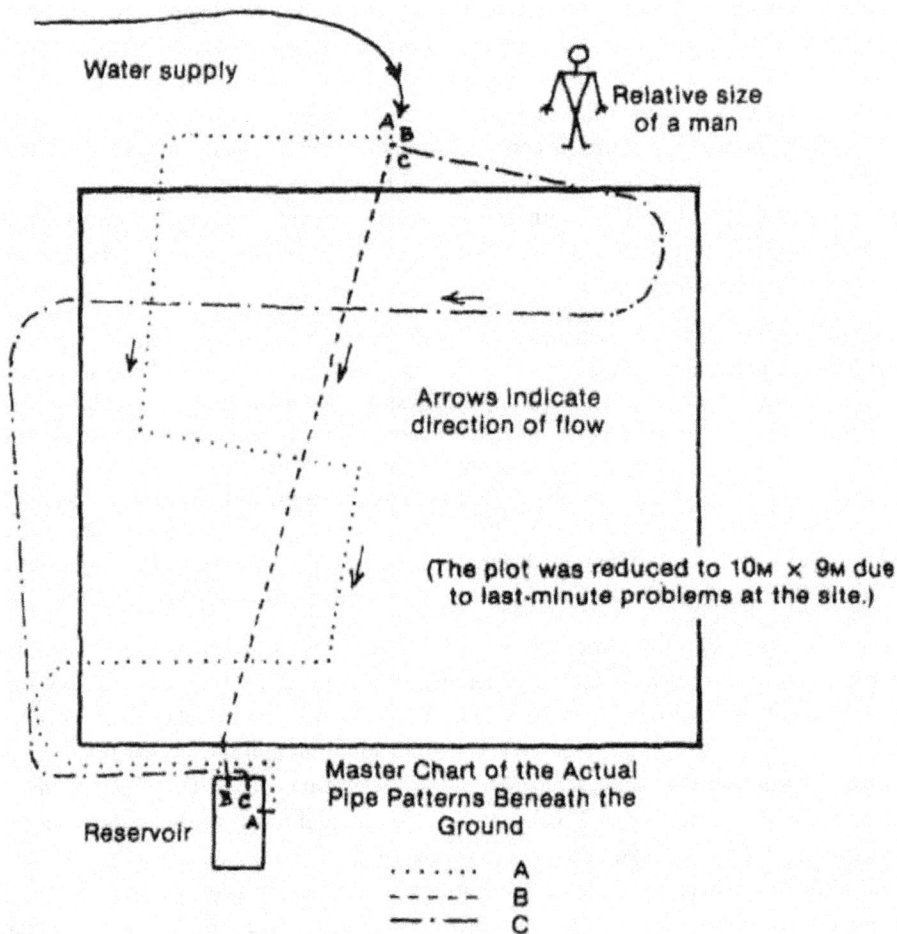

Figure 13.3. Layout of the water pipes used by Randi to test the claims of several dowsers. From Randi 1979–1980. Reprinted with permission

sample was reduced to forty-three individuals who were then more extensively tested. These forty-three were chosen because they showed some slight evidence of an ability to detect water in the pipes at a level above chance. None of the other 457 showed above-chance performance. How many of them showed below-chance performance was not reported.

A total of 843 tests were performed on the remaining forty-three dowsers. Of these, 833 tests showed no above-chance results. Only ten showed any effect that might be interpreted as evidence for the reality of dowsing. It was these ten that the experimenters, proponents of dowsing, used to argue that their study supported the reality of dowsing. Enright (1999, 46, emphasis in original) was certainly correct to conclude that "it is difficult to imagine a set of experimental results that would represent a more persuasive *disproof* of the ability of dowsers to do what they claim."

Dowsers typically try to find underground water. But other targets such as precious metals have also been sought for. At the more bizarre end of the dowsing spectrum is dowsing for corpses. Some dowsers claim to be able to find unmarked graves with the help of their dowsing rods. Whittaker (2006) reviewed instances where dowsers tried to find unmarked graves at archeological sites in Iowa. They couldn't. The dowsers did have a very high rate of false positives—they were excellent at "detecting" graves that weren't graves at all. Not one dowser detected any real, and previously unknown, grave. Whitaker (2006, 5) quotes one dowser as saying that when dowsing it was "useful to have two persons working together as one person continuously confirmed or challenged the findings of the other." Whitaker cogently comments that "in other words, dowsers obtained different, incompatible results if they did not constantly keep each other in check."

Especially when trying to detect water or metallic substances, dowsers claim that they are detecting, through their divining rods, some sort of changes in electromagnetic fields caused by the nearby water or metals. This claim was put to the test by Foulkes (1971). Dowsers were not able to find a buried highly magnetized cable even though the strength of the field exceeded almost any found in nature. Foulkes also tested what is known as "map dowsing." This is the presumed ability to locate objects by dowsing using a map rather than going to the bother of visiting an actual location. Studies were carried out by the British military to see whether dowsers could detect inert mines by dowsing a map of the area in which the mines were buried. They could not. The dowsers in these experiments had agreed in advance that the procedures were fair and that they would be highly accurate.

Smith (1981–1982) tested an Australian dowser named Holmes who claimed to be able to find both water and gold. The dowser failed to find water. During the testing of his ability to find gold, a significant occurrence took place:

> As is traditional in such tests, in full view of Holmes I placed the gold ingot in a box and asked him to see if his powers were working. Instead of going directly to the chosen box (as we expected him to), he walked up and down the row of boxes showing us that he received no reading from the empty boxes. He then mistook the correct box to be the one next to it and promptly divined the wrong box. His wife called out to him to "remember which box it was put in," but to no avail. (36–37)

Although it would be easy to laugh at this dowser who can't even find something when he's been shown where it is, this incident illustrates an important point. Dowsers' predictions are based on their beliefs. Holmes believed that the gold was in an empty box, and the rod promptly pointed to that empty box. If a dowser believes that water is to be found at a particular location, for whatever reason, the small muscular movements that cause the rod to move become more likely to occur at that location. Thus, both the movement of the rod and the place where those movements occur are internally generated although, because of the nature of the physiology of the kinesthetic system, the dowser will have no conscious appreciation of this fact.

Some dowsers don't use the traditional rod but rely on a pendulum, which can be any small object suspended from a string. A single key will do. The pendulum is held at arm's length and is said to swing back and forth under its own power, with no attempt to induce swinging on the part of the dowser. It swings when the dowser is over water or whatever substance is being searched for. The pendulum can also be used, it is said, to divine the sex of an unborn child: hold the pendulum over the mother's belly, and it will swing one way for a boy, the other for a girl. The pendulum has also been used to determine the guilt or innocence of an accused person and to reveal all sorts of hidden knowledge.

The pendulum seems to be swinging back and forth under its own power, and the one holding it claims, quite honestly, to be making no conscious attempts to influence its movement. As with the dowsing rod, small arm movements, which are not consciously registered in the brain, are responsible for the pendulum's movement. This can be demonstrated quite neatly by having the string that suspends the pendulum draped over some stationary object. Movement stops, even though the person is still holding the string and the pendulum is still free to swing. If there really were psychic forces causing its movement, it would continue to swing, but it does not. In an interesting experiment, Easton and Shor (1975) further demonstrated the nature of the pendulum's movement. In one condition, subjects could see the pendulum they were holding, in another they couldn't. Movement was greater when they could see it. Movement was even greater, by a factor of ten, when subjects were asked to imagine that the pendulum was moving, as opposed to when they were asked to imagine that it was not. Observing some other type of oscillating motion also increased the amount of pendulum movement. None of these effects would be expected if the pendulum's movement were caused by some psychic force. It was the French scientist Michel-Eugene Chevreul who, in 1812, carried out similar experiments showing that the movement of the pendulum was self-generated by the holder. A full English translation of his 1833 report of those experiments was published by Spitz and Marcuard (2001).

Tragically, dowsing-like devices have been marketed worldwide for detecting hidden bombs and explosives such as are used by terrorists. They were purchased and used by several governments in the Middle East and Africa. These devices, such as the ADE 651 manufactured in Great Britain, sold for upwards of thirty thousand dollars each. It had a movable wand attached to a small box that was said to contain sensitive electronic circuits that enabled it to detect explosives. In fact, the boxes "had no working electronics in them that could detect bombs or anything else" (Radford 2017b, 7). The complete failure of these devices led to numerous deaths. Happily, the "inventor" of the ADE 651, Jim McCormick, was sentenced to ten years in prison in 2013.

FIREWALKING

For years people have been amazed, or at least puzzled, by the ability of people in some "primitive" cultures to walk across beds of hot coals, usually during a religious celebration, without burning their feet. This ability is usually attributed to some vague power of "mind over matter." It was self-help huckster Tony Robbins who popularized firewalking in the United States in the 1970s. Robbins, one of numerous self-help gurus based in California, used firewalking as the gimmick in his self-help seminars. He persuaded thousands of people to walk across beds of red-hot coals without suffering burns. This was said to show the amazing power of the mind to prevent the feet from being burned as the basic laws of physics surely dictate they must.

In reality, it is those very basic laws of physics that prevent people's feet from being burned while firewalking. The power of the mind has nothing to do with it. Leikind and McCarthy (1985–1986) described the physics of firewalking and found that two well-known physical principles account for the rarity of burned feet. First there is the *Leidenfrost effect*. This is the effect seen when a drop of water darts about on a hot skillet. Between the skillet and the drop is a layer of steam that insulates the drop from the full heat of the skillet and prevents it from boiling away. In the firewalking situation, the soles of the feet are often damp from water on the grass surrounding the bed of coals. In many demonstrations of mass firewalking, the grass is hosed down around the bed of coals. The water on the soles provides a layer that helps to insulate the foot from the full heat of the coals.

But the Leidenfrost effect is not sufficient to explain the lack of burning. The material upon which one walks is a very important factor. Consider an example given by Leikind and McCarthy (1985–1986). You're baking something in a pan in the oven at 400 degrees. You open the oven to remove the pan. Naturally, you use a potholder to pick up the pan. If you were to try to pick it up with your bare hands, you'd be burned because it's at a temperature of 400 degrees—but so is the air in the oven, and that air certainly doesn't burn your hand, even if you leave it in the oven for a minute or so. Why not? The answer is that "different materials at the same temperature contain different amounts of thermal or heat energy and also have different abilities to carry the energy from one place to another" (29). Metal is high in both heat capacity and thermal conductivity, while air is low in both these variables. Thus, metal at 400 degrees will burn you immediately, while exposure to 400-degree air will have almost no immediate effect. What about the coals one walks on at a Robbins demonstration? Coals are hot (up to 1,200 degrees), but they have low heat capacity and thermal conductivity. Thus, if one walks rapidly over them, no burns will occur. Of course, if one lingers, burns can and do occur. Leikind and McCarthy found that firewalking as practiced by other cultures involves walking on material (coals or porous stone) that is low in both heat capacity and thermal conductance. It would be interesting to see if believers in the "mind over matter" explanation of firewalking would accept a challenge to walk barefoot over fifty feet of solid metal plates heated to 1,000 degrees. In the first season of their program *Bullshit* (episode 9, "Self-Helpless") Penn and Teller illustrate how firewalking can convince people that something amazing and life-changing is happening when they walk on hot coals.

POLYGRAPHY AND LIE DETECTION

The polygraph is used to measure three physiological parameters, heart rate, skin conductance, and breathing rate. The idea is that when a person is telling a lie they will become physiologically aroused and these three measures will change and be observable by the examiner. Polygraphs probably can detect nervousness, which leads to physiological arousal some of the time. However, it is obvious that not everyone is nervous when telling a lie and not everyone is calm when telling the truth. There is no simple correlation between a person's physiological state and whether they are telling the truth or not. Studies carried out both in a laboratory situation and in field situations, sometimes using actual criminals (e.g., Kleinmuntz and Szucko 1984), have shown that the polygraph is very inaccurate. In 2003 the National Research Council of the National Academy of Sciences published a comprehensive review of the studies of polygraph lie detection. Among the conclusions of this review was that "almost a century of research in scientific psychology and physiology provides little basis for the expectation that a polygraph test could have extremely high accuracy" (National Research Council 2003, 212). Further, the field of polygraph research "has not progressed over time in the manner of a typical scientific field. It has not accumulated knowledge or strengthened its scientific underpinnings in any significant manner" (213). This is one of the characteristics of a pseudoscience. Even if a polygraph test could be better than chance at detecting deception, it would not add any "incremental validity . . . that is, its ability to add predictive value to that which can be achieved by other methods" (214).

The major reason that polygraph examinations are so problematic is the way the results of the test are interpreted. The results are patterns of squiggly lines, either on physical paper or on a computer screen. There is no objective, quantifiable measure or measures associated with these squiggly lines. The "expert" polygraph examiner looks at the whole record, which may consist of many minutes of squiggly lines, and judges whether the person is truthful or not. Here again selective perception can and does play a huge role. An examiner primed to believe that a person is deceptive can easily pick out, from the great quantity of squiggly lines, segments that "prove" deception. Conversely, if the examiner feels that the individual is truthful, segments of the record that show "truthfulness" will be highlighted.

Until the late 1980s, one common use of polygraphs was not in criminal investigations but in employment situations. Firms, especially those like jewelry stores and banks, where employee theft could be a large problem, used polygraphs to assess prospective employees' honesty. Polygraphs were also used in internal investigations within a company. In 1986 the CBS television program *60 Minutes* broadcast an excellent example of the problems with such polygraph use. Several polygraph firms were called by CBS and told that there had been a theft of some valuable television equipment and that several CBS employees were suspected. Each firm was asked to come and examine the suspects. In fact, there had been no theft, and all the "suspects" knew that they were taking part in an experiment. Each polygraph operator was given a hint that one person was the leading suspect, but the hint concerned a different employee for each operator. The operators in each case identified the "leading suspect" as the guilty party. Not one operator failed to make this incorrect judgment. They interpreted the squiggly lines to confirm their preconceived beliefs. A 1988 federal law prohibited the use of polygraphs for employment decisions or for evaluations, such as for honesty, during employment. Exceptions to the law allowed the use of polygraphs by some government agencies.

Polygraphs are still often used by police in criminal investigations. This is more to frighten suspects into confessing than to produce evidence. The National Research Council (2003) review concluded that "polygraph examinations may have utility to the extent that they can elicit admissions and confessions. . . . However, such utility is separate from polygraph validity" (214). It should be recognized that in 2003, when the report was published, the problem of false confessions had not yet been widely recognized. Polygraph results have limited admissibility in United States courts. In the case of *U.S. v. Scheffer* (523 US 303), the Supreme Court left the decision as to whether to admit polygraph evidence to the discretion of the individual courts. Such evidence is banned in many states.

Unjustified reliance on polygraph examinations has let numerous criminals go undetected. Aldrich Ames was a CIA officer who, in the 1980s, passed several lie detector tests while he was betraying at least ten Russians who were working for the CIA to the Soviet KGB. Several of these agents were executed. Various other American traitors also passed lie detector tests. Gary Ridgeway, the Green River serial killer (Guillen 2006), passed a lie detector test when he was suspected and went on to kill several more women in the 1990s. Polygraphs were widely used to intimidate innocent U.S. government scientists in an investigation of the supposed release of nuclear secrets from government laboratories in 1999 (Zelicoff 2001).

Despite the serious problems with lie detectors as indicators of truthfulness, one will hear that some defendant in a criminal or civil case took and "passed" a lie detector test. Lie detectors have also been used in alleged cases of UFO abductions and sightings where passing a lie detector test is said to verify that the UFO encounter really took place. Such claims are without foundation.

Closely related to the polygraph is the voice stress analyzer, which had a period of popularity in the 1970s. By detecting certain frequencies in the human voice, it was said to be possible to determine whether people were telling the truth. The beauty of such a system was that the person didn't even have to be present for the method to be used. It could be used on a voice coming in by phone or even on a tape recording of a voice. Highly exaggerated claims for the validity of voice stress analysis were made, largely by representatives of firms selling voice stress analyzers at up to $4,400 each. Lykken's (1981) review of the research showed that voice stress analysis was useless. Biddle's (1986, 25) comment that the polygraph is "an unreliable, pseudo-scientific thingamabob" applies with even greater force to the voice stress analyzer. Making polygraph use illegal in private employment has not eliminated the use of this pseudoscientific gadget in other circumstances. It seems that in almost every high-profile case (e.g., O. J. Simpson, Chandra Levy, etc.) one or more of the participants asks to take a lie detector test.

The results are then used to "prove" the individual's lack of involvement. Of course, if the test turned out negative, we would never hear of the results. In either case, the results are worthless as an indication of the truth.

Employers eager for a quick fix to the problem of dishonest workers can replace the mechanical lie detector with equally dubious paper-and-pencil tests for honesty. These tests "suffer from the same shortcomings" as their mechanical cousins (Lilienfeld 1993–1994, 32).

Attempts have also been made to use functional neuroimaging (fMRI) as a lie detector. fMRI is one of the great advances in the study of the human brain. It shows which brain areas are active when people are doing cognitive (or motor) tasks. fMRI studies have provided an incredible amount of information on brain function in general and the different areas of the brain that are involved in specific cognitive processes. However, the use of fMRI relies on studies of groups of individuals. This is because there is some variance in the location of the brain areas that underly different cognitive functions in different people. It is this variance that prevents the fMRI from being any better than the old low-tech polygraph. Just as some people will show certain physiological changes when lying and some won't, in some people certain brain areas may become active when they're not telling the truth, but in some those areas will not respond. The problems with ensuring that the results of scans on individuals determine whether they're telling the truth are daunting. Although several firms have marketed what they claim are valid fMRI measures of truthfulness, the science shows these claims to be bogus. Rusconi and Mitchener-Nissen (2013, 1) conclude that the use of fMRI technology "meets neither basic legal nor scientific standards" and that the technology is "unlikely to constitute a viable lie detector for criminal courts." Similarly, Roskies (2015, 692) argues that fMRI technology is "not sufficiently well developed to use [as] lie detection for incrimination or even for screening." It seems to me that it never will be.

THE SHROUD OF TURIN

The Shroud of Turin (see figure 3.4) is said to be the burial cloth of Jesus Christ and to have on it a miraculous image of Christ that could not have been produced by any nonsupernatural method. The Shroud of Turin Research Project claims that scientific analysis of the shroud substantiates its miraculous nature. But the claims made for the shroud do not stand up to close inspection. The following discussion is based on Nickell's (1999) book-length evaluation of the evidence for the shroud's authenticity and his later article (Nickell 2001b). McCrone (1999) is another excellent source.

Where did the shroud come from? If it is genuine, it should be possible to trace its history back to the time of Christ. But this is not possible. The shroud first appeared in Lirey, France, during the 1300s, where it was displayed in a church and the claim was made that it was the burial cloth of Christ. As might be expected, it attracted considerable attention—so much attention, in fact, that Henri de Poitiers, the bishop of Troyes, ordered an investigation of the shroud. A report of this investigation was sent to the pope in 1389. Parts of that report are quoted by Nickell (1999, 12):

> The case, Holy Father, stands thus. Some time since in this diocese of Troyes the Dean of a certain collegiate church, to wit, that of Lirey, falsely and deceitfully, being consumed with the passion of avarice, and not from any motive of devotion but only of gain, procured for his church a certain cloth cunningly painted, upon which by a clever sleight of hand was depicted the twofold image of one man, that is to say, the back and front, he falsely declaring and pretending that this was the actual shroud in which our Saviour Jesus Christ was enfolded in the tomb. This story was put about not only in the kingdom of France, but, so to speak, throughout the world, so that from all parts people came together to view it. And further to attract the multitude so that money might be cunningly wrung from them, pretended miracles were worked, certain men being hired to represent themselves as healed at the moment of the exhibition of the shroud, which all believed to be the shroud of our Lord.

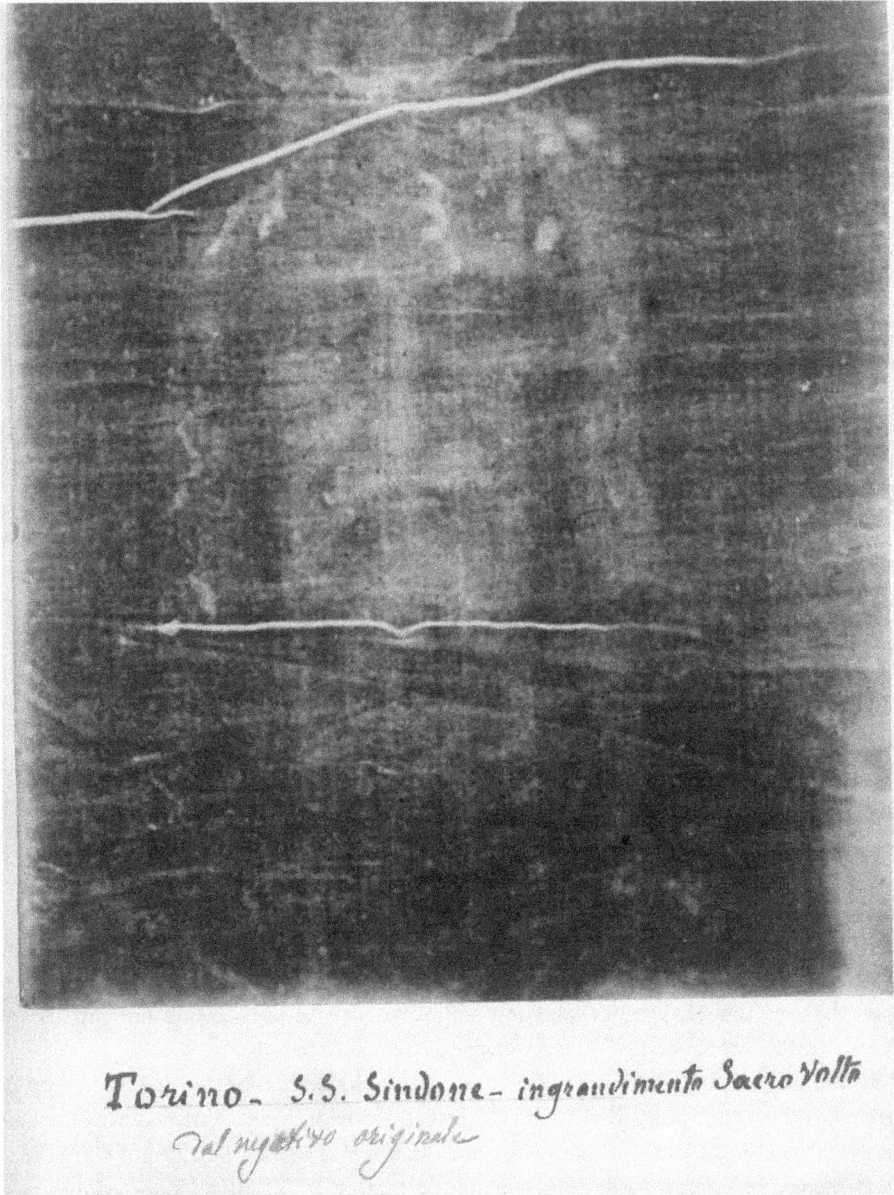

Figure 13.4. Shroud of Turin: an 1898 photographic negative by Secondo Pia of the head on the shroud. Photo by Secundo Pia from Musée de l'Élysée, Lausanne, 1898, Wikimedia Commons (https://en.m.wikipedia.org/wiki/File:Secundo_Pia_Turinske_platno_1898.jpg). PD-US

Thus, the Shroud of Turin came into existence.

Even if this report were not available, one fact would cast strong doubt on the authenticity of the shroud: it is not mentioned in the Bible. The Bible does mention that Christ's body was wrapped for burial, but the type of burial cloth used at the time in Jewish burials was very different from the shroud. The shroud is a single fourteen-foot-long piece that would have had to cover the body over the head, according to the position of the images. Jewish burial custom dictated that a separate cloth had to be used to cover the face of the dead. Further, the Bible does not mention any finding of an image on Christ's burial garments after the Resurrection. Presumably the existence of such a miraculous image would not have escaped the notice of those who entered the tomb following Christ's rising. One aspect of the image itself also poses serious problems for claims that the shroud is authentic. The image shows the hair on the head in fairly well-defined curls. But Christ had bled from the application of the crown of thorns to his scalp. The scalp bleeds profusely, and the application of liquid of any kind to the hair causes it to mat down. Thus, the curls in the hair would not be visible, either because of the blood matting the hair or because any fluid used to clean the body for burial would have had the same matting effect.

Red bloodstains are said to be present on the shroud. There are red markings on the shroud, but they are not blood. For one thing, as blood ages and dries it rapidly (within days) turns black. Precise analysis of the material that makes up the "bloodstains" on the shroud reveals that it is made up of vermilion and a red iron earth, the "two most popular red pigments" used by artists in the 1300s (Nickell 1999, 130). Shroud of Turin Research Project scientists Pellicori (1980) and Heller and Adler (1980) have claimed to find actual blood on the shroud. This finding, even if true, would not prove the shroud authentic, as the artist could easily have added blood, even human blood, to the other pigments used to create the image. However, the tests used that were claimed to indicate the presence of blood are not specific to blood. The tests will react positively in the presence of other organic materials—and organic materials that cause the tests to react positively were widely used by artists of the 1300s. For example, pigments were often put in a solution of egg tempera and then painted on whatever surface was to have an image applied. Egg tempera produces test results like those produced by blood in the tests used by Pellicori (1980) and Heller and Adler (1980), as noted by Fischer (1983).

Nickell's (1999) analysis shows that the image on the shroud was not just painted on. To paint such an image would be very difficult. How, then, was the image produced? A simple rubbing technique was used in which a piece of cloth is placed over a bas relief and pigment is then applied. Using just such a simple technique, Nickell (1978, 1999) was able to produce images that look exactly like the image on the shroud. They even duplicate the "photographic negative" quality of the shroud image that proponents of the authenticity of the shroud state could not have been produced by any artistic means. The rubbing technique was known to artists as early as the 1100s (Mueller 1981–1982), more than two hundred years before the shroud appeared.

The shroud appeared at a time when the manufacture, sale, and collection of Christian relics was big business (Nickell 1993). It has been said that there were enough pieces of the True Cross floating around Europe at the time to build the ark. Wealthy nobles and merchants collected relics. There were many other shrouds to be found in Europe; the Shroud of Turin is simply the most famous.

The conclusion from the historical and scientific analysis of the shroud is clear: it is a fake relic created sometime in the early or mid-1300s. In 1989 this conclusion was dramatically confirmed by carbon dating of the shroud (Damon et al. 1989). Until that time the church had not permitted any such testing of the shroud. The results dated the shroud to the year 1325, plus or minus sixty-five years.

In the Middle Ages the collection and veneration of religious relics of all sorts, from images of Christ to the bones of saints, were important religious activities. The Shroud of Turin is far from the only supposedly miraculous relic related to Christ to be found. Nickell (2007b) discusses numerous other relics of Christ. Weeping icons, the blood of saints that miraculously turns from a solid to a liquid, and other supposedly paranormal religious objects that have attracted attention through the ages. When investigated carefully, they turn out to be hoaxes or to have nonparanormal explanations (Nickell 1993).

REFERENCES

Aaronovitch, D. 2010. *Voodoo histories*. New York: Riverhead.

Abbott-Imboden, C., Y. Gonzalez, and A. Utley. 2023. Efficacy of the nootropic supplement Mind Lab Pro on memory in adults: Double blind placebo-controlled study. *Human Psychopharmacology: Clinical and Experimental* 38 (4): e2872.

Abell, G. 1981a. Astrology. In *Science and the paranormal*, ed. G. Abell and B. Singer, 70–94. New York: Charles Scribner's Sons.

———. 1981b. Moon madness. In *Science and the paranormal*, ed. G. Abell and B. Singer, 95–104. New York: Charles Scribner's Sons.

Abell, G., and B. Greenspan. 1979. Human births and the phase of the moon. *New England Journal of Medicine* 300:96.

Abell, G., and B. Singer, eds. 1981. *Science and the paranormal*. New York: Charles Scribner's Sons.

Abheiden, H., M. Teut, and A. Berghofer. 2020. Predictors of the use and approval of CAM: Results from the German General Social Survey. *BMC Complementary Medicine and Therapies* 20:183.

Acunzo, D. J., R. Evard, and T. Rabeyron. 2013. Anomalous experiences, psi and functional imaging. *Frontiers in Human Neuroscience* 7:893.

Adair, R. K. 1991. Constraints of biological effects of weak, extremely low-frequency electromagnetic fields. *Physical Review A* 43:1039–48.

———. 2003. Biophysical limits on athermal effects of RF and microwave radiation. *Bioelectromagnetics* 24:39–48.

Aggeborn, L., and M. Ohman. 2016. The effects of fluoride in the drinking water. In *Essays in cognitive development and medical care*, ed. M. Ohman. Uppsala, Sweden: Uppsala University Publications.

Ahuja, A. 2019. An evidence deficit haunts the billion-dollar brain training industry. *Financial Times*, January 23.

Akers, C. 1984. Methodological criticisms of parapsychology. In *Advances in parapsychological research*, ed. S. Krippner, vol. 4, 112–64. Jefferson, NC: McFarland.

Alberini, C. M., and A. Travaglia. 2017. Infantile amnesia: A critical period of learning to learn and remember. *Journal of Neuroscience* 37:5783–95.

Alcock, J. E. 1978–1979. Psychology and near-death experiences. *Skeptical Inquirer* 3 (3): 23–41.

———. 1981. *Parapsychology: Science or magic?* Oxford: Pergamon Press.

———. 1985. Parapsychology: The "spiritual" force. *Free Inquiry* 5 (2): 25–35.

———. 2011. Back from the future: Parapsychology and the Bem affair. *Skeptical Inquirer* 35 (2): 31–39.

———. 2018. *Belief: What it means to believe and why our convictions are so compelling*. Amherst, NY: Prometheus Books.

Alexander, D. 1990. Giving the devil more than his due. *Humanist* 50 (2): 5–14, 34.

Alexander, E. 2012. *Proof of heaven*. New York: Simon & Schuster.

Alison, L., C. Bennell, and A. Mokros. 2002. The personality paradox in offender profiling: A theoretical review of the processes involved in deriving background characteristics from crime scene actions. *Psychology, Public Policy, and Law* 8:115–35.

Allen, J., S. S. Mak, M. Begashaw, J. Larkin, I. Miake-Lye, J. Beroes-Severin, J. Olson, and P. G. Shekelle. 2022. Use of acupuncture for adult health conditions, 2013 to 2021: A systematic review. *JAMA Network Open* 5 (11): e2243665. doi:10.1001/jamanetworkopen.2022.43665.

Alter, A. 1973. The pyramid and food dehydration. *New Horizons* 1:92–94.

Anastasi, A. 1988. *Psychological testing.* 6th edition. New York: Macmillan.

Andreotti, G., S. Koutros, J. N. Hofmann, D. P. Sandler, J. H. Lubin, C. F. Lynch, C. C. Lerro, et al. 2018. Glyphosate use and cancer incidence in the Agricultural Health Study. *Journal of the National Cancer Institute* 110:509–16.

Angell, M. 1997. *Science on trial.* New York: Norton.

Angell, M., and J. P. Kassirer. 1998. Alternative medicine: The risks of untested and unregulated remedies. *New England Journal of Medicine* 339:839–41.

Angus, M. 1973. The rejection of two explanations of belief in a lunar influence on behavior. Master's thesis, Simon Fraser University.

Anonymous. 1882. *Confessions of a medium.* London: Griffith and Farran.

———. 1990. Unproven methods of cancer management: "Psychic surgery." *CA: A Cancer Journal for Clinicians* 40:184–88.

———. 2002. New York in quarantine? Failed predictions for 1999. *Skeptical Inquirer* 24 (2): 6.

Anson, J. 1977. *The Amityville horror.* Englewood Cliffs, NJ: Prentice-Hall.

Antrobus, J. 1978. Dreaming for cognition. In *The mind in sleep: Psychology and psychophysiology*, ed. A. Arkin, J. Antrobus, and S. Ellman, 569–81. Hillsdale, NJ: Lawrence Erlbaum Associates.

Apaydin, E. A., A. R. Maher, R. Shanman, M. S. Booth, J. N. V. Miles, M. E. Sorbero, and S. Hempel. 2016. A systematic review of St. John's wort for major depressive disorder. *Systematic Reviews* 5:148.

Arnetz, B., J. Wasserman, B. Petrini, S.-O. Brenner, L. Levi, P. Eneroth, H. Salovaara, R. Hjelm, L. Salovaara, and T. Theorell. 1987. Immune function in unemployed women. *Psychosomatic Medicine* 49:3–12.

Atkins, T., and J. Baxter. 1976. *The fire came by.* Garden City, NY: Doubleday.

Atwood, K. C., IV. 2003. Naturopathy: A critical appraisal. *Medscape General Medicine* 5 (4): 39.

Augustine, K. C. 2015. Near death experiences are hallucinations. In *The myth of an afterlife*, ed. M. Martin and K. Augustine, 529–69. Lanham, MD: Rowman & Littlefield.

Augustine, K., and Y. I. Fishman. 2015. Dualist's dilemma. In *The myth of an afterlife*, ed. M. Martin and K. Augustine, 203–92. Lanham, MD: Rowman & Littlefield.

Baggoley, C. 2015. *Review of the Australian government rebate on natural therapies for private health insurance.* Canberra, Australia: Australian Department of Health.

Baker, R. A. 1996. *Hidden memories: Voices and visions from within.* Amherst, NY: Prometheus Books.

———, ed. 1998. *Child sexual abuse and false memory syndrome.* Amherst, NY: Prometheus Books.

Baloh, R. W., and R. E. Bartholomew. 2022. *Havana syndrome.* Cham, Switzerland: Springer.

Balon, J., P. D. Aker, E. R. Crowther, C. Danielson, P. G. Cox, D. O'Shaughnessy, C. Walker, C. H. Goldsmith, E. Duku, and M. R. Sears. 1998. A comparison of active and simulated chiropractic manipulation as adjunctive treatment for childhood asthma. *New England Journal of Medicine* 339:1013–20.

Bandura, A. 1969. *Principles of behavior modification.* New York: Holt, Rinehart and Winston.

Barbarawi, M., B. Kheiri, Y. Zayed, O. Barbarawi, H. Dhillon, B. Swaid, A. Yelangi, et al. 2019. Vitamin D supplementation and cardiovascular disease risks in more than 83000 individuals in 21 randomized clinical trials. *JAMA Cardiology* 4 (8): 765–76.

Barber, P. 2010. *Vampires, burial, and death.* New Haven, CT: Yale University Press.

Barden, R. C. 2018. Multi-disciplinary, science intensive litigation reforms protect the integrity of the legal system. In *The psychology and sociology of wrongful convictions*, ed. W. J. K. Koen and C. M. Bowers, 129–50. London: Academic Press.

Barker, D. 1956. *They knew too much about flying saucers.* New York: University Books.

———. 1979a. Correspondence. *Journal of Parapsychology* 43:268–69.

———. 1979b. Rakesh Gaur: A case of reincarnation in India. *Journal of Parapsychology* 43:56.

Barnes, J. 2022. Many U.F.O. sightings are just drones or trash. *New York Times*, October 29, A17.

Barrett, S. 1985. Commercial hair analysis: Science or scam? *JAMA* 254:1041–45.

Barrett, S., and R. E. Gots. 1998. *Chemical sensitivity: The truth about environmental illness*. Amherst, NY: Prometheus Books.

Bartholomew, R. E. 1998. Michigan and the great mass hysteria episode of 1897. *Michigan Historical Review* 24 (1): 133–40.

———. 2001. *Little green men, meowing nuns, and head-hunting panics: A study of mass psychogenic illness and social delusion*. Jefferson, NC: McFarland.

———. 2012. *The untold story of Champ: A social history of America's Loch Ness monster*. Albany: State University of New York Press.

Bartholomew, R. E., and G. S. Howard. 1998. *UFOs and alien contact*. Amherst, NY: Prometheus Books.

Bartholomew, R. E., and B. Rickard. 2014. *Mass hysteria in schools*. Jefferson, NC: McFarland.

Bartholomew, R. E., and J. S. Victor. 2004. A social-psychological theory of collective anxiety attacks: The "Mad Gasser" reexamined. *Sociological Quarterly* 45:229–48.

Bass, E., and L. Davis. 1988. *Courage to heal: A guide for women survivors of child sexual abuse*. New York: Harper & Row.

Battista, C., N. Gauvrit, and E. LeBel. 2015. Madness in the method: Fatal flaws in recent mediumship experiments. In *The myth of an afterlife*, ed. M. Martin and K. Augustine, 615–30. Lanham, MD: Rowman & Littlefield.

Bauer, H. H. 1986. *The enigma of Loch Ness: Making sense of a mystery*. Eugene OR: Resource Publications.

Baum, R., and W. Sheehan. 1997. *In search of planet Vulcan*. New York: Plenum Press.

Beaumont, J., A. Young, and I. McManus. 1984. Hemisphericity: A critical review. *Cognitive Neuropsychology* 1:191–212.

Beck, J., A. E. Elsner, and C. Silverstein. 1977. Position uncertainty and the perception of apparent motion. *Perception and Psychophysics* 21:33–38.

Beck, R. 2015. *We believe the children: A moral panic in the 1980s*. New York: Public Affairs.

Becquerel, J. 1934. *Notice sur les travaux scientific de M. Jean Becquerel*. Paris: Gauthier-Villars.

Bediou, B., D. M. Adams, R. E. Mayer, E. Tipton, C. S. Green, and D. Bavelier. 2018. Meta-analysis of action video game impact on perceptual, attentional and cognitive skills. *Psychological Bulletin* 144:77–110.

Beischel, J., and G. Schwartz. 2007. Anomalous information reception by research mediums demonstrated using a novel triple blind protocol. *Explore: The Journal of Science and Healing* 3:23–27.

Beloff, J. 1973. *Psychological sciences*. London: Crosby Lockwood Staples.

Belvedere, E., and D. Foulkes. 1971. Telepathy and dreams: A failure to replicate. *Perceptual and Motor Skills* 33:783–89.

Bem, D. 2011. Feeling the future: Experimental evidence for anomalous retroactive influences on cognition and affect. *Journal of Personality and Social Psychology* 100:407–25.

Bem, D., and C. Honorton. 1994. Does psi exist? Replicable evidence for an anomalous process of information transfer. *Psychological Bulletin* 115:4–18.

Ben, J. C. 1970. Photographs from Cradle Hill. *Flying Saucer Review* 16 (4): 4–5.

Benedetti, F. 2014. *Placebo effects*. 2nd ed. Oxford: Oxford University Press.

Ben-Shakhar, G., M. Bar-Hillel, Y. Bilu, E. Ben-Abba, and A. Flug. 1986. Can graphology predict occupational success? Two empirical studies and some methodological ruminations. *Journal of Applied Psychology* 71:645–53.

Ben-Shakhar, G., M. Bar-Hillel, and A. Flug. 1986. A validation study of graphological evaluation in personnel selection. In *Scientific aspects of graphology*, ed. B. Nevo, 175–91. Springfield, IL: Charles C. Thomas.

Benson, H., J. A. Dusek, J. B. Sherwood, P. Lam, C. F. Bethea, W. Carpenter, S. Levitsky, et al. 2006. Study of the therapeutic effects of intercessory prayer (STEP) in cardiac bypass patients. *American Heart Journal* 151:934–42.

Benveniste, J. 1988. Benveniste on *Nature* investigation. *Science* 241:1028.

Berde, C. B., and N. F. Sethna. 2002. Analgesics for the treatment of pain in children. *New England Journal of Medicine* 347:1094–1103.

Berentson, Q. 2012. *Moa: The life and death of New Zealand's legendary bird*. Nelson, New Zealand: Craig Potton.

Berlinger, D. 1977. Project Blue Book. *Science Digest*, August, 24–28.

Berlinguette, C. P., Y.-M. Chiang, J. N. Munday, T. Schenkel, D. K. Fork, R. Koningstein, and M. D. Trevithick. 2019. Revisiting the cold case of cold fusion. *Nature* 570:45–51.

Berlitz, C. 1974. *The Bermuda Triangle mystery*. Garden City, NY: Doubleday.

———. 1977. *Without a trace*. Garden City, NY: Doubleday.

Berman, J., and N. Norton. 1985. Does professional training make a therapist more effective? *Psychological Bulletin* 98:401–7.

Bernstein, E. 1982. Lourdes. In *Encyclopaedia Britannica 1982 Medicine and Health Yearbook*, 129–47. Chicago: Encyclopaedia Britannica.

Bernstein, M. 1956. *The search for Bridey Murphy*. Garden City, NY: Doubleday.

Bettelheim, B. 1967. *Empty fortress: Infantile autism and the birth of the self*. New York: Free Press.

Beyerstein, B. L. 1997. Why bogus therapies seem to work. *Skeptical Inquirer* 21 (5): 29–34.

———. 1999. Social and judgmental biases that make inert treatments seem to work. *Scientific Review of Alternative Medicine* 3 (2): 20–34.

———. 2007. Graphology—a total write-off. In *Tall tales about the mind and brain*, ed. S. Della Sala, 232–70. Oxford: Oxford University Press.

Beyerstein, B. L., and D. F. Beyerstein. 1992. *The write stuff: Evaluations of graphology—the study of handwriting analysis*. Amherst, NY: Prometheus Books.

Beyerstein, B. L., and S. Downie. 2000. Naturopathy. In *Science meets alternative medicine*, ed. W. Sampson and L. Vaughn, 141–63. Amherst, NY: Prometheus Books.

Beyerstein, D. 2000. Replication of TT research: A case study. In *Therapeutic Touch*, ed. B. Scheiber and C. Selby, 245–61. Amherst, NY: Prometheus Books.

Biddle, W. 1986. The deception of detection. *Discover*, March, 24–26, 28–31, 33.

Bierman, D. J., and H. S. Scholte. 2002. A fMRI brain imaging study of presentiment. *Journal of the International Society of Life Information Science* 20:380–89.

Biesiekierski, J. R., S. L. Peters, E. D. Newnham, O. Rosella, J. G. Muir, and P. R. Gibson. 2013. No effects of gluten in patients with self-reported non-celiac gluten sensitivity after dietary reduction of fermentable, poorly absorbed, short-chain carbohydrates. *Gastroenterology* 145:320–28.

Binns, R. 1984. *The Loch Ness mystery solved*. Amherst, NY: Prometheus Books.

Blackmore, S. 1983. Divination with tarot cards: An empirical study. *Journal of the Society for Psychical Research* 52:97–101.

———. 1985. Belief in the paranormal: Probability judgements, illusory control, and the "chance baseline shift." *British Journal of Psychology* 76:459–68.

———. 1986a. *Adventures of a parapsychologist*. Amherst, NY: Prometheus Books.

———. 1986b. Making of a skeptic. *Fate*, April, 69–75.

———. 1986–1987. The elusive open mind: Ten years of negative research in parapsychology. *Skeptical Inquirer* 11:244–55.

———. 1992. *Beyond the body*. Chicago: Academy Press.

———. 1993. *Dying to live*. Amherst, NY: Prometheus Books.

Blanke, O., and S. Arzy. 2005. The out-of-body experience: Disturbed self-processing at the temporo-parietal junction. *Neuroscientist* 11:16–24.

Blanke, O., T. Landis, L. Spinelli, and M. Seeck. 2004. Out-of-body experience and autoscopy of neurological origin. *Brain* 127 (2): 243–58.

Blanke, O., S. Ortigue, T. Landis, and M. Seeck. 2002. Stimulating illusory own-body perceptions. *Nature* 419:269–70.

Blease, C., and I. Kirsch. 2016. The placebo effect in psychotherapy: Implications for theory, practice and research. *Psychology of Consciousness: Theory, Research and Practice* 3:105–7.

Blinderman, C. 1986. *The Piltdown inquest*. Amherst, NY: Prometheus Books.

Blume, E. S. 1990. *Secret survivors: Uncovering incest and its aftereffects in women*. New York: Ballantine.

Blumenthal, R. 2013. Alien nation—have humans been abducted by extraterrestrials? *Vanity Fair*, May 10.

Bolland, M. J., A. Grey, and A. Avenell. 2018. Effects of vitamin D supplementation on musculoskeletal health. *Lancet: Diabetes and Endocrinology* 6:847–58.

Bonanno, G. A., A. D. Mancini, J. L. Horton, T. M. Powell, C. A. Leardmann, E. J. Boyko, T. S. Wells, et al. 2012. Trajectories of trauma symptoms and resilience in deployed US military service members: Prospective cohort study. *British Journal of Psychiatry* 200:317–23.

Bootzin, R., G. Bower, R. Zajonc, and E. Hall. 1986. *Psychology today: An introduction*. 6th edition. New York: Random House.

Bornschein, S., C. Hausteiner, H. Rommelt, D. Nowak, H. Förstl, and T. Zilker. 2008. Double-blind placebo-controlled provocation study in patients with subjective multiple chemical sensitivity (MCS) and matched control subjects. *Clinical Toxicology* 46:443–49.

Bouvet, R., and J.-F. Bonnefon. 2015. Non-reflective thinkers are predisposed to attribute supernatural causation to uncanny experiences. *Personality and Social Psychology Bulletin* 41:955–61.

Bowers, C. M. 2017. Bite mark evidence. In *Forensic science reform: Protecting the innocent*, ed. W. J. Koen and C. M. Bowers, 145–65. Amsterdam: Elsevier/Academic.

Bowes, S. M., T. H. Costello, W. Ma, and S. O. Lilienfeld. 2021. Looking under the tinfoil hat: Clarifying the personological and psychopathological correlates of conspiracy beliefs. *Journal of Personality* 89:422–36.

Bowes, S. M., T. H. Costello, and A. Tasimi. 2023. Conspiratorial mind: A meta-analysis of motivational and personological correlates. *Psychological Bulletin* 149 (5–6): 259–93.

Boyle, E. W. 2013. *Quack medicine: A history of combating health fraud in twentieth-century America*. Santa Barbara, CA: Praeger.

Brainerd, C. J., and V. F. Reyna. 2005. *The science of false memory*. New York: Oxford University Press.

Braithwaite, J. J., and H. Dewe. 2015. Occam's chain saw: Neuroscientific nails in the coffin of dualist notions of the near-death experience (NDE). *Skeptic* 25 (2): 24–31.

Brandon, R. 1983. *The spiritualists*. New York: Alfred A. Knopf.

Brascher, A.-K., K. Raymaekers, O. Van den Bergh, and M. Witthoft. 2017. Are media reports able to cause somatic symptoms attributed to WiFi radiation? An experimental test of the negative expectation hypothesis. *Environmental Research* 156:265–71.

Bratt, B. 1989. *No time for Jello*. Cambridge, MA: Brookline Books.

Breger, L., I. Hunter, and R. Lane. 1971. Effect of stress on dreams. *Psychological Issues* 7 (3): monograph 27.

Brien, S., L. LaChance, P. Prescott, C. McDermott, and G. Lewith. 2011. Homeopathy has clinical benefits on rheumatoid arthritis patients that are attributable to the consultation process but not the homeopathic remedy: A randomized controlled clinical trial. *Rheumatology* 50:1070–82.

Brierley, J., and D. Graham. 1984. Hypoxia and vascular disorders of the central nervous system. In *Greenfield's neuropathology*, ed. J. Adams, J. Corsellis, and L. Duchen, 4th ed., 125–207. New York: Wiley.

Bright-Birnbaum, K. L. 2017. The fingerprint expert: Do you really have one? In *Forensic science reform: Protecting the innocent*, ed. W. J. Koen and C. M. Bowers, 338–61. Amsterdam: Elsevier/Academic.

Broadbent, J. M., W. M. Thomson, S. Ramrakha, T. E. Moffitt, J. Zeng, L. A. Foster Page, and R. Poulton. 2015. Community water fluoridation and intelligence. *American Journal of Public Health* 165:72–76.

Brock, P. 2008. *Charlatan*. New York: Crown.

Brodeur, P. 1977. *The zapping of America*. New York: Norton.

———. 1989. *Currents of death: Power lines, computer terminals, and the attempts to cover up their threat to your health*. New York: Simon & Schuster.

———. 1993. *The great power-line cover-up: How the utilities and the government are trying to hide the cancer hazard posed by electromagnetic fields*. Boston: Little, Brown.

Brody, H. 2010. Ritual, medicine and the placebo response. In *The problem of ritual efficacy*, ed. W. S. Sax, J. Quack, and J. Weinhold, 151–67. Oxford: Oxford University Press.

Brotherton, R. 2015. *Suspicious minds: Why we believe conspiracy theories*. New York: Bloomsbury.

Brotherton, R., and C. C. French. 2014. Belief in conspiracy theories and susceptibility to the conjunction fallacy. *Applied Cognitive Psychology* 28:238–48.

Brown, A. 2004. *The déjà vu experience.* New York: Psychology Press.

Brown, R., and D. McNeill. 1966. The "tip of the tongue" phenomenon. *Journal of Verbal Learning and Verbal Behavior* 5:325–37.

Bruck, M., and S. J. Ceci. 1999. The suggestibility of children's memory. *Annual Review of Psychology* 50:419–39.

Bruck, M., S. J. Ceci, E. Francoeur, and R. J. Barr. 1995. "I hardly cried when I got my shot": Influencing children's reports about a visit to their pediatrician. *Child Development* 66:193–208.

Bruck, M., S. J. Ceci, and H. Hembrooke. 1997. Children's reports of pleasant and unpleasant events. In *Recollections of trauma: Scientific research and clinical practice*, ed. D. Read and S. Lindsay, 199–219. New York: Plenum Press.

Buchwald, W. F. 1975. *Handbook of iron meteorites: Their history, distribution, composition, and structure.* Vol. 1: *Iron meteorites in general.* Berkeley: University of California Press.

Buie, T. 2013. The relationship of autism and gluten. *Clinical Therapeutics* 35:578–83.

Bullough, V. L., and B. Bullough. 1998. Should nurses practice therapeutic touch? Should nursing schools teach therapeutic touch? *Journal of Professional Nursing* 14:254–57.

Burke, J. 2006. Lourdes miracles get a little easier. *Guardian*, April 2.

Butler, A. C., J. E. Chapman, E. M. Forman, and A. T. Beck. 2006. The empirical status of cognitive-behavioral therapy: A review of meta-analyses. *Clinical Psychology Review* 26:17–31.

Byrd, R. C. 1988. Positive therapeutic effects of intercessory prayer in a coronary care unit population. *Southern Medical Journal* 81:826–29.

Byrne, R. 2006. *The secret.* New York: Simon & Schuster.

Cabanillas, F. 2010. Vitamin C and cancer: What can we conclude—1609 patients and 33 years later? *Puerto Rico Health Science Journal* 29:215–17.

Cameron, E., and L. Pauling. 1976. Supplemental ascorbate in the supportive treatment of cancer. *Proceedings of the National Academy of Sciences* 73:3685–89.

Campbell, D., and J. Beets. 1978. Lunacy and the moon. *Psychological Bulletin* 85:1123–29.

Campbell, N. K. J., and A. Raz. 2016. Placebo science in medical education. In *Placebo talks*, ed. A. Raz and C. S. Harris, 83–96. New York: Oxford University Press.

Campbell, S. 1997. *The Loch Ness monster: The evidence.* Amherst, NY: Prometheus Books.

Campbell, T. W. 1998. *Smoke and mirrors.* New York: Insight Books.

Campion, E. W. 1997. Power lines, cancer, and fear. *New England Journal of Medicine* 337:44–46.

Campion, N. 2008. *A history of western astrology.* Vol. 1: *The ancient world.* London: Continuum Books.

Canadian Press. 2016. P.E.I. father accused of sexually assaulting daughter: A timeline of events. CTV News, June 30. https://atlantic.ctvnews.ca/p-e-i-father-accused-of-sexually-assaulting-daughter-a-timeline-of-events-1.2968354.

Cardena, E. 2018. The experimental evidence for parapsychological phenomena: A review. *American Psychologist* 73:663–77.

Carlson, S. 1985. A double-blind test of astrology. *Nature* 318:419–25.

Carlson, S., and G. Larue. 1989. *Satanism in America: How the devil got much more than his due.* El Cerrito, CA: Gaia Press.

Cathey, J., and R. Harrington. 2007. *The veil: Heidi Wyrick's story.* Lincoln, NE: Universe.

Center for Countering Digital Hate. 2020. *Anti-vax playbook.* https://counterhate.com/wp-content/uploads/2022/05/210106-The-Anti-Vaxx-Playbook.pdf.

Cerullo, J. 1982. *Secularization of the soul.* Philadelphia: Institute for the Study of Human Issues.

Cha, K. Y., D. P. Wirth, and R. A. Lopo. 2001. Does prayer influence the success of in vitro fertilization–embryo transfer? *Journal of Reproductive Medicine* 46:781–87.

Chaibi, A., J. Š. Benth, P. J. Tuchin, and M. B. Russell. 2016. Chiropractic spinal manipulative therapy for migraine: A three armed, single-blinded, placebo, randomized controlled trial. *European Journal of Neurology* 24:143–53.

Chambless, D. L., and T. H. Ollendick. 2001. Empirically supported psychological interventions: Controversies and evidence. *Annual Review of Psychology* 52:685–716.

Chan, J., M. Hallett, C. Zalewski, C. C. Brewer, C. Zampieri, M. Hoa, S. M. Lippa, et al. 2024. Clinical, biomarker, and research tests among US government personnel and their family members involved in anomalous health incidents. *JAMA* 331 (13): 1109–21.

Chan, J., and K. Nankervis. 2015. Stolen voices: Facilitated communication is an abuse of human rights. *Evidence Based Communication Assessment and Intervention* 8 (3): 1–6.

Chapman, L. 1967. Illusory correlation in observational report. *Journal of Verbal Learning and Verbal Behavior* 6:151–55.

Chapman, L., and J. Chapman. 1967. Genesis of popular but erroneous psychodiagnostic observations. *Journal of Abnormal Psychology* 72:193–204.

———. 1969. Illusory correlation as an obstacle to the use of valid psychodiagnostic signs. *Journal of Abnormal Psychology* 74:271–80.

Charemboon, T., and K. Jaisin. 2015. Ginkgo biloba for prevention of dementia: A systematic review and meta-analysis. *Journal of the Medical Association of Thailand* 98:508–13.

Cherkin, D. C., R. A. Deyo, M. Battié, J. Street, and W. Barlow. 1998. A comparison of physical therapy, chiropractic manipulation and provision of an educational booklet for the treatment of patients with low back pain. *New England Journal of Medicine* 339:1021–29.

Child, I. 1985. Psychology and anomalous observations: The question of ESP in dreams. *American Psychologist* 40:1219–30.

Choi, A. L., G. Sun, Y. Zhang, and P. Grandjean. 2012. Developmental fluoride neurotoxicity: A systematic review and meta-analysis. *Environmental Health Perspectives* 120:1362–68.

Christopher, K. 2001. Skeptics challenge psychic mediums on CNN's *Larry King Live*. *Skeptical Inquirer* 25 (3): 5–6.

Christy, M. M. 1994. *Your own perfect medicine: The incredible proven miracle cure that medical science has never revealed.* Scottsdale, AZ: Wishland.

Clancy, F., and H. Yorkshire. 1989. The Bandler method. *Mother Jones*, February/March, 22–28, 63–64.

Clancy, S. A. 2005. *Abducted: How people come to believe they were kidnapped by aliens.* Cambridge, MA: Harvard University Press.

Clark, J., and L. Coleman. 1978. *Creatures of the outer edge.* New York: Warner Books.

Clark, P., and M. Clark. 1984. Therapeutic touch: Is there a scientific basis for the practice? *Nursing Research* 33:37–41.

Clark, S. E., and E. F. Loftus. 1996. The construction of space alien abduction memories. *Psychological Inquiry* 7:140–43.

Clarke, D. 2015. *How UFOs conquered the world.* London: Aurum.

Clifasefi, S. C., M. Garry, and E. Loftus. 2007. Setting the record (or video camera) straight on memory. In *Tall tales about the mind and brain*, ed. S. Della Sala, 60–75. New York: Oxford University Press.

Close, F. 1991. *Too hot to handle: The race for cold fusion.* Princeton, NJ: Princeton University Press.

Cockburn, A. 1990. The McMartin case. *Wall Street Journal*, February 8, A17.

Coghlan, M. L., G. Maker, E. Crighton, J. Haile, D. C. Murray, N. E. White, and R. W. Byard. 2015. Combined DNA, toxicological and heavy metal analyses provides an auditing toolkit to improve pharmacovigilance of traditional Chinese medicine (TCM). *Nature Scientific Reports* 5, article 17475.

Cohen, D. 1981. *The great airship mystery: A UFO of the 1890s.* New York: Dodd, Mead.

Cohen, P. A., B. Avula, K. Katragunta, J. C. Travis, and I. Khan. 2023. Presence and quantity of botanical ingredients with purported performance-enhancing properties in sports supplements. *JAMA Network Open* 6:e2323879.

Cohen, P. A., B. Avula, Y. H. Wang, I. Zakharevich, and I. Khan. 2021. Five unapproved drugs found in cognitive enhancement supplements. *Neurology: Clinical Practice* 11:e303–e307.

Colavito, J. 2005. *The cult of ancient aliens.* Amherst, NY: Prometheus Books.

———. 2021. How Washington got hooked on flying saucers. *New Republic*, May 21.

Colligan, M., J. Pennebaker, and L. Murphy, eds. 1982. *Mass psychogenic illness: A social psychological analysis.* Hillsdale, NJ: Lawrence Erlbaum Associates.

Collins, H., and T. Pinch. 1982. *Frames of meaning: The social construction of extraordinary science*. London: Routledge & Kegan Paul.

Collins, P. 2001. *Banvard's folly*. New York: Picador.

Colquhoun, D., and S. Novella. 2013. Acupuncture is theatrical placebo. *Anesthesia and Analgesia* 116:1360–63.

Committee to Review the Scientific Evidence on the Polygraph. 2002. *The polygraph and lie detection*. Washington, DC: National Academy Press.

Condon, E. 1969. *Scientific study of unidentified flying objects*. New York: Bantam Books.

Consumer Reports. 1987. Homeopathic remedies. *Consumer Reports* 52:60–62.

Cooper, C., L. R. Lyketsos, and G. Livingston. 2013. A systematic review of treatment for mild cognitive impairment. *British Journal of Psychiatry* 203:527–33.

Cooper, H., R. Blumenthal, and L. Kean. 2017. Glowing auras and "black money": The Pentagon's mysterious U.F.O. program. *New York Times*, December 16.

———. 2019. "Wow, what is that?" Navy pilots report unexplained flying objects. *New York Times*, May 26.

Cooper, J. 1982. Cottingley: At last the truth. *Unexplained* 117:2338–40.

Corballis, M. C. 2007. The dual-brain myth. In *Tall tales about the mind and brain: Separating fact from fiction*, ed. S. Della Sala, 291–314. Oxford: Oxford University Press.

Coren, S. 1972. Subjective contours and apparent depth. *Psychological Review* 79:359–67.

Corinda, T. 1968. *Thirteen steps to mentalism*. New York: Tannen Magic.

Cortex Editorial Board. 2018. Responsibility of neuropsychologists: The case of the "sonic attack." *Cortex* 108:A1–A2.

Costain, T. 1947. *Moneyman*. Garden City, NY: Doubleday.

Coulter, X., A. Collier, and B. Campbell. 1976. Long-term retention of early Pavlovian fear conditioning in infant rats. *Journal of Experimental Psychology: Animal Behavior Processes* 2:48–56.

Crawley, G. 2000. Photographing fairies. *British Journal of Photography*, January 5, 71–74.

Crelin, E. 1985. Chiropractic. In *Examining holistic medicine*, ed. D. Stalker and C. Glymour, 197–220. Buffalo, NY: Prometheus Books.

Crews, F. 1984. The Freudian way of knowledge. *New Criterion*, June.

———. 1995. *The memory wars: Freud's legacy in dispute*. New York: New York Review.

———, ed. 1998. *Unauthorized Freud*. New York: Viking.

———. 2017. *Freud: The making of an illusion*. New York: Metropolitan Books.

Crowe, M. J. 1986. *The extraterrestrial life debate 1750–1900*. Cambridge: Cambridge University Press.

Crumbaugh, J. 1966. A scientific critique of parapsychology. *International Journal of Neuropsychiatry* 5:521–29.

Cuijpers, P., E. Driessen, S. D. Hollon, P. van Oppen, J. Barth, and G. Andersson. 2012. The efficacy of non-directive supportive therapy for adult depression: A meta-analysis. *Clinical Psychology Review* 32:280–91.

Culver, R. B., and P. A. Ianna. 1984. *The gemini syndrome: A scientific evaluation of astrology*. Buffalo, NY: Prometheus Books.

Cumberland, S. 1888. *A thought-reader's thoughts*. New York: Arno Press, 1975.

Cummings, S. R., and C. Rosen. 2022. VITAL findings—a decisive verdict on vitamin D supplementation. *New England Journal of Medicine* 387:368–70.

Cupp, M. J. 1999. Herbal remedies: Adverse effects and drug interactions. *American Family Physician* 59:1239–44.

———, ed. 2000. *Toxicology and clinical pharmacology of herbal products*. Totowa, NJ: Humana Press.

Dagnall, N., A. Parker, and G. Munley. 2007. Paranormal belief and reasoning. *Personality and Individual Differences* 43:1406–15.

Dallenbach, K. 1955. Phrenology versus psychoanalysis. *American Journal of Psychology* 68:511–25.

Damon, P. E., D. J. Donahue, B. H. Gore, A. L. Hatheway, A. J. T. Jull, T. W. Linick, P. J. Sercel, et al. 1989. Radiocarbon dating of the Shroud of Turin. *Nature* 337:611–15.

Darvill, T., E. Lonky, J. Reihman, P. Stewart, and J. Pagano. 2000. Prenatal exposure to PCBs and infant performance on the Fagan test of infant intelligence. *Neurotoxicology* 21:1029–38.

Darwin, H., N. Neave, and J. Holmes. 2011. Belief in conspiracy theories: The role of paranormal belief, paranoid ideation and schizotypy. *Personality and Individual Differences* 50:1289–93.

Davenas, E., F. Beauvais, J. Amara, M. Oberbaum, B. Robinzon, A. Miadonna, A. Tedeschi, et al. 1988. Human basophil degranulation triggered by very dilute antiserum against IgE. *Nature* 333:816–18.

Davidson, P. W., G. J. Myers, and B. Weiss. 2004. Mercury exposure and child development outcomes. *Pediatrics* 113:1023–29.

Davies, J. 1955. *Phrenology: Fad and science.* New Haven, CT: Yale University Press.

Davis, W. 1985. *The serpent and the rainbow.* New York: Simon & Schuster.

Dawes, R. M. 1994. *House of cards: Psychology and psychotherapy built on myth.* New York: Free Press.

———. 2001. *Everyday irrationality.* Boulder, CO: Westview Press.

Dawes, R. M., D. Faust, and P. F. Meehl. 1989. Clinical versus actuarial judgment. *Science* 243:1668–74.

Dean, G. A. 1977. *Recent advances in natal astrology.* Subiaco, Australia: Analogic.

———. 1986–1987a. Does astrology need to be true? Part 1: A look at the real thing. *Skeptical Inquirer* 11:166–84.

———. 1986–1987b. Does astrology have to be true? Part 2: The answer is no. *Skeptical Inquirer* 11:257–73.

———. 1992. The bottom line: Effect size. In *The write stuff: Evaluations of graphology*, ed. B. L. Beyerstein and D. F. Beyerstein, 269–341. Buffalo, NY: Prometheus Books.

———. 2016. Does astrology need to be true? A thirty-year update. *Skeptical Inquirer* 40 (4): 38–45.

Dean, G. A., and I. W. Kelly. 2003. Is astrology related to consciousness and psi? *Journal of Consciousness Studies* 10:175–98.

Dean, G. A., A. Mather, D. Nias, and R. Smit. 2016. *Tests of astrology: A critical review of hundreds of studies.* Amsterdam: AinO Publications.

———. 2023. *Understanding astrology.* Amsterdam: AinO Publications.

DeBakesy, D. 2014. Stop Heisenberg abuse: Three outrageous misappropriations of quantum physics. *Skeptical Inquirer* 38 (3): 40–43.

Deer, B. 2011. Secrets of the MMR scare. *BMJ* 342:77–82, 136–42, 200–204.

———. 2020. *The doctor who fooled the world.* Baltimore, MD: Johns Hopkins University Press.

Delaney, J., and H. Woodward. 1974. Effects of reading an astrological description on responding to a personality inventory. *Psychological Reports* 34:1214.

de Moraes, L. 2001. Medium crosses the line. *Washington Post*, October 26.

Dendle, P. 2006. Cryptozoology in the medieval and modern worlds. *Folklore* 117:190–206.

Dennett, M. 1981–1982. Bermuda Triangle, 1981 model. *Skeptical Inquirer* 6 (1): 42–52.

———. 1982–1983. Bigfoot jokester reveals punchline—finally. *Skeptical Inquirer* 7 (1): 8–9.

DeRidder, D., K. Van Laere, P. Dupont, T. Menovsky, and P. Van de Heyning. 2007. Visualizing out-of-body experience in the brain. *New England Journal of Medicine* 357:1829–33.

De Wohl, L. 1947. *The living wood, a novel.* Philadelphia: J. B. Lippincott.

Dickey, C. 2020. *The unidentified.* New York: Viking.

Dickson, D., and I. Kelly. 1985. The "Barnum effect" in personality assessment: A review of the literature. *Psychological Reports* 57:367–82.

Dingwall, E., K. Goldney, and T. Hall. 1956. *The haunting of Borley Rectory.* London: Gerald Duckworth.

Dittrich, L. 2012. The prophet. *Esquire*, August 2013, 88–95.

Dobbs, H. 1967. The feasibility of a physical theory of ESP. In *Science and ESP*, ed. J. Smythies. New York: Humanities Press.

Dobson, B. 1982–1983. On the trail of the Buena foot "monster." *Skeptical Inquirer* 7 (4): 8–10.

Doctorow, C. 2010. Electrosensitives tortured by a radio tower that had been switched off for six weeks. *Boing Boing*, January 15. https://boingboing.net/2010/01/15/electrosensitives-to-html.

Dolnick, E. 1998. *Madness on the couch: Blaming the victim in the heyday of psychoanalysis.* New York: Simon & Schuster.

Doman, G. 2003. *What to do about your brain-injured child, or your brain-damaged, mentally retarded, mentally deficient, cerebral-palsied, epileptic, autistic, athetoid, hyperactive, attention deficit disordered, developmentally delayed, Down's child.* Towson, MD: Gentle Revolution Press.

Dommeyer, F. 1975. Book review. *Parapsychology Review* 6:11–12.

Domotor, Z., B. K. Doering, and F. Koteles. 2016. Dispositional aspects of body focus and idiopathic environmental intolerance attributed to electromagnetic fields (IEI—EMF). *Scandinavian Journal of Psychology* 57:136–43.

Douglas, K. M., R. M. Sutton, M. J. Callan, R. J. Dawtry, and A. J. Harvey. 2016. Someone is pulling the strings: Hypersensitive agency detection and belief in conspiracy theories. *Thinking and Reasoning* 22:57–77.

Dowling, S. 1984. Lourdes cures and their mental assessment. *Journal of the Royal Society of Medicine* 77:634–38.

Doyle, A. 1922. *The coming of the fairies.* New York: George H. Doran.

Drory, A. 1986. Graphology and job performance: A validation study. In *Scientific aspects of graphology*, ed. B. Nevo, 165–73. Springfield, IL: Charles C. Thomas.

Dunning, B. 2017. There is no Finland: Birth of a conspiracy theory. *Skeptoid Podcast*, May 30, episode 573.

Durkman, D., and R. Bjork, eds. 1991. *In the mind's eye: Enhancing human performance.* Washington, DC: National Academy Press.

Durlak, J. 1979. Comparative effectiveness of paraprofessional and professional helpers. *Psychological Bulletin* 86:80–92.

Dyer, N. L., A. L. Baldwin, and W. L. Rand. 2019. A large-scale effectiveness trial of reiki for physical and psychological health. *Journal of Alternative and Complementary Medicine* 25 (12): 1156–62.

Dywan, J., and K. Bowers. 1983. The use of hypnosis to enhance recall. *Science* 222:184–85.

Easton, R., and R. Shor. 1975. Information processing analysis of the Chevreul pendulum illusion. *Journal of Experimental Psychology: Human Perception and Performance* 1:231–36.

Eberle, P., and S. Eberle. 1993. *The abuse of innocence: The McMartin preschool trial.* Amherst, NY: Prometheus Books.

Edwards, F. 1956. *Strangest of all.* New York: Citadel.

———. 1959. *Stranger than science.* New York: Lyle Stuart.

Edwards, P. 1986. The case against reincarnation: Part 1. *Free Inquiry* 6 (4): 24–34.

———. 1996. *Reincarnation: A critical examination.* Amherst, NY: Prometheus Books.

Eldredge, N. 2000. *Triumph of evolution and the failure of creationism.* New York: W. H. Freeman.

Elk, M. 2013. Paranormal believers are more prone to illusory agency detection than skeptics. *Consciousness and Cognition* 22:1041–46.

Ellamil, M., C. Dobson, M. Beeman, and K. Christoff. 2012. Evaluative and generative modes of thought during the creative process. *Neuroimage* 59:1783–94.

Ellis, B. 1988. The varieties of alien experience. *Skeptical Inquirer* 12:263–69.

———. 1995. Alien autopsy show-and-tell: Long on tell, short on show. *Skeptical Inquirer* 19 (6): 15–16, 55.

———. 1998. Psychic forecasts were a big flop (again). *Skeptical Inquirer* 22 (1): 6–8.

———. 2001. Cracked crystal balls? *Skeptical Inquirer* 25 (1): 7–8.

Ellis, B., and M. Hicken. 2018. *A deal with the devil.* New York: Atria Books.

Emre, M. 2018. *The personality brokers: The strange history of the Myers-Briggs and the birth of personality testing.* New York: Doubleday.

Engber, D. 2015. The strange case of Anna Stubblefield. *New York Times Magazine*, October 20.

Enright, J. T. 1999. Testing dowsing. The failure of the Munich experiments. *Skeptical Inquirer* 23 (1): 39–46.

Ernst, E. 1999. Clinical effectiveness of acupuncture: An overview of systematic reviews. In *Acupuncture: A scientific appraisal*, ed. E. Ernst and A. White, 107–27. Oxford: Butterworth-Heinemann.

———. 2006. Spiritual healing: More than meets the eye. *Journal of Pain Symptoms and Management* 32:393–95.

———. 2012. Craniosacral therapy: A systematic review of the clinical evidence. *Focus on Alternative Complementary Therapies* 17:197–201.

———. 2017. *Homeopathy. The undiluted facts.* Cham, Switzerland: Springer.

———. 2018. *SCAM: So-called alternative medicine.* Exeter, UK: Imprint Academic.

———. 2019. *Alternative medicine: A critical assessment of 150 modalities.* Cham, Switzerland: Springer.

Ernst, E., P. Posadzki, and M. S. Lee. 2011. Reflexology: An update of a systematic review of randomized clinical trials. *Maturitas* 68:116–20.

Ernst, E., and K. Smith. 2018. *More harm than good.* Cham, Switzerland: Springer.

Ernst, E., and A. White, eds. 1999. *Acupuncture: A scientific appraisal.* Oxford: Butterworth-Heinemann.

Erwin, E. 1980. Psychoanalytic therapy: The Eysenck argument. *American Psychologist* 35:435–43.

———. 1986. Psychotherapy and Freudian psychology. In *Hans Eysenck: Consensus and controversy*, ed. S. Modgil and C. Modgil, 179–203. Philadelphia: Falmer Press.

Everson, T., and W. Cole. 1966. *Spontaneous regression of cancer.* Philadelphia: W. B. Saunders.

Eysenck, H. 1952. The effects of psychotherapy: An evaluation. *Journal of Consulting Psychology* 16:319–24.

Eysenck, H., and D. Nias. 1982. *Astrology: Science or superstition?* New York: St. Martin's Press.

Ezzo, J., B. Berman, V. A. Hadhazy, A. R. Jadad, L. Lao, and B. B. Singh. 2000. Is acupuncture effective for the treatment of chronic pain? A systematic review. *Pain* 86:217–25.

Faraday, M. 1853. Experimental investigation of table-moving. *Athenaeum*, July 2, 801–2.

Fasce, A., and A. Pico. 2018. Conceptual foundations and validation of the Pseudoscientific Belief Scale. *Applied Cognitive Psychology* 33:617–28.

Faust, D., and J. Ziskin. 1988. The expert witness in psychology and psychiatry. *Science* 241:31–35.

Fein, G. G., J. L. Jacobson, S. W. Jacobson, P. M. Schwartz, and J. K. Dowler. 1984. Prenatal exposure to polychlorinated biphenyls: Effects on birth size and gestational weight. *Journal of Pediatrics* 105:315–20.

Festinger, L., H. Riecken, and S. Schachter. 1956. *When prophecy fails.* New York: Harper & Row.

Feychting, M., and A. Ahlbom. 1993. Magnetic fields and cancer in children residing near Swedish high-voltage power lines. *American Journal of Epidemiology* 138:467–81.

Finefield, K. 2011. A ghostly image: Spirit photographs. *Picture This*, October 31. https://blogs.loc.gov/picturethis /2011/10/a-ghostly-image-spirit-photographs/.

Fischer, J. 1983. A summary critique of analysis of the "blood" on the Turin "Shroud." In *Inquest on the Shroud of Turin*, ed. J. Nickell. Amherst, NY: Prometheus Books.

Fischer, M. A. 1989. McMartin: A case of dominoes? *Los Angeles* 34 (10): 126–35.

Flamm, B. L. 2002. Faith healing by prayer. *Scientific Review of Alternative Medicine* 5:47–50.

———. 2004. The Columbia University "miracle" study: Flawed and fraud. *Skeptical Inquirer* 28 (5): 25–31.

———. 2005. The bizarre Columbia University "miracle" saga continues. *Skeptical Inquirer* 29 (2): 52–53.

Flournoy, T. 1900. *From India to the planet Mars.* Princeton, NJ: Princeton University Press, 1994.

Fodor, N. 1964. *Between two worlds.* West Nyack, NY: Parker Publishing.

Fombonne, E. 2008. Thimerosal disappears but autism remains. *Archives of General Psychiatry* 65:15–16.

Forlano, G., and V. Ehrlich. 1941. Month and season of birth in relation to intelligence, introversion-extroversion, and inferiority feelings. *Journal of Education Research* 32:1–2.

Foroughi, C. K., S. S. Monfort, M. Paczynski, P. E. McKnight, and P. M. Greenwood. 2016. Placebo effects in cognitive training. *Proceedings of the National Academy of Sciences* 113:7470–74.

Foulkes, D., F. Belvedere, R. E. Masters, J. Houston, S. Krippner, C. Honorton, and M. Ullman. 1972. Long distance "sensory-bombardment" ESP in dreams: A failure to replicate. *Perceptual and Motor Skills* 35:731–34.

Foulkes, R. A. 1971. Dowsing experiments. *Nature* 229:163–68.

Fox, B., and D. P. Farrington. 2018. What have we learned from offender profiling? A systematic review and meta-analysis of 40 years of research. *Psychological Bulletin* 144:1247–74.

Foxon, F. 2024. Bigfoot: If it's there, could it be a bear? *Journal of Zoology* 323 (1): 1–8.

Foxx, R. M., and J. A. Mulick. 2016. *Controversial therapies for autism and intellectual disabilities.* 2nd ed. New York: Routledge.

Franklin, W. 1976. Metal fracture physics using scanning electron microscopy and the theory of teleneural interactions. In *The Geller papers*, ed. C. Panati, 83–106. Boston: Houghton Mifflin.

———. 1977. Letter. *Humanist*, September/October, 54–55.

Franks, C., ed. 1969. *Behavioral therapy: Appraisal and status.* New York: McGraw-Hill.

Franks, F. 1981. *Polywater.* Cambridge: MIT Press.

Frazier, K. 1979–1980. Amityville hokum: The hoax and the hype. *Skeptical Inquirer* 4 (2): 2–4.

———. 1980–1981. Mummy's curse tut-tutted. *Skeptical Inquirer* 5 (1): 13.

———, ed. 1981. *Paranormal borderlands of science.* Amherst, NY: Prometheus Books.

———. 1981–1982. Judge rebuts Tut suit. *Skeptical Inquirer* 6 (4): 12.

———. 1986. *Science confronts the paranormal.* Amherst, NY: Prometheus Books.

———. 2024. *Shadows of science.* Lanham, MD: Prometheus.

Frazier, K., and J. Randi. 1981–1982. Prediction after the fact: Lessons of the Tamara Rand hoax. *Skeptical Inquirer* 6 (1): 4–7.

Frederick, C. 1965. Some phenomena affecting handwriting analysis. *Perceptual and Motor Skills* 20:211–18.

———. 1968. An investigation of handwriting of suicidal persons through suicide notes. *Journal of Abnormal Psychology* 73:263–67.

French, C. C., H. O'Donnell, and L. Williams. 2001. Hypnotic susceptibility, paranormal belief and reports of "crystal power." Paper presented at the British Psychological Society Centenary Annual Conference, Glasgow, March 28.

French, C. C., J. Santomauro, V. Hamilton, R. Fox, and M. A. Thalbourne. 2008. Psychological aspects of the alien contact experience. *Cortex* 44:1387–95.

French, C. C., and A. Stone. 2014. *Anomalistic psychology.* New York: Palgrave-Macmillan.

French, C. C., and L. Williams. 1999. Crystal clear: Paranormal powers, placebo, or priming? Paper presented at the Sixth European Congress of Psychology, Rome.

Freud, S. 1950. *The interpretation of dreams.* Trans. A. Brill. New York: Modern Library.

Frontline. 1995. Currents of fear. June 13.

Fuller, J. 1966. *The interrupted journey.* New York: Dell.

———. 1974. *Arigo: Surgeon of the rusty knife.* New York: Crowell.

Furnham, A., and S. Schofield. 1987. Accepting personality test feedback: A review of the Barnum effect. *Current Psychological Research and Review* 6:162–78.

Gadad, B. S., W. Li, U. Yazdani, and D. C. German. 2015. Administration of thimerosal-containing vaccines to infant rhesus macaques does not result in autism-like behavior or neuropathology. *Proceedings of the National Academy of Sciences* 112:12498–12503.

Gaddis, V. 1965. *Invisible horizons.* Philadelphia: Chilton.

Galak, J., R. A. LeBoeuf, L. D. Nelson, and J. P. Simmons. 2011. Correcting the past: Failures to replicate psi. *Journal of Personality and Social Psychology* 101:933–48.

Galton, F. 1872. Statistical inquiries into the efficacy of prayer. *Fortnightly Review* 12:125–35.

Gardiner, J. M., and A. Richardson-Klavehn. 2000. Remembering and knowing. In *Oxford Handbook of Memory*, ed. E. Tulving and F. I. M. Craik, 229–44. New York: Oxford University Press.

Gardner, H. 1983. *Frames of mind.* New York: Basic Books.

Gardner, M. 1957. *Fads and fallacies in the name of science.* New York: Dover.

———. 1981. Parapsychology and quantum mechanics. In *Science and the paranormal*, ed. G. Abell and B. Singer. New York: Charles Scribner's Sons.

———. 1984. Cruel deception in the Philippines. *Discover*, August, 8.

———. 1987a. Isness is her business. *New York Review of Books* 34 (6): 16–19.

———. 1987b. Science-fantasy religious cults. *Free Inquiry* 7 (3): 31–35.

———. 1988–1989. Water with memory? The dilution affair. *Skeptical Inquirer* 13:132–41.

———. 1997. Heaven's Gate: The UFO cult of Bo and Peep. *Skeptical Inquirer* 21 (4): 15–17.

———. 1999. Urine therapy. *Skeptical Inquirer* 23 (3): 13–15.

———. 2000. The brutality of Dr. Bettelheim. *Skeptical Inquirer* 24 (6): 12–14.

Garelik, G. 1984. The great Hudson Valley UFO mystery. *Discover*, November, 18–24.

———. 1986. Exorcising a damnable disease. *Discover*, December, 74–84.

General Medical Council. 2010. Fitness to practice hearing. London, January 25.

Gennaro, R. J., and Y. I. Fishman. 2015. The argument from brain damage vindicated. In *The myth of an afterlife*, ed. M. Martin and K. Augustine, 105–33. Lanham, MD: Rowman & Littlefield.

Gerbic, S. 2020. Operation lemon meringue—Thomas John. *Skeptical Inquirer*, September 28. https://skepticalinquirer.org/exclusive/operation-lemon-meringue-thomas-john/.

Gerlich, N. 1998. Tragedy on Elm Street. *Skeptic* 6 (4): 40–50.

Ghahremani, M., E. E. Smith, H-Y. Chen, B. Creese, Z. Goodarzi, and Z. Ismail. 2023. Vitamin D supplementation and incident dementia: Effects of sex, APOE, and baseline cognitive status. *Alzheimer's and Dementia*, 15, e12404.

Gibney, E. 2019. Google revives controversial cold-fusion experiments. *Nature* 569:611.

Gish, D. 1977. *Dinosaurs: Those terrible lizards.* San Diego, CA: Creation-Life.

Gissurarsson, L., and A. Gunnarsson. 1997. An experiment with the alleged human aura. *Journal of the American Society for Psychical Research* 91:33–49.

Gittelson, B. 1982. *Biorhythm: A personal science.* New York: Warner Books.

Gladen, B. C., and W. J. Rogan. 1991. Effects of perinatal polychlorinated biphenyls and dichlorodiphenyl dichloroethylene on later development. *Journal of Pediatrics* 119:58–63.

Gladen, B. C., W. J. Rogan, P. Hardy, J. Thullen, J. Tingelstad, and M. Tully. 1988. Development after exposure to polychlorinated biphenyls and dichlorodiphenyldichloroethylene transplacentally and through human milk. *Journal of Pediatrics* 113:991–95.

Glassner, B. 1999. *The culture of fear.* New York: Basic Books.

Gleick, J. 1986. Moon's creation now attributed to giant crash. *New York Times*, June 3, C1, C3.

Glick, P., and M. Snyder. 1986. Self-fulfilling prophecy: The psychology of belief in astrology. *Humanist* 46 (3): 20–25, 50.

Glickman, R., and E. J. Gracely. 1998. Therapeutic touch: Investigation of a practitioner. *Scientific Review of Alternative Medicine* 2 (1): 43–47.

Globus, G., P. Knapp, J. Skinner, and J. Healey. 1968. An appraisal of telepathic communication in dreams. *Psychophysiology* 4 (3): 365.

Godfrey, L., and J. Cole. 1986. Blunder in their footsteps. *Natural History*, August, 4–12.

Goetz, B. 2017. Bloodstain pattern analysis. In *Forensic science reform: Protecting the innocent*, ed. W. J. Koen and C. M. Bowers, 279–97. Amsterdam: Elsevier/Academic.

Goldacre, B. 2010. *Bad science.* New York: Farber & Farber.

———. 2013. *Bad pharma: How drug companies mislead doctors and harm patients.* New York: Faber & Faber.

Goldberg, L. 1985. Some informal explorations and ruminations about graphology. In *Scientific aspects of graphology*, ed. B. Nevo, 281–93. Springfield, IL: Charles C. Thomas.

Goldsmith, D., ed. 1979. *Scientists confront Velikovsky.* Ithaca, NY: Cornell University Press.

Goode, E. 2000. *Paranormal beliefs: A sociological introduction.* Prospect Heights, IL: Waveland Press.

Goodman, L. 1968. *Linda Goodman's sun-signs.* New York: Bantam Books.

———. 1971. *Linda Goodman's sun-signs.* New York: Bantam Books.

———. 1982. *Love signs.* New York: Fawcett.

Goodman, M. J., and J. Nordin. 2006. Vaccine adverse event reporting system reporting source: A possible source of bias in longitudinal studies. *Pediatrics* 117:387–90.

Gordon, A., J. H. Merenstein, F. D'Amico, and D. Hudgens. 1998. Effects of therapeutic touch on patients with osteoarthritis of the knee. *Journal of Family Practice* 47:271–77.

Gorski, D. 2016. No, a rat study with marginal results does not prove that cell phones cause cancer, no matter what *Mother Jones* and *Consumer Reports* say. *Science Based Medicine*, May 30.

Gould, R. 1944. *The stargazer talks.* London: Geoffrey Bles.

Gould, S. 1980. The panda's thumb. In *The panda's thumb*, ed. S. Gould, 19–26. New York: Norton.

Grandjean, P., P. Weihe, V. W. Burse, L. L. Needham, E. Storr-Hansen, B. Heinzow, F. Debes, et al. 2001. Neurobehavioral deficits associated with PCB in 7-year old children prenatally exposed to seafood neurotoxins. *Neurotoxicology and Teratology* 23:305–17.

Green, C., C. W. Martin, K. Bassett, and A. Kazanjian. 1999. *A systematic review and critical appraisal of the scientific evidence on craniosacral therapy.* Vancouver, BC: British Columbia Office of Health Technology Assessment.

Green, S., and W. Sampson. 2002. EDTA chelation therapy for atherosclerosis and degenerative disease. *Scientific Review of Alternative Medicine* 6:17–22.

Green, W. M. 1993. Therapeutic effects of distant intercessory prayer and patients' enhanced positive expectations on positive recovery rates and anxiety levels of hospitalized neurosurgical pituitary patients: A double blind study. *Dissertation Abstracts International* 54 (5-B): 2752.

Grieve, D. 1972. Report on the film of a supposed sasquatch. In *Bigfoot*, ed. J. Napier, 217–22. New York: Dutton.

Gross, M. 1978. *The psychological society.* New York: Random House.

Grove, W. M., and R. C. Barden. 1999. Protecting the integrity of the legal system: The admissibility of testimony from mental health experts under *Daubert/Kumho* analysis. *Psychology, Public Policy, and Law* 5:224–42.

Grove, W. M., R. C. Barden, H. N. Garb, and S. O. Lilienfeld. 2002. Failure of Rorschach-comprehensive-system-based testimony to be admissible under the *Daubert/Kumho* standard. *Psychology, Public Policy, and Law* 8:216–34.

Gruneberg, M., and R. Sykes. 1978. Knowledge and retention: The feeling of knowing and reminiscence. In *Practical aspects of memory*, ed. M. Gruneberg, P. Morris, and R. Sykes, 189–96. London: Academic Press.

Guallar, E., S. Stranges, C. Mulrow, L. J. Appel, and E. R. Miller III. 2013. Enough is enough: Stop wasting money on vitamin and mineral supplements. *Annals of Internal Medicine* 159:850–51.

Guerin, P. 1970. The Warminster photographs: A tentative interpretation. *Flying Saucer Review* 16 (November–December): 6.

Guillen, T. 2006. *Serial killers: Issues explored through the Green River Murders.* New York: Prentice Hall.

Hadingham, E. 1987. *Lines to the mountain gods.* New York: Random House.

Hafer, A. 2015. *The not-so-intelligent designer.* Eugene, OR: Cascade Books.

Hagen, M. A. 1997. *Whores of the court.* New York: HarperCollins.

Halkides, C., and K. Lott. 2017. Presumptive and confirmatory blood testing. In *Forensic science reform: Protecting the innocent*, ed. W. J. Koen and C. M. Bowers, 246–69. Amsterdam: Elsevier/Academic.

Hall, C. 1954. *A primer of Freudian psychology.* New York: World.

———. 1963. Strangers in dreams: An empirical confirmation of the Oedipus complex. *Journal of Personality* 31:336–45.

Hall, H. 2021. Does public water fluoridation make children less intelligent? *Skeptical Inquirer* 45 (3): 18–20.

Hall, R., ed. 1964. *The UFO evidence.* Washington, DC: NICAP.

Hall, T. 1978. *Search for Harry Price.* London: Gerald Duckworth.

———. 1985. A note on Borley Rectory: "The most haunted house in England." In *A skeptic's handbook of parapsychology*, ed. P. Kurtz, 327–38. Amherst, NY: Prometheus Books.

Halperin, D. J. 2020. *Intimate alien: The hidden story of the UFO.* Stanford, CA: Stanford University Press.

Hamilton, D. 1986. *The monkey gland affair.* London: Chatto & Windus.

Hand, D. J. 2014. *The improbability principle.* New York: Scientific American.

Hansel, C. 1966. *ESP: A scientific evaluation.* New York: Charles Scribner's Sons.

———. 1980. *ESP and parapsychology: A critical re-evaluation.* Amherst, NY: Prometheus Books.

Hansson, S. O. 2017. Science and pseudo-science. *Stanford Encyclopedia of Philosophy*, https://plato.stanford.edu/entries/pseudo-science/.

Hapgood, C. 1966. *Maps of the ancient sea kings.* New York: Chilton.

Hare, R. 1855. *Experimental investigation of spirit manifestations, demonstrating the existence of spirits and their communion with mortals: Doctrine of the spirit world respecting heaven, hell, morality, and god; Also, the influence of scripture on the morals of Christians.* New York: Partridge and Brittan.

Hargrave, C. 1966. *History of playing cards and a bibliography of cards and gaming.* New York: Dover.

Harris, J., and K. Weeks. 1973. *X-raying the pharaohs.* New York: Charles Scribner's Sons.

Harris, M. 1986. Are "past-life" regressions evidence of reincarnation? *Free Inquiry* 6 (4): 18–23.

Harris, W. S., M. Gowda, J. W. Kolb, C. P. Strychacz, J. L. Vacek, P. G. Jones, A. Forker, J. H. O'Keefe, and B. D. McCallister. 1999. A randomized, controlled trial of the effects of remote, intercessory prayer on outcomes in patients admitted to the coronary care unit. *Archives of Internal Medicine* 159:2273–78.

Hart, J., and M. Graether. 2018. Something's going on here: Psychological predictors of belief in conspiracy theories. *Journal of Individual Differences* 39:229–37.

Hattie, J., C. Sharpley, and H. Rogers. 1984. Comparative effectiveness of professional and paraprofessional helpers. *Psychological Bulletin* 95:534–41.

Haygarth, J. 1800. Of the imagination, as a cause and as a cure of disorders of the body; Exemplified by fictitious tractors, and epidemical convulsions. Bath, UK: R. Cruttwell. (Reproduced by Gale ECCO Print. *Note:* There is also an 1801 edition of this work that is slightly longer [58 pages vs. 43 pages].)

Hegstad, R. 1974. *Rattling the gates.* Washington, DC: Review and Herald.

Heider, F., and M. Simmel. 1944. An experimental study of apparent behavior. *American Journal of Psychology* 57:243–59.

Heinzen, T. E., S. O. Lilienfeld, and S. A. Nolan. 2015. *The horse that won't go away.* New York: Worth.

Helgertz, J., and K. Scott. 2020. The validity of astrological predictions on marriage and divorce: A longitudinal analysis of Swedish register data. *Genus* 76: article 34.

Heller, J., and A. Adler. 1980. Blood on the Shroud of Turin. *Applied Optics* 19:2742–44.

Hellmuth, J., G. D. Rabinovici, and B. L. Miller. 2019. The rise in pseudomedicine for dementia and brain health. *JAMA* 321:543–44.

Hemila, H., and E. Chalker. 2013. Vitamin C for preventing and treating the common cold. *Cochrane Database Systematic Reviews* 1: article CD000980.

Hemsley, B., L. Bryant, R. W. Schlosser, H. C. Shane, R. Lang, D. Paul, M. Banajee, and M. Ireland. 2018. Systematic review of facilitated communication 2014–2018 finds no new evidence that messages delivered using facilitated communication are authored by the person with disability. *Autism and Developmental Language Impairments* 3:1–8.

Hendry, A. 1979. *The UFO handbook*. Garden City, NY: Doubleday.

Henningsen, G. 1980. *The witches' advocate*. Reno, NV: University of Nevada Press.

Hilgard, E. 1980–1981. Hypnosis gives rise to fantasy and is not a truth serum. *Skeptical Inquirer* 5 (3): 25.

Hilgard, J., G. Sala, W. R. Boot, and D. J. Simons. 2019. Overestimation of action-game training effects: Publication bias and salami slicing. *Collabra: Psychology* 5 (1): 30.

Hill, C., and F. Doyon. 1990. Review of randomized trials of homeopathy. *Revue d'epidemiologie et de Sante Publique* 38:139–47.

Hill, S. 2012. Amateur paranormal research and investigation groups doing "sciencey" things. *Skeptical Inquirer* 36 (2): 38–41.

———. 2013a. The Ketchum project: What to believe about bigfoot DNA "science." *Skeptical Briefs* 23 (1): 1–6, 13.

———. 2013b. UFO research is up in the air. *Skeptical Inquirer*, August 28. http://www.skepticalinquirer.org/exclusive/ufo-research-is-up-in-the-air/.

———. 2017. *Scientific Americans: The culture of amateur paranormal researchers*. Jefferson, NC: McFarland.

Hines, T. M. 1976. Attended and unattended processing in hemispheric activation. Master's thesis, University of Oregon.

———. 1988. *Pseudoscience and the paranormal: A critical examination of the evidence*. Amherst, NY: Prometheus Books.

———. 1996. Whatever happened to N-rays? *Skeptic* 4 (4): 85–87.

———. 1998. Comprehensive review of biorhythm theory. *Psychological Reports* 83:19–64.

———. 2001. The Doman-Delacato patterning treatment for brain damage. *Scientific Review of Alternative Medicine* 5:80–89.

———. 2008. Zombies and tetrodotoxin. *Skeptical Inquirer* 32 (3): 60–62.

———. 2015. Brain, language and survival after death. In *The myth of an afterlife*, ed. M. Martin and K. Augustine, 183–94. Lanham, MD: Rowman & Littlefield.

———. 2017. Delusions of the imagination. *Skeptic Magazine* 22:18–21.

Hines, T., and T. Dennison. 1988. A reaction time test of extrasensory perception. *Skeptical Inquirer* 13:161–65.

Hines, T., P. Lang, and K. Seroussi. 1987. Extrasensory perception examined using a reaction time measure. *Perceptual and Motor Skills* 64:499–502.

Hintzman, D., S. Asher, and L. Stern. 1978. Incidental retrieval and memory for coincidences. In *Practical Aspects of Memory*, ed. M. Gruneberg, P. Morris, and R. Sykes, 61–68. London: Academic Press.

Hoagland, R. C. 2001. *The monuments of mars: A city on the edge of forever*. Berkeley, CA: North Atlantic Books.

Hodge, D. R. 2007. A systematic review of the literature on intercessory prayer. *Research on Social Work Practice* 17:174–87.

Hoebens, P. H. 1981–1982a. Croiset and Professor Tenhaeff. *Skeptical Inquirer* 6 (2): 32–40.

———. 1981–1982b. Gerald Croiset: Investigation of the Mozart of "psychic sleuths." *Skeptical Inquirer* 6 (1): 17–28.

———. 1982–1983. Modern revival of "Nostradamitis." *Skeptical Inquirer* 7 (1): 38–45.

Holden, P. 1977. Biorhythms: The flow of energy. *Oregon Daily Emerald*, October 26, 5.

Hollon, S. D., and K. Ponniah. 2010. A review of empirically supported psychological therapies for mood disorders in adults. *Depression and Anxiety* 27:891–932.

Hollon, S. D., M. E. Thase, and J. C. Markowitz. 2002. Treatment and prevention of depression. *Psychological Science in the Public Interest* 3:39–77.

Holmes, D. 1974. Investigations of repression: Differential recall of material experimentally or naturally associated with ego threat. *Psychological Bulletin* 81:632–53.

Hönel, H. 1977. Grundrhythmus und kriminelle Disposition in der Handschrift. *Zeitschrift für Menschenkunde* 41:1–55.

Honorton, C. 1985. Meta-analysis of psi ganzfeld research: A response to Hyman. *Journal of Parapsychology* 49:51–91.

Hoover, D. W., and R. Milich. 1994. Effects of sugar ingestion expectancies on mother-child interactions. *Journal of Abnormal Child Psychology* 22:501–15.

Hopkins, B. 1987. *Intruders*. New York: Random House.

Houdini, H. 1924. *A magician among the spirits*. New York: Harper & Row.

Houran, J., and R. Lange. 1996. Dairy of events in a thoroughly unhaunted house. *Perceptual and Motor Skills* 83:499–502.

Howard-Jones, P. A. 2014. Neuroscience and education: Myths and messages. *Nature Reviews Neuroscience* 15:817–24.

Hubbard, T. L. 2005. Representational momentum and related displacements in spatial memory: A review of the findings. *Psychonomic Bulletin and Review* 12:822–51.

Hubbard, T. L., J. L. Hutchison, and J. R. Courtney. 2010. Boundary extension: Findings and theory. *Quarterly Journal of Experimental Psychology* 63:1467–94.

Huber, P. W. 1977. Early cuneiform evidence for the existence of the planet Venus. In *Scientists confront Velikovsky*, ed. P. Goldsmith, 117–44. Ithaca, NY: Cornell University Press.

———. 1993. *Galileo's revenge: Junk science in the courtroom*. New York: Basic Books.

Hufford, D. J. 1982. *The terror that comes in the night*. Philadelphia: University of Pennsylvania Press.

Huizenga, J. R. 1992. *Cold fusion: The scientific fiasco of the century*. Rochester, NY: University of Rochester Press.

Humphrey, N. 2000. The power of prayer. *Skeptical Inquirer* 24 (3): 61.

Hvidd, A., J. Vinsløv Hansen, M. Frisch, and M. Melbye. 2019. Measles, mumps, rubella vaccination and autism: A nationwide cohort study. *Annals of Internal Medicine* 170:513–20.

Hyman, R. 1976–1977. "Cold reading": How to convince strangers that you know all about them. *Zetetic* 1 (2): 18–37.

———. 1980–1981. Further comments on Schmidt's PK experiments. *Skeptical Inquirer* 5 (3): 34–40.

———. 1985a. A critical historical overview of parapsychology. In *A skeptic's handbook of parapsychology*, ed. P. Kurtz, 3–96. Amherst, NY: Prometheus Books.

———. 1985b. The ganzfeld psi experiment: A critical appraisal. *Journal of Parapsychology* 49:3–49.

———. 2003. How not to test mediums. *Skeptical Inquirer* 27 (1): 20–30.

———. 2007. Ouija, dowsing and other seductions of ideomotor action. In *Tall tales about the mind and brain*, ed. S. Della Sala, 411–24. Oxford: Oxford University Press.

Hyman, R., and C. Honorton. 1986. A joint communique: The psi ganzfeld controversy. *Journal of Parapsychology* 50:350–64.

Hyman, S. L., P. A. Stewart, J. Foley, U. Cain, R. Peck, D. D. Morris, H. Wang, and T. Smith. 2016. The gluten-free/casein-free diet: A double blind challenge trial in children with autism. *Journal of Autism and Developmental Disorders* 46:205–20.

Hynek, J. A. 1972. *The UFO experience*. New York: Ballantine.

———. 1976–1977. Comments. *Zetetic* 1 (2): 77–79.

Hynek, J. A., P. J. Imbrogno, and B. Pratt. 1987. *Night siege: The Hudson Valley UFO sightings*. New York: Ballantine Books.

Hynek, J., and J. Vallee. 1975. *The edge of reality: A progress report on unidentified flying objects*. Chicago: Henry Regnery.

Imhoff, R., and P. K. Lamberty. 2017. Too special to be duped: Need for uniqueness motivates conspiracy beliefs. *European Journal of Social Psychology* 47:724–34.

Inskip, P. D., R. E. Tarone, E. E. Hatch, T. C. Wilcosky, W. R. Shapiro, R. G. Selker, H. A. Fine, P. M. Black, J. S. Loeffler, and M. S. Linet. 2001. Cellular-telephone use and brain tumors. *New England Journal of Medicine* 344:79–86.

Ioannidis, J. P. A. 2005. Why most research findings are false. *PLoS Medicine* 2 (8): e124.

Irwin, H. 1985. *Flight of mind*. Metuchen, NJ: Scarecrow Press.

Iverson, J. 1977. *More lives than one?* London: Pan Books.

Jacobs, D. 1975. *The UFO controversy in America*. Bloomington: Indiana University Press.

Jacobs, J., L. M. Jimenez, S. S. Gloyd, J. L. Gale, and D. Crothers. 1994. Treatment of acute childhood diarrhea with homeopathic medicine: A randomized clinical dual trial in Nicaragua. *Pediatrics* 93:719–25.

Jacobson, J. L., and S. W. Jacobson. 1996. Intellectual impairment in children exposed to polychlorinated biphenyls in utero. *New England Journal of Medicine* 335:783–89.

Jacobson, J. L., S. W. Jacobson, P. M. Schwartz, G. G. Fein, and J. K. Dowler. 1984. Prenatal exposure to an environmental toxin: A test of the multiple effects model. *Developmental Psychology* 20:528–32.

Jacobson, J. W., J. A. Mulick, and A. A. Schwartz. 1995. A history of facilitated communication: Science, pseudoscience, and antiscience. *American Psychologist* 50:750–65.

Jacobson, M. 1978. *Developmental neurobiology*. 2d edition. New York: Plenum.

Jacobson, S. W., G. G. Fein, J. L. Jacobson, P. M. Schwartz, and J. K. Dowler. 1985. The effect of intrauterine PCB exposure on visual recognition memory. *Child Development* 56:853–60.

James, L. E., M. M. Gottschlich, J. K. Nelson, L. C. Cone, and J. E. McCall. 2019. Pediatric perioperative measures of sleep, pain, anxiety and anesthesia emergence: A healing touch proof of concept randomized clinical trial. *Complementary Therapies in Medicine* 42:264–69.

Jansen, A. 1973. *Validation of graphological judgments: An experimental study*. The Hague, Netherlands: Mouton.

Janssen, W. 1980. The gadgeteers. In *The health robbers*, ed. S. Barrett, 93–197. Amherst, NY: Prometheus Books.

Jaroff, L. 2001. Talking to the dead. *Time*, March 5, 52.

JASON. 2018. *Acoustic signals and physiological effects on U.S. diplomats in Cuba*. McLean, VA: MITRE Corporation.

Jeffers, S. 2003. Physics and claims for anomalous effects related to consciousness. In *Psi wars: Getting to grips with the paranormal*, ed. J. Alcock, J. E. Burns, and A. Freeman, 135–54. Charlottsville, VA: Imprint Academic.

———. 2006. The PEAR proposition: Fact of fallacy. *Skeptical Inquirer* 30 (3): 54–57.

Jerome, L. 1977. *Astrology disproved*. Amherst, NY: Prometheus Books.

———. 1989. *Crystal power: The ultimate placebo effect*. Buffalo, NY: Prometheus.

Johansen, C., J. D. Boice, J. K. McLaughlin, and J. H. Olsen. 2001. Cellular telephones and cancer—a nationwide cohort study in Denmark. *Journal of the National Cancer Institute* 93:203–207.

Johnson, S. B., H. S. Park, C. P. Gross, and J. B. Yu. 2018. Complementary medicine, refusal of conventional cancer therapy, and survival among patients with curable cancers. *JAMA Oncology* 4:1375–81.

Jones, S. L., B. Campbell, and T. Hart. 2019. Laboratory tests commonly used in complementary and alternative medicine: A review. *Annals of Clinical Biochemistry* 56:310–25.

Jones, T. F., A. S. Craig, D. Hoy, E. W. Gunter, D. L. Ashley, D. B. Barr, J. W. Brock, and W. Schaffner. 2000. Mass psychogenic illness attributed to toxic exposure at a high school. *New England Journal of Medicine* 342:96–100.

Jordan, J. B. 2006. Acupuncture treatment for opiate addiction: A systematic review. *Journal of Substance Abuse and Treatment* 30:309–14.

Jorgensen, T. J. 2016. *Strange glow: The story of radiation*. Princeton, NJ: Princeton University Press.

Jung, C., and W. Pauli. 1955. *The interpretation of nature and the psyche*. New York: Pantheon.

Jureidini, J., and L. B. McHenry. 2020. *The illusion of evidence-based medicine*. Mile End, South Australia: Wakefield Press.

Kabat, G. C. 2008. *Hyping health risks*. New York: Columbia University Press.

———. 2017. *Getting risk right: Understand the elusive science of health risks*. New York: Columbia University Press.

———. 2021. Glyphosate on trial: In an "unequal contest" between science and emotion, can evidence overcome pesticide-cancer fears? Genetic Literacy Project, March 16. https://geneticliteracyproject.org/2021/03/16/glyphosate-on-trial-in-an-unequal-contest-between-evidence-and-emotion-can-evidence-overcome-pesticide-fears/.

Kabat, G. C., W. J. Price, and R. E. Tarone. 2021. On recent meta-analyses of exposure to glyphosate and risk of non-Hodgkin's lymphoma in humans. *Cancer Causes and Control* 32 (4): 409–14.

Kagan, D., and I. Summers. 1983. *Mute evidence*. New York: Bantam Books.

Kakalios, J. 2016. *The amazing story of quantum mechanics*. New York: Penguin.

Kanthamani, H., and R. S. Broughton. 1994. Institute for parapsychology ganzfeld-ESP experiments: The manual series. In *Proceedings of presented papers: The Parapsychological Association, 37th Annual Convention*, 182–89. Durham, NC: Parapsychological Association.

Karsch-Volk, M., B. Barrett, D. Kiefer, R. Bauer, K. Ardjomand-Woelkart, and K. Linde. 2014. Echinacea for preventing and treating the common cold. *Cochrane Database Systematic Reviews* 2: article CD000530.

Kasper, S. 2001. Hypericum perforatum—a review of clinical studies. *Pharmacopsychiatry* 34 (suppl. 1): S51–S55.

Kean, S. 2010. *The disappearing spoon*. New York: Little, Brown and Company.

Keene, M., and A. Spraggett. 1997. *The psychic mafia*. Amherst, NY: Prometheus Books.

Keinan, G. 1986a. Can graphologists identify individuals under stress? In *Scientific Aspects of Graphology*, ed. B. Nevo, 141–51. Springfield, IL: Charles C. Thomas.

———. 1986b. Graphoanalysis for military personnel selection. In *Scientific Aspects of Graphology*, ed. B. Nevo, 193–201. Springfield, IL: Charles C. Thomas.

Keller, J. J. 1993. Cellular phone safety concerns hammer stocks. *Wall Street Journal*, January 25, B1.

Kelly, I. W., J. Rotton, and R. Culver. 1985–1986. The moon was full and nothing happened: A review of studies on the moon and human behavior and lunar beliefs. *Skeptical Inquirer* 10:129–43.

Kemper, T. 1984. Asymmetrical lesions in dyslexia. In *Cerebral dominance: The biological foundations*, ed. N. Geschwind and A. Galaburda, 75–89. Cambridge, MA: Harvard University Press.

Kempson, I. M., and E. Lombi. 2011. Hair analysis as a biomarker for toxicology, disease and health status. *Chemical Society Reviews* 40:3915–40.

Kennedy, J. 2018. *Fighting chemophobia*. Indianapolis: CreateSpace.

Kennedy, J. L. 1939. A methodological review of extra-sensory perception. *Psychological Bulletin* 36:59–103.

Kennefick, D. 2019. *No shadow of a doubt*. Princeton, NJ: Princeton University Press.

Kimbrough, R. D. 1993. The human health effects of polychlorinated biphenyls. In *Phantom risk: Scientific inference and the law*, ed. K. R. Foster, D. E. Bernstein, and P. W. Huber, 211–28. Cambridge, MA: MIT Press.

Kimbrough, R. D., M. L. Doemland, and M. E. LeVois. 1999. Mortality in male and female capacitor workers exposed to polychlorinated biphenyls. *Journal of Environmental Medicine* 41:161–71.

King, S. V. 1977. *Pyramid energy handbook*. New York: Warner Books.

King, T. 1973. *Love, sex, and astrology*. New York: Harper & Row.

Klasco, R. 2018. Ask well. *New York Times*, October 9, D4.

Klass, P. J. 1974. *UFOs identified*. New York: Random House.

———. 1977–1978. Review of C. Berlitz, *Without a trace*. *Zetetic* 2 (1): 97–102.

———. 1978–1979. The Gallup UFO polls. *Skeptical Inquirer* 3 (2): 5–7.

———. 1980–1981. Hypnosis and UFO abductions. *Skeptical Inquirer* 5 (3): 16–24.

———. 1981. UFOs. In *Science and the paranormal*, ed. G. Abell and B. Singer, 310–28. New York: Charles Scribner's Sons.

———. 1983. *UFOs explained*. New York: Random House.

———. 1984–1985. Radar UFOs: Where have they gone? *Skeptical Inquirer* 9:257–60.

———. 1987–1988a. "Intruders of the mind": Review of B. Hopkins. *Intruders*. *Skeptical Inquirer* 12:85–89.

———. 1987–1988b. The MJ-12 crashed-saucer documents. *Skeptical Inquirer* 12:137–46.

———. 1987–1988c. The MJ-12 papers: Part 2. *Skeptical Inquirer* 12:279–89.

———. 1988. *UFO abductions: A dangerous game*. Amherst, NY: Prometheus Books.

———. 1997. *The real Roswell crashed-saucer coverup*. Amherst, NY: Prometheus Books.

———. 2000. The new bogus Majestic-12 documents. *Skeptical Inquirer* 24 (3): 44–46.

Kleijnen, J., P. Knipschild, and G. ter Riet. 1991. Clinical trials of homeopathy. *BMJ* 302:316–23.

Kleinmuntz, B., and J. Szucko. 1984. A field study of the fallibility of polygraphic lie detection. *Nature* 308:449–50.

Klimoski, R. J. 1992. Graphology and personnel selection. In *The write stuff: Evaluations of graphology*, ed. B. L. Beyerstein and D. F. Beyerstein, 232–68. Buffalo, NY: Prometheus Books.

Kline, P. 1968. Obsessional traits, obsessional symptoms, and anal erotism. *British Journal of Medical Psychology* 41:299–305.

Kling, S. 1977. *Pyramid energy handbook*. New York: Warner Books.

Klotz, I. 1980. The N-ray affair. *Scientific American* 242 (5): 168–75.

Knowles, L., and R. Jones. 1974. Police altercations and the ups and downs of life cycles. *Police Chief* (November): 51–54.

Koen, W. J., and C. M. Bowers, eds. 2017. *Forensic science reform: Protecting the innocent.* Amsterdam: Elsevier/ Academic Press.

Kolata, G. 1998. A child's paper poses a medical challenge. *New York Times*, April 1, A1, A20.

Koppl, R., and D. E. Krane. 2016. Minimizing and leveraging bias in forensic science. In *Blinding as a solution to bias*, ed. C. T. Robertson and A. S. Kesselheim, 151–65. Amsterdam: Elsevier/Academic.

Korownyk, C., M. R. Kolber, J. P. McCormack, V. Lam, K. Overbo, C. Cotton, C. Finley, et al. 2014. Televised medical talk shows—what they recommend and the evidence to support their recommendations: A prospective observational study. *BMJ* 349:g7346.

Kosok, P., and M. Reiche. 1949. Ancient drawings on the desert of Peru. *Archaeology* 2:206–15.

Kottmeyer, M. 1989. Gauche encounters: Bad films and the UFO myth. Unpublished manuscript.

Kramer, P. D. 2016. *Ordinarily well: The case for antidepressants.* New York: Farrar, Straus & Giroux.

Krane, D. E., and S. Ford. 2017. Essential elements of a critical review of DNA evidence. In *Forensic science reform: Protecting the innocent*, ed. W. J. Koen and C. M. Bowers, 211–38. Amsterdam: Elsevier/Academic Press.

Krieger, D., E. Peper, and S. Ancoli. 1979. Therapeutic touch, searching for evidence of physiological change. *American Nurses' Association* 79:660–62.

Krucoff, M. W., S. W. Crater, D. Gallup, J. C. Blankenship, M. Cuffe, M. Guarneri, R. A. Krieger, et al. 2005. Music, imagery, touch and prayer as adjuncts to interventional cardiac care. *Lancet* 366:211–17.

Krummenacher, P., C. Mohr, H. Haker, and P. Brugger. 2010. Dopamine, paranormal belief and the detection of meaningful stimuli. *Journal of Cognitive Neuroscience* 22:1670–81.

Krupp, E., ed. 1978. *In search of ancient astronomies.* Garden City, NY: Doubleday.

———. 1981. Recasting the past: Powerful pyramids, lost continents, and ancient astronauts. In *Science and the paranormal*, ed. G. Abell and B. Singer, 253–95. New York: Charles Scribner's Sons.

Kuban, G. 1986. A summary of the Taylor site evidence. *Creation/Evolution* 6 (1): 10–18.

Kundtson, M. I., D. G. Wyse, P. D. Galbraith, R. Brant, K. Hildebrand, D. Paterson, D. Richardson, C. Burkart, E. Burgess, and PATCH Investigators. 2002. Chelation therapy for ischemic heart disease: A randomized controlled trial. *JAMA* 287:481–86.

Kurtz, P. 1976–1977. The aims of the Committee for the Scientific Investigation of the Paranormal. *Zetetic* 1 (1): 6–7.

———. 1980–1981. Bigfoot on the loose: Or how to create a legend. *Skeptical Inquirer* 5 (1): 49–54.

———. 1985. Spiritualists, mediums, and psychics: Some evidence of fraud. In *A skeptic's handbook of parapsychology*, ed. P. Kurtz, 177–223. Amherst, NY: Prometheus Books.

———. 1986. Does faith-healing work? *Free Inquiry* 6 (2): 30–36.

———. 1997. UFO mythology: Escape to oblivion. *Skeptical Inquirer* 21 (4): 12–14.

Kurtz, R., and S. Garfield. 1978. Illusory correlation: A further exploration of Chapman's paradigm. *Journal of Consulting and Clinical Psychology* 46:1009–15.

Kurtzke, J. 1968. Clinical manifestations of multiple sclerosis. In *The epidemiology of multiple sclerosis*, ed. J. F. Kurtzke and M. Alter, 161–216. Springfield, IL: C. C. Thomas.

Kusche, L. 1975. *The Bermuda Triangle mystery—solved.* New York: Harper & Row.

———. 1977–1978a. Critical reading, careful writing, and the Bermuda Triangle. *Zetetic* 2 (1): 36–40.

———. 1977–1978b. Review of C. Berlitz, *Without a trace.* Zetetic 2 (1): 93–97.

———. 1979–1980. Review of W. Moore and C. Berlitz, *The Philadelphia experiment: Project invisibility.* Skeptical Inquirer 4 (1): 58–62.

———. 1980. *The disappearance of Flight 19.* New York: Harper & Row.

———. 1981. The Bermuda Triangle. In *Science and the paranormal*, ed. G. Abell and B. Singer, 296–309. New York: Charles Scribner's Sons.

Kvasnytsya, V., R. Wirth, L. Dobrzhinetskaya, J. Matzel, B. Jacobsen, I. Hutcheon, R. Tappero, and M. Kovalyukh. 2013. New evidence of meteoritic origin of the Tunguska cosmic body. *Planetary and Space Science* 84:131–40.

Lacy-Hulbert, A., J. C. Metcalfe, and R. Hesketh. 1998. Biological responses to electromagnetic fields. *FASEB Journal* 12:395–420.

Ladendorf, B., and B. Ladendorf. 2018. Wildlife apocalypse. *Skeptical Inquirer* 42 (4): 30–39.

Lai, Y.-Y., and J. M. Siegel. 1999. Muscle atonia in REM sleep. In *Rapid eye movement sleep*, ed. B. N. Mallick and S. Inoue, 60–90. New York: Marcel Dekker.

Lange, R., and J. Houran. 1997. Context induced paranormal experiences: Support for Houran and Lange's model of haunting phenomena. *Perceptual and Motor Skills* 84:1455–58.

Lanning, K. V. 1991. Ritual abuse: A law enforcement view or perspective. *Child Abuse and Neglect* 15:171–73.

Larsen, C. F. 2015. Conjecturing up spirits in the improvisations of mediums. In *The myth of an afterlife*, ed. M. Martin and K. Augustine, 585–614. Lanham, MD: Rowman & Littlefield.

Laudan, L. 1983. The demise of the demarcation problem. In *Physics, philosophy and psychoanalysis*, ed. R. S. Cohen and L. Laudan, 111–27. Dordrecht: D. Reidel.

Lawrence, J., and C. Perry. 1983. Hypnotically created memory among highly hypnotizable subjects. *Science* 222:523–24.

Laws, K. R., H. Sweetnam, and T. K. Kondel. 2012. Is ginkgo biloba a cognitive enhancer in healthy individuals? A meta-analysis. *Human Psychopharmacology: Clinical and Experimental* 27:527–33.

Laycock, J. 2009. *Vampires today.* Westport, CT: Praeger.

———. 2015. *Dangerous games.* Berkeley: University of California Press.

Lazarus, A. 1986. On sterile paradigms and the realities of clinical practice: Critical comments on Eysenck's contribution to behavior therapy. In *Hans Eysenck: Consensus and controversy*, ed. S. Modgil and C. Modgil, 247–57. Philadelphia: Falmer Press.

Lee, E. E. 2008. A trial design that generates only "positive" results. *Journal of Postgraduate Medicine* 54:214–16.

Lee, M. S., M. H. Pittler, and E. Ernst. 2009. Effects of reiki in clinical practice: A systematic review of randomized clinical trials. *International Journal of Clinical Practice* 62:947–54.

Lee, R. A. 2002. *The bizarre careers of John R. Brinkley.* Louisville, KY: University Press of Kentucky.

Lehn, W. 1979. Atmospheric refraction and lake monsters. *Science* 205:183–85.

Leibovici, L. 2001. Effects of remote, retroactive, intercessory prayer on outcomes in patients with blood stream infections. *BMJ* 323:1450–51.

Leichty, E. 1975. *The omen series Shumma izbu.* Locust Valley, NY: J. J. Augustine.

Leikind, B, and W. McCarthy. 1985–1986. An investigation of firewalking. *Skeptical Inquirer* 10:23–24.

Lentini, J. J. 2017. Confronting inaccuracies in fire cause determinations. In *Forensic science reform: Protecting the innocent*, edited by W. J. Koen and C. M. Bowers, 66–94. Amsterdam: Elsevier.

Leon, M. E., L. H. Schinasi, P. Lebailly, L. E. Beane Freeman, K.-C. Nordby, G. Ferro, A. Monnereau, et al. 2019. Pesticide use and risk of non-Hodgkin lymphoid malignancies in agricultural cohorts from France, Norway and the USA. *International Journal of Epidemiology* 48:1519–35.

Leonard, G. 1976. *Somebody else is on the moon.* New York: David McKay.

Leoni, E. 1982. *Nostradamus and his prophecies.* New York: Bell.

Leonidou, C., and G. Panayiotou. 2018. How do illness-anxious individuals process health-threatening information? A systematic review of evidence for the cognitive-behavioral model. *Journal of Psychosomatic Research* 111:100–115.

Lerner, R. 1968. Maimonides' letter on astrology. *History of Religions* 8 (2): 143–58.

Levenson, T. 2015. *The hunt for Vulcan.* New York: Random House.

Levine, K., H. C. Shane, and R. H. Wharton. 1994. What if . . . : A plea to professionals to consider the risk-benefit ratio of facilitated communication. *Mental Retardation* 32:300–304.

Levine, M., and J. Shefner. 1981. *Fundamentals of sensation and perception.* New York: Random House.

Levy, L. 1979. Handwriting and hiring. *Dun's Review* 113:72–79.

Li, B., T. L. Forbes, and J. Byrne. 2018. Integrative medicine or infiltrative pseudoscience? *Surgeon* 16:271–77.

Lie, Y.-W., M. T. Liong, Y.-C. E. Chung, H.-Y. Huang, W.-S. Peng, Y.-F. Cheng, Y.-S. Lin, Y.-Y. Wu, and Y.-C. Tsai. 2019. Effects of *Lactobacillus plantarum* PS128 on children with autism spectrum disorder in Taiwan: A randomized, double-blind, placebo-controlled trial. *Nutrients* 11:820.

Lieber, A., and J. Agel. 1978. *The lunar effect: Biological tides and human emotions.* Garden City, NY: Doubleday.

Lieber, A., and C. Sherin. 1972. Homicides and the lunar cycle: Toward a theory of lunar influence on human emotional disturbance. *American Journal of Psychiatry* 129:69–74.

Lilienfeld, S. O. 1993–1994. Do "honesty" tests really measure honesty? *Skeptical Inquirer* 18:32–41.

———. 2017. Potentially harmful treatments. *Oxford Research Encyclopedia of Psychology.* https://doi.org/10.1093/acrefore/9780190236557.013.68.

Lilienfeld, S. O., and K. Landfield. 2008. Science and pseudoscience in law enforcement. *Criminal Justice and Behavior* 35:1215–30.

Lilienfeld, S. O., S. J. Lynn, J. Ruscio, and B. L. Beyerstein. 2010. *50 Great myths of popular psychology.* Malden, MA: Wiley-Blackwell.

Lilienfeld, S. O., J. Marshall, J. T. Todd, and H. C. Shane. 2015. The persistence of fad interventions in the face of negative scientific evidence. *Evidence Based Communication Assessment and Intervention* 8 (2): 1–40.

Lilienfeld, S. O., J. M. Wood, and H. N. Garb. 2000. The scientific status of projective techniques. *Psychological Science in the Public Interest* 1:25–66.

Lim, R. 1975. Zodiacal sign polarities as an index of introversion-extroversion. Master's thesis, San Francisco State University.

Linde, K., L. Kriston, G. Rücker, S. Jamil, I. Schumann, K. Meissner, K. Sigterman, and A. Schneider. 2015. Efficacy and acceptability of pharmacological treatments for depressive disorders in primary care: Systematic review and network meta-analysis. *Annals of Family Medicine* 13:69–79.

Linet, S. L., E. E. Hatch, R. A. Kleinerman, L. L. Robison, W. T. Kaune, D. R. Friedman, R. K. Severson, et al. 1997. Residential exposure to magnetic fields and acute lymphoblastic leukemia in children. *New England Journal of Medicine* 337:1–7.

Linn, R. 1976. *The last chance diet.* Secaucus, NJ: Lyle Stuart.

Lionetti, E., A. Pulvirenti, M. Vallorani, G. Catassi, A. K. Verma, S. Gatti, and C. Catassi. 2017. Re-challenge studies in non-celiac gluten sensitivity: A systematic review and meta-analysis. *Frontiers in Physiology* 8:621.

Lipsey, M. W. 2009. The primary factors that characterize effective interventions with juvenile offenders: A meta-analytic overview. *Victims and Offenders* 4:124–47.

Lobell, M. 1975. Letter. *Science News* 108 (14): 223.

Loeb, M., M. L. Russell, B. Neupane, V. Thanabalan, P. Singh, J. Newton, and E. Pullenayegum. 2018. A randomized, blinded, placebo-controlled trial comparing antibody responses to homeopathic and conventional vaccines in university students. *Vaccine* 36:7423–29.

Loftfield, E., C. P. O'Connell, C. C. Abnet, B. I. Graubard, L. M. Liao, L. E. Beane Freeman, J. N. Hofmann, N. D. Freedman, and R. Sinha. 2024. Multivitamin use and mortality risk in 3 prospective US cohorts. *JAMA Network Open* 7 (6): e2418729.

Loftin, R. W. 1980–1981. A Maltese cross in the Aegean? *Skeptical Inquirer* 5 (4): 54–57.

———. 1989–1990. Auras: Searching for the light. *Skeptical Inquirer* 14:403–9.

Loftus, E. 1975. Leading questions and eyewitness report. *Cognitive Psychology* 7:560–72.

———. 1979. *Eyewitness testimony.* Cambridge, MA: Harvard University Press.

———. 1993. The reality of repressed memory. *American Psychologist* 48:518–37.

———. 1995. Remembering dangerously. *Skeptical Inquirer* 19 (2): 20–29.

———. 1997. Creating false memories. *Scientific American* 277 (3): 70–75.

Loftus, E., and K. Ketcham. 1994. *The myth of repressed memory.* New York: St. Martin's Press.

Loftus, E., D. Miller, and H. Burns. 1978. Semantic integration of verbal information into a visual memory. *Journal of Experimental Psychology: Human Learning and Memory* 4:19–31.

Loftus, E., and J. Palmer. 1974. Reconstruction of automobile destruction: An example of the interaction between language and memory. *Journal of Verbal Learning and Verbal Behavior* 13:585–89.

Lohr, J. M., R. Gist, B. Deacon, G. J. Devilly, and T. Varker. 2015. Science-and non-science based treatments for trauma-related stress disorders. In *Science and pseudoscience in clinical psychology*, 2nd ed., ed. S. O. Lilienfeld, S. J. Lynn, and J. M. Lohr, 277–321. New York: Guilford Press.

Long, R., P. Bernhardt, and W. Evans. 1999. Perception of conventional sensory cues as an alternative to the postulated "human energy field" of therapeutic touch. *Scientific Review of Alternative Medicine* 3 (2): 53–61.

Lonky, E., J. Reihman, T. Darvill, J. Mather Sr., and H. Daly. 1996. Neonatal behavioral assessment scale performance in humans influenced by maternal consumption of environmentally contaminated Lake Ontario fish. *Journal of Great Lakes Research* 22:198–212.

Lorenzen, J., and C. Lorenzen. 1980. *Abducted! Confrontations with beings from outer space*. New York: Berkley.

Lowell, P. 1908. *Mars as the abode of life*. New York: Macmillan.

Loxton, D. 2020. QAnon is just a warmed over witch panic—and it's also very dangerous. *Skeptic* 25 (4): 36–40.

Loxton, D., and D. R. Prothero. 2013. *Abominable science*. New York: Columbia University Press.

Lykken, D. 1981. *A tremor in the blood*. New York: McGraw Hill.

MacDougall, C. 1983. *Superstition and the press*. Amherst, NY: Prometheus Books.

Macfarlane, G. J., P. Paudyal, M. Doherty, E. Ernst, G. Lewith, H. MacPherson, J. Sim, and G. T Jones. 2012. A systematic review of evidence for the effectiveness of practitioner-based complementary and alternative therapies in the management of rheumatic diseases: Osteoarthritis. *Rheumatology* 51:2224–33.

Mack, J. E. 1997. *Abduction: Human encounters with aliens*. New York: Ballantine.

———. 1999. *Passport to the cosmos: Human transformation and alien encounters*. New York: Crown.

MacKay, C. 1980. *Extraordinary popular delusions and the madness of crowds*. New York: Bonanza Books.

Macmillan, M. 1997. *Freud evaluated*. Cambridge, MA: MIT Press.

MacRobert, A. 1982. A skeptic's guide to new age hokum. *Vermont Vanguard Press*, September 2, 46–49, 62.

Malarkey, K., and A. Malarkey. 2010. *The boy who came back from heaven*. Carol Springs, IL: Tyndale House.

Mallardi, V. 1978. *Biorhythms and your behavior*. Philadelphia: Running Press.

Mancini, A. D. 2012. A postwar picture of resilience. *New York Times*, February 6, A23.

Mann, J., and M. Stanley, eds. 1986. *Psychobiology of suicidal behavior*. New York: New York Academy of Sciences.

Manson, J. E., N. R. Cook, I-M. Lee, W. Christen, S. S. Bassuk, S. Mora, H. Gibson, et al. 2019a. Marine n-3 fatty acids and prevention of cardiovascular disease and cancer. *New England Journal of Medicine* 380:23–32.

———. 2019b. Vitamin D supplements and prevention of cancer and cardiovascular disease. *New England Journal of Medicine* 380:33–44.

Marcus, D. M., and A. P Grollman. 2003. Ephedra-free is not danger-free. *Science* 301:1669–71.

Margolin, A., S. K. Avants, and H. D. Kleber. 1998. Rationale and design of the Cocaine Alternative Treatments Study (CATS): Randomized, controlled trial of acupuncture. *Journal of Alternative and Complementary Medicine* 4:405–18.

Margolin, A., H. D. Kleber, S. K. Avants, J. Konefal, F. Gawin, E. Stark, J. Sorensen, et al. 2002. Acupuncture for the treatment of cocaine addiction. *JAMA* 287:55–63.

Margolin, K. N. 1994. How shall facilitated communication be judged? Facilitated communication and the legal system. In *Facilitated communication: The clinical and social phenomenon*, ed. H. C. Shane, 227–58. San Diego, CA: Singular Press.

Mari-Bauset, S., I. Zazpe, A. Mari-Sanchis, A. Llopis-González, and M. Morales-Suárez-Varela. 2014. Evidence of the gluten-free and casein-free diet in autism spectrum disorders: A systematic review. *Journal of Child Neurology* 29:1718–27.

Marks, D. 2000. *The psychology of the psychic*. 2nd ed. Amherst, NY: Prometheus Books.

Marks, D., and R. Kammann. 1980. *The psychology of the psychic*. Amherst, NY: Prometheus Books.

Marks, D., and C. Scott. 1986. Remote viewing exposed. *Nature* 319:444.

Marmot, A. F., J. Eley, M. Stafford, S. A. Stansfeld, E. Warwick, and M. G. Marmot. 2006. Building health: An epidemiological study of "sick building syndrome" in the Whitehall II study. *Occupational and Environmental Medicine* 63:283–89.

Markwick, B. 1978. The Soal-Goldney experiments with Basil Shackleton: New evidence of data manipulation. *Proceedings of the Society for Psychical Research* 56:250–77.

———. 1985. Establishment of data manipulation in the Soal-Shackleton experiments. In *A skeptic's handbook of parapsychology*, ed. P. Kurtz, 287–311. Amherst, NY: Prometheus Books.

Marsh, M. 2010. *Out-of-body and near-death experiences*. New York: Oxford University Press.

Maslow, A. 1966. *The psychology of science: A reconnaissance*. New York: Harper & Row.

Masters, K. S., and G. I. Spielmans. 2007. Prayer and health: Review, meta-analysis, and research agenda. *Journal of Behavioral Medicine* 30:329–38.

Masters, K. S., G. I. Spielmans, and J. T. Goodson. 2006. Are their demonstrable effects of intercessory prayer? *Annals of Behavioral Medicine* 32:21–26.

Matthews, M. R. 2019. *Feng shui: Teaching about science and pseudoscience.* Cham, Switzerland: Springer.

Matthews, P. 1982. Where does Sherrington's "muscle sense" originate? Muscles, joints, corollary discharges? *Annual Review of Neuroscience* 5:189–218.

Matthews, W. J., J. Conti, and T. Christ. 2000. God's HMO: Prayer, faith, belief, and physical well-being. *Skeptic* 8 (2): 64–68.

May, A. 2017. *Pseudoscience and science fiction.* Cham, Switzerland: Springer International.

Mayo, J., O. White, and H. Eysenck. 1978. An empirical study of the relation between astrological factors and personality. *Journal of Social Psychology* 105:229–36.

McAndrews, J. 1997. *The Roswell report: Case closed.* Washington, DC: U.S. Government Printing Office.

McCrone, W. 1999. *Judgment day for the Shroud of Turin.* Amherst, NY: Prometheus Books.

McKenzie, B. 2019. *Placebos for pets?* Aberdeen, UK: Ockham Press.

McLeod, C. C., B. Corbisier, and J. E. Mack. 1996. A more parsimonious explanation for UFO abduction. *Psychological Inquiry* 7:156–68.

McNally, R. J. 2003. *Remembering trauma.* Cambridge, MA: Harvard University Press.

McNamara, P. 2019. *The neuroscience of sleep and dreams.* New York: Cambridge University Press.

Medalia, N., and O. Larsen. 1958. Diffusion and belief in a collective delusion: The Seattle windshield pitting epidemic. *American Sociological Review* 23:180–86.

Medhurst, R. 1971. The origin of "prepared random numbers" used in the Shackleton experiments. *Journal of the Society for Psychical Research* 46:39–55. (*Note:* A short correction to this paper appeared in the same journal, 46:203.)

Meehl, P. E. 1954. *Clinical versus statistical predictions.* Minneapolis: University of Minnesota Press.

Megargie, E. 1972. *The CPI handbook.* San Francisco: Jossey-Bass.

Mehl-Madrona, L. 1997. *Coyote medicine: Lessons from Native American healing.* New York: Scribner.

Melby-Lervag, M., T. S. Redick, and C. Hulme. 2016. Working memory training does not improve performance on measures of intelligence or other measures of "far transfer." *Perspectives on Psychological Science* 11:512–34.

Menger, H. 1959. *From outer space.* New York: Pyramid Books.

Menzel, D. 1972. UFOs—the modern myth. In *UFOs—a scientific debate*, ed. C. Sagan and T. Page, 123–82. Ithaca, NY: Cornell University Press.

Menzel, D., and E. Taves. 1977. *The UFO enigma.* Garden City, NY: Doubleday.

Mercer, J., L. Sarner, and L. Rosa. 2003. *Attachment therapy on trial.* Westport, CT: Praeger.

Mercier, H. 2017. Confirmation bias—myside bias. In *Cognitive illusions*, 2nd ed., ed. R. F. Pohl, 99–114. London: Routledge.

Mielczarek, E. V., and B. D. Engler. 2013. Nurturing non-science. *Skeptical Inquirer* 37 (3): 32–39.

Mihura, J. L., G. J. Meyer, N. Dumitrascu, and G. Bombel. 2013. Validity of individual Rorschach variables: Systematic review and meta-analyses of the comprehensive system. *Psychological Bulletin* 139:548–605.

Millar, K., and N. Watkinson. 1983. Recognition of words presented during general anaesthesia. *Ergonomics* 36:585–94.

Miller, K. R. 1999. *Finding Darwin's god.* New York: HarperCollins.

Miller, L. 1986. In search of the unconscious. *Psychology Today*, December, 60–64.

Milton, J., and R. Wiseman. 1999. Does psi exist? Lack of replication of an anomalous process of information transfer. *Psychological Bulletin* 125:387–91.

Mishkin, M., and T. Appenzeller. 1987. The anatomy of memory. *Scientific American*, June, 80–89.

Mnookin, S. 2011. *The panic virus.* New York: Simon & Schuster.

Montgomery, R. 1965. *A gift of prophecy: The phenomenal Jeane Dixon.* New York: William Morrow.

———. 1985. *Aliens among us.* New York: Putnam.

Moody, R. 1976. *Life after life.* New York: Bantam Books.

Moore, C. B. 1997. The early New York University balloon flights. In *UFO crash at Roswell*, ed. B. Saler, C. A. Ziegler, and C. B. Moore, pp. 74–114. Washington, DC: Smithsonian Institution Press.

Moore, R. 1983. The impossible voyage of Noah's ark. *Creation/Evolution* 4 (1): 1–43.

Moore, W., and C. Berlitz. 1979. *The Philadelphia experiment: Project invisibility.* New York: Grossett and Dunlap.

Moran, R., and P. Jordan. 1978. The Amityville horror hoax. *Fate*, May, 43–47.

Morris, R. 1977–1978. Review of *The Amityville horror. Skeptical Inquirer* 2 (2): 95–102.

———. 1978. Survey of methods and issues in ESP research. In *Advances in parapsychological research 2: Extrasensory perception*, ed. S. Krippner, 7–58. New York: Plenum.

———. 1982. An updated survey of methods and issues in ESP research. In *Advances in Psychological Research 3*, ed. S. Krippner, 5–40. New York: Plenum.

Mossman, B. T., J. Bignon, M. Corn, A. Seaton, and J. B. Gee. 1990. Asbestos: Scientific developments and implications for public policy. *Science* 247:294–301.

Mostert, M. P. 2001. Facilitated communication since 1995. A review of published studies. *Journal of Autism and Developmental Disorders* 31:287–313.

Moulton, S. T., and S. M. Kosslyn. 2008. Using neuroimaging to resolve the psi debate. *Journal of Cognitive Neuroscience* 20:182–92.

Muckli, L., F. De Martino, L. Vizioli, L. S. Petro, F. W. Smith, K. Ugurbil, R. Goebel, and E. Yacoub. 2015. Contextual feedback to superficial layers of V1. *Current Biology* 25:2690–95.

Mueller, M. 1981–1982. The Shroud of Turin: A critical appraisal. *Skeptical Inquirer* 6 (3): 15–34.

Muhmenthales, M. C., M. Dubravac, and B. Meier. 2022. The future failed: No evidence for precognition in a large scale replication attempt of Bem (2011). *Psychology of Consciousness: Theory, Research and Practice*, advance online publication.

Murch, S. H., A. Anthony, D. H. Casson, M. Malik, M. Berelowitz, A. P. Dhillon, M. A. Thomson, A. Valentine, S. E. Davies, and J. A. Walker-Smith. 2004. Retraction of an interpretation. *Lancet* 363:750.

Muri, I. H., A. L. Fernandes, L. P. Sales, A. J. Pinto, K. F. Goessler, C. S. C. Duran, C. B. R. Silva, et al. 2021. Effect of a single high dose of Vitamin D3 on hospital length of stay in patients with moderate to severe COVID-19. *JAMA* 325:1053–60.

Muscat, J. E., M. G. Malkin, S. Thompson, R. E. Shore, S. D. Stellman, D. McRee, A. I. Neugut, and E. L. Wynder. 2000. Handheld cellular telephone use and risk of brain cancer. *JAMA* 284:3001–7.

Nadis, F. 2013. *The man from mars.* New York: Penguin.

Nair, A., R. Jalal, J. Liu, T. Tsang, N. M. McDonald, L. Jackson, C. Ponting, S. S. Jeste, S. Y. Bookheimer, and M. Dapretto. 2021. Altered thalamocortical connectivity in 6-week-old infants at high familial risk for autism spectrum disorders. *Cerebral Cortex* 31:4191–4205.

Napier, J. 1972. *Bigfoot.* New York: Dutton.

Nash, M. R. 1987. What, if anything, is regressed about hypnotic age regression? A review of the empirical literature. *Psychological Bulletin* 102:42–52.

———. 2001. The truth and hype about hypnosis. *Scientific American* 285 (1): 47–55.

Nathan, D. 2011. *Sybil exposed.* New York: Free Press.

Nathan, P. E., and J. M. Gorman, eds. 2015. *A guide to treatments that work.* 4th ed. New York: Oxford University Press.

Nation, P. N., and E. S. Williams. 1989. Maggots, mutilations and myth: Patterns of postmortem scavenging of the bovine carcass. *Canadian Veterinary Journal* 30:742–47.

National Academy of Sciences. 1999. *Science and creationism: A view from the National Academy of Science.* Washington, DC: National Academy Press.

National Health and Medical Research Council. 2015. *NHMRC information paper: Evidence on the effectiveness of homeopathy for treating health conditions.* Canberra: NHMRC.

National Research Council. 1997. *Possible health effects of exposure to residential electric and magnetic fields.* Washington, DC: National Academy Press.

———. 2003. *The polygraph and lie detection.* Washington, DC: National Academy Press.

———. 2009. *Strengthening forensic science in the United States: A path forward.* Washington, DC: National Academy Press.

National Toxicology Program. 2016. Report of partial findings from the National Toxicology Program carcinogenesis study of cell phone radiofrequency radiation in Hsd: Sprague Dawley R rates (whole body exposures). http://dx.doi.org/10.1101/055699.

Negida, A., A. Menshawy, G. El Ashal, Y. Elfouly, Y. Hani, Y. Hegazy, S. El Ghonimy, S. Fouda, and Y. Rashad. 2016. Coenzyme Q10 for patients with Parkinson's disease: A systematic review and meta-analysis. *CNS Neurological Disorders: Drug Targets* 15:45–53.

Nelson, G. 1970. Preliminary study of the electroencephalograms of mediums. *Parapsychologica* 4:30–35.

Nelson, K. B., and M. L. Bauman. 2003. Thimerosal and autism? *Pediatrics* 111:674–79.

Nelson, K. M., J. L. Dahlin, J. Bisson, J. Graham, G. F. Pauli, and M. A. Walters. 2017. Essential medical chemistry of curcumin. *Journal of Medical Chemistry* 60:1620–37.

Nelson, N. A., J. D. Kaufman, J. Burt, and C. Kall. 1995. Health symptoms and the work environment in four nonproblem United States office buildings. *Scandinavian Journal of Work Environment and Health* 21:51–59.

Nelson, T. 1978. Detecting small amounts of information in memory: Savings for nonrecognized items. *Journal of Experimental Psychology: Human Learning and Memory* 4:453–68.

Ness, M. A., and C. Phillips. 2015. Auditory pareidolia: Effects of contextual priming on perception of purportedly paranormal and ambiguous auditory stimuli. *Applied Cognitive Psychology* 29:129–34.

Newman, L. S., and R. F. Baumeister. 1996. Towards and explanation of the UFO abduction phenomenon: Hypnotic elaboration, extraterrestrial sadomasochism, and spurious memories. *Psychological Inquiry* 7:99–126.

Newport, F. 2014. In U.S., 42% believe creationist view of human origins. Gallup. https://news.gallup.com/poll/170822.

Nguyen, L., K. Murphy, and G. Andrews. 2022. A game a day keeps cognitive decline away? *Neuropsychological Review* 32:601–30.

Nichols, T. 2017. *The death of expertise.* New York: Oxford University Press.

Nickell, J. 1978. The Shroud of Turin—solved! *Humanist* 38 (6): 30–32.

———. 1982–1983. The Nazca drawings revisited: Creation of a full sized duplicate. *Skeptical Inquirer* 7 (3): 36–44.

———. 1993. *Looking for a miracle: Weeping icons, relics, stigmata, visions and healing cures.* Amherst, NY: Prometheus Books.

———, ed. 1994. *Psychic sleuths.* Amherst, NY: Prometheus Books.

———. 1995a. Alien autopsy hoax. *Skeptical Inquirer* 19 (6): 17–19.

———. 1995b. Crop circle mania wanes: An investigative update. *Skeptical Inquirer* 19 (3): 41–43.

———. 1996. Crop circles. In *The encyclopedia of the paranormal*, ed. G. Stein, 181–86. Amherst, NY: Prometheus Books.

———. 1999. *Inquest on the Shroud of Turin.* Amherst, NY: Prometheus Books.

———. 2001a. John Edward: Hustling the bereaved. *Skeptical Inquirer* 25 (6): 19–22.

———. 2001b. Scandals on follies of the "Holy Shroud." *Skeptical Inquirer* 25 (5): 17–20.

———. 2002. Benny Hinn: Healer or hypnotist? *Skeptical Inquirer* 26 (3): 14–17.

———. 2005. *Secrets of the sideshows.* Lexington, KY: University Press of Kentucky.

———. 2007a. "John of God": Healings by entities? *Skeptical Inquirer* 31 (5): 20–22.

———. 2007b. *Relics of the Christ.* Amherst, NY: Prometheus Books.

———. 2009. Demons in Connecticut. *Skeptical Inquirer* 33 (3): 25–27.

———. 2014. The conjuring. *Skeptical Inquirer* 37 (2): 22–25.

Nickell, J, and K. Biddle. 2020. So, you have a ghost in your photo. *Skeptical Inquirer* 40 (4): 39–43.

Nielsen, J. A., B. A. Zielinski, M. A. Ferguson, J. E. Lainhart, and J. S. Anderson. 2013. An evaluation of the left-brain vs. right-brain hypothesis with resting state functional connectivity magnetic resonance imaging. *PLOS One* 8 (8): e71275.

Nogrady, H., K. McConkey, and C. Perry. 1985. Enhancing visual memory: Trying hypnosis, trying imagination, and trying again. *Journal of Abnormal Psychology* 94:195–204.

Nogueira, F. 2019. The not so divine acts of medium "John of God." *Skeptical Inquirer* 43 (4): 11–13.

Nolan, J. M., E. Loskutova, A. Howard, R. Mulcahy, R. Moran, J. Stack, M. Bolger, et al. 2015. The impact of supplemental macular carotenoids in Alzheimer's Disease: A randomized clinical trial. *Journal of Alzheimer's Disease* 44:1157–69.

Nolen, W. 1974. *Healing: A doctor in search of a miracle.* New York: Random House.

Nortier, J. L., M.-C. M. Martinez, H. H. Schmeiser, V. M. Arlt, C. A. Bieler, M. Petein, M. F. Depierreux, et al. 2000. Urothelial carcinoma associated with the use of a Chinese herb (*Aristolochia fangchi*). *New England Journal of Medicine* 342:1686–92.

Norvell, A. 1975. *Astrology—your wheel of fortune*. New York: Harper & Row.

Nowack, N., J. Wittsiepe, M. Kasper-Sonnenberg, M. Wilhelm, and A. Schölmerich. 2015. Influence of low-level prenatal exposure to PCDD/Fs and PCBs on empathizing, systematizing and autistic traits: Results from the Duisburg birth cohort study. *PLOS One* 10:c0129906.

Numbers, R. L., and J. M. Butler, eds. 1987. *The disappointed: Millerism and millenarianism in the nineteenth century*. Bloomington: Indiana University Press.

Nye, M. 1980. N-rays: An episode in the history and psychology of science. *Historical Studies in the Physical Sciences* 11 (1): 125–56.

Oberg, J. 1977a. Astronauts and UFOs: The whole story. *Space World*, February, 4–28.

———. 1977b. Modern moon myths and UFO folklore. *Search*, Fall, 5–8, 52–62.

———. 1978–1979a. Astronaut "UFO" sightings. *Skeptical Inquirer* 3 (1): 39–46.

———. 1978–1979b. Tunguska echoes. *Skeptical Inquirer* 3 (1): 49–57.

———. 1982. *UFOs and outer space mysteries*. Norfolk, VA: Donning.

Oberg, J., and R. Sheaffer. 1977–1978. Pseudoscience at *Science Digest*. *Zetetic* 2 (1): 41–44.

Offit, P. A. 2008. *Autism's false prophets*. New York: Columbia University Press.

———. 2013. *Do you believe in magic?* New York: HarperCollins.

Offit, P. A., and S. Erush. 2013. Skip the supplements. *New York Times*, December 12, SR7.

Offit, P. A., J. Quarles, M. A. Gerber, C. J. Hackett, E. K. Marcuse, T. R. Kollman, B. G. Gellin, and S. Landry. 2002. Addressing parents' concerns: Do multiple vaccines overwhelm or weaken the infant's immune system? *Pediatrics* 109:124–29.

Ofshe, R., and E. Watters. 1994. *Making monsters: False memories, psychotherapy, and sexual hysteria*. New York: Scribner's.

Olshansky, S. J., B. A. Carnes, and R. N. Butler. 2001. If humans were built to last. *Scientific American* 284 (3): 50–55.

Omarr, S. 1972. *Astrology, you, and your love life*. New York: Pyramid Books.

Omohundro, J. 1976–1977. Von Dänkien's chariots: A primer in the art of cooked science. *Zetetic* 1 (1): 58–68.

Ongley, P. 1948. New Zealand diviners. *New Zealand Journal of Science and Technology* 30:38–54.

Oppenheimer, M. 2017. Peter Popoff, the born-again scoundrel. *GQ*, February 27.

Orne, M. T., W. G. Whitehouse, E. C. Orne, and D. F. Dinges. 1996. "Memories" of anomalous and traumatic autobiographical experiences: Validation and consolidation of fantasy through hypnosis. *Psychological Inquiry* 7:168–72.

Osis, K., and E. Haraldsson. 1977. Deathbed observations by physicians and nurses: A cross-cultural survey. *Journal of the American Society for Physical Research* 71:237–59.

Otani, D., and P. Dixon. 1976. Power function between duration of friendly interaction and conformity in perception and judgments. *Perceptual and Motor Skills* 43:975–78.

Otgaar, H., M. L. Howe, L. Patihis, H. Merckelbach, S. J. Lynn, S. O. Lilienfeld, and E. F. Loftus. 2019. The return of the repressed: The persistent and problematic claims of long-forgotten trauma. *Perspectives in Psychological Science* 14:1072–95.

Palmer, J. 1978. Extrasensory perception: Research findings. In *Advances in parapsychological research 2: Extrasensory perception*, ed. S. Krippner, 59–243. New York: Plenum.

———. 1982. ESP research findings: 1976–1978. In *Advances in parapsychological research 3*, ed. S. Krippner, 41–82. New York: Plenum.

Palmer, R. 2022. The great Australian psychic prediction project. *Skeptical Inquirer* 46 (2): 14–16.

Park, R. 2000. *Voodoo science: The road from foolishness to fraud*. New York: Oxford University Press.

———. 2008. *Superstition: Belief in the age of science*. Princeton, NJ: Princeton University Press.

Patihis, L., L. Y. Ho, I. W. Tingen, S. O. Lilienfeld, and E. F. Loftus. 2014. Are the memory wars over? A scientist-practitioner gap in beliefs about repressed memory. *Psychological Science* 25:519–30.

Patihis, L., and M. H. Pendergrast. 2019. Reports of recovered memories of abuse in therapy in a large age-representative U.S. national sample: Therapy type and decade comparisons. *Clinical Psychological Science* 7:3–21.

Patterson, J. 1983. Thermodynamics and evolution. In *Scientists confront creationism*, ed. L. Godfrey, 99–116. New York: Norton.

Peebles, C. 1994. *Watch the skies: A chronicle of the flying saucer myth*. Washington, DC: Smithsonian Institution Press.

Pehek, J., H. Kyler, and D. Faust. 1976. Image modulation in corona discharge photography. *Science* 194:263–70.

Pellicori, S. 1980. Spectral properties of the Shroud of Turin. *Applied Optics* 19:1913–20.

Penman, A. 2015. Two very different charlatans both selling the divine right to get rich quick. *Daily Mirror*, September 24.

Pennock, R. T. 1999. *Tower of Babel: The evidence against the new creationism*. Cambridge, MA: MIT Press.

Pennycook, G., J. A. Cheyne, N. Barr, D. J. Koehler, and J. A. Fugelsang. 2015. On the reception and detection of pseudo-profound bullshit. *Judgment and Decision Making* 10:549–63.

Pepper, C. 1984. *Quackery: A $10 billion scandal*. Washington, DC: U.S. Government Printing Office.

Perez, B. M., and T. Hines. 2011. The aura: A brief review. *Skeptical Inquirer* 35 (1): 38–40.

Perillo, J. T., and S. M. Kassin. 2011. Inside interrogation: The lie, the bluff and false confessions. *Law and Human Behavior* 35:327–37.

Persinger, M., and K. Makarec. 1987. Temporal lobe epileptic signs and correlative behaviors displayed by normal populations. *Journal of General Psychology* 114:179–95.

Pervin, L. A., ed. 1996. *Psychological Inquiry* 7 (2): 99–197.

Pessah, I. N., P. J. Lein, R. F. Seegal, and S. K. Sagiv. 2019. Neurotoxicity of polychlorinated biphenyls and related organohalogens. *Acta Neuropathologica* 138:363–87.

Petrie, K. J., B. Sivertsen, M. Hysing, E. Broadbent, R. Moss-Morris, H. R. Eriksen, and H. Ursin. 2001. Thoroughly modern worries: The relationship of worries about modernity to reported symptoms, health and medical care utilization. *Journal of Psychosomatic Research* 51:395–401.

Pfungst, O. 1956. *Clever Hans: The horse of Mr. von Osten*. New York: Hold, Rinehart and Winston.

Piccinini, G., and S. Bahar. 2015. No mental life after brain death. In *The myth of an afterlife*, ed. M. Martin and K. Augustine, 135–70. Lanham, MD: Rowman & Littlefield.

Pierpaoli, C., A. Nayak, R. Hafiz, A. Nayak, R. Hafiz, M. Okan Irfanoglu, G. Chen, P. Taylor, M. Hallett, et al. 2024. Neuroimaging findings in US government personnel and their family members involved in anomalous health incidents. *JAMA*, 331 (13): 1122–34.

Pigliucci, M., and M. Boudry, eds. 2013. *Philosophy of pseudoscience*. Chicago: University of Chicago Press.

Pignotti, M., and B. A. Thyer. 2015. New age and related novel unsupported therapies in mental health practice. In *Science and pseudoscience in clinical psychology*, 2nd ed., ed. S. O. Lilienfeld, S. J. Lynn, and J. M. Lohr, 191–209. New York; Guilford Press.

Piper, A. 1993. "Truth serum" and "recovered memories" of sexual abuse: A review of the evidence. *Journal of Psychiatry and Law* 21:447–71.

Pittler, M. H., E. M. Brown, and E. Ernst. 2007. Static magnets for reducing pain: Systematic review and meta-analysis of randomized trials. *CMAJ* 117:736–42.

Pleasonton, A. J. 1876. *The influence of the blue ray of the sunlight and of the blue color of the sky*. Philadelphia: Claxton, Remsen and Haffelfinger.

Plummer, M. 1986. Current investigations. *Skeptic* 6 (2): 2–5.

Pollack, J. 1964. *Croiset the clairvoyant: The story of an amazing Dutchman*. Garden City, NY: Doubleday.

Posey, T., and M. Losch. 1983–1984. Auditory hallucinations of hearing voices in 375 normal subjects. *Imagination, Cognition and Personality* 3:99–113.

Posner, G. P. 1998. Talking to the living loved ones of the dearly departed. *Skeptics* 6 (1): 94–95.

———. 2000. The face behind the "face" on mars. *Skeptical Inquirer* 24 (6): 20–26.

———. 2020. *Pharma*. New York: Avid Reader Press.

Power, R., R. F. Coen, S. Beatty, R. Mulcahy, R. Moran, J. Stack, A. N. Howard, and J. M. Nolan. 2018. Supplemental retinal carotenoids enhance memory in healthy individuals with low levels of macular pigment in a randomized, double-blind, placebo-controlled clinical trial. *Journal of Alzheimer's Disease* 61:947–61.

Pratt, J. 1978. Statement. *Proceedings of the Society for Psychical Research* 56:279–81.

Price, H. 1940. *The most haunted house in England: Ten years' investigation of Borley Rectory*. London: Longman, Green and Co.

Prioleau, L., M. Murdock, and N. Brody. 1983. An analysis of psychotherapy versus placebo studies. *Behavioral and Brain Sciences* 6:275–310.

Prothero, D. R. 2007. *Evolution: What the fossils say and why it matters*. New York: Columbia University Press.

———. 2020. *Weird earth: Debunking strange ideas about our planet*. Bloomington, IN: Red Lightning Books.

Prothero, D. R., and T. D. Callahan. 2017. *UFOs, chemtrails and aliens*. Bloomington: Indiana University Press.

Rabin, S. J. 2008. Pico on magic and astrology. In *Pico della Mirandola: New Essays*, ed. M. V. Dougherty, 152–78. New York: Cambridge University Press.

Rachman, S. 1971. *The effects of psychotherapy*. New York: Pergamon Press.

Rachman, S., and G. Wilson. 1980. *The effects of psychological therapy*. Oxford: Pergamon Press.

Radford, B. 2006. Art Bell's show broadcasts Sylvia Browne failure about mine tragedy. *Skeptical Inquirer* 30 (2): 8.

———. 2007. Sylvia Browne's biggest blunder. *Skeptical Inquirer* 31 (3): 12.

———. 2009. Ghosts, doughnuts, and a *Christmas Carol*. *Skeptical Inquirer* 33 (3): 45–55.

———. 2010. *Scientific paranormal investigation: How to solve unexplained mysteries*. Corrales, NM: Rhombus Books.

———. 2011. *Tracking the chupacabra*. Albuquerque, NM: University of New Mexico Press.

———. 2012a. Are pet psychics real? Cult Education Institute, April 24. https://culteducation.com/group/1104 -psychics/22854-are-pet-psychics-real.html.

———. 2012b. The psychic and the serial killer. *Skeptical Inquirer* 34 (2): 32–37.

———. 2013. Did psychic visions locate missing California boy? *Skeptical Inquirer* 37 (5): 26–27.

———. 2017a. *Investigating ghosts: The scientific search for spirits*. Corrales, NM: Rhombus Books.

———. 2017b. The legacy of fake bomb detectors in Iraq. *Skeptical Inquirer* 41 (1): 7.

Radford, B., and J. Nickell. 2006. *Lake monster mysteries*. Lexington: University Press of Kentucky.

Radner, D., and M. Radner. 1982. *Science and unreason*. Belmont, CA: Wadsworth.

Rae, A. 1986. Extrasensory quantum physics. *New Scientist*, November 27, 36–39.

Rafaeli, A., and R. Klimoski. 1983. Predicting sales success through handwriting analysis: An evaluation of the effects of training and handwriting sample content. *Journal of Applied Psychology* 68:212–17.

Ramey, D. W. 1998. Magnetic and electromagnetic therapy. *Scientific Review of Alternative Medicine* 2 (1): 13–19.

Randall, J. 1975. *Parapsychology and the nature of life: A scientific appraisal*. London: Souvenir Press.

Randi, J. 1978. King Tut's revenge. *Humanist* 28 (2): 44–47.

———. 1979–1980. A controlled test of dowsing abilities. *Skeptical Inquirer* 4 (1): 16–20.

———. 1982a. *Flim-flam! Psychics, ESP, unicorns and other delusions*. Buffalo, NY: Prometheus Books.

———. 1982b. *The truth about Uri Geller*. Amherst, NY: Prometheus Books.

———. 1982–1983a. Allison and the Atlanta murders: A follow-up. *Skeptical Inquirer* 7 (2): 7.

———. 1982–1983b. Nostradamus: The prophet for all seasons. *Skeptical Inquirer* 7 (1): 30–37.

———. 1982–1983c. Project alpha experiment: Part 1, the first two years. *Skeptical Inquirer* 7 (4): 24–33.

———. 1983–1984. Project alpha experiment: Part 2, beyond the laboratory. *Skeptical Inquirer* 8:36–45.

———. 1984–1985. The Columbus poltergeist case: Part I. *Skeptical Inquirer* 9:221–35.

———. 1986a. An answer to Peter Popoff. *Free Inquiry* 6 (4): 46–48.

———. 1986b. "Be healed in the name of God!" An exposé of the Reverend W. V. Grant. *Free Inquiry* 6 (2): 8–19.

———. 1986c. Peter Popoff reaches heaven via 39.17 Megahertz. *Free Inquiry* 6 (3): 6–7.

———. 1987. *The faith healers*. Amherst, NY: Prometheus Books.

———. 1988–1989. The case of the remembering water. *Skeptical Inquirer* 13: 142–46.

———. 1993. *The mask of Nostradamus*. Amherst, NY: Prometheus Books.

———. 2000. John Edward and the art of cold reading. *Skeptic* 8 (3): 6.

Randolph, G. 1984. Therapeutic and physical touch: Physiological response to stressful stimuli. *Nursing Research* 33:33–36.

Ransom, C. 2015. A critique of Ian Stevenson's rebirth research. In *The myth of an afterlife*, ed. M. Martin and K. Augustine, 571–74. Lanham, MD: Roman & Littlefield.

Rao, K. 1978. Theories of psi. In *Advances in parapsychological research 2: Extrasensory perception*, ed. S. Krippner, 245–95. New York: Plenum.

Raskin, J. 2000. Rogerian nursing theory: A humbug in the halls of higher learning. *Skeptical Inquirer* 24 (5): 31–35.

Raso, J. 1993. *Mystical diets: Paranormal, spiritual, and occult nutrition practices*. Amherst, NY: Prometheus Books.

Rathus, S. A. 1999. *Psychology in the new millennium*. 7th ed. Fort Worth: Harcourt Brace.

Ratzon, H. 1986. Handwriting analysis of Holocaust survivors. In *Scientific aspects of graphology*, ed. B. Nevo, 127–39. Springfield, IL: Charles C. Thomas.

Rawlings, M. 1978. *Beyond death's door*. New York: Thomas Nelson.

Raz, A., T. Hines, J. Fosella, and D. Casto. 2008. Paranormal experience and the COMT dopaminergic gene. *Cortex* 44:1336–41.

Razdan, R., and A. Kielar. 1984–1985. Sonar and photographic searches for the Loch Ness monster: A reassessment. *Skeptical Inquirer* 9:147–58.

Reber, A. S., and J. E. Alcock. 2020. Searching for the impossible: Parapsychology's elusive quest. *American Psychologist* 74:391–99.

Reber, R. 2017. Availability. In *Cognitive illusions*, 2nd ed., ed. R. F. Pohl, 185–203. London: Routledge.

Redelmeier, D. A., and E. Shafir. 2017. The full moon and motorcycle related mortality; population based double control study. *BMJ* 359:5367.

Redick, T. S. 2019. The hype cycle of working memory. *Current Directions in Psychological Science* 28:423–29.

Regal, B., and F. J. Esposito. 2018. *The secret history of the Jersey devil*. Baltimore, MD: Johns Hopkins University Press.

Reid, J. 1983. Use of graphology. *Personnel Management* 14 (10): 71.

Reilly, N. R. 2016. The gluten-free diet: Recognizing fact, fiction, and fad. *Journal of Pediatrics* 175:206–10.

Reiser, M., L. Ludwig, S. Saxe, and C. Wagner. 1979. An evaluation of the use of psychics in the investigation of major crimes. *Journal of Police Science and Administration* 7:18–25.

Reiterman, T. 1982. *Raven: The untold story of the Reverend Jim Jones and his people*. New York: Dutton.

Relman, A. 1998. A trip to Stonesville. *New Republic*, December 14, 28–37.

———. 2000. Andrew Weil: Public perception and reality. In *Science meets alternative medicine*, ed. W. Sampson and L. Vaughn, 119–40. Amherst, NY: Prometheus Books.

Rennie, J. 2002. 15 answers to creationist nonsense. *Scientific American* 287 (1): 78–85.

Repacholi, M. H., A. Lerchl, M. Röösli, Z. Sienkiewicz, A. Auvinen, J. Breckenkamp, G. d'Inzeo, et al. 2012. Systematic review of wireless phone use and brain cancer and other head tumors. *Bioelectromagnetics* 33:187–206.

Rhine, J., and J. Pratt. 1962. *Parapsychology: Frontier science of the mind*. Oxford: Blackwell.

Rhine, J., and L. Rhine. 1929. An investigation of a mind-reading horse. *Journal of Abnormal and Social Psychology* 23:449–66.

Rhine, J. B., and L. E. Rhine. 1929. Second report on Lady, the "mind-reading" horse. *Journal of Abnormal and Social Psychology* 24:287–92.

Richmond, S. J., S. R. Brown, P. D. Campion, A. J. L. Porter, J. A. Klaber Moffett, D. A. Jackson, V. A. Featherstone, and A. J. Taylor. 2009. Therapeutic effects of magnetic and copper bracelets in osteoarthritis: A randomized placebo-controlled crossover trial. *Complementary Therapies in Medicine* 17:249–56.

Richmond, S. J., S. Gunadasa, M. Bland, and H. Macpherson. 2013. Copper bracelets and magnetic wrist straps for rheumatoid arthritis. *PLOS One* 8 (9): e71529.

Riekki, T., M. Lindeman, M. Aleneff, A. Halme, and A. Nuortimo. 2013. Paranormal and religious believers are more prone to illusory face perception than skeptics and non-believers. *Applied Cognitive Psychology* 27:150–55.

Righter, C. 1977. Your astrological signs tell if you've picked the right mate. *National Enquirer*, February 8, 49.

Rines, R. H., H. E. Edgerton, C. W. Wyckhoff, and M. Klein. 1975–1976. Search for the Loch Ness monster. *Technology Review* 78 (5): 25–40.

Ring, K. 1980. *Life at death: A scientific investigation of the near-death experience*. New York: Coward, McCann and Geoghegan.

Ritchie, S. J., R. Wiseman, and C. C. French. 2012. Failing the future: Three unsuccessful attempts to replicate Bem's "retroactive facilitation of recall" effect. *PLOS One* 7 (3): e33423.

Roach, M. 2005. *Spook.* New York: Norton.

Robbins, R. 1959. *Encyclopedia of witchcraft and demonology.* New York: Crown.

Robertson, C. T., and A. S. Kesselheim, eds. 2016. *Blinding as a solution to bias.* Amsterdam: Academic Press.

Robertson, C. T., and M. A. Rodwin. 2016. "Money blinding" as a solution to biased design and conduct of scientific research. In *Blinding as a solution to bias,* ed. C. T. Robertson and A. S. Kesselheim, 115–31. Amsterdam: Academic Press.

Rogan, W. J., and B. C. Gladen. 1991. PCBs, DDE, and child development at 18 and 24 months. *Annals of Epidemiology* 1:407–13.

Rogan, W. J., B. C. Gladen, J. D. McKinney, N. Carreras, P. Hardy, J. Thullen, J. Tingelstad, and M. Tully. 1987. Polychlorinated biphenyls (PCBs) and dichlorodiphenyldichloroethylene (DDE) in human milk: Effects on growth, morbidity, and duration of lactation. *American Journal of Public Health* 77:1294–97.

Rogo, D. 1986. Making of a psi failure. *Fate,* April, 76–80.

Rogo, D., and R. Bayless. 1979. *Phone calls from the dead.* Englewood Cliffs, NJ: Prentice-Hall.

Rommel, K. 1980. *Operation animal mutilation.* Albuquerque, NM: District Attorney, First Judicial District, State of New Mexico.

Röösli, M. 2008. Radiofrequency electromagnetic field exposure and non-specific symptoms of ill-health: A systematic review. *Environmental Research* 107:277–87.

Rorschach, H. 1942. *Psychodiagnosis: A diagnostic test based on perception.* New York: Grune and Stratton.

Rosa, L., E. Rosa, L. Sarner, and S. Barrett. 1998. A close look at therapeutic touch. *JAMA* 279:1005–10.

Rose, L. 1968. *Faith healing.* London: Penguin.

Rosen, R. 1977. *Psychobabble.* New York: Atheneum.

Roskies, A. L. 2015. Mind reading, lie detection and privacy. In *Handbook of neuroethics,* ed. J. Clausen and N. Levy, 679–93. Dordrecht: Springer Netherlands.

Roth, B. J. 2022. *Are electro-magnetic fields making me ill?* Cham, Switzerland: Springer.

Rothleitner, C. 2021. Ultra-weak gravitational field detected. *Nature* 591:209–10.

Rothman, M. A. 1989–1990. Cold fusion: A case history in "wishful science"? *Skeptical Inquirer* 14:161–70.

Rotton, J., and I. Kelly. 1985. Much ado about the full moon: A meta-analysis of lunar-lunacy research. *Psychological Bulletin* 97:286–306.

Rubin, G., M. Burns, and S. Wessely. 2017. Possible psychological mechanisms for "wind turbine syndrome." *Noise and Health* 16:116.

Rubin, G. J., R. Nieto-Hernandez, and S. Wessely. 2010. Idiopathic environmental intolerance attributed to electromagnetic fields (formerly "electromagnetic hypersensitivity"): An updated systematic review of provocation studies. *Bioelectromagnetics* 31:1–11.

Rusconi, E., and T. Mitchener-Nisser. 2013. Prospects of functional magnetic resonance imaging as lie detector. *Frontiers in Human Neuroscience* 7:594.

Rush, J. 1982. Problems and methods in psychokinesis research. In *Advances in parapsychological research 3,* ed. S. Krippner, 83–114. New York: Plenum.

Russell, D., and W. Jones. 1980. When superstition fails: Reactions to disconfirmation of paranormal beliefs. *Personality and Social Psychology Bulletin* 6:83–88.

Rutherford, M. D., and V. A. Kuhlmeier, eds. 2014. *Social perception: Detection and interpretation of animacy, agency and intention.* Cambridge, MA: MIT Press.

Sacks, O. 2015. Seeing god in the third millennium. *Atlantic,* December 12, 2012.

Sagan, C. 1972. UFOs: The extraterrestrial and other hypotheses. In *UFOs—a scientific debate,* ed. C. Sagan and T. Page, 265–75. Ithaca, NY: Cornell University Press.

———. 1977. An analysis of "Worlds in Collision." In *Scientists confront Velikovsky,* ed. D. W. Goldsmith, 41–105. Ithaca, NY: Cornell University Press.

Sagan, C., and P. Fox. 1975. The canals of Mars: An assessment after Mariner 9. *Icarus* 25:602–12.

Saitsu, Y., A. Nishide, K. Kikushima, K. Shimizu, and K. Ohnuki. 2019. Improvement of cognitive functions by oral intake of *Hericium erinaceus*. *Biomedical Research* 40:125–31.

Sala, G., K. S. Tatlidil, and F. Gobet. 2017. Video game training does not enhance cognitive ability: A comprehensive meta-analytic investigation. *Psychological Bulletin* 144:111–39.

Salas, C., and D. Salas. 1996. Report of the commissioners charged by the king to examine animal magnetism. [Translation from the French.] *Skeptic* 4 (3): 68–83.

Saler, B., C. A. Ziegler, and C. B. Moore. 1997. *UFO crash at Roswell: The genesis of a modern myth*. Washington, DC: Smithsonian Institution Press.

Salerno, S. 2005. *Sham: How the self-help movement made America helpless*. New York: Crown.

Salzberg, S. 2017. Gwyneth Paltrow wants to heal you with magic stickers. *Forbes*, June 26.

Sampson, W., and W. London. 1995. Analysis of homeopathic treatment of childhood diarrhea. *Pediatrics* 96:961–64.

Sanderson, I. 1970. *Invisible residents*. New York: World Books.

Sanduleak, N. 1984–1985. The moon is acquitted of murder in Cleveland. *Skeptical Inquirer* 9:236–42.

Saunders, D. 1975. To Steven Soter and Carl Sagan. *Astronomy*, August, 20.

Saxon, A. H. 1989. *P. T. Barnum: The legend and the man*. New York: Columbia University Press.

Saxon, K. 1974. *Keeping score on our modern prophets*. Eureka, CA: Atlan Formularies.

Schacter, D. 2021. *The seven sins of memory*. Boston: Houghton Mifflin.

Schantz, S. L., D. M. Gasior, E. Polverejan, R. J. McCaffrey, A. M. Sweeney, H. E. Humphrey, and J. C. Gardiner. 2001. Impairments of memory and learning in older adults exposed to polychlorinated biphenyls via consumption of Great Lakes fish. *Environmental Health Perspectives* 109:605–11.

Scheiber, B. 1997. Therapeutic touch: Evaluating the "growing body of evidence" claim. *Scientific Review of Alternative Medicine* 1 (1): 13–15.

Scheiber, B., and C. Selby, eds. 2000. *Therapeutic touch*. Amherst, NY: Prometheus Books.

Schmack, K., H. Rossler, M. Sekutowicz, E. J. Brandl, D. J. Müller, P. Petrovic, and P. Sterzer. 2015. Linking unfounded beliefs to genetic dopamine availability. *Frontiers in Human Neuroscience* 9:521.

Schmidt, S. 1970. *Astrology 14*. New York: Pyramid Books.

Schnabel, J. 1993. *Round in circles*. London: Hamish Hamilton.

Schneider, E., and J. Reed. 1985. Life extension. *New England Journal of Medicine* 312:1159–68.

Schneiderman, L. J. 2000. The ethics of alternative medicine. In *Science meets alternative medicine*, ed. W. Sampson and L. Vaughn, 203–26. Amherst, NY: Prometheus Books.

Schreiber, F. R. 1973. *Sybil*. Chicago: Regnery.

Schulberg, H. C., W. Katon, G. E. Simpson, and A. J. Rush. 1998. Treating major depression in primary care practice. *Archives of General Psychiatry* 55:1121–27.

Schuller, D., and K. Pennachio. 1998. Therapeutic touch can't be dismissed. *White Plains* (NY) *Reporter Dispatch*, April 24, 14A.

Schur, M. 1966. Some additional "day residues" of the specimen dream of psychoanalysis. In *Psychoanalysis, a general psychology: Essays in honor of Heinz Hartmann*, ed. R. M. Loewenstein, L. M. Newman, M. Schur, and A. J. Solnit, 45–85. New York: International Universities Press.

Schwab, I. R. 2012. *Evolution's witness: How eyes evolved*. New York: Oxford University Press.

Schwarcz, J. 2013. Dr. Oz's questionable wizardry. *Skeptical Inquirer* 37 (5): 28–29.

Schwartz, G. 2002. *The afterlife experiments*. New York: Pocket Books.

Science and Technology Committee, United Kingdom House of Commons. 2010. *Evidence check 2: Homeopathy*. London: House of Commons.

Scofield, A. M. 1984. Homeopathy and its potential role in agriculture: A critical review. *Biological Agriculture and Horticulture* 2:1–50.

Scoles, S. 2020. *They are already here: UFO culture and why we see saucers*. New York: Pegasus.

Scott, C., and P. Haskell. 1973. "Normal" explanations of the Soal-Goldney experiments in extrasensory perception. *Nature* 245:52–54.

———. 1974. Fresh light on the Shackleton experiments? *Proceedings of the Society for Psychical Research* 56:43–72.

Seabrook, W. 1941. *Doctor Wood*. New York: Harcourt, Brace.

Sebeok, T., and R. Rosenthal, eds. 1981. *The clever Hans phenomenon: Communication with horses, whales, apes, and people*. New York: New York Academy of Sciences.

Seidel, S., R. Kreutzer, D. Smith, S. McNeel, and D. Gilliss. 2001. Assessment of commercial laboratories performing hair mineral analysis. *JAMA* 285:67–72.

Shaffer, R. 2010. Spiritual healing revisited. *Free Inquiry* 30 (6): 37–40.

———. 2013. The psychic defective: Revisited. *Skeptical Inquirer* 37 (5): 30–35.

Shaffer, R., and A. Jadwiszczok. 2010. Psychic defective: Sylvia Browne's history of failure. *Skeptical Inquirer* 34 (2): 38–42.

Shanteau, J. 1992. Competence in experts: The role of task characteristics. *Human Decision Processes* 53:252–66.

Shapiro, A., and E. Shapiro. 1997. *The powerful placebo: From ancient priest to modern physician*. Baltimore, MD: Johns Hopkins University Press.

Sharpless, B. A., and K. Doghramji. 2015. *Sleep paralysis: Historical, psychological and medical perspectives*. New York: Oxford University Press.

Sharpley, C. F. 1987. Research findings on neurolinguistic programming: Nonsupportive data or an untestable theory. *Journal of Counseling Psychology* 34:103–7.

Sharps, M. J. 2018. Percival Lowell and the canals of Mars. *Skeptical Inquirer* 42 (3): 41–46.

Shaw, J., and A. Vredeveldt. 2019. The recovered memory debate continues in Europe: Evidence from the United Kingdom, the Netherlands, France and Germany. *Clinical Psychological Sciences* 7:27–28.

Sheaffer, R. 1977–1978. Do fairies exist? *Zetetic* 2 (1): 45–52.

———. 1978. The Cottingley fairies: A hoax? *Fate*, June, 76–81.

———. 1978–1979. Review of J. Hynek's *Hynek UFO report*. *Skeptical Inquirer* 3 (2): 64–67.

———. 1981. *The UFO verdict*. Amherst, NY: Prometheus Books.

———. 1982–1983. Creationist cosmology. *Skeptical Inquirer* 7 (1): 7–8.

———. 1983–1984. Psychic vibrations. *Skeptical Inquirer* 8:117–20.

———. 1998a. E-mailed antigens and iridium's iridescence. *Skeptical Inquirer* 22 (1): 19–20.

———. 1998b. *UFO sightings: The evidence*. Amherst, NY: Prometheus Books.

———. 2015. Dr. Simon reveals his real thoughts on the Hill "UFO abduction" case. *Bad UFOs* blog, December 23.

———. 2016. *Bad UFOs*. Middletown, DE: CreateSpace.

———. 2019. The Pentagon's UFOs. *Skeptic* 24 (3): 14–17.

Sheehan, W. 1988. *Planets and perception*. Tucson: University of Arizona Press.

———, ed. 2021. *Neptune: From grand discovery to a world revealed*. Cham, Switzerland: Springer.

Shelton, R. C., M. B. Keller, A. Gelenberg, D. L. Dunner, R. Hirschfeld, M. E. Thase, J. Russell, et al. 2001. Effectiveness of St. John's wort in major depression: A randomized, controlled trial. *JAMA* 285:1978–86.

Shermer, M. 1996. Testing claims of mesmerism. *Skeptic* 4 (3): 66–67.

———. 1998. Talking twaddle with the dead. *Skeptic* 6 (1): 48–53.

———. 2011. *The believing brain*. New York: Times Books.

———. 2022. *Conspiracy*. Baltimore, MD: Johns Hopkins University Press.

Shic, F., S. Macari, and K. Chawarska. 2014. Speech disturbs face scanning in 6-month old infants who develop autism spectrum disorder. *Biological Psychiatry* 75:231–37.

Shiel, L. A. 2006. *Backyard bigfoot*. Lake Linden, MI: Slipdown Mountain.

Shinn, E. 1978. Atlantis: Bimini hoax. *Sea Frontiers* 24:130–41.

Shumaker, W. 1972. *Occult sciences in the Renaissance*. Berkeley: University of California Press.

Siegel, R. 1980. The psychology of life after death. *American Psychologist* 35:911–31.

Simmons, D. 1973. Experiments on the alleged sharpening of razor blades and the preservation of flowers by pyramids. *New Horizons* 1:95–101.

Simmons, D. J., W. Boot, N. Charness, S. E. Gathercole, C. F. Chabris, D. Z. Hambrick, E. A. L. Stine-Morrow. 2016. Do "brain-training" programs work? *Psychological Science in the Public Interest* 17 (3): 103–86.

Simmons, W. P., J. Boynton, and T. Landman. 2021. Facilitated communication, neurodiversity and human rights. *Human Rights Quarterly* 43:138–67.

Simon, A., D. Worthen, and J. Mitas. 1979. An evaluation of iridology. *JAMA* 242:1385–89.

Simpson, D. 1979–1980. Controlled UFO hoax: Some lessons. *Skeptical Inquirer* 4 (3): 32–39.

Singer, B. 1981. Kirlian photography. In *Science and the paranormal*, ed. G. Abell and B. Singer, 196–208. New York: Charles Scribner's Sons.

Singh, R. D., S. R. Jimerson, T. Renshaw, E. Saeki, S. R. Hart, J. Earhart, and K. Stewart. 2011. A summary and synthesis of contemporary empirical evidence regarding the effects of the Drug Abuse Resistance Education Program (DARE). *Contemporary School Psychology* 15:93–102.

Slater, E. 1985a. Conclusions on nine psychologies. In *Final report on the psychological testing of UFO "abductees,"* ed. R. Westrum, 17–31. Mt. Rainier, MD: Fund for UFO Research.

———. 1985b. Addendum to "Conclusions on nine psychologies." In *Final report on the psychological testing of UFO "abductees,"* ed. R. Westrum, 32–40. Mt. Rainier, MD: Fund for UFO Research.

Small, G. W., and J. F. Borus. 1983. Outbreak of illness in a school chorus: Toxic poisoning or mass hysteria? *New England Journal of Medicine* 308:632–35.

Small, G. W., and A. M. Nicholi. 1982. Mass hysteria among schoolchildren. *Archives of General Psychiatry* 39:721–24.

Small, G. W., M. W. Propper, E. T. Randolph, and S. Eth. 1991. Mass hysteria among student performers: Social relationship as a symptom predictor. *American Journal of Psychiatry* 148:1200–1205.

Smith, A. M., and C. Messier. 2014. Voluntary out-of-body experience: An fMRI study. *Frontiers in Human Neuroscience* 80: article 70.

Smith, D. 1981–1982. Two tests of divining in Australia. *Skeptical Inquirer* 6 (4): 34–37.

Smith, J. 1956. *The search beneath the sea: The story of the coelacanth.* New York: Holt.

Smith, M. 1983. Hypnotic memory enhancement of witnesses: Does it work? *Psychological Bulletin* 94:387–407.

Smith, M., G. Glass, and T. Miller. 1980. *The benefits of psychotherapy.* Baltimore, MD: Johns Hopkins University Press.

Smith, W., E. Dagle, M. Hill, and J. Mott-Smith. 1963. Testing for extrasensory perception with a machine. Data Sciences Laboratory Project 4610, AFCRL-63-141, May.

Snook, B., J. Eastwood, P. Gendreau, C. Goggin, and R. M. Cullen. 2007. Taking stock of criminal profiling: A narrative review and meta-analysis. *Criminal Justice and Behavior* 34:437–53.

Snyder, C., and R. Shenkel. 1975. The P. T. Barnum effect. *Psychology Today*, March, 52–54.

Soal, S., and K. Goldney. 1943. Experiments in precognitive telepathy. *Proceedings of the Society for Psychical Research* 47:21–150.

———. 1960. Correspondence. *Journal of the Society for Psychical Research* 40:378–81.

Sommer, B. 1973. Effect of menstruation on cognitive and perceptual-motor behavior: A review. *Psychosomatic Medicine* 35:515–34.

Sommers, C. H., and S. Satel. 2005. *One nation under therapy.* New York: St. Martin's Press.

Soter, S., and C. Sagan. 1975. Pattern recognition Zeta Retuculi. *Astronomy*, July, 39–41.

Spanos, N. P., P. A. Cross, K. Dickson, and S. C. DuBreuil. 1993. Close encounters: An examination of UFO experiences. *Journal of Abnormal Psychology* 102:624–32.

Spear, N. 1979. Experimental analysis of infantile amnesia. In *Functional disorders of memory*, ed. J. Kihlstrom and F. Evans, 75–102. Hillsdale, NJ: Lawrence Erlbaum Associates.

Spitz, H. H. 1997. *Nonconscious movements: From mystical messages to facilitated communication.* Mahwah, NJ: Erlbaum.

Spitz, H. H., and Y. Marcuard. 2001. Chevreul's report on the mysterious oscillations of the hand-held pendulum. *Skeptical Inquirer* 25 (4): 35–39.

Stahlman, J. 2000. A brief history of therapeutic touch. In *Therapeutic touch*, ed. B. Scheiber and C. Selby, 21–51. Amherst, NY: Prometheus Books.

Standage, T. 2000. *The Neptune file.* New York: Walker.

Steiner, R. A. 1986–1987. Exposing the faith healers. *Skeptical Inquirer* 11 (1): 28–31.

Stenger, V. J. 2000. The pseudophysics of therapeutic touch. In *Therapeutic touch*, ed. B. Scheiber and C. Selby, 302–11. Amherst, NY: Prometheus Books.

Stevens, S. S. 1968. Measurement, statistics and the Schempiric view. *Science* 161:849–56.

Stevenson, I. 1974. *Xenoglossy: A review and report of a case*. Charlottesville: University Press of Virginia.

———. 1975. *Cases of the reincarnation type*. Vol. 1: *Ten cases in India*. Charlottesville: University Press of Virginia.

———. 1977. *Cases of the reincarnation type*. Vol. 2: *Ten cases in Sri Lanka*. Charlottesville: University Press of Virginia.

Stewart, P., J. Reihman, E. Lonky, T. Darvill, and J. Pagano. 2000. Prenatal PCB exposure and Neonatal Behavioral Assessment Scale (NBAS) performance. *Neurotoxicology and Teratology* 22:21–29.

Stiebing, W. 1984. *Ancient astronauts, cosmic collisions, and other popular theories about man's past*. Amherst, NY: Prometheus Books.

Stojanoski, B., C. J. Wild, M. E. Battista, E. S. Nichols, and A. M. Owen. 2020. Brain training habits are not associated with generalized benefits to cognition: An online study of over 1000 "brain trainers." *Journal of Experimental Psychology: General* 150:729–38.

Story, R. 1976. *The space-gods revealed*. New York: Harper & Row.

———. 1977–1978. Von Däniken's golden gods. *Zetetic* 2 (1): 22–35.

———. 1980. *Guardians of the universe?* New York: St. Martin's Press.

Strauss, A. Y., J. D. Huppert, H. B. Simpson, and E. B. Foa. 2018. What matters more? Common or specific factors in cognitive behavioral therapy for OCD. *Behavioural Research and Therapy* 105:43–51.

Streitberger, K., and J. Kleinhenz. 1998. Introducing a placebo needle into acupuncture research. *Lancet* 352:364–65.

Strieber, W. 1978. *Wolfen*. New York: Bantam Books.

———. 1987a. *Communion*. New York: Morrow.

———. 1987b. Open Letter to Dr. Swords. *MUFON UFO Journal*, May, 7–8.

Stromberg, J., and E. Caswell. 2015. Why the Myers-Briggs test is totally meaningless. *Vox*, October 8.

Stubbs, A. L., and F. Montealegre. 2019. Recording of "sonic attacks" on U.S. diplomats in Cuba spectrally match the echoing call of a Caribbean cricket. *bioRxiv*. https://doi.org/10.1101/510834.

Summers, D. 2017. Troubling examples of pseudoscience at the Cleveland Clinic. *Washington Post*, January 11.

Swan, R. 1983. Faith healing, Christian Science, and the medical care of children. *New England Journal of Medicine* 309:1639–41.

Swanson, R. L., II, S. Hampton, J. Green-Mckenzie, R. Diaz-Arrastia, M. S. Grady, R. Verma, R. Biester, D. Duda, R. L. Wolf, and D. H. Smith. 2018. Neurological manifestations among US government personnel reporting directional audible and sensory phenomena in Havana, Cuba. *JAMA* 319:1125–33.

Swiss, J. I. 2020. *Conjurer's conundrum*. N.p.: Vanishing.

Swords, M. 1987. *Communion*: A reader's guide. *MUFON UFO Journal*, May, 3–6.

Szabo, L. 2018. Shadows on a sunny fad. *New York Times*, August 19, Business Section, 1 and 6.

Talbot, N. 1983. The position of the Christian Science Church. *New England Journal of Medicine* 309:1641–44.

Tankard, J. W., Jr. 1984. *The statistical pioneers*. Cambridge, MA: Schenkman.

Tarazona, J. V., D. Court-Marques, M. Tiramani, H. Reich, R. Pfeil, F. Istace, and F. Crivellente. 2017. Glyphosate toxicity and carcinogenicity: A review of the scientific basic of the European Union assessment and it differences with IARC. *Archives of Toxicology* 91:2723–43.

Targ, R., and H. Puthoff. 1974. Information transfer under conditions of sensory shielding. *Nature* 251:602–7.

———. 1977. *Mind reach*. New York: Delacorte Press.

Tarone, R. E. 2018. On the International Agency for Research on Cancer classification of glyphosate as a possible human carcinogen. *European Journal of Cancer Prevention* 27:82–87.

Tart, C. 1976. *Learning to use extrasensory perception*. Chicago: University of Chicago Press.

———. 2009. *End of materialism*. Oakland, CA: New Harbinger.

Tart, C., H. Puthoff, and R. Targ. 1980. Information transmission in remote viewing experiments. *Nature* 284:191.

Taubes, G. 1993. *Bad science: The short life and weird times of cold fusion*. New York: Random House.

Taylor, B. A., L. Lorson, C. M. White, PharmD, and P. D. Thompson. 2015. A randomized trial of coenzyme Q10 in patients with confirmed statin myopathy. *Atherosclerosis* 238:329–35.

Taylor, M. A., D. Reilly, R. H. Llewellyn-Jones, C. McSharry, and T. C. Aitchison. 2000. *BMJ* 321 (7259): 471–76.

Templer, D., R. Brooner, and M. Corgiat. 1983. Geophysical variables and behavior: 14. lunar phase and crime—fact or artifact? *Perceptual and Motor Skills* 57:993–94.

Templer, D., D. Veleber, and R. Brooner. 1982. Geophysical variables and behavior: 6. lunar phase and accident injuries—a difference between night and day. *Perceptual and Motor Skills* 55:280–82.

Tessman, I., and J. Tessman. 2000. Efficacy of prayer: A critical examination of claims. *Skeptical Inquirer* 24 (2): 31–33.

Thomason, S. 1984. Do you remember your previous life's language in your present incarnation? *American Speech* 59:540–50.

———. 1986–1987. Past tongues remembered? *Skeptical Inquirer* 11:367–75.

Thomson, K. S. 1991. *Living fossil: The story of the coelacanth*. New York: Norton.

Thouless, R. 1974. Some comments on "Fresh light on the Shackleton experiments." *Proceedings of the Society for Psychical Research* 56:88–92.

Thulborn, T. 1986. On the tracks of men and money. *Nature* 320:308.

Thyer, B. A., and M. G. Pignotti. 2015. *Science and pseudoscience in social work practice*. New York: Springer.

Tompkins, M. I. 2019. *The spectacle of illusion*. London: Thames & Hudson.

Torrey, E. F. 1986. *Witchdoctors and psychiatrists*. Northvale, NJ: Jason Aronson.

Tostanoski, A., R. Lang, T. Raulston, A. Carnett, and T. Davis. 2014. Voices from the past: Comparing the rapid prompting method and facilitated communication. *Developmental Neurorehabilitation* 17:219–23.

Toth, M., and G. Nielsen. 1976. *Pyramid power*. New York: Warner Books.

Tracey, T. J. G., B. E. Wampold, R. K. Goodyear, and J. W. Lichtenberg. 2015. Improving expertise in psychotherapy. *Psychotherapy Bulletin* 50:7–13.

Tracey, T. J. G., B. E. Wampold, J. W. Lichtenberg, and R. K. Goodyear. 2014. Expertise in psychotherapy. *American Psychologist* 69:218–29.

Turnbull, C. 1961. Some observations regarding the experiences and behavior of the Bambuti pygmies. *American Journal of Psychology* 74:304–8.

Turner, J. G., A. J. Clark, D. K. Gauthier, and M. Williams. 1998. The effects of therapeutic touch on pain and anxiety in burn patients. *Journal of Advanced Nursing* 28:10–20.

Tyler, H. 1977. The unsinkable Jeane Dixon. *Humanist* 38 (3): 6–9.

Ukai, M., S. McGrath, and J. Wakshlag. 2023. The clinical use of cannabidiol and cannabidiolic acid-rich hemp in veterinary medicine and lessons from human medicine. *Journal of the American Veterinary Medicine Association* 261:623–31.

Vallbona, C., C. F. Hazlewood, and G. Jurida. 1997. Response of pain to static magnetic fields in postpolio patients: A double-blind pilot study. *Archives of Physical Medicine and Rehabilitation* 78:1200–1203.

Vallee, J. 1975. *The invisible college: What a group of scientists has discovered about UFO influences on the human race*. New York: E. P. Dutton.

Van der Waerden, B. 1974. *Science awakening II: The birth of astronomy*. New York: Oxford University Press.

Van Deventer, W. 1983. Graphoanalysis as a management tool. *United States Banker*, November, 74–76.

Van Helsing, A. 1863. Comparative effects of three species of garlic for repelling vampires. *Zeitschrift fur Vampirstudien* 27:432–67.

Van Prooijen, J.-W., and M. Acker. 2015. The influence of control on belief in conspiracy theories. *Applied Cognitive Psychology* 29:753–61.

Van Prooijen, J.-W., K. M. Douglas, and C. De Inocencio. 2018. Connecting the dots: Illusory pattern perception predicts belief in conspiracies and the supernatural. *European Journal of Social Psychology* 48:320–35.

Victor, J. S. 1993. *Satanic panic*. Chicago: Open Court.

Verma, R., R. L. Swanson, D. Parker, A. A. O. Ismail, R. T. Shinohara, J. A. Alappatt, J. Doshi, et al. 2019. Neuroimaging findings in US government personnel with possible exposure to directional phenomena in Havana, Cuba. *JAMA* 322:336–47.

Vitaliano, D. 1973. *Legends of the earth.* Bloomington: Indiana University Press.

Voas, D. 2008. The million marriages. *Skeptical Inquirer* 32 (2): 52–55.

Vogt, E. 1952. Water witching: An interpretation of a ritual pattern in a rural American community. *Scientific Monthly*, September, 175–86.

Vogt, E., and R. Hyman. 1979. *Water witching U.S.A.* 2nd ed. Chicago: University of Chicago Press.

Vokey, J. R., and J. D. Read. 1985. Subliminal messages. *American Psychologist* 40:1231–39.

von Däniken, E. 1970. *Chariots of the gods?* New York: Putnam.

———. 1984. *Pathways to the gods.* New York: Berkley.

Von Franz, M.-L. 1964. The process of individuation. In *Man and his symbols,* ed. C. Jung, 158–229. Garden City, NY: Doubleday.

Wagenmakers, E.-J., R. Wetzels, D. Borsboom, and H. van der Maas. 2011. Why psychologists must change the way they analyze their data: The case of psi. *Journal of Personality and Social Psychology* 100:426–32.

Wagner, H., H. D. Betz, and H. L. Konig. 1990. Schlussbericht 01 KB8602. Bundesministerium fur Forschung und Technologie.

Wagner, M. W. 1997. Is homeopathy "new science" or "new age"? *Scientific Review of Alternative Medicine* 1 (1): 7–12.

———. 2000. Recent research on therapeutic touch. In *Therapeutic touch,* ed. B. Scheiber and C. Selby, 262–74. Amherst, NY: Prometheus Books.

Wakefield, A. J., S. H. Murch, A. Anthony, J. Linnell, D. M. Casson, M. Malik, M. Berelowitz, et al. 1998. Ileal-lymphoid-nodular hyperplasia, non-specific colitis and pervasive developmental disorder in children. *Lancet* 351 (9103): 637–41. (Retracted.)

Wakshlag, J., S. Cital, S. J. Eaton, R. Prussin, and C. Hudalla. 2020. Cannabinoid, terpene, and heavy metal analysis of 29 over-the-counter commercial veterinary hemp supplements. *Veterinary Medicine: Research and Reports* 11:45–55.

Walker, A. C., M. H. Turpin, J. A. Stolz, J. A. Fugelsang, and D. J. Koehler. 2019. Finding meaning in the clouds: Illusory pattern perception predicts receptivity to pseudo-profound bullshit. *Judgment and Decision Making* 14:109–19.

Walkowlak, J., J. Wiener, A. Fastabend, B. Heinzow, U. Krämer, E. Schmidt, H. J. Steingrüber, S. Wundram, and G. Winneke. 2001. Environmental exposure to polychlorinated biphenyls and quality of the home environment: Effects on psychodevelopment in early childhood. *Lancet* 358:1602–7.

Wallace, A. R. 1878. Psychological curiosities of skepticism: A reply to Dr. Carpenter. In *Psycho-physiological sciences and their assailants,* ed. A. R. Wallace, 37–55. Boston: Colby and Rich.

Waller, R., and S. Keeley. 1978. Effects of explanation and information feedback on the illusory correlation phenomenon. *Journal of Consulting and Clinical Psychology* 46:342–43.

Walsh, J. J. 1923. *Cures.* New York: Appleton.

Walzer, E. 1984. Mystery UFOs are identified. *White Plains* (NY) *Reporter Dispatch,* November 1, A1, A5.

Warren, E., L. Warren, A. Snedeker, C. Snediker, and R. Garton. 1992. *In a dark place: The story of a true haunting.* New York: Villard Books.

Watkins, A. J., and W. S. Bickel. 1988–1989. The Kirlian technique: Controlling the wild cards. *Skeptical Inquirer* 13:172–84.

Weber, C. 1980. The bombardier beetle myth exploded. *Creation/Evolution* 1 (3): 1–5.

Weil, A. 1995a. *Natural health, natural medicine.* Boston: Houghton Mifflin.

———. 1995b. *Spontaneous healing.* New York: Knopf.

———. 1997. *Eight weeks to optimum health.* New York: Random House.

———. 1998. *Health and healing.* Boston: Houghton Mifflin.

Weinberg, S. 2000. *A fish caught in time: The search for the coelacanth.* New York: HarperCollins.

Welch, P. 1967. A man who thinks pictures. *Life,* September 22, 112–14.

Wertheimer, N., and E. Leeper. 1979. Electrical wiring configurations and childhood cancer. *American Journal of Epidemiology* 109:273–84.

West, M. 2017. Curated crowd sourcing in UFO investigations. *Skeptical Briefs* 27 (1): 1–5.

———. 2021. I study UFOS and I don't believe the alien hype. Here's why. *Guardian*, June 11.

———. 2022. The Gimbal video: Genuine UFO or camera artifact? *Skeptic Magazine* 27 (2): 58–62.

Westra, H. A., and A. A. DiBartolomeo. 2024. Developing expertise in psychotherapy: The case for process coding as clinical training. *American Psychologist* 79:163–74.

Westrum, R. 1985. Introduction: Putting abduction reports into perspective. In *Final report on the psychological testing of UFO "abductees,"* ed. R. Westrum, 1–5. Mt. Rainier, MD: Fund for UFO Research.

Whelan, E. M. 1993. *Toxic terror: The truth behind the cancer scares.* Amherst, NY: Prometheus Books.

White, A. 1999. Neurophysiology of acupuncture analgesia. In *Acupuncture: A scientific appraisal*, ed. E. Ernst and A. White, 60–92. Oxford: Butterworth-Heinemann.

White, S., and D. Pillemer. 1979. Childhood amnesia and the development of a socially accessible memory system. In *Functional disorders of memory*, ed. J. Kihlstrom and F. Evans, 29–73. Hillsdale, NJ: Lawrence Erlbaum Associates.

Whitson, J. A., and A. D. Galinsky. 2008. Lacking control increases illusory pattern perception. *Science* 322:115–17.

Whittaker, W. E. 2006. *Grave dowsing reconsidered.* Iowa City: Office of the State Archaeologist.

Whooley, M. A., and G. E. Simon. 2000. Primary care: Managing depression in medical outpatients. *New England Journal of Medicine* 343:1942–50.

Wilford, J. N. 1986. Fossils of "man tracks" shown to be dinosaurian. *New York Times*, June 17.

Wilhelm, J. 1976. *Search for superman.* New York: Pocket Books.

Will, C. M. 2018. *Theory and experiment in gravitational physics.* 2nd ed. New York: Cambridge University Press.

Willin, M. J. 1996. A ganzfeld experiment using musical targets. *Journal of the Society for Psychical Research* 61:1–17.

Wilson, I. 1982. *All in the mind.* Garden City, NY: Doubleday.

Wilson, M. 2015. Fortuneteller cost him fortune after fortune. *New York Time*, June 6, A1.

Wimmer, M. 2012. *The complete guide to children's drawings.* Stuttgart: Ibidem Verlag.

Wing, A., and A. Baddeley. 1978. A simple measure of handwriting as an index of stress. *Bulletin of the Psychonomic Society* 11:245–46.

Winter, D. E. 1985. *Faces of fear.* New York, NY: Berkley Trade.

Winters, W., S. Devriese, I. Van Diest, B. Nemery, H. Veulemans, P. Eelen, K. Van de Woestijne, and O. Van den Bergh. 2003. Media warnings about environmental pollution facilitate the acquisition of symptoms in response to chemical substances. *Psychosomatic Medicine* 65:332–38.

Wirth, D. P. 1990. Effect of noncontact therapeutic touch on the healing rate of full thickness dermal wounds. *Subtle Energies* 1:1–20.

———. 2000. Complementary healing intervention and dermal wound reepithelialization: An overview. In *Therapeutic touch*, ed. B. Scheiber and C. Selby, 292–301. Amherst, NY: Prometheus Books.

Wiseman, R. 2010. Heads I win, tails you lose: How parapsychologists nullify null results. *Skeptical Inquirer* 34 (1): 36–39.

———. 2011. *Paranormality.* London: Pan Books.

Wiseman, R., and C. O'Keeffe. 2001. A critique of Schwartz et al.'s after-death communication studies. *Skeptical Inquirer* 25 (6): 26–30.

Wiseman, R., and C. Watt. 2006. Belief in psychic ability and the misattribution hypothesis: A qualitative review. *British Journal of Psychology* 97:323–38.

Witkowski, T. 2010. Twenty five years of research on neuro-linguistic programming. *Polish Psychological Bulletin* 41:58–66.

Witthoft, M., I. Freitag, C. Nassbaum, A.-K. Bräscher, F. Jasper, J. Bailer, and G. J. Rubin. 2018. On the origin of worries about modern health hazards: Experimental evidence for a conjoint influence of media reports and personality traits. *Psychology and Health* 33:361–80.

Witthoft, M., and G. J. Rubin. 2013. Are media warnings about the adverse health effects of modern life self-fulfilling? An experimental study on idiopathic environmental intolerance attributed to electromagnetic fields (IEI-EMF). *Journal of Psychosomatic Research* 74:206–12.

Wolfner, G., D. Faust, and R. Dawes. 1993. The use of anatomically detailed dolls in sexual abuse evaluations: The state of the science. *Applied and Preventive Psychology* 2:1–11.

Wolraich, M. L., D. B. Wilson, and J. W. White. 1995. The effect of sugar on behavior or cognition in children. *JAMA* 274:1617–21.

Wood, J. M., H. N. Garb, M. T. Nezworski, S. O. Lilienfeld, and M. C. Duke. 2015. A second look at the validity of widely used Rorschach indices: Comment on Mihura, Meyer, Dumitrascu and Bobmel (2013). *Psychological Bulletin* 141:236–49.

Wood, J. M., M. T. Nezworski, and H. N. Garb. 2023a. The Rorschach inkblot test. *Skeptical Inquirer* 47 (6): 39–45.

Wood, J. M., M. T. Nezworski, and H. N. Garb. 2023b. Rorschach inkblots. In *Investigating clinical psychology*, ed. N. Stea and S. Hupp, 45–57. New York: Routledge.

Wood, J. M., M. T. Nezworski, S. O. Lilienfeld, and H. N. Garb. 2003. *What's wrong with the Rorschach.* San Francisco: Jossey-Bass.

Wood, R. W. 1904. The N-rays. *Nature*, September 29, 530–31.

Woodhead, M. 2016. 8% of China's clinical trial data are fraudulent, investigation finds. *BMJ* 355:i5396.

World Animal Protection US. 2019. *Trading cruelty: How captive big cat farming fuels the traditional Asian medicine industry.* New York: World Animal Protection US.

Wright, L. 2013. *Going clear.* New York: Knopf.

Wylie, K. 1980. *Bigfoot: A personal inquiry into a phenomenon.* New York: Viking Press.

Yirmiya, N., and T. Charman. 2010. The prodrome of autism: Early behavioral and biological signs, regression, peri- and post-natal development and genetics. *Journal of Child Psychology and Psychiatry* 51:432–58.

Yoon, D.-E., S. Lee, J. Kim, H.-J. Park, V. Napadow, I.-S. Lee, and Y. Chae. 2023. Graded brain fMRI response to somatic and visual acupuncture stimulation. *Cerebral Cortex* 33:11269–78.

Young, R. R. 1990–1991. Old mysteries: The Kecksburg incident. *Skeptical Inquirer* 15 (3): 281–85.

Yuan, Q., C.-W. Wang, J. Shi, Z.-X. Lin. 2017. Effects of ginkgo biloba on dementia: An overview of systematic reviews. *Journal of Ethnopharmacology* 195:1–9.

Zdep, S., and H. Weaver. 1967. The graphoanalytic approach to selecting life insurance salesmen. *Journal of Applied Psychology* 51:295–99.

Zelicoff, A. P. 2001. Polygraphs and the national labs: Dangerous ruse undermines national security. *Skeptical Inquirer* 25 (4): 21–23.

Zhang, L., I. Rana, R. M. Shaffer, E. Taioli, and L. Sheppard. 2019. Exposure to glyphosate-based herbicides and risk of non-Hodgkin lymphoma: A meta-analysis and supporting evidence. *Mutation Research* 781:186–206.

Ziegler, C. A. 1997. Mythogenesis: Historical development of the Roswell narratives. In *UFO crash at Roswell*, ed. B. Saler, C. A. Ziegler, and C. B. Moore, 1–29. Washington, DC: Smithsonian Institution Press.

Zimmer, C. 2000. *Parasite rex.* New York: Free Press.

Ziskin, J. 1995. *Coping with psychiatric and psychological testimony.* 5th ed. 3 vols. Los Angeles: Law and Psychology Press.

Zusne, L., and W. Jones. 1982. *Anomalistic psychology.* Hillsdale, NJ: Lawrence Erlbaum Associates.

INDEX

3; on unfair skeptics demand for proof, 4–5; unwillingness to look closely at phenomenon, 3; on usual rules of science being too strict, 23

prosperity gospel, 214; Oliver on, 215; Popoff as preacher of, 215

pseudopsychologies: Freudian theory, 101–8; graphology, 124; humanistic psychology, 131–34; Myers-Briggs Type Indicator, 124–26; projective tests, 118–24; psychology of Jung, 130–31; psychotherapy, 125–30

pseudoscience: argument from ignorance logical fallacy, 4; astrology classification of, 3; biorhythm theory classification as, 3; failure to change theory with new evidence, 6; failure to contribute to knowledge advancement, 3; Frazier definition of, 1; Hitler racial theories as, 23, 24; major characteristics of, 2; myths used as support for, 5; Popper on nonfalsifiability of, 1; proponent unwillingness to look closely at phenomenon, 3; unchanging theories of, 6

pseudoscientific beliefs: antivaccine movement and measles increase, 21; dangers of, 22–24; human perceptual and cognitive systems acceptance of, 15; intelligence not factor in, 20; meaningful patterns in randomness perceptions, 17; nonreflective thinking and, 20; personality factors role in, 20; study of, 17–21

pseudoscientific claims: on beliefs determination of reality, 23–24; cognitive psychologists on belief in false, 18; consumer fraud for, 20; CSICOP/CSI on, 17; importance of testing of beliefs of, 18; important psychological issues in examination of, 17; increase in rejection of basic scientific establishment of reality, 17; market for, 20; media and websites support of, 20; perception as constructive process in, 18; possible false and public deprived of information, 17; possible truth with important knowledge, 17; psychological mechanisms supporting belief in, 20; study of, 17–20; unthinking acceptance and real dangers of, 17

psi phenomenon: belief in, 96–99; believer suggestibility and, 98; cognitive processes and, 97; COMT neurochemical and believers of, 98; ESP, 75, 96–99; jealous phenomena point of view, 77; magician on investigating team, 84–85; one-hundred-year investigations on, 94; persistence reasons for, 95

psi theory: of quantum mechanics, 96, 133–34, 229; of synchronicity, 96, 131

Psychical Research Foundation, Roll of, 64–65

psychic crime detection: Allison and, 47–48; Croiset incorrect information on Zwenne, 48; Ragland and, 47; Renier and, 49; study on, 48–49; Weber and, 47, 49

The Psychic Mafia (Keene), 34

psychic predictions of future, 47; Australian Psychic Prediction Project, 44; Australian Skeptics on, 44; Dixon on Kennedy election and assassination, 46; of Nostradamus, 44–45; of Rand on Reagan attempted assassination, 46

psychic readings, 34; billet reading trick by, 35–36; cold reading technique and, 36–39; detailed victim files for, 36; multiple out technique in, 37–38, 44, 48; for parents of children with serious illnesses, 41–42; private detective or information sources for, 36; P.T. Barnum effect, 39; stock spiel vague descriptions in, 40, 41

psychics: Browne as, 38; Browne on missing persons cases, 42; Center for Inquiry "Paranormal Challenge" prize, 43; direct mail use by, 49, 50; Edward as, 38–39; JREF one-million-dollar prize money for, 43; online scams for, 43–44, 49; online Zoom platforms for, 43; Penn and Teller's Show *Bullshit* on tricks of, 41; pet, 43; Project Alpha study and, 85; van Praagh as, 37–38

psychics and psychic phenomena: prophetic dreams and hunches, 49–53, 103; psychic crime detection, 47–49; psychic predictions of future, 44–47; psychic readings, 34–44, 48, 290; spiritualism, 25–34

psychic surgery: Agpaoa arrest for fraud, 216; of Arigo, 215; deaths from, 22; Fuller, W. as psychic dentist, 216; of John of God, 214; Nolen and Randi on, 216; Philippines as location of, 215–16; sleight of hand used in, 215

psychoanalysis, nonfalsiability of, 1–2, 101, 122

psychokinesis (PK), 75, 89; Hydrick and, 92; SPR on spiritualism and, 26

psychological mechanisms, for support of beliefs, 20

psychology, 81; behind alien abduction reports, 181–83; humanistic, 131–34; of Jung, 130–31

The Psychology of the Psychic (Mark), 81

psychosexual development theory, of Freud, 106–7

psychotherapies: animal magnetism, 125–26; behavioral modification techniques, 130; double-

ABOUT THE AUTHOR

Terence Hines did his undergraduate work as a psychology major at Duke University, class of 1973. He went on to obtain his master's and Ph.D. (1977) in cognitive psychology from the University of Oregon, working in Mike Posner's laboratory. The topic of his dissertation was the organization of language in bilingual memory. It was at Oregon that he became interested in examining the psychology of paranormal and pseudoscientific claims and experience through contact with Professor Ray Hyman, a founding member of what is now the Committee for Skeptical Inquiry (CSI). Hines has been a fellow of the CSI since 2013.

After graduate school, he went to Boston as a postdoctoral student in the Veterans Administration Geriatric Research Education and Clinical Center (GRECC). After a year there, he moved to the Division of Cognitive Neuroscience, directed by Michael Gazzaniga, at the Cornell University Medical School in New York City (1979–1980).

In 1981 he took a position in the Psychology Department at Pace University in Pleasantville, New York, where he remains professor of psychology. In 1992–1993 he was a visiting professor in the Department of Neurophysiology of the Nencki Institute of Experimental Biology in Warsaw, Poland. While in Warsaw, he was also a visiting professor in the Psychology Department at the University of Warsaw. Since 1996, he has been an adjunct professor of neurology at New York Medical College in Valhalla, New York.

www.ingramcontent.com/pod-product-compliance
Lightning Source LLC
Chambersburg PA
CBHW081735270326
41932CB00020B/3275